American
Jewish
Year Book

American

Jewish

Year Book 1983

VOLUME   83

Prepared by THE AMERICAN JEWISH COMMITTEE

Editors

MILTON HIMMELFARB

DAVID SINGER

THE AMERICAN JEWISH COMMITTEE
NEW YORK
THE JEWISH PUBLICATION SOCIETY OF AMERICA
PHILADELPHIA

ISBN 0-8276-0221-9

Library of Congress Catalogue Number: 99-4040

PRINTED IN THE UNITED STATES OF AMERICA
BY THE HADDON CRAFTSMEN, INC., SCRANTON, PA.

Preface

The present volume features two articles dealing with religious developments in Israel: "Religiosity Patterns in Israel" by Calvin Goldscheider and Dov Friedlander and "Reform and Conservative Judaism in Israel: A Social and Religious Profile" by Ephraim Tabory.

Articles focusing on Jewish life in the United States include Murray Friedman's "Intergroup Relations"; George Gruen's "The United States, Israel, and the Middle East"; Steven Cohen's "The 1981–1982 National Survey of American Jews"; Alan Fisher's "The National Gallup Polls and American Jewish Demography"; and U.O. Schmelz's and Sergio DellaPergola's "The Demographic Consequences of U.S. Jewish Population Trends." Alvin Chenkin provides revised U.S. Jewish population estimates.

Jewish life around the world is reported on in a series of articles dealing with Israel, Canada, Great Britain, France, the Soviet Union, Poland, Rumania, Bulgaria, and South Africa. Estimates for the world Jewish population are given.

Carefully compiled directories of national Jewish organizations, periodicals, and federations and welfare funds, as well as religious calendars and obituary notices, round out the 1983 AMERICAN JEWISH YEAR BOOK.

We are very grateful to our colleague Carol Sue Davidson for technical and editorial assistance. Thanks are also due to Joan Margules for her proofreading efforts and to Diane Hodges for compiling the index. We acknowledge the aid of Cyma M. Horowitz, director of the Blaustein Library, Lotte Zajac, and all our other co-workers in the Information and Research Department.

THE EDITORS

Contributors

BERNARD BASKIN: rabbi, Temple Anshe Sholom, Hamilton, Ontario.

ALVIN CHENKIN: research consultant, CJFWF, New York.

STEVEN MARTIN COHEN: associate professor, sociology, Queens College, CUNY, New York.

SERGIO DELLAPERGOLA: senior lecturer, Jewish demography, Institute of Contemporary Jewry, Hebrew University, Jerusalem.

DENIS DIAMOND: associate director, World Jewish Congress, Israel branch, Jerusalem.

ALAN M. FISHER: assistant professor, political science, California State University: Dominguez Hills, Carson.

DOV FRIEDLANDER: professor, statistics and demography, Hebrew University, Jerusalem.

MURRAY FRIEDMAN: director, middle Atlantic region, AJC, Philadelphia.

CALVIN GOLDSCHEIDER: professor, sociology and demography, Hebrew University, Jerusalem.

GEORGE E. GRUEN: director, Israel and Middle East affairs, AJC, New York.

LIONEL E. KOCHAN: Bearsted Reader in Jewish history, University of Warwick, Oxford.

MIRIAM KOCHAN: journalist, translator, Oxford.

ARNOLD MANDEL: novelist, reporter, literary critic, Paris.

RALPH MANDEL: journalist, translator, Jerusalem.

U. O. SCHMELZ: associate professor, Jewish demography, Institute of Contemporary Jewry, Hebrew University, Jerusalem.

LEON SHAPIRO: Rutgers University, retired, New York.

EPHRAIM TABORY: lecturer, sociology and anthropology, Bar Ilan University, Ramat-Gan.

Table of Contents

Special
Articles

Religiosity Patterns in Israel

by CALVIN GOLDSCHEIDER and DOV FRIEDLANDER

AN ANALYSIS OF RELIGION (religious institutions, culture, and groups) and religiosity (religious identification, ritual observances, and the intensity of religious commitment) in Israeli society involves a variety of complex political, ideological, and cultural-historical issues. Religious identification and behavior are major facets of differentiation in Israel. Institutionally, the influence of religion is conspicuous in politics, education, marriage and divorce regulations, the military, and cultural activities. Ideologically, Judaism and Zionism are intimately connected. At the same time, many religious organizations and leaders are anti-Zionist or, at the least, skeptical about Zionism as a form of secular nationalism. Moreover, many leading Zionist figures are secularists who wish to substitute nationalism for religion or, at a minimum, reject the traditional dominance of religion.

Of key importance is the growing differentiation between religious and national identities in the process of modernization. In the pre-modern period there was little separation of Judaism from Jewishness; religious observance, ritual performance, and identification were tied to a sense of peoplehood, ethnicity, and community. In contrast, one of the distinguishing features of the societal changes associated with modernization is the process of differentiation of various aspects of social life. In our context, modernization involves the potential for differentiating religion from nationalism. On the individual level, this means that one can be religious without being nationalistic and *vice versa.*

While the modernization of Jews, particularly in Israel, allows for the separation of religious and national identities, it also generates new forms of interdependence. Novel types of religious expression emerge in celebration of national occasions and secular events; nationalistic interpretation (or reinterpretation) is applied to traditional religious symbols. The sanctification of the national-secular and the desanctification of the holy-religious are

Note: The authors acknowledge with gratitude the support of grant no. HD 06721 from the U.S. National Institutes of Health in the collection of data reported in this paper. Hagit Weiss and Eliahu Ben Moshe ably assisted in the preparation and tabulation of the statistical data. Revisions of this paper were prepared while the senior author was visiting professor of contemporary Jewish studies and associated with The Center for Modern Jewish Studies at Brandeis University.

3

clear expressions of the reintegration of religion and nationalism in the old-new Israeli society.

Previous research has focused primarily on the relationship between religious and political institutions, and has included the study of such issues as church-state relations, legal-political definitions of who is a Jew, religious conflict over autopsies and public transportation on *shabbat,* and the control of marriage and divorce by the religious establishment.[1] Aside from the institutional analysis, there are selected studies of religious ritual from an anthropological perspective, and recent research, some not yet published, on civil religion in Israel.[2] Still other studies have examined the influence of religiosity on personal hopes and fears, fertility, political attitudes, authoritarianism, and occupational interests.[3]

Surprisingly little reliable and systematic empirical information is available on the dimensions of religiosity, as well as the variations and changes over time in religiosity among the diverse segments of Israel's Jewish population. Most studies have been limited to descriptions of religiosity in terms of one dimension (religious, secular, and a mixed intermediate group). Recent research, based on public opinion surveys, has lacked essential background information necessary for in-depth analysis.[4]

Before turning to a detailed investigation of the available data, it is instructive to set up several theoretical models as guidelines for our analysis. There are three reasonable, though somewhat contradictory, theoretical

---

[1]For a general review see Samuel Eisenstadt, *Israeli Society* (New York, 1967), pp. 309–320; Zvi Yaron, "Religion in Israel," AJYB, Vol. 76, 1976, pp. 41–90 and references cited therein. See also the review in Leon Weller, *Sociology in Israel* (Westport, 1974), chapter 7; Stephen Sharot, *Judaism: A Sociology* (London, 1976); Sammy Smooha, *Israel: Pluralism and Conflict* (Los Angeles, 1978); Charles Liebman, "Religion and Political Integration in Israel," *Jewish Journal of Sociology,* June 1975, pp. 17–27; and Emanuel Gutmann, "Religion in Israeli Politics," in Jacob Landau, (ed.), *Man, State and Society in the Contemporary Middle East* (New York, 1971), pp. 122–134.

[2]See H. Goldberg, "Culture and Ethnicity in the Study of Israeli Society," *Ethnic Groups,* Vol. 1, 1977, pp. 163–186; Shlomo Deshen and Moshe Shokeid, *The Predicament of the Homecoming* (Cornell, 1974); Shlomo Deshen, "Israeli Judaism: Introduction to the Major Patterns," *International Journal of Middle Eastern Studies,* 1978; see also Charles Liebman, *Civil Religion in Israel,* unpublished manuscript.

[3]See Leon Weller, *op. cit.,* chapters 7 and 8; Aaron Antonovsky and Alan Arian, *Hopes and Fears of Israelis* (Jerusalem, 1972), chapter 6; and Solomon Poll and Ernest Krausz, (eds.), *On Ethnic and Religious Diversity in Israel* (Ramat-Gan, 1975), *passim.*

[4]For a recent attempt to describe various social-psychological and ideological aspects of religiosity in Israel, see Yehuda Ben-Meir and Peri Kedem, "Index of Religiosity of the Jewish Population of Israel," *Megamot* (Hebrew), February 1979, pp. 353–362. For a more social-psychological approach to the issues of Jewish identity in Israel, see Simon Herman, *Jewish Identity* (New York, 1977). Other empirical studies include Judah Matras, *Social Change in Israel* (Chicago, 1965); Judah Matras, "Religious Observance and Family Formation in Israel," *American Journal of Sociology,* March 1964, pp. 464–475; and Alan Arian, *The Choosing People* (Cleveland, 1973), chapter 4.

expectations about changing patterns of religiosity in Israel which reflect common-sense notions. (1) Israel is like all other modern societies. As such, Jews in Israel have become less traditional as socioeconomic and political modernization have taken place. We therefore expect a process of secularization to be evident over time for the Jewish population of Israel. (2) The options for Jewish religious expression are unique in Israel; issues of *kashrut* and *shabbat* observance, Jewish education, etc. are relatively less problematic there. In Israel there is little opportunity for assimilation. Hence, we might expect general stability in religiosity over the several decades, and even possibly some increase in religious observance. (3) The expected picture of religiosity in Israel is similar to the American Jewish model of greater polarization. Modernization creates options for both secularization and new religious expression, and these options are selectively exercised in either a more religious or a more secular direction. Israeli society has become polarized into two conflicting segments—the religious and the secular—with fewer persons remaining in the middle. There is an obvious need to systematically analyze empirical evidence in order to test the relative accuracy of each of these models.

The analysis of religiosity patterns presented here is based on data obtained from a random sample of Israel's urban Jewish population, as part of a larger study of social and demographic change in the country. Included in the sample were Jewish men and women in their first marriage, aged 55 or less, living in areas of over 30,000 population. The field work took place between mid-1974 and early 1975. A total of 3,000 interviews were completed; from the checks available, the sample appears to be representative of the urban Jewish population defined as eligible.[5]

In addition to extensive background information, six basic questions were included to explore the structure of religiosity in Israel. Two subjective questions were asked: (1) How would you define the religiosity of your home today? (2) How important is Judaism in your daily life? Three questions were asked about specific religious observances: (A) *kashrut* (maintaining separate utensils for meat and dairy); (B) *shabbat* (travelling on *shabbat*); (C) *mikveh* for women (regular use of the ritual bath). A final question was asked about the frequency of the husband's synagogue attendance.[6]

---

[5]For details of the sample, see Calvin Goldscheider and Dov Friedlander, "Patterns of Jewish Fertility in Israel," in Paul Ritterband, (ed.), *Modern Jewish Fertility* (Leiden, 1981), pp. 232–254; and Dov Friedlander and Calvin Goldscheider, "Immigration, Social Change and Cohort Fertility in Israel," *Population Studies,* July 1978, pp. 299–317.

[6]The alternatives for the self-definition of religiosity were: very religious, religious (or traditional), not religious, very not religious. For the importance of Judaism, the alternative responses were: very important, important, not so important, not important at all. For synagogue attendance, the alternatives were: at least once a week, several times a year or holidays, only on the high holy days, never.

There are areas of religiosity that are clearly not covered by these questions (e.g., religious beliefs, political-religious ideologies, and membership and participation in religious organizations). Nevertheless, these questions, in combination with the background socioeconomic information collected, allow for a detailed analysis of variation and change in critical aspects of religiosity. In particular, the data allow for a systematic examination of the following issues: (1) What is the structure of religiosity in Israel today? How are the various aspects of religious identification and observance inter-related? (2) What have been the processes and directions of change in religiosity in Israel? (3) How do religiosity patterns vary by ethnic origin? Have changes in religiosity levels characterized the different ethnic Jewish subcommunities? (4) How is exposure to Israeli society related to religious identification and observance? Are there indications of religiosity convergences among the Israeli-born of different ethnic subcommunities? (5) What is the relationship between educational attainment and religiosity? Have increases in educational levels equalized ethnic group differences in religious identification and behavior? (6) What have been the effects of exposure to religious education in Israel on levels of religiosity?

The Structure of Religiosity

The first and most elementary question that may be addressed relates to the overall pattern of religious identification and observance in Israeli society. In terms of the two subjective measures of religious identification, data in Table 1 show that over half of the respondents define their homes as either very religious or religious (traditional), and indicate that Judaism plays a very important or important role in their daily lives. A slightly smaller proportion (47 per cent) observes *kashrut* to the extent that separate meat and dairy utensils are maintained. In contrast, less than one-fourth go to the *mikveh* (women), attend synagogue services regularly (men), and abstain from riding on *shabbat*.

Fully 47 per cent of the total Jewish population are either religious or secular on all six measures, with over twice as many secular as compared to religious. Equally important, the remaining population is not distributed randomly over the range of individual item combinations; nor, for that matter, are all possible combinations of religious observance and identification to be found in Israel. Indeed, when the total theoretical range of possible combinations of religiosity on the six measures are examined, 15 combinations out of a possible 64 cover 95 per cent of all cases and result in the following typology (see Table 2): (1) The "secular" who rank themselves non-religious and non-observant on all six measures (35 per cent of all cases included in the typology); (2) The "moderately secular" who consider Judaism important in their daily lives and/or define their

TABLE 1. PROPORTION RELIGIOUS FOR SIX MEASURES OF RELIGIOSITY BY MAR-
RIAGE COHORT, JEWISH POPULATION OF ISRAEL, 1974–1975

| | | Marriage Cohort | |
	Total	Before 1954	1955–64	1965–74
Self Definition **of Home**				
Very Religious	9.0	11.6	8.8	5.9
Religious	45.9	49.7	45.3	41.7
Not Religious	36.2	32.0	36.6	41.2
Not at All Religious	8.9	6.7	9.3	11.2
Daily Importance **of Religion**				
Very Important	14.6	18.2	14.3	10.1
Important	37.4	37.4	39.3	35.6
Not Very Important	28.6	26.4	28.8	31.4
Not at All Important	19.4	18.0	17.5	22.9
Separate Utensils For Dairy and Meat	47.0	52.4	45.8	41.2
Husband Attends **Synagogue**				
Once a Week	24.2	31.3	22.6	16.5
On Holidays	22.5	22.8	23.1	21.5
Three Times a Year	27.5	24.8	29.6	29.0
Never	25.8	21.0	24.8	32.9
Does Not Ride On Shabbat	24.1	29.9	23.2	17.2
Woman Goes to Mikveh	21.1	24.6	20.6	17.1
Per Cent Religious on All Six Measures	13.9	17.1	13.6	9.8
Per Cent Secular on All Six Measures	32.8	27.0	33.8	39.6
Number of Cases	2,951	1,177	872	902

households as religious and/or maintain separate meat and dairy dishes. This group does not observe *mikveh*, travels on *shabbat*, and does not attend synagogue regularly. The moderately secular category accounts for 38 per cent of the total sample. Almost three-fourths of the Israeli population may be categorized as moderately secular or secular. (3) The "moderately religious" who identify themselves as religious, consider Judaism important in their daily lives, maintain separate dishes for meat and dairy, and selectively observe one or two of the following: *mikveh;* do not travel on *shabbat;* attend synagogue regularly. Fourteen per cent of the total population may be classified as moderately religious. (The moderately secular and moderately religious categories may be subdivided as noted in Table 2.) (4) The "religious" (14 per cent of the population) who define their homes as religious, consider Judaism important in their daily lives, observe *kashrut, shabbat,* and *mikveh,* and attend synagogue regularly.

The evidence suggests that those who define their homes as religious or who consider Judaism important in their daily lives observe *kashrut* regulations, but do not necessarily observe *mikveh, shabbat,* or regular synagogue attendance. On the other hand, the observance of *mikveh, shabbat,* and regular synagogue attendance almost always implies the observance of *kashrut,* the definition of the home as religious, and the evaluation of Judaism as important in daily life.

Variation by Marriage Cohort

This empirically descriptive typology provides a first approximation of the structure of religiosity among Israeli Jews. The analytic questions we posed, however, were related to the dynamics of variation and change in religiosity. The cross-sectional data may be used to clarify some of the dynamics. In particular, we can examine variations in religious identification and observances for marriage cohorts (i.e., groups of families married at specific time periods) as clues to change processes. These data show (Table 1) that the most recent marriage cohort (1965–74) has the lowest level of religiosity, while the oldest marriage cohort (before 1954) has the highest level of religiosity. Part of this variation by marriage cohort may reflect the impact of life cycle, more specifically, length of marriage, on religious identification and observances. More likely, the systematic variations by cohort reflect the process of change toward lowered levels of religiosity that characterizes the younger generation. This interpretation of the marriage cohort data remains inferential since the information on religiosity is based on cross-sectional rather than longitudinal observations. More detailed and direct analysis of the changes in religiosity will be presented in a subsequent section.

TABLE 2.   TYPOLOGY OF RELIGIOSITY COMBINING SIX MEASURES BY ETHNICITY, JEWISH POPULATION OF ISRAEL, PER CENT DISTRIBUTION

	Total	East Europe	West Europe	Asia	Africa	Israel–Europe	Israel–Asia/Africa
Religious on All Measures	14	7	19	19	26	11	7
Moderately Religious	14	8	9	21	25	4	12
All Except Mikveh	4	5	5	4	3	3	4
All Except Shabbat	2	0	0	4	5	0	0
All Except Synagogue	2	0	0	2	5	0	3
All Except Shabbat & Mikveh	2	2	1	3	3	0	2
All Except Shabbat & Synagogue	2	0	0	4	6	0	3
All Except Mikveh & Synagogue	2	1	3	4	3	1	0
Moderately Secular	38	35	30	43	36	32	52
Kashrut Plus 2 Subjective Measures	10	8	8	16	15	6	12
Just 2 Subjective Measures	7	6	4	8	5	5	13
Kashrut Plus Religon is Important	4	1	1	2	1	1	3
Kashrut Plus Self-Definition	2	3	4	3	4	4	7
Just Kashrut	4	4	3	3	3	5	6
Just Self-Definition	5	7	6	4	5	5	5
Just Religion is Important	6	7	4	7	3	6	6
Secular on All Measures	35	47	43	17	13	53	27
Proportion Covered by Typology	95	97	96	95	92	96	93

Although the most recent marriage cohort is characterized by the lowest level of religiosity for all six indicators, the extent of variation is different among the measures of religiosity. *Shabbat* observance, synagogue attendance, and the two subjective measures of religious identification are lower by about 45 per cent for the youngest marriage cohort as compared to the oldest cohort. For *mikveh*, the proportion is 31 per cent, and for *kashrut*, 21 per cent. The relatively small declines in *kashrut* observance by cohort may reflect the greater ease of such observance in Israel, but most likely relates to the strong extended family ties in the country and the desire to maintain appropriate facilities for family members who are more observant. This is particularly true with respect to older family members who are more likely to observe traditional dietary regulations.

There appears to be no indication from these cohort data that religious-secular polarization has increased for the youngest cohort. Although there are clear patterns of increasing proportions of secular identification and non-observance among the more recent marriage cohorts, the decline in the per cent religious on all six measures of religiosity is somewhat sharper. There is no pattern of greater concentration at the two extremes of the religiosity continuum among the most recent cohort. As such, these cohort patterns suggest secularization rather than polarization.

Ethnic Variation

A striking feature of Israeli society is the pattern of ethnic Jewish variation that is tied to the history and sources of immigration to the country.[7] Ethnicity is perhaps the most significant, and surely the most conspicuous, basis of social, cultural, and economic differentiation within the Jewish population. In terms of religiosity, ethnic origin takes on particular significance, since Israeli Jews born in Europe were exposed to a more modern-secular environment than Jews born in Asian or African countries. Indeed, European Jews had already undergone a much more extensive transformation of religiosity prior to their coming to Israel. An examination of contemporary Israeli patterns of religiosity must therefore take account of the religiosity "origins" of the various ethnic groups.

Ethnic origin relates to religiosity change in yet another way. Comparisons between foreign-born and native-born Israelis provide clues as to the direction of change and the extent of ethnic convergence among the Israeli-born.

Four ethnic subgroups among the foreign-born Jewish population may be identified based on place of birth: (1) East European; (2) West European (including North America); (3) Asian (mainly Iraq and Yemen, but also Iran and Turkey); and (4) African (mainly Morocco, but also Algeria, Tunisia, and Libya). Jews born in Israel were classified as those of European and those of Asian or African origin. The data in Table 3 clearly show that the pattern of religiosity varies significantly among the ethnic subgroups, and is consistent for each of the six measures of religiosity. The relative ranking of religiosity from the most to the least religious is as follows:

---

[7]For a detailed discussion, see Dov Friedlander and Calvin Goldscheider, *The Population of Israel* (New York, 1979), chapters 3 and 4.

TION OF ISRAEL, 1974-1975

Ethnicity and Marriage Cohort	Defines Home as Religious	Religion is Important	Observes Kashrut	Attends Synagogue Regularly	Does Not Ride on Shabbat	Woman Goes to Mikveh	Per Cent Religious	Per Cent Secular	Number of Cases
East Europe	40.2	37.1	32.6	16.0	15.7	8.3	6.6	45.7	744
Before 1954	45.7	39.7	37.5	18.8	19.2	9.0	7.5	40.3	468
1955–1964	38.9	40.2	30.2	14.1	10.7	8.1	6.7	47.7	149
1965–1974	21.6	23.8	17.5	7.9	8.7	6.3	3.2	63.2	126
West Europe	50.2	44.2	43.4	26.3	27.8	18.9	17.9	41.1	287
Before 1954	58.6	48.1	47.7	34.6	36.4	23.7	22.3	33.8	131
1955–1964	50.7	44.9	42.0	24.6	27.5	17.4	17.4	42.0	69
1965–1974	36.0	38.4	37.2	15.1	15.1	12.9	11.8	51.8	86
Asia	70.3	71.0	60.1	32.9	31.1	29.9	18.3	16.1	602
Before 1954	73.3	74.3	67.2	43.6	38.2	37.7	24.1	10.5	241
1955–1964	69.9	71.2	55.3	27.9	29.7	26.0	16.4	19.6	219
1965–1974	65.7	64.3	55.0	21.4	20.0	21.6	10.1	20.1	140
Africa	80.9	73.9	71.8	38.1	37.8	43.3	24.0	12.2	472
Before 1954	88.0	79.3	78.3	51.1	46.7	52.5	32.8	6.6	184
1955–1964	76.5	73.2	70.6	34.6	35.5	38.8	19.9	15.9	153
1965–1974	75.6	67.4	64.4	23.4	27.3	35.1	15.4	16.2	132
Israel–Europe	36.4	34.3	31.6	15.4	17.3	12.7	10.8	50.8	538
Before 1954	49.5	40.7	36.3	14.3	20.9	13.1	9.9	40.7	91
1955–1964	34.7	32.2	29.6	16.3	17.9	13.8	11.3	52.8	196
1965–1974	33.2	34.0	31.6	15.2	15.6	11.6	10.8	52.8	250
Israel–Asia/Africa	57.7	52.9	47.1	17.5	15.7	16.1	7.0	27.1	274
Before 1954	76.1	67.4	65.2	39.1	28.3	22.2	13.3	13.3	46
1955–1964	45.8	51.3	38.9	9.7	9.7	9.7	4.2	29.2	72
1965–1974	57.7	49.4	45.5	14.7	14.7	17.3	6.4	30.1	156

African, Asian, West European, and East European. Not unexpectedly, the sharpest religiosity differences are between the European-born and the Asian/African-born.

While ethnic differences in religiosity are significant for all six measures, differences in the observance of *mikveh* are particularly large. Comparing the two extreme ethnic group patterns of religiosity, we see that the proportion classified as religious is about twice as high among the African-born as among the East Europeans. However, the proportion of African women going to the *mikveh* is over five times higher than that of East European women (43 per cent compared to 8 per cent). This may reflect the traditional significance of *mikveh* within the cultural system of African-born women, and may have meaning that goes beyond purely religious considerations.[8]

Additional insight into the ethnic differences in religiosity emerges from an examination of the typology constructed earlier (Table 2). The structure of religiosity for the East and West Europeans is strikingly similar despite differences in levels. However, differences between the European-born and the Asian/African-born appear not only in terms of religiosity levels, but also in terms of structure. Thus, for example, the proportion religious on all six items is identical for the West European-born and Asian-born. However, the proportion moderately religious is significantly higher for the Asian-born (21 per cent compared to 9 per cent for the West Europeans), while the proportion secular is higher among the West European-born (43 per cent as compared to 17 per cent of the Asian-born). The Asian-born are much more concentrated within the more religious segment of the moderately secular category. The structure of religiosity among the African-born is more similar to that of the Asian-born than that of the European-born, but at a higher level of religiosity. None of the European-born appear in several sub-categories of the moderately religious, while 10 per cent of the Asian-born and 16 per cent of the African-born fall into these groups. Again, the implication is that the retention of *mikveh* observance may have a different religio-cultural meaning for the Asian-born and African-born than for the Europeans. For the Europeans, the non-observance of *mikveh* implies non-observance of *shabbat* and/or synagogue attendance, while for the Asian-born and African-born the observance of *mikveh* is independent of these other ritual observances.

Comparing the Israeli-born of different ethnic origins to each other and to the first-generation foreign-born adds another dimension to the analysis of religiosity in Israel. First, the data indicate that ethnic differences among the Israeli-born are considerably smaller than among the foreign-born. Nevertheless, for five of the six measures (*shabbat* excepted) the Israeli-born of Asian/African origin have a higher proportion religious than those of

---

[8]See Matras, *Social Change in Israel, op. cit.,* pp. 68–73.

European origin, and the proportion secular is considerably higher among the Israeli-born of the European group (53 per cent compared to 27 per cent among those of Asian/African origin). Thus, these data point to an unmistakable pattern of ethnic convergence in the level of religious identification and observance among native-born Israelis.

These data facilitate another type of comparison—between the foreign-born and native-born of each ethnic group. For the Europeans, only small differences in the religiosity patterns emerge, with the general trend toward somewhat lower levels for the Israeli-born. Much sharper generational differences characterize the Asian/African group. For each measure of religiosity, a smaller proportion of the Israeli-born of Asian/African origin are religious than are first-generation Asian/Africans. Thus, ethnic convergence in religiosity among the Israeli-born is the consequence of greater generational change among Asian/Africans, who are moving toward the lower levels of religiosity characteristic of the Europeans in Israel.

Ethnicity and Cohort

The basic findings are reinforced when ethnicity and cohort are combined, as shown in Table 3. Four patterns clearly emerge: (1) Decreasing levels of religiosity among the more recent marriage cohorts characterizes each ethnic and generation group and each of the measures of religiosity. (2) Greater generational changes in religiosity characterize the Asian/African group than the Europeans for each of the marriage cohorts. (3) Significant ethnic convergences in religiosity among the Israeli-born characterize each of the marriage cohorts. (4) Ethnic differences in religiosity, while weakened, continue to characterize the more recently married, Israeli-born cohorts.

The ethnicity-cohort data also clarify the polarization issue. Although the overall cohort data provide no evidence of religious-secular polarization for the total Jewish population, an examination of the religious and secular extremes among Israel's ethnic subpopulations qualifies that conclusion. These data point unmistakably to polarization for the European groups. In contrast, for the Asian-born and African-born, the declines in the per cent religious by cohort are sharper than the increases in the per cent secular. While two-thirds of the European-born of the younger cohort are at the extremes of religious or secular (a clear majority are secular), the majority of the Asian-born and African-born are at intermediate levels of religiosity. Of particular interest is the fact that the Israeli-born of Asian and African origin follow the European pattern of increasing polarization due to increases in the per cent secular, rather than decreases in the per cent religious. While the proportions secular and religious among the oldest cohort are equal, the proportion secular is four-and-a-half times higher than the proportion religious among the youngest marriage cohort. In sum, the cohort data suggest that increased secularization characterizes all ethnic groups in Israel, whereas polarization characterizes the European sub-groups and is increasingly characteristic of second-generation Israelis of African/Asian origins. While there is greater *ethnic* homogeneity in religiosity patterns among the Israeli-born, there is greater *religious* polarization.

Changes in Religiosity: Direct Measures

From the marriage-cohort and generation data, inferences were made about change in the level of religiosity in Israel. Given the basic cross-sectional nature of the data source, these data are only approximations of change. A more direct examination of the issue may be made from two additional questions that were included in the survey. Each female respondent was asked to identify the extent of religiosity in her parents' home when she was growing up, and whether her mother was accustomed to going to the *mikveh*. These data, in aggregate distributional form (compared to the aggregate data presented earlier on the self-definition of the woman's own home and her observance of *mikveh*) and in the individual combinations, provide a direct basis for a detailed investigation of change processes in religiosity.[9]

The data in aggregate form point up the significant generational declines in religiosity that have characterized Israeli society. Data in Table 4 indicate that over 75 per cent of the women define their parents' homes as either very religious or religious. This compares to 44 per cent who define their own homes as very religious or religious (Table 1). These aggregate comparisons are even more striking when the details are examined. About one-third of the women define their parents' home as very religious whereas only nine per cent define their own homes as very religious. Moreover, about half the women report that their mothers were accustomed to going to the mikveh, whereas only 21 per cent report that they themselves observe *mikveh* regulations.

Adding the data by marriage cohort confirms these general patterns of decline in religiosity. The changes inferred from the cohort pattern are clear and consistent: the more recent marriage cohorts report lower levels of religiosity in their parents' homes (and smaller proportions of mothers who went to the *mikveh*) than do the older marriage cohorts, and for each

---

[9]There is a clear overlap between these direct generational data and the pattern by marriage cohort. To the extent that religiosity varies little by life cycle, the cohort data should be reasonable approximations of these direct measures. Data were also obtained on the extent of religiosity of the husband's parents' home when he was growing up. The patterns are the same as for the wife and are not presented in tabular form.

TABLE 4. PROPORTION VERY RELIGIOUS AND RELIGIOUS OF WIFE'S PARENTAL HOUSEHOLD AND PROPORTION OF MOTHERS GOING TO MIKVEH BY ETHNICITY AND MARRIAGE COHORT, JEWISH POPULATION OF ISRAEL

| | Wife's Parents' Home | | Mother Went |
	Very Religious	Religious	to Mikveh
Total	32.0	43.2	49.5
Marriage Cohort			
Before 1954	39.9	42.5	58.6
1955–1964	32.1	42.8	51.1
1965–1974	21.5	44.4	36.2
Ethnicity and Cohort			
East Europe	21.2	43.7	35.2
Before 1954	27.0	46.9	45.0
1955–1964	17.4	39.6	26.0
1965–1974	4.0	36.8	11.2
West Europe	25.6	40.7	33.0
Before 1954	37.1	40.2	43.0
1955–1964	19.1	41.2	26.9
1965–1974	13.1	40.5	22.9
Asia	42.6	47.7	70.9
Before 1954	51.5	41.8	79.4
1955–1964	41.6	48.4	73.0
1965–1974	28.6	57.1	52.9
Africa	53.6	41.1	76.8
Before 1954	60.3	37.0	79.9
1955–1964	55.3	36.8	78.1
1965–1974	42.0	51.9	71.1
Israel–Europe	15.6	39.4	22.6
Before 1954	29.7	37.4	38.5
1955–1964	15.3	41.8	24.1
1965–1974	10.8	38.0	15.6
Israel–Asia/Africa	38.3	44.9	61.0
Before 1954	56.5	39.1	84.1
1955–1964	37.5	50.0	67.6
1965–1974	33.3	44.2	51.3

marriage cohort the proportion of parents who are defined as religious is larger than the proportion who define their own homes as religious.

These aggregate comparisons support our earlier inference about significant generational reductions in religiosity levels. However, the value of these data resides in the possibility of tracing directly the influence of parental religious background on the religiosity of the children. For each level of parental religiosity, we can examine the religiosity distribution of the children. The analysis of these "outflows" serves as a basis for evaluating the "inheritance" of religiosity.[10]

One way to summarize these generational data (see Table 5) is to examine the proportion of those whose current level of religious identification is lower than their parents, or higher, or the same. These summary data do not indicate the specific levels of decline, or whether stability reflects high or low levels of religiosity. They are revealing, however, particularly when the details on specific outflows are taken into consideration. (For outflows, see Table A in the Appendix.)

Overall, 44 per cent of the respondents have a lower level of religious self-definition than their definition of the religiosity of their parental home. About half have the same level, and only four per cent indicate a higher level. When we take into account that stability is more likely to be at lower levels of religiosity, it is clear that the population of Israel has experienced major processes of religious secularization, at least in terms of the self-definition of the home.

There is significant variation among Jewish ethnic groups in Israel in the extent of generational decline in religious identification. Israeli-born Jews of Asian/African origin have experienced the greatest declines generationally in religiosity (55 per cent), followed by the Asian/African-born, with the Israeli-born of European origin experiencing the least amount of generational change. Thus, while ethnic differences in religiosity have narrowed among the Israeli-born, religiosity origins vary significantly by ethnic origin. Clearly, the processes that have led to relatively similar levels of religiosity among the native-born have differed by ethnicity. The greater generational stability of the Israeli-born of European origin (61 per cent with the same level of religiosity as their parents) tends to be at lower levels of religiosity, while the Israeli-born of Asian/African origin have the lowest level of generational stability of all ethnic subpopulations.

Consistent with these findings and those presented earlier are the data by marriage cohort. The declines generationally in religiosity are highest among the earlier cohorts. These patterns generally characterize each of the ethnic groups.

---

[10]To the extent that fertility and survivorship vary by religiosity (and there is evidence for the former), the patterns may be biased upward. Clearly a variety of factors affect the representativeness of the parental generation.

TABLE 5. INTERGENERATIONAL CHANGES IN RELIGIOSITY, COMPARING WIFE'S PARENTS' RELIGIOSITY WITH CURRENT RELIGIOSITY, SUMMARY MEASURE, BY ETHNICITY AND MARRIAGE COHORT, JEWISH POPULATION OF ISRAEL

	Decline	Increase	Stability
Total	43.8	4.4	51.6
Before 1954	48.8	4.0	47.2
1955–64	44.6	4.6	51.0
1965–74	36.6	5.1	58.1
East Europe	42.4	5.4	52.4
Before 1954	48.3	4.8	47.1
1955–64	36.2	7.4	56.4
1965–74	28.0	5.6	66.4
West Europe	36.2	6.4	57.4
Before 1954	42.4	5.3	52.3
1955–64	28.1	5.9	66.0
1965–74	33.1	8.4	58.4
Asia	50.7	2.6	46.7
Before 1954	53.4	1.6	44.9
1955–64	52.1	3.2	44.7
1965–74	43.6	3.5	52.9
Africa	48.9	2.6	48.5
Before 1954	48.3	2.6	48.9
1955–64	52.0	2.0	46.0
1965–74	47.4	3.0	49.7
Israel–Europe	32.0	6.7	61.3
Before 1954	41.8	7.7	50.6
1955–64	34.2	5.6	60.2
1965–74	26.4	7.2	66.4
Israel–Asia/Africa	54.8	2.6	42.6
Before 1954	63.0	0.0	36.9
1955–64	66.7	2.8	30.5
1965–74	46.7	3.2	50.0

Taken together, these data document that Israeli society as a whole, and the ethnic subpopulations within it, have undergone a transition toward lower levels of religiosity. But the extent of the transition varies depending on the religious origins of the parents, being greater for those whose parents are more religious, and being continuous for those whose parents are less religious. Moreover, these data suggest that a major part of the explanation of current ethnic differences in religiosity relates to differential religiosity origins. As these religiosity origins change—and the evidence for ethnic convergence in the religiosity of the second generation is clear—the ethnic differential in religiosity should diminish further for third-generation Israelis.

The direct data on changes in *mikveh* point to similar conclusions (Table 6). Overall, the proportion of generational increase in *mikveh* observance is very low (one to two per cent). The proportion of generational decline is highest for the Asian/African group. The degree of *mikveh* observance over two generations is highest for the African-born women, while nonobservance of *mikveh* over two generations is highest for the Israeli-born of European background. If these ethnic groups are viewed in terms of some transition model, it seems reasonable to argue that the shift is from continuous *mikveh* observance (African-born) to continuous non-observance of *mikveh* (Israeli-born of European origin), with a middle, transition group in which the proportion of both generations who observe *mikveh* is equal to the proportion of both generations who do not observe *mikveh*. In this context, the Israeli-born of Asian/African origin are much closer to the European groups than to the Asian/African-born.

The Effects of Israeli Society

Part of the complexity in understanding and analyzing Israeli society arises from the confounding effects of background factors associated with place of origin and the specific effects of Israeli society. We have already noted that ethnic groups have been differentially exposed to modernization before arrival in Israel and have undergone different degrees of religiosity change. In this section, we will focus specifically on the effects of exposure to Israeli society for those who are foreign-born.

Variation in exposure to Israeli society can be measured in several ways. The most direct measure relates to age at arrival. The four ethnic groups were subdivided into those who arrived before and after age 18. If Israeli society has a secularizing effect, we would expect those whose primary socialization is in Israel (i.e., those who arrived in Israel before age 18) to be less religious those who are socialized outside of Israel. These data are presented in Table 7. In general, the hypothesis is confirmed for all six measures and for each of the four ethnic groups.

TABLE 6. OUTFLOW PERCENTAGES AND DISTRIBUTION OF MIKVEH OBSERVANCES OF TWO GENERATIONS BY ETHNICITY, JEWISH POPULATION OF ISRAEL

	Total	East Europe	West Europe	Asia	Africa	Israel–Europe	Israel–Asia/Africa
Outflow							
Mikveh (mother)							
Mikveh (daughter)	40.3	22.0	52.2	39.1	54.1	50.4	26.1
No Mikveh (daughter)	59.7	78.0	47.8	60.9	45.9	49.6	73.9
No Mikveh (mother)							
Mikveh (daughter)	2.5	1.3	2.7	5.3	7.5	1.7	1.0
No Mikveh (daughter)	97.5	98.7	97.3	94.7	92.5	98.3	99.0
Distribution							
Decline	29.6	27.5	15.9	43.2	35.2	11.2	45.1
Increase	1.3	0.8	1.8	1.5	1.7	1.3	0.4
Stability	69.2	71.7	82.3	55.3	73.1	87.4	54.5
A. Two Generational Mikveh	19.9	7.8	17.3	27.7	41.5	11.4	15.9
B. Two Generational No Mikveh	49.3	63.9	65.0	27.6	21.6	76.0	38.6
Ratio: A/B	0.40	0.12	0.27	1.00	1.92	0.15	0.41

TABLE 7. PROPORTION RELIGIOUS FOR SIX MEASURES OF RELIGIOSITY BY AGE AT ARRIVAL IN ISRAEL, ETHNICITY, AND MARRIAGE COHORT, FOREIGN-BORN JEWISH POPULATION OF ISRAEL

Ethnicity, Age at Arrival, and Marriage Cohort	Defines Home as Religious	Religion is Important	Observes Kashrut	Attends Synagogue Regularly	Does Not Ride on Shabbat	Woman Goes to Mikveh
East Europe						
Before Age 18	38.8	39.6	29.7	13.1	12.5	8.3
Before 1954	44.9	47.1	36.0	14.7	14.0	9.6
1955–1964	45.6	44.3	35.4	15.2	12.7	10.1
1965–1974	24.7	25.5	16.3	9.2	10.2	5.1
After Age 18	41.5	35.3	34.6	18.0	18.0	8.4
Before 1954	46.1	36.7	37.8	20.2	21.1	8.8
1955–1964	31.8	36.2	24.6	13.0	8.2	5.8
1965–1974	11.1	18.5	27.3	3.7	3.7	11.1
West Europe						
Before Age 18	41.5	38.8	38.8	20.0	21.6	12.8
Before 1954	44.6	38.2	38.2	23.2	27.3	13.0
1955–1964	48.2	48.2	48.3	31.0	31.0	24.1
1965–1974	32.6	34.7	32.7	10.2	10.2	6.1
After Age 18	57.6	49.4	47.7	31.8	33.1	24.7
Before 1954	68.8	55.3	54.5	42.9	42.9	31.2
1955–1964	52.5	42.5	37.5	20.0	25.0	12.5
1965–1974	38.3	44.1	44.1	20.6	20.6	24.2

Asia						
Before Age 18	70.3	68.4	59.0	27.9	28.2	26.4
Before 1954	77.5	72.5	70.0	41.2	36.2	35.4
1955–1964	68.5	70.8	56.2	28.1	30.9	25.8
1965–1974	67.6	61.4	55.3	17.5	17.5	20.4
After Age 18	71.3	76.1	62.6	41.9	36.5	36.7
Before 1954	71.1	75.2	65.8	44.7	39.1	38.7
1955–1964	73.7	71.0	50.0	26.3	23.7	28.9
1965–1974	68.2	90.9	59.1	45.5	36.4	31.8
Africa						
Before Age 18	74.4	68.1	64.7	23.7	26.4	29.1
Before 1954	79.5	74.3	69.2	38.5	41.0	44.7
1955–1964	72.2	70.0	67.8	24.4	27.0	25.8
1965–1974	74.3	64.7	60.8	17.6	20.6	26.5
After Age 18	87.3	79.3	78.9	52.7	49.4	57.6
Before 1954	91.0	80.5	81.3	54.9	48.6	54.9
1955–1964	82.5	77.8	74.6	49.2	47.6	57.1
1965–1974	78.6	75.0	75.0	46.4	53.6	70.4

The data show that ethnic differences in religiosity levels are clear and consistent only among those who arrive in Israel after age 18. For those socialized in Israel, however, the detailed ethnic pattern of religiosity is not clear for all religiosity measures. There is nevertheless a clear two-fold ethnic differential in religiosity (European vs. Asian/African) among the foreign-born socialized largely in Israel. This pattern parallels that noted earlier among native-born Israelis.

The effects of Israel on the religiosity of the foreign-born may also be observed when the ethnic groups are subdivided into those married in Israel and those married abroad, or when the per cent of time in Israel is examined. This latter measure is based on the number of years spent in Israel divided by the age of the woman (Table B in the Appendix). We shall not repeat the details except to note the consistency of these data with those based on age at arrival.

It seems clear from these data that socialization, marriage, and time spent in Israel have a secularizing effect on Jews from a variety of ethnic backgrounds, and that exposure to Israeli society has resulted in processes of ethnic convergence in religiosity. In general, it may be argued that the greater the exposure to Israeli society, the lower the level of religiosity. Hence, the least religious are the Israeli-born; the most religious are the foreign-born socialized and married abroad; and the intermediate groups are the foreign-born socialized and married in Israel. These conclusions most clearly apply to those of Asian and African origins, whose changes in religiosity are most dramatically associated with exposure to Israel.

These patterns suggest that two major factors are involved in the understanding of ethnic differentials in religiosity and the processes of secularization in Israel: the religiosity of the parental household and exposure to Israeli society.

Educational Attainment and Religiosity

One of the most important indicators of social change and differentiation in Israeli society is the level of educational attainment. Not only does the latter affect socioeconomic status and stratification, but is also associated with secularization and the declining importance of religious identification and observance. Educational levels have increased for all ethnic groups in Israel, and ethnic differences in educational attainment have narrowed, particularly for the Israeli-born.[11]

---

[11]See Calvin Goldscheider, "The Demography of Asian and African Jews in Israel," in Joseph Maier and Chaim Waxman, (eds.), *Ethnicity, Identity, and History: Essays in Memory of W. Cahnman* (New Brunswick, 1983).

The most direct question that may be addressed with the data relates to the overall pattern of religiosity for various levels of education. Data in Table 8 (as in subsequent tables) present these patterns for the education of women, although the data for men show virtually identical results. Overall, the data indicate that those with less than eight years of schooling have the highest levels of religiosity on all measures. As the level of education increases, the per cent of those religious declines from 20 to 12, while the per cent of those secular more than doubles from 19 to 47.

Nevertheless, the relationship between years of education and religiosity is not monotonic, and the patterns are not similar for all religiosity indicators. For the two subjective measures and *kashrut* observance, the pattern of religiosity by educational level tends to be relatively smooth, declining gradually as the years of education increase, up to high school completion (12 years). For the other three measures (synagogue attendance, *shabbat,* and *mikveh*) the distinction is largely between those with the lowest level of education (0–8 years) and higher levels. Most interestingly, for five out of the six measures there is a pattern of increase in religiosity between those with 12 and those with 13 or more years of education. This upturn in religiosity among the most educated characterizes only the most recent marriage cohort for all measures. Illustrative of these patterns are comparisons between the per cent religious by cohort for the highest and lowest educational categories. For those with 13 or more years of education, the per cent who are religious *increases* from 8.6 to 15 from the oldest to the youngest cohort; for those with less than eight years of education the per cent who are religious *decreases* from 23 to 13.5 from the oldest to the youngest cohort.

In order to further clarify this upturn in religiosity among the most educated of the youngest cohort, an analysis of ethnic variation is necessary. We have already suggested that the factors associated with ethnic differences in religiosity are complex and relate in part to the differential religious origins of the various ethnic groups. Another element that may be involved in ethnic variation and change in religiosity is differential educational attainment. The question may be posed whether ethnic differences in religiosity remain when educational differences between ethnic groups are equalized.

Data in Table 9 show that, almost without exception, for each of the six ethnic-generation groups and for each of the six measures of religiosity, the least educated have a higher proportion who are religious than do those with nine or more years of education. At the same time, the upturn in religiosity among the more educated characterizes all ethnic groups and each measure of religiosity. Hence, the general relationship between educational attainment and religiosity is not specific to particular ethnic groups in Israel nor to particular dimensions of religiosity.

TABLE 8. PROPORTION RELIGIOUS FOR SIX MEASURES OF RELIGIOSITY BY EDUCATION OF WOMEN AND MARRIAGE COHORT

Years of Education	Defines Home as Religious	Religion is Important	Observes Kashrut	Attends Synagogue Regularly	Does Not Ride on Shabbat	Woman Goes to Mikveh	Per Cent Religious	Per Cent Secular
Total								
0–8	68.8	64.7	60.4	34.8	34.7	32.1	20.0	19.2
9–11	51.4	51.3	42.3	16.5	16.4	12.4	7.3	33.9
12	43.1	38.1	34.0	16.7	15.9	14.1	10.6	46.8
13+	41.8	38.8	37.0	18.2	19.2	15.3	12.3	47.0
Before 1954								
0–8	69.3	65.6	61.5	39.3	38.0	33.9	22.8	17.7
9–11	51.7	47.4	45.3	22.7	21.6	12.2	9.6	35.1
12	51.4	39.2	38.7	20.4	17.1	14.4	11.1	41.7
13+	48.3	37.9	34.5	14.7	19.8	10.3	8.6	42.2
1955–1964								
0–8	69.5	65.2	60.1	31.1	31.7	30.3	17.3	20.3
9–11	52.3	58.8	42.1	16.7	16.7	12.0	8.4	31.2
12	43.0	42.2	33.9	19.8	20.7	19.8	16.5	45.5
13+	37.4	35.3	32.8	16.4	17.4	13.5	11.0	52.5
1965–1974								
0–8	64.4	59.7	56.1	23.8	26.8	28.0	13.5	23.3
9–11	50.7	49.0	40.2	11.1	11.8	13.0	4.5	34.7
12	35.4	34.4	29.6	11.1	11.6	10.1	6.4	52.7
13+	42.4	41.6	40.9	21.0	20.3	18.8	14.9	45.8

The question as to whether religiosity differences among ethnic groups in Israel reflect differentials in educational attainment is more complex. In part, the answer depends on which ethnic differences are examined, which measures of religiosity are used, and which generation is studied. For example, comparing ethnic differences in religiosity among the foreign-born reveals that religiosity differences between West European women and East European women are not a function of educational levels. In contrast, religiosity differences between Asian-born women and African-born women only characterize the lowest level of education. For those with nine or more years of education, the level of religiosity of Asian-born women is as high or higher than that of African-born women for most religiosity measures. Thus, the overall higher level of religiosity of African-born women as compared to Asian-born women is clearly related to the generally lower educational levels of the former. As educational levels increase, the level of religiosity of African-born women declines significantly, to below that of Asian-born women.

Comparing the religiosity of European-born women to that of Asian/ African-born women reveals significantly different patterns among the six measures of religiosity. For the two subjective measures of religiosity and *kashrut* observance, the Asian/African-born women are consistently more religious than European-born women at all educational levels. The impact of educational level on ethnic differences is most significant for synagogue, *mikveh,* and *shabbat* observance. At the upper levels of educational attainment, even the broad distinctions between European-born women and African/Asian-born women are blurred for *kashrut* and *mikveh* observance, and regular synagogue attendance.

If higher levels of education have an equalizing effect on the religiosity differences between foreign-born Asian women and foreign-born African women as well as between foreign-born European women and foreign-born Asian/African women, what effects do they have on the Israeli-born? Comparing the religiosity levels of the Israeli-born of different ethnic groups shows that Israeli-born women of Asian/African origin are more likely than those of European origin to define their homes as religious at all educational levels. However, for all other measures of religiosity, the more educated among the Israeli-born of Asian/African origin (particularly those with 12 years of education) have similar or lower levels of religiosity than do those of European origin. Thus, among the foreign-born, higher education reverses the levels of synagogue attendance, as well as *shabbat* and *mikveh* observance between European and Asian/Africans; among the Israeli-born, ethnic differences among the more educated are reversed for these measures as well as for *kashrut* observance.

TABLE 9. PROPORTION RELIGIOUS FOR SIX MEASURES OF RELIGIOSITY BY ETHNICITY AND EDUCATION OF WOMEN

Ethnicity and Years of Education	Defines Home as Religious	Religion is Important	Observes Kashrut	Attends Synagogue Regularly	Does Not Ride on Shabbat	Woman Goes to Mikveh	Per Cent Religious	Per Cent Secular
East Europe								
0–8	50.2	45.2	40.4	22.6	22.3	10.9	8.3	33.2
9–11	40.8	38.3	36.5	16.0	16.0	7.8	6.8	42.9
12	29.9	26.3	22.2	10.4	9.0	7.6	6.3	60.4
13+	31.6	30.9	24.3	9.2	9.9	5.3	3.9	57.9
West Europe								
0–8	58.7	52.1	52.2	39.1	32.6	28.3	26.1	34.8
9–11	46.5	45.1	40.3	24.7	27.8	14.1	12.7	42.3
12	49.2	45.9	37.7	23.0	24.6	13.3	13.3	43.3
13+	50.0	38.9	45.4	24.1	27.8	21.3	20.4	41.7
Asia								
0–8	72.1	72.6	64.5	36.5	37.9	35.1	21.8	14.6
9–11	65.1	70.6	46.5	21.7	18.6	16.4	9.4	18.0
12	62.5	54.2	54.2	18.8	8.3	12.5	6.3	22.9
13+	75.0	72.2	58.3	36.1	25.0	36.1	22.2	22.2

Africa								
0–8	86.1	78.4	78.4	46.6	47.6	52.9	31.3	8.5
9–11	68.0	63.1	56.3	17.5	13.7	17.6	5.9	21.8
12	78.0	68.0	62.0	36.0	34.0	36.7	20.4	14.3
13+	73.3	72.3	72.2	5.6	16.7	33.3	5.6	16.7
Israel–Europe								
0–8	56.4	48.7	46.2	17.9	23.1	15.4	12.8	28.2
9–11	29.8	33.4	24.6	9.6	10.5	6.1	4.4	54.4
12	35.3	31.7	29.4	14.0	16.2	14.7	13.2	55.1
13+	36.7	33.9	33.9	18.5	20.2	14.2	12.1	50.6
Israel–Asia/Africa								
0–8	64.3	57.2	52.0	27.6	21.4	20.6	8.2	20.6
9–11	61.7	58.9	52.3	12.1	14.0	15.9	5.6	23.4
12	38.7	31.8	22.7	9.1	6.8	4.5	2.3	47.7
13+	45.8	50.0	45.8	16.7	16.7	16.7	16.7	33.3

The narrowing of some specific ethnic differences in religiosity at higher levels of education raises the issue of greater or lesser polarization for different levels of education. The evidence seems to suggest that greater religious polarization is more characteristic of those with higher than lower levels of education. While some of the traditional ethnic differences in religiosity characteristic of the less educated are altered as educational levels increase, new patterns seem to be emerging which widen ethnic differences in religiosity. Hence, the gap between the religious and the secular (defined in terms of each measure and in terms of the combined index) is greater for the two higher levels of education than for the two lower levels of education.

It should be noted that detailed data on the relationship between education and religiosity among ethnic groups within marriage cohorts (Table C, Appendix) do not alter these basic findings.

The lack of monotonic decline in religiosity with increasing levels of education for almost all measures and among all ethnic-generational groupings, and the striking upturn in religiosity among the more educated of the most recent marriage cohort, suggest that other factors in addition to increasing levels of educational attainment function to reduce religiosity levels. One possibility is that we have conceptualized the issue incorrectly. The argument has been made that educational attainment "determines" religiosity. Perhaps, the relationship should be viewed in reverse, i.e., the more religious are as likely or more likely to emphasize higher levels of education. It is not that "the higher the education, the lower the religiosity" but "the more religious, the greater the emphasis on educational attainment." Indirect tests of this alternative view, however, suggest that this is not the case. Data in Appendix D show that for each ethnic group, a higher proportion of those from more religious homes have lower levels of education than do those from less religious homes.

The upturn in religiosity among the most educated of the youngest marriage cohort for all ethnic groups and all measures of religiosity remains puzzling. It is difficult to attribute this increase to events in Israel during the time when these families were formed (i.e., 1965–74), particularly the Six Day War and its aftermath, since it is not clear why these events would have affected the religiosity only of those with 13 or more years of education. Nor can we attribute this pattern to recent selective immigration of the more religious Jews from Western countries, since the patterns characterize the native-born Israelis of both ethnic groups. This upturn in religiosity, therefore, remains unexplained. Future research should attempt to clarify in more detail its importance and sources.[12]

---

[12]One possibility relates to the problems associated with years of education as a measure. This includes an unknown number of cases where 13 or more years may include advanced

Religious Education and Religiosity

One dimension of the educational experience in Israel that is a basis for continuity of religiosity patterns is exposure to religious education. Religious institutions at all educational levels, from elementary school to universities and technical colleges, are available to provide specific religious instruction as well as a religious context for formal socialization. The relationship between exposure to religious education and subsequent religiosity may be viewed in two theoretical contexts. First, and most simply, exposure to religious values and ideas through formal education may result directly in higher levels of religiosity in adult life. Secondly, those who are exposed to religious education are more likely to come from more religious origins than those not exposed to religious education. Hence, the greater religiosity of those exposed to religious education may largely reflect religiosity origins rather than the specific effects of religious education.

The data available for analysis relate to whether the respondent has been exposed to formal religious education and not to the intensity or type of exposure. These data will be presented only for those born in Israel. This is done to eliminate the confounding influences of the sole availability or non-availability of religious educational institutions in various countries of origin. Thus, the question that we shall investigate relates to the effects of religious education on religiosity among those whose educational experience was in Israel.

Twenty-six per cent of Israeli-born women of European origin and 41 per cent of Israeli-born women of Asian/African origin have had at least some exposure to formal religious education. The data in Table 10 indicate significant differences in all measures of religiosity between those with some exposure to religious education and those with none. For both ethnic origin populations, the effects of religious education are much sharper for synagogue attendance, *shabbat* travel, and *mikveh* observance than for the other three measures.

The critical question relates to the impact of religious education on religiosity, controlling for religiosity origins. The data show that the *net* impact of religious education on religiosity is significant. This characterizes both ethnic origin groups and each of the six measures of religiosity. Thus, the effects of religious education on current religiosity reflect more than the fact that those who are exposed to religious education tend to come from more religious backgrounds. Neither variable can be reduced simply to the other.

---

religious studies. In any case, 13 years or more of education does not necessarily imply college or university attendance. Our data do not allow for the separation of these various types of secular and religious educational experiences.

TABLE 10. PROPORTION RELIGIOUS FOR VARIOUS MEASURES OF RELIGIOSITY BY RELIGIOUS EDUCATION (WOMEN), RELIGIOSITY ORIGINS, AND ETHNICITY, ISRAELI-BORN JEWISH POPULATION OF ISRAEL

	Defines Home as Religious	Religion is Important	Observes Kashrut	Attends Synagogue Regularly	Does Not Ride on Shabbat	Woman Goes to Mikveh	N
Israel—Europe							
Religious Education	76.1	73.2	70.3	51.4	55.1	42.8	138
No Religious Education	22.7	20.9	18.3	3.0	4.3	2.3	398
Origins—Religious							
Religious Education	82.4	76.8	75.2	56.0	60.0	47.2	125
No Religious Education	41.5	28.6	26.3	4.1	5.3	3.5	171
Origins—Non-Religious							
Religious Education	15.4	38.5	23.1	7.7	7.7	0.0	13
No Religious Education	8.4	14.9	12.3	2.2	3.5	1.3	227
Israel—Asia/Africa							
Religious Education	64.2	60.5	58.7	29.4	28.4	23.9	109
No Religious Education	52.2	47.2	38.4	8.2	5.7	9.4	159
Origins—Religious							
Religious Education	68.0	61.0	62.0	31.0	31.0	26.0	100
No Religious Education	63.9	56.5	47.5	9.0	7.4	11.5	122
Origins—Non-Religious							
Religious Education	22.2*	55.6*	22.2*	11.1*	0.0*	0.0*	9
No Religious Education	13.5	16.2	8.1	5.4	0.0	2.7	37

*Less than ten cases.

The effects of religious education on religiosity are more pronounced for Israelis of European origin than for Israelis of Asian/African origin; there is a much stronger selectivity effect among the former, and the correlation between religious education and religiosity origins is higher for them. Indeed, the level of religiosity of Israelis of European origin is higher than that of Israelis of Asian/African origin among those with some exposure to religious education (for those defining their parental homes as religious). For those with no exposure to religious education, the religiosity level of the Asian/African group is higher than that of the European group.

In sum, the evidence clearly points to the important influence of religious education on current religiosity, whether the parental home is defined as religious or not religious. The impact of religious education on the religiosity of European-origin Israelis is greater than the impact on Israelis of Asian/African origin, thus implying that for the latter, religiosity origins is the key factor in shaping current religiosity. The combined effects of religiosity origins and religious education on current levels of religiosity are substantial, more so for Israelis of European origin than for Israelis of Asian/African origin, and more so for subjective measures of religiosity and *kashrut* than for synagogue attendance, and *shabbat* and *mikveh* observance.

Conclusion

This analysis of structure and change in religiosity in Israel provides systematic evidence about a matter that has been referred to as "potentially the sharpest dividing line in [Israeli] society."[13] There is no claim that we have examined all the various aspects of religiosity; the data presented are limited by their focus on specific dimensions and their cross-sectional character. Nevertheless, we have moved beyond the one-dimensional and much oversimplified analysis of religiosity characteristic of previous research. We have emphasized the importance of examining separately and in detail the subjective as well as behavioral aspects of religious identification and observance. The analysis of religious origins, however limited by its perceptional-*post facto* rationalization biases, has added a dynamic dimension to the cross-sectional character of the data. Comparisons between first-generation (foreign-born) and second-generation (Israeli-born) Israelis and between various marriage cohorts reflect, inferentially, processes of change and continuity in religiosity.

Several major themes emerge from the empirical details that have been presented. One is that religiosity is clearly multidimensional and complex

---

[13]Elihu Katz, "Culture and Communication in Israel: The Transformation of Tradition," *Jewish Journal of Sociology,* June 1973, p. 9.

in Israeli society. Subjective measures of religious self-definition and the importance of Judaism in everyday life obviously have a different meaning than do such observances as *mikveh, shabbat,* and synagogue attendance. While those who observe these aspects of Judaism tend in large part to see religion as important and to define their households as religious, the reverse is not true. The only measure that is similar structurally to subjective measures of religiosity is *kashrut* observance. No doubt, this is related to the relative ease of *kashrut* observance in Israel and its familial implications. In contrast, the other ritual items tend to be much more individualistic. Indeed, travel on *shabbat,* which has become the accepted norm for the large majority of Israel's population, may be related to familial visits or to leisure activities of the nuclear family unit. An analysis of religiosity that ignores these dimensions or combines them artificially into an overall index will obscure rather than clarify the nature of religious identification and observance in Israel.

A second theme that emerges from this study is the process of change in religiosity that may be described as secularization. Secularization clearly has been greater for some rituals than others, but the decline in religiosity seems to be a broad societal characteristic, specific neither to particular ethnic groups nor to selected dimensions of religiosity. The modernization of Israeli society has clearly resulted in the secularization of the various subgroups that make up Israel's heterogeneous Jewish population. Nevertheless, secularization is a process that does not necessarily result in the total abandonment of all forms of religiosity, at the same pace, by all groups. Placed in a broader perspective, the secularization process implies the transformation of traditional religious observances, rather than assimilation or the loss of Jewish identification. Perhaps new forms of religious expression are emerging that are more closely attuned to the national experiences of Jews in Israel. These phenomena have not been studied in this context, but must be included in order to clarify the broader picture.

A third theme that emerges from the data is the importance of ethnic differences in religiosity. Differences in religiosity origins, educational attainment, and exposure to religious education account for a large part of the overall ethnic differences in religiosity. Ethnic differences not only characterize the broad categories of European and Asian/African Jews, but differentiate within both groups—between Jews from Western and Eastern Europe and between Jews from Asia and Africa. All indicators of change reveal dramatic declines in religiosity among the Asian/African group, and continuing reductions in religious identification and observance among the Europeans. Indeed, ethnic differences in religiosity among the Israeli-born have narrowed considerably. Given the powerful effects of religious origins on religiosity, it seems reasonable to expect even further reductions in religiosity by ethnic origin among the third generation, as their religious origins become much more similar. Indeed, convergences in religiosity patterns may be viewed as yet another dimension of general processes of convergence in Israeli society.[14]

Our findings on the relationship between years of education and changing religiosity patterns are only partly what might have been expected. While the least educated have the highest levels of religiosity, systematic declines in religiosity with higher levels of education are not observed. Indeed, the upturn in religiosity among the most educated of the youngest cohort remains puzzling and unexplained by our analysis. Neither selective recent migration nor events in Israel in the post-1967 period account satisfactorily for the upturn. While educational attainment equalizes some of the traditional ethnic differences in religiosity, ethnic variation and change are not solely a reflection of educational attainment.

The secularization of Israeli society has not only blurred the traditional ethnic differences in religiosity, but has also resulted in greater concentration of the population at the extremes of religious and secular identification and observance. The evidence suggests that the ethnic factor in religiosity will diminish in the future. At the same time, religious-secular divisions will become sharper. To the extent that these processes continue into the future, we can expect social and political issues associated with religiosity to become more pronounced and divisive in Israeli society.

---

[14]On fertility convergence, see Friedlander and Goldscheider, "Immigration, Social Change, and Cohort Fertility," *op. cit.*

APPENDIX TABLE A. OUTFLOW PERCENTAGES (INHERITANCE) FROM RELIGIOSITY OF WIFE'S PARENTAL HOME TO CURRENT RELIGIOSITY BY ETHNICITY, JEWISH POPULATION OF ISRAEL

	Total	East Europe	West Europe	Asia	Africa	Israel–Europe	Israel–Asia/Africa
Parents' Home Very Religious							
Very Religious	26.7	22.7	42.5	22.0	28.6	47.6	8.6
Religious	60.4	56.1	49.3	67.7	62.7	41.7	68.6
Not Religious	10.5	17.8	6.8	7.9	7.9	8.3	17.1
Very Not Religious	2.3	3.2	1.4	2.4	0.8	2.4	5.7
Parents' Home Religious							
Very Religious	1.3	1.5	1.7	0.7	3.1	0.5	0.0
Religious	54.9	44.4	54.3	62.6	71.5	46.2	56.9
Not Religious	37.2	43.5	31.9	33.2	22.3	47.2	39.0
Very Not Religious	6.6	10.5	12.1	3.5	3.1	6.1	4.1
Parents' Home Not Religious							
Very Religious	0.0	0.0	0.0	0.0	0.0	0.0	0.0
Religious	10.9	9.0	14.7	15.0	23.8	9.0	10.5
Not Religious	81.3	82.5	72.0	85.0	71.4	82.4	86.8
Very Not Religious	7.9	8.5	13.3	0.0	4.8	8.2	2.6
Parents' Home Very Not Religious							
Very Religious	0.0	0.0	0.0	0.0	*	0.0	*
Religious	1.7	14.0	4.8	27.8	*	8.3	*
Not Religious	17.9	18.0	19.0	16.7	*	21.7	*
Very Not Religious	67.9	68.0	76.0	55.6	*	70.0	*

*Less than ten cases.

APPENDIX TABLE B. MEASURES OF RELIGIOSITY BY PLACE OF MARRIAGE AND PER CENT TIME SPENT IN ISRAEL*, ETHNICITY, FOREIGN-BORN JEWISH POPULATION IN ISRAEL

	Defines Home as Religious	Religion is Important	Observes Kashrut	Attends Synagogue Regularly	Does Not Ride on Shabbat	Woman Goes to Mikveh
East Europe						
Married in Israel	38.5	38.1	28.1	11.7	10.3	7.1
Married Abroad	43.8	36.8	39.5	22.7	23.7	10.7
Majority Israel	40.4	37.7	29.3	13.1	12.4	6.9
Majority Abroad	39.7	36.2	37.3	19.7	20.4	10.0
West Europe						
Married in Israel	43.0	40.9	39.2	19.5	21.1	12.1
Married Abroad	65.4	51.2	51.2	41.7	41.7	33.7
Majority Israel	47.6	43.4	43.1	24.4	26.9	16.3
Majority Abroad	55.5	46.4	45.5	30.9	30.9	24.8
Asia						
Married in Israel	70.9	69.2	58.5	28.6	26.8	26.2
Married Abroad	68.4	75.9	64.5	46.8	44.7	40.7
Majority Israel	70.8	69.7	60.6	30.5	29.8	29.0
Majority Abroad	69.2	76.2	58.5	40.8	34.0	34.2
Africa						
Married in Israel	74.6	69.4	65.5	26.1	29.7	33.1
Married Abroad	90.0	81.2	82.3	56.9	49.7	58.6
Majority Israel	76.1	67.3	64.0	25.1	26.4	29.1
Majority Abroad	86.5	81.5	81.0	53.7	52.6	61.4

*Majority equals more than 50 per cent of total years spent in Israel (or Abroad).

APPENDIX TABLE C. PROPORTION RELIGIOUS FOR SIX MEASURES OF RELIGIOSITY BY ETHNICITY, MARRIAGE COHORT, AND EDUCATION* OF WOMEN

Ethnicity, Education, and Marriage Cohort	Defines Home as Religious	Religion is Important	Observes Kashrut	Attends Synagogue Regularly	Does Not Ride on Shabbat	Woman Goes to Mikveh	Per Cent Religious	Per Cent Secular
East Europe								
Low Educ.								
Before 1954	51.7	47.8	41.5	24.2	25.1	11.1	8.7	30.9
1955–1964	52.2	39.1	37.0	19.6	13.0	10.9	6.5	37.0
1965–1974	16.6	25.0	33.3	8.3	8.3	8.3	8.3	58.3
High Educ.								
Before 1954	40.5	33.3	34.2	14.2	14.2	7.3	6.6	48.2
1955–1964	33.3	40.2	27.5	11.8	9.8	6.9	6.9	52.9
1965–1974	22.1	23.7	15.8	7.9	8.8	6.1	2.7	63.7
West Europe								
Low Educ.								
Before 1954	71.0	64.5	67.7	51.6	45.2	35.5	35.5	19.4
1955–1964	—	—	—	—	—	—	—	—
1965–1974	—	—	—	—	—	—	—	—
High Educ.								
Before 1954	55.5	42.4	42.0	29.7	34.0	20.2	18.2	38.4
1955–1964	50.8	45.9	44.3	24.6	29.5	18.0	18.0	41.0
1965–1974	37.9	40.5	39.2	16.5	16.5	12.8	12.8	48.7

Asia								
Low Educ.								
Before 1954	73.0	75.4	67.5	44.0	41.9	41.8	26.7	11.2
1955–1964	71.6	70.2	61.0	29.8	33.3	27.7	16.3	19.1
1965–1974	69.1	66.6	61.9	23.8	33.3	28.6	16.7	14.3
High Educ.								
Before 1954	71.1	65.8	57.9	28.9	13.7	13.2	7.9	10.5
1955–1964	66.2	72.7	44.2	24.7	23.4	22.1	16.9	20.8
1965–1974	64.3	63.2	52.0	20.4	14.3	18.6	7.2	22.7
Africa								
Low Educ.								
Before 1954	90.0	80.7	82.9	54.3	53.6	58.6	37.9	5.7
1955–1964	81.0	76.0	76.0	43.0	43.0	48.5	25.3	11.1
1965–1974	84.6	77.4	71.7	32.1	39.6	45.3	23.1	11.5
High Educ.								
Before 1954	80.5	73.2	61.0	36.6	24.4	27.5	15.0	16.0
1955–1964	67.3	67.3	59.6	17.3	19.6	19.2	7.8	25.5
1965–1974	69.2	60.2	59.0	16.7	17.9	27.3	9.1	19.5
Israel–Europe								
Low Educ.								
Before 1954	59.1	45.5	50.0	18.2	27.3	18.2	13.6	27.3
1955–1964	45.5	54.6	36.4	9.1	18.2	9.1	9.1	27.3
1965–1974	—	—	—	—	—	—	—	—
High Educ.								
Before 1954	45.6	38.3	32.4	13.2	19.1	11.8	8.8	45.6
1955–1964	34.1	30.8	29.2	16.8	17.8	14.1	11.4	54.3
1965–1974	32.3	33.6	31.1	14.8	15.6	11.5	10.7	53.3

Israel–Asia/Africa

Low Educ.								
Before 1954	74.3	68.5	60.0	42.9	31.4	29.4	17.6	14.7
1955–1964	60.0	55.0	50.0	15.0	15.0	15.0	5.0	20.0
1965–1974	58.1	48.8	46.5	20.9	16.3	16.3	2.3	25.6
High Educ.								
Before 1954	81.8	63.6	81.8	27.3	18.2	0.0	0.0	9.1
1955–1964	40.4	50.0	34.6	7.7	7.7	7.7	3.8	32.7
1965–1974	57.2	50.0	44.6	12.5	14.3	17.0	8.0	32.1

*Low Education equals less than eight years; High Education equals more than nine years.

RELIGIOSITY PATTERNS / 39

APPENDIX TABLE D. PROPORTION OF WOMEN WITH ONLY AN ELEMENTARY SCHOOL EDUCATION AND WITH 13 YEARS OR MORE OF EDUCATION BY RELIGIOUS ORIGINS AND ETHNICITY

Years of Education	Parental Household of Women			
	Very Religious	Religious	Not Religious	Very Not Religious
East Europe				
0–8	49.7	36.8	29.9	12.0
13+	14.6	18.1	22.3	48.0
West Europe				
0–8	23.3	14.8	12.0	9.5
13+	28.8	38.3	44.0	42.9
Asia				
0–8	70.1	60.2	61.5	33.3
13+	5.3	6.3	5.1	16.7
Africa				
0–8	72.6	53.1	52.0*	—
13+	3.2	4.7	4.0*	—
Israel—Europe				
0–8	19.0	8.0	2.2	3.3
13+	38.1	45.3	49.2	51.7
Israel—Asia/Africa				
0–8	39.4	31.7	39.1*	—
13+	6.7	8.1	15.2*	—

*Not Religious includes Very Not Religious.

Reform and Conservative Judaism in Israel: A Social and Religious Profile

by EPHRAIM TABORY

POWERFUL FORCES are currently at work in Israeli society to modify Orthodox Judaism in the direction of greater conservatism.[1] On a state level, efforts are being made to apply the *halakhah* to many spheres of public life—to enforce Sabbath prohibitions against public entertainment, soccer games, and El Al flights.[2] The Orthodox *yeshivot* and the chief rabbis are also becoming increasingly militant in their demands. It is in this atmosphere that the Reform and Conservative denominations in Israel are seeking to become established Jewish movements on an equal footing with Orthodoxy.

There would appear to be a market for Reform and Conservative Judaism in Israel. While about 17 per cent of Israel's Jews classify themselves as "religious" (basically co-terminous with Orthodox),[3] it is estimated that 75 per cent of the population observe a "non-secular" life style.[4] Many among the latter group could presumably be attracted to the more liberal forms of religion offered by Reform and Conservative Judaism. In fact, however, these movements have met with only a limited response in Israel. Of the

Note: This study was supported, in part, by a grant from the National Institute of Mental Health, United States Health Service (grant number IR 03 MH 24972-01A1). Appreciation is also expressed to the Memorial Foundation for Jewish Culture and Bar-Ilan University for fellowships during the study period. Bernard Lazerwitz made many useful suggestions during the course of this study, and I am very much indebted to him. Thanks are also extended to the leaders and members of the Reform and Conservative movements in Israel for their full cooperation.

[1] On Judaism and Jewish practices in Israel, see Ervin Birnbaum, *The Politics of Compromise: State and Religion in Israel* (Rutherford, 1970); Samuel Clement Leslie, *The Rift in Israel: Religious Authority and Secular Democracy* (London, 1971); Norman L. Zucker, *The Coming Crises in Israel: Private Faith and Public Policy* (Cambridge, 1973); S. Zalman Abramov, *Perpetual Dilemma, Jewish Religion in the Jewish State* (Rutherford, 1976); and Zvi Yaron, "Religion in Israel," AJYB, Vol. 76, 1976, pp. 41–90.

[2] Fifty-six of the 83 items contained in the coalition agreement to the tenth Knesset (signed on August 4, 1981 by representatives of the Likud, National Religious, Agudat Israel, and Tami parties) deal, directly or indirectly, with religious matters.

[3] Yehuda Ben Meir and Peri Kedem, "Index of Religiosity of the Jewish Population of Israel," *Megamot* (Hebrew), February 1979, pp. 353–362.

[4] See Sammy Smooha, *Israel, Pluralism and Conflict* (London, 1978), p. 73.

more than 6,000 synagogues in the country,[5] only 40 (with a total membership of about 2,000 families) are affiliated with either the Israel Movement
for Progressive Judaism (Reform) or the Movement of Masorati Judaism
(Conservative).[6] The purpose of this article is to describe the social and
religious characteristics of these movements and to analyze their possible
impact on the future of religious life in Israel.

Establishment of Reform and Conservative Judaism in Israel

An initial attempt to establish a non-Orthodox form of Judaism in Israel
was made by Rabbi Max Elk, an immigrant from Germany. In 1935 he
founded a liberal congregation, Beth El, in Haifa, where he also set up the
Leo Baeck School in 1939.[7] The school maintains close ties with Reform
Judaism (it came under the formal auspices of the World Union for Progressive Judaism in 1971) and is currently headed by an American expatriate
Reform rabbi, Robert Samuels.

Beth El congregation existed for only a few years. The generally anti-
Zionist attitude of early Reform Judaism[8] was a primary cause of its dissolution.[9] A pamphlet describing the Reform movement in Israel does not even
mention its pre-state history.[10] In any event, it is clear that the Reform
movement in Israel had its "modern" beginnings only in 1958, with the
founding of the Harel synagogue in Jerusalem. There are now about 12
Reform congregations which hold regular Saturday services; all but four
were founded before 1970.

The first Conservative congregation was also established by a liberal
immigrant rabbi from Germany. David Wilhelm founded the Emet
Ve'Emuna congregation in Jerusalem in 1937. The World Council of Synagogues (Conservative) sought to establish a presence in Jerusalem in the
1930's, by constructing what is today one of Jerusalem's most prestigious
synagogues, Yeshurun. The religious adherence of the congregants,
however, led the synagogue to adopt an Orthodox pattern of worship. The

---

[5]Eliezer Don-Yehiya, *Religion in Israel* (Hebrew), (Jerusalem, 1975), p. 37.

[6]Mevakshe Derech ("Seekers of the Way"), a congregation established in Jerusalem in 1962,
is an independent liberal synagogue that encompasses several dozen families. Its style of service
is similar to that found in Reform synagogues, but the congregation is unaffiliated with any
religious organization.

[7]Meir Elk, "First Steps in the History of Our Movement in Israel," *Shalhevet* (Hebrew), 1,
1969, pp. 9–12.

[8]See David Polish, *Renew Our Days: The Zionist Issue in Reform Judaism* (Jerusalem, 1976),
for a discussion of the changes that have taken place in the attitude of Reform Judaism toward
Zionism.

[9]Ze'ev Harari, "Chapters in the History of the Movement for Progressive Judaism in Israel,"
(Hebrew), seminar paper, Hebrew Union College, Jerusalem, 1974.

[10]Shlomo Cohen, *Not to Negate Have We Come, But Rather to Pave the Way* (Hebrew),
(Ramat Gan, n.d.).

Conservative movement in Israel is larger, though younger, than the Reform movement; about 30 Conservative congregations hold regular services, and all but three of these were founded after 1970.

The manner in which Reform and Conservative synagogues have been founded is indicative of the demand for such congregations in Israel. The driving force behind the creation of many of the Reform congregations has been either a movement rabbi (one rabbi was responsible for the establishment of four different congregations) or personnel from the national movement office. In contrast, Conservative synagogues have generally been founded by a nucleus of American expatriates who, desirous of establishing such congregations, approached the national movement for assistance.

Only a few congregations have their own facilities; most Reform and Conservative groups use rented halls and school buildings. This situation has enabled state-religious authorities to hinder the congregations. Some institutions have allegedly been threatened with removal of *kashrut* certification, if they allowed non-Orthodox congregations the use of their facilities.[11] The efforts of Reform Jews in Tel Aviv to obtain permission to build a synagogue were thwarted for years by the religious parties in the municipal coalition. In one instance, permission to perform a wedding was withheld from an Orthodox rabbi because the ceremony was to be held in the hall of a Conservative congregation.[12]

The Israeli government has no "official" policy with regard to the Reform and Conservative movements in Israel. Local religious officials and local councils either render assistance or seek to impede developments, depending on the personalities and coalition politics prevailing at given times and places. In some communities, congregations have been sold land for the construction of synagogues for mere nominal sums. Even the national ministry of religious affairs has granted money to congregations for educational purposes, although the sums involved have not been listed under the ministry's regular budget lines.[13]

The legal system in Israel entrusts issues of personal status to the religious courts of the various religious communities.[14] Reform and Conservative

---

[11]A letter from the mayor of Rishon LeZion (dated January 16, 1977) to the founder of the Reform congregation in that town stated it was impossible to allocate a place of worship to the congregation because of the "danger of increased public and social tension."

[12]These examples, and others, are discussed in Abramov, *op. cit.,* p. 350 ff.

[13]Some persons involved in the Reform and Conservative movements are opposed to the acceptance of such sums. They feel that the receipt of any government aid prevents them from arguing that they are discriminated against. At the same time, the manner in which the funds are transferred does not enable the movement to argue convincingly that this is a form of governmental recognition, especially given the small amounts awarded.

[14]See Zerach Warhaftig *et al.,* (eds.), *Religion and State in Legislation* (Hebrew), (Jerusalem, 1973); Menahem Elon, *Religious Legislation* (Hebrew), (Tel Aviv, 1964); and Pinchas Shifman, "Religious Affiliation in Israeli Interreligious Law," *Israel Law Review,* January 1980, pp. 1–48.

rabbis are *ipso facto* enjoined from being considered as designates of the state for these purposes. Likewise, at times they have been prevented from conducting funerals. The conversions they perform are not recognized. For the past several years, the Orthodox rabbinate has placed advertisements in the press prior to the high holy days stating that the prayers of persons who worship in Conservative synagogues are not valid, and that individuals cannot fulfill the commandment of *shofar* in such houses of worship.[15]

While some Reform and Conservative congregations have had difficulties in renting facilities, and their rabbis are not recognized by the state, it would be a mistake to attribute the limited progress of the movements to these factors. First, in every case facilities have eventually been found. Secondly, movement leaders are aware that they would not necessarily attract more members to their congregations even if Reform and Conservative rabbis were permitted to conduct wedding services. While it might be argued that the actions taken against the rabbis are an infringement of civil rights, their actual effect on the growth of the Reform and Conservative movements has been limited.

Organizational Structure of the Movements

The Reform and Conservative movements in Israel, like those in the United States, are better characterized as federations of synagogues than as satellite congregations of united organizations.

The Israel Movement for Progressive Judaism is formally composed of representatives of all congregations, as well as such affiliated bodies as the youth movement, Leo Baeck School, Hebrew Union College–Jewish Institute of Religion, and the Council of Progressive Rabbis in Israel. A national council makes the major policy decisions that affect the movement on a day to day basis. One of the main responsibilities of the Council of Progressive Rabbis is the preparation of a new Israeli Reform prayer book. The rabbinic body also occasionally deals with religious questions posed to it by members of the Reform kibbutz.

In the Conservative movement the main division is between the synagogue body, the United Synagogue of Israel, and the rabbinic group, the Rabbinical Assembly in Israel. Working together, the two organizations have established a Movement of Masorati (Traditional) Judaism in Israel. The name was carefully chosen because of its compatibility with the philosophy of Conservative Judaism and its potential appeal to the many Jews in Israel who characterize themselves, religiously, as *masorati*.[16]

---

[15]Some Reform leaders have been disheartened by the fact that they have not been included in the Orthodox rabbinate's denunciations. Apparently, the Orthodox do not take them all that seriously.

[16]Forty-one per cent of the respondents in Ben-Meir's and Kedem's study, *op. cit.*, stated that they were *masorati*.

The leaders of Reform and Conservative Judaism in Israel want their movements to be seen as indigenous to the country. At the same time, they are affiliated with counterpart movements abroad. In the case of Conservative Judaism, it is the World Council of Synagogues; in the case of Reform Judaism, it is the World Union for Progressive Judaism. The main branches of both of these world movements are in the United States.

The Reform and Conservative movements in Israel are quite dependent on financial support from abroad. Over half of the Reform movement's budget is covered by the World Union for Progressive Judaism, which also subsidizes the salaries of several Reform rabbis. In general, the Reform movement in Israel appears to be subject to considerable outside influence. Thus, the vice-president of the Israel executive of the World Union for Progressive Judaism holds *ex officio* membership in the national council of the Israel movement. Publicly at least, the holder of this position, rather than the actual chairman of the Israel Movement for Progressive Judaism, is often perceived to be the leader of Reform Judaism in Israel. The Conservative movement in Israel has had some unpleasant arguments with the United Synagogue of America over the question of financial support. The perceived lack of greater support from abroad has led Conservative leaders in Israel to adopt a more independent course.

Demographic Profile of the Movements

A survey of the members of Reform and Conservative congregations, conducted in 1978, provides data on their demographic composition. While there has been some fluctuation in membership in the interim period (more Conservative congregations have been founded), the basic picture has not changed.[17] For comparative purposes, data from the United States National Jewish Population Study will also be presented.[18]

An initial difference between the movements relates to the number of families that have joined them. There were about 2,049 family units in the

---

[17]Inasmuch as neither of the movements maintained a national membership list from which respondents for the survey could be drawn, it was necessary to obtain lists from each of the congregations. These lists accounted for 815 family units in the Reform synagogues and 1,500 in the Conservative houses of worship. A sample of adults in these households was sent a questionnaire dealing with a variety of synagogue-related issues as well as demographic characteristics. The questionnaires were accompanied by requests for cooperation from the heads of the movements. A total of 977 questionnaires (517 in the Reform movement and 460 in the Conservative movement) were obtained. The response rate in both movements was 85 per cent.

[18]The National Jewish Population Study was commissioned by the Council of Jewish Federations and Welfare Funds. Data relevant to this study are found in Bernard Lazerwitz, "Past and Future Trends in the Size of American Jewish Denominations," *Journal of Reform Judaism,* Summer 1979, pp. 77–82, and in Bernard Lazerwitz and Michael I. Harrison, "American Jewish Denominations: A Social and Religious Profile," *American Sociological Review,* August 1979, pp. 656–666.

two movements in 1978; 64 per cent (1,308 units) belonged to Conservative synagogues and 36 per cent (741 units) to Reform synagogues.

Table 1 presents the family life cycle (a composite picture of the age of the members, their marital status, and the age of their children) of Reform and Conservative Jews in Israel, as well as comparable data for Reform and Conservative denomination members in the United States.

The Conservative movement in Israel is composed of younger members, and more members with younger children, than is the Reform movement. The Reform movement has a larger percentage of members with children no longer at home. The significance of these findings is evident when com-

TABLE 1. FAMILY CYCLE OF MEMBERS OF ISRAELI REFORM AND CONSERVATIVE SYNAGOGUES, BY PER CENT

| | | | NJPS[a] | |
Family Cycle	Reform	Con-servative	Reform	Con-servative
Under 36 and Single	2	3	1	1
Under 36, Married, No Children	1	2	1	6
Married, One or More Children Aged 13 or Younger	18	37	42	36
Married, One or More Children Aged 14–18	12	13	15[b]	18[b]
Married, All Children Over 18 (or No Children)	41	30	35[c]	31[c]
Not Married, Aged 31–54, No Children at Home	2	2	1	1
Not Married, Aged 60 or Over, No Children at Home	22	12	3	5
One-Parent Families	1	1	2	2
NA	1	0	–	–
Total Per Cent	100	100	100	100
N	517	460	841	1,160

[a]Source: Bernard Lazerwitz, "Jewish Denominations, Synagogue Membership, and Attendance," mimeographed, Bar Ilan University, Ramat Gan, Israel. Data refer to synagogue members.
[b]Married couples with children 14 years and older.
[c]Married, 36 years or older, no children now at home.

paring the Israeli members with Reform and Conservative members in the United States. Lazerwitz and Harrison report that 57 per cent of Reform and Conservative members in the United States are married and have children under 16 years old in their households.[19] Whereas the Conservative membership in Israel closely resembles the American group (50 per cent of the Israeli members are married with children under 19 in the household), the Reform membership does not (only 30 per cent of the Reform members in Israel are married with children under 19 in the household). Another difference between the Israeli and American data is that a greater percentage of persons in the Reform and Conservative movements in Israel are elderly, with no immediate family members in the household. The implications of this situation will be discussed below.

The continents of birth of the members, presented in Table 2, show that a smaller percentage of Conservative than Reform Jews are of European origin. The basic difference between the movements is the relatively large number of persons in the Conservative movement born in North America (Canada and the United States). Jews of Asian-African and Latin American origins are virtually unrepresented in the two groups. Within Israeli society, Asian-Africans comprise about 46 per cent of the Jewish population.[20]

Over ten per cent of the members in each of the movements are native-born Israelis. These persons are younger than the other members—their average age in each of the movements is 42. The average age of the non-Israeli-born in the Reform movement is 61, and in the Conservative, 55.

The data in Table 2 point up the fact that Reform and Conservative Judaism in Israel are basically ethnic movements. Ethnic here is taken to mean that the members have a relatively homogeneous cultural background.[21] This common background is further underscored by looking at the members' continents of emigration in Table 3. It should be noted that the North American presence in the Reform and Conservative movements is embedded in a broad "Anglo-Saxon" framework; 11 per cent of the members are from English-speaking countries other than the United States and Canada. In all, one out of three members of the two movements is from an English-speaking country. These persons account for close to half of all Conservative members, but only for about 20 per cent of the Reform members.[22]

Following the English-speaking countries, the country contributing the largest percentage of members is Germany. Thirty per cent of the Reform

---

[19]See Lazerwitz and Harrison, *op. cit.,* p. 659.

[20]Israel Central Bureau of Statistics (CBS), *Statistical Abstract of Israel,* 1978, Table ii/23.

[21]See Shlomo Deshen, "Political Ethnicity and Cultural Ethnicity in Israel During the 1960's," in Ernest Krausz, (ed.), *Studies of Israeli Society: Migration, Ethnicity, and Community* (New Brunswick, 1980), pp. 117–163.

[22]*Cf.,* CBS, *op. cit.,* Table ii/23.

TABLE 2. CONTINENT OF BIRTH OF MEMBERS OF ISRAELI REFORM AND CONSERVATIVE SYNAGOGUES, BY PER CENT

Continent	Reform	Conservative	Israel Jewish Population[a]
Israel	11	14	12
East Europe	32	20	} 40
West Europe	45	29	
Asia–Africa	2	2	46
North America	8	24	
Latin America	1	3	} 2
Oceania	1	8	
Total Per Cent	100	100	100
N	512	455	3.1m

[a]Source: Israel Central Bureau of Statistics, *Statistical Abstract of Israel 1978,* Volume 29, Table ii/23. First-generation Israel-born are classified according to father's continent of birth.

members and ten per cent of the Conservative members immigrated directly from that country. It is possible that the differences between the movements, with regard to "Anglo-Saxon" members in the Conservative group and the Germans in the Reform group, is due less to the intrinsic attraction of the movements than to the nature of immigration to Israel. The German immigrants to Israel brought Reform Judaism with them. In addition, the nature of Reform Judaism abroad would not lead one to expect a large immigration of Reform Jews to Israel. In fact, Orthodox and Conservative Jews are overrepresented among American *olim* to Israel.[23] For that reason the number of "Anglo-Saxons" in the Reform movement is not higher. Supporting this contention is the fact that the average Reform immigrant has been in Israel 31 years, whereas the average Conservative immigrant has been in the country for 19 years. Over half of the non-Israeli-born Reform members came to Israel before 1944, whereas the median year of immigration for the non-Israeli-born Conservative members is 1965.

The ethnic nature of the Reform and Conservative movements is particularly evident in the synagogues. In only three of the twelve Conservative congregations does the percentage of "Anglo-Saxons" fall below 50 per cent; in only two of the ten Reform congregations does the "Anglo-Saxon"

---

[23]See Bernard Lazerwitz and Arnold Dashefsky, "Success and Failure in Ideological Migration: American Jews in Israel," paper presented at the annual meeting of the American Sociological Association, 1979.

presence rise above 50 per cent. Most members of German origin are found principally in one of the Conservative and three of the Reform synagogues.

Members of Reform synagogues in the United States are generally of higher social status than Conservative Jews, although the difference between them is diminishing.[24] This study measures such social status by education and occupation.[25]

The data in Table 4 show that the members of the Reform and Conservative movements have higher educational levels than the general Israeli public. The differences are considerably diminished when Asian/North African Jews are excluded from the Israeli data, but the contrast remains. The differences between Reform and Conservative Jews themselves are attributable to the specific countries of emigration of the members, and to their periods of immigration. Formal education probably received greater emphasis among the many "Anglo-Saxon" members in the Conservative movement than among the European members of the Reform movement. In addition, Reform members generally immigrated to Israel before the Conservative members, and conditions in Europe prior to their immigration were not conducive to formal education. The needs of Israel at the time also worked against their seeking higher education; there was a greater demand for laborers than for academicians. Thus, while many Reform Jews do have some higher education, their number is surpassed by the Conservative Jews.

TABLE 3. IMMIGRANT MEMBERS' CONTINENT OF EMIGRATION, BY PER CENT

Continent	Reform	Conservative	Israel Jewish Population[a]
East Europe	26	11	38
West Europe	54	30	
Asia–Africa	1	2	54
North America	14	40	4
Latin America	3	5	4
Oceania	2	12	
Total Per Cent	100	100	100
N	450	384	3.1 m

[a]Source: Israel Central Bureau of Statistics, *Immigration to Israel, 1948–1972, Part II, Composition by Period of Immigration,* Special Series No. 489, Table 2.

---

[24]See Lazerwitz and Harrison, *op. cit.*

[25]No attempt was made to assess family income because of the problems involved in obtaining a valid response in a mail survey. In Israel's inflationary society, where monthly salaries are supplemented by "bonuses" and extra payments throughout the year, it is particularly difficult to measure income accurately.

TABLE 4. MEMBERS' HIGHEST LEVEL OF FORMAL EDUCATION, BY PER CENT

Education	Reform	Conser-vative	NJPS[a] Reform	NJPS[a] Conser-vative	Israel Jewish Population[b]
High School or Less	43	26	23	40	82[c]
Partial College	16	20	24	25	5[d]
B.A. Degree	12	15	25	11	
Some Advanced Studies	10	10	14	10	9
Advanced Degree	14	27	14	14	
NA	5	2	—	—	4[e]
Total Per Cent	100	100	100	100	100
N	517	460	841	1,160	1.1 m

[a]Source: Bernard Lazerwitz, "Jewish Denominations, Synagogue Membership, and Attendance," mimeographed, Bar Ilan University, Ramat Gan, Israel. Data refer to synagogue members.

[b]Source: Israel Central Bureau of Statistics, *Statistical Abstract of Israel 1978*, Volume 29, Table xxii/3. Data are for Jewish population age 14 and over.

[c]Includes primary, heder, yeshiva, vocational school, and secondary schools. Corresponds to 81.3% of the Jewish population having 0–12 years of education (in *ibid.*, Table xii/2).

[d]Includes teacher training colleges and other post-secondary schools.

[e]Referred to as "other."

With regard to education, there is a reversal of patterns between the movements in Israel and the United States. In the U.S., a significantly larger percentage of Conservative Jews than Reform Jews have no more than a high school education. There is a corresponding difference between those holding a B.A. degree. In Israel, the differences relate to the graduate level, and it is the Conservative Jews who have higher levels of education.

Table 5 presents the occupational distribution of three groups: Reform and Conservative Jews in Israel; Israel's general Jewish population; and members of Reform and Conservative synagogues in the United States. The occupations are ranked from those of highest social prestige to those of lowest.[26] There is a basic difference in occupational distribution of Reform and Conservative Jews in Israel—a much larger percentage of Conservative Jews are professionals. This pattern, a reversal of that found in the United States, is apparently explained by the differential immigration of American

[26]See Moshe Hartman, *Occupation as a Measure of Social Status in Israeli Society* (Hebrew), Part A., (Tel Aviv, 1975).

Reform and Conservative Jews to Israel. Twenty-three per cent of the professionals in the two movements are American-born, and 70 per cent of the American-born in the Israeli Conservative movement are professionals.[27]

Having examined the general demographic characteristics of Reform and Conservative members in Israel, we now turn to their Jewish traits. The first question to be dealt with is the synagogue affiliation of the members prior to their immigration to Israel. Are they merely continuing an institutional affiliation initiated abroad? Sixty per cent of the Reform members and 70 per cent of the Conservative members did attend some synagogue abroad on a regular basis prior to their immigration. The data in Table 6 refer to these persons.

TABLE 5. OCCUPATIONAL DISTRIBUTION OF HEADS OF HOUSEHOLDS, BY PER CENT

| Occupation | Reform | Conser-vative | NJPS[a] | | Israel Jewish Population[d] |
			Reform	Conser-vative	
Professionals	51	71	39	30	21
Managers	8	6	20[b]	44[b]	5
Clerical	16	8	20	14	20
Sales	11	6	15	8	8
Services	1	1	6[c]	4[c]	11
Agriculture	3	1	–	–	5
Skilled Workers	10	7	–	–	24
Unskilled Workers	0	0	–	–	6
Total Per Cent	100	100	100	100	100
N	384	366	841	1,160	1.04 m

[a]Source: Bernard Lazerwitz and Michael I. Harrison, "Denominationalism: What Remains After Americanization," mimeographed, Bar Ilan University, Ramat Gan, Israel.
[b]Owners and managers.
[c]Blue Collar.
[d]Source: Israel Central Bureau of Statistics, *Statistical Abstract of Israel 1978*, Volume 29, Table xii/18. Data relate to population aged 14 and above who are employed or have actively sought employment.

---

[27]The percentage of professionals among American-born Reform members (46 per cent) is higher than that among non-American-born Reform Jews (37 per cent). However, the small sample (n=41) of American-born in the Reform movement limits the generalizations to be inferred.

Over 20 per cent of the members in both movements regularly attended an Orthodox synagogue abroad. This denominational "switch" is somewhat surprising, since it refers to the members' own behavior and not to a comparison of intergenerational change. Several possible explanations for this finding may be offered. First, "Orthodox" congregations in one area of the United States may be similar to Conservative congregations in another.[28] Thus some members might have attended synagogues in the United States that were quite like Conservative congregations in Israel, despite the different nominal affiliation. Second, some members might have attended Orthodox congregations abroad out of choice, but were looking for an alternative to the religious services held in contemporary Israeli Orthodox congregations. Indeed, about one-third of the Reform and Conservative members in Israel attended a synagogue of a different denomination on a regular basis subsequent to their immigration; for over one-half of these persons, that synagogue was Orthodox. Additional analysis shows that 80 per cent of those persons in each of the movements who attended an Orthodox congregation abroad at some time also regularly attended an Orthodox synagogue in Israel. This accounts for ten per cent of the total Conservative membership, and six per cent of all Reform respondents.

At least 50 per cent of the members in each of the movements who attended a synagogue abroad on a regular basis did not attend a synagogue affiliated with their current denomination. Furthermore, the members generally come from similar synagogue movements abroad, or from ones which may be considered "more" religious. This finding about the members' own synagogue attendance is matched by data concerning the synagogues their fathers attended. About half of all Reform and Conservative members come from homes in which the father attended an Orthodox synagogue. The pattern of an institutional "decline" from Orthodox to Conservative to Reform appears to be quite characteristic of modern Jewry.[29]

Overall, the data suggest that previous synagogue attendance on a regular basis is a prerequisite for affiliation with Reform or Conservative Judaism in Israel. Still, about 30 per cent of the Reform members, and about 20 per cent of the Conservative members, did not attend services regularly.

Aside from previous synagogue affiliation, there is the question of the members' present religious behavior. Table 7 shows the distribution of ritual practices of Reform and Conservative Jews in Israel. Comparable data for the adult, urban Ashkenazic population are also presented.

---

[28]See Daniel J. Elazar, *Community and Polity: The Organizational Dynamics of American Jewry* (Philadelphia, 1976), p. 110.

[29]See Morris Axelrod *et al., A Community Survey for Long Range Planning: A Study of the Jewish Population of Greater Boston* (Boston, 1967).

TABLE 6. MOVEMENT AFFILIATION OF SYNAGOGUES MEMBERS ATTENDED
ABROAD, BY PER CENT

Synagogue Attended Abroad	Reform	Conservative
Orthodox	28	37
Conservative	19	42
Liberal	28	7
Reform	16	3
Other (+ More than 1)	9	11
Total Per Cent	100	100
N	319	327

TABLE 7. RELIGIOUS BEHAVIOR OF MEMBERS, BY PER CENT

Religious Behavior	Reform	Conservative	Israel Pop.[a]	NJPS[b]
Refrain from Eating Bread on Passover	82	89	78	
Fast All Day on Yom Kippur	74	84	56	51
Light Shabbat Candles in Home Each Shabbat	72	82	60	
Make Kiddush in Home Each Shabbat	41	65	34[c]	19
Eat Only Kosher in Home	41	65	33[d]	22
Separate Dishes for Meat and Dairy in Home	23	49		
Eat Only Kosher Outside Home	23	36	32	
Refrain from All Travel on Shabbat	6	18	15	
N	517	460	784	—

[a]Data on the general Ashkenazic Israeli population were provided by Dr. Peri Kedem, and are based on special computer runs. Missing data are excluded from these calculations. For details on her study see Ben-Meir and Kedem (supra, footnote 3).

[b]Source: B. Lazerwitz, "Minority Jews Contrasted to Majority Jews," unpublished paper, 1979. Data refer to all American Jews surveyed in the National Jewish Population Study (NJPS).

[c]Includes 9%—"occasionally" and "usually."

[d]Question asked was whether there is separation of meat and dairy in the home.

Both in Israel and the United States, Conservative Jews perform more ritual practices than do Reform Jews. The most striking feature of the findings in Table 7, however, is the high level of religious observance of Reform Jews in Israel relative to both the Ashkenazic population and the general Jewish population in the United States. The finding in Israel is all the more significant in that Orthodox persons are included in the Ashkenazic population data. Indeed, it is probable that Israeli Reform members comprise the most observant Reform Jewish body in the world.

A multiple classification analysis of the factors leading to affiliation with either a Reform or a Conservative synagogue was undertaken.[30] This analysis, which accounts for 26 per cent of the variance observed, confirms the importance of ethnicity as a differentiating factor in the movements. (The beta value of the continents of emigration was .23.) Likewise, the type of synagogue attended abroad has a relatively strong impact (beta of .21) on the synagogue attended in Israel. Religious behavior and occupation have a moderate impact (beta values of .16 and .14, respectively). The age of the members has a barely moderate effect (beta of .12).

The differences between the Reform and Conservative movements in Israel may be highlighted by comparing the multiple classification analysis results with those relating to Jewish denominational choice in the United States.[31] In the U.S., education and occupation (as well as income) are not significant factors differentiating the two movements (their beta values are below .07). In Israel, however, the Conservative movement is composed of persons of higher social status than those who join the Reform movement, although the beta values associated with these variables are only of moderate (or only approach moderate) strength. Since the members of Conservative synagogues are also relatively young, the Conservative movement has a distinct advantage over the Reform movement in attracting young, socially mobile Israelis. The Western, "American" nature of the Conservative movement also works to its advantage inasmuch as Anglo-Saxons enjoy the highest prestige of all immigrant groups in Israel.

A factor influencing affiliation with Reform and Conservative Judaism in the United States, at least in the formative years of the movements, was the rising social status of the members.[32] A social status higher than that of the Israeli population in general also characterizes the native Israeli members

---

[30]See Frank M. Andrews *et al., Multiple Classification Analysis: A Report on a Computer Program for Multiple Regression Using Categorical Predictors* (Ann Arbor, 1973). The absence of interaction between variables was ascertained by using the AID III program of Osiris. See John A. Sonquist *et al., Searching for Structure* (Ann Arbor, 1974).

[31]See Lazerwitz and Harrison, *op. cit.*

[32]Marshall Sklare, *Conservative Judaism: An American Religious Movement* (New York, 1972), pp. 26–28.

(the majority of whom are of Western background). They are five times as likely as the general population to have had at least a college education; a much larger percentage are in professional occupations (57 per cent in the Reform movement, 61 per cent in the Conservative movement, in contrast with 21 per cent among the general Israeli population). How did these persons come to attend Reform or Conservative synagogues? Some married Anglo-Saxon expatriates (7 per cent in the Reform group and 14 per cent in the Conservative group), and their spouses may have been instrumental in their joining the Reform or Conservative movement. Some Israeli members (26 per cent in the Reform group and 19 per cent in the Conservative group) came into contact with non-Orthodox Judaism while on visits or extended stays abroad. Over 30 per cent of the Israeli Reform members and 35 per cent of their Conservative counterparts say that they first heard about the movements from their family or friends. In this connection (but not limited to it), the bar and bat mitzvah services held in these congregations are important in attracting native Israelis. Twenty-eight per cent of the Israeli-born in the Reform movement and 34 per cent in the Conservative movement say that attendance at such celebrations (including those of their own children) first led them to attend their current congregations. It should be noted that membership and periodic attendance are requirements for the conduct of bar and bat mitzvah celebrations in most of the synagogues. Many families apparently do not maintain their membership beyond the requisite year.

It is very rare to encounter a Reform or Conservative congregation that has more than half of its registered membership in attendance on any *shabbat*. Still, the difference between Israeli-born and other members in this regard is noteworthy. Table 8 indicates that Israeli-born members attend religious services much less frequently. In the course of discussions with them, some native Israelis stated that they joined one of the movements only because they wished to indicate their support of religious pluralism, rather than because they were specifically interested in Reform or Conservative Judaism *per se*.

An important indicator of the future of Reform and Conservative Judaism in Israel is the ability of the movements to attract the children of present members. Only about half of the grown children of current members prefer the denomination of their parents; 32 per cent of the children of Reform members and 22 per cent of the children of Conservative members have no denominational preference. Only a minority of children of Reform and Conservative members who no longer live at home attend synagogues of the same denomination as their parents (27 per cent in the Reform movement and 42 per cent in the Conservative movement). Inasmuch as the average number of children of the current members is small (1.9 in the Reform

TABLE 8. FREQUENCY OF SYNAGOGUE ATTENDANCE OF ISRAELI-BORN MEMBERS, BY PER CENT

Synagogue Attendance	Reform		Conservative	
	Israeli-Born	Born Else-where	Israeli-Born	Born Else-where
Each Shabbat (or Almost Each Shabbat) and Holidays	38	49	24	38
Holidays, and Occasionally on Shabbat	24	23	26	30
On Holidays (Including High Holy Days)	6	6	14	13
On Just the High Holy Days	4	9	17	12
Rarely or Never	28	13	19	7
Total Per Cent	100	100	100	100
N	47	470	62	398

movement and 2.3 in the Conservative movement), they cannot be counted upon to maintain current membership levels in the future.

Responses to the Israeli Setting

The demographic data help clarify the charge occasionally made in Israeli Orthodox circles that the Reform and Conservative movements are "imported."[33] Of course, an ideological element is present in this accusation, as well as in the offshoot argument that the movements are geared to the Diaspora and thus religiously "non-authentic." Nevertheless, Reform and Conservative leaders are well aware that they have not succeeded in attracting large numbers of native Israelis. In the hope of doing so, they have sought to alter some behavioral patterns and to undertake specific activities of an "Israeli" nature. This section focuses on some of these activities and analyzes their implications for the movements themselves.[34]

---

[33]See David Telsner, *The Sinai Covenant and Cincinnati "Religion"* (Hebrew), (Jerusalem, 1978).

[34]Berger's "market" theory of religion, which analyzes the need of religious movements to adapt to local "market" conditions in order to "compete" with alternative movements, is relevant here. See Peter L. Berger, *The Sacred Canopy: Elements of a Sociological Theory of Religion* (New York, 1967).

An interesting linguistic issue has arisen in the Conservative movement because of the unavailability of a Conservative prayer book containing only Hebrew. Several congregations prefer using an Orthodox prayer book rather than a Conservative prayer book with an English translation. While the liturgical differences between the two prayer books are not great, some congregants wish to avoid too obvious a manifestation of a largely Anglo-Saxon membership.[35]

Several Hebrew-only Reform prayer books have been published in Israel, and they have been clearly affected by the country's traditional Orthodox environment. The Reform movement has decided to issue a uniform prayer book for adoption by all congregations, although it is an open question (given Reform's stress on autonomy in matters of prayer and ritual) how many will choose to make use of it. Interestingly, one compiler of the new Reform prayer book has commented that it will have to be "fat" like the Orthodox prayer book, so that Reform Judaism will not be perceived as merely non-Orthodox. "People generally treat Progressive Judaism as 'abridged Judaism'. The Orthodox pray from a 'fat' *siddur,* while we pray from a shortened 'thin' one," he stated.[36]

The movement has established a Reform kibbutz (Yahel, in the Negev, some 70 kilometers north of Eilat) to demonstrate Reform Judaism's rootedness in Israeli society and its break with its anti-Zionist past. Rabbi Alexander Schindler, president of the Union of American Hebrew Congregations, stated at Yahel's ground-breaking ceremony in November 1976: "We demonstrate Reform's full flowering in its return to Israel—the people and the land."[37] The cover of a brochure describing the kibbutz features the words "Israel Reform Judaism" and "Rooted in the Land," and shows a smiling *kova tembel* hatted girl holding a cluster of grapes. The text of the brochure reads in part: "With the establishment of the new Reform kibbutz this winter, Israel Reform Judaism becomes, literally, rooted in the soil. . . . Israeli Reform Judaism is not only in the land. It is of the land. . . ." The brochure also states: "Israeli Reform Judaism grows because it meets the spiritual needs of a growing number of Israelis who seek a satisfying alternative to empty secularism and rigid Orthodoxy. It inspires those Israelis who wish to experience the beauty of Judaism."

Publicity wise, the kibbutz has been a great asset to the Reform movement. However, the members of Yahel have felt that the Reform movement,

---

[35]Plans to print a Hebrew-only version of the Conservative prayer book, using plates provided by the Rabbinic Assembly in the United States, have not materialized for technical reasons.

[36]See Moshe Chaim Weiler, "On the Eve of Rosh Hashana 5737" (Hebrew), *Telem,* 10, 1976, pp. 1–2.

[37]Jerusalem *Post,* November 19, 1976, p. 2.

and particularly the rabbinic leadership, have been slow in prescribing behavioral norms suitable to their needs. (The kibbutz has decided to observe *shabbat* in all public spheres, but not to interfere with what the members do in their private lives. Nevertheless, members who turn air-conditioners and lights on and off in their rooms have begun doing so in the kitchen and dining-room as well.) A greater question relates to what a kibbutz as a Reform institution means. Inasmuch as prayer and rituals are dispensed with on a daily basis, what distinguishes the kibbutz as a Reform enterprise?

The kibbutz has encountered difficulty in recruiting a sufficient number of suitable members. The Reform movement in Israel does not yet have a large number of youth interested in a Reform kibbutz. With the permission of the leaders of the movement, therefore, the kibbutz has turned to other youth organizations in Israel to recruit youngsters who are in the *nachal* program (combining military training and work in a developing kibbutz) of the army. But the persons recruited to Yahel in this manner have almost no religious background and are not interested in a specifically Reform Jewish outlook. There are Americans willing to settle on the kibbutz, but Yahel's present members fear that the kibbutz (which in 1982 had only about 60 members, about half of whom were American) will become "hopelessly" American if they are permitted to do so. This is one of the reasons why the Reform movement has decided to establish another kibbutz in the same area—to absorb the Americans. At the same time, the new kibbutz will have to absorb those native Israelis who wish to join a Reform kibbutz, so that a balance can be maintained. This means that Yahel will have to do without new members for the next few years.

The Reform and Conservative movements in Israel hope to create a core of dedicated youth through the development of national youth organizations. These organizations are still in the formative stage; in 1981 they claimed a total membership of less than one thousand. In order to reach a wider audience, the Reform youth organization, Telem Noar has affiliated with the Boy Scouts of Israel (Tsofim), and been assigned several lodges. The challenge facing the organization is to turn these youth, who have little, if any, religious background, into Reform Jews. The Conservative youth groups, attached to local congregations, are composed primarily of the children of current synagogue members. Regional and national activities serve to integrate Conservative youth into a united organization, Noam. The Conservative movement, in response to the demands of the high-school age youth, is planning the establishment of a kibbutz, so that young people will be able to devote their army service to the *nachal* (soldier-pioneer) program.

No survey of the youth organizations has been undertaken, but the directors note that many of the current members are either Anglo-Saxon, or the children of Anglo-Saxons. The movements are clearly serving an important integrative function in Israeli society. It appears, though, that the Conservative movement will have the edge in retaining its young people as members. Many Conservative congregations are well attended by children, thus completing their socialization as Conservative Jews. This is in contrast to the situation in Reform synagogues.

A very significant development in the Reform movement has been the inauguration of a rabbinical studies program for native Israelis. At the time that this study was carried out, five students (all men) were registered. (One of them has since been ordained.) Two of the student rabbis came into initial contact with the movement through the Leo Baeck School in Haifa. Another two became aware of Reform Judaism while they were exchange high school pupils in the United States. The fifth student became active in the movement as a result of having attended a Reform high holy day service (which he had learned about through a newspaper advertisement). None of these persons come from an Orthodox background; their families are either secular or traditional. The father of one student had been a member of the liberal movement in Germany. Two are married to Americans. The high visibility of the student rabbis greatly strengthens the Reform movement's claim of being part and parcel of Israeli society.[38]

While the rabbinical students are being trained to administer to the needs of established congregations, they may be better able than expatriate American rabbis to attract native Israeli youth to the Reform movement. They are very much interested in ideological issues, and participate actively in debates during national conferences. Some of the student rabbis are involved in editing *Shalhevet,* the Reform movement's publication. Their religious leanings and views (still in the formative stage at this point, since they have come to the Reform movement with only limited Jewish knowledge) can be expected to have a significant impact on Reform Judaism in Israel as they assume greater leadership responsibilities in the coming years.

Conclusion

A key feature of both Reform and Conservative Judaism is that they facilitate the "privatization" of religion, the isolation of religious life from public practice. They thus enable Jews to take part in secular social life without undue restrictions. As Sklare and Greenblum note, the practices retained by Reform and Conservative Judaism in the United States tend to be those that are compatible with the American social environment.[39] Many

---

[38]Wide publicity, including press and television coverage, was given to the ordination of the first Israeli Reform rabbi in February 1980.

[39]Marshall Sklare and Joseph Greenblum, *Jewish Identity on the Suburban Frontier* (New York, 1967).

American Jews who want to be part of the general society and yet retain a degree of Jewish identification affiliate with the non-Orthodox branches of Judaism.

Obviously, in Israel adherence to Orthodoxy is less of an impediment to active participation in the mainstream of society than it is in the United States. Israel is geared to the observance of Jewish holidays; *kashrut* is observed in government institutions and many other places as well. Thus, there is less social pressure pushing Jews in the direction of the more liberal Jewish denominations.

In the United States, Reform and Conservative Judaism function as a vehicle for ethnic as well as religious identification. Non-affiliation with a religious denomination in America appears to lead to (as well as to indicate) marginality in the Jewish ethnic community. Thus, even persons who are religiously lax are motivated to attend, or at least affiliate with, the Reform or Conservative denominations (or other institutionalized forms of Judaism) in order to retain and demonstrate an ethnic Jewish identity. In Israel, however, a full Jewish ethnic life is quite possible; there is little fear of "assimilation" and thus less of a need for affiliation with a synagogue. In addition, the use of Hebrew as the vernacular in Israel and the incorporation of Jewish symbols into Israel's "civic" religion[40] negate or, at least, modify the function that the Reform and Conservative movements might play in strengthening Jewish identity.

A recent development in Israel might be noted, inasmuch as it points to a possible direction that the Reform and Conservative movements might take in the future. In accordance with government regulations enabling such action, some parents of children attending a non-religious state school in Jerusalem petitioned for the replacement of part of the curriculum with a richer program of Jewish studies following a basically Conservative syllabus. Many of the parents initially involved in this project were Conservative Jews who had immigrated from the United States. Significantly, however, the program has met with strong approval from parents unconnected with any Jewish denomination and not of Anglo-Saxon background. Enrollment in the school has consistently increased over the past three years, and there have been attempts by parents to establish similar programs in two other locations.

The desire to establish such institutions suggests that the need for religious modification in Israel might manifest itself in ways other than through synagogue forms and ritual practices. Perhaps there is a role for Reform and Conservative Judaism in transmitting a Jewish heritage that is less coercive

---

[40]See Charles Liebman and Eliezer Don-Yehiya, "Israel's Civil Religion," *The Jerusalem Quarterly*, Spring 1982, pp. 57–69.

than that demanded in Orthodox state religious schools, while richer than that provided in non-religious state institutions. The pattern of many Americans to "return" to the synagogue when their children come of school age in order to socialize them into Judaism may, in Israel, be transformed into a desire for a richer Jewish program in the school system.

One last point remains to be discussed in the light of this study's findings. Both the Reform and Conservative movements in Israel are more "traditional" than their counterpart movements in the United States, in that their religious practices are less "deviant" from Orthodox practices. The range of practices found in the synagogues of both movements is no greater than that observed within either of the movements in the United States. Is there, then, a need for two separate non-Orthodox movements in Israel? This question was posed to Reform and Conservative leaders in the course of the interviews with them. Some replied that the Reform and Conservative movements in Israel should combine forces and develop an indigenous, innovative responses to Jewish life in a Jewish society unfettered by institutional affiliations carried over from the past. This feeling, though, is much more prevalent among the leaders of the Reform movement, which has proven less successful than Conservative Judaism. On the other hand, many if not most of the Conservative leaders believe there should be only one movement, but that it should be their own. They feel that any cooperation with the Reform movement will further antagonize the Orthodox establishment. Furthermore, many Conservative leaders emphasize the basic incompatiblity of the movements with regard to the acceptance of *halakhah* as authoritative law. Some Conservative rabbis have gained a measure of official recognition (including the occasional right to conduct weddings) in the communities in which they serve, and this, too, strengthens their determination to retain their independence.

Review
of
the
Year

UNITED STATES
OTHER COUNTRIES

Civic and Political

Intergroup Relations

IN "THE EXPOSED AMERICAN JEW," written in *Commentary* in June 1975, Nathan Glazer took note of the factors that were bringing American Jews into the public eye. Chief among them was the following: "American Jews must ask a very big thing of their country: they must ask the United States to support Israel and do whatever is in its power to see that Israel survives." In 1981 this issue moved to the center of the political arena, as the Reagan administration sought to sell AWACS (air warning) planes and other advanced weaponry to Saudi Arabia. For Jews, the AWACS struggle marked a serious break with the popular Republican president, whom they had given an unprecedented 39 per cent of their vote the year before, in part because of their dissatisfaction with the handling of the Middle East situation by President Carter. The Jewish community locked horns with the administration and the military-industrial complex, and, for the first time since World War II, there were attacks on Jews at the highest governmental levels.

The AWACS Fight

Pressures on American Jews in 1981 were foreshadowed even before the AWACS fight. The Israeli bombing of an Iraqi nuclear reactor in June, followed by the bombing of PLO facilities in Beirut in July, stimulated a strong anti-Israel reaction, particularly in the media. In the summer issue of the influential journal *Foreign Affairs,* Senator Charles Mathias (R., Md.) was critical of the "Israel lobby," whose members, he declared, sometimes acted for "reasons not always related either to personal conviction or careful reflection on the national interest." Simultaneously, Representative Paul McCloskey (R., Calif.) told a group of retired naval officers, "We have got to overcome the tendency of the Jewish community in America to control the actions of Congress and force the president and the Congress not to be even-handed in the Middle East."

In the fall the Reagan administration moved to implement the AWACS deal. Recognizing that it stood no chance of winning in the House of Representatives, the administration placed pressure mainly on the Senate, where 51 members, led by Robert Packwood (R., Ore.), had signed a resolution announcing opposition to the sale. According to a major investigative article in the *New Republic* (Feb. 17, 1982), President Reagan's decision and his advisors to lay the prestige of the administration on the line in the AWACS deal may have been influenced by an unprecedented lobbying campaign launched by American business organizations and oil companies.

Jews soon came under attack from the administration as the single, most powerful interest group seeking to bar a sale that the White House defined as beneficial to American interests. Secretary of State Alexander Haig spoke of "an independent foreign policy" not held hostage to "external veto," while an unnamed national security council aide was widely quoted as challenging American Jews to choose "between Begin and Reagan." In a news conference on October 1, President Reagan declared, "It is not the business of other nations to make American foreign policy." Asked if this meant that Israel should "keep her hands off" American national security matters, he said, "Well, or anyone else." Former president Richard Nixon stated that "if it were not for the intense opposition" of Prime Minister Menachem Begin of Israel and "parts of the American Jewish community," the AWACS sale would go through. All in all, there were innuendos from high places that it was improper, disloyal, or, at the very least, counter-productive for Jews to speak out forcefully way on so controversial an issue.

As the AWACS debate peaked, reports came out of Washington that the issue had stimulated considerable antisemitic feelings. Senator Mark Hatfield (R., Ore.) declared several days before the vote that his office mail indicated a "resurgence of antisemitism," while Senator David F. Durenberger (R., Minn.) said, "I have never experienced anything like this, in terms of basic prejudice." Senator Walter S. Cohen (R., Ma.), an original signer of the Packwood resolution, received considerable public attention when he switched his vote at the last moment, saying it would be better for Jews to lose than to suffer the consequences of winning. An Anti-Defamation League survey of mail received by senators shortly after the vote showed that seven per cent was antisemitic and 32 per cent critical of Israel for alleged "interference" in the controversy. The American Jewish Committee later reported, however, that the extent of anti-Jewish feeling had been exaggerated. Moreover, many congressional assistants indicated that the sale of AWACS was not an important issue to their constituents.

President Reagan's narrow victory when the vote came in the Senate on October 28 was almost anti-climactic for the Jewish community in the light of the intense public discussion of its role. Jewish officials were deeply concerned. "It would be a very long step backward for us to start looking over our shoulders out of fear that our participation in debate is going to bring antisemitism out of the woodwork," Nathan Perlmutter, national director of the Anti-Defamation League, declared a day after the vote. In fact, virtually all segments of the Jewish community remained strongly opposed to the AWACS deal. This was highlighted when a group of influential Republican Jews publicly spoke out against the sale. Their willingness to do so led Rabbi Irving Greenberg to declare, in a column in a number of

Anglo-Jewish publications, that the Jewish community had come of age. The defeat, nevertheless, marked the second time—the first was in 1978 when Jews opposed the sale by President Carter of F-15's to Saudi Arabia—that Jews strenuously opposed an administration matter involving Israel and had lost.

As the year drew to a close, members of the Conference of Presidents of Major Jewish Organizations and major Republican Jewish leaders met with President Reagan to assess the damage done to the administration's relations with the Jewish community and to urge him to publicly denounce antisemitism and defend the right to dissent. Reagan indicated that he would. Asked by CBS News about antisemitism growing out of the AWACS fight, Senate majority leader Howard Baker said, "I think the leadership on both sides of the aisle and the White House and throughout the country would realize that such a devastating consequence is just simply unacceptable."

Antisemitism

For the third consecutive year, the number of reported antisemitic incidents in the United States more than doubled. According to a survey released by the Anti-Defamation League, there were 974 cases of assault against property and 350 attacks against individual Jews or Jewish institutions in 1981. Once again, New York, California, New Jersey, and Massachusetts reported the most vandalism incidents. In Philadelphia at least 20 incidents occurred in the last six months of the year, among them a bomb threat against a Jewish business, a cross burning on a synagogue lawn, tire slashings, and swastika daubings. Police patrols were increased at all six synagogues in Fairlawn, New Jersey, in November, following the spraying of swastikas and antisemitic slogans on two of them. However, police and Jewish community relations officials tended to see most of these episodes as acts of youthful defiance rather than the work of organized hate groups.

Responses to the increase in antisemitic activities took a number of forms. The New York State legislature enacted two measures providing parental penalties for youths who defiled or damaged houses of worship and increasing penalties for discrimination or harassment because of race, creed, color, or national origin. New Jersey passed a measure making racial or ethnic terror a state crime of the third degree, punishable by fines and prison sentences. Jewish community relations agencies stepped up their efforts to persuade schools to teach about prejudice and discrimination in general and about the horrors of the Holocaust in particular. *Newsweek* reported that the Jewish Defense League was offering ten-week training courses in Southern California, Michigan, and upstate New York to meet the threat of antisemitic groups like the Nazis and the Ku Klux Klan.

Despite mounting pressures on Jews, highlighted by the AWACS fight, a survey conducted by the opinion research company of Yankelovich, Skelly, and White for the American Jewish Committee, released on July 28, reported that antisemitism in the United States had declined significantly over a 17-year period. Some 34 per cent of Americans could be categorized as antisemitic today, as against 45 per cent in 1964. The survey found, however, that the percentage of non-Jewish respondents who believed that Jews held too much power in the United States rose to 23 per cent, as against 13 per cent in 1964. Moreover, the percentage of non-Jews who believed Jews were more loyal to Israel than to America climbed to 48 per cent, from 39 per cent in 1964. According to a Gallup poll conducted in late November (after the AWACS debate), 53 per cent of the public expressed the belief that Israel wielded "too much influence" in American foreign policy, but only 10.5 per cent felt this way about American Jews. Higher percentages of the public believed that Saudi Arabia, the oil companies, and labor unions possessed too much influence. All in all, there was little reason to believe that the AWACS debate had changed popular perceptions of Jews. It was possible, however, that the insinuations about Jews made during the AWACS fight at the highest levels of government might make it easier to repeat them if and when some new crisis involving Israel or Jews developed.

Extremism

Earlier predictions of an increase in extremist activity proved accurate as the Ku Klux Klan and similar groups stepped up their actions. A six-month investigation by the American Jewish Committee revealed that a significant number of militant Klan activists had broken away from the main groups and, joined by Nazis, were planning more drastic actions than the standard cross burnings and rallies. Two Klan members and a neo-Nazi were convicted in November of an attempt to bomb Nashville's largest Reform congregation, as well as a transmission tower of a television station supposedly owned by Jews. Several Jewish businessmen in Nashville were also threatened with violence. In Catonsville, Maryland, a Klansman was convicted of conspiring to bomb the residence of a local NAACP official. A federal jury found six avowed Nazis guilty of conspiracy to blow up sections of Greensboro, North Carolina.

Women, hitherto relegated to a passive position in the Klan, were assuming a key role in the new militancy. One Klan member taken into custody in Nashville was a 50-year-old woman. A woman was also in the forefront of the Alabama Klan schismatics.

In an attempt to counteract Klan efforts to recruit members and exploit racial tensions in the public schools, the National Education Association planned to distribute a new curriculum guide about the white supremacist group to its 1.7 million teachers. While agreeing about the need for such materials, the Anti-Defamation League executive committee publicly took issue with portions of the guide "for indicting American society as innately racist." Children should be taught that the Klan is "an aberration" rather than "the tip of the iceberg of entrenched racism in America," the Anti-Defamation League argued. The Anti-Defamation League also filed an *amicus curiae* brief with the U.S. district court in Houston backing the constitutionality of a Texas law that banned the Klan from operating paramilitary training camps.

The extremist, antisemitic Liberty Lobby continued to remain in the news. Its weekly tabloid, *The Spotlight,* held a gala at the National Press Club in Washington in late 1980 to celebrate the claimed achievement of a circulation goal of 300,000. The *New Republic* charged in September 1981 that the credibility of Liberty Lobby had been enhanced by the casual way in which Capitol Hill legislators cited *The Spotlight* and appeared on Liberty Lobby radio and television broadcasts. The group's former lawyer, Warren Richardson, was nominated by President Reagan as assistant secretary for legislation in the U.S. department of health and human services. However, Richardson withdrew his name from consideration when he was sharply attacked by Jewish groups.

The New Right

Pressures generated by the New Right and Christian Right troubled many Jews. Groups such as the Moral Majority, generally associated with Bible Belt sections of the country, began to move East. The Reverend Jerry Falwell, head of Moral Majority, declared early in the year that he would focus his attention on 17 states, including New York, New Jersey, and Connecticut, which were "not yet mature and developed." (The head of Moral Majority's fledgling New York State chapter, the Reverend Dan C. Fore, shocked many people when he was quoted on February 5 as saying, "I love the Jewish people deeply. . . . Jews have a God-given ability to make money." Later in the year Fore resigned, apparently under pressure from the national organization.) The president of the Religious Roundtable announced that his organization hoped to establish branches in all 50 states.

There were indications that the Reagan administration, which had received strong support from New Right and Christian Right groups in the 1980 election, was seeking to put some distance between itself and them. In January the new chairman of the Republican National Committee warned those on the right not to exaggerate their role or try to tell the president what to do in office. President Reagan and the Republican leadership focused their attention on reviving the badly deteriorating economy and attempted to subordinate such issues as abortion and prayer in the public schools. However, the New Right groups and their congressional allies continued to press forward. Spearheaded by Senators John East (R., N.C.) and Jesse Helms (R., N.C.) and Representative Henry Hyde (R., Ill.), legislation was introduced defining a fertilized human egg as "a person" entitled to the full protection of the 14th Amendment's "due process" clause. Anti-abortion forces were buoyed when, at a March 6 press conference, President Reagan stated that it was necessary to determine "when and what is a human being." Three Republican senators introduced a family protection act with the aim of achieving a number of Christian Rights goals; among other things, the legislation required that parents of pregnant teenagers be notified before contraceptive and abortion information could be provided by government-financed agencies.

In June the Coalition for Better Television, a group of more than 100 right-wing organizations, including Moral Majority, launched a campaign to monitor television programs and boycott advertisers who sponsored shows that were deemed offensive. Falwell declared that his organization would spend at least $2 million to promote the campaign. In response, NBC's president, Fred Silverman, described the boycott tactic as "a sneak attack on the foundation of democracy." Simultaneously, Procter and Gamble revealed that it had withdrawn sponsorship from 50 television programs because they depicted sex and violence in a gratuitous manner. Late in June, following a meeting between New Right leaders and a number of companies, including Smith Kline and Warner Lambert, the Coalition for Better Television cancelled its projected boycott. The group stated that it had reason to believe that sexual themes and violence would be reduced in the network's new fall line-up.

The movement to couple the teaching of evolution in the public schools with the Bible-backed theory of creationism continued, as Louisiana joined Arkansas in enacting legislation requiring this. Early in the year, a California superior court judge ruled that the state's policy on the teaching of evolution did not violate the rights of fundamentalists who believed in the biblical version of creation. Out of respect for the latter, however, he ordered the state to underscore to local schools the official policy forbidding dogmatism in the treatment of the origins of life. At year's end, the Arkansas chapter of the ACLU was challenging creationism in the courts. The effect of the movement was also felt in the publishing industry; many textbooks were revised, reducing the space given to evolution, and presenting the subject in more tentative terms.

There were indications that parents groups across the country, using sophisticated lobbying techniques and backed by organizations like Moral Majority, the Eagle Forum, and the Christian Broadcasting Networks, were banding together to remove certain books from libraries, replace school textbooks, and eliminate sex education courses. The number of censorship cases took a five-fold leap during the first months of the Reagan administration. In June the Republican party leadership conceded that it had failed to keep anti-busing and other social legislation out of Congress while it focused on the president's economic recovery program. At year's end there were more than 20 bills pending to limit the jurisdiction of the federal courts in such areas as school desegregation, prayer in the public schools, and abortion.

Jews and the New Right

Most Jewish groups were critical of the activities of the New Right. Testifying at public hearings before a Senate subcommittee on the proposed human life bill, Rabbi Henry Siegman, executive director of the American Jewish Congress, argued that the view that fetal life is human life "is a view unique, primarily though not exclusively, to the Catholic Church." The ACLU challenge of Arkansas' creationism law was initiated by a dozen ministers and two rabbinical groups; the American Jewish Committee joined the suit as a plaintiff. In June the National Council of Jewish Women criticized Congress for restricting federal abortion funds to only those situations in which the life of the woman was threatened. A Los Angeles court ruled in November, in a case brought by the Anti-Defamation League on behalf of two Jewish businessmen, that the publisher of the Christian Yellow Pages business directory could not limit advertising to those willing to declare that they are "born-again Christians."

While there was concern in the Jewish community about many of the New Right's positions, there was also recognition that many elements within the movement were supportive of Israel. Prime Minister Begin phoned Jerry Falwell, seeking his support, following the sharp, negative reaction to Israel's attack on the nuclear reactor in Iraq. Falwell visited Israel in September, and announced his uncompromising support for the embattled Jewish state. As the debate over the sale of AWACS reached its climax, however, there was some indication that the Christian Right and many of the senators associated with it had backed away from their announced opposition to the sale. In December the Anti-Defamation League sponsored a trip to Israel by the Reverend Bailey Smith, the president of the Southern Baptist Convention, who had stirred a storm of protest the year before with his statement that "God almighty does not hear the prayer of a Jew." While in Israel, Smith said that he had been "wrong" in singling out the Jewish people for not accepting Jesus. Anti-Defamation League officials attributed Smith's remark about Jewish prayer to his narrow experience, rather than to any malice toward Jews.

Blacks and Jews

The Reagan administration's economic program, which featured cuts in social services aimed at relieving the problems of the poor and racial minorities, caused concern among Jews. The American Jewish Congress published a full-page advertisement in the New York *Times* headlined "America Must Not Quit on Social Justice." Rabbi Alexander Schindler, head of the Union of American Hebrew Congregations, stated that "the war against poverty has become a war against the poor." At its annual meeting in May, the American Jewish Committee expressed concern about the cuts.

Black-Jewish tensions continued, although largely beneath the surface. In March the New York *Times* reported friction between the two groups in the Democratic party in Detroit, Miami, and the District of Columbia. On March 18 Washington mayor Marian Barry, Jr. declared, in response to a series of child murders in Atlanta, that if the black children of that city "had been Jewish, the federal government would have moved faster" to provide aid. Jewish groups protested, but Barry refused to apologize; privately he sought to assuage their concerns. Benjamin Hooks, executive director of the NAACP, announced at a September news conference that he was "very alarmed by the closeness of the relationship between Israel and South Africa."

The running battle between Mayor Koch and the black leadership of New York City continued. In the mayoral primary, which Koch won handily, blacks voted 2 to 1 against him. At a Democratic party conference in Baltimore, Koch spoke out against racial quotas, engendering a sharp attack by black congressman Charles Rangel (D., N.Y.).

There were some signs of blacks and Jews uniting out of concern about President Reagan's economic program, his attempts to modify existing civil rights programs, the growth of the New Right, and antisemitic and Klan activities. Sixteen of the seventeen members of the Black Caucus in the House of Representatives voted against the sale of AWACS. In September the leaders of the NAACP and of Reform Judaism met in Washington, and called for joint activities to support extension of the Voting Rights Act and strong affirmative action programs.

Quotas

As the new administration in Washington sought to determine its civil rights stance, the American Jewish Committee, American Jewish Congress, and Anti-Defamation League appealed in April for a national policy reaffirming the U.S. commitment to "genuine equal opportunity for all" and "legitimate affirmative action in every field" without "the many abuses and excesses" that had developed from distortions of the affirmative action principle. In March the Anti-Defamation League criticized the Reagan administration for adopting a new civil service scheme that would allegedly give preferential treatment to blacks and Hispanics. Earlier in the year, amid considerable controversy, the *Harvard Law Review* adopted a plan to consider a student's race, ethnic background, or sex in filling some editorial positions. The plan replaced an earlier one which established a strict quota for minorities and women in an effort to diversify the journal's make-up.

Church-State Relations

In March the supreme court left intact a ruling barring a "motorist's prayer" that appeared on state maps in North Carolina. On November 16 the Senate voted to endorse programs of voluntary prayer and meditation in the public schools by barring the justice department from using federal funds to interfere with this matter. At one point in the debate, Senator Ernest Hollings (D., S.C.) referred to Senator Howard Metzenbaum (D., Ohio) as "the Senator from B'nai B'rith." Hollings later apologized.

At year's end the supreme court ruled that the University of Missouri must allow student religious groups to meet for worship and religious study. Both the National Jewish Commission on Law and Public Affairs (COLPA) and the American Jewish Congress, which had submitted friend-of-the-court briefs in the case, expressed concern that Christian missionary groups would be strengthened by the ruling. A week later the supreme court left intact a lower court ruling that voluntary prayer had no place in public high schools. In refusing to hear an appeal in the Albany, N.Y. case, the justices did not explain their routine dismissal, but it seemed likely that the court continued to make a distinction between public schools and colleges or universities, where religious views could be freely aired.

A split within the Jewish community was evident during two days of hearings before a subcommittee of the Senate finance committee on the proposal to provide tuition tax credits for private education. The major American Jewish organizations continued to oppose aid to parochial schools, but Orthodox groups demonstrated their growing militancy, as more parents were sending their children to Jewish day schools. Rabbi Moshe Sherer, president of Agudath Israel of America, noted that there were 101,000 students in Jewish day schools in the United States. In a set-back for proponents of tax credits, District of Columbia voters overwhelmingly rejected a $1,200 per pupil education tax credit proposal that had received national attention.

Cults

Jewish organizations continued their attempts to counter the cult phenomenon and its in-roads among Jewish youth. In Baltimore two Jewish groups obtained funding from the Jacob and Hilda Katz Blaustein Foundation to establish Project Friend, intended to provide counseling and information about cults. B'nai B'rith's commission on adult Jewish education received a grant to hold seminars on cults around the country.

California enacted legislation, believed to be the first in the nation, allowing former cult members to sue those cults for financial deprivation while they were involved as members. The New York chapters of the American Jewish Committee and the American Jewish Congress, however, opposed on constitutional grounds two "cult bills" proposing the appointment of temporary guardians for "adults over 16" who might have been influenced by religious cults.

MURRAY FRIEDMAN

The United States, Israel, and the Middle East

IN 1981 RELATIONS BETWEEN THE UNITED STATES AND ISRAEL were marked by sharp fluctuations. The new year and the new administration in Washington began auspiciously with declarations by President Ronald Reagan that he considered Israel not simply a friend but a "force in the Middle East that actually is of benefit to us." During a visit to Washington in September, Prime Minister Menachem Begin proclaimed that the traditional friendship between the United States and Israel had reached the level of a strategic alliance. The areas of defense cooperation were to be formalized in a memorandum of understanding on strategic cooperation.

Yet the ink had scarcely dried on the agreement, signed at the end of November by Defense Secretary Caspar Weinberger and Defense Minister Ariel Sharon, when the United States announced that it was suspending implementation of the agreement. This was a demonstrative sign of Washington's pique at Begin's action in rushing through the Knesset a measure to apply Israeli "law, jurisdiction, and administration" to the Golan Heights, in effect unilaterally annexing the territory Israel had captured from Syria in the 1967 Six Day War. Twice before during the year, the Reagan administration had temporarily suspended scheduled military aircraft shipments to Israel; once when the Israelis attacked an Iraqi nuclear installation outside Baghdad and a second time when they bombed high-rise buildings in the heart of Beirut containing the operational headquarters of the Palestine Liberation Organization (PLO).

Washington and Jerusalem clashed most sharply over the Reagan administration's plan to sell Saudi Arabia some $8.5 billion worth of highly sophisticated airborne warning and control system surveillance planes (AWACS) and highly advanced missiles, fuel tanks, and other equipment to enhance the military capability of the 60 F-15's the United States had originally agreed to sell the Saudis in 1978.

The controversy over the Saudi weapons sale illustrated two paradoxes. First, despite sharp differences between the Reagan and Carter administrations in their overall foreign policy outlooks, when it came to practical responses to the situation in the Persian Gulf/Arabian Peninsula, the Reagan administration followed its predecessor's practice of courting Saudi favor through the sale of American weapons and equipment. Second, the Reagan administration's emphasis on Saudi Arabia also helps explain why so much friction developed between Begin and Reagan, despite the seemingly far greater ideological rapport between the two men than between Begin and Carter.

Reagan Administration's Views on the Middle East

In a press interview on February 2, Reagan was asked whether he had "any sympathy toward the Palestinians or any moral feeling toward them and their aspirations?" The president replied, "That's got to be a part of any settlement," but then listed the obstacles to a solution: "There is the outspoken utterance that Israel doesn't have a right to exist; there is the terrorism that is being practiced by the PLO." He added, "I never thought the PLO had ever been elected by the Palestinians," and reiterated that before there could be any Palestinian participation in the peace process there had to be "the acceptance of Israel as a nation." Asked whether he approved of the reported acceleration of Israeli settlement activity in the West Bank, Reagan replied, "I disagreed when the previous administration referred to them as illegal; they're not illegal." However, he added that "this rush to do it . . . is ill-advised because if we're going to continue with the spirit of Camp David to try and arrive at a peace, maybe this, at this time, is unnecessarily provocative."

The Israelis concluded from President Reagan's remarks and other indications that, in contrast to the Carter administration, the Reagan administration would not quickly embark on a major initiative of its own to tackle the thorny Palestinian issue or to press toward a comprehensive settlement of the Arab-Israel conflict. There were both practical and philosophical reasons for this caution. With regard to the former, the first priority of the new administration was to deal with the country's pressing domestic economic problems. In any case, it would take several months before the new administration team became familiar with the intricacies of Middle East diplomacy. Finally, the elections scheduled in Israel for the end of June seemed to offer the possibility that the Likud government of Prime Minister Begin would be replaced by the Labor Alignment, which would have more flexible views regarding the nature of autonomy, the rationale for settlements, and the prospects for a territorial compromise with Jordan on the West Bank.

On a philosophical level, the Reagan administration viewed foreign policy as a struggle by the free world against Soviet expansionism. Emphasis was placed on building America's military strength so as to counter the threat posed by growing Soviet conventional and nuclear capabilities. Moreover, President Reagan and Secretary of State Alexander Haig underscored the need to combat international terrorism, which they saw as largely organized and directed by Moscow with the aim of destabilizing and ultimately overthrowing pro-Western and democratic societies. Given the PLO's Soviet ties, then, it could be expected that there would be a significant shift away from the Palestinians in the official attitude in Washington.

It appeared to the Israelis that the Reagan administration, which recognized Israel's value as a strategic ally, would also be more understanding than the Carter administration might have been of a vigorous Israeli campaign to disrupt and even uproot PLO terrorism from its operational bases in Lebanon. The Israeli view was strengthened by the remarks of National Security Affairs Advisor Richard Allen, who told an ABC-TV interviewer on April 2, "There is no question that we must identify the PLO as a terrorist organization—until it provides convincing evidence to the contrary." Allen compared Israel's policy of pre-emptive strikes against PLO bases in southern Lebanon to the internationally accepted principle of "hot pursuit." He did not hesitate to express his personal judgment that "there is ample justification" for Israel's action in reaching to the source of PLO terrorism, since such action constitutes "hot pursuit."

It soon became apparent, however, that under the Reagan administration there was no single vicar of foreign policy. Secretary Haig's contention that he was "in charge" was belied by a number of facts. The president placed Vice President George Bush in charge of crisis management and Defense Secretary Caspar Weinberger made policy pronouncements and undertook initiatives on his own. Moreover, within the national security council, Richard Allen lacked the formal authority of a Kissinger or a Brzezinski, having less regular access to the president than such White House advisors as James Baker, Michael Deaver, and Edwin Meese. Given the president's own lack of expertise in foreign affairs and his emphasis on domestic issues, the generally pro-Israel sympathies of Haig and Allen were often diluted in the formulation of U.S. policy by the concerns of other advisors, whose previous business connections made them more sensitive to the interests of the Arab oil producers.

Haig's Efforts to Promote a "Strategic Consensus"

The Israelis soon discovered that they were mistaken in assuming that Washington would give them operational *carte blanche* in the Middle East. The Reagan administration never accepted Jerusalem's thesis that Israel was the only reliable American ally in the region. Indeed, the very emphasis on the Soviet global threat, which had heightened the administration's appreciation of Israel's value as a strategic ally, also prompted the Reagan administration to labor mightily to develop what Secretary of State Haig termed "a consensus of strategic concerns throughout the region among Arab and Jew" in order to be sure that "the overriding dangers of Soviet inroads into this area are not overlooked." In his testimony before the House foreign affairs committee on March 18 and before the Senate foreign relations committee the following day, Haig said that while the Reagan administration had not rejected the idea of reviving Arab-Israel peace talks, he planned to give top priority to regional security questions during his forthcoming visit to Egypt, Israel, Jordan, and Saudi Arabia.

Haig quickly learned during his trip in April that even those countries, such as Egypt and Israel, which were deeply concerned about the threat of Soviet expansionism, were not eager to have permanent U.S. military bases on their soil. Israel had proposed that the major military airfields in Sinai (Eitam and Etzion) that it was relinquishing as part of the withdrawal, be turned over for use by the U.S. rapid deployment force to serve as the nucleus for a permanent American presence in the region. The Egyptians rejected this idea. However, when President Anwar Sadat met with President Reagan in Washington in August, he agreed to sign a contract to permit the emergency American use of the Egyptian strategic military base at Ras Banas on the Red Sea, if the United States paid the cost of the extensive renovation that was required. Israel offered to make its naval facilities at Haifa available to the U.S. sixth fleet as needed, but Jerusalem did not wish to have any U.S. forces based within Israel, so as not to depart from the principle that Israel would defend itself solely with its own men.

In the Persian Gulf/Arabian Peninsula, Haig was even less successful in selling his strategic cooperation concept. In Jordan, King Hussein told Haig that Israel's intransigence toward the Palestinians was the chief issue in the Middle East, since it had "opened the door to turbulence [and] instability." Yet only a few days earlier, on March 21, Hussein had accused Syrian president Hafez al-Assad of involving the Middle East in East-West rivalries and had charged Damascus with betrayal of the Arabs by supporting Iran in its continuing war with Iraq. In May Hussein went to Moscow on an arms-purchasing mission and supported a Soviet proposal for an international conference on the Arab-Israel conflict, with the participation of the Soviet Union, the United States, the Arabs (including the PLO), and Israel.

After Haig completed his visit to Saudi Arabia on April 8, Saudi foreign minister Saud al-Faisal reiterated his view that Israel was "the main cause of instability" in the Middle East. The Saudis were reportedly pressuring the sheikhdom of Oman to deny permanent bases to the U.S. rapid deployment force. On April 25 the Soviet Union and Kuwait issued a joint statement opposing the establishment of military bases in the Gulf area. On June 6 United Arab Emirates president Sheikh Zayed bin Sultan al-Nahiyan said that the U.S. rapid deployment force, not the USSR, constituted the chief threat to the Gulf.

Israel's Destruction of Iraqi Nuclear Plant

On June 7 Israeli planes bombed and destroyed the Osirak atomic reactor near Baghdad, which Israel claimed was about to go critical, enabling Iraq to manufacture nuclear weapons. The Reagan administration's reaction to the raid ranged from strong condemnation to passive acquiescence. The day after the attack, Dean Fischer, spokesman for the state department, said, "The United States government condemns the reported Israeli air strike on the Iraqi nuclear facility, the unprecedented character of which cannot but seriously add to the already tense situation in the area." At the same time, the New York *Times* reported that state department and intelligence officials believed "that Iraq had acquired enough enriched uranium and sensitive technology to make one nuclear weapon by the end of this year, and several bombs by the mid-1980's." At a press conference on June 16, President Reagan said, "I do think that one has to recognize that Israel had reason for concern in view of the past history of Iraq, which . . . does not even recognize the existence of Israel as a country." Israel, he added, "might have sincerely believed its action was defensive in nature." Prime Minister Begin told the Knesset that United States officials had provided Israel with a document expressing American concern that Iraq was preparing to use the French-built Osirak reactor to manufacture nuclear weapons. The document, based on American intelligence reports, had reportedly been given to Begin in January by U.S. ambassador Samuel Lewis. In Washington, the state department confirmed that information on the Iraqi nuclear program had been exchanged at various times with Israel and other Middle East countries, but the department would not comment specifically on the document Ambassador Lewis had allegedly given Begin.

Because of the close ties between the United States and Israel and the use of American-supplied planes, the United States was vulnerable to charges of collusion in the attack. The Soviet Union and the Arab states were quick to contend that the United States knew of the plans for the raid and had supported it. A prime United States concern was that the Israeli raid would discredit the peacemaking mission of Philip Habib, the United States envoy in the Middle East, who at the time was trying to mediate between Israel and Syria over the presence of Soviet-made SAM missiles manned by Syrian forces in Lebanon. Another concern was that the raid would complicate United States-Saudi relations just when the AWACS deal was heading for a vote in the Senate. The United States also feared a possible Iraqi move toward the Soviets, which would end the gradual bettering of Iraqi-United States relations which had begun early in 1980.

On June 19 the UN security council unanimously condemned the Israeli air attack and called on Israel to refrain from such acts or threats in the future. The council also stated that Iraq was entitled to reparations from Israel. American Jewish organizations criticized the United States for joining in the vote. Maynard Wishner, president of the American Jewish Committee, stated that "the resolution again demonstrates the United Nations' double standard applied against Israel. Iraq recently invaded a neighboring sovereign state (Iran) and today occupies much of its territory, but the United Nations has yet to breathe a word of condemnation." Howard Squadron, chairman of the Conference of Presidents of Major American Jewish Organizations, said, "It is distressing to find this country appearing to uphold a claim of injury by Iraq, a nation that has persistently proclaimed itself to be at war with Israel and that has continuously committed itself to the destruction of Israel."

In a column in the New York *Times* on June 10, James Reston expressed concern over the broad implications of Israel's actions. He contended that Prime Minister Begin "has produced a storm of protest in a world that fears he may have set a precedent for all nations to act on their own to bomb their opponents at will—and this has worried even the friends of Israel, and added to that country's isolation in the world community." However, Arthur Goldberg, former supreme court justice and United States ambassador to the United Nations, defended the Israeli raid. He pointed out that Iraq had maintained a declared state of war against Israel since 1948. Israel, therefore, was allowed under international law to destroy any facility —industrial as well as military—which aided its opponent. Goldberg recalled that during World War II the United States had bombed German power plants and factories.

On July 11 Secretary of State Haig notified Congress that Israel may have violated a mutual defense assistance agreement of 1952, and asked the Senate foreign relations committee to examine this possibility. The committee was asked to determine whether Israel's act was one of self-defense or aggression. Under the 1952 agreement, Israel had promised to use arms sold by the U.S. only for "legitimate self-defense" and pledged that it would "not undertake any act of aggression against any other state." The United States arms export control act required that no military credits or sales be provided to a country in "substantial violation" of an arms supply agreement. The scheduled shipment of four United States F-16 fighter planes to Israel was halted while Congress debated whether Israel had violated the agreement. In the end, neither Congress nor the administration ever formally concluded that Israel's raid definitely constituted a violation.

Israel Bombs PLO Headquarters in Beirut

On July 17, the day the U.S. was scheduled to resume the supply of F-16's delayed because of the Osirak raid, Israel bombed the PLO headquarters in downtown Beirut. The act met with severe criticism internationally because of the high number of civilian casualties. Prime Minister Begin justified the raid as an act of self-defense against Palestinian terrorist groups responsible for many civilian deaths in northern Israel. Kuwait, Syria, the United Arab Emirates, and Iran condemned both Israel and the United States—the former for doing the bombing and the latter for supplying the weaponry. Egypt and Saudi Arabia focused only on Israel, denying Israel's claim of self-defense. Egypt warned that Israel was threatening Cairo's peacemaking efforts; Egyptian deputy UN delegate Nabil Elaraby declared on July 21, "The new edifice of peace which Egypt is faithfully striving to construct in the Middle East is being undermined with the continuation of such policies and bloodshed."

The Reagan administration's immediate reaction to the raid was to again postpone indefinitely the shipment to Israel of F-16's, as well as F-15's scheduled for delivery in August, due to what it termed the "escalating level of violence" in the Middle East. Two high Reagan administration officials criticized Prime Minister Begin, suggesting that Israel's recent military actions had damaged American diplomatic efforts in the Middle East. Secretary of Defense Weinberger said that Begin's policies "cannot really be described as moderate at this point, and it is essential that there be some moderation." Deputy Secretary of State William Clark said that Prime Minister Begin "is making it difficult for us to help Israel. Our commitments are not to Mr. Begin, but to the nation he represents." He added that Begin had caused "disappointment and maybe some embarrassment" in bombing targets in Beirut on the heels of a visit to Israel by state department counselor Robert McFarlane. Secretary of State Haig sought to temper the severity of the U.S. reaction by stressing, in an appearance on ABC-TV's *Nightline* on July 20, that despite the indefinite delay in the shipment of ten F-16 military planes to Israel, the United States had in no way altered its conviction that Israel was a staunch ally and a strategic asset which America had a continuing moral obligation to support. The practical impact of the United States criticism was limited, and the shipment of the planes was resumed in August.

According to a national NBC poll conducted on August 11 and 12, in which some 1,600 persons were asked whether Israel's recent military actions had raised or lowered their opinion of Prime Minister Begin, 51 per cent of the respondents indicated a lowered opinion of him, 14 per cent a raised opinion, 21 per cent said it made no difference, and 14 per cent were not sure. Asked about the level of United States military aid to Israel, 38 per cent thought it too much, 42 per cent the right amount, 7 per cent not enough, and 14 per cent were not sure. These figures had not changed much from previous polls; in December 1979, for example, an NBC poll found that 38 per cent thought the United States gave too much aid, 38 per cent the right amount, 5 per cent not enough aid, and 19 per cent were not sure.

A poll conducted by *Newsweek* in August indicated that "a majority (69 per cent) of United States Jews think that Israel was justified in bombing Palestine Liberation Organization bases." However, many Jews faulted Prime Minister Begin for showing little remorse for the civilian casualties. A majority (53 per cent) of the Jewish sample agreed with the view that "Begin's policies are hurting support for Israel in the United States." Jews feared in particular that repetition of actions such as the Beirut raid would antagonize Congress and the administration, making it more difficult to maintain United States assistance to Israel.

U.S.-Israeli Strategic Cooperation

When Secretary of State Haig welcomed Prime Minister Begin on his arrival in Washington in September for his first meeting with President Reagan, he assured him that the administration regarded recent events as "behind us." According to Begin, neither the Baghdad nor Beirut raids were mentioned at the White House talks. However, the prime minister spent much of his time with Congressional leaders, the media, and Jewish leadership in justifying Israel's actions. Begin acknowledged that the Beirut raid had aroused a great deal of concern even within the American Jewish community. At a meeting of the Conference of Presidents of Major Jewish Organizations on September 12, he expressed regret that civilians had been killed, and emphasized that the Beirut "counterattack" was a unique event and did not mean that Israel had abandoned its policy of avoiding civilian targets. Begin was convinced that without the Beirut raid the PLO would not have agreed to the ceasefire that U.S. envoy Philip Habib had negotiated through Lebanese intermediaries.

Begin hailed his meeting with President Reagan as "a turning point" in relations between Israel and the United States. He noted that for a number of years there had been discussions between Israeli and American defense experts, but that they had never resulted in a formal agreement on strategic cooperation. Now, however, President Reagan had accepted the idea. On September 11, Secretary of Defense Weinberger and Minister of Defense Sharon announced the formation of joint groups to discuss strategic problems and means of countering Soviet aggression in the Middle East, and to prepare a formal document dealing with the matter.

The AWACS Sale

Knowing of the traditional reluctance of American diplomats and defense planners to offend the Arabs by having the United States publicly identify with Israel, Prime Minister Begin counselled Washington to tell the Arabs that the proposed American-Israeli strategic cooperation had nothing to do with the Arab-Israel conflict and was intended solely to strengthen common defense against the international Communist danger. The problem was that the administration proceeded to use the same logic to justify the proposed AWACS sale to Saudi Arabia, arguing that it was necessary to protect the Saudis from the growing threat of Soviet and radical expansionism, and that the sale would not undermine Israel's security or the American commitment to maintain Israel's qualitative military edge.

The Begin government faced a dilemma. It did not wish to jeopardize the movement toward a strategic partnership with the Reagan administration or to appear to be interfering in American domestic politics. Yet, Israel was deeply concerned over the proposed military sales to Saudi Arabia. When reports first reached Jerusalem in February that President Reagan was planning to support the Carter administration's decision to furnish enhancement equipment for the F-15's the Saudis had contracted for in 1978, the Begin government had asked the United States to modify the Carter package, e.g., to eliminate the multiple ejection bomb racks, and requested that they give Israel additional F-15's to compensate for the increased Arab strength. Once it became clear, however, that the Reagan administration also intended to sell the Saudis five AWACS, Israel decided to strongly oppose the entire package.

Prime Minister Begin observed the diplomatic niceties by telling American Jewish and general audiences that the proposed sales to Saudi Arabia were matters for the U.S. government to decide, and that he would not intervene in the discussions between the executive and legislative branches. However, whenever he was asked his personal opinion, as he was by President Reagan, the Congressional foreign relations committees, and the media, Begin stated bluntly that he regarded the enhancement of the Saudis' offensive capacity as "a grave threat to Israel's security." He contended that the 1,177 advanced AIM 9-L sidewinder air-to-air missiles the Reagan administration planned to sell the Saudis would change the qualitative edge that Israel held. The proposed F-15 enhancement sale also included six KC-707 aerial refueling tanker aircraft, with an option for the Saudis to buy two more, and

101 pairs of "conformal fuel tanks" that greatly extend the F-15's range and combat endurance. Begin stressed that this meant the 62 Saudi F-15's would be able to reach Tel Aviv and the entire Dan region from any part of Saudi Arabia.

The five AWACS and 22 ground radar stations combined with the increased offensive capacity of the F-15's would create a formidable integrated air combat team. Begin said that General Sagui, Israel's chief of military intelligence, had demonstrated on maps that five of Israel's seven major airfields would be completely exposed to surveillance by Saudi AWACS. The Saudis cooperated closely with Jordan, which in turn had recently been helping Iraq, Israel's most implacable foe. This raised the spectre of the AWACS equipment and intelligence being made available as part of a *jihad* (holy war) to "liberate Jerusalem and the occupied Arab lands," which had been proclaimed as a major objective of the Islamic summit conference which the Saudis had hosted in Taif at the end of January.

Virtually all major American Jewish organizations engaged in a strong lobbying campaign opposing the sale. Already on April 1, Presidents Conference chairman Howard Squadron had written to Secretary of State Haig, arguing that proceeding with the sale would convey a "misleading signal." Noting that the Reagan administration had been elected on a two-fold promise to pursue a global anti-communist strategy and to demand consideration of U.S. interests from the international community, Squadron pointed out that Saudi Arabia and other Arab states which gave first priority to their conflict with Israel were "clearly acting at cross purposes" with American goals. The interests of the United States required that the Arab world cease its support of PLO terrorism and holy war against Israel. Arms for Saudi Arabia or other Arab states, Squadron said, should be made conditional upon their agreeing to "come to the peace table with Israel, to enter the Camp David process, and to deal cooperatively in the pursuit of this country's global strategy." Squadron concluded that "in the absence of such an agreement by Saudi Arabia, the American Jewish community will be obliged to oppose vigorously the proposed sale."

Groups like the American Israel Public Affairs Committee and the American Jewish Committee argued that the proposed sale was contrary to American interests. The American Jewish Committee acknowledged the U.S. interest in protecting the Saudi airfields from foreign attack and in keeping the Persian Gulf shipping lanes open, but pointed out that these interests were already well served by the four United States AWACS that had been sent to Saudi Arabia in October 1980 at the start of the Iraq-Iran war. The crucial difference was that these planes and their sophisticated equipment remained under American operational control and the intelligence gathered could not be diverted to anti-Israeli use.

It was widely suspected that prestige rather than security was the real motivation for the request by the Saudis, who wanted the latest and best equipment to enhance their standing among their Arab neighbors. The Saudis also made the deal a litmus test of American friendship. Having won approval in principle for the sale from the Carter administration, the Saudis would have regarded a reversal by the Reagan administration as an act of bad faith. Within the United States Senate, however, the

Carter administration's agreement to sell the F-15 enhancement package was itself seen as a violation of a solemn commitment. In February Senators Thomas Eagleton (D., Mo.), Daniel Inouye (D., Hawaii), and Patrick Leahy (D., Vt.) had written to the president pointing out that they had voted to support the 1978 Middle East arms sale package only after receiving assurance that Saudi Arabia would not receive equipment of the type now proposed. They added that they had informed President Carter as soon as the new request had surfaced that "we consider any modification of the planes to enhance offensive capabilities to be a direct violation of that earlier understanding." The senators said that they appreciated that the heightened tension in the Middle East and Persian Gulf area necessitated a review of Saudi defense policy, but they rejected the argument of both the Carter and Reagan administrations that the changed circumstances justified a reneging on the pledge to the Senate. They concluded that "the spirit of the [1978] arms sale agreement precludes the transfer of any offensively enhanced F-15's to Saudi Arabia."

The Saudis, aided by powerful allies in the business community, especially the ARAMCO oil partners and the numerous defense and building contractors operating in Saudi Arabia, such as Boeing, Bechtel, and Westinghouse, lobbied actively for the sale in Washington. The lobbying effort was led by Prince Bandar bin Sultan, assisted by the National Association of Arab Americans, several public relations firms, and four former American ambassadors to Saudi Arabia. It was not generally realized, but the United States had already concluded $34.4 billion in military sales to Saudi Arabia, not counting the proposed $8.5 billion AWACS and F-15 enhancement package. Most of the funds were for the construction of "military cities," base facilities, and infrastructure. Moreover, American companies had a large share in the nearly $200 billion spent on the Saudi development plan for 1975–1980, and were eager to participate in the new development plan for 1980–1985, which budgeted a colossal $391 billion.

The Saudi "Peace" Plan and the AWACS Deal

When Crown Prince Fahd first revealed a Saudi "peace" plan in an interview over Riyadh radio on August 7, President Sadat—then meeting with President Reagan in Washington—dismissed it as nothing new. Many observers speculated that the Saudis' timing had been determined by a desire to impress Congress, which was about to consider the AWACS deal. Saudi Arabia officially explained its "peace" initiative as designed to produce an Arab consensus and win international support for a plan that could replace the Camp David accords, "whose failure has been proven." Fahd hoped the Reagan administration would accept "the uselessness of the Camp David agreements" and initiate "a drastic change in American policy" which would demonstrate that the U.S. was "less biased toward Israel and more equitable toward the Arabs."

There were eight points in the Fahd plan: (1) Israel should withdraw from all Arab territory occupied in 1967, including Arab Jerusalem; (2) Israeli settlements built on Arab land after 1967 should be dismantled; (3) freedom of worship for all religions in the holy places should be guaranteed; (4) the right of the Palestinian people to return to their homes, and to compensation for those who do not wish to return, should be reaffirmed; (5) there should be a transitional period, under the auspices of the United Nations and not exceeding several months, for the West Bank and the Gaza Strip; (6) an independent Palestinian state should be set up, with Jerusalem as its capital; (7) the states of the region should be able to live in peace; and (8) the United Nations or its member states should guarantee to execute these principles. Fahd called on the UN security council to consolidate these points in a new and binding resolution.

While the Reagan administration sought to depict the Fahd plan as a positive trend in the evolution of the Saudi position, it soon became clear that the Saudis were still not prepared to recognize Israel officially or establish normal diplomatic relations with it. The Saudi plan did not specifically endorse security council resolution 242, which recognized Israel's right to exist within "secure and recognized boundaries," or resolution 338, which called for direct negotiations among the parties to implement resolution 242. Indeed, doubt remained that the Saudis were prepared to include Israel among the nations with a legitimate right to a permanent existence within the Middle East. Thus, when Saudi foreign minister Saud al-Faisal officially presented the Fahd plan to the United Nations in the course of a major address to the general assembly on October 5, he stated, "Ever since the forces of East and West combined to partition Palestine and establish the *so-called* State of Israel, that state has decided to adopt expansion as its principle and aggression as its way of life." (Emphasis added.) In another passage the Saudi foreign minister spoke of the "blind arrogance" that led Israel to proclaim Jerusalem as the capital "of its *racist entity.*" (Emphasis added.)

If the Fahd plan was intended to demonstrate Saudi moderation, it certainly failed to convince the members of Congress. Under a 1974 amendment to the arms export control act, Congress was empowered to block a proposed sale if both houses passed a joint resolution of disapproval. When such a resolution opposing the Saudi sale was first introduced in the House by Representatives Clarence Long (D., Md.) and Norman Lent (R., N.Y.) in July, it drew 228 co-sponsors. The number continued to grow over the summer, and when the matter finally came to a vote in the House on October 14, the Reagan proposal was defeated by 301 to 111. A majority of Republicans voted against the president (108 opposed and 78 for); among the Democratic opposition the tally was even more lopsided, with 193 disapproving and only 33 supporting the sale. The House vote was in line with popular sentiment around the country. A nationwide Louis Harris poll conducted in late September found that 59 per cent of the respondents were against the sale, 28 per cent in favor, and 13 per cent undecided.

The Reagan administration now concentrated all its efforts on winning a majority for the sale within the Senate. This was by no means an easy task. In early July the president had received a letter signed by 52 senators—an absolute majority of its 100 members—saying, "It is our deep belief that this sale is not in the best interest of the United States, and therefore recommend that you refrain from sending this proposal to the Congress." The Senate opposition was led by Republicans Robert Packwood (Ore.) and Rudy Boschwitz (Minn.) and Democrats William Roth (Del.), Roger Jepsen (Iowa), Henry Jackson (Washington), Howell Helfin (Ala.), David Pryor (Ark.), and Daniel Inouye (Hawaii).

Responding to the fear that the Saudi regime would go the way of the Shah of Iran, President Reagan declared at a press conference on October 1 that the United States "will not permit" Saudi Arabia "to be an Iran" and implied that the U.S. was prepared to use its own forces to intervene since "there's no way [the U.S.] could stand by and see [Saudi Arabia] taken over by anyone who would shut off the oil." Yet, this significant restatement of the American commitment to Saudi Arabia received far less prominence than Reagan's assertion that "it is not the business of other nations to make American foreign policy." Although there was heavy lobbying by Saudi Arabia in favor of the sale, the media universally regarded the president's criticism as directed against Israel. The New York *Daily News* ran a front page banner headline: "Reagan to Begin: Butt Out!" Administration lobbyists for the Saudi sale had been attempting to cast the issue as one of Begin versus Reagan, implying that the opponents of the president's position were guilty of disloyalty. There were warnings of a backlash against Israel if Saudi displeasure resulted in negative foreign policy and domestic economic consequences. Although the president disclaimed any such intention, sources close to the administration did not discourage the fear that antisemitism might be stirred up within the United States if Jews maintained too high a profile in opposing the Saudi sale. Former president Richard Nixon, whose White House tapes had disclosed a propensity for antisemitic remarks, sharply criticized and suggestively linked "intense opposition by Begin and parts of the American Jewish community" to the AWACS sale.

Assassination of President Sadat and the AWACS Debate

On October 6, while reviewing a military parade commemorating the 1973 war with Israel, Egyptian president Sadat was assassinated by a group of Muslim fanatics who had infiltrated the army. Vice President Hosni Mubarak, upon being sworn in as the new president, reaffirmed Egypt's commitment to its international obligations, including peace with Israel and the continuation of the Camp David process. While maintaining close ties with the United States, Mubarak also held out an olive branch to the Soviet Union and to the various Arab states, most significantly Saudi Arabia, which had broken off relations with Egypt after Sadat had made peace with Israel.

Sadat's death became yet another element in the AWACS debate. Opponents of the sale cited the assassination as proof of the instability and unreliability of the Arab world. The administration, however, tried to make the sale a posthumous referendum on the highly popular Egyptian president. Secretary of State Haig declared that defeat of the sale to the Saudis would "make a mockery of all that President Sadat stood for," ignoring the fact that the Saudi rulers had been at odds with Sadat personally and had opposed his peace efforts and strategic cooperation with the United States. The administration also argued that with the Shah and Sadat both gone, Saudi Arabian friendship had become even more important to the United States, if it wished to maintain influence in the Middle East.

The major effect of President Sadat's assassination was psychological. Several heretofore undecided senators now argued that irrespective of the merits of the AWACS arguments pro and con, it would be inappropriate to abandon President Reagan at a time of crisis. In the crucial final days before the vote, the president personally spoke to most of the senators and stressed that a defeat on the AWACS sale would cripple his effectiveness as a leader in foreign affairs. To help allay the fears of opponents to the sale, the president also sent a letter to Congress stating that the United States would retain close involvement in the security of the AWACS equipment and information for many years, that the Saudis would in any case require a long period of training and American assistance in the handling of the F-15's, and finally that the AWACS would not be delivered to Saudi Arabia until the president had certified that "significant progress" toward peaceful resolution of the Arab-Israel conflict had been accomplished "with the substantial assistance of Saudi Arabia." (However, the day after the vote, White House chief-of-staff James Baker said that the president's letter was binding only as a "moral commitment," but probably did not have the "technical legal effect" to stop the AWACS deliveries if Riyadh failed to support American peace initiatives.)

On October 28, after months of heated debate and intense lobbying, the administration managed to garner 52 votes in the Senate to defeat the resolution of disapproval. Yet the fact that 48 Senators held firm in opposition to the Saudi sale despite the combination of presidential arm-twisting and assurances indicated the depth of the misgivings about the American arms sales policy to Saudi Arabia.

U.S. Agrees to Participate in MFO

Almost lost in the furor over the AWACS debate was an important Congressional action in support of American participation in the Sinai peace-keeping force. The Camp David accords had provided for a UN force to undertake this task, but the threat of a Soviet veto led to the creation of a multinational force and observers unit (MFO), with half of the 2,500-man force consisting of Americans. The United States agreed to pay $125 million, or 60 per cent of the initial cost of facilities and deployment, with Egypt and Israel splitting the remaining $80 million. Starting in fiscal 1983 each of the three countries would pay a third. U.S. participation in the MFO received unanimous Senate approval on October 7, the day after Sadat's assassination. Senator Charles Percy (R., Ill.), chairman of the foreign relations committee, had strongly urged his colleagues to "support this resolution and thereby give tangible evidence of our support for the peace process which President Sadat so courageously set in motion." The House approved the MFO resolution on November 19 by a vote of 368 to 13.

Memorandum of Understanding on Strategic Cooperation

On November 30 the United States and Israel signed a memorandum of understanding on strategic cooperation to deter Soviet threats in the Middle East. The memorandum called for joint military exercises, "including naval and air exercises in the eastern Mediterranean Sea," and the establishment and maintenance of joint readiness activities. The agreement also proposed the formation of joint working groups to address specific military issues.

The memorandum received a mixed reaction in Israel. While members of the ruling Likud government praised it as "another stage in the friendly relations between Israel and the United States," opponents saw the memorandum as a one-sided deal whereby the United States gained Israeli military strength to help deter the Soviets, while Israel gained nothing new from America and needlessly provoked Moscow. Article 1:1 of the memorandum stated, "United States-Israeli strategic cooperation, as set forth in this memorandum, is designed against the threat to peace and security of the region caused by the Soviet Union or Soviet-controlled forces from outside the region introduced into the region." Reaction in the Arab states was harshly critical of the United States' strategic venture. The United States, it was claimed, could not arbitrate the Middle East conflict as a neutral third party while maintaining a strategic alliance with Israel. The Reagan administration denied that the memorandum addressed any country other than the Soviet Union.

Golan Heights Law

The issue of the memorandum was complicated when, on December 14, the Knesset voted to extend its "law, jurisdiction, and administration" to the occupied Golan Heights. What followed in America and the world at large was condemnation of Israel's action. On December 18 the United States joined with the rest of the UN security council in a resolution opposing Israel's action, stressing that it lacked international legal effect. Furthermore, because Israel had not consulted the United States before acting, the United States postponed indefinitely discussions intended to implement the memorandum of understanding signed only two weeks earlier. The state department spokesman claimed that "the spirit of that agreement obliged each party to take into consideration in its decisions the implications for the broad policy concerns of the other. We do not believe that spirit was upheld in the case of Israel's decision on the Golan." The United States also suspended its plans to purchase $200 million worth of Israeli-produced goods and services.

Secretary of Defense Weinberger called the annexation "provocative and destabilizing." Secretary of State Haig said the Israeli action "is not consistent with [UN security council resolution] 242, which is the fundamental United Nations resolution underlying the peace process itself." Prime Minister Begin challenged this view. In a statement issued to U.S. ambassador Lewis after the United States' harsh criticism of Israel, he said, "The essence of the resolution (242) is negotiations for the determination of recognized, secure borders. Syria announced that it would not negotiate with us, that it does not recognize us, and that it will not recognize us. And thus it took the essence out of 242. How could we therefore harm 242?"

Begin was furious that the U.S. government had over the last six months "punished Israel three times" and had in fact "breached a signed contract." Referring to American criticism of the Israeli raid on the PLO headquarters in Beirut, Begin said, "You don't have the right, from a moral perspective, to preach to us regarding civilian loss of life." Noting that the Knesset had passed the Golan Heights law by a decisive two-thirds majority, he bristled at the renewed talk of "punishing Israel." Begin asked rhetorically: "Are we a vassal state of yours? Are we a banana republic?" The U.S., he warned, would find Israel deaf to threats and amenable only to "rational arguments." Begin further charged that the effort to win a Senate majority for the arms deal for Saudi Arabia was "accompanied by an ugly antisemitic campaign."

Within the American Jewish community the initial response to Begin's Golan Heights action was confusion and quiet questioning. Yet, when the United States reacted by suspending the memorandum of understanding, the Jewish community tended to side with Israel in characterizing the American response as inappropriate and excessive. Howard Squadron, chairman of the Conference of Presidents of Major American Jewish Organizations, strongly criticized the United States. He said that Prime Minister Begin's bitter attack on the Reagan administration in the wake of the suspension of the strategic cooperation memorandum was "perfectly understandable." The strategic cooperation agreement, he added, was a pact of mutual defense and "not a favor to Israel." Other American Jews, while opposed to United States criticism of Israel, were embarrassed by the vitriolic character of the prime minister's public attack on the United States. They called for moderation on both sides and a quick resumption of friendly relations. The American Jewish Committee said it understood "American disappointment over the annexation as well as Mr. Begin's anguish over the response," but added, "It is less important now to assess blame for the present disarray than to get the two governments back to positive trusting discussions." This, in fact, proved to be the case; Israel and the United States sought to smooth over this latest conflict. Nevertheless, the memorandum of understanding on strategic cooperation remained in limbo at the end of the year. Moreover, the Habib mission failed to bring about the removal of Syrian missiles or to stop the continuing buildup of PLO forces in southern Lebanon. Despite professed agreement on overall objectives, the Reagan and Begin administrations seemed destined to clash over the methods and tactics required to remove these threats.

GEORGE E. GRUEN

Communal

The 1981–1982 National Survey of American Jews

A<small>CCURATE</small> <small>INFORMATION ON</small> American Jews has been both difficult and costly to obtain. Since Jews comprise a mere 2.7 per cent of the total American population, very few of them appear in most standard national surveys. Moreover, aside from one occasion in recent history (1957), the U.S. Census has not provided a breakdown of data along religious lines. Researchers have relied on several less than ideal sources for data on the social and demographic characteristics of American Jews, as well as their politics, religious practices, and communal affiliations. These sources include widely scattered Jewish community surveys conducted irregularly by local federations; post-election "exit polls"; nationwide social surveys amalgamated so as to obtain sufficient quantities of Jewish respondents for reliable statistics; and the highly costly and, by now, somewhat dated National Jewish Population Study (1970–1971).

To fill the need for current information on the country's Jewish population, the American Jewish Committee recently sponsored a study using an experimental, low-cost sampling technique to survey a representative group of American Jews. In the fall of 1981, a six-page questionnaire was mailed to approximately 1,700 people having about a dozen Distinctive Jewish Names (such as Cohen, Kaplan, Levine, etc.) who were listed in the telephone directories of over 40 communities of all sizes throughout the continental United States.[1] The sample was constructed so as to

Note: This study was supported by the American Jewish Committee as well as by Calculogic, Inc., which donated its very capable data processing services. Milton Himmelfarb and Geraldine Rosenfield of the AJC consulted in the design and execution of the study. A.B. Data Corporation of Milwaukee supplied much of the sample, and Calvin Goldscheider offered useful comments on the findings. The support of CUNY Research Foundation Grant #13654 (1981–82) is gratefully acknowledged.

[1]Roughly two-thirds of the sample resided in eight major metropolitan areas: New York, Chicago, Los Angeles, Philadelphia, Miami, Boston, Washington, and Baltimore. In addition to these areas of 90,000 or more Jews (including their surrounding suburbs), questionnaires were sent to appropriate numbers of respondents living in 24 Jewish communities of at least 20,000: Providence, Hartford/New Britain, New Haven, Rochester, Buffalo, Rockland Co.

roughly approximate the geographic distribution of American Jews as reported in the 1980 *American Jewish Year Book*.

Of the 1,700 questionnaires that were initially mailed out, about 300 were returned as undeliverable. Out of a pool of 1,400 potential respondents, about half eventually completed and returned the questionnaires at the conclusion of four mailings (February, 1982).

Comparisons With Other Studies

For several reasons, the procedure that was employed might be expected to yield results that were less than representative of American Jewry. People with Distinctive Jewish Names may be different from Jews without such names (although previous research[2] has shown this is not the case); those listed in telephone directories may differ from those who are unlisted; and those who return questionnaires may be different from those who do not. To assess the representativeness of the mail-back sample of Distinctive Jewish Names, Table 1 presents data from the National Survey of American Jews alongside comparable data from two other recent studies using more sophisticated and more costly sampling techniques—the 1975 Greater Boston Jewish population study and the 1981 Greater New York Jewish population study.[3]

Comparison of the results of the three studies demonstrates that the respondents in the National Survey hardly differ from those in the New York and Boston studies. Jews in the National Survey are somewhat older than Boston Jews, and slightly less Orthodox and observant than New York Jews. The other characteristics of the respondents in the three studies are virtually identical.

Findings

The table reports several well-known features of American Jews. They are extraordinarily well-educated (four-fifths have been to college; one-third have a

---

(N.Y.), Monmouth Co. (N.J.), Cincinnati, Cleveland, Detroit, Milwaukee, Minneapolis, St. Louis, Kansas City (Mo.), Fort Lauderdale, Palm Beach Co. (Fla.), Dallas, Houston, Denver, San Diego, Phoenix, San Francisco, Orange Co. (Cal.), and Alameda and Contra Costa Cos. (Cal.). Within each of the nine census regions, one community was chosen at random with a Jewish population size of 5,000 to 20,000 and another with fewer than 5,000 Jews; these 18 representative localities were: Bridgeport, Conn.; Meriden, Conn.; Union City, N.J.; Glen Falls, N.Y.; Indianapolis; Peoria; St. Paul; Sioux City; Orlando; Greensboro, N.C.; Memphis; Nashville; San Antonio; Tulsa; Las Vegas; Salt Lake City; Ventura, Cal.; and Eugene, Ore.

[2]See Harold S. Himmelfarb and R. Michael Loar, "How Distinctive Are Jews With 'Distinctive Jewish Names'?," unpublished manuscript.

[3]See Floyd J. Fowler, *1975 Community Survey: A Study of the Jewish Population of Greater Boston* (Boston, 1973). The New York study is now being conducted under the auspices of the Federation of Jewish Philanthropies of New York by Paul Ritterband and Steven M. Cohen of the City University of New York.

TABLE 1.   COMPARISON OF SELECTED DEMOGRAPHIC CHARACTERISTICS AND
MEASURES OF JEWISH IDENTIFICATION ACROSS THREE SURVEYS OF
AMERICAN JEWS,[a] BY PER CENT

	1981 NSAJ	1981 New York	1975 Boston
<u>Median Age</u> (Adult Respondents)	49	49	37
<u>Current Marital Status</u>			
Never-Married	21	15	32
Married	62	65	56
Separated or Divorced	8	8	4
Widowed	9	11	8
	100	100	100
<u>Ever-Divorced</u>	14	11	12
<u>Educational Attainment</u>			
H.S. Grad., or less	20	28	25
Some College	21	19	16
B.A.	26	25	27
Graduate School	33	28	33
	100	100	100
<u>Median Income</u>	$27,500	$27,500	n.a.
<u>Denomination</u>			
Orthodox	6	13	5
Conservative	36	36	36
Reform	26	29	36
Other (not affiliated, secular)	32	23	23
	100	100	100
<u>Jewish Education As A Child</u>			
Yeshiva, Day School	4	11	7
Hebrew School	53	49	57
<u>Ritual Practices</u>			
Attend a Passover Seder	77	87	85
Light Hanukkah Candles	67	74	n.a.
Regularly Light Sabbath Candles	22	(39)[b]	(43)[b]
Fast on Yom Kippur	54	64	55

	1981 NSAJ	1981 New York	1975 Boston
Attend Services on Yom Kippur	59	n.a.	n.a.
Attend Services on Rosh Hashanah	54	59	61
Have different dishes for meat and dairy products	15	26	17
Refrain from shopping or working on the Sabbath	5	13	n.a.
Belong to a synagogue	51	41	38
Belong to another Jewish organization	38	n.a.	27
Give to the UJA/Federation every year	49	52	52
Have been to Israel	37	37	20
Closest Friends Jewish			
All	12	n.a.	n.a.
Almost All	27	n.a.	n.a.
Most	22	n.a.	n.a.
About Half	24	n.a.	n.a.
Fewer Than Half	8	n.a.	n.a.
Few or None	7	n.a.	n.a.
	100		
Children's Jewish Education			
Expect no Children	11	n.a.	n.a.
Children will be Non-Jews	2	n.a.	n.a.
None	12	n.a.	n.a.
Bar/Bat Mitzvah Lessons	9	n.a.	n.a.
Sunday School	18	n.a.	n.a.
Hebrew School	40	n.a.	n.a.
Yeshiva, Day School	7	n.a.	n.a.

[a]The three surveys are: (1) The 1981 National Survey of American Jews; (2) The 1981 Greater New York Jewish Population Study (sponsored by the UJA/Federation of New York; Paul Ritterband, Steven M. Cohen, directors); (3) The 1975 Greater Boston Jewish Population Study (sponsored by the CJP of Boston; Floyd J. Fowler, director). Question wording for comparable items differ somewhat. The notation n.a. means not available.

[b]Parentheses denote question wordings which differ considerably from those used in the National Survey.

graduate degree). They are also fairly affluent (median income = $27,500), although Jews have extremely heterogeneous incomes: almost a third earn under $20,000, and almost a quarter earn over $50,000 a year. Only a small number (six per cent) of the national sample identify as Orthodox, with the rest divided among the Conservative and Reform denominations and the unaffiliated. Barely a majority attended Hebrew school, and only four per cent went to a yeshivah or day school.

Results for ritual practices mirror those reported time and again in previous studies. The Passover Seder and the lighting of Hanukkah candles are the most popular practices (77 and 67 per cent, respectively), followed by Yom Kippur fasting, and Yom Kippur and Rosh Hashana service attendance (between 54 and 59 per cent). Much less often practiced are regular Sabbath candle lighting (22 per cent as compared with noticeably higher rates in the two other studies where the word "regular" was omitted), having two sets of dishes for meat and dairy products (15 per cent), and eschewing shopping or working on the Sabbath (five per cent).

In the area of communal affiliation, we find that half of the national sample belong to a synagogue (as compared with 70 per cent of Americans who belong to a house of worship), and about the same number claim to contribute to the UJA-Federation every year. (Interestingly, in the New York data, only about 25 per cent of the total sample say that they contribute more than $25 to the federation campaign.)

One of the most startling findings in the study concerns the large number of adult respondents (37 per cent) who report that they have been to Israel. The figure is the same as that reported in the New York study, lending credibility to the finding. The 1970 National Jewish Population Study reported that, at that time, only 16 per cent had been to Israel;[4] in 1975 only 20 per cent of Boston Jews had traveled there (a figure probably lower than that year's national average, owing to the youthfulness of Boston Jewry).

Table 1 reports the large extent to which Jews restrict their closest friends to fellow Jews. Nearly two out of five respondents (39 per cent) report that "all" or "almost all" of their closest friends are Jewish; 22 per cent say that "most" of their friends are Jewish; and 24 per cent indicate that "half" of their friends are Jewish. Only one in seven (15 per cent) report that fewer than half of their friends are Jews.

Annual censuses of Jewish school enrollment have reported growth in the number of full-time students and in the number of youngsters receiving little or no schooling (Sunday school and bar/bat mitzvah lessons fall into this category);[5] enrollment in Hebrew schools has been declining. The respondents were asked to identify the predominant form of Jewish education they had given, were giving, or would be giving their children. We may compare these answers with the educational background of the respondents themselves to ascertain trends in Jewish schooling. In so doing, we find a near doubling in the proportion of yeshivah or day school students (from four per cent among respondents to seven per cent among their children), a

---

[4]See Table 3, p. 662, in Bernard Lazerwitz and Michael Harrison, "American Jewish Denominations: A Social and Religious Profile," *American Sociological Review,* August 1979, pp. 656–666.

[5]See Walter Ackerman, "Jewish Education Today," AJYB, Vol. 80, 1980, pp. 130–148.

decline in Hebrew school students (from 53 to 40 per cent), and a commensurate increase in those with little or no Jewish schooling (from 43 to 53 per cent).

Trends in Jewish Identification

More detailed information on trends in Jewish identification can be gleaned from Table 2 which presents various measures of Jewish identity broken down by age,

TABLE 2.   SELECTED MEASURES OF JEWISH IDENTIFICATION BY RESPONDENTS' AGE AND AMONG RESPONDENTS' PARENTS, BY PER CENT

	Age			Parental Observance
	18–39	40–59	60+	
Orthodox or Conservative	30	44	52	n.a.
Passover Seder	79	81	71	67
Hanukkah Candles	68	70	61	65
Fast Yom Kippur	55	59	47	60
Regularly Light Sabbath Candles	12	26	29	52
Yom Kippur Services	56	64	58	62
Rosh Hashanah Services	52	59	52	61
Kosher Dishes	8	17	20	40
No Sabbath Shopping/Working	3	5	8	22
Synagogue Member	38	60	57	n.a.
Jewish Organization Member	20	47	48	40
UJA/Federation Donor	31	56	62	37
Been to Israel	31	37	47	n.a.
Most Friends Jewish	45	56	76	n.a.

alongside figures for parental observance as reported by the respondents. Generally, measures which decline by age (as we move from older to younger respondents) also decline by generation (i.e., when we compare the previous generation of parents with the current generation of respondents). The table demonstrates a significant decline in the proportion who identify as Orthodox or Conservative, as well as in the proportion who light Sabbath candles, have Kosher dishes, and refrain from shopping or working on the Sabbath. Moreover, on all measures of communal activity —synagogue or other organization membership, UJA giving, traveling to Israel— younger respondents (ages 18–39) score considerably lower than their elders. To some extent these associations of lower Jewish activity with youth reflect the effects of early family life cycle stage; these effects will inevitably subside as the young adults marry and bear children.[6] But, to some degree, the differences between old and young signify more enduring declines in Jewish identification, and reflect growing assimilation among later-generation, younger Jews. The decline in the proportion with mostly Jewish friends—from 76 per cent among those 60 and over, to under half (45 per cent) among those under 40—suggests that a significant and enduring trend toward lower levels of Jewish identification is indeed underway. At the same time, all is not unequivocally gloomy for Jewish survivalists as some practices are indeed holding steady with age. These include the Passover Seder, Hanukkah candle lighting, and high holy day observance.

Israel and Zionism

Historically, American Jews have distinguished between support for Israel (and, before 1948, the Jewish settlement in Palestine) and endorsement of classical Zionist ideology. According to the latter, the very existence of Israel—the Jewish national home—implies that Jews everywhere should "return" from Galut—the Exile—and come "home" to Israel. This view contrasts sharply with one of the cardinal tenets of American Jewish belief, i.e., that the United States is "home" to American Jews.

In the 1981 National Survey, an overwhelming majority of the respondents (81 per cent) *disagree* with the statement that "each American Jew should give serious thought to settling in Israel" (Table 3). Only a tiny minority (12 per cent) agree with this classical Zionist position. (See also the data in Table 4 on the sample's rejection of the Zionist contention that Jewish life in the Diaspora is precarious or untenable.) However, reservations about classical Zionism do not inhibit deep, passionate, and widespread concern for Israel. Fully 83 per cent agree that "if Israel were destroyed, I would feel as if I had suffered one of the greatest personal tragedies in my life." The deep caring for Israel emerges in other findings as well. Over three-quarters of the respondents (76 per cent) concur that "Jews should not vote for candidates who are unfriendly to Israel." Over two-thirds (71 per cent) say they do not believe "Israel's future is secure," and almost as many (67 per cent) say they "often talk about Israel with friends and relatives." Moreover, consistent with other studies, more than nine Jews out of ten (94 per cent) regard themselves as "very pro-Israel" (44 per cent) or "pro-Israel" (50 per cent); almost all the rest are "neutral."

Clearly, American Jews continue to distinguish support for Israel from endorsement of classical Zionist thinking. They may be developing yet another distinction between concern for Israel and support for Israeli government policy. The vast majority of the respondents are convinced that the Palestinians and the PLO seek to destroy Israel. They line up with the majority of Israeli political leaders in rejecting (by 74 to 18 per cent) negotiations with the PLO. By a smaller, though

---

[6]See Steven M. Cohen, "The American Jewish Family Today," AJYB, Vol. 82, 1982, pp. 136–154.

TABLE 3.   ATTITUDES TOWARD ISRAEL AND ZIONISM, BY PER CENT

Agree—Disagree Questions	Agree	Undecided	Disagree
Classical Zionism Each American Jew should give serious thought to settling in Israel.	12	7	81
Concern For Israel If Israel were destroyed, I would feel as if I had suffered one of the greatest personal tragedies in my life.	83	5	13
Jews should not vote for candidates who are unfriendly to Israel.	76	5	20
Israel's future is secure.	12	17	71
I often talk about Israel with friends and relatives.	67	2	31
Support for Israel's Policies Israel is right not to agree to sit down with the Palestine Liberation Organization (PLO), because the PLO is a terrorist organization that wants to destroy Israel.	74	9	18
If the West Bank became an independent Palestinian state, it would probably be used as a launching pad to endanger Israel.	64	25	11
If the alternatives are permanent Israeli annexation of the West Bank or an independent Palestinian state, then an independent Palestinian state is preferable.	28	30	42
If Israel could be assured of peace and secure borders, she should be willing to return to Arab control most of the territories she has occupied since 1967.	41	18	41

Agree—Disagree Questions	Agree	Undecided	Disagree

Other Questions
In general, how would you characterize
your feelings about Israel?

Very Pro-Israel	44		
Pro-Israel	50		
Neutral	6		
Anti-Israel	1		
	100		

In general, do you think Israel's
policies in its dispute with
the Arabs have been:

Too "Hawkish"	23		
About Right	74		
Too "Dovish"	4		
	100		

still lopsided majority (64 to 11, with 25 per cent undecided), they fear that an independent Palestinian state on the West Bank of the Jordan "would probably be used as a launching pad to endanger Israel." At the same time, the respondents divide over whether Israel should permanently annex territories occupied in the Six Day War. By a small majority (42 to 28, with fully 30 per cent undecided), the sample prefer annexation to an independent Palestinian state; the many "undecideds" reveal considerable difficulty with this question. Even more telling, the respondents split evenly (41 to 41, with 18 per cent undecided) over whether Israel should trade occupied territory for assurances of peace. Clearly, annexationist policies are less popular among American Jews than are actions taken to defend Israel against perceived Palestinian threats.

A summary question asked the respondents to characterize "Israel's policies in its disputes with the Arabs." Almost a quarter (23 per cent) emerge as "doves"; they believe Israel's policies are "too hawkish." Almost all the other respondents (74 per cent) think Israel's policies are "about right."

More detailed analyses (see Table 6, below) reveal the types of Jews most likely to express concern for Israel, or to support its policies. In broad terms, there is less concern for Israel among young people, the better educated, and the more assimilated. Support for specific Israeli policies is also weakest among the young and most assimilated, and declines particularly among those with a post-graduate education. Moreover, although political liberals are as concerned about Israel as are conservatives, the liberals are more likely to take issue with Israeli government policies (see Table 9).

These results suggest a refinement of some observers' perception of growing American Jewish alienation from Israel.[7] Alienation, at least at this point, is limited to disagreement with Israeli policy; there is no general disillusionment with Israel. Significantly, the greatest disenchantment is found among Jews who are far removed from organized Jewish life. The more committed Jews find far less to fault in Israeli policies. As of now, hard-core critics of Israeli policy form only a small but noticeable minority of American Jews.

The American Jewish Situation

At the heart of American Jewish faith in the United States has been a sense that Jewish survival and interests are fully compatible with integration into America and the advancement of American interests.[8] Consistent with these sentiments, the sample is virtually unanimous (94 per cent) in declaring that "U.S. support for Israel is in America's interest." A sizeable majority (61 to 13 per cent) believe (in line with their rejection of classical Zionism) that "there is a bright future for Jewish life in America." An equally lopsided majority (72 to 25 per cent) reject the thought that "there are times when my devotion to Israel comes into conflict with my devotion to America." Thus, on an abstract level, Jews see America as basically hospitable to Jewish life and to the exercise of Jewish group interests.

However, more pointed questions uncover substantial anxieties about America's benevolence toward its Jewish community. Even though most Jews are optimistic about "Jewish life in America" (at a time when there are more Jewish senators, corporate directors, and Ivy League law school presidents than ever before,[9] and when public opinion polls show non-Jewish stereotyping of Jews at an all-time low[10]), a substantial majority (62 versus 34 per cent) reject the proposition that

---

[7]See, for example, Arthur Hertzberg, "Begin and the Jews," *New York Review of Books,* February 18, 1982, pp. 11–12.

[8]This point is argued at length in Charles Liebman, *The Ambivalent American Jew: Politics, Religion, and Family in American Jewish Life* (Philadelphia, 1973).

[9]See Charles Silberman, "The Jewish Community in Change: Challenge to Professional Practice," *Journal of Jewish Communal Service,* Fall 1981, pp. 4–11.

[10]See Yankelovich, Skelly, and White, "Anti-Semitism in the United States," prepared for the American Jewish Committee, mimeograph, 1981.

TABLE 4. ATTITUDES TOWARD JEWS AND JEWISH LIFE IN THE UNITED STATES,
BY PER CENT

	Agree	Undecided	Disagree
There is a bright future for Jewish life in America.	61	17	13
There are times when my devotion to Israel comes into conflict with my devotion to America.	25	3	72
U.S. support for Israel is in America's interest.	94	5	2
Most Americans think that U.S. support for Israel is in America's interest.	46	15	39
American Jews should not criticize Israel's policies publicly.	38	5	57
Virtually all positions of influence in America are open to Jews.	34	5	62

"virtually all positions of influence in America are open to Jews." Moreover, the respondents are evenly divided (46 per cent agree; 39 per cent disagree) as to whether most Americans share their rosy view of Israeli-American compatibility.

The respondents were asked to evaluate the importance of five "issues or problems confronting American Jews": assimilation, antisemitism in America, the security of Israel, the quality of Jewish education, and Soviet Jewry. Two of these—Israeli security and American antisemitism—are endorsed by at least two-thirds of the sample as "very important." The other issues garner considerably less support.

While concern for Israel's security is certainly consistent with previously reported findings and the very obvious support rendered Israel by organized Jewry, the concern with American antisemitism is, at first glance, more anomalous. As noted above, popular prejudice toward Jews and discrimination against individuals have fallen considerably. The growth since 1965 in Jewish-gentile intermarriage (which itself causes survival-conscious Jews much consternation) indicates the increasing interpersonal acceptance afforded Jews. However, it must be borne in mind that popular prejudice—the kind of antisemitism measured in standard social surveys—constitutes only one component of America's overall receptivity to Jews and their interests. American Jews have become increasingly aware that opposition to Israel and Zionism may mask outright antisemitism. Moreover, acts of vandalism against

TABLE 5. JEWISH CONCERNS,[a] BY PER CENT

	Very Important	In Between	Somewhat Important	In Between	Not Important
Assimilation	39	19	22	9	11
Antisemitism in America	66	17	13	3	1
Security of Israel	69	19	9	2	1
Quality of Jewish Education	38	23	26	8	5
Soviet Jewry	33	27	26	11	4

[a]"How important is each of the following issues or problems confronting American Jews?"

synagogues and other Jewish communal property have become more frequent of late,[11] stirring fears among many Jews.

Table 6 examines how age, education, and ritual observance influence concern for Israel (a composite of items discussed earlier—see Table 3), support for Israeli policies (an index made up of items found in Table 3 as well), and the importance attached to American antisemitism/Israel's security.

Findings contained in the columns regarding concern for Israel and support for its policies have already been noted. (To repeat, both measures decline with young age, increased education, and diminished ritual observance.) The last panel tries to discern whether particular population groups are more prone to evince concern about antisemitism, about Israel, or both. We find that those who are concerned about one issue are also concerned about the other; moreover, the types of Jews who are most pro-Israel (however measured) are also apt to regard American antisemitism as a very important issue.

The number of those who regard both antisemitism and Israel's security as very important rises with age, from 42 per cent among those under 40 years old to 60 per cent among those 60 or over. Consistent with the findings for Israel support, the better educated are much less apt to be concerned with either issue; only 39 per cent of those with a post-graduate degree regard both antisemitism and Israel's security as very important issues, compared with 67 per cent of those with no more than a high school education. As one would expect, the least observant ("secular") Jews are much less concerned with the two issues than are those with "minimal," "moderate," or "observant" levels of ritual practice (see below for explanations of

[11]See Anti-Defamation League of B'nai B'rith, "The 1981 Audit of Anti-Semitic Incidents," mimeograph, 1981.

TABLE 6. CONCERN FOR ISRAEL,[a] SUPPORT FOR ISRAELI POLICIES,[b] AND IMPORTANCE OF ANTISEMITISM IN AMERICA AND THE SECURITY OF ISRAEL,[c] BY AGE, EDUCATION, AND RITUAL OBSERVANCE

	Concern for Israel	Support For Israeli Policies	Neither	Antisemitism or Israel "Very Important?"		
				Antisemitism	Israel	Both
Age						
18–39	33	53	28	16	14	42
40–59	46	65	21	11	17	51
60+	55	73	16	10	15	60
Education						
H.S. Grad.	61	75	14	8	11	67
Some College	50	70	21	13	12	54
B.A.	38	65	21	13	19	48
Grad. School	35	50	27	16	18	39
Ritual Observance						
Secular	17	45	41	16	18	25
Minimal	48	61	19	15	14	52
Moderate	51	68	16	10	15	59
Observant	60	75	18	7	17	58

[a] Per cent expressing concern for Israel on at least three out of five questions: (1) Being very pro-Israel; (2) Security of Israel ("very important"); (3) Talking about Israel ("Agree strongly"); (4) Not voting for anti-Israel candidates ("Agree strongly"); (5) Tragedy if Israel destroyed ("Agree strongly"). See Table 3 for wording of questions.

[b] Per cent supporting Israeli policies or analyses on at least three out of five questions: (1) Not talking with the PLO ("Agree"); (2) A Palestinian state's threat to Israel ("Agree"); (3) Desirability of a Palestinian state ("Disagree"); (4) Return of Arab territories ("Disagree"); and (5) View on Israeli policies ("About Right" or "Too Dovish"). See Table 3 for wording.

[c] See Table 5 for wording.

these categories). Among the latter three groups, the extent of concern is about the same.

Social and Political Views

Table 7 presents the distribution of responses to several questions dealing with social and political issues. The table also presents reasonably comparable data from recent national studies of the American population, where such data are available.

With full appreciation of the hazards involved in making comparisons across surveys of different populations, carried out at different times, and using different methods, we can nevertheless make some tentative inferences from the broad patterns emergent in the findings. Jews, apparently, remain more liberal than the rest of society, but their marked liberalism is of a selective nature. They are much more liberal than others in their support for the equal rights amendment (73 versus 45 per cent among all Americans) and in permitting homosexuals to teach in the public schools (67 versus 45 per cent). They are also somewhat more liberal than others in supporting government expenditures for abortions (52 versus 40 per cent). These three issues involve, in varying degrees, civil liberties that have historically been dear to American Jews. None of these issues can be said to entail salient current Jewish group interests; thus there is little restraint on Jewish liberalism.

In the area of affirmative action, Jews (56 per cent) are somewhat less inclined than others (66 per cent) to adopt a liberal stance. Here some combination of historically induced sensitivity to quotas and current anxieties about the probable impact of affirmative action on Jewish access to jobs and universities probably helps to diminish Jewish enthusiasm. However, despite their relatively weak support for affirmative action, Jews—in comparison with non-Jews—are relatively more supportive of such extreme measures for alleviating racial inequality as outright quotas in jobs and universities, and school busing.

Further evidence of Jewish sympathy for the political agenda of minority groups is found in reactions to proposed changes in government spending. Despite their relative affluence, a majority of the sample (58 versus 35 per cent) reject substantial cuts in social spending. At the same time, most of those with definite opinions (49 versus 33 per cent) also rejected the Reagan administration's call for substantial increases in defense spending.

Somewhat more exact comparisons of Jews and other Americans can be drawn from the results of the questions dealing with political identification, party identification, and presidential preference in the last election. Over one-third of the sample identify themselves as liberal (or radical) as compared with only 21 per cent of those in a recent national study. Similarly, many fewer Jews (17 per cent) than non-Jews (43 per cent) say that they are conservative. The shading of Jewish politics toward the liberal end of the spectrum is further documented by the respondents' relatively disproportionate identification as Democrats (66 as compared with 47 per cent for

TABLE 7. COMPARISON OF JEWS' POLITICAL VIEWS WITH ANALAGOUS
NATIONAL DATA, BY PER CENT

Public Opinion Items (Liberal Responses)	1981 NSAJ	National Data
Should the Equal Rights Amendment (ERA) be passed? (Yes)	73	45[a]
Should declared homosexuals be allowed to teach in the public schools? (Yes)	67	45[b]
Should the government pay for abortions? (Yes)	52	40[c]
Should the death penalty be abolished? (Yes)	19	20[b]
Should affirmative action be used to help disadvantaged groups? (Yes)	56	66[d]
Should quotas be used to help disadvantaged groups? (Yes)	20	10[e]
Should school children be bused when other means of integrating schools have failed? (Yes)	23	12[f]
Should the U.S. substantially cut spending on social welfare? (No)	58	n.a.
Should the U.S. substantially increase defense spending? (No)	49	n.a.
Political Identification		
Liberal (and Radical)	34	21[g]
Moderate	49	36
Conservative (and Very Conservative)	17	43
	100	100
Party Identification		
Democratic	66	47[h]
Republican	11	27
Independent, None, Other	24	26
	100	100
Presidential Preference		
Reagan	37 (34)[i]	55[j]
Carter	40 (47)	36

Public Opinion Items (Liberal Responses)	1981 NSAJ	National Data
Anderson	20 (17)	8
Others	4 (2)	2
	100	100

[a]NBC News/Associated Press National Survey, Fall 1980; reported in Milton Himmelfarb, "Are Jews Becoming Republican?," *Commentary,* August 1981, pp. 27–31.

[b]ABC News/Washington *Post* survey, May 18–20, 1981.

[c]Gallup Organization survey, July 11–14, 1980.

[d]ABC News/Louis Harris survey, November 11–13, 1980.

[e]Gallup Organization survey, December 5–8, 1980.

[f]CBS News/New York *Times* survey, June 22–27, 1980.

[g]Computed from Yankelovich *et al.,* "Anti-Semitism in the United States," New York, July 1981, p. 81.

[h]*Time*/Yankelovich survey, September 15–17, 1981.

[i]Jewish voters as reported on p. 333 of Alan Fisher, "Jewish Political Shift?"; computed from an adjusted New York *Times*/CBS News Election Day Poll, 1980.

[j]Whites only, *ibid.*

the country as a whole), and their commensurate under-identification as Republicans (11 versus 27 per cent). Similarly, Jews are roughly ten per cent more likely than other Americans to claim they favored Jimmy Carter and/or John Anderson for president in 1980; they are about 20 per cent less likely to claim they supported Ronald Reagan for president.[12]

Sources of Jewish Liberalism

Some understanding of the sources of Jewish liberalism can be gleaned from examining political variation among major population sub-groups. Table 8 reports how four measures of political orientation vary by age, education, and ritual observance. The four measures are: an index of liberalism constructed out of nine public opinion items and the question on self-identification; political self-identification (as liberal or radical, moderate, conservative or very conservative); party identification; and 1980 presidential preference.

Age, education, and ritual observance bear fairly consistent relationships with the various measures of liberalism. Thus, in three out of four instances, the young (ages 18–39) are between five and 15 per cent more liberal than the middle-aged or elderly.

[12]Exit polls are reported in Alan Fisher, "Jewish Political Shift? Erosion, Yes; Conversion, No," in Seymour Lipset, (ed.), *Party Coalitions in the 1980's* (New Brunswick, 1981), pp. 327–340. Fisher indicates that 34 per cent of Jews voted for Reagan, whereas the National Survey reports a figure of 37 per cent. Sampling error, the distinction between actual voting and mere "favoring," as well as over-reporting of support for a winner are partial explanations for this small discrepancy.

TABLE 8. LIBERAL PUBLIC OPINION INDEX,[a] POLITICAL IDENTIFICATION, PARTY IDENTIFICATION, AND PRESIDENTIAL PREFERENCE, BY AGE, EDUCATION, AND RITUAL OBSERVANCE, BY PER CENT

	Liberal Index	Political Identification			Party Identification			Presidential Preference		
		Lib./Rad.	Mod.	Cons.	Dem.	Rep.	Other	Reagan	Carter	And.
Age										
18–39	55	44	42	15	61	9	30	32	39	25
40–59	41	28	52	19	60	16	24	42	36	19
60+	38	29	53	18	76	7	17	37	46	15
Education										
H.S. Grad.	35	31	47	22	76	9	15	40	42	14
Some College	35	26	57	18	61	13	26	47	33	18
B.A.	51	31	48	18	64	12	24	35	41	20
Grad. School	57	37	48	12	63	10	27	29	42	24
Ritual Obs.										
Secular	45	42	39	20	49	21	30	37	47	12
Minimal	52	39	49	11	68	7	25	29	47	20
Moderate	41	26	56	19	68	12	20	42	34	22
Observant	41	27	48	25	72	10	18	46	28	23

[a]Per cent giving Liberal (or Radical) answers to at least five out of ten questions on Public Opinions and Political Identification.

Party preference constitutes the single exception to this generalization, in that fewer young Jews identify as Democrats. They—like young Americans generally—are less likely than their elders to identify as either Republicans or Democrats (30 per cent of the under-40 respondents fail, in fact, to do so).

One reason for the greater liberalism among younger Jews is their lead over their elders in educational attainment. Better educated people in the general population are more liberal, and such is the case with Jews also. Respondents with a graduate degree score high on the liberal index 20 per cent more often than do those without a B.A. Similar but less dramatic differences obtain for political self-identification and presidential preference. Interestingly, the party preference question is out of line with the three ideological indicators. In fact, the least well-educated—those with no more than a high school education—are the most Democratic group, even as they are the least liberal. Overall, though, the association between education and liberalism is direct, much as one would expect.

More significant is the relationship between liberalism and ritual observance. Respondents were classified into four ritual observance groups based on their answers to six questions about ritual and one on synagogue membership. These groups are: (1) the "observant"—almost all of whom have Passover Seders, light Hanukkah candles, fast on Yom Kippur, attend Rosh Hashanah services, and belong to a synagogue, while the overwhelming majority also light Sabbath candles, and have meat and dairy dishes; (2) the "moderately observant"—who differ from the "observant" in that only a small minority light Sabbath candles or keep Kosher at home; (3) the "minimally observant"—who perform only one or two of the activities mentioned above, usually attending a Passover Seder or lighting Hanukkah candles; and (4) the "secular"—who perform none of the six rituals mentioned.

According to conventional wisdom, liberalism should increase uniformly as observance declines. Table 8's lowest panel shows that this is largely, but not totally, true. Liberalism does increase with diminishing ritual observance, but only up to a point, that demarked by the "minimally observant." Thus, the "observant" are generally less liberal than the "moderately observant," and both are clearly less liberal than the "minimally observant." But then, continuing to move down the observance continuum, the increase in liberalism ceases: "secular" respondents are considerably *less* liberal than the "minimally observant." They score seven per cent lower than the "minimally observant" on the liberalism index, are three times as likely to identify as Republicans (21 versus 7 per cent), are 12 per cent more likely to have voted for (or favored) Ronald Reagan for president (37 versus 29 per cent), and are nine per cent more likely to call themselves conservative (20 versus 11 per cent).

The liberalism-observance relationship, then, can be characterized as a lopsided, inverted U-shaped contour. Liberalism reaches a peak among Jews who are only somewhat less observant than the "average" Jew. Both the more observant ("observant" and "moderately observant" respondents) and the least observant ("secular" Jews) are less liberal than the "minimally observant."

Several theories that have been advanced to explain why modern Jews generally identify with the political left have been subjected to criticism by Charles Liebman.[13] My own view—drawn in part from Liebman's thinking on the matter—is that Jewish liberal tendencies are bound up with the process of assimilation and integration into the larger society. Liberalism is both a strategy for, and a reflection of, the successful entry of Jews into the social mainstream. For years, liberal politics signified successful integration; more assimilated Jews viewed their universalist politics as a sign of sophistication, while they saw the particularism of their parents and other less well-educated Jews as an indication of incomplete adjustment to American modernity. Beyond that, Jews have entered—and have probably significantly influenced—the highly-educated free professions, becoming part of what some have called the "new class," those who work in the world of ideas and communication. Public opinion analysts have portrayed this "class" as especially liberal. Finally, and not least relevant to the integration argument, Jews remain a minority group with considerable insecurities. Many Jews continue to believe that there is a definite Jewish stake in supporting the civil rights and civil liberties of all Americans.

While these considerations impel the bulk of American Jews to lean leftward in their overall political stance, still other factors restrain Jewish liberalism. Significantly, these restraints operate most effectively among Jews at either end of the assimilation-identification continuum, that is, among the most observant and least observant Jews.

The more observant are less liberal (or more conservative) for at least two sorts of reasons. In the first place, traditional Jewish teaching in many areas is, in fact, quite conservative. Secondly, more observant Jews—Orthodox or not—are more likely to think politically in terms of the particularist group interests of American and world Jewry. As such, they are less committed to unqualified universalism; they are more prepared to make alliances with powerful conservative elites if, in their view, it is "good for the Jews."

At the other extreme of the identification-assimilation continuum are the largely assimilated Jews. They are represented in this study by the 15 per cent or so who qualify as "secular" Jews on the ritual observance scale. Not only are these people ritually uninvolved and much less likely to belong to a synagogue (only ten per cent of the "secular" respondents do belong, as opposed to over half of the rest), but they are considerably less likely to have mostly Jewish friends (only about a quarter do, as opposed to roughly three-quarters of the others). As such, they are highly integrated into non-Jewish society, are distant from the semi-segregated Jewish subsociety, and are relatively untouched by the liberal Jewish political subculture fostered by Jewish social networks. When Jews assimilate, they move toward the politics of the mainstream to which they assimilate. Thus, while the "minimally

---

[13]See Liebman, *op. cit.*

observant" are the most liberal group, the "secular" Jews manifest more moderate and sometimes even conservative political views. (In analyses whose results are not shown here, I further subdivided the "secular" group into two roughly equal segments, consisting of those with mostly non-Jewish friends and those with at least half Jewish friends. The former are considerably more conservative than the latter, and they are about as conservative as the "observant.")

In sum, as with many other aspects of social behavior, Jews act politically in line with the rest of society and yet in a distinctly Jewish fashion as well. Like other Americans, Jews who are younger and better educated are more liberal. No doubt part of the Jews' preponderance in liberalism can be traced to their extraordinary educational achievements and their concentration in the "new class" professions. But Jews also act distinctively; their Jewishness still operates in a special fashion to alternately induce or restrain their left-of-center proclivities. The most liberal are those who identify as Jews, but participate minimally in Jewish life. They are not so assimilated as to have left the essentially liberal Jewish subculture or to no longer feel the group identification and insecurity which impels many Jews to the liberal side of the political spectrum. Nor are they so thoroughly identified as Jews that they feel comfortable either with unabashed particularism or with the social conservatism of the more religiously observant.

Liberalism and Pro-Israelism

During the last decade, several commentators have suggested that the tradition of dual American-Jewish support for Israel and liberalism has come under increasing strain. Some liberals have claimed that many Jews are leaving the liberal coalition because of their commitment to Israel. At the same time, conservative and neo-conservative supporters of Israel charge Jewish liberals with failing to rally to Israel's cause with sufficient fervor because of their universalist commitments. If, in fact, there has been either erosion of support for Israel among liberals or a disproportionate retreat from liberalism among supporters of Israel, then we would expect to find greater support for Israel among conservatives than among liberals. Table 9 examines the extent to which liberalism and pro-Israelism are actually incompatible among our nationwide sample of American Jews. Respondents are divided into three political groups—low, medium, and high liberals—based on their answers to nine issue questions and the question on political self-identification. The left panel of the table reports differences among these groups in three measures of pro-Israelism: concern for Israel, support for Israel's policies (see Table 6 for details on these two indices), and having traveled to Israel.

While travel to Israel is level across all three political groupings, both concern for Israel and support for its policies decline (and the latter more so) as liberalism increases. Since both political views and the Israel measures are subject to influences which causally precede them, it would be erroneous to infer a causal association between liberalism and any of the pro-Israel measures simply on the basis of the

TABLE 9. PRO-ISRAEL MEASURES BY LIBERALISM, UNADJUSTED AND AD-JUSTED FOR AGE, EDUCATION, INCOME, AND RITUAL OBSERVANCE, BY PER CENT

Liberalism	Unadjusted			Adjusted		
	Low	Med.	High	Low	Med.	High
Concern for Israel	47	44	39	45	42	45
Support for Israel's Policies	70	66	46	69	65	51
Have Been to Israel	37	38	39	37	37	41

unadjusted figures on the left. The right panel in Table 9 adjusts for such antecedent factors as age, education, income, and ritual observance. Since both supporters of Israel and the less liberal tend to be older and less well-educated, controlling for these factors in particular should help to explain the association between liberalism and pro-Israelism. After controls are introduced, we find absolutely no relationship between liberalism and either concern for Israel or travel to Israel. However, as before, significantly fewer "high" liberals are supportive of Israeli policies than are "medium" or "low" liberals.

The distinction between support for Israeli policies and other forms of pro-Israeli thinking and action proves to be quite crucial in this analysis of the putative incompatibility between liberalism and pro-Israelism. Liberal political views do not in any way inhibit concern for Israel, or travel there, which is a very concrete manifestation of concern. Liberals, though, are more ready than moderates and conservatives (i.e., "low" liberals) to part company with hard-line Israeli government policies. Insofar as liberals are more prone to adopt conciliatory rather than confrontational approaches to settling international disputes in general, they apply the same perspective to Israeli-Arab differences. As a result, they more readily criticize Israel for being too hawkish, more easily contemplate negotiations with the PLO, and more frequently consider territorial concessions as a way of bringing peace and security to Israel. These political positions do not necessarily imply weaker commitment to Israel in the abstract, although those most supportive of Israeli policies are more likely to evince strong concern for Israel as well (data not shown). In sum, American Jewish liberalism is not incompatible with pro-Israeli feelings or certain expressions of support (such as travel). It does, however, restrain concurrence with certain hard-line policies of the Israeli government.

Conclusion

The 1981/1982 National Survey of American Jews replicates many previously reported findings pertaining to American Jews (especially in the demographic area), documents characteristics and trends noted earlier by astute observers of American Jewry, and clarifies some issues by sharpening our understanding of the thinking and practices of American Jews. The experience of this first survey has shown that it is possible to collect reasonably representative survey data on American Jews at relatively low cost. This successful experiment with the mail-back Distinctive Jewish Name technique may ultimately spur other researchers to collect additional data on these and other matters, thereby contributing to improved and expanded quantitative research on American Jewry.

STEVEN MARTIN COHEN

The National Gallup Polls and American Jewish Demography

T HE BEGINNING OF SOCIAL SCIENCE is demography, and the beginning of demographic studies is the national census. Because of the absence of up-to-date national census data on religio-ethnic groups, the demographic map of American Jewry is often sketchy. Lacking an authoritative base for comparison, estimates become risky.

Two studies of American Jewish demography stand out: the one-shot National Bureau of the Census study of March 1957 and the National Jewish Population Study (NJPS) of 1971.[1] Published reports on the NJPS are incomplete.[2] Moreover, the NJPS is based on parameters established by the Council of Jewish Federations and Welfare Funds which, at best, provide a rough estimate of the Jewish population. In the past, the methods used by various Jewish federations have overestimated religiously-affiliated Jews and minimized the number of non-affiliated Jews.[3]

Figures for American Jewry as a whole have often been projections from local studies or guesses based on personal observation. Because of the costs involved, Jewish organizations have been reluctant to underwrite national studies. Those which have been undertaken suffer from two serious shortcomings: small sample sizes and inadequate sampling methods. The most accepted contemporary methods —multi-stage cluster sampling and random digit telephone dialing—are particularly expensive for studying a group which constitutes less than three per cent of the total population.

One obvious source of data on American Jews consists of the large national polls conducted by both private and academic groups. However, national polls rarely

---

Note: Some of the data utilized in this paper were made available by the Inter-University Consortium for Political and Social Research. Most of the data are from various issues of *Gallup Opinion Index* or were generously made available by the Gallup Organization, to which I am indebted. Neither the original collectors of any of the data, nor the consortium or other sources bear any responsibility for the analyses presented here.

[1]See U.S. Bureau of the Census, "Religion by the Civilian Population of the United States, March 1957," *Current Population Reports,* Series P-20, No. 79, 1958, also reported in Sidney Goldstein, "Socio-Economic Differences Among Religious Groups in the United States," *American Journal of Sociology,* May 1969, pp. 612–631; Fred Massarik and Alvin Chenkin, "United States National Jewish Population Study: A First Report," AJYB, Vol. 74, 1973, pp. 264–306.

[2]The best report is in Bernard Lazerwitz, "An Estimate of a Rare Population Group—the United States Jewish Population," *Demography,* August 1978, pp. 389–394.

[3]For an historical overview, see Jack Diamond, "A Reader in the Demography of American Jews," AJYB, Vol. 77, 1977, pp. 251–319.

encompass more than 1500–2000 respondents, including a Jewish sample of 35–60, which is too small to ensure accurate results. One solution, which has already been tried for very small groups, including Southern Jews, is to merge a set of coterminous studies to create a larger Jewish sample.[4] By merging ten sets of samples, each with forty Jews, it is possible to create a respectable Jewish sample with an error margin of about ±6 percentage points—still high, but better than much of what we have now. With repeated sampling of a relatively constant number over an extended time period, we can hope to trace patterns of stability and change.

Given the advantages of such a procedure, why has it not been widely used? First, the total number of national studies is relatively small; many are sponsored by private businesses, hence not available for secondary analysis at reasonable fees. Second, merging requires similar sampling procedures and the exact duplication of questions. (For a variety of reasons, competing survey organizations have not reached a consensus on exact question wording and response categories.) Thus it is not possible to equate responses to even elementary questions like "In what place (e.g., state) were you born?" with those for "In what place did you spend most of the years before age 12?" (The first would overrepresent the population of Jews in New York and underrepresent those in Los Angeles.) Uniformity of sampling and question wording is typically found for the same survey organization. But using only one accessible survey organization limits the total number of surveys and thus lessens the accuracy of trend analysis.

The only ongoing, widely-disseminated national sources of demographic information on American Jews that have Jewish samples larger than 150 per year and that repeat the same questions over time are the Gallup and Harris polls. Partly because of the interest shown in religious demography by George Gallup, Jr., and because of the cooperation of the Gallup Organization in making available unpublished information, the Gallup Poll was selected for this study. The Gallup Poll has a large sample (normally about 1500 people, of whom 35–40 are Jews), and the basic demographic questions are repeated in exactly the same form in every poll. The polls are conducted on a biweekly average. Furthermore, the Gallup Poll has from time to time published figures on religious (including Jewish) demography based on reasonably-sized samples.[5]

The information is presented in two sections—(A) and (B)—divided roughly by sample size. Generally, we can be more confident about the findings in the first section, although even here the sample sizes are not as large as would be desirable.

---

[4] See John Shelton Reed, "Needles in Haystacks: Studying Rare Populations by Secondary Analysis of National Sample Surveys," *Public Opinion Quarterly,* Winter 1975–1976, pp. 514–522; Lazerwitz, *op. cit.*

[5] In some instances, where the Gallup samples are small and National Opinion Research Center or University of Michigan Survey Research Center data match the Gallup or Census questions and answer categories, the cases for the Jews have been combined, although the additional data do not appear in the tabular presentations.

For a sample size of 1500, the error margin is ±3 points at the 95 per cent confidence level; when the size is reduced to 600, the error margin increases to ±5. For variables which have many categories, the error margin increases as the number of respondents in any category decreases. For variables with two categories, e.g., sex, confidence increases.

First, we shall look at the changes that took place among the national population in the 1970's.[6] Then we shall examine the changes among Jews. What are the trends? For statistical reasons, trends are often more meaningful than absolute percentage differences. Is the Jewish population different from the country as a whole? (In the Gallup presentation, Jews are not compared with non-Jews but rather with the population as a whole. This slightly underestimates the differences between Jews and non-Jews.) How do the Gallup data compare with our previous information? Is there a need to radically revise our estimates, or do the new facts support our working figures?

The published findings for 1979 are based on all the polls taken during the year, not just a sample half-dozen polls spaced evenly throughout the year. As a consequence, except for Tables 1 and 4, the sample size of Jews in 1979 is considerably larger than in previous studies and hence more trustworthy. The existence of previous Gallup national data makes it possible to scan major demographic changes among American Jews and to take a somewhat blurred picture of the community at any given moment. Over the period of a year, that picture becomes clearer.

Findings (A)

FAMILY

Although Gallup figures dealing with family status are available only from 1973 on, they bear out some common observations about the national population, particularly the steady decline in the percentage of married people (from 72.6 in 1973 to 66.0 in 1979)[7] and a smaller increment in the percentage of never-married people (from 14.6 to 18.7). Observations about the escalation of separation and divorce are

---

[6]In all cases Gallup rather than Census and NJPS data have been used for national figures in order to control whatever bias might exist for the Jewish sample. A separate check against Census data suggests the accuracy of the Gallup figures for most of the items. Comparisons with the NJPS are more problematic because Gallup data in the early 1970's are sparse, whereas the more numerically-based findings from the late 1970's may reflect either changes over time or population differences. Where the Gallup data are available, however, they are generally comparable with those from the NJPS.

[7]Compare with a decline from 71.1 (1973) to 67.0 (1978) according to the Census Bureau. But these figures should be increased slightly because the Census sample includes persons over 14 years of age compared to 18 and over for Gallup data.

TABLE 1.   FAMILY STATUS FOR THE NATION (N) AND JEWS (J), BY PER CENT[a]

		1973	1974	1975	1976	1977	1978	1979
(Sample size)	(N)	(21,000)	(27,000)	(33,000)	(31,500)	(33,000)	(27,000)	(41,500)
	(J)	(571)	(597)	(818)	(711)	(879)	(702)	(991)
Family								
Married	N	72.6	71.8	69.9	69.0	67.6	66.2	66.0
	J	67.6	69.6	71.0	67.2	63.9	62.5	60.9
Never-	N	14.6	14.7	15.6	16.3	17.5	18.0	18.7
Married	J	19.9	19.2	18.4	22.3	21.2	25.2	22.9
Widowed*	N					8.3	7.8	8.6
	J	12.4	13.4	13.6	12.7	8.4	7.0	10.2
Divorced*	N					3.9	3.9	4.8
	J	12.2	10.7	10.0	9.3	3.1	3.2	4.8
Separated	N	.5	.1	1.0	1.9	2.3	4.0	1.9
	J	.3	.5	.7	1.1	1.9	2.1	1.2

*Numbers for Widowed and Divorced are combined from 1973–1976.

[a]Sources: *Gallup Opinion Index: Religion in America:* Report Nos. 130 (1976); 145 (1977–78); 184 (1981); and (1979–80); also unpublished polls, nos. 862–881 (1973); 886–920 (1974); 921–943 (1975); 944–964 (1976); 965–991 (1977); 992–1119 (1978); 120–145 (1979).

not clearly proven by the data because the differentiation between widowhood and divorce was not made until 1977, and the numbers are too small to allow confidence in small differences. These questions tap only the current marital status and not whether an individual was previously separated or divorced. There is no pattern for the widowed population.

Except for 1975, a similar family-status pattern obtains for Jews, especially if we take 1974 as the base year.[8] The married population declined from 67.6 to 60.9 per cent; the percentage of never-marrieds increased from 19.9 to 22.9 per cent. Divorce also seemed to be on the rise, although data are very sketchy. The figures for the separated are too small to evaluate, and no pattern appears for the widowed. With the exception of 1975, Jews were consistently less likely than other Americans to be married and more likely to have never married. Between 1977 and 1979 Jews averaged 4.2 per cent fewer married people than did Americans in general.

---

[8]No exact numerical comparison with the NJPS is possible because that study takes as its sample "head of household," which understates the proportion of never-marrieds and overstates the proportion of marrieds in the population.

SYNAGOGUE MEMBERSHIP

Nationally, there was a very slight but consistent decline in church membership —a drop from 72 to 69 per cent over eight years. These figures call into question reports of the widespread revival of religion among people formerly outside the church, although the measure of church membership omits the phenomenon of non-denominational, non-churched Christian believers who turn to extra-church religious groups.

No pattern is visible for synagogue membership since there are too few observations. (Data were excluded for years in which there were fewer than 100 cases.) What is clear is that Jews are significantly less likely than their neighbors to be identified with religious institutions. In the three years for which sizeable observations are available, Jewish enrollment is 60 per cent of the national figure.

TABLE 2: CHURCH/SYNAGOGUE MEMBERSHIP FOR THE NATION (N) AND JEWS (J), BY PER CENT[a]

Church/Synagogue Membership		1973	1974	1975	1976	1977	1978	1979
(Sample size)	(N)	(6,000)	(6,000)	(6,000)	(6,000)	(6,000)	(6,000)	(9,000)
	(J)	X	X	(150)	X	(311)	X	(193)
Yes	N	72	71	71	70	70	69	69
	J	X	X	34	X	51	X	40
No	N	28	29	29	30	30	31	31
	J	X	X	66	X	49	X	60

X = Sample size too small for reliable figures.

[a]Sources: *Gallup Opinion Index: Religion in America:* Report Nos. 114 (1975); 130 (1976); 145 (1977–78); 184 (1981); and (1979–80); also unpublished polls, nos. 924 (1974); 958, 962, 964 (1975); 967–970, 973, 978, 989–990 (1977).

SYNAGOGUE ATTENDANCE

Church/synagogue attendance is measured in Gallup surveys by asking people if they have attended church/synagogue sometime in the previous week. The Gallup figures are higher than those found in the National Opinion Research Center or University of Michigan data, which are based on differently worded questions. There is no guarantee that a positive response indicates attendance at prayer rather than at a business or social meeting, but the same question has been asked for many years, so that any distortion which exists is likely to be constant. For both Christians and Jews, attendance increases at holiday periods, suggesting a significant religious impulse for church/synagogue attendance.

Nationally, church attendance has been almost constant over the last decade, at about 40 per cent. There is, then, no obvious widespread religious revival involving church attendance. However, modern technology has affected religion and given rise, especially among the elderly, the ill, and the isolated, to a generation of the television faithful, many of whom believe but do not attend church. (This option is not readily available to many Jews.)

The figures for synagogue attendance fluctuate and are not clear; most of the variance is explained by random error. There appears to be a slight increase in synagogue attendance from the early to late 1970's, but the 1979 figure—the largest sample and hence most accurate— indicates a return to the earlier level. Regardless of the exact percentage, it is clear that Jews are much less likely than non-Jews to attend synagogue/church.

TABLE 3.   CHURCH/SYNAGOGUE ATTENDANCE FOR THE NATION (N) AND JEWS (J) BY PER CENT[a]

Church/Synagogue Attendance		1970	1971	1973	1974	1975	1976	1977	1978	1979
(Sample size)	(N)	(16,500)	(7,500)	(7,500)	(6,000)	(6,000)	(12,000)	(6,000)	(6,000)	(14,700
	(J)	(475)	(180)	(179)	(175)	(240)	(160)	X	(140)	(347
Yes	N	42	40	40	40	40	42	41	41	40
	J	19	19	19	16	21	23	X	27	20
No	N	58	60	60	60	60	58	59	59	60
	J	81	81	81	84	79	77	X	73	80

X = Sample size too small for reliable figures.

[a]Sources: *Gallup Opinion Index: Religion in America:* Report Nos. 70 (1971); 114 (1975); 130 (1976); 145 (1977–78); 184 (1981); and (1979–80); unpublished Report (Feb., 1980); also unpublished polls, nos. 861 (1973); 918 (1974); 924, 935, 942, 943 (1975); 946–948, 950, 953, 958, 960, 962–964 (1976); 978, 981, 982, 984, 988–990 (1977); 993 (1978).

POLITICAL AFFILIATION

In dealing with party preference, the Gallup data reveal a picture—supported by other national polls—radically different from popular impressions. In the second half of the 1970's, the national Democratic preference increased slightly, then declined back to the 1975 level. Republican support oscillated slightly in a strangely regular pattern of $+2$, -2, $+2$, -2 over five years, but no substantive transformation occurred. Independents fluctuated irregularly, but the rate is very close to the 1975 figure.

NATIONAL POLLS / 117

Jewish political affiliation also showed no meaningful change. The increase in Republican identifiers was almost nil (from 7.8 to 9.0 per cent), while the Democratic identifiers increased slightly between 1975 and 1977 (from 55.0 to 58.2 per cent), and thereafter declined. The independent vote seemed to be declining. Most of the fluctuation is easily explained by sampling error. Clearly, Jews have not (yet) realigned their party orientation.

For all the years surveyed, Jews remained regularly and significantly more Democratic (average of about 30 per cent) and less Republican (average 40 per cent) than other Americans. From 1975 to 1977 (when these data were available), Jewish independents who stated a preference were decidedly Democratic (75.6 per cent), more so than other independents (62.4 per cent).

TABLE 4: PARTY AFFILIATION FOR THE NATION (N) AND JEWS (J), BY PER CENT[a]

Political Affiliation		1970	1975	1976	1977	1978	1979
(Sample size)	(N)	(16,500)	(16,500)	(18,000)	(19,500)	(30,000)	(41,500)
	(J)	(475)	(241)	(783)	(1,028)	(712)	(991)
Democrat	N	43	43.9	45.4	46.1	45.9	43.6
	J	63	55.0	57.4	62.4	62.0	58.2
Republican	N	28	20.8	22.0	20.5	22.2	20.7
	J	6	7.8	8.6	8.4	8.8	9.0
Independent	N	28	32.1	29.9	29.9	28.1	31.8
	J	29	35.2	32.0	26.0	26.9	28.8
Don't Know/Other	N	Y	3.4	2.6	3.4	3.5	3.8
	J	Y	1.9	2.0	3.2	2.1	4.1

Y = Categories not used in this year.

[a]Sources: *Gallup Opinion Index: Religion in America:* Report Nos. 70 (1971); 114 (1975); 130 (1976); 145 (1977–78); 184 (1981); and (1979–80); unpublished Report (Feb., 1980); George Gallup, *The Gallup Poll: Public Opinion 1972–1977* (Wilmington, 1978), pp. 453; *The Gallup Poll: Public Opinion 1976–1977*, p. 1174; also unpublished polls, nos. 916 (1974); 924, 926, 928, 929, 932, 939, 940, 942, 943 (1975); 944–947, 949–964; 965–973 (1977).

Findings (B)

The findings in this section are taken directly from various issues of *Gallup Opinion Index.* The sample sizes are generally small—about 150 (except 1979). With a sample size of 150, the margin of error is ±10. However, these samples are still considerably larger than those found in almost all other national studies of Jews. The Gallup Poll uses a weighting formula for sex, education, age, and region to match Census figures. These variables, therefore, are already partly adjusted for in the Jewish samples. While community size is accounted for nationally in the (cluster) sampling procedure, the effects on the Jewish figures are less certain because of the high concentration of Jews in a few localities.

NATIONAL PERCENTAGES AND NUMBERS

The first datum reads the simplest: the percentage of Jews in the country has dropped from three to two. However, this is rounded ±0.49, i.e., the actual difference may be from 0.01 to 0.99 percentage points. The figure reflects conscious, semi-public religious self-identification. If, therefore, Jews are less likely now than in the past to declare their religious status—and there is some weak evidence to this effect—the percentages will decline even if the population remains the same. Of course, we are dealing with relative, not absolute, change, and Jews may simply be growing at a slower rate than other Americans. Counterbalancing these qualifications is the Gallup sample framework: if Jews have fewer children than non-Jews, interviewing people over age 18 will tend to overrepresent the Jewish share of the entire population.

The sampling error, the process of rounding fractions to integer percentages, and the under-identification by Jews make it impossible to project anything but a very rough estimate of the number of Jews in the United States. These data, however, suggest support for (or at least do not contravene) the *American Jewish Year Book* (AJYB) total percentage estimates of 3.1 per cent in 1960, 2.9 per cent in 1970, and 2.7 per cent in 1975 and 1979. Given the slight increase of the national population, this would mean a relatively stable number of Jews, probably not radically different from the AJYB estimate of about 5.8 million in 1979.[9]

SEX

Because of the weighting procedure for sex, national figures are likely to be accurate (at least to approximate Census data), as are the figures for Jews (slightly less so because of the smaller sample size). Except for 1975, the figures for Jews are close to the national distribution—a slight majority (51:49) of women, the same proportion found by the NJPS in 1970. Differences between Jews and non-Jews, though consistent, are too small to indicate any pattern; a much larger sample size would be needed to test for any significant differences.

RACE

Nationally, the percentage of non-whites has been growing very slightly in the 1970's, and may increase due to the influx of Southeast Asians. However, this has

[9]Estimates are from "Jewish Population in the United States," AJYB, Vols. 70–80, 1969–1980. For a tabular display, see Sidney Goldstein, "Jews in the United States: Perspectives from Demography," AJYB, Vol. 81, 1981, p. 9, Table 1.

TABLE 5: PERCENTAGE OF JEWS (J) IN THE NATION (N), BY PER CENT[a]

Percentage of Nation		1970	1971	1974	1975	1976	1979
(Sample size)	(N)	(16,000)	(U)	(7,000)	(6,500)	(6,000)	(41,500)
	(J)	(475)	(U)	(170)	(160)	(150)	(991)
	N	100	100	100	100	100	100
	J	3	3	2	2	2	2

U = Numbers not available.
[a]Sources: *Gallup Opinion Index: Religion in America:* Report Nos. 70 (1971); 114 (1975); 130 (1976); 145 (1977–78); 184 (1981); and (1979–80).

TABLE 6: DISTRIBUTION OF THE SEXES FOR THE NATION (N) AND JEWS (J), BY PER CENT[a]

Sex		1970	1971	1974	1975	1976	1979
(Sample size)	(N)	(16,500)	(U)	(6,000)	(6,000)	(6,000)	(41,500)
	(J)	(475)	(U)	(170)	(160)	(150)	(991)
Male	N	48	47	47	48	48	48
	J	49	49	49	52	48	49
Female	N	52	53	53	52	52	52
	J	51	51	51	48	52	51

U = Numbers not available.
[a]Sources: *Gallup Opinion Index: Religion in America:* Report Nos. 70 (1971); 114 (1975); 130 (1976); 145 (1977–78); 184 (1981); and (1979–80).

TABLE 7: DISTRIBUTION BY RACE FOR THE NATION (N) AND JEWS (J), BY PER CENT[a]

Race		1970	1971	1974	1975	1976	1979
(Sample size)	(N)	(16,500)	(U)	(6,000)	(6,000)	(6,000)	(41,500)
	(J)	(475)	(U)	(170)	(160)	(150)	(991)
White	N	91	89	87	89	88	88
	J	99	99	99	99	98	99
Non-White	N	9	11	13	11	12	12
	J	1	1	1	1	2	1

U = Numbers not available.
[a]Sources: *Gallup Opinion Index: Religion in America:* Report Nos. 70 (1971); 114 (1975); 130 (1976); 145 (1977–78); 184 (1981); and (1979–80).

little impact on the Jewish group, which is almost completely white. Still, in the 1970's about one per cent of the Jews in the Gallup surveys consistently showed up as non-white. Little is known about this almost invisible group, which may number as many as 40,000–50,000 individuals.

AGE

Unfortunately, there are no good Gallup data available on the age distribution of Jews until 1974. This leaves us with only a six-year period for comparison, which is too short for measuring definite trends. The Gallup national figures closely approximate Census data for 1974–1979; however, the latter show a very small but consistent increase (1.2 per cent) in the population over age 55 and an even smaller increase in people under 30.

TABLE 8: AGE DISTRIBUTION FOR THE NATION (N) AND JEWS (J), BY PER CENT[a]

Age		1971	1974	1975	1976	1979
(Sample size)	(N)	(U)	(6,000)	(6,000)	(6,000)	(41,500)
	(J)	(U)	(170)	(160)	(150)	(991)
18–24	N	Y	17	17	17	18
	J	Y	16	13	18	13
25–29	N	Y	10	11	12	11
	J	Y	6	7	13	9
Under 30	N	25	27	28	29	28
	J	20	22	20	31	22
30–49	N	31	34	34	34	34
	J	32	35	33	32	34
Over 50	N	43	39	38	37	36
	J	48	43	47	37	43

U = Numbers not available.

Y = Categories not used in this year.

[a]Sources: *Gallup Opinion Index: Religion in America:* Report Nos. 114 (1975); 130 (1976); 145 (1977–78); 184 (1981); and (1979–80).

The Gallup figures clearly show that Jews are older than the rest of the population. Over five different years, the proportion of Jews over age 50 averages eight percentage points higher than that of the rest of the population—a difference considerably greater than that found in the 1957 Census and the 1971 NJPS. Like both these studies, however, Gallup observations suggest that age differences between Jews and other Americans have been increasing.

If we exclude 1976, which looks like an exception, Jews in the age bracket of 30 or under score an average of six percentage points less than the rest of the population. Thus there are fewer young people and more old people among Jews than among the population at large. For the middle group, 30 to 59, virtually no diff

GEOGRAPHY

In comparison with NJPS and Census data projections, geography is the least accurate item for Jews in the Gallup Poll. Since it is divided into four areas, the sample size in each category is reduced, thus increasing the error margin.

The data bear out popular impressions of a general population shift from the North and Midwest to the sun belt, with the largest gain in the South. Changes in the Jewish population closely parallel national changes, although they are of greater magnitude, e.g., the proportion of Jews living in the South tripled, from 5 to 17 per cent. The 1971 figures for Jews are drastically different from those of 1974, after which change becomes considerably more moderate. If 1971 figures for Jews are distorted, the conclusions are not very dramatic. Nevertheless, even if differences between 1971 and 1974 are halved, change among Jews is still greater than that among the rest of the population. Using a mean 1971/1974 base, the percentage of Jews residing in the East declined from 72.5 to 60 per cent in 1979, while the Jewish population of the South increased from 9 to 17 per cent. Jewish population increase in the West was almost as great as that in the South (from about 10.5 per cent to 18 per cent).

TABLE 9. GEOGRAPHICAL DISTRIBUTION FOR THE NATION (N) AND JEWS (J), BY PER CENT[a]

Geography		1970	1971	1974	1975	1976	1979
(Sample size)	(N)	(16,500)	(U)	(6,000)	(6,000)	(6,000)	(41,500)
	(J)	(475)	(U)	(170)	(170)	(150)	(991)
East	N	30	29	28	28	27	27
	J	83	82	63	64	65	60
Mid-West	N	28	28	28	28	27	27
	J	6	5	11	10	5	5
South	N	27	26	27	27	28	28
	J	6	5	13	19	13	17
West	N	16	17	17	17	18	18
	J	6	8	13	7	17	18

U = Numbers not available.

[a]Sources: *Gallup Opinion Index: Religion in America:* Report Nos. 70 (1971); 114 (1975); 130 (1976); 145 (1977–78); 184 (1981); and (1979–80); also unpublished Report (Feb., 1980).

The most dependable Gallup Poll, that of 1979, matches AJYB findings for the same year only in broad outline.[10] For the South and Northeast, differences between the two estimates are within two percentage points. However, for the Midwest, the Gallup percentage (5) is considerably lower than AJYB's (11.9); for the West, the order is reversed: Gallup shows 18 per cent, while the AJYB indicates 14 per cent. The population figures are probably between the two estimates.

SIZE OF COMMUNITY

In the 1970's, according to the Gallup data and categories, the only noticeable gross national changes (two percentage points) in community size were the decline of highly rural areas and the growth of moderate-sized (50,000–500,000) cities. From other sources, we know that there were additional changes: sizeable losses in old cities, e.g., Philadelphia and Detroit, and gains in others, viz., Houston and Phoenix. (Census data indicate a slight decline in the proportion of cities with more than a million residents.) But the overall national percentages are generally stable.

Observable trends appear in the Jewish figures. More Jews lived in rural or unincorporated areas in 1979 than in 1957 or 1970, although they were still a very

TABLE 10: DISTRIBUTION BY COMMUNITY SIZE FOR THE NATION (N) AND JEWS (J), BY PER CENT[a]

Size of Community		1970	1971	1974	1975	1976	1979
(Sample size)	(N)	(16,500)	(U)	(6,000)	(6,000)	(6,000)	(41,500)
	(J)	(475)	(U)	(170)	(170)	(150)	(991)
1,000,000+	N	20	19	18	18	19	20
	J	66	65	66	54	52	58
5,000–1,000,000	N	13	13	12	13	13	13
	J	18	17	10	11	16	14
50,000–500,000	N	23	24	25	26	25	26
	J	14	14	14	23	16	20
2,500–20,000	N	15	15	16	16	16	16
	J	3	3	1	6	5	4
Less than 2,500 (rural)	N	29	28	29	27	27	26
	J	1	1	9	6	11	5

U = Numbers not available.

[a]Sources: *Gallup Opinion Index: Religion in America:* Report Nos. 70 (1971); 114 (1975); 130 (1976); 145 (1977–78); 184 (1981); and (1979–80); also unpublished Report (Feb., 1980).

---

[10]See Alvin Chenkin and Maynard Miran, "Jewish Population in the United States, 1979," AJYB, Vol. 80, 1980, pp. 159–171.

small minority. There was a striking decline in big-city dwelling, and an increase in residence in moderate-sized cities, reflecting a continual move to the suburbs. Still, Jews were much more likely than other Americans (about 58:20) to live in large cities and much less likely to live in rural areas and small towns (9:42). They remain a largely cosmopolitan population (almost three-quarters live in or immediately around cities of half a million or more people), although most Jews have left the inner city.

EDUCATION

The Gallup categories include respondents who have had some, but who have not necessarily finished, education at the indicated level. Nationally, there was a dramatic change during the 1970's: a decrease of 40 per cent (from 25 to 15 per cent) in the proportion of those with only a grade school education, and an increase of 33 per cent (from 22 to 29 per cent) in the proportion of people with at least some college training. Such a sudden leap reflects not only high rates of college enrollment for recent high school graduates, but includes older people as well.

TABLE 11: LEVELS OF EDUCATION FOR THE NATION (N) AND JEWS (J), BY PER CENT[a]

Education		1970–1971	1974	1975	1976	1979
(Sample size)	(N)	(16,500)	(6,000)	(6,000)	(6,000)	(41,500)
	(J)	(475)	(170)	(170)	(150)	(991)
College	N	22	25	26	29	29
	J	42	49	54	58	56
High School	N	53	54	55	55	55
	J	42	43	35	34	35
Grade School	N	25	21	19	16	15
	J	16	8	11	8	9

[a]Sources: *Gallup Opinion Index: Religion in America:* Report Nos. 70 (1971); 114 (1975); 130 (1976); 145 (1977–78); 184 (1981); and (1979–80).

College involvement across age groups is even more prevalent among Jews; the almost linear increase (14 percentage points, from 42 to 56 per cent) of Jews with college experience is greater than that among non-Jews, who start at a lower rung. In addition, the percentage of Jews with only high school education declined from 42 to 35 per cent. With the slight exception of 1976, the comparison between the education levels of Jews and non-Jews is consistent in all the Gallup surveys, as well as with the 1957 Census data. Figures for Jews, probably as accurate as any in this study, suggest that NJPS data slightly inflate Jewish educational attainment. The

NJPS (1971) configuration does not appear in the Gallup study until 1975. Both surveys agree that Jews still have much stronger educational backgrounds than do Americans at large.

OCCUPATION

Nationally, the proportion of professional and business people increased from 21 to 27 per cent, and the proportion of farm workers was halved (6 to 3 per cent)—an ongoing process since before the turn of the century. Changes in the other areas were small and irregular, except for a slight decline in the clerical-sales force.

For Jews—as for all Americans—the percentage point increase (13) in professional and business careers closely parallels the increase (14 percentage points) among those with college education. (Unfortunately, there is no breakdown between professionals and business executives and between salaried and non-salaried professionals. There is also no indication of business size.) There was a significant decline in the percentage of Jewish manual workers, but all of the change occurred between 1971 and 1974 and is dependent upon the accuracy of the 1971 findings; after 1973 the figures are stable. Even by 1970, however, considerably fewer Jews than other Americans (1:2) were manual laborers. By 1979 this proportion widened to 1:3.5; the percentage of manual laborers remained constant for non-Jews while declining among Jews. The figures for 1974 and afterward closely resemble those found in the NJPS, although that sample is slightly older.

TABLE 12.   OCCUPATIONAL DISTRIBUTION FOR THE NATION (N) AND JEWS (J), BY PER CENT[a]

Occupation		1970–1971	1974	1975	1976	1979
(Sample size)	(N)	(16,500)	(6,000)	(6,000)	(6,000)	(41,500)
	(J)	(475)	(170)	(170)	(150)	(991)
Professional/Business	N	21	21	21	25	27
	J	40	41	46	53	53
Clerical/Sales	N	10	11	11	9	7
	J	22	24	15	15	7
Manual	N	40	42	40	42	41
	J	21	12	13	11	12
Non-Labor	N	21	19	20	19	21
	J	16	16	20	18	24
Farmer	N	6	4	3	3	3
	J	1	1	X	1	X

X = Sample size too small for reliable figures.
[a]Sources: *Gallup Opinion Index: Religion in America:* Report Nos. 70 (1971); 114 (1975); 130 (1976); 145 (1977–78); and (1979–80) ; also unpublished Report (Feb., 1980).

To no one's surprise, we find few if any Jewish farmers. Of interest is the increase of the non-labor force—significantly higher in 1979 than in 1971 and 1974. The obvious explanation is an increased number of retired persons. If we exclude 1971 data, we see the same development, but on a smaller scale, for the nation as a whole. What needs to be asked, however, is why the Jewish figures were equal to or lower than the national figures for the non-labor force between 1971 and 1976. Probably, most of those differences can be attributed to sample error.

INCOME

Measurement of family income entails two special problems: the large number of categories and the rapidly changing meaning of the categories because of inflation. Five thousand dollars a year, once marginal, is now well below the poverty line. Comparison with NJPS data becomes tenuous because of dissimilar income

TABLE 13: INCOME LEVELS FOR THE NATION (N) AND JEWS (J), BY PER CENT[a]

Income		1970–1971	1974	1975	1976	1979
(Sample size)	(N)	(16,500)	(6,000)	(6,000)	(6,000)	(41,500)
	(J)	(475)	(170)	(170)	(150)	(991)
More than $20,000	N	Y	15	15	21	32
	J	Y	42	34	43	49
$15,000–$19,999	N	Y	14	14	17	17
	J	Y	16	13	16	14
$10,000–$14,999	N	24	25	22	23	20
	J	26	18	17	21	11
$7,000–$9,999	N	21	12	11	11	11
	J	16	8	8	4	8
$5,000–$6,999	N	14	13	11	11	8
	J	11	9	7	7	8
$3,000–$4,999	N	14	10	9	9	6
	J	9	2	6	5	6
Less than $3000	N	12	11	18	8	5
	J	7	5	15	4	3
More than $15,000	N	15	29	29	38	49
	J	31	58	47	59	63
Less than $7,000	N	40	34	38	28	19
	J	27	16	28	16	17

Y = Categories not used in this year.
[a]Sources: *Gallup Opinion Index: Religion in America:* Report Nos. 70 (1971); 114 (1975); 130 (1976); 145 (1977–78); 184 (1981); and (1979–80); also unpublished Report (Feb., 1980).

categories and the NJPS focus on household head. (Nevertheless, the findings for 1971 are generally congruent.)

Changes in income generally reflect educational and occupational factors as well as inflation. Over the decade the proportion of Americans with a family income of more than $15,000 more than tripled, and in the second half of the decade the percentage of families with incomes of more than $20,000 more than doubled. In general, families making less than about $12,000 decreased, whereas those above that level increased.

As a group, Jews are still considerably wealthier than their neighbors, but these differences have begun to narrow significantly. The percentage of Jewish families making more than $20,000 increased from 42 to 49 per cent, whereas among the total population it more than doubled, from 15 to 32 per cent. For $15,000 and above, the ratio of Jewish to all families changed from 58:29 (1974) to 63:49 (1979). At the lower end of the scale (less than $7,000), there was no comparable reduction for Jews, from 16:34 (1974) to 17:19 (1979). In 1979 one-quarter of the Jewish families earned less than $12,000 a year, an amount insufficient to secure decent housing in most cities.

Conclusion

The Gallup data provide an important check on other American Jewish demography sources, particularly the NJPS and the materials gathered in Sidney Goldstein's review articles.[11] Differences with NJPS data and Goldstein's summaries are generally minor, the most noticeable having to do with region and education. Gallup data overstate the number of Jews in the Northeast, whereas NJPS estimates probably inflate those in the Midwest. (AJYB figures are in between for both regions.) Gallup figures tend to be higher—and perhaps more accurate—than other sources for the South, but this partially reflects later Gallup studies. Gallup and 1957 Census data suggest that the NJPS slightly overestimates the level of Jewish education, although all agree that it is significantly higher than that of other Americans.

For income the samples are picked in a slightly different manner, so that some minor differences exist between NJPS and Gallup data. But even for this trait, like almost all the others, Gallup data generally complement earlier studies. There is a close fit among Gallup and the other major national (and international) studies on population increase, age, sex, and the political party preference of Jews.[12]

ALAN M. FISHER

---

[11]See Goldstein, "Jews in the United States: Perspectives from Demography," *op. cit.*, and "American Jewry, 1970: A Demographic Profile," AJYB, Vol. 72, 1971, pp. 3–88.
[12]See Goldstein, "Jews in the United States: Perspectives from Demography," *op. cit.*, and U.O. Schmelz, "Jewish Survival: The Demographic Factors," AJYB, Vol. 81, 1981, pp. 61–117. For party identification, see Alan M. Fisher, "Realignment of the Jewish Vote?," *Political Science Quarterly,* Spring 1979, pp. 111–113.

Demographic

Jewish Population in the United States, 1982

T HE JEWISH POPULATION in the United States in 1982 is estimated to be 5.725 million. The drop from the 1981 figure of 5.921 million is due almost entirely to a lower estimate of the size of the Jewish population of Greater New York City, a figure derived from a newly-conducted demographic study. (See below.)

The convention employed in this and previous articles for "Jewish population" is that used by almost all Jewish federations providing estimates, *viz.*, the number of individuals in households with one or more self-identified Jews. The 1970 National Jewish Population Study found that approximately seven per cent of the persons in such households were non-Jews. If in 1982 the figure remained the same, the number of Jews identifying as such would be in the neighborhood of 5.325 million.

The reason for adopting the broad definition of "Jewish population" is inherent in the process of obtaining the local estimates which are shown in Table 3 and which form the basis of the state and regional totals in Table 1 and Table 2. (In the latter two tables, known areas with less than 100 Jews and estimates for "unknowns" have been added. Adjustments have also been made for local estimates which overlap or cover more than one state.) In most cases, local estimates were developed by starting with known Jewish households, adjusting for non-listed Jewish households (i.e., "unknowns"), and finally, multiplying by an average size of household figure. In only a small number of cases did federations have available information which could produce estimates limited only to "Jews." Since the more inclusive figure can be reported on a comparable basis for all communities, this procedure has been adopted.

Each year all Jewish federations are asked to provide current Jewish population estimates. In 1982, 114 federations responded, with a total population estimate of almost 5.1 million, or 89 per cent of the total national figure. It should be noted that in the last decade there has been an expansion in the use of computerized files of federation contributors and prospects. These provide a firmer base for estimates than existed in earlier decades.

In addition to the inquiries addressed to federations, there is a periodic survey made of areas not covered by them. In the main, this is handled through inquiries sent to local synagogues. While the resulting estimates may lack precision, they do provide valuable information about Jewish population pockets that might otherwise be overlooked. The next survey of the unaffiliated areas will be done for the 1983 estimates.

Except in those cases where a current population study has been carried out, the local estimates shown for 1982 do not vary a great deal from the figures indicated over the past several years. However, many federations have conducted population studies at some point in time, and these serve as benchmarks in the ongoing estimation process. Comparisons of figures on the local, state, and regional levels are best done over some span of time, preferably a minimum of five years. The following chart shows the regional proportions reported in the AJYB for 1977 and 1982, demonstrating the marked population shift to the Sun Belt.

Region	Proportion of Total Jewish Population	
	1977	1982
Northeast	59.8	54.3
North Central	12.4	12.2
South	14.1	17.2
West	13.7	16.3
Total	100.0	100.0
Number	5,776,000	5,725,000

Greater New York Area Estimate

Previous volumes of the AJYB carried an estimate of 1,998,000 for Greater New York, while pointing out that this figure, derived from the National Jewish Population Study, was probably, with the passage of time, overstated. The first results of a demographic study of New York Jewry, sponsored by the New York Federation of Jewish Philanthropies, provide a new estimate of 1,734,800. This figure represents a 13.4 per cent decline from the 1970 estimate or, approximately, an annual decrease of one per cent. The current estimate is shown on a basis comparable to the 1970 figure, i.e., it *includes* approximately six per cent non-Jews and *excludes* the institutionalized population. Excluding non-Jews and including the institutionalized population, New York reported a total of 1,668,700 Jewish persons.

The following chart shows the county estimates for the New York area in 1970 and 1982.

	1970	1982
Bronx	143,000	93,260
Brooklyn	514,000	420,840
Manhattan	171,000	297,230
Queens	379,000	314,600
Staten Island	21,000	33,150
Nassau	⎰ 605,000	253,670
Suffolk	⎱	192,320
Westchester	165,000	125,935
Total	1,998,000	1,734,800*

*The difference between the sum of the counties shown and the total is the result of rounding the average household size in each county.

In Queens, Nassau, Suffolk, and Westchester counties, the average household size decreased in the twelve-year period by 14 to 15 per cent. In the latter three counties, the number of households also decreased substantially, resulting in a population difference of approximately 198,100 persons between 1970 and 1982; Queens showed a smaller loss in households.

In the Bronx, the loss in population is due almost entirely to a drop in households. This is also largely true in the case of Brooklyn. Manhattan is the one county showing a substantial population increase since 1970; there, the average household size increased by 9.5 per cent, and the number of households by 59 per cent.

Initial census reports for 1980 show that 1.16 million more people moved out of New York City proper than moved into it. There was no significant growth in the New York suburbs. These trends are consistent with the data reported here, except for Manhattan. When detailed characteristics of Manhattan's Jewish population become available, it will be possible to evaluate the reasons for Manhattan's growth since 1970.

ALVIN CHENKIN

APPENDIX

TABLE 1. JEWISH POPULATION IN THE UNITED STATES, 1982

State	Estimated Jewish Population	Total Population*	Estimated Jewish Per Cent Of Total
Alabama................	8,960	3,917,000	0.2
Alaska.................	960	412,000	0.2
Arizona................	46,285	2,794,000	1.7
Arkansas	2,885	2,296,000	0.1
California..............	775,995	24,196,000	3.2
Colorado...............	44,365	2,965,000	1.5
Connecticut	102,075	3,134,000	3.3
Delaware	9,500	598,000	1.6
District of Columbia.....	30,000	631,000	4.8
Florida	478,180	10,183,000	4.7
Georgia................	38,855	5,574,000	0.7
Hawaii	5,625	981,000	0.6
Idaho	505	959,000	0.1
Illinois	266,985	11,462,000	2.3
Indiana................	25,610	5,468,000	0.5
Iowa..................	7,470	2,899,000	0.3
Kansas	11,260	2,383,000	0.5
Kentucky	12,285	3,662,000	0.3
Louisiana	16,625	4,308,000	0.4
Maine.................	7,800	1,133,000	0.7
Maryland	195,915	4,263,000	4.6
Massachusetts	248,545	5,773,000	4.3
Michigan	85,735	9,204,000	0.9
Minnesota..............	33,790	4,094,000	0.8
Mississippi	3,080	2,531,000	0.1
Missouri...............	85,835	4,941,000	1.7
Montana...............	640	793,000	0.1
Nebraska	7,850	1,577,000	0.5
Nevada................	19,200	845,000	2.3
New Hampshire.........	5,380	936,000	0.6
New Jersey.............	435,165	7,404,000	5.9
New Mexico............	5,305	1,328,000	0.4
New York	1,872,150	17,602,000	10.6

State	Estimated Jewish Population	Total Population*	Estimated Jewish Per Cent Of Total
North Carolina	14,740	5,953,000	0.3
North Dakota	1,085	658,000	0.2
Ohio	138,795	10,781,000	1.3
Oklahoma.............	6,860	3,100,000	0.2
Oregon	11,940	2,651,000	0.5
Pennsylvania	415,125	11,871,000	3.5
Rhode Island..........	22,000	953,000	2.3
South Carolina	8,760	3,167,000	0.3
South Dakota	605	686,000	0.1
Tennessee.............	18,100	4,612,000	0.4
Texas	73,960	14,766,000	0.5
Utah	2,300	1,518,000	0.2
Vermont..............	2,465	516,000	0.5
Virginia	59,265	5,430,000	1.1
Washington	21,885	4,217,000	0.5
West Virginia..........	4,295	1,952,000	0.2
Wisconsin.............	31,295	4,742,000	0.7
Wyoming	310	492,000	0.1
U.S. TOTAL	5,724,600**	229,307,000	2.5

N.B. Details may not add to totals because of rounding.

*Resident population, July 1, 1981, Provisional. (Source: *Provisional Estimates of the Population of States: July 1, 1981,* Bureau of the Census, Series P-25, No. 911, issued April 1982.)

**Exclusive of Puerto Rico and the Virgin Islands, which reported Jewish populations of 1,800 and 510, respectively.

TABLE 2. DISTRIBUTION OF U.S. JEWISH POPULATION BY REGIONS, 1982

Region	Total Population	Per Cent Distribution	Jewish Population	Per Cent Distribution
Northeast:	49,320,000	21.5	3,110,705	54.3
New England	12,444,000	5.4	388,265	6.8
Middle Atlantic	36,876,000	16.1	2,722,440	47.6
North Central:	58,893,000	25.7	696,315	12.2
East North Central	41,656,000	18.2	548,420	9.6
West North Central	17,237,000	7.5	147,895	2.6
South:	76,944,000	33.6	982,265	17.2
South Atlantic	37,751,000	16.5	839,510	14.7
East South Central .	14,723,000	6.4	42,425	0.7
West South Central.	24,470,000	10.7	100,330	1.8
West:	44,150,000	19.3	935,315	16.3
Mountain	11,694,000	5.1	118,910	2.1
Pacific	32,456,000	14.2	816,405	14.3
TOTALS	229,307,000	100.0	5,724,600	100.0

N.B. Details may not add to totals because of rounding.

TABLE 3. COMMUNITIES WITH JEWISH POPULATIONS OF 100 OR MORE, 1982
(ESTIMATED)

State and City	Jewish Population	State and City	Jewish Population	State and City	Jewish Population
ALABAMA		*Eureka	250	Tulare & Kings County	
Anniston	100	Fontana	165	(incl. in Fresno)	
**Birmingham	4,000	*Fresno	2,500	Vallejo	400
*Dothan	205	Kern County	850	Ventura County	5,000
Gadsden	180	Lancaster (incl. in			
*Huntsville	550	Antelope Valley)		**COLORADO**	
**Mobile	1,250	**Long Beach	13,500	Colorado Springs	1,000
**Montgomery	1,700	**Los Angeles Metropoli-		**Denver	42,600
Selma	210	tan Area	500,870	Pueblo	375
*Tri-Cities[a]	150	Merced	100		
Tuscaloosa	315	Modesto	260	**CONNECTICUT**	
		Monterey	1,500	**Bridgeport	18,500
ALASKA		*Oakland (incl. in		Bristol	250
*Anchorage	600	Alameda & Contra		Colchester	525
*Fairbanks	210	Costa Counties)		*Danbury (incl. New Mil-	
		Ontario (incl. in Pomona		ford)	3,500
ARIZONA		Valley)		Greenwich	2,200
*Phoenix	30,000	**Orange County	50,000	**Hartford (incl. New	
**Tucson	16,000	**Palm Springs	4,950	Britain)	23,500
		Pasadena (also incl. in		Lebanon	175
ARKANSAS		Los Angeles Metropol-		Lower Middlesex	
*Fayetteville	120	itan Area)	2,000	County[d] (incl. in	
Ft. Smith	160	*Petaluma	800	New London)	
Hot Springs (incl. in		Pomona Valley[c]	3,500	Manchester (incl. in	
Little Rock)		*Riverside	1,200	Hartford)	
**Little Rock	1,600	**Sacramento	7,000	Meriden	1,400
Pine Bluff	175	*Salinas	350	Middletown	1,300
Southeast		San Bernardino	1,900	Milford (incl. in	
Arkansas[b]	140	*San Diego	33,230	New Haven)	
Wynne-Forest		**San Francisco	75,000	Moodus	150
City	110	**San Jose	25,000	*New Haven	20,000
		*San Luis Obispo	450	**New London	3,500
CALIFORNIA		San Pedro	300	Newtown (incl. in	
*Alameda & Contra Costa		*Santa Barbara	3,800	Danbury)	
Counties	28,000	*Santa Cruz	1,000	**Norwalk	4,000
Antelope Valley	375	Santa Maria	200	Norwich	2,500
Bakersfield (incl. in Kern		Santa Monica	8,000	Putnam	110
County)		Santa Rosa	750	Rockville (incl. in	
El Centro	125	Stockton	1,050	Hartford)	
Elsinore	250	Sun City	800	**Stamford	12,000
				*Torrington	450

State and City	Jewish Population
Valley Area[c]	700
Wallingford	440
**Waterbury	2,800
Westport	2,800
Willimantic	400
Winsted	110

DELAWARE
*Wilmington (incl. rest of state)	9,500

DISTRICT OF COLUMBIA
**Greater Washington[f]	160,000

FLORIDA
**Boca Raton– Delray	15,000
*Brevard County	2,250
**Daytona Beach	2,000
**Fort Lauderdale	80,000
Fort Myers	300
Fort Pierce	270
*Gainesville	1,000
*Hollywood	55,000
**Jacksonville	7,200
Key West	170
Lakeland	800
Lehigh Acres	125
**Miami	225,000
*Orlando	15,000
**Palm Beach County (excl. Boca Raton)	45,000
Pensacola	725
Port Charlotte	150
**Sarasota	6,500
St. Augustine	100
**St. Petersburg (incl. Clearwater)	9,000
Tallahassee	1,000
**Tampa	11,500

GEORGIA
*Albany	525

State and City	Jewish Population
Athens	250
**Atlanta	30,000
**Augusta	1,500
Brunswick	120
*Columbus	1,000
Dalton	235
Fitzgerald-Cordele	125
*Macon	900
**Savannah	2,600
Valdosta	145

HAWAII
*Hilo	100
*Honolulu	5,000
*Kona	100
*Maui	200

IDAHO
*Boise	120

ILLINOIS
Aurora	400
Bloomington	125
**Champaign– Urbana	2,000
**Chicago Metropolitan Area	253,000
Danville	240
*Decatur	350
East St. Louis (incl. in So. Ill.)	
*Elgin	830
*Galesburg (incl. in Peoria)	
*Joliet	800
*Kankakee	260
**Peoria	1,900
**Quad Cities[g]	1,800
Quincy	200
Rock Island (incl. in Quad Cities)	
**Rockford	975
**Southern Illinois[h]	950
**Springfield	1,250

State and City	Jewish Population
Sterling-Dixon	110
Waukegan	1,200

INDIANA
Anderson	105
Bloomington	300
*Elkhart (incl. in South Bend)	
Evansville	1,200
**Ft. Wayne	1,350
Gary (incl. in Northwest Indiana–Calumet Region)	
**Indianapolis	13,800
*Lafayette	600
Marion	170
**Michigan City	425
Muncie	175
**Northwest Indiana–Calumet Region[i]	4,300
*Richmond	110
Shelbyville	140
**South Bend	1,900
Terre Haute	450

IOWA
Cedar Rapids	330
Council Bluffs	245
Davenport (incl. in Quad Cities, Ill.)	
**Des Moines	3,500
Dubuque	105
Fort Dodge	115
*Iowa City	750
Mason City	110
Muscatine	120
Ottumwa	150
**Sioux City	845
*Waterloo	450

KANSAS
Topeka	500
**Wichita	900

State and City	Jewish Population	State and City	Jewish Population	State and City	Jewish Population
KENTUCKY		Fitchburg	300	Grand Rapids	1,500
**Lexington	2,100	*Framingham	9,500	Iron County	160
**Louisville	9,200	Gardner	100	Iron Mountain	105
Paducah	175	Gloucester	400	Jackson	375
		Great Barrington	105	*Kalamazoo	700
LOUISIANA		Greenfield	250	Lansing	1,800
**Alexandria	700	*Haverhill	1,650	Marquette County	175
**Baton Rouge	1,500	Holyoke	1,100	Mt. Clemens	420
Lafayette	600	Hyannis	1,200	*Mt. Pleasant	100
Lake Charles	250	Lawrence	2,550	*Muskegon	235
*Monroe	550	*Leominster	750	*Saginaw	550
**New Orleans	10,600	*Lowell	2,000	South Haven	100
**Shreveport	1,600	**Lynn (incl. Beverly,			
		Peabody, and		**MINNESOTA**	
MAINE		Salem)	19,000	Austin	125
Augusta	215	Medway (incl. in Fra-		*Duluth	900
*Bangor	1,500	mingham)		Hibbing	155
**Southern Maine (excl.		Milford (incl. in Fra-		**Minneapolis	22,000
Portland)	950	mingham)		Rochester	240
Calais	135	Mills (incl. in Framing-		*St. Paul	9,250
**Lewiston-Auburn	700	ham)		Virginia	100
**Portland	3,550	**New Bedford	3,100		
Waterville	300	Newburyport	280	**MISSISSIPPI**	
		North Berkshire	675	*Biloxi-Gulfport	100
MARYLAND		*Northampton	700	Clarksdale	160
Annapolis	2,000	Peabody	2,600	Cleveland	180
**Baltimore	92,000	**Pittsfield (incl. all Berk-		Greenville	500
*Cumberland	265	shire County)	3,500	Greenwood	100
Easton Park Area[j]	100	Plymouth	500	Hattiesburg	180
Frederick	400	Salem	1,150	*Jackson	650
Hagerstown	275	Southbridge	105	Meridian	135
*Hartford County	500	**Springfield	11,250	Natchez	140
**Montgomery and		Taunton	1,200	Vicksburg	260
Prince Georges		Webster	125		
County[f]	100,000	**Worcester	10,000	**MISSOURI**	
Salisbury	300			Columbia	350
		MICHIGAN		Joplin	115
MASSACHUSETTS		Ann Arbor (incl. all		**Kansas City	20,000
Amherst	750	Washtenaw		Kennett	110
Athol	110	County)	3,000	Springfield	230
Attleboro	200	Battle Creek	245	**St. Joseph	430
Beverly	1,000	Bay City	650	**St. Louis	53,500
**Boston (incl.		Benton Harbor	650		
Brockton)	170,000	**Detroit	70,000	**MONTANA**	
*Fall River	1,780	**Flint	2,430	Billings	160

State and City	Jewish Population	State and City	Jewish Population	State and City	Jewish Population
NEBRASKA		Morristown (incl. in		Auburn	315
**Lincoln	750	Morris County)		Batavia	165
**Omaha	6,500	Mt. Holly	300	*Beacon	315
		Newark (incl. in Essex		*Binghamton (incl.	
NEVADA		County)		all Broome	
**Las Vegas	18,000	New Brunswick (incl. in		County)	4,000
Reno	1,200	Raritan Valley)		*Brewster (incl. in Dan-	
		North Hudson		bury, Ct.)	300
NEW HAMPSHIRE		County[p]	7,000	**Buffalo	20,000
Claremont	130	**North Jersey[q]	32,500	Canandaigua	135
Concord	350	**Northern Middlesex		Catskill	200
Dover	425	County[r]	22,000	Corning	125
Keene	105	*Ocean County	8,100	Cortland	440
*Laconia	150	**Passaic-Clifton	7,500	*Dunkirk	150
*Manchester	2,500	Paterson (incl. in North		Ellenville	1,450
Nashua	450	Jersey)		**Elmira	1,100
*Portsmouth	1,000	Perth Amboy (incl.		Geneva	300
		in North Middlesex		Glens Falls	360
NEW JERSEY		County)		Gloversville	535
*Atlantic City		Plainfield (incl. in Union		Herkimer	185
(incl. Atlantic		County)		Highland Falls	105
County)	12,000	Princeton	2,600	Hudson	470
*Bayonne	5,500	**Raritan Valley[s]	22,500	Ithaca	1,000
Bergen County[k]	100,000	Salem	230	Jamestown	185
Bridgeton	375	*Somerset County[t]	6,000	**Kingston	3,000
**Camden[l]	28,000	Somerville (incl. in Som-		Liberty	2,100
Carteret	300	erset County)		Loch Sheldrake–	
Elizabeth (incl. in Union		Toms River (incl. in		Hurleyville	750
County)		Ocean County)		Monroe	400
**Englewood (also incl.		**Trenton[u]	8,500	Monticello	2,400
in Bergen		**Union County	39,500	Mountaindale	150
County)	9,300	Vineland[v]	3,335	**New York City	
**Essex County[m]	95,000	Wildwood	425	Metropolitan	
Flemington	875	Willingboro (incl. in		Area[w]	1,734,800
Gloucester		Camden)		New Paltz	150
County[n]	165			Newark	220
*Hoboken	350	**NEW MEXICO**		**Newburgh-	
**Jersey City	3,500	**Albuquerque	4,500	Middletown	4,900
Metuchen (incl. in North		Las Cruces	100	**Niagara Falls	900
Middlesex County)		Santa Fe	300	Norwich	120
Millville	240			Olean	140
*Monmouth		**NEW YORK**		Oneonta	175
County	32,000	**Albany	13,000	Oswego	100
**Morris-Sussex		Amenia	140	Parksville	140
Counties[o]	16,000	Amsterdam	595	Pawling	105

State and City	Jewish Population	State and City	Jewish Population	State and City	Jewish Population
Plattsburg	275	**OHIO**		Ambridge	250
Port Jervis	560	**Akron	6,000	Beaver (incl. in	
Potsdam	175	**Canton	2,850	Pittsburgh)	
Poughkeepsie	4,900	**Cincinnati	21,500	Beaver Falls	350
**Rochester	19,600	**Cleveland	70,000	Berwick	120
Rockland		**Columbus	13,000	Bethlehem	960
County	25,000	**Dayton	6,000	Braddock	250
Rome	205	*East Liverpool	300	Bradford	150
Saratoga Springs	500	Elyria	275	Brownville	150
*Schenectady	5,400	Hamilton	560	*Butler	350
Sharon Springs	165	*Lima	290	Carbon County	125
South Fallsburg	1,100	Lorain	1,000	Carnegie	100
**Syracuse	9,000	Mansfield	600	Central Bucks	
Troy	1,200	Marion	150	County	400
**Utica	2,250	Middletown	140	Chambersburg	340
Walden (incl. in New-		New Philadelphia	140	Chester	2,100
burg–Middletown)		Newark	105	Coatesville	305
Warwick	100	Piqua	120	Connellsville	110
Watertown	250	Portsmouth	120	Donora	100
White Lake	425	Sandusky	150	Easton	1,300
Woodbourne	200	Springfield	340	Ellwood City	110
Woodridge	300	**Steubenville	230	**Erie	930
		**Toledo	7,500	Farrell	150
NORTH CAROLINA		*Warren	500	Greensburg	300
*Asheville	1,000	Wooster	200	**Harrisburg	4,750
*Chapel Hill–		*Youngstown	5,200	*Hazleton	575
Durham	1,850	Zanesville	350	Homestead	300
**Charlotte	3,700			Indiana	135
*Fayetteville (incl. all		**OKLAHOMA**		**Johnstown	550
Cumberland		Muskogee	120	Kittanning	175
County)	500	**Oklahoma City	2,600	*Lancaster	1,800
Gastonia	220	Oklahoma City		Lebanon	425
Goldsboro	120	Zone^y	190	Lock Haven	140
*Greensboro	3,200	**Tulsa	2,900	*Lower Bucks	
*Hendersonville	105			County^z	18,000
High Point	400	**OREGON**		*McKeesport	2,000
Raleigh	1,375	Corvallis	140	Monessen	100
*Rocky Mount	110	Eugene	1,500	Mt. Pleasant	120
*Whiteville Zone^x	160	*Portland	9,845	New Castle	400
Wilmington	500	Salem	200	*New Kensington	560
Winston-Salem	440			Norristown	2,000
		PENNSYLVANIA		North Penn	200
NORTH DAKOTA		Aliquippa	400	Oil City	165
Fargo	500	**Allentown	4,980	Oxford–Kennett	
Grand Forks	100	**Altoona	580	Square	180

State and City	Jewish Population	State and City	Jewish Population	State and City	Jewish Population
**Philadelphia Metropolitan Area....	295,000	**Memphis	9,000	County, and urban Fairfax County)[f]	30,000
*Phoenixville.	340	**Nashville	4,925	Arlington (incl. in	
**Pittsburgh	50,000	Oak Ridge	240	Alexandria)	
Pottstown	700			*Charlottesville	800
Pottsville	500	**TEXAS**		Danville	180
**Reading	2,800	Amarillo	300	Fredericksburg	140
Sayre	100	**Austin	2,700	Hampton (incl. in	
**Scranton.	3,800	Baytown.	300	Newport News)	
*Sharon	330	*Beaumont	400	Harrisonburg.	115
State College	450	Brownsville	160	Hopewell	140
Stroudsburg.	410	**Corpus Christi.	1,200	Lynchburg.	275
*Sunbury	200	**Dallas.	21,000	Martinsville	135
Uniontown.	290	De Witt County[bb]	150	*Newport News (incl.	
Upper Beaver	500	**El Paso	5,000	Hampton)	2,575
Washington (incl. in		*Ft. Worth	3,000	*Norfolk (incl. Virginia	
Pittsburgh)		**Galveston.	620	Beach)	11,000
Wayne County	210	**Houston	28,000	Petersburg	600
West Chester	300	Laredo	420	*Portsmouth (incl.	
**Wilkes-Barre	4,000	Longview	185	Suffolk)	1,100
*Williamsport	415	Lubbock.	350	**Richmond	10,000
*York.	1,600	McAllen.	295	*Roanoke.	1,200
		North Texas Zone[cc]	100	Williamsburg.	120
RHODE ISLAND		Odessa	150	Winchester.	110
**Providence (incl. rest of state)	22,000	Port Arthur.	260		
		**San Antonio	6,500	**WASHINGTON**	
SOUTH CAROLINA		Texarkana	100	Bellingham	120
**Charleston	3,500	*Tyler	450	Bremerton (incl. in	
*Columbia.	2,300	*Waco	750	Seattle)	
*Florence.	350	Wharton	170	**Seattle	19,500
Greenville	600	Wichita Falls.	260	Spokane.	800
Orangeburg				Tacoma	750
County.	105	**UTAH**			
Spartanburg.	295	Ogden	100	**WEST VIRGINIA**	
Sumter	190	*Salt Lake City.	2,200	*Bluefield–Princeton.	250
				*Charleston	1,105
SOUTH DAKOTA		**VERMONT**		*Clarksburg.	205
**Sioux Falls.	125	Bennington	120	*Huntington	450
		Burlington	1,800	Morgantown	200
TENNESSEE		Rutland	350	Parkersburg.	155
**Chattanooga	2,000	St. Johnsbury	100	Weirton	150
Johnson City[aa]	210			Wheeling	650
*Knoxville.	1,350	**VIRGINIA**			
		**Alexandria (incl. Falls Church, Arlington		**WISCONSIN**	
				*Appleton	250

State and City	Jewish Population	State and City	Jewish Population	State and City	Jewish Population
Beloit	120	*Manitowoc	115	Waukesha (incl. in	
Eau Clair	120	**Milwaukee	23,900	Milwaukee)	
Fond du Lac	100	*Oshkosh	150	Wausau	155
*Green Bay	350	Racine	405		
*Kenosha	250	*Sheboygan	250	WYOMING	
**Madison	4,500	Superior	165	Cheyenne	255

*Denotes estimate submitted within the previous three years.

**Denotes estimate submitted in 1982.

[a]Florence, Sheffield, Tuscumbia.

[b]Towns in Chicot, Desha, Drew Counties.

[c]Includes Alta Loma, Chino, Claremont, Cucamonga, La Verne, Montclair, Ontario, Pomona, San Dimas, Upland.

[d]Centerbrook, Chester, Clinton, Deep River, Essex, Killingworth, Old Lyme, Old Saybrook, Seabrook, Westbrook.

[e]Ansonia, Derby–Shelton, Oxford, Seymour.

[f]Greater Washington includes urbanized portions of Montgomery and Prince Georges Counties, in Maryland; Arlington County, Fairfax County (organized portion), Falls Church, Alexandria, in Virginia.

[g]Rock Island, Moline (Illinois); Davenport, Bettendorf (Iowa).

[h]Towns in Alexander, Bond, Clay, Clinton, Crawford, Edwards, Effingham, Fayette, Franklin, Gallatin, Hamilton, Hardin, Jackson, Jasper, Jefferson, Jersey, Johnson, Lawrence, Mascoupin, Madison, Marion, Massac, Montgomery, Perry, Pope, Pulaski, Randolph, Richland, St. Clair, Saline, Union, Wabash, Washington, Wayne, White, Williamson Counties.

[i]Includes Crown Point, East Chicago, Gary, Hammond, Munster, Valparaiso, Whiting, and the Greater Calumet region.

[j]Towns in Caroline, Kent, Queen Annes, Talbot Counties.

[k]Allendale, Elmwood Park, Fair Lawn, Franklin Lakes, Oakland, Midland Park, Rochelle Park, Saddle Brook, Wykoff also included in North Jersey estimate.

[l]Includes Camden and Burlington Counties.

[m]Includes contiguous areas in Hudson, Morris, Somerset, and Union Counties.

[n]Includes Clayton, Paulsboro, Woodbury. Excludes Newfield; see Vineland.

[o]See footnote (m).

[p]Includes Guttenberg, Hudson Heights, North Bergen, North Hudson, Secaucus, Union City, Weehawken, West New York, Woodcliff.

[q]Includes Paterson, Wayne, Hawthorne in Passaic County, and nine towns in Bergen County. See footnote (k).

[r]Includes Perth Amboy, Metuchen, Edison Township (part), Woodbridge.

[s]Includes in Middlesex County, Cranbury, Dunellen, East Brunswick, Edison Township (part), Jamesburg, Matawan, Middlesex, Monmouth Junction, Old Bridge, Parlin, Piscataway, South

River, Spottswood; in Somerset County, Kendall Park, Somerset; in Mercer County, Hightstown.

'Excludes Kendall Park and Somerset, which are included in Raritan Valley.

"Includes Mercer County in New Jersey; and Lower Makefield, Morrisville, Newtown, and Yardley in Pennsylvania.

'Includes in Cumberland County, Norma, Rosenheim, Vineland; in Salem County, Elmer; in Gloucester County, Clayton, Newfield; in Cape May County, Woodbine.

"See text for discussion of alternate estimate. Includes the Bronx, Brooklyn, Manhattan, Queens, Staten Island, Nassau, Suffolk, and Westchester Counties.

'Elizabethtown, Fairmont, Jacksonville, Lumberton, Tabor City, Wallace, Warsaw, and Loris, S.C.

'Towns in Alfalfa, Beckham, Cadelo, Canadian, Cleveland, Custer, Jackson, Kingfisher, Kiowa, Lincoln, Logan, Oklahoma, Payne, Roger Mills, Tillman, Washita Counties.

'Bensalem Township, Bristol, Langhorne, Levittown, New Hope, Newtown, Penndel, Warington, Yardley.

ᵃᵃIncludes Kingsport and Bristol (including the portion of Bristol in Virginia).

ᵇᵇIncludes communities also in Colorado, Fayette, Gonzales, and La Vaca Counties.

ᶜᶜDenison, Gainesville, Greenville, Paris, Sherman, and Durant (Oklahoma).

The Demographic Consequences of U.S. Jewish Population Trends

T HE 1981 AMERICAN JEWISH YEAR BOOK (AJYB) carried Sidney Gold-stein's comprehensive study "Jews in the United States: Perspectives from Demography." The picture drawn there is here extended in two directions: (a) further investigation of nuptiality, fertility, and mixed marriage. These processes and their demographic consequences stand at the core of Jewish population dynamics in the United States and deserve special attention; (b) quantitative assessments of the dynamics of the U.S. Jewish population, expressed in projections according to alternative assumptions and in demographic balance sheets. This information on U.S. Jewry forms part of, and is briefly compared with, the results of similar research on all the regional Jewries of the world.

Because of space considerations most of this study is confined to reporting the population dynamics of U.S. Jews on the country-wide scale in comparison to all U.S. whites, and to ascertaining the demographic factors which directly induce the changes noted. We cannot enter here into an analysis of the underlying societal processes affecting U.S. Jews—trends in their socio-economic structure, residential mobility,[1] and Jewish identity, and institutions—or the general societal transformations in America which may influence Jewish demography.

The main data source on American Jewry used here both in the analysis of recent demographic dynamics and as a basis for population projections is the 1970–1971 National Jewish Population Study (NJPS). NJPS is the only recent documentation of the U.S. Jewish population that combines two important features: country-wide representativeness and a large sample size. Although many NJPS findings have already been published, the study has not been exhausted as a source of information. The tabulations presented in this article have been derived in the main from a special NJPS data file that has been created by amalgamating two separate data sets: the census-type characteristics of all the persons included in the survey and the

---

Note: The research activities which supplied the findings reported in this article have been mainly conducted in the division for Jewish demography and statistics at the Institute of Contemporary Jewry, Hebrew University. Research by Sergio DellaPergola for this article was partially undertaken during stays as visiting research associate at the population studies and training center, department of sociology, Brown University (1978–1979), and at the Institute for Advanced Studies, Hebrew University (1980–1981). The authors wish to thank Sidney and Alice Goldstein for kindly reading a draft of this article and making valuable suggestions.

[1]See Sidney Goldstein, "Population Movement and Redistribution among American Jews," in U.O. Schmelz, Paul Glikson, and Sergio DellaPergola, (eds.), *Papers in Jewish Demography, 1981* (Jerusalem, forthcoming).

particulars of each marriage and of each birth event relating to the ever-married persons included in NJPS. The amalgamated file was obtained by matching each individual in the census-type file with his/her detailed marriage record and, for women, fertility history in the vital events file. The few ever-married individuals for whom this record linkage could not be established have been excluded from the analysis.[2]

Size and Composition of U.S. Jewry

SIZE OF JEWISH POPULATION

The official U.S. decennial censuses do not supply information on the total number of Jews in the United States. The yearly estimates published in the AJYB have had an irregular course, both because of the great difficulties inherent in compiling consistent national totals from a multitude of local estimates and because of changes in sources and methodology. In March 1957 the U.S. Bureau of the Census inserted a question on religion in its Current Population Survey, and came up with a figure of 5,030,000 Jews. While the contemporary AJYB estimate stood at about 5,250,000, the difference between that figure and the Survey result is within the range of a reasonable sampling error. From that level, subsequent AJYB estimates rose substantially year after year, reaching 6,115,000 by the end of 1972. It was pointed out at the time, however, that this rise seemed exaggerated in light of what was known about the probable differences in the growth rates of the Jewish and general white populations.[3]

In 1970–1971, NJPS was conducted. This large-scale socio-demographic study led to a reduction in the estimate of Jewish population size in the United States. However, the results, as presented in different publications, raised serious conceptual and estimation problems: (a) the population size of 5,800,000, which was

---

[2]NJPS yielded 5,790 households net, at a 79 per cent response rate. (See Bernard Lazerwitz, "An Estimate of a Rare Population Group—the U.S. Jewish Population," *Demography*, August 1978, pp. 389–394. The amalgamated file comprises 4,719 ever-married males and 5,303 ever-married females. The authors gratefully acknowledge the cooperation of Fred Massarik of the University of California, Los Angeles, the scientific director of NJPS, who provided the census-type data file, and Bernard Lazerwitz, now of Bar-Ilan University, the statistical supervisor of NJPS, who provided the vital events data file. Record matching was executed at the computer center, Brown University, by Sergio DellaPergola and Robert Novy. Sidney Goldstein of Brown University, himself a member of the NJPS scientific committee, gave his advice on the file merging procedures. In evaluating NJPS data, attention should be paid to the limitations in statistical significance that are inherent in sampling and data-weighting procedures. See Bernard Lazerwitz, *Sampling Errors and Statistical Inference for the National Jewish Population Survey* (New York, 1974).

[3]See U.O. Schmelz, "Evaluation of Jewish Population Estimates," AJYB, Vol. 70, 1969.

published in AJYB and elsewhere as a result of NJPS, included 430,000 non-Jewish members of "Jewish households." At the same time, it did not include long-term institutionalized Jews, whose number was estimated at 50,000.[4] In this framework the actual number of Jews in 1970–1971 was about 5,420,000; (b) an analysis of the statistical implications of the methodology and implementation of NJPS led to three estimates of the number of Jews, excluding those institutionalized on a long-term basis: low—5,555,000; medium—5,779,000; high—6,002,000.[5]

A reasoned demographic adjudication between all the various versions discussed above would require comprehensive research that might well retrace the evolution of the U.S. Jewish population since the inception of large-scale immigration in the last century.[6] In the meantime, however, we can do no more than propose a provisional estimate which is so calibrated as to reasonably reconcile the principal pieces of evidence that are currently available.

On the basis of the 1957 Current Population Survey and our knowledge of the demographic dynamics of U.S. Jewry between 1957 and 1970, a moderate estimate of Jewish population size according to NJPS appears indicated. We have therefore provisionally proposed the figure of 5,600,000 for the total number of Jews in the United States at the end of 1970 (i.e., at the mid-date of NJPS).[7]

The number of Jews in the United States may be considered to have remained rather stable until the middle of the 1970's, with a modestly positive balance of external migrations offsetting a modestly negative balance of internal dynamics (i.e., natural movement and affiliative changes). However, in the second half of the 1970's the positive migratory balance of U.S. Jewry increased, due to the arrival of many Soviet Jews.[8] On the basis of 5,600,000 Jews in 1970, therefore, we estimate the Jewish population at the end of 1980 to have been 5,690,000.[9] The corresponding proportions of Jews in the total U.S. population in 1970 and 1980 were 2.73 per cent

---

[4]See Fred Massarik, "National Jewish Population Study," AJYB, Vol. 75, 1974–75, pp. 296–302.

[5]See Lazerwitz, "An Estimate of a Rare Population Group—The U.S. Jewish Population," *op. cit.*

[6]Initial steps along these lines have been taken by Jack Diamond, "A Reader in the Demography of American Jews," AJYB, Vol. 77, 1977, pp. 251–317 and Ira Rosenwaike, "A Synthetic Estimate of American Jewish Population Movement over the Last Three Decades," in U.O. Schmelz, Paul Glikson, and Sergio DellaPergola, (eds.), *Papers in Jewish Demography, 1977* (Jerusalem, 1980), pp. 83–102.

[7]See U.O. Schmelz, *World Jewish Population—Regional Estimates and Projections* (Jerusalem, 1981).

[8]For this and other factors of change, see below the section on the balance of demographic dynamics. For trends in U.S. Jewry and in other Jewish populations, see U.O. Schmelz, "Jewish Survival: the Demographic Factors," AJYB, Vol. 81, 1981, pp. 61–117.

[9]See U.O. Schmelz and Sergio DellaPergola, "World Jewish Population," AJYB, Vol. 82, 1982, pp. 277–290.

and 2.54 per cent, respectively; the ratios of Jews per 100 U.S. whites were 3.10 per cent and 2.95 per cent, respectively.

COMPOSITION ACCORDING TO SOME DEMOGRAPHIC CHARACTERISTICS

Jews as a group are more aged than the entire white population of the United States; they comprise a smaller proportion of young people and a larger share of the elderly. In the 1970's demographic aging increased among Jews and all whites; the percentage of children dropped, while that of the elderly (65+ years old) rose. The latter change has been much stronger among Jews. The non-Jewish household members of Jews are, as a group, far younger than the Jewish population, since they are largely composed of relatively recent spouses, especially wives, and children of mixed marriages (Table 1).

TABLE 1. JEWS AND OTHER POPULATION GROUPS, BY AGE, 1970 AND 1980

| | 1970 | | | | 1980[a] | |
| | Persons in Jewish Households | | | U.S. | | U.S. |
Age	Jews	Others	Total	Whites	Jews	Whites
Total	100.0	100.0	100.0	100.0	100.0	100.0
0–14	21.2	35.0	22.3	27.4	16.2	21.7
15–29	23.5	32.8	24.2	24.2	26.0	26.8
30–44	16.8	14.9	16.6	17.1	18.2	19.1
45–64	26.5	15.6	25.7	21.1	24.1	20.6
65+	12.0	1.7	11.2	10.2	15.5	11.8

[a]1979 for all whites.

Sources: for persons in Jewish households, 1970—NJPS, authors' tabulations; for Jews, 1980—medium projection (see below); for all whites—U.S. Bureau of the Census, *Estimates of the Population of the United States, by age, race, and sex: 1976 and 1979,* Current Population Reports, Series P-25, No. 870, 1980.

The recent age composition of U.S. Jews is to be understood as largely resulting from changing fertility levels in the past, whether in the United States itself or in Europe, from whence most of the immigrants came. This can be demonstrated by identifying the birth cohorts corresponding to the 5-yearly age groups as estimated for 1980 (Table 2).[10] Of course, above age 60 the extant cohorts are already much depleted by deaths, and even below this age the effects of cumulative mortality are not negligible. Nonetheless, it can be seen from inspection of the cohort frequencies that substantial fertility prevailed until the 1920's, when birth control intensified.

---

[10]The estimates for 1980 were developed as part of the projections presented below.

Natality was particularly reduced during the period 1930–1945, which corresponded to the great depression and World War II. After the weak cohorts born in those years came the strong ones of the "baby boom," which in the United States extended from the mid-1940's to the end of the 1950's. Beginning in the 1960's, a drastic fertility decline set in, which, for Jews, was probably compounded by increasing losses of newborn due to mixed marriages.[11] These shifts in fertility trends run parallel to similar ones among the general white population of the United States, though Jews have shown peculiarities of timing and levels (see below).

Among other things, the age estimates for Jews in 1980 (which are an update of the empirical data of NJPS) make it clear that (a) there has been rapid progress in demographic aging. In 1980 the 65+ year olds were nearly as numerous as the children below age 15; (b) the potential exists for a further increase of the 65+ year olds, since the age group 50–64 was comparatively large in 1980; (This theme will be taken up again in the section which presents the results of projections into the future.) (c) paradoxically there likewise exists a potential for a temporary rise in the number of Jewish newborn, because of the increased frequency of Jews in the most

TABLE 2.   JEWS, BY AGE AND BIRTH COHORT (ESTIMATES), 1980

Age	Birth Cohort	Jews (per cent)
Total	Total	100.0
0–4	1976–80	6.1
5–9	1971–75	5.4
10–14	1966–70	4.7
15–19	1961–65	6.8
20–24	1956–60	10.0
25–29	1951–55	9.2
30–34	1946–50	8.2
35–39	1941–45	5.4
40–44	1936–40	4.6
45–49	1931–35	5.2
50–54	1926–30	6.3
55–59	1921–25	6.0
60–64	1916–20	6.6
65–69	1911–15	5.7
70–74	1906–10	4.2
75+	Up to 1905	5.6

Source: medium projection (see below).

---

[11]The data in Table 2 which show the age distribution of Jews reflect only the results of "effectively Jewish" births, excluding children from mixed marriages who are not Jews.

procreative ages. By 1980 the cohorts born in the 1945–1959 "baby boom" occupied ages 20–34. As an echo effect of that "baby boom," the number of young Jewish children has probably risen and may remain on a somewhat raised level for several years. However, the transitory nature of this phenomenon should be realized. By 1995 all of the ages 20–34 will be occupied by weak cohorts born since 1961.

According to NJPS, 51 per cent of all Jews in 1970 were females. In middle age the proportion of women was also about one-half, but it amounted to 54 per cent among the elderly. This is in conformance with the biological tendency for lower mortality among women.

According to NJPS, the native-born constituted 85 per cent of all U.S. Jews, and more than 90 per cent of those up to approximately age 40. By now the former percentage must have risen further, while the latter applies up to age 50. This signifies strong objective prospects for integration into the American way of life, especially its middle- and upper middle-class metropolitan variants as consonant with most Jews' socio-economic and residential situations. These prospects also exist with regard to demographic matters which depend on decisions of the persons concerned, such as marriage and fertility.

Family Formation

PROPORTION EVER-MARRIED

Nuptiality trends and levels are important factors in population growth because of their relationship to fertility levels, and, in the case of the Jewish minority, to the balance of cohesive and assimilatory forces affecting the choice of marriage partners and the religious composition of households. During the last decades, typical Jewish marriage patterns in Western countries have included a lower than average propensity to marry at young ages, but higher than average overall marriage propensities.[12] This, indeed, is the picture that emerges from an examination of past Jewish family formation trends in the United States (Table 3). According to NJPS, high proportions of the ever-married, ranging between 96 and 99 per cent, appear among both sexes between ages 35 and 49, and also among older males. The proportions of Jews ever-married at these ages in 1970–1971 were slightly but consistently higher than those found among the total white population. On the other hand, the percentages of ever-married Jews below age 30 were much lower than those found among all whites. The higher ages at marriage did not prevent the eventual attainment of virtually universal marriage among the Jewish population—at least until the recent past.

A better understanding of the dynamics of Jewish family formation is obtained by comparing the marital status of persons of different ages at similar points in the

---

[12]See Roberto Bachi, *Population Trends of World Jewry* (Jerusalem, 1977).

TABLE 3. PER CENT EVER-MARRIED AMONG JEWISH POPULATION AND ALL WHITES BY AGE AND SEX, 1970–1971.

Year of Birth	Age at End 1970	Per Cent Ever-Married At Exact Ages:					Total	All Whites
		19	22	25	30	35		
Males								
1949–51	19–21	0.0					2.9	22.8
1946–48	22–24	0.1	10.5				34.4	56.8
1941–45	25–29	0.9	17.1	64.4			75.0	81.3
1936–40	30–34	0.3	19.1	49.0	89.1		93.0	90.0
1931–35	35–39	1.2	18.5	55.0	84.9	94.3	96.3	92.4
1926–30	40–44	3.5	15.8	45.0	83.9	93.1	96.0	93.0
1921–25	45–49	3.7	14.2	45.9	84.9	94.1	98.4	93.8
Females								
1949–51	19–21	1.2					22.0	43.4
1946–48	22–24	13.8	39.9				52.5	75.3
1941–45	25–29	5.6	46.3	80.6			85.2	89.1
1936–40	30–34	13.2	57.8	80.0	94.4		95.3	93.3
1931–35	35–39	13.3	65.3	87.9	94.9	97.3	97.6	94.6
1926–30	40–44	6.7	51.9	78.5	93.4	96.2	98.6	94.8
1921–25	45–49	10.3	50.2	80.8	92.6	94.6	97.6	94.8

Sources: for Jews—NJPS, authors' tabulations; for all whites—U.S. Bureau of the Census, *1970 Census of Population, Subject Reports* PC(2)–4C; *Marital Status*, 1972.

lifecycle. Among the younger cohorts, whose marital experience is yet incompletely described in the data reported here, a marked decline can be observed in the proportions of the ever-married at younger ages.[13] While 65 per cent of Jewish women aged 35–39 in 1970–1971 had been married before reaching age 22, this was true of only 40 per cent of those aged 22–24. This marked the transition from the peak of the post-war increase in marriages to the declining marriage propensity of the early 1970's. Among males, the proportion married by age 25 apparently reached a peak among the cohort aged 25–29 in 1970–1971; the declining proportion married by age 22 among younger Jewish males suggests that a trend reversal was beginning.

The available data for both sexes point to less inter-cohort variation in the past at the older end of the marriage age range. Thus, the declining proportion married at younger ages might be interpreted as being due to a shift in the timing of marriage, which could be counter-balanced by more marriages at older ages, rather than in the propensity to marry at all. However, the more recent trends among the total U.S. white population do not support such an assumption. Since the 1960's, a marked general increase in singlehood has occurred, partially reflecting also an increase in the cohabitation of unmarried adults.[14] For example, the proportion of women still single at age 22 increased from 26 per cent in 1960 to 48 per cent in 1980.[15] There has been, moreover, an increase in the proportion of currently separated or divorced persons. Some of these trends, which may also have affected the Jewish population, recall changes in family formation that occurred during the years of the great depression. Many persons—in the case of the U.S. Jewish population, especially females—who reached prime marriage age during that unfavorable period, not only postponed marriage, but eventually ended up never-married. Part of the more recent changes, even if determined by temporary causes, such as cyclical constraints in labor market opportunities and income, may turn out to be irreversible in the long run for the currently marriageable population.

On the basis of the available evidence, it seems likely that there has been a substantial increase in the proportion of never-married American Jews in recent years, a trend that probably reflects normative changes in the relative position of the "parents and children" family vis à vis alternative life-styles in contemporary society.

AGE AT MARRIAGE

With regard to young Jewish adults marrying for the first time, age at marriage has been declining for both males and females since the end of World War II (Table

---

[13]For marriage-age-specific sex imbalances, see below.

[14]See Paul Glick and Arthur Norton, "Marrying, Divorcing, and Living Together in the U.S. Today," Population Bulletin, October 1977, pp. 3–39.

[15]See U.S. Bureau of the Census, Marital Status and Living Arrangements—March 1980, Current Population Reports, Series P-20, No. 365, 1981.

4). Mean age at first marriage for Jews of each sex has been consistently higher—
by one to three years—than among total whites. Higher Jewish educational attainment and the related longer period of schooling are major factors in this differential.
Jewish age at marriage declined from 28.1 for grooms and 24.0 for brides in 1945–
1949—when many weddings postponed in previous years were celebrated—to, respectively, 27.1 and 23.2 in 1955–1959, 25.7 and 23.0 in 1965–1969, and 24.9 and
22.9 in the last two years covered by NJPS data. The age gap between Jews and the
general population at marriage has been narrowed for males. The speedier decline
in age at marriage among Jewish males caused a reduction in the mean age difference
between spouses from 4.1 years in 1945–1949 to 2.0 in 1970–1971. Hence the
difference in average marriage age between the sexes, which was much greater
among Jews than among all whites in the late 1940's, diminished and became similar
for both these population groups.

TABLE 4.   MEAN AGE AT FIRST MARRIAGE AMONG JEWISH POPULATION AND
           ALL WHITES, BY YEAR OF MARRIAGE AND SEX, 1970–1971

Year of	Jews			All Whites		
Marriage	Males	Females	Difference	Males	Females	Difference
1970–71	24.9	22.9	2.0	23.4	21.2	2.2
1965–69	25.7	23.0	2.7	23.6	21.1	2.5
1960–64	26.7	22.9	3.8	23.7	21.0	2.7
1955–59	27.1	23.2	3.9	24.1	21.3	2.8
1950–54	26.5	23.0	3.5	24.4	21.7	2.7
1945–49	28.1	24.0	4.1	25.0	22.3	2.7

Sources: for Jews—NJPS, authors' tabulations; for all whites—U.S. Bureau of the Census, *1970 Census of Population, Subject Reports PC (2)-4D; Age at First Marriage,* 1973.

The trend toward lower age at marriage can in part be explained by the improved
quality of, and access to, contraception, which has led to a weakening of the previous
linkage between marriage and childbearing and has reduced the importance of
delayed marriage as a means of controlling family growth. At the same time, the
age patterns observed here and in the preceding section seem also to reflect important fluctuations in the pool of Jewish candidates for marriage, fluctuations which
are determined by the changing sex ratio of persons reaching marriageable ages in
different years. Such sex ratios can be assessed by examining the age-sex composition
of the Jewish population in 1970–1971[16] (see Table 5). The customary age difference
between somewhat older grooms and somewhat younger brides combined with wide
fluctuations in the number of Jewish births before, during, and after World War II
in generating alternate phases in the relative size of the cohorts of each sex which

[16]Adjusted data.

reached that stage in the lifecycle when young adults started considering marriage, exploring the available pool of candidates, and forming relationships that later led to marriage. In Table 5 this is exemplified by an age of 22.5 for males and 20 for females. With regard to this age-sex combination, a relative shortage of Jewish females prevailed during the 1950's as a consequence of the declining number of Jewish births during the years of the great depression. The young adult sex-ratio was reversed in the early 1960's, when the reduced male cohorts born during the depression and World War II confronted more numerous female cohorts born during the early stages of the post-war "baby boom." This shortage continued in the 1970's. However, during the 1980's young Jewish adult males born toward the end of the "baby boom" will again outnumber the somewhat younger Jewish females born in the low fertility years.

Other things being equal, an excess of persons of one sex on the "marriage market" will mean greater competition and reduced chances of success in finding suitable partners of the opposite sex. This may induce prolonged and perhaps definitive celibacy and later ages at marriage. Moreover, from the perspective of a given subpopulation within a total national population—as is the case with U.S. Jewry—a deficiency of potential spouses of a given sex within that subpopulation may stimulate the quest for partners from outside. Since sex imbalance may occur more or less at the same time among different subpopulations, mixed marriage is likely to increase in such periods, other things being equal. On the other hand, to counterbalance these internal pressures generated by changing population structures, mechanisms of demographic adjustment may emerge. Since the "marriage

TABLE 5. SEX RATIOS AMONG JEWISH POPULATION REACHING MARRIAGEABLE AGE, BY YEAR OF BIRTH, 1970–1971

Year of Birth		Approximate Years When Reaching: Males = Age 22.5 Females = Age 20	Ratios[a]	
Males	Females		Males / Females	Females / Males
1928–32	1931–35	1951–55	105.4	94.9
1933–37	1936–40	1956–60	104.8	95.4
1938–42	1941–45	1961–65	90.4	110.7
1943–47	1946–50	1966–70	81.7	122.4
1948–52	1951–55	1971–75	94.4	105.9
1953–57	1956–60	1976–80	96.0	104.1
1958–62	1961–65	1981–85	125.3	79.8
1963–67	1966–70	1986–90	125.8	79.5

[a]Balance between sexes = 100.0.
Source: NJPS, adjusted data, authors' tabulations.

squeeze" stems from the age differences between spouses (the number of men and women born during the same year being quite similar), variations in those differences are apt to reduce the imbalance between the number of potential grooms and brides. This is precisely what occurred among U.S. Jews between 1950 and 1971—on top of a general trend of declining ages at first marriage, the decline was speedier among males, who became outnumbered by females. It can be presumed that the reverse situation of the early 1980's, as pointed out in Table 5, i.e., the more privileged "market" position of Jewish females, might lead to a rise in male age at marriage and/or in male celibacy among U.S. Jews.

MARRIAGE DISRUPTION AND REMARRIAGE

Marriage can be terminated through the death of one of the spouses, or through divorce or separation. According to NJPS, in 1970–1971, 2.2 per cent of the Jewish male population aged 20–54 were currently divorced or separated, and 0.3 per cent were widowed. The percentages for females were 3.3 and 1.5, respectively. This type of information, conventionally available in census-type data, is of limited value because it results from a combination of variable levels of marriage disruption and remarriage. The incidence of these two factors should be investigated separately (see Table 6). The proportion of ever-married Jews aged 20–54 who had a terminated marriage was substantially lower than the proportion among the total white U.S. population. In 1970–1971, 9 to 15 per cent of ever-married Jewish males aged 35–54, and 10 to 16 per cent of females in these ages had an ever-terminated marriage.[17] The corresponding levels for total whites in 1975 were 20 to 23 per cent among males, and 26 to 30 per cent among females. These findings confirm the generally known pattern of greater marital stability among Jews in Western countries.

The recent high frequencies of marital disruption in the United States—which have led to the prediction that 50 per cent of currently performed weddings in the general population might end in divorce[18]—find some support in the higher percentages of Jews with terminated marriages at ages 40–44, as compared to ages 50–54. The percentages of younger people with terminated marriages are higher than those of older ones observed at comparable ages. Moreover, these percentages are bound to increase in future years, following further exposure to the risk of marital disruption.[19]

---

[17]Inclusive of both divorce or widowhood. The predominant factor was divorce. Because of the low mortality levels at ages 20–54, differentials in survival of Jews and of all whites cannot have more than a very marginal effect on the observed differences in marital disruption.

[18]See U.S. Bureau of the Census, *Number, Timing, and Duration of Marriages and Divorces in the United States: June 1975,* Current Population Reports, Series P-20, No. 297, 1976.

[19]An increase in the proportion of previously divorced individuals among Jews currently marrying in Canada—from less than 10 per cent in 1971 to 18 per cent in 1979—is reported by Leo Davids, "Divorce and Remarriage among Canadian Jews," *Journal of Comparative Family Studies,* Spring 1982, pp. 34–47.

TABLE 6.   PERCENTAGES OF PREVIOUSLY MARRIED AND OF REMARRIED PER-
SONS AMONG JEWISH POPULATION AND ALL WHITES, BY AGE AND
SEX, 1970–1971

	Jews		All Whites	
Age	Per Cent With Ever-Terminated Marriages Among All Ever-Married	Per Cent Re-married Among Persons With Terminated Marriages	Per Cent With Ever-Terminated Marriages Among All Ever-Married	Per Cent Re-married Among Persons With Terminated Marriages
Males				
20–24	2.4	16.7	11.4	36.4
25–29	18.9	16.2	15.6	53.6
30–34	3.5	66.7	18.6	70.1
35–39	9.0	75.6	21.9	74.8
40–44	14.7	89.0	20.3	76.4
45–49	10.5	82.7	20.4	76.6
50–54	10.0	82.8	23.0	76.6
Females				
20–24	7.4	74.5	15.8	37.4
25–29	10.5	60.9	21.6	53.3
30–34	11.6	71.4	23.9	61.2
35–39	9.6	67.3	25.8	65.3
40–44	16.1	69.6	26.1	63.8
45–49	16.3	46.5	30.1	60.1
50–54	9.9	38.3	30.5	58.0

Sources: for Jews—NJPS, authors' tabulations; for all whites—U.S. Bureau of the Census, *Number, Timing and Duration of Marriages and Divorces in the United States, June 1975,* Current Population Reports, Series P-20, No. 297, 1976.

Greater Jewish familism also appears in the generally higher frequencies of remarriage among persons with terminated marriages. Among Jewish males the remarriage rates below age 30 were low, partly in connection with their higher ages at first marriage; but over 80 per cent of the relevant persons aged 40–54 had remarried, as against 76 to 77 per cent among all whites. Among females below age 45, Jewish remarriage rates were higher than those of total whites; in the older age groups in which widowhood tends to become the predominant factor in marital disruption, they were lower.

It can be noted, in evaluating these findings, that, on the whole, mixed couples involving Jews have had higher rates of divorce than homogamous Jewish couples.[20]

___

[20]See Larry Bumpass and James Sweet, "Differentials in Marital Instability, 1970," *American Sociological Review,* 1972. Another indicator of greater instability of mixed marriages, at

Remarriages, in turn, have been more often heterogamous than first marriages. These tendencies should be kept in mind in the interpretation of increasing frequencies of both divorce and mixed marriage (see below) among U.S. Jews.

Family Growth

RECENT TRENDS

In recent decades two main patterns have characterized the fertility trends of U.S. Jews in comparison to those of the total white population:[21] (a) a generally lower than average completed family size, whether estimated through analysis of the natality level of a given period or ascertained from the cumulative number of children born to women by the end of their reproductive cycle; (b) greater responsiveness to those periodic societal changes that have stimulated upward or downward swings in the general levels of American fertility. Jews have usually anticipated these changes by a few years.

The total fertility rate (TFR) (a synthetic expression of the level of reproductivity in a given period) of Jews reached an all-time minimum of 1.3 children around 1935 (as against 2.1 among total whites), climbed to 2.8 around 1955 (versus 3.5 among total whites), and declined again to 1.5 (versus 2.2 among total whites) around 1970.[22] Similar, though less pronounced, fluctuations are apparent in the cumulative childbearing experiences of Jewish women who had completed reproduction in 1970–1971: a minimum average of 1.4 children among women born in 1901–1905, followed by relatively higher levels of 2.2 to 2.4 children on the average among women born between 1921–1925 and 1931–1935, and a subsequent decline of fertility among later born women. These data relate to all women, regardless of marital status; the mean completed fertility of ever-married women was slightly higher, ranging between 1.5 and 2.4 children, according to the birth cohorts involved. Fluctuations indicated here reflect the evolution of total white American fertility over the last 50 years.[23] Some lack of synchronization in the pace of change is revealed by the varying ratio of Jewish fertility to all white fertility as expressed by

least in the past, is the shorter duration of interfaith, as compared to intrafaith, marriages ending in a divorce. See, e.g., State of California, Department of Public Health, Bureau of Vital Statistics, *Divorce in California: Initial Complaints for Divorce, Annulment, and Separate Maintenance, 1966* (Berkeley, 1967).

[21]See Sidney Goldstein, "Jewish Fertility in Contemporary America," in Paul Ritterband, (ed.), *Modern Jewish Fertility* (Leiden, 1981), and Sergio DellaPergola, "Patterns of American Jewish Fertility," *Demography*, August 1980, pp. 261–273. For a description of similar trends in Canada and comparisons between Jews and many other ethnic groups, see K. Basavarajappa and S. Halli, "Are Ethnic Fertility Differences in Canada Disappearing? An Examination of the Period 1926–1971," paper presented at IUSSP general conference, Manila, 1981.

[22]See DellaPergola, "Patterns of American Jewish Fertility," *op. cit.,* Table 1.

[23]See Ronald Rindfuss and James Sweet, *Postwar Fertility and Differentials in the United States* (New York, 1977).

period measures (TFR): 59 per cent around 1935; 87 per cent around 1945; and 66 per cent around 1970.

Recent developments in Jewish fertility should be seen against the background of the continuing decline in general U.S. fertility. An assessment of the trend between 1971 and 1976 can be made by comparing the 1970–1971 NJPS data with the small Jewish subsample included in cycle 2 of the National Survey of Family Growth (NSFG), carried out in 1976 by the U.S. National Center for Health Statistics.[24] By comparing the number of children born on the average to women belonging to the same birth cohort and surveyed at different ages in 1970–1971 and 1976, we can roughly estimate the number of additional children born during this approximate five-year period to each such group of mothers (Table 7). By summing the age-specific additions to family size, a total marital fertility of 1.5 is obtained, which corresponds to a TFR (relative to all women, regardless of marital status) of 1.3 to 1.4 in 1970–1976. This compares with a total white TFR of 1.8 in the same period. Thus, Jewish fertility, by the mid-1970's, was again very close to the bottom levels of the inter-war period. However, since total white fertility in the 1970's was substantially lower than during the 1930's, the ratio of Jewish to total fertility (72 to 78 per cent) was higher than in the past.

These age-specific fertility estimates provide a tentative empirical basis for estimating a crude birthrate (CBR) for the U.S. Jewish population in the years 1971–1975. By multiplying the average number of additional children born to each age-group by the number of women in the respective age-group and adding up the results, a rough CBR estimate of nine to ten per 1,000 Jewish population is obtained.[25] This compares with a general U.S. birthrate of 15 per 1,000 during the same period. Assuming invariance in the age-specific fertility schedule of Jewish women, the changed female age composition alone would produce an increase of 10 to 15 per cent in the Jewish CBR in 1976–1980, bringing it to 11 to 12 per 1,000.

On the basis of such data, no firm conclusion can be reached as to the ultimate family size of Jewish and total women that were at childbearing ages during the 1970's. The possibility of an upward fertility swing, which might at least partially compensate for the effects of the recent prolonged phase of low fertility, has been extensively discussed in the United States and elsewhere.[26] It has been hypothesized by some economists and demographers that the entrance into the labor force of the small cohorts born since 1960 might stimulate easier employment, relatively better wages, more marriage opportunities, and, in consequence, larger families in the 1980's. But, even if the assumed conditions materialize, there are weak points in the hypothesis of a consequent rise in fertility. Because of changing sex norms, the link

---

[24]The data are presented in Schmelz, "Jewish Survival," op. cit.

[25]A similar CBR for 1967–1969 has been estimated by Sidney Goldstein. See "Jewish Fertility in Contemporary America," op. cit.

[26]See, for example, Richard Easterlin, "What Will 1984 be Like? Socioeconomic Implications of Recent Twists in Age Structure," Demography, November 1978, pp. 397–432.

TABLE 7.   AGE-SPECIFIC FERTILITY AMONG JEWISH WOMEN, 1970–1971 TO 1976

Year of Birth	1970–71		1976		Additional Children, 1971–76, Ever-Married Women	Per Cent Ever-Married[a]	Additional Children 1971–76, All Women
	Age	Average Children, Ever-Married Women	Age	Average Children, Ever-Married Women			
1956–60	10–14	0.0	15–19	—	0.0[a]	1	0.00
1951–55	15–19	0.3	20–24	—	0.4[a]	35	0.14
1946–50	20–24	0.5	25–29	1.1	0.6	85	0.51
1941–45	25–29	1.3	30–34	1.7	0.4	95	0.38
1936–40	30–34	2.2	35–39	2.4	0.2	98	0.20
1931–35	35–39	2.4	40–44	2.5	0.1	99	0.10
1926–30	40–44	2.2	45–49	—	0.0[a]	98	0.00
					Total marital fertility rate = 1.5		Total fertility rate = 1.33

[a]Our estimates, assuming additional children born to women of respective age, were slightly below total white levels.
Sources: for Jews—NJPS, authors' tabulations (see DellaPergola, "Patterns of American Jewish Fertility," op. cit.); for all whites—U.S. National Center for Health Statistics, National Survey of Family Growth, Cycle 2. Data reported by Schmelz, "Jewish Survival: The Demographic Factors," op. cit.

between marriage and fertility has become less clear than it was in the past, particularly during the great post-war fertility increase. More marriages, made possible by improved economic conditions, still do not guarantee that many more children will be born.[27] Moreover, relatively "old" mothers (aged 30–39) had an important role in the increased natality of the late 1940's and 1950's. The changes in contraceptive patterns that have emerged in the United States in more recent years include a growing diffusion of voluntary sterilization, especially toward the later stages of the reproductive span.[28] Consequently, for a rising number of households, including substantial proportions of Jewish couples, the currently achieved low fertility levels might become irreversible even in the hypothetical case of future renewed demand for larger families.

By the end of the 1970's, after 20 years of decline, U.S. white fertility had actually stabilized, and there were even modest signs of recovery. But the somewhat higher birthrates among women aged 30 and over—pointing to delayed childbearing—could not compensate for the low birthrates that had characterized the same women in the preceding years. It appears that the eventual completed family size of all white and, by inference, of Jewish women who around 1980 were already at central or terminal ages of their reproductive life-span is bound to be rather small.

FERTILITY EXPECTATIONS AND THE PACE OF FAMILY GROWTH

Data on the total number of children expected by Jewish women provide another way of assessing the recent and expected level of fertility among American Jews. In an efficiently contracepting population, such as the American Jewish community, birth expectation data may provide a useful indication of current trends for aggregate cohorts, even if not for individual women. A substantial decline in Jewish birth expectations took place between 1970–1971 (according to NJPS) and 1976 (according to NSFG). The 2.7 children expected on average by Jewish women aged 15–19 in 1970–1971 had declined to 2.1 among women aged 20–24 some five years later. Among the women aged 20–24 in 1970–71, who were roughly 25–29 years old by 1976, birth expectations declined from 2.5 to 2.2; among women aged 25–29, from

---

[27]See Larry Bumpass, "The Changing Linkage of Nuptiality and Fertility in the United States," in Lado Ruzicka, (ed.), *Marriage and Fertility* (Liège, 1981), pp. 195–209.

[28]According to the 1975 Boston Jewish Community Survey, 23 per cent of couples with 31–39-year-old wives, and 22 per cent of couples married for 10 to 15 years, included a husband or wife that had undergone a sterilization operation. Among older couples, and at longer marriage durations—whose fertility levels are minimal in any case—the per cent sterilized was nearly twice as high. See Calvin Goldscheider, "Contraceptive Use among American Jewish Families," in Schmelz, Glikson, and DellaPergola, (eds.), *Papers in Jewish Demography, 1981, op. cit.* For general discussions of trends and prospects in sterilization in the United States, see Charles Westoff and Norman Ryder, *The Contraceptive Revolution* (Princeton, 1977) and Kathleen Ford, "Contraceptive Use in the United States, 1973–1976," *Family Planning Perspectives,* 1978.

2.3 to 2.0; and among those aged 30–34, from 2.4 to 2.1. These changes are partly explained by the fact that women who join the married population at older ages tend to have lower birth expectations, and to depress the averages expressed by women who had married earlier. Moreover, there may have been an actual revision of reproductive targets, consistent with the general lowering of fertility during the 1970's. Jewish birth expectations in 1976 were lower by five to 25 per cent, according to age-groups, than those of all white women.

Marriage cohorts provide more stable data on the expected fertility of younger women, since each marriage cohort is unaffected by marriages occurring subsequently. The evidence of the later marriage cohorts covered by NJPS points, in fact, to declining expectations: from 2.4 children on average among women married in 1955–1959, to 2.1 to 2.2 among those married in 1965–1969, who were at the peak of reproduction during the 1970's (see Table 8). The data on the number of final births expected by ever-married Jewish women reveal an evident convergence toward an expectation of two children. This was the case among 64 per cent of Jewish women married in 1965–1969, as against 41 per cent of those married in 1950–1954. Steady decline has occurred with regard to the proportion of women preferring only one child. The trend in expected childlessness is more irregular, though there may have been some increase in the latest marriage cohorts studied. On the other hand, there has been a decline in the proportion of Jewish women expecting relatively large families of four and more children. Additional NJPS data —not presented here—on the fertility expectations of the marriage cohort of the late 1960's show that the higher fertility standards which prevailed in the past in the religiously more observant and segregated sections of American Jewry have settled at relatively moderate levels, around three to four children on the average per married woman.

These fertility expectation data quite naturally raise the question whether the observed current—and so far incomplete—fertility schedules of younger Jewish women are actually adequate to achieve the expectations. An answer can be outlined by comparing the pace of family growth of younger women with that of women with completed fertility. Delayed beginning of family growth, has generally characterized U.S. Jewish households as compared to the total white population. Among Jewish women married between 1920 and 1964, the proportion having a child by the end of the first year of marriage ranged between 25 per cent (as against 30 per cent of total whites) in 1920–1924 marriages and four per cent (versus 24 per cent) in wartime marriages (1940–1944); among Jewish women married in 1965–1964, eight per cent had a child during the first year of marriage (as against 37 per cent of total whites).[29] The latter figure includes 20 per cent of white women who had their first

---

[29]The data on total whites are taken from U.S. Bureau of the Census, *Marriage, Fertility, and Childspacing: August 1959,* Current Population Reports, Series P-20, No. 108, 1961 and U.S. Bureau of the Census, *Trends in Childspacing: June 1975,* Current Population Reports, Series P-20, No. 315, 1978.

TABLE 8. COMPLETED FAMILY SIZES EXPECTED BY EVER-MARRIED JEWISH WOMEN, BY YEAR OF MARRIAGE, 1970–1971

Year of Marriage	Total	Expected Final Births						Mean	Actual Births, Mean
		0	1	2	3	4	5+		
1965–69	100.0	8.0	3.1	64.4	17.7	6.0	0.8	2.15	0.87
1960–64	100.0	10.7	5.7	44.9	32.0	5.3	1.4	2.20	1.89
1955–59	100.0	3.8	9.5	46.8	29.3	7.6	3.0	2.36	2.27
1950–54	100.0	8.0	9.8	41.3	24.4	15.2	1.3	2.34	2.34

Source: NJPS, authors' tabulations.

child not later than seven months after marriage (five per cent were born before marriage), i.e., more than twice the proportion of contemporary Jewish wives having a child by the end of their first year of marriage. Rarer premarital conceptions resulting in a birth, and more stringent marital contraception among Jews, in particular in the early stages of marriage, underlie these differentials. They, in turn, may be related to differences in socioeconomic structure—e.g., different enrollment rates in higher education—as well as cultural norms and values of Jews and members of other subpopulations in the United States. The progression of family growth at increasing marriage duration (Table 9) leads to a narrowing of these very substantial initial differentials. Taking an average of all the marriage cohorts examined, Jewish women achieved 28 per cent of their total marital fertility after three years of marriage, 49 per cent after five years (virtually the same as among recent total white cohorts), 72 per cent after eight years, and 93 per cent after 15 years (above

TABLE 9. CUMULATIVE NUMBER OF CHILDREN BORN TO EVER-MARRIED JEWISH WOMEN UP TO SELECTED MARRIAGE DURATIONS, 1970–1971

Year of First Marriage	Exact Years Since First Marriage				
	3	5	8	15	Total
Average Births					
1965–69	0.48				2.15[a]
1960–64	0.69	1.18	1.64		2.20[a]
1955–59	0.73	1.41	1.86		2.36[a]
1950–54	0.59	1.04	1.75	2.21	2.34[a]
1945–49	0.66	1.15	1.64	2.07	2.17
1940–44	0.52	1.03	1.57	2.19	2.35
1935–39	0.49	0.83	1.26	1.83	2.00
1930–34	0.47	0.72	1.12	1.56	1.72
1925–29	0.60	0.92	1.26	1.61	1.71
1920–24	0.60	0.94	1.37	1.64	1.84
Per Cent of Total Births (Actual or Expected) Already Achieved					
1965–69	22				100[a]
1960–64	31	54	75		100[a]
1955–59	31	60	79		100[a]
1950–54	25	44	75	94	100[a]
1945–49	30	53	76	95	100
1940–44	22	44	67	93	100
1935–39	25	42	63	92	100
1930–34	27	42	65	91	100
1925–29	35	54	74	94	100
1920–24	33	51	74	89	100

[a]Final birth expectations.
Source: NJPS, authors' tabulations.

total whites). There has been variation around these averages, pointing to the adaptation of childbearing patterns to changing societal circumstances in the United States. Women married during the economic depression and World War II were "slow starters" in the family building process, but displayed more rapid family growth at longer marriage durations. Women married after World War II have tended to achieve higher proportions of their total marital fertility at relatively lower marriage durations. Correspondingly, the mean age of the women at the time of their terminal birth has tended to decline.

A comparison of the actual incomplete fertility schedules of women recently married (1965–1969) with their reported fertility expectations reveals a particularly slow pace of family growth at short marriage durations. A greater reproductive effort would thus be required at later stages of family growth to attain the expected fertility. This, however, contrasts with the pattern of declining fertility at longer marriage durations that emerges from an examination of the previous marriage cohorts.[30] The initial birth history of the 1965–1969 marriages resembles that of the 1940–1944 cohort, whose fertility was later swept upward during the American post-war "baby boom." However, the declining levels of general fertility in the United States during the 1970's are not likely to have stimulated greater fertility at later marriage durations among the young American Jewish women.[31] Rather, their already low birth expectations in 1970–1971 may have been revised still further downward in the years that have followed.

What emerges clearly from the analysis is that the differences between Jewish and other women are even greater in the timing of fertility onset and in the spacing of successive births than in the cumulative number of children born. Jewish women reach the peak of childbearing at ages 25–29, *inter alia* because of their higher age at marriage and longer first birth intervals, and not at 20–24, as among the total white population.[32] This fact, in itself, is of some demographic significance: given the same final average number of children, a higher age at motherhood, i.e., greater generation length, makes for slower population growth.

In considering family growth among American Jews, it must be borne in mind that measurements of period fertility (Table 7) may differ from those of cohort fertility. Moreover, differences between marital fertility and the fertility of all women, including the unmarried, must be duly taken into account. The role of changing marriage patterns may be very significant in this context. When marital fertility is anyway very low, age at marriage may have only minor effects on the final number of children ever born (at least for that large majority of women who marry between ages 19 and 34);[33] but a momentous question is which proportion of the many young Jewish adults who were single in 1970–1971 actually married in subsequent years. If the probably

[30]See DellaPergola, "Patterns of American Jewish Fertility," *op. cit.*

[31]See, however, concluding remarks in the previous section.

[32]See DellaPergola, "Patterns of American Jewish Fertility," *op. cit.*

[33]See Sergio DellaPergola, "Contemporary Jewish Fertility: An Overview," in Schmelz, Glikson, and DellaPergola, (eds.), *Papers in Jewish Demography, 1981, op. cit.*

exaggerated expectations of the latest marriage cohorts studied in NJPS are critically evaluated, fertility is found to have recently been below replacement level, which, at minimal mortality, is 2.1 children on average for all women, including the unmarried. While fluctuations are quite possible, continuation of essentialy low fertility among U.S. Jews seems to be the most likely trend for the forseeable future.

Out-Marriage and its Implications

PAST AND EXPECTED LEVELS

Out-marriage[34] is one of the most intriguing factors in the demographic development of subpopulations. Its study involves numerous definitional and measurement problems, the solution of which may influence both the reading and interpretation of the observed trends. Different analysts have used somewhat different approaches for computing the frequency of out-marriage among households that were surveyed in the NJPS.[35] In this report we present a new set of NJPS estimates of the extent of out-marriage, by period of marriage. The data presented in Table 10 illustrate the religious composition of first marriages among ever-married persons, regardless of current marriage status. The frequencies of marriage with originally non-Jewish spouses are given, broken down according to whether conversion to Judaism took place (prior to the date of the survey or the termination of the marriage through the death of the spouse or divorce).

In 1970–1971 altogether 11.0 per cent of ever-married Jewish men and 5.1 per cent of Jewish women had contracted their first marriage with an originally non-Jewish partner. This corresponded to 8.1 per cent of Jewish spouses of both sexes together, and to 15.0 per cent of all couples with at least one Jewish partner.[36]

After reducing these initial out-marriage rates because of conversions to Judaism, the overall frequencies of mixed marriage are somewhat lower: 6.8 per cent of Jewish spouses (8.5 per cent of Jewish husbands, and 4.9 per cent of Jewish wives), and 12.5 per cent of couples with at least one Jewish partner. A significant increase in the extent of mixed marriage is shown by comparing the latter data with an earlier nationwide study. In 1957, according to the U.S. Current Population Survey, the

---

[34]The term "out-marriage" is used throughout with reference to all weddings in which one of the spouses was not born Jewish or was not Jewish at the time the two partners first met. When the non-Jewish partner does not change his/her original identification, the term "mixed marriage" applies. In case of conversion, use of the term "intermarriage" may be appropriate.

[35]See Fred Massarik, "Explorations in Intermarriage," AJYB, Vol. 74, 1973, pp. 292–306; Dov Lazerwitz, "Current Jewish Intermarriages in the Unites States," in Schmelz, Glikson, and DellaPergola, (eds.), Papers in Jewish Demography, 1977, op. cit., pp. 103–114; and Bernard Lazerwitz, "Jewish-Christian Marriages and Conversions," Jewish Social Studies, Winter 1981, pp. 31–46.

[36]"Couple" rates of out-marriage are higher than "individual" rates because homogamous Jewish couples are entered in the denominator once in the former case and twice in the latter.

TABLE 10. PER CENT OF OUT-MARRIAGES, BY SEX OF JEWISH SPOUSE, CONVERSION STATUS OF ORIGINALLY NON-JEWISH SPOUSE, AND YEAR OF MARRIAGE, EVER-MARRIED PERSONS, FIRST MARRAGES, 1970–1971

Year of Marriage	All Ever-Married Jews[a]			Per Cent of Jews with Originally Non-Jewish Spouse						Per Cent of Couples with Originally Non-Jewish Spouse[a]		
				Jewish Husbands			Jewish Wives					
	Total	Spouse Converted to Judaism		Total	Spouse Converted to Judaism		Total	Spouse Converted to Judaism		Total	Spouse Converted to Judaism	
		Yes	No		Yes	No		Yes	No		Yes	No
	(1)	(2)	(3)	(4)	(5)	(6)	(7)	(8)	(9)	(10)	(11)	(12)
Total	8.1	1.3	6.8	11.0	2.5	8.5	5.1	0.2	4.9	15.0	2.5	12.5
1965–71	29.2	6.7	22.5	41.1	10.8	30.6	10.3	0.4	9.9	45.1	10.3	34.8
1960–64	11.6	1.7	9.8	13.0	3.1	9.9	10.0	0.3	9.7	20.7	3.1	17.6
1955–59	6.6	1.7	4.9	10.1	3.1	7.0	2.8	0.1	2.7	12.3	3.1	9.2
1950–54	5.1	0.6	4.5	7.5	1.0	6.5	2.5	0.2	2.3	9.7	1.2	8.5
1945–49	6.5	0.3	6.2	5.1	0.5	4.6	7.9	0.2	7.7	12.2	0.6	11.6
1940–44	5.9	0.2	5.7	5.3	0.4	4.9	6.5	0.1	6.4	11.2	0.4	10.8
1935–39	3.9	0.5	3.4	6.5	0.9	5.6	1.2	0.0	1.2	7.5	0.9	6.6
1930–34	3.4	0.4	3.0	3.9	0.8	3.1	2.6	0.4	2.2	6.6	0.8	5.8
1925–29	2.6	0.5	2.1	2.0	0.5	1.5	3.0	0.0	3.0	5.0	0.9	4.1
Up to 1924	1.7	0.3	1.4	2.1	0.6	1.5	1.4	0.0	1.4	3.4	0.5	2.9

a"Couple" rates of out-marriage are higher than "individual" rates, because homogamous Jewish couples are entered in the denominator once in the former case and twice in the latter.

Source: NJPS, authors' tabulations.

overall extent of mixed marriage among the currently married was: 4.0 per cent of Jewish spouses (5.2 per cent of Jewish husbands, and 2.7 per cent of Jewish wives), and 7.6 per cent of couples with at least one Jewish partner.[37]

Let us now focus on the net frequency of mixed marriage after any conversions to Judaism took place, and examine more closely the changes that occurred over time in the rate of formation of mixed households. On the assumption that most conversions occur before marriage, our data reflect the composition of couples at the moment of marriage (see columns 3, 6, 9, and 12 in Table 10). Mixed marriage was relatively rare among U.S. Jews, as compared to other Jewries in Western countries, from the beginning of the century until the late 1950's. Over that half century, the proportion of Jewish spouses in first marriages marrying a partner who was not originally Jewish, and had not been converted to Judaism, passed from less than 1 per cent around 1900 to 3 per cent during the 1930's, about 6 per cent during the 1940's, and slightly lower levels (4 to 5 per cent) during the 1950's. A marked increase has occurred since the 1960's in the levels of Jewish heterogamy, bringing it to 10 per cent in 1960–1964, and reaching 22 to 23 per cent in the latest marriage cohorts reflected in NJPS (1965–1971). Translated into couple rates, these data indicate that the proportion of mixed couples among current weddings with at least one Jewish spouse passed from 6 to 7 per cent in the 1930's to 11 to 12 per cent in the 1940's, 8 to 9 per cent in the 1950's, 17 to 18 per cent in 1960–1964, and 35 per cent in 1965–1971.

It is interesting to compare these estimates with the official data routinely available for neighboring Canadian Jewry. In Canada, the proportion of mixed couples among all new marriages involving at least one Jewish partner was 9 per cent in the 1940's, 13 per cent in the 1950's, 17 per cent in 1961–1965, 21 per cent in 1966–1970, 31 per cent in 1971–1976, and 40 per cent in 1978.[38] In terms of the individual Jewish spouses involved, the rates increased from 3 per cent during the 1930's to 5 per cent in the late 1940's, 7 per cent in the 1950's, 9 per cent in 1961–1965, 12 per cent in 1966–1970, 19 per cent in 1971–1975, and 25 per cent in the late 1970's. In other words, the previously moderate levels of mixed marriage among Canadian Jews more than doubled between the mid-1960's and late 1970's. If allowance is made for the fact that the steep increase in out-marriage among U.S. Jews began a few years earlier, the NJPS data do not differ much from the Canadian data.

In evaluating the trends of the recent past and determining those most likely to occur in the near future, the interplay of identificational and demographic factors must be carefully considered. Even if the level of out-marriage is primarily shaped

---

[37]U.S. Bureau of the Census, *Tabulations of Data on the Social and Economic Characteristics of Major Religious Groups, March 1957,* 1967, mimeographed. Spouses with religion not reported were excluded from the computations; spouses reporting no religion were included in the percentages. Out-marriages which had led to conversion in either direction were not reflected in these data.

[38]Statistics Canada, *Vital Statistics,* various issues. See also the detailed statistical appendix in Sergio DellaPergola, *Jewish and Mixed Marriages in Milan, 1901–1968* (Jerusalem, 1972).

by the degree of cultural, social-structural, and ideological assimilation of a minority group within the surrounding majority, demographic factors such as changing size and composition of the "marriage market" (already discussed above) may play an important role in determining individual chances to choose a spouse within one's own group. Thus there is a need to separately inspect the out-marriage trends of Jewish males and females. According to NJPS, the out-marriage rates have generally been higher for males than for females. Yet, growth of female out-marriage was more rapid than that of males between the early 1950's and the mid-1960's. In Canada, too, the increase in Jewish out-marriage since the 1960's has been more substantial among females than among males. It can be presumed that the excess of marriageable Jewish females over marriageable Jewish males contributed to this narrowing of the male-female differential in out-marriage. On the other hand, among the latest NJPS marriage cohorts (1965–1971) over 30 per cent of Jewish husbands and about 10 per cent of Jewish wives had unconverted non-Jewish–born spouses.

A considerable excess of young adult males expected during the 1980's (Table 5) may have the effect of bolstering their already high out-marriage level, while moderating somewhat the out-marriage rate of Jewish females. Whether this in fact occurs depends also, of course, on normative-ideological factors. In the past, out-marriage by Jewish women was relatively rare, indicating non-conformist social behavior. However, once established on a larger scale, under the influence of temporary "marriage market" constraints, it may have become socially more acceptable and thus irreversible.

CONVERSION PATTERNS OF THE OUT-MARRIED

The pattern of conversion in U.S. Jewish households has been examined in previous research.[39] Here we shall briefly trace the evolution over time of a factor that is increasingly perceived as a potentially important component in Jewish population change. The data reported in Table 10 relate to first marriages of all ever-married persons included in the NJPS definition of Jewish or mixed households, regardless of their marital status at the time of the survey. The NJPS data report on the religion of the spouses both at the time they first met and at the time of the survey. This makes it possible to give alternative estimates of out-marriage rates—before or after conversion—as well as rates of conversion among the originally non-Jewish partners of Jewish spouses. However, NJPS does not constitute an adequate source for assessing the extent of conversions or informal dropouts from Judaism in connection with marriage or otherwise. Both alienated Jews who converted out or severed their links with the Jewish group and Jews, whether ideologically estranged or not, who lived in areas completely isolated from the existing

---

[39]See Massarik, "Explorations in Intermarriage," *op. cit.* and Lazerwitz, "Current Jewish Intermarriages in the United States," *op. cit.*

network of Jewish community organizations had fewer chances of being investigated in NJPS.[40]

With regard to the population for which information is available, the propensity of originally non-Jewish marriage partners to convert to Judaism has been much greater among females than among males. Of all ever-married originally non-Jewish wives covered by NJPS, 22 per cent were converted to Judaism, as against only 3 per cent of the husbands. Declining rates of conversion to Judaism characterized the females as long as the frequency of out-marriage was generally low. While the percentage of Jewish husbands outmarrying—regardless of the conversion of the spouse—passed from less than 4 per cent in weddings up to 1939 to 5 per cent among the marriage cohorts of the 1940's, conversions declined from 19 per cent to 8 per cent[41] of the originally non-Jewish wives. Later on, when Jewish male out-marriage rose from 7 per cent in 1950–1954 to 13 per cent in 1960–1964, the proportion of originally non-Jewish wives converting to Judaism followed a parallel course, increasing from 14 per cent to 24 per cent. However, the more recent increase in male out-marriage (41 per cent in 1965–1971) failed to be matched by a parallel response in the propensity of non-Jewish wives to convert to Judaism (26 per cent in the same period). Conversions to Judaism of originally non-Jewish husbands of Jewish women broadly followed a similar pattern, though at a far lower level.

EFFECTS ON JEWISH FERTILITY[42]

The relevance of out-marriage for Jewish population trends is probably greatest in terms of its impact on "effectively Jewish" fertility. Thus it is vital to know if there are fertility differentials between homogamous and mixed couples. Moreover, we need to determine the proportion of children of out-marriages who are reported as Jews by their parents or will identify themselves with the Jewish group later in life. These factors, combined with the frequency of mixed couples, may determine the long-run gains or losses for the Jewish population as a consequence of out-marriage.

Table 11 presents an attempt to evaluate the overall effect of out-marriage on U.S. Jewish fertility and to disaggregate this effect into its various components.[43] The data relate to all ever-married women included in NJPS and to their current or former husbands. The religious identification of the spouses or ex-spouses relates to the time

---

[40]See Fred Massarik, "National Jewish Population Study: A New United States Estimate," AJYB, Vol. 75, 1974–75, p. 300 and Lazerwitz, "An Estimate of a Rare Population Group," op. cit.

[41]Per cent ratios of columns (5) and (4) in Table 10.

[42]For brevity's sake, "Jewish" fertility has been used in this specific section instead of the fuller term "effectively Jewish" fertility, which has been employed elsewhere in this article.

[43]For a more detailed presentation of the computation technique, and for analogous data on Jewish communities in other countries, see Sergio DellaPergola, "L'effet des mariages mixtes sur la natalité dans une sous-population: quelques problèmes et resultats concernant la diaspora juive," in Demographie et Destin des Sous-Populations (Paris, forthcoming).

TABLE 11. EFFECTS OF OUT-MARRIAGE ON JEWISH FERTILITY, BY SELECTED CHARACTERISTICS OF WIVES,* 1970-1971

Characteristics of Wives	Per Cent of Out-Married Couples Among All Couples in Given Category[a]	Per Cent Difference of Fertility of Out-Married Couples as Compared to Jewish Couples[b]	Per Cent Jewish Among All Children of Out-Married Couples[c]	Per Cent Difference of Jewish Fertility of Out-Married Couples as Compared to Jewish Couples[d]	Total Per Cent Effect on Jewish Fertility[e]
Total	14[f]	−24	49	−26	−4
Year of Marriage					
1965–71	45	+33	25	−34	−15
1955–64	15	−36	76	−3	0
1945–54	11	−13	46	−21	−2
1935–44	10	+57	53	+66	+6
1925–34	6	−24	53	−19	−1
Up to 1924	3	−52	38	−63	−2
Conversion Patterns					
Husband Jewish, wife converted to Judaism	2[g]	−52	94	−10	0
Husband Jewish, wife non-Jewish	7[g]	−14	27	−72	−5
Wife Jewish, husband non-Jewish	5[g]	−19	86	+39	+2

Preferred Denomination

Orthodox, Conservative,										
Reform	6		−25		87		+36		+2	
Other and none	53		−4		22		−57		−30	

*Includes marriages of a Jew/Jewess with a converted or unconverted originally non-Jewish spouse; excludes out-marriages in which the (ex-) Jew/Jewess could not be covered by NJPS.

ᵃEver-married, first marriages. Percentages relate to total in specified category, unless otherwise stated. This column corresponds to column (10) in Table 10.

ᵇFertility relates to average number of children ever born. Fertility of out-married couples, regardless of religious identification of children.

ᶜPercentages above 50 indicate a "gain" and below 50 a "loss" (see text).

ᵈCombined effects of fertility differentials between out-married and homogamous Jewish couples, and of religious identification of children of out-marriages. Obtained by comparing *twice* the average number of Jewish children of out-married couples with the average number of children of Jewish couples.

ᵉProduct of the percentages in columns (4) and (1) in this table.

ᶠThe corresponding value in Table 10, column (10) is 15 per cent. The difference is due to percentage rounding and missing cases.

ᵍPercentages relate to total couples.

Source: NJPS, authors' tabulations.

they first met. Both converted and unconverted originally non-Jewish spouses are included in this analysis, conversion being considered as one of the elements affecting the relationship between out-marriage and Jewish fertility. The religious identification of the children—as reported by the parents—was ascertained by examining the individual records of each of about 10,000 births reported in the detailed fertility histories of NJPS.

While the data reflect the out-marriages ascertainable from NJPS (if the wife or ex-wife was included in that survey) and show a net loss for the reproduction of the Jewish population, they still give too optimistic a picture because of the limitations of the survey. There is an asymmetry in the coverage of out-marriage in NJPS. Out-marriages may be divided into three categories: "mixed" marriages where each partner preserves his/her religious identification; matches involving the conversion to Judaism[44] of the originally non-Jewish partner; and matches involving the out-conversion (or informal dropping out) of the originally Jewish partner. The first two categories may be considered to be adequately represented in NJPS. However, the third category is insufficiently covered—because of a lack of information, no statement can be made about the fertility of couples comprising an ex-Jewish spouse, even though the bias produced by them with regard to the ascertainable identification of the children of out-marriages is obvious. Our analysis relates to the original composition of the couples. Hence it was assumed that for originally out-married couples, i.e., those composed of a Jew/Jewess and an initially non-Jewish spouse, the expected probability of the identificational distribution of the children between Jews and non-Jews was an even one (50:50). In those households in which a conversion to Judaism took place, a very great majority of the children were raised as Jews, thus attaining a gain for the Jewish population. On the other hand, in those households in which the Jewish-born spouse left the Jewish group, it must be presumed that the children were raised as non-Jews. However, the losses caused thereby to the Jewish population in the second generation are hardly reflected in the NJPS data.[45]

The first component examined is the overall fertility (i.e., average number of children ever born) of out-married couples compared to that of Jewish couples,

---

[44]There may be some instances of self-identification as Jew/Jewess without any formal conversion, though the NJPS questionnaire was rather specific on the topic of conversion.

[45]If the current composition of out-married couples—and not the original one—had been taken as the reference situation, the expected probabilities of Jewish identification for the children would have been: (a) mixed marriages—50 per cent; (b) originally non-Jewish spouses converted to Judaism—100 per cent; (c) originally Jewish spouses who left the Jewish group —0 per cent (this last category is, as stated, largely undocumented in NJPS). With this approach, a gain to the Jewish population in (b) (or the loss in (c), if recorded) would have already been attained in the parent generation. However, according to the actual NJPS data, situation (b) resulted in a serious loss of fertility—the gain in the first generation and the loss in the second generation roughly cancelling each other out, and thus replicating the zero effect shown in Table 11. We have preferred to display the more comprehensive picture that emerges when out-marriages are traced to their roots.

regardless of the religion of the children. The former has generally been much lower —24 per cent less on the average; there have been few exceptions to this pattern of lower fertility among the out-married. With regard to the fertility of families formed after 1965, whose fertility was still incomplete by the time of NJPS, out-married couples displayed relatively higher levels, but this may have been due to differences in the timing of initial childbearing.

The second component is the proportion Jewish among all children of out-married couples and the variation from a hypothetical split into equal parts (50:50) as between the two different parental identifications. In the American Jewish community, unlike Jewish communities elsewhere, this factor had caused only a minor loss by 1970–1971, if all out-marriages are considered together: 49 per cent of all children of out-married couples were identified as Jewish. For several older marriage cohorts, Jewish children even formed a majority among the children of the out-married couples. However, only 25 per cent of the children were Jewish among the out-marriages contracted since 1965.

On the whole, considering the combined effects of the two previous components, the Jewish fertility[46] of out-married couples was lower by 26 per cent than the fertility of Jewish couples. Since out-married couples constituted 14 per cent of the total,[47] the overall effect of out-marriage on fertility of the Jewish population[48] was to diminish its level by 4 per cent. The mid-1960's apparently constituted a turning point with regard to both the rapid increase in out-marriage and its effect on Jewish fertility as examined here. While this effect had been only marginally negative or even moderately positive in the case of the marriage cohorts formed prior to 1964, the most recent cohort (1965–1971) displayed a net fertility loss of 15 per cent.

The effect of out-marriage on Jewish fertility must also be specified in terms of the conversion status of the originally non-Jewish spouse. The fertility of couples in which originally non-Jewish women converted to Judaism was much below that of Jewish couples, but since most of their children were Jewish, no overall effect on Jewish fertility resulted. Out-married Jewish women ended up with a higher than average Jewish fertility, because their relatively low fertility (in general) was more than compensated for by the predominant Jewishness of their children. The losing element consisted of couples made up of Jewish husbands and unconverted non-Jewish wives, where low fertility was associated only seldom with the Jewishness of the children. In the United States, the religious identification of the children of out-married couples mostly follows that of the mother, unlike in continental

---

[46]Obtained by comparing *twice* the average number of Jewish children of out-married couples (assuming only half of the children of these couples should be expected to be Jewish) with the average number of children of homogamous Jewish couples.

[47]See note (f) to Table 11.

[48]Computed by multiplying the per cent of differences between *Jewish* fertility of out-married and homogamous Jewish couples, and the percentage of out-married couples among all couples with at least one Jewish partner, i.e., column (5) in Table 11 was obtained by multiplying columns (1) and (4).

European Jewish communities, where it mainly follows the father's religion.[49] It should be stressed again that a full inclusion of couples in which the out-married Jewish partner converted or dropped out of Jewish life would have affected the patterns reported here, revealing a stronger erosion of Jewish fertility in connection with out-marriage.

The processes described here are further clarified by examining fertility differentials by the Jewish denominational preference of the mother. There is a basic difference between the level of out-marriage and its effect on Jewish fertility among married women in Jewish households who are willing to express a preference for any of the three main ideological streams in American Jewry (Orthodox, Conservative, Reform), and among those who are not. The former, who represented 83 per cent of ever-married women in NJPS, experienced relatively low rates of out-marriage. The low fertility of the out-married was more than compensated for by the Jewish identification of most of the children, which resulted in a moderate raising of Jewish fertility.[50] On the other hand, nearly two-thirds of all recorded out-marriages involved couples in which the wife did not express any denominational preference,[51] and fully half of the recorded denominationally undefined couples were out-married. Fertility losses among the denominationally undefined wives in the Jewish population as a consequence of out-marriage are very substantial—30 per cent as compared to the respective homogamous couples. Lack of denominational preference might be explained as the consequence of mixed marriage, rather than as its background. Yet it appears that internal mobility between the more and the less identified may have remarkable consequences for the current and future demographic trends of American Jewry by changing the proportion between the stable and losing sections.[52]

Actual achievement of fertility expectations, already discussed above in general terms, may be of relevance in this context. We have indicated that out-marriage had a reductive effect on Jewish fertility among the 1965–1971 marriage cohort, even after account was taken of the conversion of originally non-Jewish wives to Judaism. These converts, however, whose fertility at early marriage durations was very low,

---

[49]See DellaPergola, "L'effet des mariages mixtes sur la natalité dans une sous-population," *op. cit.*

[50]There are very few out-married couples that are Orthodox-oriented. Differences between Conservative and Reform-oriented out-married couples are more apparent in fertility levels than in the percentage of children reported as Jewish. Interdenominational differences in conversion requirements and in recognizing the validity of conversions performed by other denominations have been left out of consideration here.

[51]Or, in a few cases, indicated a label other than the three major ones.

[52]For further extended discussions of these topics, see Bernard Lazerwitz and Michael Harrison, "American Jewish Denominations: A Social and Religious Profile," *American Sociological Review,* August 1979, pp. 656–666 and Fred Massarik, "Socio-Ideological Differentiation in the U.S. Jewish Population," in Schmelz, Glikson, and DellaPergola, (eds.), *Papers in Jewish Demography 1977, op. cit.,* pp. 143–162.

expressed higher than average final fertility expectations. Should these targets be achieved, the overall impact of out-marriage on the fertility of the more recently out-married American Jews might become slightly positive. Nonetheless, in view of the reservations we have already expressed about the predictive value of the fertility expectations of the women who in 1970–1971 were recently married, we suggest that the evidence of actual current fertility loss seems to outweigh the promise of possible future gain.

Summary of Family Processes

Summing up the interrelated dynamics of the several family processes reviewed in the previous sections, it appears that the late 1960's and the 1970's witnessed considerable internal demographic erosion among American Jews. In part, this reflected the diffuse redirection of marriage and fertility patterns in the United States from the predominance of stable parents-children families toward a greater frequency of smaller households headed by single or divorced, and often childless, adults.[53] The combination of fewer marriages and few children (actual or expected) per married woman was already experienced during the years of the great depression. The renewed impact of these trends has recently been accompanied by higher rates of marriage disruption, though the frequency of remarriage, relative to the ever-divorced, has been quite high too. An additional factor shaping current Jewish population dynamics, whose weight was relatively unimportant during the earlier decades of the century, is assimilation. Higher out-marriage rates, even at stable rates of conversion to Judaism, have meant growing absolute numbers of mixed households, which, in turn, have been associated with greater losses in the affiliative balance of children of the out-married. Consequently, further significant attritional elements have been added to the already low Jewish fertility.

A recurring question in the preceding analysis has been whether trends described are irreversible or rather follow a wave-like pattern in which phases of slower population growth may be followed by phases of relative recovery. This is a very complex question, relating as it does to the interplay of values and norms (which may be changing and continue to change) in the Jewish population with more mechanical demographic processes, whose unfolding depends upon cyclical transformations in population structure, which themselves are determined by conditions in the past. Keeping in mind certain apparent contradictions between actual demographic behavior and the future expectations of the younger cohorts covered in NJPS, one may detect fluid and unstable elements in the demographic and identificational patterns shaping the quantitative evolution of U.S. Jewry. However, the

---

[53]For a discussion of the possible implications of these changes on Jewish family community life in the United States, see Steven Cohen, "The American Jewish Family Today," AJYB, Vol. 82, 1982, pp. 136–154.

cumulative evidence of all the relevant factors that have been assessed points in the direction of negative population growth in the future.

Balance of Demographic Dynamics

It has been indicated that in recent years, the fertility of Jews has been very low and by itself insufficient for demographic replacement.

Jewish population trends have also been negatively affected by out-marriage, which has most likely increased in the decade since the NJPS survey was carried out.

There are no recent large-scale data on mortality among U.S. Jews, but life expectancy at birth is certainly high. In the 19th and early 20th centuries, Jews in Europe and North America had an impressive record of comparatively low age-specific mortality, especially in the case of children. It is probable that the differentials in life expectancy at birth between Jews and non-Jews have meanwhile been largely bridged by the general progress of public health. Among the white population of the United States, life expectancy has recently gone up, after stalling in the 1960's. Jews may be assumed to have achieved analogous progress in their mean length of life. Yet, because of the considerably higher proportion of persons in late middle and old age in the Jewish population, the crude death rate[54] of Jews must have been greater than that of the general population.

The external migration balance of Jews in the United States was mildly positive in the first half of the 1970's. It became more positive in the second half, with the arrival of many Soviet Jews in addition to immigrants from other Diaspora regions and *yordim* from Israel. While the total number of Jewish immigrants during 1971–1975 was estimated at about 40,000,[55] with about 11,000 coming from the Soviet Union, Soviet Jewish arrivals alone ran to 69,000 during 1976–1980.[56]

Exaggerated figures are often mentioned with regard to *yordim* in the United States. Admittedly their number is not accurately known and the whole issue is beset with definitional difficulties. However, upper limits can be established by using Israel's official statistics. Taking the period 1971–1980, the total external migration balance of Jews permanently resident in Israel (excluding the first arrival of new immigrants) was negative to the extent of 71,000. This figure is based on the registration of border crossings, which is quite reliable because of tight frontier control. In Israeli statistics, "permanent population" includes residents absent for less than one year; thus the figure is the difference between the number of

---

[54]Crude rates relate to the entire population, both sexes and all ages together.

[55]HIAS reports. See also, Diamond, "A Reader in the Demography of American Jews," *op. cit.,* p. 319.

[56]HIAS reports. See also, Joseph Edelman, "Soviet Jews in the United States: An Update," AJYB, Vol. 82, 1982, pp. 155–164.

permanently resident Jews who departed for abroad and did not return within 12 months, and between the number of such returnees after an absence of 13 months or longer.[57] The total of 71,000 extends to all countries of the world, and it is unlikely that more than 50,000 went to the United States.

Figures on the emigration of Jews from the United States are available only for *aliyah* to Israel. American *olim,* most of whom contented themselves at first with the status of "potential immigrants," amounted only to 23,300 in 1971–1975, and 13,500 in 1976–1980. Re-emigration has been frequent among them. According to the immigration absorption survey, a longitudinal study regularly conducted by Israel's Central Bureau of Statistics throughout the 1970's, about 30 per cent of the "potential immigrants" and immigrants from North America[58] left Israel permanently or for a long period within three years of taking up residence in the country. On the one occasion that this matter was looked into after five years, nearly half were reported to have left Israel.

A demographic balance sheet for U.S. Jewry has been tentatively computed for 1976–1980 (Table 12). It is based on the age-sex-distribution indicated in NJPS and the available updating information, and attempts to account empirically or conjecturally for all direct factors of change. The purpose is to illustrate the order of magnitude of the factors involved and to compare Jews to all whites in the United States. It should be emphasized that the figures on assimilatory losses are conjectures resting on very fragmentary evidence. However, without these figures the balance sheet would remain incomplete.

The tentative findings are as follows:

(a) Assuming that the low fertility diagnosed for the early 1970's continued approximately, the "effectively Jewish" birth rate[59] may have gone up somewhat in 1976–1980. Such an occurrence would be explained by the frequency of Jews in the most procreative ages as an echo effect of the "baby boom" which took place around 1945–1959. In fact, around 1980 the percentage of females aged 20–34 was higher in the Jewish population than in the entire white population of the United States.[60] Even so, the "effectively Jewish" crude birth rate of Jews must have remained

---

[57]The figure includes Israelis who had been abroad uninterruptedly for more than one year by the end of 1980 but returned later, e.g., students and professional trainees. On the other hand, it does not include holders of Israeli passports who stayed abroad in process of *yerida* but came on a "home visit" in 1980 and, after renewed departure, did not yet again reach a continuous absence of 12 months before the end of 1980. Recent immigrants, *inter alia* from the Soviet Union, who failed to strike roots and left Israel are included. However, "potential immigrants" (compare the next paragraph in text) are excluded.

[58]Nearly 90 per cent of them came from the United States.

[59]The "effectively Jewish" birth rate excludes those newborn, mostly from mixed marriages, who are not identified as Jews by their parents.

[60]This percentage was estimated at 27 per cent of Jewish females in 1980 as against 24 per cent of all white females in 1979. The higher proportion of "baby boom" cohorts among the Jews was due *inter alia* to their more intensive fertility reduction before and after the "baby boom."

beneath that of all whites, because of lower fertility and assimilatory losses of the newborn.

(b) The crude death rate of Jews has exceeded that of all whites, because of greater aging.

(c) The crude rate of natural increase among Jews has been lower than that of all whites, and only barely positive.

(d) Jews are a small minority in an open, secularized society. Consequently, they are exposed to affiliative changes whose net effect is the assimilatory loss of persons who were Jews. The loss of alienated ex-Jews, through informal dropping-out or formal conversion, is estimated to have at least offset the anyway modest natural increase during 1976–1980, so that the Jewish population's balance of internal dynamics was perhaps slightly negative.

(e) The external migration balance of U.S. Jewry has been positive and, per 1,000 of respective population, larger than that of all whites.

(f) Yet the overall demographic balance of all whites has been relatively more positive than that of Jews.

(g) According to this analysis, the growth in the number of U.S. Jews from 1975 to 1980 was largely due to the then prevailing positive migration balance. It was assisted by a temporary rise in the number of persons in the procreative ages and by a consequent rise in the birth rate.

(h) At the bottom of Table 12, the assimilatory losses of the newborn have been estimated. They are incurred if less than 50 per cent of the newborn of mixed

TABLE 12. COMPONENTS OF POPULATION CHANGE AMONG JEWS AND ALL WHITES, 1976–1980[a]

	Jews (Estimates)	All Whites
	Annual Rates per 1,000 of Population	
a) "Effectively Jewish" births	+12	+14
b) Deaths	−11	−9
c) Natural increase (a−b)	+1	+5
d) Assimilatory losses	−2	not applicable
e) Balance of internal dynamics (c−d)	−1	+5
f) Balance of external migrations	+4	+1
g) Total balance (e+f)	+3	+6
h) Assimilatory losses of newborn	−2	not applicable
i) Total assimilatory losses (d+h)	−4	not applicable

[a]1976–1978 for all whites.

Sources: for Jews—authors' estimates; for all whites—U.S. Bureau of the Census, *Statistical Abstract of the United States 1980*, 1982.

marriages, or any of the newborn of homogamously Jewish marriages,[61] are not considered Jews by their parents.[62] These losses of the newborn figure outside the body of the just summarized demographic balance sheet in which the birth rate was given at its "effectively Jewish" level, i.e., as reflecting the net of such losses of the newborn. Adding together the conjectured net affiliative losses above infancy and the losses of the newborn, their total may have approximated—and therefore offset —the increasingly positive migratory balance of U.S. Jews in the quinquennium considered.

(i) The balances of the three types of demographic changes—natural, affiliative, and migratory—were all rather small. In 1976–1980, the increased positive migratory balance was perhaps able to cancel the immediate effect of total assimilatory losses on Jewish population size.[63] Writing these lines in 1982, it seems necessary to add that the migratory balance of U.S. Jewry has meanwhile dwindled because of the virtual stoppage of Jewish emigration from the Soviet Union.

While this article was being finalized for publication, important new empirical information became available.[64] The "1981 Greater New York Jewish Population Survey," carried out by Paul Ritterband and Steven Cohen, has yielded a preliminary estimate of four per cent children in ages 0–4, including the non-Jewish children of mixed marriages. This would imply a gross average for the annual Jewish birth rate of 0.8 per cent (or eight per thousand) of the Jewish population during the five years preceding the survey. The "effectively Jewish" birth rate, excluding the non-Jewish children of the surveyed Jews, must have been even lower. Since the age composition of New York Jewry was somewhat older than that indicated in Table 1 and Table 2 for all U.S. Jews in 1980, the death rate is also likely to have been somewhat greater and to have exceeded even more the death rate of the general white population (see Table 12). The inevitable conclusion is a deficit in the natural movement of New York's Jews.

---

[61]Whether the couple was homogamously Jewish from the outset or was made so by the conversion of the non-Jewish spouse.

[62]The lower fertility of mixed couples as compared to Jewish ones (see Table 11) has here been accounted for in the "effectively Jewish" birth rate. As for the expected identification of the children, see footnote 45.

[63]It did not offset all the long-term effects of the assimilatory losses; in the long-range demographic view, the lost newborn are not compensated for by the immigration of, for instance, elderly persons.

[64]Kindly communicated by the authors.

Projections to The Year 2000

GENERAL EXPLANATIONS

The demographic projections for U.S. Jewry that are outlined here are part of a larger complex of projections for world Jewry.[65] The projections are based on estimates of Jewish population, by age and sex, in 1975. In the case of U.S. Jewry, these estimates have been derived from the 1970–1971 NJPS.

The various versions used in computing the projections for U.S. Jewry are briefly set out in Table 12A. Versions A to E are "complete" insofar as they account for all factors of change. Versions A, C, and E correspond, respectively, to the principal versions—medium, high, and low—of our regional projections for world Jewry. Versions B and D are additional variants whose informative value will be set out below. The remaining versions are hypothetical, as they deliberately take into consideration only an incomplete range of demographic factors: F—natural movement alone; G and H—natural movement and assimilatory losses, but not external migrations. The purpose of versions F to H is to make possible, through comparison with other versions, an assessment of the separate influence of various factors. While Table 12A gives only a general indication of the level of each factor, concise information on parameter size can be found in the Appendix.

TABLE 12A. VERSIONS USED IN COMPUTING PROJECTIONS FOR U.S. JEWRY

Symbol and Name of Version	Fertility	Mortality	Assimilation	Immigration
A—Medium	Low	Low	Moderate	Moderate
B—	Low	Low	Moderate	Stronger
C—High	Rising	Low	Moderate	Moderate
D—	Rising	Low	Stronger	Moderate
E—Low	Low	Low	Stronger	Moderate
F—	Low	Low	—	—
G—	Low	Low	Moderate	—
H—	Low	Low	Stronger	—

[65]See Schmelz, *World Jewish Population—Regional Estimates and Projections, op. cit.*; U.O. Schmelz, "Evolution and Projection of World Jewish Population," in U.O. Schmelz, Paul Glikson, and Julius Gould, (eds.), *Studies in Jewish Demography: Survey for 1972–1980* (Jerusalem, forthcoming); and U.O. Schmelz, "World Jewish Population Trends: Projections and Implications," in Schmelz, Glikson, and DellaPergola, (eds.), *Papers in Jewish Demography, 1981, op. cit.*

PROJECTED SIZE OF U.S. JEWRY

In Table 13 the eight versions of the projections for the future size of U.S. Jewry have been listed in ascending order of magnitude as of the year 2000. In most instances the same order is also found in 1990 and 1995. The index numbers on the right-hand side of Table 13 compare future population size with the 1975 estimate of 5,600,000 (a figure close to the one that already held good for U.S. Jews in 1970). It should be borne in mind that the updated estimate as of 1980 has risen to 5,690,000,[66] a figure closely approached by the medium projection.

The demographic dynamics underlying the projection results can be summarized as follows:

(a) If low fertility continues at approximately its recent level, the outcome of natural movement will turn negative, despite high life expectancy at birth, and deaths will increasingly outnumber births. This trend will be intensified by the aggravation of aging in the Jewish population. Consequently, version F, which accounts for natural movement alone, indicates that a modest temporary rise in the total number of Jews will be followed, toward the end of the projection period, by a decline below the initial level.

(b) The negative trend in the evolution of population size is much accelerated if, in addition to natural movement, assimilatory losses—moderate or strong—are taken into account (versions G and H, respectively).

(c) However, these negative tendencies can be offset, at least partly and temporarily, through a positive migration balance (versions A to E).

(d) This is exemplified by the medium projection (A), which assumes low fertility and moderate levels of both assimilatory losses and a positive migration balance. The two latter factors largely cancel each other out, so that the results of the medium projection toward the end of our century are close to those of the version allowing for natural movement alone.[67] The medium projection leads to a population figure of roughly 5,650,000 by 1990, which is less than the 1980 estimate of 5,690,000, though still above the initial 1975 level of 5,600,000. The figure projected for year 2000 approaches 5,300,000, which is five per cent lower than the initial level.

(e) Among the modifications of parameters in the complete projections, version C—rising fertility combined with moderate assimilation and migration—delays the drop of Jewish population below the initial level until the end of the century. Rising fertility has been so calibrated as to lead up to the "replacement level" of 2.1 children on average per woman by 1996–2000. The projected decline in population size which nevertheless occurs is due mainly to the following causes: (1) The level of 2.1 children per woman assures replacement at minimal mortality, if this fertility is continued for a long time. In the short run, which may extend over several decades,

---

[66]See the section on Jewish population size.

[67]The change in ranking of the results of these two versions between 1995 and 2000 is due to the assumption that immigration operates with decreasing strength, while assimilation functions with increasing strength.

the actual birth rate and rate of natural increase/decrease also depend on age composition. The great aging which prevails among U.S. Jews depresses these rates. (2) The level of 2.1 children is only reached at the end of the projection period. (3) Among Diaspora Jews, fertility has to contend not only with mortality, but also with assimilatory losses, which are on the increase—including the loss of offspring of mixed marriages.

(f) A more strongly positive migration balance (B) will boost Jewish population size in a manner similar to rising fertility (compare with version C).

(g) In versions D and E, stronger assimilation has been assumed together with a moderate migration balance. If stronger assimilation is combined with rising fertility (D), it tends to cancel the latter's positive influence on Jewish population size. The combination of stronger assimilation, low fertility, and low immigration constitutes the low projection (E), which, according to the actual assumptions used, implies a decrease of 11 per cent in the U.S. Jewish population between 1975 and 2000.

The future levels of the parameters used in computing the projections are necessarily conjectural. Yet all the versions of the projections presented here point to a decrease in the size of the U.S. Jewish population before the end of the century. At the assumed intensities of the various parameters (see Appendix), only the conjunction of rising fertility with stronger immigration and moderate assimilation would prevent this from happening.

Maintenance of the size of U.S. Jewry, or even its increase, could be produced if fertility or immigration were to reach levels beyond those assumed in the higher variants of the parameters. However, even the low fertility used in the projections —1.5 children on average per woman—exceeds the level of 1.3–1.4 attributed to all Jewish women in 1970–1976.[68] Moreover, the rise of Jewish fertility up to 2.1 in versions C and D equals the future rise of fertility assumed by the Bureau of Census in its medium projection for all U.S. whites (see below), whereas empirically Jewish fertility in the United States has long been below that of total whites. Both the moderate and stronger variants of the positive migration balance for U.S. Jews, as applied in the projections, have resulted from computations of the worldwide potential for international Jewish migration. Hence, if constant age-specific emigration rates are applied to the future Jewish population projected for Eastern Europe and other emigration regions in the Diaspora, the expected volume of migrants contracts rather sharply. At any rate, the assumptions for stronger immigration imply a net intake of more than 600,000 Jews during the 25 years of projections, which is 11 per cent of the initial population. Yet even this may not be enough to offset the negative balance of internal dynamics at the end of the century.

The projections presented here should be viewed primarily as illustrating trends in U.S. Jewish population size rather than as reporting absolute levels. It has been

---

[68]This is the more so, as further inroads on fertility *per se,* irrespective of the identification of the children, may be caused by the increase of out-marriage which is anticipated in the projections (see Table 11).

TABLE 13. PROJECTIONS OF JEWS UP TO YEAR 2000

Symbol[a] and Name of Version	In Thousands			Index Numbers (1975 = 100)		
	1990	1995	2000	1990	1995	2000
	Versions Arranged According to Assumptions					
A—Medium, regular	5,645	5,503	5,321	101	98	95
B—Medium, stronger immig.	5,785	5,700	5,571	103	102	99
C—High, regular	5,739	5,665	5,563	102	101	99
D—High, stronger assim.	5,519	5,364	5,178	98	96	92
E—Low	5,435	5,222	4,972	97	93	89
F—No immig., no assim.	5,619	5,498	5,345	100	98	95
G—No immig., moderate assim.	5,393	5,197	4,974	96	93	89
H—No immig., stronger assim.	5,188	4,925	4,639	93	88	83
	Versions Arranged in Rising Order of Estimates for Year 2000					
H—No immig., stronger assim.	5,188	4,925	4,639	93	88	83
E—Low	5,435	5,222	4,972	97	93	89
G—No immig., moderate assim.	5,393	5,197	4,974	96	93	89
D—High, stronger assim.	5,519	5,364	5,178	98	96	92
A—Medium, regular	5,645	5,503	5,321	101	98	95
F—No immig., no assim.	5,619	5,498	5,345	100	98	95
C—High, regular	5,739	5,665	5,563	102	101	99
B—Medium, stronger assim.	5,785	5,700	5,571	103	102	99

*Estimated number of Jews (in thousands): 1970—5,600; 1975—5,600; 1980—5,690.
[a]See Table 12A.
Source: authors' projections.

stated before that even the present size of U.S. Jewry is not clearly known; the necessarily conjectural magnitude of the parameters of demographic change during the projection period is obvious. If any parameter should exceed the assumed magnitude in a positive or negative direction, the projected population size would change accordingly. The actual future size of the Jewish population in the United States may turn out to be either higher or lower than some or even all the complete versions of the projection.

While the future levels of U.S. Jewish population size are contingent and conjectural, as is implied in the presentation of numerous alternatives within the projections, the direction in which each relevant demographic factor operates *per se* is certain. Moreover, the result of the interplay of these trends is fairly evident for the not too distant future. If fertility is by far insufficient for demographic replacement, even at minimal mortality, and has moreover to contend with assimilatory losses and with the effects of pronounced aging, a population decrease is bound to come, unless there is large and ever-increasing immigration. In other words, for U.S. Jewry, in the long run, to achieve growth or even maintain its size ("zero population growth"), it would be necessary to either raise fertility, curb assimilatory losses, attract immigration, or attain a combination of these positive influences, and moreover do so very substantially.

To date, a decrease of U.S. Jewry has been prevented by the direct and indirect effects of the extended "baby boom" of 1945–1959 and by the immigration of Soviet Jews in the second half of the 1970's. The first influence is transitory. As for the second, emigration of Jews from the Soviet Union has been virtually discontinued at the time that these lines are being written.[69] However, it is important to realize that any migratory reinforcement, even if it should come, can have no more than a temporary effect on population size, unless the negative trends in the internal dynamics of U.S. Jews should change. If these trends continue to prevail and are also adopted by the new immigrants—or if the latter bring with them and maintain in America the even more negative demographic trends now characteristic of East European Jewry—the effects of such migratory transfusions on U.S. Jewish population size can only delay, but not in the long run prevent, renewed decreases.

AGE COMPOSITION

An increase in the number of elderly Jews (65+) is inevitable in the near future because of the age structure of the adult Jews as reflected in the 1970–1971 NJPS and updated to 1980 in Table 2. The strong cohorts born ca.1916–1930, which occupied the late middle-age range in 1980, will penetrate into the old-age range.

The elderly constituted 12 and 15.5 per cent, respectively, of the U.S. Jewish population in 1970 and 1980 (Table 1 above). According to the three principal versions of the projections for Jews, the percentage will rise to 16 to 18 per cent by the end of the century (Table 14). This compares to 12 to 13.5 per cent 65+ year olds among all whites in the United States by the year 2000, according to official projections.

Tables 14 and 1 show, furthermore, that not only the proportion of the elderly but also the proportion of persons in later middle age (45–64 years old) will continue to be greater among Jews than among all whites. On the other hand, the percentage of children (aged 0–14) will keep on being much smaller in the Jewish population. Among all whites as well as among Jews, the proportion above age 30 will rise, while the proportion below that age will drop, due to the reduction in size of the cohorts

[69]See the section on the balance of demographic dynamics.

TABLE 14. PROJECTIONS OF JEWS AND ALL WHITES, BY AGE (PER CENT), 2000

Age	Jews			All Whites		
	Medium Proj.	High Proj.	Low Proj.	Medium Proj.	High Proj.	Low Proj.
Total	100.0	100.0	100.0	100.0	100.0	100.0
0–14	13.9	17.0	12.7	21.5	25.6	18.5
15–29	18.8	18.6	18.9	19.7	20.3	19.1
30–44	22.5	21.6	22.6	22.6	20.8	24.0
45–64	27.7	26.4	28.1	23.3	21.4	24.8
65+	17.1	16.4	17.7	12.7	11.8	13.5

Sources: for Jews—authors' projections; for all whites—U.S. Bureau of the Census, *Projections of the Population of the United States: 1977 to 2050,* Current Population Report, Series P-25, No. 704, 1977.

born successively during the post-World War II "baby boom" and after its termination.

Since the absolute number of the elderly for decades ahead is mainly determined by the alternating size of the already living birth cohorts, one can expect a decrease at the beginning of the next century, because of the penetration of the weak cohorts born in 1930–1945 into this age range. This will be followed by a strong rise and, afterward, by a renewed drop, due to the penetration of the strong "baby boom" cohorts born in 1946–1960 and the subsequent weaker ones, respectively. However, on the whole, the trend for aging, i.e., for a marked proportion of the elderly in the population, will increase if fertility remains low and if, in addition, assimilation makes its normal inroad, especially among the younger age groups.[70]

Projections of the Jewish school age population, i.e., of children and youngsters between the ages of 3 and 25,[71] are given in Table 15. These persons constitute the maximum potential for enrollment in Jewish educational institutions. The data are broken down into age groups which correspond, respectively, to kindergarten, elementary school, junior high school, senior high school, and college and university students. If the frequencies of these age groups are compared in the data base year 1975, the declining trend of Jewish births in the preceding two decades is once again revealed—from the 18–21 year olds, who were born at the peak of the "baby boom," down to the 3–5 year olds. Compared to the 1975 figures there is a marked decline, on the whole, in the projection period. However, there are also counter-currents: (a) the increase of Jews in the procreative ages, which is apt

[70]See U.O. Schmelz, *Elderly Jews in the World—Regional Estimates and Projections* (Jerusalem, forthcoming).
[71]I.e., inclusive of age 17, but below age 18.

TABLE 15. PROJECTION OF JEWISH SCHOOL AGE POPULATION, 1975–2000

	3–17 Total	3–5	6–11	12–14	15–17	18–25 Total	18–21	22–25
Jewish children, 1975	1,108	172	365	229	342	840	435	404
				In Thousands				
				Index Numbers (1975 = 100)				
Medium projection								
1990	91	110	116	91	54	56	53	59
2000	75	74	84	79	62	65	64	66
High projection								
1990	96	128	123	91	54	56	53	59
2000	91	101	106	94	68	67	67	66
Low projection								
1990	85	100	108	87	53	55	52	57
2000	65	62	73	69	56	61	59	63

Source: authors' projections.

to raise the number of Jewish newborn from approximately the mid-1970's to the end of the 1980's,[72] makes itself felt through a rise in ages 3–5 and 6–11 until about 1990. This will also mitigate the decrease of the 12–25 year olds toward the end of the century. Otherwise this decrease would be even stronger, especially for the 15–25 year olds, who in the base year 1975 still belonged to the strong "baby boom" cohorts; (b) in the high projection, the assumed rise in fertility has a boosting effect on the frequencies after 1980. In the college and university ages of 18–25, the decrease will be very strong—to 59–67, according to projection levels, in the year 2000, per 100 in 1975. This is due, on the one hand, to the high initial frequencies in 1975, when these ages were occupied by persons born in the "baby boom," and, on the other hand, to the fact that these ages will be barely reached until the year 2000 by the again increased cohorts born as of the mid-1970's as an echo of the original "baby boom."[73]

These examples illustrate both the underlying tendency toward aging and the marked degree of instability in the short run, as stronger and weaker cohorts pass alternatively through certain stages. The negative impact of the shifts in cohort size on the "marriage market," given the age differential between grooms and brides, has been mentioned above.

COMPARISONS

Table 16 compares the results for the year 2000 of the principal projections for Jews with the Bureau of the Census projections for all whites in the United States. While the former do not indicate a numerically positive outcome, the latter do. It is instructive to examine the reasons for this difference in anticipated evolution, particularly since the fertility assumptions of the medium projection for all whites and the high projection for Jews are the same—2.1 children by the end of the century —and the fertility assumptions of the low projection for all whites and the medium and low projections for Jews are not very different—about 1.7 in the former, instead of 1.5 in the two latter, throughout the projection period. Moreover, a relatively more positive external migration balance has been assumed for Jews (Table 16). Analysis shows that the main reasons for the difference in outcome are (a) the much greater aging of Jews (Tables 1 and 14), which depresses their crude birth rate and raises their crude death rate and (b) the Jews' assimilatory losses (which have no parallel among all whites), which diminish the number of Jewish persons and reduce the "effectively Jewish" birth rate if less than half the children of mixed marriages are not raised as Jews.[74]

---

[72]See above.

[73]See U.O. Schmelz, *Jewish School Age Population—Regional Estimates and Projections* (Jerusalem, forthcoming).

[74]In the medium projection the ratio of lost newborn per 1,000 of Jewish population (row H) does not grow appreciably from 1976–1980 to 1996–2000 (see Tables 12 and 16). This

TABLE 16. PROJECTIONS AND COMPONENTS OF POPULATION CHANGE AMONG JEWS AND ALL WHITES, 1996–2000

	Jews			All Whites		
	Medium Proj.	High Proj.	Low Proj.	Medium Proj.	High Proj.	Low Proj.
Population, 2000	95	99	89	117	128	111
	Index Numbers (1975 = 100)					
Fertility, 1996–2000	1.5	2.1	1.5	2.1	2.7	1.7
	Average Number of Children per Woman					
	Annual Rates per 1,000 of Population					
Components of Change, 1996–2000:						
a) "Effectively Jewish" births	+ 7.5	+10	+ 6.5	+ 13.5	+ 17	+ 11.5
b) Deaths	−14	−13.5	−14.5	− 10	− 9.5	− 10.5
c) Natural increase (a−b)	− 6.5	− 3.5	− 8	+ 3.5	+ 7.5	+ 1
d) Assimilatory losses (excluding newborn)	− 2	− 2	− 4	not applicable		
e) Balance of internal dynamics (c−d)	− 8.5	− 5.5	−12	+ 3.5	+ 7.5	+ 1
f) Balance of external migrations	+ 2	+ 2	+ 2	+ 1	+ 1	+ 1
g) Total balance (e+f)	− 6.5	− 3.5	−10	+ 4.5	+ 8.5	+ 2
h) Assimilatory losses of newborn	− 2	− 3	− 3.5	not applicable		
i) Total assimilatory losses (d+h)	− 4	− 5	− 7.5	not applicable		

Sources: see Table 14.

Table 17 shows the evolution of U.S. Jews in comparison to the Jewries of the Diaspora, Israel, and the whole world (according to the medium version of our regional projections). U.S. Jews are expected to decrease far less so than the rest of Diaspora Jewry; their number will evolve similarly to world Jewry as a whole, while Israel's Jews will grow markedly. The joint share of Jews in the United States and Israel among world Jewry is anticipated by the projections to increase from about two-thirds in 1975 to 80 per cent by year 2000. Thus, a bipolar configuration in world Jewry will increasingly manifest itself.

TABLE 17. PROJECTIONS OF JEWS IN THE U.S., DIASPORA, AND WORLD (MEDIUM VERSION), 1975 AND 2000

	Index Numbers[a] 2000	Per Cent Distributions			
		Diaspora		World	
		1975	2000	1975	2000
World	96	—	—	100	100
Diaspora, Total	79	100	100	77	64
U.S.	95	56	67	43	43
Other countries	59	44	33	34	21
Israel	152	—	—	23	36
U.S. and Israel	115	—	—	66	79

[a]1975 = 100.
Sources: authors' projections.

The reasons for the more marked decrease in Jewish population in the rest of the Diaspora as compared to the United States are even greater aging and assimilatory losses and the even lower fertility in other Diaspora areas. Moreover, some Diaspora regions have a very negative migration balance, whereas U.S. Jewry is assumed to have a positive one.

The marked growth foreseen for Israel's Jews, alone among all large Jewries of the world, is due primarily to considerable fertility and the absence of net assimilatory losses, and only secondarily to a rapidly dwindling positive migration balance.[75] While the majority status of Jews in Israel of necessity precludes assimilation, the evolution of fertility among Israel's Jews has been quite remarkable.[76] Thirty years

---

happens despite the rising proportion of assimilatory losses among the newborn (see specifications in Appendix), and is due to the decrease in the Jewish birth rate. This decrease exercises an analogous influence in the other projection versions.

[75]Israel's external migration balance, like that of U.S. Jews, has been fitted to global assumptions about Jewish migration streams in the projection period.

[76]See Schmelz, "Jewish Survival," op. cit., pp. 61–117.

ago, a striking difference of three to four children existed between the fertility levels of the two origin groups (Asian-African and European) of which Israel's Jews are composed. At present, however, the fertility differential has virtually disappeared; Asian-African Jews have rapidly reduced their fertility in acceleration of an anyway expected demographic transition; European Jews have increased their fertility, which has stood for the last 15 years at about 2.75 children on average per woman. All of Israel's Jews, including those of European provenance, have a fertility which not only exceeds by far that of Diaspora Jews, but also the recent fertility of the general populations in all the advanced countries.[77]

Conclusion

The decrease anticipated in the number of Jews in the United States is less acute than that anticipated in most Diaspora regions. Yet the balance of the internal population dynamics of U.S. Jewry may already be slightly negative and, despite immigration, is expected to become overtly negative in the foreseeable future. Moreover, this quantitative problem is closely linked to qualitative problems prevalent in large sections of American Jewry with regard to the maintenance and transmission of Jewish identity.

Should there be a sizeable upswing in general U.S. fertility, Jewish fertility may be carried along with it, though, judging by the experience of the past, probably at a lower level. This might still fall short of the replacement needs of the Jewish population. Moreover, by itself a fertility upswing would neither change the trend toward cumulative assimilatory losses nor rapidly alter the tendency toward further aging.

Demographic policies are difficult to devise and apply. All the more so is this true when one is dealing with a minority group that must act on a voluntary basis. Failing shifts in the pattern of general society toward increased nuptiality and fertility, any change in the respective behavior of American Jews would seem conditional on making a wide Jewish public aware of the demographic situation and prospects. This study supplies some of the relevant information, though, for lack of space, the manifold implications of the demographic trends could not be discussed.

This study has called attention to the complexity and fluidity of such phenomena as nuptiality, fertility, mixed marriage, etc., in the modern, largely secularized American Jewish community. There is a clear need for frequent monitoring and systematic research so that they can be better understood. The same holds true for the seemingly more straightforward matter of the changing size of U.S. Jewry.

---

[77]The "total fertility rate" of all whites in the United States was about 1.7 during 1975–1978. Even the high projection for whites by the Bureau of the Census assumes that only at the end of the century will there be a return to the fertility level that is currently prevalent among European Jews in Israel.

APPENDIX

CONCISE SPECIFICATIONS FOR THE PROJECTIONS
(Compare Table 12A)

Method: component method, applied age-sex-specifically.
Projection period: 1975–2000.
Base population in 1975: (a) size: 5,600,000; (b) age-sex composition: NJPS figures updated to 1975, with adjustments.
Fertility: "low": total fertility rate = 1.5; "rising": from 1.5 to 2.1. Appropriate age-specific fertility rates were applied to the Jewish women.[1]
Mortality: life expectancy at birth: 72.9 years for males; 76.1 for females.[2]
Assimilatory losses (implying, *inter alia*, intensification of the consequences of out-marriage for the Jewish population): "moderate": the number of newborn, computed according to the fertility levels, was reduced increasingly from 2.5 per cent in 1976–1980 to 12.5 in 1996–2000; above infancy, average loss of two per thousand per annum, with enhanced impact in ages 20–34; "stronger": losses of newborn rising from 5 to 25 per cent; above infancy, average loss of four per thousand per annum. The estimates in Tables 12 and 16 of the assimilatory losses of the newborn try to account for both the losses already prevalent by 1975 and for their relative increase during the projection period.[3]
External migration balance:[4] "moderate": positive, though declining from 105,000 in 1976–1980 to 50,000 in 1996–2000; a total of 365,000 from 1975 to 2000; "stronger": ranging between 122,000 in 1976–1980 and 137,000 in 1981–1985 to 110,000 in 1996–2000; a total of 627,000 between 1975 and 2000. Different age-sex schedules have been applied to immigrants from the Diaspora, to *yordim,* and to emigrants from the United States.

U. O. SCHMELZ
SERGIO DELLAPERGOLA

[1]Conceptually, in the computation of births according to these fertility assumptions, the non-Jewish wives of out-married Jews were replaced by proxies, *viz,* by that group of out-married Jewesses who were estranged, but had not yet seceded from the Jewish community, and who themselves hardly contributed to "effectively Jewish" fertility. Experimentation with different realistic schedules of age-specific fertility rates, at the same level of total fertility (TFR), has shown that the resulting variations in the Jewish population size by year 2000 are quite minor.
[2]This is in accordance with the world projections. It is modeled on Israeli experience, which provides the only reliable life-tables for a large Jewish population. Control computations of the mortality of U.S. Jews, using the life-table of all U.S. whites in 1975 (males—69.4, females —77.2), yielded results similar to those in the projections.
[3]The differential fertility of out-married couples is, in principle, accounted for by the fertility assumptions.
[4]Fitted to global estimates of Jewish migration streams, accounting for reduced potentials from the main emigration regions (at constant age-specific emigration rates), because of shrinkage and aging of the respective Jewish populations.

Canada

National Affairs

DESPITE A YEAR of unusual political achievement, Prime Minister Trudeau's Liberal government appeared to be out of favor with the electorate in 1981. After Trudeau secured the agreement of nine out of ten provinces to transform the 114-year-old British North America act into a fully Canadian constitution, a Gallup poll jolted the Liberal leadership; it showed the Liberals trailing the Progressive Conservatives by four points among decided voters. An ambitious energy program was begun, following the agreement of the provinces that produced the nation's oil to a policy of compromise and accommodation. Any political benefit to the Liberals, however, was largely nullified by a severe recession. With 70 per cent of Canadian trade tied to the American market, the downturn in the United States economy meant hard times for Canadian businesses. Real GNP growth in 1981 was projected at one to two per cent. The year ended with unemployment at 8.6 per cent and inflation at 12.6 per cent.

There was a widespread feeling among Canadians that the United States dominated their country economically, polluted it with acid rain, and bullied it in the area of foreign policy. But Canada was coming of age. As a resource-rich country in a resource-hungry age, Canada would no longer accept being treated as the 51st American state.

JEWISH COMMUNITY

Demography

The Jewish population of Canada in 1981 was estimated at 308,000. Leading Jewish centers were Toronto, Montreal, Winnipeg, Vancouver, and Ottawa.

The Canadian office of the Council of Jewish Federations and Welfare Funds announced the initiation of a national Jewish population study, funded by a grant from Secretary of State Jim Fleming's multi-culturalism directorate. The project aimed at compiling a national Jewish census. This was to be followed by an examination of communal needs.

With little fanfare, the Winnipeg Jewish community had been absorbing a steady stream of Soviet Jewish immigrants; since 1974 approximately 300 families had been resettled in Winnipeg. The Jewish Child and Family Service, supported financially by the Winnipeg Jewish Community Council, took the lead in the resettlement process. New arrivals were provided with orientation as well as basic needs, including housing. On average, most families became self-sufficient within three months.

As a result of an influx of newcomers, the Jewish population of Edmonton and Calgary had grown to 3,500–4,000 and 6,000–7,000, respectively.

Communal Activities

Irwin Cotler, president of the Canadian Jewish Congress (CJC), hailed the constitutional accord struck between the federal government and the nine provinces as "a notable achievement." He warned, however, that the "notwithstanding" clause in the charter, which allowed any province to bypass guarantees of freedom, posed a potential threat to Jews and other groups. He stated, "The theory of the charter is that the rights of the people will precede the power of government, but the 'notwithstanding' clause reserves power for governments to override these rights."

According to CJC executive vice-president Alan Rose, the Canadian government had agreed to accept 184 Argentine Jewish political prisoners whose release from jail was being negotiated.

Rose Wolfe, past president of the Toronto Jewish Congress (TJC), warned that enormous financial problems lay ahead for Toronto's Jewish community. She said that the rising costs of Jewish education and social services, and the expenditures involved in counteracting antisemitic forces, were imposing a heavy financial burden that would increase due to government cutbacks in spending for social benefits and health services.

Wolfe noted the changing makeup of Toronto Jewry since the World War II period. Waves of immigration had brought European Holocaust survivors, Sephardic North Africans, Israelis, Russians, South Africans, and Quebecers into the community. "They come from different cultures with varying degrees of identification with our way of life," Wolfe said, "and we have not done a particularly good job in helping to integrate them. . . . The Israelis are completely alienated, and we are struggling with the problem of the Russians who know nothing of our system . . . of Jewishness."

Only 50 per cent of the 5,500 Soviet Jewish immigrants in Toronto had any Jewish affiliation. This was one of the findings of a TJC survey taken to determine how effectively Russian Jews were being integrated into the fabric of Jewish communal life. The survey revealed that formal Jewish education was being provided to 205 children, and that some 100 immigrant families attended holiday celebrations at synagogues.

A total of $6,708,632 was allocated for local and national services by TJC for the July 1980-June 1981 budget year. This represented a 2.4 per cent increase over the previous year. (However, because expenditures were lower than anticipated, the increase amounted to 7.5 per cent over what was actually spent the year before. Remaining funds were sent to Israel.) In presenting his report to the executive, TJC treasurer Murray Segal said that the committee "was faced with especially difficult challenges of recognizing the community's responsibility and commitment to Israel; of funding the budgetary requirements of the local and national agencies; and of recommending allocations of those local and national agencies not exceeding a global limit of five per cent over expenditures during the past year." Of the total allocations, $3,695,470 went for education; $1,238,460 to local agencies; $449,750 to TJC for administration; $1,390,152 to national agencies; and $39,800 for special items. In the national allocations, CJC was granted $528,973 for national programs, $493,465 for immigrant relief, and $22,080 for Network. The Jewish Immigrant Aid Service received $147,807.

The 1981 Montreal Combined Jewish Appeal recorded a 9.7 per cent increase in contributions over the previous year. The total raised was the highest ever in Montreal, excluding 1973, the year of the Yom Kippur War. The number of contributors was about 35,000.

Employment opportunities were a critical factor in determining whether young Jewish men and women remained in Quebec, according to a survey conducted by Montreal's community programming department of the Allied Jewish Community Services. The survey, involving a sample of 500 young people aged 18 to 35, showed that a majority (59 per cent) planned to stay in Quebec. However, 30 per cent remained undecided on their future in the province.

The number of disabled Jews across Canada was said to be about 36,000, with 12,000 to 14,000 residing in the metropolitan Toronto area. In Toronto the mentally handicapped had access to the Reena Foundation, which provided a broad variety of services. For other disabled Jews throughout Canada, the situation was very bleak.

CJC set up a national law and social action committee to focus on the needs of the handicapped, the aged, and the poor in the Jewish community. At its initial meeting, Fred Zemans of Toronto, the chairman, said that the requirements of the elderly for residential help were growing every day. He disclosed that Jewish social agencies in Toronto were dealing with an increasing number of elderly people abandoned by younger family members. The majority of the Jewish elderly were women, many of whom were living below the poverty line.

The Toronto vocational rehabilitation center of Jewish Vocational Service (JVS) continued its activities. In a 19-week program, approximately 65 people were taught new skills and work habits. About 20 per cent of those in the program were physically handicapped; 80 per cent suffered emotional disorders. With the encouragement and support of the Ontario government, the vocational rehabilitation center was gradually being opened to all Torontonians. About 50 agencies in the area referred their discharged patients to the JVS center.

The Ottawa Jewish community paid tribute to Canada's six Jewish senators—David Croll, Sidney Buckwold, Carl Goldenberg, Jack Austin, Jack Marshall, and Nathan Nurgitz—at the annual public service division dinner of the United Jewish Appeal.

"You can still be Jewish and live in a small community," Mark Scharf of Barrie told participants from across Canada who attended the first small communities conference in Oshawa. Many topics were discussed at the gathering, which was sponsored by the small communities committee of CJC. Among the participants were Jews from Owen Sound, Sudbury, Barrie, Burlington, Brantford, Sarnia, Kitchener-Waterloo, Cambridge, Niagara Falls, and Oshawa.

Community Relations

The financially troubled Canadian Council of Christians and Jews (CCCJ) reported a deficit of $250,000 in 1980. In 1981 the deficit was expected to be $400,000. Nevertheless, CCCJ's president, Victor Goldbloom, and the newly-appointed fundraising chairman, George Cohon, president of McDonald's Restaurants of Canada, were hopeful that the financial situation would improve.

The much hailed charter of rights of the new Canadian constitution contained a serious flaw in the view of CJC. Section 2 of the charter, which guaranteed "freedom of expression," could give a license to racists to peddle hatred without any legal restraint. CJC's committee on the Canadian constitution, headed by Maxwell Cohen, asked Parliament to provide a qualifying clause that would align the charter with the UN covenant on civil and political rights, which removed race-hatred dissemination from the category of a protected right.

Ernest Zundel, 42, a Toronto artist of German descent, was identified as the principal author, publisher, and distributor of a large quantity of neo-Nazi material. He had been turning out Nazi hate literature for 18 years, but was believed to have little support among Canada's German community. A two-hour demonstration outside Zundel's house climaxed a community-wide anti-Nazi rally.

The Jewish War Veterans (JWV) of Canada asked the federal government to establish a special branch of the justice ministry to "institute a study of law and conventions as a basis for a public report on war crimes prosecution possibilities in Canada." JWV pointed out that Nazis implicated in the Holocaust were living in Canada as Canadian citizens. JWV alleged that these Nazis had succeeded "by lies and deceit in continuing to take refuge in our country, thereby gaining immunity from deportation and trial." CJC also submitted a brief asking for the removal of legal impediments to the prosecution of Nazi war criminals resident in Canada.

For the second time within a year, the House of Commons passed a motion condemning the Ku Klux Klan.

Hugh McCullum, editor of the *United Church Observer,* expressed regret for the publication of an antisemitic letter.

The Ukrainian Canadian Committee adopted a resolution condemning the planned publication in the Ukraine of *Judaism and Zionism—Adherents of Racism,* by Trofym Kichko, a notorious antisemite. The Committee charged that Soviet authorities were attempting to sow discord between the Jewish and Ukrainian communities in Canada and elsewhere.

Exactly a year after the Beth Shalom synagogue in Edmonton was burned down, the culprit, 32-year-old Daniel Kautz, was sentenced to four years in jail. The Shaar Shalom synagogue in Chomedey, Quebec was desecrated by vandals. As congregants arrived at the synagogue for Saturday morning services, they found the exterior walls covered with Nazi slogans and hate messages. Montreal's Bourret Avenue synagogue was also the target of antisemitic attacks.

Zionism and Israel

Close observers of Canadian external affairs, such as the Canada-Israel Committee (CIC), got a whiff of new winds in 1981 that indicated a deeper sympathy for the Palestinian cause and a willingness—unofficially—to deal with the PLO. There was, however, no indication that recognition would be extended to the PLO until it had demonstrated a willingness to accept the existence of the State of Israel.

During a "private" visit to Ottawa, Khaled al-Hassan, foreign affairs advisor to Yasir Arafat, met with top Canadian officials, including Michael Shenstone, assistant under-secretary of state of the bureau of African and Middle Eastern affairs. Shenstone affirmed Canada's intention of developing substantial commercial links with the Arabs. He stated, however, that this would not affect Canada's traditional support for the security of Israel.

In January, during the general assembly of the United Nations, CIC took the Canadian government to task for two votes that were seen as prejudicing future negotiations on Jerusalem. CIC also blasted Canada's abstention on a resolution favoring the efforts of a committee working for the "inalienable rights of the Palestinians."

On his trip to the Middle East in November, Prime Minister Trudeau spelled out the prevailing attitudes in Ottawa. "There is no dialogue between the PLO and Canada at the present moment," he noted, adding that such a dialogue, even if it did come, would not "destroy our friendship with Israel." Trudeau also reiterated Canada's opposition to Israeli settlements in the West Bank and Israel's annexation of Jerusalem.

In a move to broaden its commitment to Project Renewal, the United Jewish Appeal of metropolitan Toronto undertook to twin itself to the central Israel village of Beit Dagan.

The labor Zionist movement in Canada celebrated its 75th anniversary at the Borochov Center in Toronto.

The fourth annual Israel Day in Toronto attracted a crowd that exceeded 22,000. Sponsored by the Canadian Zionist Federation, central region, the event included various presentations by Toronto day school students. A special award was given to the mayor of Amsterdam, Win Polak, who was present, and to the Dutch people, who played a large role in protecting Jews during World War II.

The Canadian Zionist Federation (CZF) was making a concerted effort to boost its membership past 50,000. If this goal were achieved, Canada would be able to send at least 20 delegates, a record number, to the world Zionist congress in Jerusalem in December 1982. At the last congress, in 1978, 17 Canadian delegates, representing 45,000 CZF members, attended.

A Palestine Information Office, operating out of the headquarters of the French teachers' union, opened in Montreal. It was affiliated with the Palestine Information Office in Ottawa, which was part of Arab League operation in that city. The Palestine Information Office, in conjunction with the local Arab community association, opened an art exhibit at Ottawa's city hall. Mayor Marion Dewar told the 150 invited guests, including various third world representatives, "that all Canadians who are aware of their heritage and have roots and attachments going back to another land can understand the attachment to one's roots." The purely cultural exhibit of paintings and Palestinian artifacts was coupled with a large map of the Middle East that listed "Palestine" in the place of Israel.

Soviet and Ethiopian Jewry

A one-day conference on Soviet Jewry in Ottawa, organized by the Canadian Committee for Soviet Jewry, attracted some 500 people. The highlight of the meeting was the appearance of former "prisoner of Zion" Iosif Mendelevich. In a major address, Serge Joyal, federal minister of state, pointed out that human rights violations by the Soviet Union angered all members of parliament, regardless of party affiliation.

The Israel Aliyah Center and CZF brought Iosif Mendelevich to Toronto, where, after a full day of interviews with the press and a meeting with students, he spoke at Shaarei Shomayim synagogue.

About 500 of the delegates to the Canadian Hadassah-WIZO convention in Ottawa staged a rally outside the Soviet embassy to protest the declining number of exit visas being issued to Soviet Jews and the repression of Jewish religious and cultural life in the Soviet Union. The delegates were joined by David Berger, the Liberal MP from the Montreal riding of Laurier.

Humanitarian concern for Soviet Jewry at the federal level was expressed through a parliamentary committee on Soviet Jewry, House of Commons resolutions on behalf of refuseniks, and calls by individual MP's to the Soviet ambassador in Ottawa.

The Canadian Association for Ethiopian Jews (CAEJ) sponsored a meeting that was attended by about 750 people. Simcha Jacobovici, the head of the group, argued that more Ethiopian Jews were rescued in 1979, when there was publicity about the issue, than in more recent years when nobody was lobbying. Joe Ain, president of the United Israel Appeal of Canada, labeled this an "unjust charge which can only be refuted at the cost of endangering those who still await rescue and patriation." He argued that Ethiopian Jews were being brought to Israel "through means and by an effort which cannot be discussed or debated in the public print. And once in Israel, they are embraced by the affection and sympathy of all who come in contact with them."

A Pacific region chapter of the Canadian Association for Ethiopian Jews was established in Vancouver.

Holocaust Observances

There was a vital need for the various Christian churches to recognize the State of Israel, declared Sister Maureena Fritz, professor of theology at the University of Toronto. Addressing Toronto's first Christian service in memory of the Holocaust at the Bloor Street United Church, she stated, "I can only mourn that my own church has not provided official recognition of the Israeli state." The service was sponsored by the Roman Catholic archdiocese, the Anglican diocese of Toronto, the Toronto conference of the United Church of Canada, and TJC's Holocaust remembrance committee.

A moving memorial meeting, sponsored by TJC's Holocaust remembrance committee, was held at the Beth Tzedec synagogue. Israeli consul-general David Ariel presented Marie DeVries, 84, and her son, Eric Wicherts, with awards in honor of their heroism in sheltering Jews during World War II. David Roskies, a professor at the Jewish Theological Seminary of America, spoke about Jewish spiritual resistance to the Nazis. The evening culminated with a presentation of Ben Steinberg's cantata, "Echoes of Children," which set to music the unedited words of young people that were found in diaries and poetry collections after the Holocaust.

In Winnipeg, Holocaust remembrance week began with a gathering of 300 people, many of them students at Jewish day schools, at the YMHA Jewish community center. Mayor William Norrie read a proclamation renaming Hargrave Street "Avenue of the Warsaw Ghetto Heroes" for the week.

The testimony of 25 Torontonians who were concentration camp survivors was videotaped at Adath Sholom synagogue as part of a Holocaust documentation project. The project, a $300,000 undertaking funded by Ottawa's multiculturalism directorate and CJC, was to provide a permanent record of the atrocities suffered by Jews during World War II. The tapes were to be deposited at the Public Archives of Canada, and at Yad Vashem and other Holocaust study centers around the world. In addition, 25 cassettes on various Holocaust-related themes were to be made available for distribution to schools and colleges.

Rallies for Raoul Wallenberg took place simultaneously in Toronto, Ottawa, and Montreal. Wallenberg was the Swedish diplomat who saved thousands of Jews from Nazi extermination camps during World War II. Toward the end of the war, he was taken into custody by the Soviets. It is believed that he may still be alive in a Russian prison.

Religion

According to *Statistics Canada,* there were 1,753 marriages involving Jews in all the provinces except Quebec in 1978; in 696 cases the spouses were not Jewish. "This is pure intermarriage with no conversion. If one included marriages following conversion, the rate would probably be closer to 45 or 50 per cent," said Rabbi Reuven Bulka, spiritual leader of Congregation Machzikei Hadas in Ottawa. However, Jean Claude Lasry, a psychologist affiliated with Jewish General Hospital, pointed out that Bulka's statistics dealt with marriages and not individuals. In fact, 20 per cent of Canadian Jews were intermarrying.

In the past decade, the number of Reform Jews had doubled and ten new temples had opened in the Toronto area and western Canada, according to Maurice Miller of Montreal, the newly-appointed president of the Canadian Council of Liberal Congregations. There were 17 Reform synagogues in Canada, representing some 6,000 families, or approximately 23,000 persons. However, Montreal's Reform membership was declining, and one synagogue, Temple Beth Sholom, had been forced to close its doors. The three Reform congregations in the prairie provinces (Winnipeg, Calgary, and Edmonton) had been established in the past two years, as had the Baycrest Terrace temple in Toronto. Other temples less than ten years old were located in Vancouver, Windsor, Willowdale, Thornhill, Mississauga, and Kitchener.

Toronto's long-standing *eruv* was extended to incorporate the Steeles Avenue area between Bayview and Leslie. The announcement was made by Rabbi Moshe Bomzer, whose Shaarei Zion synagogue was located within the enlarged area. "Now," he said, "we and other observant Jews in this newly-developing section of metropolitan Toronto will be able to avail ourselves of *eruv's* benefits."

An interfaith program in Montreal, featuring Rabbi Marc Tannenbaum of the American Jewish Committee, was organized by CCCJ. The theme of Tannenbaum's address was "Evangelicals and Jews in Conversation." Approximately 350 Christian and Jewish leaders attended the session.

Three hundred residents of the Kitchener-Waterloo area in Ontario witnessed a mass wedding ceremony, in which nine couples, newly-arrived from the Soviet Union, finally got the opportunity to be married under a *chupah*. The Kitchener-Waterloo Committee for Russian Jews, whose members included representatives of the Orthodox Beth Jacob synagogue and the local Reform synagogue, Temple Shalom, sponsored the ceremony and festivities.

Jewish Education

The Association of Jewish Day Schools asked a Quebec governmental committee to accord Jewish day schools a special status within the Quebec educational system that would permit them 100 per cent funding, rather than the present 80 per cent funding for secular studies. A $5,000,000 annual grant from Allied Jewish Community Services supplemented the government money. Parents' fees paid for Jewish studies.

After nearly two years, labor negotiations between the teachers and administration of Montreal's École Maimonide reached a successful conclusion. The two sides signed a three-year contract that was the first in the twelve-year history of the

French-language day school. Terms of the agreement included an average salary increase for teachers of 42 per cent.

A week-long teachers' strike affected about 800 students attending the United Synagogue day school at Toronto's Beth Tikvah synagogue.

Jewish Culture

The National Library of Canada opened the largest exhibition of Hebraica and Judaica in Canadian history. Some 150 works from the Lowy collection—several thousand volumes of rare printed books that once belonged to the Montreal industrialist Jacob Lowy—were put on display.

Gershon Iskowitz of Toronto was honored by the Art Gallery of Ontario with the largest exhibition of his work ever offered.

The Jewish Canadians, a National Film Board production, set itself the difficult goal of covering 200 years of Jewish settlement in Canada in 30 minutes.

The Spies Who Never Were, a two-part television film by Harry Rasky, related the dramatic story of German and Austrian nationals incarcerated as "spies" in Canadian detention camps for lengthy periods during World War II. Most of the "spies" were Jews who had fled the Nazis.

After 70 years of publication, the Winnipeg Yiddish weekly, *Dos Yiddishe Vort,* folded. Circulation had fallen to 1,600 subscribers.

The multiculturalism directorate made a grant of $10,000 to the Winnipeg Board of Jewish Education to develop an anthology of Canadian Jewish literature as an educational tool for high school and university students.

Publications

Unfinished Business is the many-sided autobiography of W. Gunther Plaut, who served as senior rabbi of Toronto's prestigious Holy Blossom temple for almost two decades.

In her autobiography, *The Errand Runner: Reflections of a Rabbi's Daughter,* 75-year-old Leah Rosenberg writes movingly of her father, who lived in Toronto and Montreal. Rosenberg is the mother of well-known Canadian author Mordecai Richler.

Anita Mayer offers a harrowing depiction of her imprisonment by the Nazis in *One Came Back.*

A Toronto taxi driver, George Gabori, describes his life under the Nazis, and then under the Communists in Hungary, in his memoirs, *When Evils Were Most Free.*

Vichy France and the Jews, by Michael Marrus of Toronto and his American associate, Robert Paxton, is an important scholarly work.

Solomon Birnbaum, 89, one of the world's greatest authorities on the Yiddish language, summarizes his life's work in *Yiddish, a Survey and a Grammar,* published by the University of Toronto Press.

A Yiddish lexicon, *A Hundred Years of Hebrew Literature,* written by H.L. Fuks, contains the biographies of 422 authors who contributed to Jewish publications in Canada in the past century.

Les Juifs de Québec, bibliographie retrospective annotée, compiled by David Rome, Judith Nefsky, and Paule Obermeir, provides extensive documentation on the Jewish community.

Susan Goldberg's *Man of Property* presents the inside story of Canada's ten largest developers.

Recent books of poetry on a variety of themes include *Europe and Other Bad News* by Irving Layton; *Apples, Nuts, and Wine* by Larry Geller; *A Small Book of Small Verse* by Sam Kusner; and *Winter Flowers* by Janis Rapoport. *A Regge Ruh Gefunen* ("To Find a Moment's Rest") is the thirteenth book of poems by the Montreal poet M.M. Shaffir.

In *The Spice Box,* edited by Gerri Sinclair and Morris Wolfe, 38 authors reflect on their Jewishness.

The Immortals, by Ed Kleiman, is a collection of 14 stories written over the past 25 years.

Eight diverse short stories, written between 1954 and 1980, are collected in Henry Kreisel's *The Almost Meeting and Other Stories.*

Anthony Renshaw's *House of Lions* is a chilling fictional picture of a neo-Nazi group which plots the downfall of parliamentary democracy in Britain.

The Third Power, by Neville Frankel, is a novel about racial and tribal conflict in South Africa.

Personalia

Senator Jack Austin of Vancouver was named the minister responsible for western Canadian affairs in Prime Minister Trudeau's cabinet reshuffle. In a long and distinguished career in Ottawa, Austin had served as executive assistant to a minister; deputy minister of energy, mines, and resources; and, finally, as the prime minister's principal secretary. He was the third Jew in the cabinet; the others were Herb Gray, minister of industry and trade, and Robert Kaplan, solicitor-general.

Three of Manitoba's best-known provincial politicians, Saul Cherniak, Sidney Green, and Saul Miller, left public office following the election in which the NDP returned to power. There were still three Jewish members in the new legislature—two on the NDP side, and one on the Conservative side.

Three Jewish candidates—two Conservatives and one Liberal—were reelected in Ontario's general election. The Conservative winners were Larry Grossman, minister of trade and tourism (St. Andrew-St. Patrick), and David Rotenberg (Wilson Heights). Stuart Smith, leader of the Liberal party, won handily in Hamilton West.

Two Jewish winners of the Order of Canada were Sydney Newman, film-maker and television executive, and Martin Goodman, president of Toronto Star Newspapers, Ltd.

Melvyn Ball, professor of neuropathology at the University of Western Ontario, was awarded $1,033,437 to research Alzheimer's disease, which affected more than 300,000 Canadians.

Joe Greenberg of Toronto became the first Canadian inductee into the prestigious Boxing Hall of Fame.

The Saidye and Samuel Bronfman Family Foundation made a $100,000 gift to McGill University to establish the Saul Hayes graduate fellowship in civil liberties and human rights. Hayes, the long-time executive director and executive vice-president of CJC, who died in 1980, was regarded as Canadian Jewry's most distinguished communal worker and elder statesman.

Edward Bronfman, regional chairman of Hebrew University's Mount Scopus development project, received the university's highest honor—the Mount Scopus Award. Two previous Canadian recipients were Louis Posluns of Toronto and Edward Winant of Montreal.

Bora Laskin, the chief justice of Canada, was honored at a national dinner tendered by the Canadian society of the Weizmann Institute of Science.

Mirial Small of Toronto was reelected national president of the 17,000-member Hadassah-Wizo of Canada at its biennial in Ottawa.

Denise Altman was chosen president of Congregation Habonim of Toronto. She was believed to be the first woman president of a Conservative synagogue in the province.

Among Canadian personalities who died in 1981 were David Lewis (71), leader of NDP, Canada's socialist party; Victor Kugler (81), who helped hide Anne Frank, her family, and four other Jews during World War II in Holland; Ruth Lowe Sandler (66), who wrote the hit song "I'll Never Smile Again"; Heinz Warschauer (68), director of the religious school at Toronto's Holy Blossom temple for more than 30 years; David Kirshenbaum (79), of London, Ontario, rabbi and author; David Newman (71), long-time chairman of the educational board of the Associated Hebrew Schools of Toronto; Mark Gayn (72), one of Canada's most distinguished newspapermen, and columnist for the Toronto *Star;* Martin Goodman (46), president of Toronto Star Newspapers, Ltd., and an eminent journalist; Morris Pulver (70), Toronto philanthropist, whose bequest of $5 million to the United Jewish Welfare Fund of Toronto may have been the largest gift ever to a Jewish federation; Harry Topper (81), known as "Mr. Yiddish," who was involved in all aspects of Jewish education; Shimson Dunsky (82), Montreal educator, writer, and translator of Jewish classics into Yiddish and Hebrew; Hyman Singer (73), physician and leader in Jewish communal life in the Niagara area; Anna Raginsky (89), organizer of Hadassah-Wizo in Toronto and life-long stalwart of Canadian Hadassah-Wizo; and Hart Wintrob (70), active in a wide range of communal organizations.

BERNARD BASKIN

Western Europe

Great Britain

National Affairs

IN 1981 THERE WAS a royal wedding, but also urban riots on an unprecedented scale. Most of the violence was centered in run-down inner-city areas in which unemployed young blacks formed a large part of the population. In April riots broke out in Brixton, South London, resulting in extensive damage and widespread looting. Early in July white "skinheads" attacked Asian youths in Southall, West London. Between July 6 and 12 there were riots in Liverpool, Manchester, Salford, Wood Green (North London), and other areas. The police bore the brunt of the violence, suffering more than 300 casualties. In November an inquiry conducted by Lord Scarman concluded that urban violence was fueled by poor police relations with the black community. Scarman called for the creation of police review boards to make the police more accountable for their actions.

In February concern over increased racial violence caused Home Secretary William Whitelaw to institute a probe of racist organizations. In May Peter Alexander, national organizer of the Anti-Nazi League (ANL), said that the activities of the extreme right-wing National Front (NF) had become more avowedly Fascist and Nazi in outlook. In November NF set up an industrial department with a special section to infiltrate and recruit members within the trade union movement. Nevertheless, in the May county council elections, NF and other racist organizations fielded fewer candidates and took a half to a third fewer votes than in 1977; in Greater London, NF's vote fell to 34,000 from 119,000; in the West Midlands, NF and British Movement (BM) candidates obtained two per cent of the total vote as against 17 per cent in 1977.

Home Secretary Whitelaw banned NF marches when he was requested to do so by chief constables. This happened in Leicester and Wolverhampton in March; in Crawley (West Sussex) and Liverpool in August; and in Brent (London) and Rochdale in December. A march by BM members in Southend in August met with violent opposition from the local Anti-Fascist Committee and ANL.

In December the director of public prosecutions decided to take action against Robert Hamilton Edwards, cartoonist for the violently antisemitic *The Stormer*, under the race relations act.

In October immigration officials at London's Heathrow airport refused to allow Rabbi Meir Kahane, leader of the Jewish Defense League, to enter the country.

The established political parties suffered declines in popularity; the Conservatives because of their failure to revive the economy in any perceptible way and Labor on account of internal disputes. The conflict within Labor reached a peak in a public row between party leader Michael Foot and left-wing spokesman Tony Benn. The growing influence of the latter led to the formation of the Social Democratic party (SDP). An early indication of the new party's appeal came at Warrington in July when Roy Jenkins, former Labor chancellor, cut the Labor majority from 10,274 to 1,759 votes. In September SDP formed an alliance with the small Liberal party and in October won its first seat with a by-election victory at Croydon, a seat previously held by the Conservatives. In the Crosby by-election in November, former Labor minister of education Shirley Williams, now a leading SDP member, made an even greater impact by overturning a Conservative majority of 19,272 votes.

Relations with Israel

Britain's Middle East policy was bound up with the Venice declaration of the European Economic Community (EEC). This was particularly so after June when Foreign Secretary Carrington took over the six-month presidency of EEC's council of ministers. Proclaiming 1981 "the year of progress in the settlement of the Arab-Israeli dispute," Carrington reiterated the argument that EEC's initiative was not meant to undercut the Camp David accords. The PLO, he argued, should be included in future peace efforts, with the PLO recognizing Israel's right to exist in secure borders and Israel recognizing the legitimate rights of the Palestinians. In December, after a year of intensive British diplomacy in the Arab world, Douglas Hurd, minister of state with special responsibility in the foreign office for the Middle East and North Africa, admitted that little progress had resulted from EEC's peace initiative.

In March Sir Ian Gilmour expressed the government's anger at "the speeding up of [Israeli] settlements on the West Bank." In June Prime Minister Margaret Thatcher condemned Israel's air attack on Iraq's nuclear installation as a "grave breach of international law." In July she described Israel's actions in Lebanon as wholly disproportionate to any attacks on Israeli territory. In November British support for a Saudi Arabian peace plan, as well as remarks by Lord Carrington on the Sinai peace-keeping force that seemed to repudiate the Camp David accords, brought a warning from Prime Minister Begin that Britain and other Common Market countries might be barred from participation in the force. In December Prime Minister Thatcher condemned Israel's annexation of the Golan Heights at a dinner celebrating the Board of Deputies of British Jews' 220th anniversary, stressing "the inadmissibility of the acquisition of territory by war," enshrined in UN resolution 242.

In January Douglas Hurd stated that British officials had maintained contact with the PLO for some time, and believed such contacts to be "in our interests and in the interest of peace." On the other hand, Hurd and Prime Minister Thatcher declined to attend a London dinner arranged by Arab diplomats in July because a PLO representative had been invited. "We quite rightly do not recognize the PLO. We do not recognize organizations, only countries," said Thatcher in Kuwait in October. Britain did not have ministerial meetings with the PLO, she continued, "first because of the association with terrorism, and secondly, because of the statements by parts of the PLO that their real objective is to drive Israel into the sea."

Jewish community fears of growing PLO influence in Great Britain were fed by the Dundee (Scotland) council's decision to twin with the West Bank city of Nablus. The PLO's flag flew over the Dundee town hall, and the mayor of the city made an Arab-financed visit to Nablus. Protest meetings against the twinning were held, and a vast "Say No to PLO" rally was organized in London's Trafalgar Square by the Board of Deputies in conjunction with the Zionist Federation (ZF).

Anti-Zionist forces were responsible for motions being debated on university campuses throughout Britain to twin with West Bank universities. Such motions were passed by the Glasgow University student representative council (Bir Zeit), the Strathclyde student union (Bethlehem), and Girton College, Cambridge. Anti-Zionist motions were passed at Sussex University and at Brighton and Middlesex Polytechnics.

In July an SDP friends of Israel group was formed with MP Bill Rodgers as president.

Trade figures announced in January showed that Israel's exports to Great Britain in 1980 (valued at £236.6 million), were up by four per cent over 1979, while British exports to Israel (valued at £231.6 million) were down by 14.4 per cent. In March new government currency regulations allowed Israel bonds to be purchased in Britain for the first time. Also in March the Egyptian ambassador and the commercial counsellor attended a thirtieth anniversary celebration of the British-Israel Chamber of Commerce, which that month had organized the first Israeli industrial exhibition in London.

JEWISH COMMUNITY

Demography

The Jewish population of Great Britain was estimated to be 390,000. Leading Jewish population centers were London, Manchester, Leeds, and Glasgow.

The Board of Deputies' research unit reported that synagogue marriages fell from 1,303 in 1979 to 1,222 in 1980, the lowest figure in 20 years. The greatest declines were among the Sephardim and the Liberals; the modern Orthodox sector grew. The majority of marriages were in London, indicating a drop in the provicial communities. However, Barry Kosmin, director of the research unit, told the *Jewish Chronicle* that a survey of the Jewish population was needed in order to obtain a clear picture of what was happening.

In July the Jewish Marriage Council decided to sponsor a marriage bureau.

Burials and cremations under Jewish religious auspices fell to 4,656 in 1980, from 4,889 in 1979.

In April Chief Rabbi Immanuel Jakobovits predicted that apathy and assimilation would reduce the Jewish population of Great Britain to around 300,000 by the year 2000. However, he argued that the community's future would be assured by building upon the successful network of Jewish day schools.

Communal Activities

Current economic conditions, in conjunction with local government spending cuts, had changed the emphasis in Jewish Welfare Board (JWB) activities to non-residential services such as social work teams based in areas of high Jewish population and day centers. Sobell House, Golders Green, London, had a register of over 900 elderly and handicapped persons. Nearly 400 pensioners met at Sylvia Leighton Day Center, Hackney, London. The Gants Hill, Essex project, that was in the process of construction, would be the last residential home for the foreseeable future. JWB currently administered 14 homes for the elderly and, through an associated housing society, maintained 293 people in seven flatlet blocks.

In August the Housing Society, established by JWB, received approval and an offer of funding from the Housing Corporation to develop 28 units of sheltered housing, including special facilities for the disabled, on a site adjoining the Sobell Center. The new housing was to be administered by JWB and the Jewish Blind Society.

In December JWB took over the affairs of the Jewish Bread, Meat, and Coal Society, the oldest Jewish charitable organization in Britain.

In October the Westlon Housing Association announced a £1 million sheltered flatlet scheme for elderly Jews to be built in Ealing, London.

In August the British ORT Trust, in collaboration with the Manpower Services Commission, announced plans for a vocational training center in North Manchester. The scheme, British ORT's first "operational" project in Great Britain since the 1940's, would provide 45 places for young people over the age of 16.

In September the Ravenswood Foundation established a visiting professorship in special education at the Bulmershe College of Higher Education, Reading, Berkshire.

Zionism

Interim reports in August and October by a commission appointed to appraise the funding of the Zionist Federation of Great Britain and Ireland (ZF) stressed the need to uphold the principle of accountability throughout the organization. The commission urged that priority be given to re-establishing the ZF department responsible for maintaining and expanding Zionist societies in London and the provinces, and to improving ZF's public relations efforts.

The Joint Israel Appeal (JIA) took several cost-cutting measures during the year. In February it withdrew financial backing and staff services from the annual Independence Day celebration; in March it put ZF on a "cash only" basis; and in September it withdrew its annual grant of £20,000 to the Hillel Foundation. JIA was "running a different campaign, reflecting the difficult economic environment," said national chairman Trevor Chinn, in June.

With one thousand emigrants, Britain was the only country in the world which maintained stable *aliyah* during 1980. Whereas youth movement graduates and retired people had previously predominated, a growing number of professional people had emigrated recently. Seventy per cent of all British *olim* in 1980 were under the age of 30.

Soviet Jewry

Prime Minister Thatcher's pledge to the Board of Deputies in December of government cooperation in the cause of Soviet Jewry was foreshadowed earlier in the year when she received the wife of Anatoly Shcharansky, supported the Wilberforce council's world-wide campaign to reunite Soviet Jews with their families, and met with a joint delegation from the Student and Academic Campaign for Soviet Jewry and the Union of Jewish Students. "We have conveyed to the Soviet Union, at a high level, our concern about the abuses of human rights. We shall continue to take every suitable opportunity to reiterate that concern," Thatcher said in December.

Jewish and non-Jewish groups in London and the provinces continued to campaign on behalf of Soviet Jews. In February senior national officers of the Association of Jewish Ex-Servicemen espoused the cause of Soviet Jewish war veterans wishing to emigrate. In March some 750 young people held a torchlight procession through Manchester to express solidarity with Soviet Jewry. In April 75 British academics signed a letter to the Soviet minister of culture protesting the repeated harassment of Hebrew teachers and their students. In May members of a new organization, Concerned Jewish Youth, disrupted a Moscow Philharmonic Orchestra concert at London's Festival Hall. In June more than 100 fellows of the Royal Society protested to the Soviet authorities over the arrest and impending trial of Viktor Brailovsky. In November a large group of MP's signed a motion expressing grave concern at the reduction in the number of exit permits being granted. In December Hull and Bristol students demonstrated in support of Russian Jewish students.

Religion

George Gee, who in June won the first contested election for the United Synagogue (US) presidency, stated his intention to "extend the scope of US discussions, encourage greater autonomy for synagogues, and invite greater participation by young people in US work."

In November the US council voted to allow four members of the Ladies' Guilds to attend its meetings; they would have the right to speak, but not to vote or move motions. In December the council warned that it would look more closely at the viability of synagogues under its administration. "We can not worship at the shrine of empty buildings," said Gee.

In August Brixton synagogue, London, no longer situated at the center of the South London Jewish community, was sold. The proceeds of the sale were to be held until Streatham synagogue was also sold and a site could be found for a new joint congregation. New synagogues were opened in such fast growing areas as Belmont (Stanmore, Middlesex) and Pinner.

In March the Spanish and Portuguese Synagogue raised membership fees by 30 per cent to meet inflation.

In May the first students graduated from Judith Lady Montefiore College, Golders Green, London.

A continuing swing to traditionalism was noted at the Liberal and Progressive Synagogues' conference in March. In December Rabbi Hugo Gryn, Reform and Liberal Rabbis' Council chairman, affirmed his adherence to the classical *halakhic* definition of a Jew. Gryn told the *Jewish Chronicle* that he was disturbed by trends in the Reform movement in the United States to actively seek converts and to regard the children of mixed marriages as Jewish regardless of the mother's faith. During 1980 the British Reform movement accepted 120 converts.

The number of functions supervised by the Kashrus Commission fell by a third in the first half of 1981. In February the meetings of the London Kashrus Commission were opened to women as observers for the first time. In May the London Board for Shechita announced plans to establish the Shechita Liaison Commission of Great Britain in conjunction with the National Council of Shechita Boards.

Jewish Education

The London Board of Jewish Religious Education was currently employing 326 Sunday and 112 midweek teachers. This compared with 408 and 165 teachers, respectively, in 1979.

In March a £90,000 deficit caused ZF's education trust to close Hillel House School, Willesden, London. The official opening of the Brodetsky primary school completed the three schools comprising the George Lyttleton Center, Leeds, sponsored by the trust. The Lyttleton Center provided Jewish education to nearly 700 children between the ages of three and 13.

The new £2 million Michael Sobell Sinai primary school in Kingsbury, London, opened in September.

In September the Akiva school, the first primary school established under the auspices of the Reform and Liberal movement, opened on a seven-acre site in Finchley, London. The property had been purchased by Leo Baeck College in January for use as a religious and educational center.

In December US vice-president Victor Lucas pledged the group's active support for a plan to make Jews' College (which in September admitted a record 13 new students) a university of Jewish studies. In September Jews' College announced that it had leased its central London premises.

Jewish studies programs at British universities were hard hit by government cuts. In August it was announced that Jewish studies would be completely eliminated at Lancaster University. In December the closure was mooted of the nearly 100-year-old Hebrew section of Leeds' University's semitic studies department.

In March, at a Cambridge conference, the Hebraica Libraries Group, concerned with Hebrew manuscript and book collections, was formed. In July it was announced that preservation work on the Taylor-Schechter genizah collection housed at Cambridge University library would be completed in the coming year.

Publications

The *Jewish Chronicle*-Harold Wingate literary awards went to Jerry White for *Rothschild Buildings—Life in an East End Tenement Block, 1887–1920* and to Mordecai Richler for his novel *Joshua Then and Now*.

Studies focusing on Anglo-Jewish communities and institutions included *The Jewish Communities of North East England, 1755–1980* by L. Olsover; *Birmingham Jewry, 1749–1914* by the Birmingham Jewish Research Group; *A History of the Jewish Working Men's Club and Institute, 1874–1912* by Harold Pollins; *East End Underworld* by Raphael Samuel; *Sheffield: Commentary on a Community* by Armin Krausz; and *Jewish Education, 1981/82* edited by Derek Taylor.

Events in Anglo-Jewish history were described in *The Battle of Stepney* by Colin Rogers (the Sidney Street siege) and *Shefford* by Judith Grunfeld (the Jewish Secondary School's evacuation to Bedfordshire).

Zionist histories included *Britain and Palestine* by Phillip Jones, a British Academy project listing unpublished documents of British industries and organizations involved in Palestine; *Britain and Zion—The Fateful Entanglement* by Frank Hardie and Irwin Herrman; and *Jews and Zionism: The South African Experience, 1910–1967* by Gideon Shimoni.

Among other historical works were *The Jews in Weimar Germany* by Donald L. Niewyk and *The Vanished Worlds of Jewry* by Raphael Patai.

Holocaust studies included *Blind Eye to Murder* by Tom Bower; *Return to Auschwitz* by Kitty Hart; and *Auschwitz and the Allies* by Martin Gilbert. *The House on Prague Street* by Hana Demetz describes life in Prague in the 1930's and 1940's.

Religious works included *Jewish Folklore and Legend* by David Goldstein; *Jewish Literature between the Bible and the Mishnah* by George W.E. Nickelsburg; *Buber on God and the Perfect Man* by Pamela Vermes; and *Isaiah XXI: A Palimpsest* by A.A. Macintosh.

Among biographies were *Days of Sorrow and Pain* by Leonard Baker (Leo Baeck) and *Righteous Gentile* by John Bierman (Raoul Wallenberg). Lewis and Jacqueline Golden compiled *Harold Reinhart, 1891–1969: A Memorial Volume.* George Clare described a segment of family history in *Last Waltz in Vienna: The Destruction of a Family, 1842–1942.*

An important volume was *The Penguin Book of Hebrew Verse,* edited and translated by T. Carmi.

Fiction included *Deceptive Cadence* by Eugenia Zukerman; *Reparations* by Rudolf Nassauer; *Farewell to Europe* by Walter Laqueur; *July's People* by Nadine Gordimer; *Birds of Passage* by Bernice Rubens; *The Patriarch* by Chaim Bermant; *The Portage to San Cristabel of A.H.* by George Steiner; and *Defy the Wilderness* by Lynne Reid Banks.

Personalia

Knighthoods went to Chief Rabbi Immanuel Jakobovits; Sidney Cyril Hamburger, chairman, North West Regional Health Authority; and Maxwell Joseph, chairman, Grand Metropolitan, Ltd.

Nigel Lawson, financial secretary to the treasury, was made a privy counsellor. Edwina Coven was appointed to serve as the first woman lieutenant of London.

British Jews who died in 1981 included Hephzibah Menuhin, musician, in January, aged 60; Godfrey Phineas Godfrey-Isaacs, expert in child delinquency, in January, aged 90; Israel Feldman, physician and communal leader, in February, aged 92; Gustav George Bunzl, treasurer, British Committee of Children and Youth Aliyah, in February, aged 64; Schlomo Baumgarten, dayan, Union of Orthodox Hebrew Congregations, in February, aged 76; Rabbi Eliezer Spector, educator, in February, aged 69; Marguerite Gollancz, prominent archivist, in March, aged 69; Pierre Gildegame, Maccabi movement leader and founder of a youth leadership award, in March, aged 77; Hugh Harris, *Jewish Chronicle* literary editor for 30 years, in March, aged 83; Felix Gluck, children's book publisher, in March, aged 58; Walter Simon, emeritus professor of Chinese at London University, in March, aged 87; Reuben Kelf-Cohen, economist and civil servant, in March, aged 85; Abraham Wix, tobacco manufacturer and philanthropist, in April, aged 86; George Bilainkin, author, lecturer, and historian, in April, aged 78; Daphne Sasieni, psychiatrist and prison medical officer, in April; Victor Waddington, art world personality, in May, aged 74; Isaac Eugene Kornberg, businessman, in May, aged 81; Maurice Ludmer, editor, anti-fascist monthly, *Searchlight,* in May, aged 54; Cyril Salmon, circuit judge, in May, aged 56; Cecil Bernstein, arts patron and philanthropist, in June, aged 76; Manuel, Lord Kissen, Scotland's first Jewish high court judge and senator of the College of Justice, in June, aged 65; Frederic Warburg, publisher, in June, aged 82; Sir Philip Wien, high court judge, in June, aged 67; Alfred Strudwick, chairman, Reform Synagogues of Great Britain, in July, aged 58; Sir Frederick Lawrence, civic and communal leader, in July, aged 91; Maurice Barbanell, founder and editor, *Psychic News,* in July, aged 79; John Maurice Shaftesley, *Jewish Chronicle* editor, 1946–1958, in August, aged 80; Harry Bloom, anti-apartheid lawyer and academic, in August, aged 64; Jakob J. Kokotek, rabbi, London's Belsize Square Reform Synagogue, in September, aged 70; Eugen Glueckauf, atomic scientist, in September, aged 75; Sam Costa, show business personality, in September, aged 71; P. Selvin Goldberg, rabbi, Manchester Reform Congregation, in October, aged 63; Cyril Carr, Lord Mayor of Liverpool and president-elect of the Liberal party, in November, aged 55; Fay Schneider, kosher caterer, in November; Jacob Teicher, lecturer in rabbinics, Cambridge University, in November, aged 77; Sir Hans Krebs, Nobel laureate and professor of biochemistry, Sheffield and Oxford Universities, in November, aged 81; Louis Michaels, impresario, in December, aged 78; Reuben Ainsztein, historian and journalist, in December, aged 64; Cecil P. Taylor, playwright, in December, aged 52; Martin Sulzbacher, Jewish bookseller, in December, aged 85; Maurice Fogel, illusionist, in December, aged 70.

LIONEL AND MIRIAM KOCHAN

France

National Affairs

DURING THE FIRST FEW MONTHS of 1981, France was caught up in the excitement of the presidential election campaign. A decrease in the number of votes for the incumbent president, Valéry Giscard d'Estaing, was expected, but it was still thought likely that he would win. Adding credibility to this view was the persistent disunity of the left coalition, manifesting itself most particularly in the Communist campaign against Socialist leader François Mitterrand. However, as the day of decision drew near, cracks appeared in the majority that were no less grave than those in the minority. Jacques Chirac, mayor of Paris and a former minister in the cabinet of Giscard d'Estaing, announced his candidacy for the presidency; he conducted an anti-Giscard campaign as violent as that of the Socialists. Other figures in the majority, including Michel Debré, prime minister in the cabinet of the late General Charles de Gaulle, also sharply criticized the president. Then, Debré too became a candidate. On the eve of the elections, the outcome remained uncertain, but Mitterrand's chances had clearly improved.

In Jewish circles the campaign was echoed in an appeal by Henri Hajdenberg, leader of the Renouveau Juif (Jewish Renewal) organization, to "vote sanctions" against Giscard d'Estaing, who was accused of pursuing a pro-Arab, anti-Israel policy. In practical terms—although it was never stated directly—Renouveau Juif sought to secure votes for Mitterrand. On the other hand, both Lionel Stoléru, the secretary of state responsible for the problems of immigrant workers and a man well-versed in Jewish culture, and Simone Veil, president of the European Parliament in Strasbourg, supported Giscard d'Estaing. Gérard Israël, a deputy in the European Parliament and editor of the Jewish quarterly *Les Nouveaux Cahiers* ("New Notebooks"), campaigned for Chirac. In general, Jews were solicited as such by all the parties except those on the extreme right; even the Communists distributed a propaganda leaflet addressed to Jews in the less affluent Paris neighborhoods.

There was some skepticism about the possibility of any real change in France's attitude toward Israel, even if the Socialists won. While Mitterrand himself was considered a friend of Israel, there were elements within the Socialist party, and even within Mitterrand's own entourage, that favored the PLO. It was also feared that Communist participation in the government might have serious implications for the conduct of foreign policy.

In the second round of the elections, on May 10, Mitterrand was elected president of the Republic by a vote of 15,708,000 (52 per cent) to 14,650,000 (48 per cent) for Giscard d'Estaing. In the new Parliament, the Socialists gained an absolute majority of 285. The Communists suffered severe losses, emerging with only 44 seats, in contrast to their previous 86. The parties making up the old majority—the Rassemblement du Peuple Républican (RDR, Rally for the Republic) and Union pour la Démocratie Française (UDF, Union for Democracy in France)—lost about 150 seats.

The Socialists could have governed alone, but, as had been predicted and feared, the new cabinet of Pierre Mauroy ended up with four Communist ministers, among them Charles Fitermann, a Jew who had never shown the slightest interest in Jewish affairs. Two other ministers, Robert Badinter and Pierre Dreyfus, were committed Jews.

Among the government's first acts were several nationalizations, including large credit institutions, such as the dynastic Rothschild Bank. There were no great changes in foreign policy; France remained faithful to the spirit of NATO. Despite Communist participation in the government, relations with the USSR were encumbered by the situations in Afghanistan and Poland.

Mitterrand had announced that he would visit Israel if he won the election, but Israel's bombing of Iraq's nuclear plant at Tamuz, which had been built with French cooperation, led him to postpone the trip. At the end of September, Mitterrand went to Saudi Arabia. Israel's annexation of the Golan Heights at the end of the year created new Franco-Israeli tensions. While Foreign Minister Claude Cheysson visited Israel in early December, he first met with Yasir Arafat, head of the PLO. Cheysson's position on the Middle East was frankly pro-PLO; on one occasion, he compared Arafat's organization to the French resistance movement during the German occupation.

Anti-Jewish and anti-Israeli graffiti increasingly appeared on the walls of the Paris subway during the year. *Le Monde,* in its January 2 issue, published a front-page article by Jean-Marie Paupert, a Catholic writer and historian, reproaching French Jews for strongly asserting their Jewishness. Paupert advised French Jewry to be more moderate and discreet, and raised the possibility of an anti-Jewish reaction. The article brought an angry response from, among others, Simone de Beauvoir, companion of the late Jean-Paul Sartre.

The Socialists' accession to power stimulated a revival of secular militancy. There were demands for the total integration of private and parochial schools into the public education system and the end of all subsidies, direct or indirect, to non-state schools anywhere in France, including Alsace-Lorraine. If these demands were met, it would effectively mean the end of full-time Jewish schools.

In February the naming of the bishop of Orléans, Jean-Marie Lustiger, as archbishop of Paris created something of a sensation in Jewish circles, where it was seen as a response to the attack on the synagogue in rue Copernic the year before. It was said that Pope John Paul II had appointed Lustiger as a way of demonstrating his regard for Jews and his categorical rejection of all antisemitism. Lustiger had been born in Paris to a family of poor Polish-Jewish immigrants. During World War II, at the age of 14, he converted to Christianity under circumstances that were still unknown. After his ordination as a priest, Lustiger not only repeatedly mentioned his Jewish origin, but insisted on identifying himself as a Jew in accordance with the classic Christian view that Christianity was the fulfillment of Judaism. Some Jews admired Lustiger for his proud acknowledgement of his Jewish roots, while others viewed him with the suspicion traditionally accorded an apostate.

JEWISH COMMUNITY

Demography

The Jewish population of France was estimated to be 535,000. Leading Jewish population centers were Paris, Marseilles, Nice, Lyons, and Toulouse.

Communal Activities

The official installation of France's chief rabbi, René Samuel Sirat, took place on April 5 in the Great Paris Synagogue in the rue de la Victoire, in the presence of many political leaders, including President Mitterrand.

In May a series of gatherings and exhibitions celebrated the 30th anniversary of the Fonds Social Juif Unifié (FSJU, United Jewish Philanthropic Fund).

Among the measures included in the new government's liberalization program was the authorization of radio broadcasts by private stations. An immediate result was the introduction of broadcasts by various groups and organizations. Thus, four programs of a Jewish nature were added to the Jewish religious programs already sponsored for several years by the Consistory and incorporated into state-run broadcasts. One new program, sponsored by FSJU, dealt mostly with political issues, but also broadcast Jewish music, cultural news, interviews with writers and artists, etc. The other three programs covered similar ground, but with different emphases. Renouveau Juif's program, for example, was almost exclusively political, and took an adamantly pro-Israel stance. Whereas the old schedule had allotted one hour a week to Jewish affairs, under the more liberal regulations, all Jewish programs were being transmitted daily. Nevertheless, they had only about 20,000 listeners.

Outside the official Jewish community there was a growing effort, inspired in the main by neo-Bundists, to reassert the value of Yiddish language and culture among young people of East European extraction. Residual leftist and, occasionally, anti-Zionist tendencies were discernible in various Yiddish broadcasts, which offered songs, theatrical performances, and folklore.

The Yiddish press was on the way to extinction, as its elderly readers passed from the scene and were not replaced by younger ones. Of the three Yiddish dailies in Paris—Zionist, Bundist, and Communist—not one actually appeared every day. The left-Zionist *Unser Wort* ("Our Word") fared the least badly, simply because it was largely subsidized by Zionist organizations and was directed by a *shaliach*, an official Israeli representative. The religious Zionist *Unser Weg* ("Our Path") had a small, relatively stable circulation among Jews who wanted to read a good commentary in Yiddish on the biblical portion of the week.

There was an upsurge of interest in Talmudic studies among university intellectuals. Professor Emmanuel Lévinas' Talmud courses attracted a large, attentive audience not limited to religious circles.

The teaching of modern Hebrew in the high schools seemed to have reached a peak and was no longer increasing. Anti-Israel political prejudice in the universities and secondary schools hindered a wider interest in Hebrew, now in competition with Arabic, which was more "up-to-date" both politically and economically.

The 22nd annual colloquium of French-speaking Jewish intellectuals, held in Paris in November, was devoted to the Bible. There were several brilliant presentations, including one by Henri Atlan, the renowned biologist and Talmudist who now lived in Israel, but was still active in Jewish intellectual life in France.

In May, during FSJU's national council meeting, a large group of Jewish intellectuals gathered to discuss the topic "intellectuals and the community." Jacques Attali, advisor to President Mitterrand, moderated the public debate. Among the participants were some who, until then, had never appeared at events connected with Jewish life, e.g., the "critical Communist" Jean Ellenstein, former professor at the Communist party's Institute of Marxist Studies.

Publications

In *Le Spectateur Engagé* ("The Committed Spectator," Julliard), Raymond Aron, one of France's most highly-esteemed political thinkers and journalists, offers a balance-sheet on his life. Among other things, he clarifies the nature of his Jewish outlook.

The reissue of *Amos* (Brin) by Andre Néher renewed interest in the work of this French-Jewish theologian, now residing in Jerusalem. Néher's writings in the post-World War II period were the point of departure for the current renaissance of Jewish culture in France.

The Médici Prize for foreign literature went to Israeli novelist Yoram Kaniuk, whose works, published by Stock, had been very well received by the critics.

Stock published a translation of Martin Buber's *Tales of Rabbi Nachman.*

Even before Elias Canetti won the Nobel Prize for literature, Albin Michel had published his *Les Voix de Marrakech* ("Voices from Marrakesh"), an evocation of the Moroccan city that reflects the author's profound Jewish consciousness.

Far from Paris, in a small village in Midi, four young intellectuals started a publishing house specializing in scientific Judaica. Editions Verdier brought out an excellent French translation of Maimonides' *Guide to the Perplexed,* and followed it with an outstanding French translation of the first part of the Zohar, which took Charles Mopsik eight years to prepare. The Zohar translation, with no publicity at all, sold very well due to an increased interest in Jewish mysticism.

The 1981 prize for literature of the Fondation du Judaïsme Français (Foundation for French Judaism) was awarded to historian Léon Poliakov.

Personalia

George Vajda, the eminent scholar of Hebrew and semitics, died in Paris on Yom Kippur, at the age of 73. He had taught at the rabbinic seminary in Paris and at the École des Haute Études (School for Higher Studies). Vajda was born in Budapest and came to France in 1920.

On April 6, 75-year-old Vladimir Rabinovitch, also known by the literary pseudonym Rabi, was killed in an automobile accident. A chronicler, literary critic, and polemicist, he played an important role in the Finaly affair (a case involving the kidnapping and attempted conversion to Catholicism of two young children of Holocaust victims) after the Liberation. Although once a Zionist in good standing, he became increasingly critical of Israel in his later years.

Julien Samuel, one of the founders and a former director of FSJU, died on September 16, at the age of 69. Born in Alsace, he began his activities on behalf of Jews during the second World War, when he worked semi-clandestinely in Marseilles in a home established by the Organisation de Secours à l'Enfance (Children's Aid Organization). He was among the principal advocates within FSJU of strong support for Jewish cultural institutions. Samuel served as editor-in-chief of the monthly *l'Arche* ("The Ark") until his retirement.

ARNOLD MANDEL

Eastern Europe

Soviet Union

Domestic Affairs

During 1981 THE SOVIET UNION faced continuing resistance in Russian-invaded Afghanistan, an unstable situation in Poland, and growing economic problems.

Agricultural production was only about 150,000,000 tons, putting the country at the mercy of foreign suppliers. In addition, poor transportation impeded efforts to deliver the available produce to the centers of industrial production. Soviet party chief Leonid Brezhnev stated in November that food was "economically and politically the central problem of the five-year plan...." For the second consecutive year, industrial growth was markedly smaller than the planned output.

While the Soviet masses lived under economic hardship, the bureaucrats—party and state functionaries, estimated to number some 700,000 individuals—were the beneficiaries of a preferential regime that supplied them with a variety of imported goods. Huge food imports greatly increased the Soviet trade deficit with the West, and created problems with the payment of short-term debts.

The sorry state of affairs in the USSR was well known in Western Europe, where it had a significant impact on the various Communist parties. Increasing disenchantment with the Soviet Union made itself felt at the 26th congress of the Soviet Communist party which was held in Moscow in February and March. Giancarlo Pajetta, one of the leaders of the Communist party in Italy, was refused the floor, because it was known that he favored such things as the withdrawal of Soviet troops from Afghanistan, dialogue with the Polish opposition, and social reforms in the USSR.

There were no significant changes in the leadership of the Communist party or in the ruling politburo. Among the newcomers to the central committee was Georgii Arbatov, the top Soviet expert on the United States and Canada. There were continuing reports of conflict within the top Soviet group, but the aged leadership maintained its power, with Brezhnev at the head.

While "socialist realism" continued to be the controlling principle in published writings, some of the themes covered in contemporary letters reflected the painful realities of Soviet life. Illustrative of this trend were the writings of the very talented Valentin Rasputin. In his popular *Farewell to Matera,* he described the horrors imposed on Russian peasants by rapid industrialization. This subject had previously been taboo; the new discussion indicated that important changes were taking place beneath the surface of Soviet society.

Paralleling the new non-conformist literature were the songs of Soviet "bards," that treated the various problems faced by the Soviet people. The popularity of the bards was such that tens of thousands of men and women of all Soviet classes came to the funeral of Vladimir Vysotski, a leading singer, when he passed away in Moscow at the age of 42. For weeks Vysotski's grave at the Vagankov cemetery attracted large crowds, even though the authorities had discouraged his artistic activities and his concerts had gone unadvertised.

Dissidence

General Semion Tsvigun (now deceased), first deputy chairman of the KGB, writing in the September issue of the party magazine *Communist,* maintained that the movement of dissent in the Soviet Union had been completely eliminated by the authorities. According to Tsvigun, the human rights movement, associated with such names as Andreii Sakharov and Yurii Orlov, no longer existed. In fact, however, severe repression by the authorities was unable to stamp out dissent, either among the general population or in the lower ranks of the Communist party. Various groups were demanding strict application of human rights principles in line with the 1975 Helsinki accords.

The police took into custody virtually all members of the Helsinki Watch Committee on Human Rights, that had sprung up in various cities after the signing of the Helsinki accords. Toward the end of the year, Ivan Kovaliov was arrested by the authorities. His father, Sergei, and his wife, Tatiana, were already serving prison terms for their activities.

In December the police arrested Evgenii Kozlovski, Nikolaii Klimontovich, Vladislav Lion, and Bakhyt Kenzheev when they attempted to establish an independent writers club. Also in December the Leningrad historian Arsenii Roginskii was brought to trial for "illegally" using the state's libraries and archives in his research work.

Socialism and Our Future, a new Samizdat magazine giving voice to the old Russian democratic socialist tradition, appeared in Moscow.

Toward the end of the year, Andreii Sakharov and his wife, Elena Bonner (who had been exiled to the city of Gorky), went on a hunger strike to protest the refusal of Soviet authorities to issue an exit visa to Elizaveta Alekseeva, wife by proxy of their stepson, Alekseii Semionov. The KGB apparently decided it was not good policy to make a martyr of Sakharov, and permitted Alekseeva to join Semionov in the United States.

Interestingly, the Hare Krishna movement suddenly appeared in various Soviet cities, winning disciples among the technical intelligentsia. Evgenii Tretiakov, a leader of the movement, was arrested by the authorities and declared a "social parasite." It was not clear whether his arrest liquidated the activities of the devotees.

The continuing resistance of the Polish workers affected the attitudes of workers within the Soviet Union. There was a strike by bus drivers in Togliatti. In Gorky there was a strike in factories producing military goods. The workers in the Leninets factory in Leningrad organized a work stoppage. Strikes were also reported in the Minsk tractor factory in Pechenga, and in Tartu in Estonia.

Nationalities

The growth of great-Russian nationalism, centering on the glorification of the Russian past, had a substantial impact on the various nationality groups inhabiting the Soviet Union. Tatar historians, for example, began to question the traditional view that the end of Tatar independence and the destruction of Tatar culture by the Russians were necessary steps in the progressive development of society. These historians called for an objective study of the history of their groups.

In November a group of Volga Germans demonstrated in Red Square, demanding the right to leave the USSR. Their banners, similar to those of Jewish protesters, read, "We want to go home." According to official sources in Bonn, some 100,000 Volga Germans had applied for exit visas, in addition to the 85,000 who had already left the Soviet Union. Other sources estimated the number of departures at around 65,000.

It was reported that the Kremlin authorities were quietly changing the upper echelon of the Communist party in the Asian, mostly Moslem, areas of the Soviet Union, where the Afghanistan invasion and the upheavals in neighboring Iran had made an impact on the local intelligentsia and some party workers. The authorities sent extra security forces to Caucasus, where disorders had taken place. A mood of dissent and discontent was also present in the Ukraine and in the Baltic republics, where the local ethnic populations were being deeply affected by the Polish upheaval. Reliable dissident sources reported that mass searches took place in many cities of Estonia, particularly in the homes of families associated with the Baptist denomination, which had official status. The authorities confiscated copies of the Bible and other religious literature. Among those arrested was Endel Rose, who had advocated the restoration of traditional names to Estonian cities that had been renamed by the Russians.

Foreign Affairs

The Soviet Union maintained 11 divisions in Afghanistan, numbering about 110,000 men.

While contacts between the USSR and China seemed to increase, there was no change in Sino-Soviet relations; both countries maintained substantial armed forces on their common border.

Following the installation of the Reagan administration in Washington, very little remained of détente, although the Geneva disarmament talks continued. Moscow endeavored to convince the West European nations that it had no covert designs against them, and pointed to the economic benefits of strong trade relations. In the course of a visit to West Germany, Brezhnev assured his hosts of the continuing friendship of the Soviet Union, and of his willingness to negotiate with the West on peace and disarmament. At the same time, the Soviet Union obtained the right to have the Russian navy enter various harbors in Malta and Greece.

Relations with Israel

In his presentation to the Communist party congress, Brezhnev devoted considerable attention to the Middle East problem. He called for an international conference in which the Soviet Union, the United States, Israel, and the PLO would participate.

During the year Moscow received a great number of Arab leaders, including President Qaddafi of Libya, King Hussein of Jordan, Kuwaiti minister Sabah el Akhmed, and PLO chief Yasir Arafat. The Soviet Union maintained substantial arms deliveries to the Arab countries. After Israel annexed the Golan Heights, Moscow promised Syria an increase in various types of modern weaponry. According to reports, Soviet military advisors were stationed in Syria.

The Soviet authorities maintained a strong anti-Israeli policy, and anti-Zionist slogans and propaganda filled the pages of the press in Moscow and in the provincial cities. On January 5 *Izvestia* informed its readers that the Israelis were endeavoring to completely wipe out the Palestinian people. Horror stories about the lives of Jews who had left the Soviet Union for Israel were printed in many publications, including the Yiddish *Sovetish Heimland.*

There were sporadic contacts between the USSR and Israel. A Soviet delegation went to Israel at the invitation of the Israeli-Soviet Friendship Society to participate in a commemoration of the victory over fascism in the Second World War. Vladimir Karpov, secretary of the Writers Union of USSR and editor of *Novyi Mir,* headed the delegation, which also included Urii Mikheev, a journalist, and Jan Frenkel, a composer. Karpov's "A Voyage to Israel," in Yiddish translation, was issued as a supplement to *Sovetish Heimland.*

Genrikas Zimans, Jewish editor of *Communistas,* an important theoretical journal published in Lithuanian, participated as a friendly delegate in the congress of the Communist party of Israel, which took place in Haifa.

The Soviet Peace Committee invited a number of Israelis to visit the USSR, among them Knesset members Rabbi Menahem Hacohen and Ora Namir, Communist party members David Chinin and Selim Jubran, and Haika Grossman, a fighter in the Bialystok ghetto uprising. During his visit, Rabbi Hacohen chanted the *haftorah* at the synagogue in Leningrad.

JEWISH COMMUNITY

Demography

The 1979 official Soviet census put the Jewish population of the Soviet Union at about 1,810,000. A more accurate figure, however, would be approximately 2,620,000, constituting about one per cent of the total population of some 268,000,000. (See the discussion in the 1982 AJYB, p. 233.)

Emigration

According to official data, some 9,500 Jews left the USSR in 1981. This was about 80 per cent less than in 1979 (over 50,000) and around 55 per cent less than in 1980 (over 21,000). Since the beginning of Jewish emigration from the Soviet Union in 1970, approximately 256,000 Jews had left the country. One interpretation of the decline in emigration was that the Soviet authorities were sending a signal to the United States about the need for improved relations.

Candidates for emigration were required to receive a request for departure *(vyzov)* from a close family member residing in Israel. Of course, many Soviet Jews did not have relatives in Israel. Moreover, many *vyzovs* were not delivered by Soviet postal authorities. The Soviet agency entrusted with matters of emigration—the so-called OVIR—often disregarded applications to leave the country or took the position that particular applicants could not depart because they had a knowledge of state secrets.

Continuing the pattern of the last several years, most of the Soviet emigrants went to the West (U.S., Canada, etc.); a minority went to Israel. The per cent of those settling outside of Israel rose from 50 in 1977 to about 66 in 1980. This situation led to a split between the government of Israel and some American Jewish organizations. The former contended that the refusal of Soviet Jewish emigrants to go to Israel jeopardized the departure of other would-be emigrants. HIAS, in charge of immigrant operations from Vienna to the United States and other countries, affirmed the principle of freedom of choice. Toward the end of the year, under increasing pressure from the Israeli government, HIAS reversed itself and accepted on a trial basis (a three-month period) a plan that effectively curtailed the flow of emigrants to countries other than Israel.

Communal and Religious Life

There were no Jewish communal or social organizations in the Soviet Union. Around the legally-constituted congregations *(dvadtsatkas),* some 50 synagogues were functioning, in addition to private *minyonim.* Soviet officials reported that the synagogue in Odessa had been repaired and that a *sukkah* had been built in the synagogue compound. Boris Gram continued as chairman of the Moscow congregation; Arkadii Zitran was the chairman in Odessa. Both men were in their middle thirties.

There were very few rabbis. In Moscow the aged Rabbi Iakov Fishman and Rabbi Adolf Shayevich, a recent graduate of the Budapest Rabbinical Seminary, ministered to the needs of the congregants. The Moscow yeshiva founded by the late Rabbi Solomon Shliefer was not successful. *Soviet Life,* the foreign propaganda publication of the Soviet embassy in Washington, reported in October that the Moscow yeshiva had five students. It was obvious, however, that under present conditions, without an adequate staff, the yeshiva could not train rabbis.

There was no formal religious or secular Jewish education; *chedorim* and other Jewish schools were forbidden. A bat mitzvah ceremony performed by Ann Kogan in Leningrad represented a rare demonstration of Jewish identification. The ceremony took place at home in the company of friends and relatives of the girl.

Novosti, the Soviet press agency, reported that the Moscow synagogue baked 130 tons of *matzot* for Passover and that *matzo shmura* was also available. Rabbi Fishman stated that *matzot* were also baked in the provincial cities.

With the help of Rabbi Pinhas Teitz of Elizabeth, New Jersey, Soviet authorities permitted a group of Braslaver hasidim to visit the grave of the rabbi of Braslav in Uman (Ukraine).

Jews attached to their ethno-religious roots developed various forms of Jewish identification. For years Jewish men and women had been gathering in large numbers outside the synagogues in Moscow, Leningrad, and other cities during the high holy days, Simchat Torah, and Passover. Soviet official sources reported that in 1981 high holy day services were held in 92 synagogues—a figure that seemed highly exaggerated—and that 5,000 Jews attended the Moscow Choral Synagogue.

New and more sophisticated forms of Jewish self-expression were being developed; there were seminars dealing with Jewish subjects, Hebrew lessons, and lectures in Jewish history, thought, and literature. While most of the participants in these activities were would-be emigrants and "refuseniks," they had been joined of late by individuals who were simply interested in obtaining a Jewish education.

The paucity of open religious life in the Soviet Union was also characteristic of other religious groups—Christian, Moslem, etc. In the 1970's, there were only some 4,500 Russian Orthodox churches openly functioning throughout the USSR. However, the Soviet government had a special relationship with the Russian Orthodox denominations. The official magazine of the Moscow Patriarchate (No. 10, 1981) reported that a new building was put at the disposal of the publishing department of the church. The opening of the building was an official affair, with P. Makartsev, the vice president of the Council of Religious Affairs, in attendance. At the same time, such Christian dissidents as Vladimir Poresh, Aleksandr Ogorodnikov, Nikolaii Goretoi, Pavel Akhterov, Ivan Fedotov, and Vladimir Murashkin were arrested.

Antisemitism and Discrimination

Anti-Jewish feelings and overt antisemitism were characteristic of Soviet life. The authorities were returning to the old quota system practiced under the Tsarist regime. Higher technical schools in the Ukraine, for example, permitted only a five per cent Jewish student enrollment. Quota systems were applied in most Soviet enterprises, in academic degree-granting, and in bureaucratic advancement. Well-qualified Jews were often told by university administrators not to seek academic careers, since they had little chance of being accepted, or, if they were, of advancing. In the last decade more than 40 top mathematicians had left the Soviet Union because of official antisemitism in the universities. Apparently, the authorities were not concerned about a "brain drain"; Lev Pontriagin, a member of the Soviet Academy of Sciences, was said to have stated, "Jewish mathematics is bad mathematics. . . ."

Maxim Shostakovich, a conductor and the son of the celebrated composer, reported, after escaping from the USSR, that it was necessary to intervene with the authorities on the highest level in order to have a Jewish musician appointed to an orchestra position.

With few exceptions, Jews had disappeared from high party posts and leading positions in the government. Veniamin Dymshits was the deputy premier and a member of the central committee of the party. Other Jews holding membership in the central committee were Lev Volodarskii, head of the Soviet central statistical office, Georgii Tsukanov, an assistant to Brezhnev, and Georgii Arbatov. Lev Shapiro of Birobidzhan and Aleksandr Chakovskii, editor of *Literaturnaia Gazeta* (Moscow), were candidate-members.

As in Tsarist Russia, Soviet newspapers and periodicals were obsessed with things Jewish. In March the armed forces magazine carried an article by Vladimir Bolshakov, the notorious author of *Zionism in the Service of Anti-Communism,* arguing that American Zionists had taken control of Lockheed, General Dynamics, and other corporations linked to the Pentagon. Roman Brodsky, in *The Truth About Zionism,* argued in the same vein. The Kiev satirical weekly *Peretz* (No. 12) carried a Nazi-like cartoon denouncing international Zionism. In a movie based on Chekhov's story, "Step," Moiseii Moiseevich, the Jewish character, was presented in the most disgusting manner. Another film, *Zionist Street,* depicted the Israelis as engaged in the genocidal destruction of the Arabs. Vadim Kozhinov, a critic, in reviewing the poetry of Unna Moritz in *Den Poezii 1981,* took note of its "Jewish" character, and threw in a reference to Shylock for good measure.

Antisemitism was present in some *Samizdat* publications. *Mnogaia Leta* ("Many More Years"), edited by G. Shimanov and supposedly presenting a Christian point of view, fulminated against the Jews. In one article Shimanov argued that the well-known Moscow priest Father Aleksandr Men, a converted Jew, was a "Zionist agent" who had penetrated the Greek Orthodox church in Russia.

Jewish Resistance

Despite severe oppression, including lengthy sentences meted out to dissidents, Soviet Jews continued the struggle for emigration and national Jewish identity. Kim Fridman, a radio operator in Kiev who had been seeking to leave the Soviet Union for nearly a decade, was sentenced to a year in prison for "parasitism." Another

Jewish activist in Kiev, Vladimir Kisik, received a three-year sentence in a labor camp on a trumped-up charge of hooliganism. Stanislav Zubko received a four-year camp sentence. Still, a group of Kiev "refuseniks" sent a letter to the Soviet authorities indicating that they would begin a hunger strike if their exit visas were not forthcoming.

In Kharkov, Aleksandr Paritski was sentenced to three years forced labor. An engineer and researcher at the Ukrainian Academy of Science, he had taken a leading role in a Jewish studies program that was functioning in the city.

The authorities prevented Moscow Jews from celebrating Israel's independence day in the Ovrazhki forest, where gatherings had been held during the last few years. Nonetheless, some "refuseniks" marked the occasion at a meeting outside the city. Also in Moscow, the police stopped a demonstration on behalf of the prisoners of Zion, among whom were Anatoly Shcharansky, Ida Nudel, Iurii Fedorov, and Aleksei Murzhenko. The latter two individuals were participants in the celebrated Leningrad trial. A third participant, Josif Mendelevich, was released from prison in February.

In Kishinev (Bessarabia) 50 "refuseniks" organized a march to protest denial of their exit visas.

Judith Lerner, wife of the well-known "refusenik" scientist Aleksandr Lerner, passed away in July. The Lerners had been denied exit visas for nearly a decade.

The authorities continued their actions against Jewish studies seminars and the Hebrew teaching programs that had sprung up. Some 80 teachers of Hebrew were threatened by the police.

Culture

Despite the negative attitude of the authorities, some Jewish cultural activities were maintained in Moscow and other cities. Since there was no central communal organization, secular Jewish activities were focused around *Sovetish Heimland,* an official Yiddish language publication now in its 21st year of existence. The magazine strictly followed the Communist party line, and its editor, Aron Vergelis, attacked Israel at every opportunity. Over the years *Sovetish Heimland* had published the works of some 100 Yiddish writers and poets; 55 novels, 63 long poems, and 25 plays had appeared in its pages. A supplement to *Sovetish Heimland* (August, No. 8) contained a detailed bibliographical index covering the years 1961–1981. The index, however, omitted those Yiddish writers who had appeared in *Sovetish Heimland* but had subsequently gone to Israel.

Because there were no Yiddish schools in the Soviet Union, there was a serious shortage of professionally-trained personnel who could be employed in Yiddish journalism, editorial work, etc. To deal with this shortage, the Gorky Institute of Literature started a two-year course of study to train young students as Yiddish language editors, proofreaders, and translators. Among the teachers involved in the program were Rivka Rubin (Yiddish classics), Chaskl Zaen (Yiddish language),

Uran Guralnik (Yiddish and Russian literature), Muni Shulman (History of Soviet Yiddish literature), and Shmuel Gordon (History of Soviet Yiddish literature).

As far as could be ascertained, 12 books in the Yiddish language were available in 1981: *Der Lebn Geit Veiter* ("Life Goes On") by Yosef Burg; *Di Viner Karete* ("The Vienna Carriage") by Moishe Altman; *Der Morgenshtern* ("The Morning Star") by Avrom Gontar; *Menchn oif der Milkhome* ("Men in the War") by David Dragunskii; *Baginen* ("At Dawn") by Shmuel Helmond; *Di Zeit* ("Times") by Aron Vergelis; *Mai in Kazan* ("May in Kazan") by Boris Mogilner; *Nochemke Esreg* by Aleksandr Lizan; *Zunike Shtamen* (poems) by Pinie Kiritchanskii; *Nechtn un Haint* ("Yesterday and Today") by Iasha Rubian; *Yiddishe Avtonome Gegent* ("Jewish Autonomous Region"), issued in Chabarovsk; and *Shtaplen* ("Steps") by Hersh Remenik. Between 1948 and 1981 a total of 90 Yiddish books, an average of some three a year, had been published in the USSR. This compared with 500–600 volumes a year allotted to some national groups in Siberia and other parts of Asia. It should be noted that in the 1979 census 14.2 per cent of the Jews in the RSFSR (Russia) listed Yiddish as their native language.

Soviet customs agents, checking the foreign books brought to the third Moscow International Book Fair, seized, among other volumes, the 1981 *American Jewish Year Book* and the youth edition of Abba Eban's *History of the Jews*.

In February and June *Sovetish Heimland* carried scholarly articles by the well-known semitics scholar Leib Wilsker, devoted to Jehuda Halevi and Saadia Gaon. Wilsker's collection of pieces on Russian Jewish history appeared in a supplement to *Sovetish Heimland* in September.

The Yiddish Musical Chamber Theater of Birobidzhan, the only legitimate Yiddish theatrical group in the Soviet Union, gave many performances in Baku (Azerbeidzhan). Freilachs, a newly-created amateur ensemble, performed in Tashkent, Bratsk, Novosibirsk, and Irkutsk. The Moscow Yiddish Drama Ensemble premiered Sholem Aleichem's *Blonzhende Shtern* ("The Straying Stars"). The Vilno Yiddish Folk Theater maintained its activities and was preparing a recording of songs at the Moscow Melodia Studio. Its new presentation, *Chelmer Chachomim* ("The Sages of Chelm"), directed by E. Khersonskii, was enthusiastically received. The Vilno group celebrated its 25th anniversary with a production of *L'Haim* ("To Life"). The Kovno Yiddish Folk Theater presented its programs in many cities. Sofia Saitan, a well-known Jewish actress, was awarded the title of "Honored Artist" of the RSFSR. Her recordings of Yiddish and Russian material had substantial success among the art-loving public.

In April and May there was a large exhibition of paintings by the late Moscow Jewish artist Meir Axelrod (1902–1970) at the Tbilisi State Museum. A catalogue of Axelrod's works was issued in the Georgian language, and posters pointed out the "national Jewish character" of his art.

An interesting aspect of Jewish cultural life was underground music. A number of composers, including Sergeii Slowinskii and Maks Goldin, wrote Jewish music that was either excluded from the approved repertoire or presented under a neutral title. Some of this music had recently been brought to Israel.

Moscow Television devoted part of its regular evening broadcast "Goodnight Children" to the songs of the Yiddish poet Shika Driz.

Birobidzhan

There were no changes in the Jewish autonomous region. The Jewish population was about 10,000, with some 13 per cent of the Jews listing Yiddish as their native language. There were reports, particularly in the Russian emigré press, that the presidium of the Supreme Soviet had abolished five autonomous regions, including Birobidzhan, in December. However, the Soviet press continued to refer to the Jewish autonomous region. A Jewish library was functioning and the *Birobidzhaner Stern* continued to appear. There were also Yiddish radio broadcasts. All in all, it was clear that Birobidzhan, which had important strategic value and a small Jewish population, was being gradually Russified.

Holocaust

In Kiev, in September, five Jews—Mikhail Elman, Pavel Astrakhan, Aleksandr Lorenson, Svetlana Efimova, and Vladimir Tereshchenko—were sentenced to 10 to 15 days in prison for trying to commemorate the 40th anniversary of the Nazi massacre at Babi Yar. In Moscow, in May, the KGB prevented a large group of Jews from commemorating the Holocaust. However, commemorative events took place in smaller cities, sometimes with the participation of local officials.

In August the "liberal" *Novyi Mir* carried a long article by the well-known Soviet translator of German poetry Lev Ginsburg, in which he described Jewish suffering under the Nazis, particularly in the Riga ghetto.

Personalia

Zinovii Kaminskii, a well-known Yiddish actor, died in Moscow at the age of 69. Moishe Altman, a veteran Yiddish writer, died in Czernovitz at the age of 91. Avrom Gontar, a Yiddish writer, died at the age of 73. Gontar was an editor of Jewish Anti-Fascist Committee publications in Moscow during the Second World War. Hersh Remenik, a Yiddish writer and critic, died at the age of 75. Gershon Kravtsov, a painter and illustrator, died at the age of 75. Aleksandra Azarch, a well-known actress and pedagogue, died in Moscow at the age of 88. Azarch was a close collaborator of the murdered Jewish actor and director Shlome Mikhoels. Yuri Trifonov, an important Soviet writer who remained in Russia despite the fact that his works were not always considered acceptable by the authorities, died at the age of 55. Anatolii Rybakov, author of *Heavy Sand,* a novel dealing sympathetically with the Jewish plight during the Nazi period, spoke at Trifonov's funeral, alluding to the tragedies of Russian life under Stalin.

LEON SHAPIRO

Soviet Bloc Nations

Introduction

THE SOVIET UNION WAS UNHAPPY with the continuing process of change taking place in its satellite empire, fearing that it would result in a loss of control over the East European Communist regimes. While Moscow accepted certain deviations in the economic program of Hungary, as well as an independent foreign policy in Rumania, it viewed the Solidarity rebellion in Poland as a "creeping counterrevolution" promoted by capitalist circles of the West. The Kremlin bosses hinted that if "law and order" were not reestablished in Poland, they might intervene directly. In the meantime, the Soviet Union was busy dealing with its own problems—falling production, a lack of food, and heavy fighting in Afghanistan.

Poland

The social and political upheaval that had begun in August 1980 continued unabated, with an increasingly large number of Communist party members joining the opposition and clamoring for reform; party membership dropped from 3,200,000 to some 2,900,000. In April 1981 the central committee of the PPZR (Communist party) ousted Joseph Pinkowski, a former prime minister, and Emil Wojtaszek, who was in charge of foreign affairs, from the politburo. Two former ministers in Edward Gierek's regime committed suicide: Jerzy Olszewski, minister of chemical industry, and Edward Barszcz, minister of construction. In the course of a party congress held in Warsaw in July 1981, Gierek himself was expelled from the party. The congress represented a watershed in post-World War II Poland, in that, for the first time, the delegates were elected by secret ballot.

In addition to Solidarity, the workers' movement headed by Lech Walesa, a union of independent peasants was established under the leadership of Jan Kulaj. The two movements together constituted a substantial force for political and social change in Poland. The Polish church, under the late Stefan Cardinal Wyshynski, and his successor, Archbishop Joseph Glemp of Gniezno and Warsaw and primate of Poland, played an important advisory role to Solidarity and the peasants' union.

The Polish situation greatly worried the Soviet Union. Moscow feared that the internal reforms that had been introduced in Poland might spread to other countries, thus endangering its rigid system of alliances and military pacts. Radio Moscow asserted that Solidarity "wants to declare war on the people's power." The Soviet press pointed to a "mass campaign by the Zionists" to destroy socialist Poland.

223

By autumn 1981 it had become clear that the Polish authorities and the elements around Solidarity were on a collision course, involving opposing ideas about the very structure and character of the state. In October, after being in office for about one year, Stanislaw Kania, in an unprecedented move, was replaced as secretary-general of the party by General Wojciech Jaruzelski, the first professional military man to be placed at the top of a Communist regime. Jaruzelski had to grapple not only with the hopeless state of the Polish economy, but also with the increasingly menacing attitude of the Kremlin. In order to quiet Soviet fears, the Committee for Self-Defense (KOR), which had been active in the launching of Solidarity, disbanded itself in Gdansk on September 28; this was announced to the public by KOR's elderly leader, Edward Lipinski. Solidarity leaders meeting in Gdansk suggested that a referendum be made on the form of the government in Poland and the nature of the Polish-Soviet relationship.

On December 13, 1981 Jaruzelski, using the army and the special police, proceeded with what was in fact a coup d'etat, placing the country under martial law. The newly-established Martial Council for National Redemption drastically restricted civil rights and suspended Solidarity and other similar groups. Among the people taken into custody were Lech Walesa, Committee for Social Self-Defense organizers Jan Kuron and Adam Michnik, Edward Gierek, former prime ministers Piotr Jaroszewicz and Edward Babiuch, and former politburo member Jerzy Lukasziewicz. Official newspapers attacked Michnik and Kuron in particular, pointing out their Jewish origin. It was clear that Jaruzelski's actions had the approval of the Kremlin leadership.

As the end of the year approached, there were strikes, confrontations, and violence in Poland. Reliable sources put the number of those arrested at over 5,000. In reaction to the repression, the United States government decided to apply sanctions against both the USSR and Poland. However, the United States permitted Poland to defer payment of 90 million dollars due on the Polish debt, which totalled about 26 billion dollars.

JEWISH COMMUNITY

The upheaval in Polish society had a considerable impact on the small community of about 6,000 Jews who identified with Jewish life. (It was estimated that another 1,500–2,000 Jews had "passed" into the surrounding population through intermarriage and conversion.) There was an effort to revive and intensify the limited activities conducted by small Jewish clubs in various cities. In 1981, according to official reports, Jewish activities of various sorts (lectures, dramatic presentations, song evenings) numbered 27 in Wroclaw, 12 in Krakow, 26 in Katowice, 13 in Lodz, 12 in Gliwice, 21 in Zary, 24 in Lignice, 10 in Szczecin, 37 in Dzierzoniow, four in Warsaw, 26 in Bielosko-Biala, eight in Lublin, and seven in Walbrzych. Indicative of the changing times was the fact that the Jewish clubs commemorated the 120th anniversary of the birth of the great Jewish historian Simon Dubnow.

The Jewish Historical Institute maintained its research activities under the direction of Maurycy Horn; its library and museum were open to interested scholars. Some of the Institute's projects were supported by the Memorial Foundation for Jewish Culture based in New York. After a lengthy interval, the *Bleter far Geschichte* (vol. XIX) reappeared with articles devoted to Jewish history. The State Yiddish Theater performed in Zagreb (Yugoslavia), Vienna (Austria), and various cities in Israel. A group of Hebrew writers from Israel, including Benzion Tomer, Gabriel Maked, Haim Gury, and Debora Emer, visited Poland at the invitation of the Polish Writers Union and the Janusz Korczak Society.

In the course of the year, the Jewish Cultural and Social Union, which conducted all secular Jewish activities, organized memorial meetings for the victims of Maidanek and Auschwitz; the group also commemorated the 38th anniversary of the Warsaw ghetto revolt. An official representative of the Communist party, Stanislaw Kociolek, participated in the proceedings. Edward Reiber was the president of the Jewish Cultural and Social Union, but he was in poor health, and the organization's activities were directed by Abraham Kwaterko, the secretary. Other Jewish activists were Shmuel Tenenblat, editor of *Folks-szytme* and vice-president of the Union; Szymon Szurmiej, the director of the Yiddish State Theater; and Joseph Gitler-Barski, who dealt with research and documentation.

Jewish religious life continued to deteriorate. There were no rabbis in Poland, nor was there any religious education for children. Organized prayer services were few and far between. According to the official community calendar, there were 19 religious congregations in Warsaw, Katowice, Krakow, Lodz, Lublin, Wroclaw, and other cities. The Union of Religious Congregations provided over 50,000 kosher meals to interested individuals. The president of the Union, Moses Finkelsztein was awarded a Golden Cross of Merit by the government on the occasion of his 70th birthday.

The Jewish Cultural and Social Union and the Union of Religious Congregations had begun to develop closer ties, with Moses Finkelsztein participating in the activities of both organizations. With the support of the government, a committee was formed to take care of Warsaw's Jewish cemetery, which was in a very poor state. Some funds had already been provided by the government, but they were insufficient for the purpose. The Jewish Cultural and Social Union participated in a meeting of the World Jewish Congress, and detailed reports about the proceedings were printed in *Folks-sztyme*.

In the spring Warsaw University and the Union of American Hebrew Congregations signed an agreement whereby important archival documents dealing with Jewish life in Poland would be made available to American scholars. The agreement also covered joint research to be undertaken in certain areas.

In July 1981 an American Jewish Joint Distribution Committee (JDC) delegation visited Warsaw. Included in the group were JDC president Henri Taub, executive vice-president Ralf Goldman, and JDC's European representative Akiva Kahane. The delegation was received by Jerzy Kubelski, minister of religious affairs. The leaders of the Jewish community suggested that the JDC renew its activities in Poland. A special coordinating committee of the Jewish Cultural and Social Union and of the Union of Religious Congregations was established to oversee the distribution of aid.

Antisemitism remained a very potent force in Poland. During the months of the political spring, crude anti-Jewish propaganda, disseminated by Grunwald, a veterans group, appeared in Warsaw and other cities. Not only was Grunwald's material openly distributed, it was endorsed by official circles. A Grunwald meeting was shown on television, and the bulletin of the Warsaw Communist party sympathetically reported the proceedings. A delegation of the Jewish Cultural and Social Union went to see Stanislaw Demianuk, secretary of the central committee of the party, demanding that the anti-Jewish actions of Grunwald be stopped, and that the Union's protest against antisemitism be made known through the press. Demianuk stated that "antisemitism has no place in Poland." However, little was done to suppress the anti-Jewish militants of the right.

Some anti-Jewish sentiments also surfaced in the Solidarity movement. Marian Jurczyk, the head of the Szczecin trade union, declared in a speech that "the government is filled with Jews who have changed their names to conceal their real identities. . . ." This was given as a reason why the government had to be changed. On the other hand, Solidarity's official publications consistently protested against acts of anti-Jewish hooliganism that took place in various cities.

Interestingly, the Jewish Cultural and Social Union, referred publicly, for the first time, to the anti-Jewish pogrom which had taken place in Kieltz in July 1946. The Union warned that strict measures had to be taken to prevent a repetition of that tragedy.

Joel Lazebnik, an old Communist stalwart and one of the leading figures in the Jewish Cultural and Social Union, died away on September 14, 1981.

Rumania

Nicolae Ceausescu, head of the Communist party and president of the state, maintained rigid political control over Rumania. At the same time, he stressed the continuity of national history as a basis for political and social development in the country. In accordance with this doctrine of "national Communism," Ceausescu dissented from Soviet foreign policy and rejected a number of Moscow's significant moves. The Rumanian government continued to maintain close relations with Israel, notwithstanding its support for some Arab demands.

Although Rumania was a member of the Council of Mutual Economic Assistance of the Soviet Bloc, it maintained close relations with the United States, which accorded it important trade concessions as a "most favored nation." This status was conditional on the maintenance of a flexible emigration policy, whereby individuals desiring to leave the country could do so without undue difficulty. Compliance with this principle was reviewed annually by the United States Congress. While there were some problems, Rumania was thought to be basically living up to its commitments. According to official sources, 1,119 people left Rumania in 1980 and 1,067 in 1981.

JEWISH COMMUNITY

Antisemitism was outlawed, and the authorities took whatever steps were necessary to prevent its occurrence. President Ceausescu, in a speech to a workers conference, condemned an antisemitic pamphlet that had been distributed in Bucharest. (It was claimed that the material had been smuggled into Rumania from abroad by fascist groups.) Ceausescu's remarks were reported in the press and on radio and television.

While Rumanian Jews enjoyed all the religious and social rights accorded other minorities, the small community of about 37,000 Jews continued to decline. Many active Jews had left the country, and the younger generation showed less interest in things Jewish. Jewish activities were coordinated by the Federation of Jewish Communities, under the chairmanship of Rabbi Moses Rosen, who was also chief rabbi; Emil Schechter was general secretary of the Federation. Under difficult conditions, Rabbi Rosen continued to provide dynamic leadership, traveling throughout the country to visit local communities. Among the active leaders of Rumanian Jewry were Theodor Blumenfeld, president of the Jewish community of Bucharest; Simion Kaufman, president of the community in Iasi; Paul Friedlander, president of the community in Timisoara; Julius Wenger, president of the community in Bacou; and Ivan Koves, president of the community in Brasov. The very small rabbinical corps included, in addition to Rabbi Rosen, rabbis Itschak Meir Marilus, Ernest Neiman, Carol Jolesz, and Srul Moscovici. Professor Chaim Rimer was editor of the *Revista Culturui Mosaic,* a semimonthly periodical published by the Federation in Hebrew, Yiddish, and Rumanian. The *Revista* devoted part of its content to rabbinic sources and ancient Jewish history, and the remainder to matters of current Jewish interest.

The Federation encompassed 68 Jewish communities and 27 smaller units. It was responsible for 118 synagogues, 45 of which held daily services, while 73 were open only on the Sabbath and holidays. There were talmud torahs and courses for young people in 23 communities. Iasi, Bucharest, and Brasov had small communal orchestras; 16 synagogues maintained choirs. Some of the communities also arranged cultural programs. In Bucharest there were weekly gatherings to discuss topical Jewish subjects. A memorial meeting for the victims of the Holocaust was held in the Bucharest Choral Synagogue. *Revista's* 25th anniversary was celebrated by the Federation, with many Jewish leaders from abroad sending greetings. Among those saluting the Rumanian Jewish community on the occasion were Yitzhak Navon, president of Israel; Zevulun Hammer, Israel's minister of education; Edgar Bronfman, head of the World Jewish Congress; Arie Dulchin, chairman of the Jewish Agency; Henri Taub, president of JDC; and the Lubavitcher Rebbe.

Collective *sedorim* were held in 30 communities, and 120,000 kg. of *matzot* and matzah-meal were distributed throughout the country. It was estimated that some 12,000 individuals participated in Hanukkah and Purim festivities. Eleven kosher canteens provided 2,500 dinners daily, either gratis or for a token payment. Kosher meat was generally available.

A difficult problem was the maintenance of Jewish cemeteries in places where Jewish communities no longer existed. In the last five years the fences surrounding 49 such cemeteries had been repaired.

The Federation's welfare program assisted 6,700 individuals, most of them senior citizens or invalids. Some 7,160 clothing packages and 46,000 food parcels were distributed among the needy. Home help was provided to 672 invalids. Rest homes offering kosher food were operated in the summer in Eforie Nord, Borsec, and Christian (Brasov). The Federation's medical center was directed by Arthur Meerson.

Part of the Federation's budget was covered by the state, which allocated money for the salaries of the clergy and the administrative personnel. The Federation's social welfare activities were funded by the JDC, while its cultural activities were financed by the New York-based Memorial Foundation for Jewish Culture.

The Rumanian Jewish community maintained close contact with Jews abroad. The Federation was affiliated with the World Jewish Congress, and participated in various Jewish projects of a general character. Rabbi Rosen went to Israel in December 1980 to attend the Labor party congress. In January 1981 he, together with Amalia Rosen and Emil Schechter, participated in the plenary meeting of the World Jewish Congress in Jerusalem; Rabbi Rosen was elected to the governing body of the organization. Rosen also participated in the work of a special committee of the Memorial Foundation for Jewish Culture that met in Paris, under the chairmanship of Nahum Goldmann.

Many prominent guests visited Bucharest, among them Nisan Harpaz, secretary of the Workers' Council of Jerusalem; Rabbi Arthur Schneier, president of the Appeal of Conscience Foundation of New York; and Jack Spitzer, president of B'nai B'rith. The latter two men were received by President Ceausescu.

In addition to the activities conducted by the Federation, there was an active secular Jewish sector, including the well-known State Yiddish Theater and a small Yiddish publication program.

Bulgaria

At age 70, Todor Zhivkov continued to serve as first secretary of the Communist party, a position that he had initially assumed in 1954. Bulgaria was the most loyal member of the Soviet empire, following Moscow's lead not only in the area of foreign policy, but also in the application of strict totalitarian rule at home. Like Moscow, Bulgaria was strongly hostile to Israel; it had no diplomatic relations with the Jewish state. Attacks on Zionism in Sofia resembled similar outbursts in Moscow.

JEWISH COMMUNITY

There were around 7,000 Jews in Bulgaria. It was likely that some Jews had "passed" into the general population, since Bulgarian Jewry as a whole was highly assimilated. Intermarriage was widespread; few Jews continued to speak Ladino. Jews were well represented in the universities: Angel Chaim Astrug held a chair in the Academy of Medicine; Elieser Iakov Gershonov was the director of the ministry of electronics; and Moritz Albert Iomtov was a faculty member of the Institute of Parasitology. Two Jews, Ruben Avramov Levi and David Solomon Elasar, were members of Parliament as well as the central committee of the Bulgarian Communist party. Elasar was also director of the Institute of Party History. Another member of Parliament was Iosif Astrukov, chairman of the secular Jewish Social, Cultural, and Educational Organization of Bulgaria. Other Jewish activists included David Vidas, Baruch Shamliev, Isa Beracha, Moise Pasi, Armand Baruch, Iako Molchov, Salvador Israel, Albert Dekalo, Iosif Baruch, Sarina Pencheva, Robert Beracha, Solomon Levi, and Moise Benaroia.

The Jewish Social, Cultural, and Educational Organization, which was centered in Sofia, had branches in many provincial cities, including Burgas, Plevni, Yambol, and Varna. The Organization conducted a program of lectures, concerts, and meetings that was largely geared to the propaganda efforts of the state. Some of the lectures, however, dealt with Jewish writers such as Isaac Babel and Sholom Aleichem. There were no Jewish educational programs for children, either secular or religious.

The Jewish Social, Cultural, and Educational Organization published *Evreiski Vesti* ("Jewish News"), a Communist party organ that appeared biweekly. This newspaper carried some material from *Sovetish Heimland* as well as from the Jewish press in other countries of the Soviet Bloc. The Organization also published *Godishnik*, a yearbook; volume 15 appeared in 1980. *Godishnik's* editor-in-chief was David Benvenisti; the editorial board included David Cohen, Jana Molhova, Israel Mayer, Isac Moscona, Iosif Conforti, Clara Pincus, Mancho Rachamimov, Renata Nathan, Salvador Israel, and Solomon Levi. Among other things, the 1980 issue contained indices to *Evreiski Vesti* (1944–1976) and *Godishnik* (1966–1980). While *Godishnik* was obviously a Communist publication, some of the material dealt with the history of Bulgarian Jews, and was thus useful to researchers.

Jewish religious life in Bulgaria continued to deteriorate. There were no qualified rabbis and few religious marriages. There were great difficulties in obtaining kosher meat and other kosher products. The government, however, did allocate a subsidy for synagogue maintenance and the salary of a cantor. It also financed the reconstruction of old buildings, including the Sofia synagogue, which was badly damaged by an earthquake in 1977.

There was no open antisemitism. The authorities paid tribute to Jewish participants in the resistance to the Nazis; there were memorials throughout the country honoring Jewish war heroes. From time to time, Jewish writers, artists, and musicians were awarded special medals and distinctions. Alexis Weissenberg, a worldrenowned pianist who was born in Sofia, was given the title, "People's Artist." Also awarded the title "People's Artist" were violinist Dina Shnaiderman and singers Mati Pinkas and Yulia Winer.

Since the Jewish Social, Cultural, and Educational Organization rejected all ties to Jewish organizations abroad, the Bulgarian Jewish community was totally isolated from world Jewry.

LEON SHAPIRO

Israel

In 1981 THE LIKUD REPEATED its election victory of four years earlier, demonstrating that a significant shift in the Israeli polity had indeed occurred. The year also witnessed events of far-reaching import in the security sphere, notably the air force's destruction of an Iraqi nuclear reactor and a "mini-war" waged across the Lebanese border which was terminated by a fragile cease-fire. In Judea and Samaria, Jewish settlement activity continued unabated, and plans were announced for a "civilian administration." Israeli law was applied to the Golan Heights. Israel's efforts to achieve harmonious relations with the new administration in Washington were set back by its actions in Iraq, Lebanon, and with respect to the Golan Heights. Relations with Western Europe, however, were a bit smoother. Normalization with Egypt went on uninterrupted, though the autonomy talks remained largely moribund. The inflation rate, while still among the world's highest, fell by nearly one-third. In an Independence Day interview, President Yitzhak Navon perhaps summed up what many Israelis felt when he asserted that the quality of life in the country would have to improve if Israel wished to attract Western immigrants and prevent its own citizens from leaving. "I can't predict if it will improve," he said, "but it must—and it must start tomorrow."

The Elections

Throughout 1980 the government of Menachem Begin had sustained a series of political blows, and as that year ended it had reached a point where it could barely carry on. (For the background, see AJYB, Vol. 82, 1982, pp. 255–256.) On January 11, 1981 the catalytic act occurred—the resignation of Finance Minister Yigael Hurvitz. He was protesting the cabinet's decision to implement the recommendations of a public committee on the status of the teaching profession. Hurvitz argued that the salary increases called for in the report would encourage a spate of similar demands from other sectors, thus generating even higher inflation. Late in January, Yoram Aridor (Herut)—who had been appointed communication minister after Yitzhak Modai, minister of energy and communications, relinquished the latter portfolio in December 1980—was named to succeed Hurvitz as finance minister.

As Hurvitz resigned not only from the cabinet but also from the Likud, taking two of his Rafi colleagues with him, the Likud was now left with only 39 members in the Knesset and the coalition with 58, though it managed to scrape through several votes of confidence with the aid of some of the defectors. For some time the opposition had been calling for fresh elections, with signs of response even from coalition quarters. Prime Minister Begin now took the initiative and the cabinet sponsored a bill for the holding of a general election on July 7. The parties ultimately agreed on June 30, four-and-a-half months before the statutory date, and the Knesset passed the necessary legislation early in February.

Meanwhile there had been other shifts on the political scene. Deputy Prime Minister Yigael Yadin announced on February 18 that he would be leaving political life when the term of the Knesset expired, and that his party, the Democratic Movement—which had aroused such great hopes upon its formation four years earlier (see AJYB, Vol. 78, 1978, p. 474; Vol. 79, 1979, pp. 261–268)—was to be officially dissolved. The formal act of dissolution followed two weeks later.

This apparent vacuum at the center of the Israeli political spectrum did not remain empty for long. On April 4 Moshe Dayan officially announced the formation of a new party, Telem (Hebrew acronym for State Renewal Movement), under his leadership. Early polls indicated that a list headed by Dayan might win as many as 19 seats, thus harming the Labor party, but the new party's prospects soon dwindled to as few as four.

The polls were very flattering to the Labor party in the waning days of the first Begin government. As late as February polls showed Labor winning 58 seats to the Likud's 20, and Labor party chairman Shimon Peres enjoying a personal seven per cent lead over Begin as the person best suited to be the country's next prime minister. These polls, however, were conducted soon after Labor's widely covered convention, with its built-in drama of Shimon Peres' election as party leader against the challenge of Yitzhak Rabin (see AJYB, Vol. 82, 1982, pp. 256–257). From that point on—indeed, virtually from the moment new elections moved from the realm of possibility to that of actuality—Labor's fortunes began to decline.

One major cause of the decline was Shimon Peres' evident inability to translate his sweeping convention victory into genuine party and national leadership. Party morale suffered a setback when, in mid-March, Bank Hapoalim chairman Yaacov Levinson, who had been widely touted as Labor's candidate for finance minister, was unable to reach agreement with Peres on the powers that would be granted him to carry out his economic policy. Peres continued to make unfavorable headlines that month in the wake of a report that he had met secretly with Morocco's King Hassan II and with a brother of Jordan's King Hussein. Cabinet ministers charged that Peres had undermined Israel's bargaining position by indicating that a Labor government under his leadership would be more willing than a Likud-led government to make concessions in the peace negotiations. Internal tension in the Labor party intensified when Haim Bar-Lev, the secretary-general, stated that he would choose to stay out of a Labor government altogether if he did not receive the defense portfolio—this in the wake of a mounting campaign by Yitzhak Rabin's supporters to have him named to that post. As Labor's lead in the polls began to shrink (a late

March survey showed it ahead of the Likud by 45 seats to 33) a Jerusalem *Post* editorial seemed to catch the prevailing mood in the party: "While the polls flash their warning signals, the party bigwigs sit around, happily quarreling over the division of the spoils of an imagined triumph."

Triumph there undoubtedly was in the Histadrut elections, held on April 7, with Labor increasing its share of the vote by about four per cent over 1977 (see below for details). However, the Likud, too, took heart from the results. Its approximately 27 per cent of the vote was virtually the same as its 1977 showing—allaying the Likud leaders' major fear, that it would suffer because of its socio-economic record since taking office. The Likud's traditional grassroots support in the development towns and among the urban disadvantaged was, it appeared, holding fast. It was also pointed out that the turnout had been low—56.7 per cent—and that Histadrut members accounted for only 65 per cent of the general electorate.

Not even Peres' naming of his shadow cabinet immediately after the Histadrut election enabled Labor to regain its momentum. The nominees themselves—among others, Abba Eban as shadow foreign minister, Haim Bar-Lev as candidate for defense minister, and Tel Aviv University president Haim Ben-Shahar for the finance portfolio—failed to generate any great excitement among the public. A similar reaction greeted the Alignment's Knesset list, which was announced in early May. For the most part, the list was comprised of long-familiar names. The only surprise was the appearance of MK Shoshana Arbeli-Almoslino in the number two slot, demoting Abba Eban to third place. Indeed, the chief reasons adduced by observers for Arbeli-Almoslino's preeminent position pointed directly to the areas of Alignment weakness and Likud strength. Iraqi-born, she was a representative of the "oriental" Jews (among whom the Likud was very strong). She was also known as a hawk on foreign affairs—a stance which would enable the party to dispel somewhat its dovish image. The Alignment was to find, however, that it could not play on the Likud's field.

Labor's decline was by no means entirely self-generated. Heartened by the Histadrut poll, the Likud, and Menachem Begin in particular, seemed to take a new lease on life. The Likud ran a three-pronged campaign. Agriculture Minister Ariel Sharon launched a program that eventually brought some 300,000 Israelis to visit Jewish settlements in Judea and Samaria. By stressing its own settlement activities, the Likud was seeking to deprive Labor of its image as the paramount settler and builder of the land. The second thrust of the Likud's campaign was more indirect in nature. Shortly after his appointment as finance minister, Yoram Aridor launched a policy which he termed "proper economics," although others claimed it was "election economics." Its main features were tax reductions on consumer durables, chiefly color television sets and automobiles, along with price freezes, greater government subsidies to prevent price rises, and elements of income tax reform. The results were a buying spree by the public on the one hand and, on the other, a May inflation rate of 3.3 per cent, one of the lowest in months—which, moreover, was announced on June 15, just two weeks before the election.

The third, and most important, element in the Likud's campaign and subsequent victory was Prime Minister Begin himself. Seemingly downcast, dispirited, and depressed throughout 1980 and the first part of 1981, as his government appeared to have lost favor with the public, Begin soon regained his ebullience and demonstrated that he had lost none of his flair for crowd-pleasing rhetorical flourishes. Formally re-elected Herut leader at the party's convention on May 11—by which time the polls showed the Alignment and the Likud running neck-and-neck— Begin proceeded to take his campaign to the people.

One of the most contentious aspects of the election campaign was the acute polarization among the Israeli public between Sephardi and Ashkenazi Jews, the former being in the main identified with the Likud and the latter with the Alignment. However, the chief victim of this phenomenon was probably the National Religious party. During the first part of 1981, Religious Affairs Minister Aharon Abuhatzeira of the NRP was on trial in connection with alleged irregularities in his ministry (see also AJYB, Vol. 82, 1982, p. 256). Abuhatzeira, along with his aide at the ministry and two religious leaders in Bnei Brak who were charged with complicity, pleaded not guilty as the court proceedings opened on February 3. During the trial the credibility of the chief prosecution witness, a former Bnei Brak mayor who had been promised immunity for turning state's evidence, was severely shaken in cross-examination. On May 24 Abuhatzeira and the other defendants were found not guilty on all counts. Two of the judges held, however, that there was a "heavy suspicion" as to the culpability of the minister and his aides on one of the charges, and the court was severely critical of the "extremely low moral standards" revealed, by Abuhatzeira's own admission, in allocating public funds to religious institutions on the basis of political criteria. While the trial was still in progress, Attorney General Yitzhak Zamir submitted to the Knesset a second set of charges against Abuhatzeira, alleging that he had misappropriated public funds during the period that he was mayor of Ramleh. After a series of delays, the Knesset in mid-May voted to lift his immunity so he could stand trial on the new charges. The actual proceedings, however, were postponed until after the elections. (Following the high court of justice's rejection of various legal maneuvers by the defense, which sought to have the minister's immunity restored because he had been re-elected to a new Knesset, the second trial opened on November 22, with Abuhatzeira pleading not guilty.)

Riding the crest of his acquittal and buoyed by the enthusiastic support of the Moroccan community in general and of the NRP's Sephardi members in particular, Abuhatzeira now demanded that the party revise its Knesset list to include greater Sephardi representation. On May 25, the day after his acquittal and the final day for submitting party slates for the elections, Abuhatzeira announced that he was breaking with the NRP to form his own independent Sephardi party, Tami (Hebrew acronym for Movement for Jewish Tradition). Joining Tami—which gained the blessing and financial support of Nessim Gaon, a resident of Switzerland and the chairman of the World Sephardi Federation—were Aharon Uzan, a former agriculture minister in the last Labor government, and Benzion Rubin, an NRP MK.

As the campaign proceeded, its tone became increasingly rancorous. Violence erupted on an unprecedented scale. With tension in the country already running high because of defense and foreign affairs developments—the missile crisis in Lebanon and the bombing of the Iraqi reactor, as well as Begin's *ad hominem* attacks on West German Chancellor Helmut Schmidt and on U.S. Secretary of Defense Caspar Weinberger, all of which were played up prominently in the Likud's campaign, along with events such as the Begin-Sadat summit meeting on June 4 and the ceremony inaugurating the Mediterranean-Dead Sea canal project (see the relevant sections below for details)—and the polls showing new Likud gains after every tough Begin pronouncement, thus encouraging even more outspoken declarations, the crowds at mass election rallies grew increasingly restive. On June 14 Peres was pelted with garbage by groups of vociferous Likud supporters in Petah Tikva. A few days later Peres and Rabin had to be escorted to their cars when they were mobbed following an election assembly in Jerusalem. A Labor party branch office in Tel Aviv was fire-bombed. Cars bearing Alignment stickers had their tires slashed and their windshields shattered. On the other side, an anonymous bomb threat was phoned in to the Herut building in Tel Aviv.

About two weeks before the election Prime Minister Begin appealed to all to show tolerance and "refrain from disrupting election meetings for any reason, regardless of the provocation." For his part, Peres accused Begin of "inciting" the violence that was marring Labor election rallies by his "inflammatory" rhetoric against the opposition and by intimating that anyone who did not back Begin to the hilt was a subversive. By election eve the police had arrested 157 persons suspected of having committed 171 election-related offenses.

The small parties, which made efforts to run on substantive issues, were overwhelmed by the intensity of the Likud-Alignment struggle. The National Religious party found itself with a greatly reduced constituency, not only due to the Abuhatzeira affair, but also because its evident vacillation on the issue of the administered areas led many of its former backers to turn to the Likud or to Tehiya (Renaissance). The latter party, formed by Likud dissidents in the wake of the Camp David accords (see AJYB, Vol. 81, 1981, p. 266), had as its main plank a call to retain all the territories; it opposed Israel's withdrawal from Sinai as stipulated in the peace treaty with Egypt. On the other side of the political spectrum, Hadash (Front for Democracy, Peace, and Equality), whose main support came from the Arab population, and Sheli (Peace and Equality for Israel) urged the establishment of a Palestinian state and called for withdrawal to the 1967 lines within the framework of a peace settlement. The left-of-center Citizens' Rights Movement, joined by a large bloc from the Peace Now group, advocated reforms in various spheres, urging particularly a total separation of religion and state. Ideologically not far removed from them was the Shinui (Change) party, composed of former members of Yigael Yadin's Democratic Movement for Change; indeed, their identification by the public with Yadin's fragmented party was to hurt them in the election. Dayan's Telem list advocated the unilateral implementation of autonomy in the administered areas, though its campaign concentrated largely on the figure of the party's leader. One non-candidate was Samuel Flatto-Sharon, who had conducted a successful one-man campaign in the 1977 Knesset elections. In mid-May he was sentenced to nine months in prison, with a 27-month suspended sentence, on two counts of election bribery, although execution of the sentence was postponed pending appeal. The trial had lasted over a year. (See also AJYB, Vol. 81, 1981, p. 271; Vol. 78, 1978, p. 478.) All told, 31 parties contested the election, including a pensioners' list and a group advocating repeal of the income tax.

The two large parties seemed to spend more time attacking each other's past records than in explaining their policies for the future. The campaign was capped by a Begin-Peres television debate on June 25 in which the Labor party appeared to make the better showing. Immediately afterward Peres announced that Yitzhak Rabin had been named shadow defense minister in place of Haim Bar-Lev. Dismissing his recent years of bitter feuding with Peres, Rabin, who had been outpolling the party leader as Labor's top vote-getter, said he and Peres would henceforth "work together." In the few days remaining before the vote, the Likud, apprehensive that Rabin's popularity and relatively hawkish stance might hurt it, charged that the move was yet another demonstration of Peres' "non-credibility" and "indecisiveness."

The results of the election, as compared with 1977, are given below. Nearly 80 per cent of the electorate went to the polls. The Alignment, with 36.6 per cent of the popular vote (well above its 1977 figure of 24.6 per cent but still 3 per cent less than it received in 1973), recouped nearly all the seats it had lost to the DMC four years earlier. The Likud also strengthened its popular vote (37.1 per cent in 1981 as compared with 35.4 per cent in 1977) and gained several seats, throwing the two parties into a virtual deadlock.

ELECTIONS TO 9TH KNESSET (May 17, 1977) AND 10TH KNESSET (June 30, 1981)

	1977	1981
Eligible voters	2,236,293	2,490,140
Jewish	2,030,734	2,224,840
Non-Jewish	205,559	247,300
Valid votes cast[a]	1,747,820	1,937,366
Valid votes cast for parties not qualifying[a]	46,969	99,903
Valid votes counting in allocation of seats[a]	1,700,851	1,837,463
Quota per Knesset seat[b]	14,173	15,312

Party	Popular Vote (%) 1977	1981	Net gain or loss	Knesset Seats 1977	1981	Net gain or loss
Likud	583,075 (33.4)	718,941 (37.1)	+(3.7)	43	48	+5
Alignment	430,023 (24.6)	708,536 (36.6)	+(12.0)	32	47[c]	+15
National Religious	160,787 (9.2)	95,232 (4.9)	−(4.3)	12	6	−6
Agudat Israel	58,652 (3.4)	72,312 (3.7)	+(0.3)	4	4	—
Democratic Front for Peace & Equality	79,733 (4.6)	64,918 (3.46)	−(1.2)	5	4	−1
Tehiya	— —	44,700 (2.3)	—	—	3	+3
Tami	— —	44,466 (2.3)	—	—	3	+3
Telem	— —	30,600 (1.6)	—	—	2	+2
Shinui[d]	— —	29,837 (1.5)	—	—	2	+2
Citizens' Rights Movement	20,621 (1.2)	27,921 (1.4)	+(0.2)	1	1[c]	—
Poalei Agudat Yisrael	23,956 (1.4)	17,090 (0.9)	−(0.5)	1	—	−1
Independent Liberals	21,277 (1.2)	11,764 (0.6)	−(0.6)	1	—	−1
United Arab	24,185(1.4)	11,590 (0.6)	−(0.8)	1	—	−1
Flatto-Sharon	35,049 (2.0)	10,823 (0.6)	−(1.4)	1	—	−1
Sheli	27,281 (1.6)	8,691 (0.5)	−(1.1)	2	—	−2
Arab Brotherhood	— —	8,304 (0.4)				
Aliya	— —	6,992 (0.4)				
Kach (Meir Kahane)	4,396 (0.2)	5,128 (0.3)				
Atzmaut	— —	4,710 (0.2)				
One Israel	— —	3,726 (0.2)				
Arab Citizens	— —	2,596 (0.1)				
Pensioners	— —	2,404 (0.1)				
Ihud	— —	1,293 (0.07)				
Ya'ad	— —	1,228 (0.06)				
Otzma	— —	839 (0.04)				
Ohalim	— —	545 (0.03)				
Income Tax Repeal ..	— —	503 (0.03)				
Amcha	— —	460 (0.02)				
Youth	— —	412 (0.02)				
Council for a Changing Society .	— —	405 (0.02)				
Yozma	— —	400 (0.02)				
Other Lists (1977) ...	42,573(2.3)					

[a] Only lists receiving at least one per cent of the valid votes cast—i.e., 19,374 in 1981—are entitled to share in the allocation of seats.

[b] The quota for one Knesset seat is the number of valid votes cast for the lists qualifying—i.e., 1,837,463 in 1981—divided by 120 (the number of Knesset seats).

[c] Shortly after the elections, the Citizens' Rights Movement formally joined the Alignment.

[d] Shinui (Change) was part of the Democratic Movement for Change in the 1977 elections; at that time the DMC won 202,265 votes (11.6% of the popular vote) and elected 15 Knesset members.

The most stunning result was the halving of the NRP's strength and the overall decline in seats for the religious parties, although it soon became apparent that their political clout was in inverse proportion to their electoral fortunes. The hopes of the left-of-center parties of all shades were severely dashed, although there was no mass swing in the other direction either, as Tehiya had counted on. Abuhatzeira's Tami party did less well than had been expected; indeed, none of the overtly ethnic lists fared well. The Communists (DFPE) suffered a decline, with Labor tripling its vote among the Arab population, while Sheli was wiped off the Knesset map altogether. The greatest disappointment was probably that of Moshe Dayan, whose vaunted charisma appeared to have faded away. The decline of the Independent Liberals continued apace and they failed to elect a single candidate. Overall, the public swung sharply away from small parties, although it was unclear whether this was the start of a long-term trend (a backlash, perhaps, following the DMC's atomization) or, as some observers suggested, a one-time phenomenon due to the intense Begin-Peres struggle.

Subsequent analyses of voting patterns only confirmed what had been strikingly apparent during the campaign: the Likud, under Menachem Begin, retained its populist support among voters of the "oriental" communities, while Labor, belying its name, was strong among the more affluent, largely "occidental" sections of the public. Many commentators attributed Labor's lack of success in regaining power to its failure, in the four years since the 1977 elections, to reform and recast itself, or to divest itself of its establishment image. The children of the early 1950's mass immigration from Arabic-speaking lands, now come of age, were evidently repaying the current Labor leaders for the mistakes their predecessors had made in the absorption of those immigrants. These children of the *ma'abarot*—the transit camps that were their initial experience of Israel and which they identified with Mapai, now the Labor party—turned to the Likud not only because their origins in Muslim countries led them to perceive the Arab world in much the same way as Menachem Begin (his own extraction notwithstanding), but because they saw themselves and Herut as having overcome, together, the Mapai machine which they believed had sought to relegate them to a perpetual second-class status.

The Histadrut Elections

The election of delegates to the 14th convention of the Histadrut, Israel's General Federation of Labor, on April 7 was widely regarded as a significant prelude to the Knesset elections. Eleven lists were submitted (three of them for the first time) representing the major political parties (except for the religious parties, which had their own labor federations). The Alignment's list was headed by MK Yeruham Meshel, who had already served two terms as secretary-general, and the Likud's list by Housing and Immigration Absorption Minister David Levy. The Likud presented Levy as the "strong man" needed by the Histadrut, while the Alignment countered by seeking to build Meshel's image as a "responsible and resolute" leader who had proved himself.

Both chief parties had some reason to be satisfied with the outcome of the election. Meshel, pointing out that the Alignment's 63 per cent of the vote had reversed Labor's downward trend in the labor federation for the first time since Herut's appearance there in 1965, termed the result a "great victory for the Labor Alignment." The Likud, however, was satisfied (and relieved) to have retained its

ELECTIONS TO THE 13TH AND 14TH CONVENTIONS OF THE HISTADRUT, 1977 AND 1981 (Percentages)

Party	1977	1981
Alignment[a]	58.35	61.96
Likud[b]	28.18	26.86
Shinui[c]	8.02	2.20
Hadash (Communists) .	3.03	3.58
Religious Workers[a]	1.80	—
Independent Liberals[d] .	1.27	1.78
Sheli	1.11	1.36
Rafi[b]	—	1.21
Others	1.28	1.05
Votes cast as percentage of eligible voters	68.47	56.72

[a] In 1981 the Alignment list included the Religious Workers and the Civil Rights Movement.
[b] In 1977 the Likud included Rafi.
[c] In 1977 Shinui was part of the Democratic Movement for Change.
[d] In 1977 the Independent Liberals ran on a joint list with the Civil Rights Movement.

strength virtually undiminished. The Alignment maintained its majority in Na'amat (Women Workers and Volunteers) and in all but four of the 71 local labor councils, for which elections were held simultaneously.

The Histadrut convention, (September 8–10), which followed the violent Knesset election campaign by just two months, was marred by brawling between Likud and Alignment delegates over a change in the federation's constitution. Police had to be summoned to break up the fighting. The convention, which was attended by 1,501 delegates, elected Yeruham Meshel to a third term as secretary-general.

The New Government

Talks on the formation of a new coalition to a large extent followed the pattern set in 1977. Although the Alignment and the Likud were virtually stalemated numerically—indeed, after the Citizens' Rights Movement joined the Alignment following the elections, both major parties had 48 seats and the Alignment actually had a larger share of the popular vote—it was clear from the outset that only the Likud would be able to put together a coalition capable of mustering a Knesset majority. Both religious parties, the NRP and Agudat Israel, asserted their readiness to join a Likud-led coalition, thus assuring Begin of 58 seats. An initial stumbling block—the NRP's refusal to serve in a government with Aharon Abuhatzeira's breakaway Tami faction—was soon overcome, though Abuhatzeira's demand to retain the religious affairs portfolio he had held in the previous cabinet presented another obstacle. Negotiations between the Likud and Moshe Dayan's Telem list quickly proved fruitless, as the two found it impossible to bridge their differences on the autonomy issue. Likud feelers to Tehiya also produced no results. The

Alignment on July 7 turned down the idea of joining a national unity government under Menachem Begin, a plan broached by the NRP.

Following the publication of the official election results and the statutory consultations with the representatives of the parties, President Navon on July 15 formally charged Menachem Begin with the task of forming a government. As he had done four years earlier, Begin went from his meeting with President Navon to the Western Wall to utter a prayer. He set a three-week deadline for forming a new government, asserting that if he failed he would not ask for an extension but would return his mandate to the president. He also ruled out a minority government.

The coalition talks were conducted against the backdrop of a "mini-war" fought across Israel's northern border (see Lebanon, below). Begin cited the unstable situation in the North as well as his forthcoming meetings with presidents Sadat and Reagan as the reasons why a new government was needed urgently. The main problems were 120 listed demands on religious, social, and economic issues put forward by the NRP, and Agudat Israel's insistence that the government undertake to amend the law of return by making it mandatory for a proselyte to have been converted "according to the *halacha*" (Jewish religious law), thus effectively disqualifying conversions performed by Conservative or Reform rabbis. In the meantime, the Tenth Knesset convened on July 20 and by a vote of 61–56 (3 abstentions) elected Menahem Savidor (Likud-Liberals) as speaker.

Just one day before Begin's self-imposed deadline, on August 4, the coalition agreement was signed by the Likud, NRP, Agudat Israel, and Tami, representing 61 members in the 120-seat House. Fifty of the agreement's 83 clauses dealt with religious matters, the others largely with socio-economic reforms and plans. A good many of the religious clauses concerned means to minimize work on the Sabbath and on Jewish holidays (a particularly controversial clause asserted that all El Al flights were to be grounded on the Sabbath and on the Jewish holy days) and the allocation of funds to religious educational institutions. The thorny "who is a Jew" issue was resolved in the agreement's final clause, with the prime minister pledging to "make every effort possible to assemble a Knesset majority" to legislate the amendment to the law of return.

Begin presented his 18-man cabinet to the Knesset on August 5. The main innovation was the creation of the post of chief economic coordinator expressly for Begin's long-time associate—and the man he replaced as commander of the Irgun underground—Yaacov Meridor. (It was only in November that the cabinet institutionalized the new post when it decided to create an office for economic and interministerial coordination, to be headed by Meridor. The new department was to deal with long-range economic forecasting and with projects for efficiency and saving.) Tourism was once again made a separate portfolio. The NRP retained the religious affairs portfolio, but as compensation Tami's Aharon Abuhatzeira was given two ministries, social betterment and immigration absorption. David Levy, a leading Herut figure who had held the latter portfolio in the outgoing government, threatened not to serve in the new cabinet, but was finally mollified by being named deputy prime minister. As in 1977, the Agudat Israel faction did not join the cabinet—this

THE BEGIN CABINET
(installed on August 5, 1981)

Prime Minister	Menachem Begin (Likud-Herut)
Deputy Prime Minister & Minister of Agriculture	Simcha Ehrlich (Likud-Liberals)
Deputy Prime Minister & Minister of Housing	David Levy (Likud-Herut)
Communications	Mordechai Zippori (Likud-Herut)
Defense	Ariel Sharon (Likud-Herut)
Economic Coordination	Yaacov Meridor (Likud-Herut)
Education & Culture	Zevulun Hammer (NRP)
Energy	Yitzhak Berman (Likud-Liberals)
Finance	Yoram Aridor (Likud-Herut)
Foreign Affairs	Yitzhak Shamir (Likud-Herut)
Health	Eliezer Shostak (Likud-La'am)
Labor and Social Betterment & Immigrant Absorption	Aharon Abuhatzeira (Tami)
Industry & Commerce	Gideon Pat (Likud-Liberals)
Interior, Police, Religious Affairs	Yosef Burg (NRP)
Justice	Moshe Nissim (Likud-Liberals)
Tourism	Avraham Sharir (Likud-Liberals)
Transport	Haim Corfu (Likud-Herut)
Without Portfolio	Yitzhak Modai (Likud-Liberals)

at the directive of the Council of Torah Sages, a group of rabbinic authorities whose rulings were binding on Agudat Israel in all spheres.

Among the new government's basic policy guidelines presented to the Knesset for approval (together with the ministerial list) was the assertion of the "right of the Jewish people to the Land of Israel, an eternal, unassailable right which is intertwined with the right to security and peace." The guidelines promised that the government would "act to strengthen, expand, and develop settlement" throughout the Land of Israel, and that it would "decide on the appropriate timing for the application of Israeli law, jurisdiction, and administration on the Golan Heights" (see also The Administered Areas, below). A series of socio-economic guidelines followed, as well as the assertion that "the status quo in matters of religion will be preserved" and, finally, a declaration that "Jerusalem is the eternal capital of Israel, indivisible, entirely under Israeli sovereignty." Following a ten-hour debate, Menachem Begin's second Likud-led government won a 61–58 vote of confidence from the Knesset.

The Election Aftermath

In its first session the new cabinet approved the appointment of ten deputy ministers (another was added two weeks later). Observers charged that this was designed solely to solve various coalition personnel problems and was a wasteful step. Among the appointees were Dov Shilansky (Likud-Herut) as deputy minister for parliamentary affairs in the prime minister's office, Yehuda Ben-Meir (NRP) as deputy foreign minister, and two Tami appointments: Aharon Uzan as deputy minister of immigrant absorption and Benzion Rubin as deputy minister of labor and social betterment.

Although the government's Knesset majority appeared fragile on paper, it proved remarkably durable throughout the remainder of 1981. While the government did lose a few parliamentary votes, they were not on key issues; when it came to major legislation or votes of confidence, the government was able to muster a majority.

The Labor party, meanwhile, was wracked by feuding in the wake of its election loss. Its internal campaign for the post of party secretary-general brought to the surface all of the party's discords and divisions. In the event, Haim Bar-Lev won the late November vote by a large majority. Late in December several left-wing Labor MKs, along with "doves" from Mapam and other parties, formed their own political group, a move which was assailed by Labor's "hawks."

On November 26 Prime Minister Begin slipped and fell in his bathroom, breaking a hip joint. He underwent 90-minute surgery during which a metal pin was inserted into the fractured joint. Three days later the cabinet met for its regular weekly session at Begin's hospital bedside. He was released from the hospital on December 14 and ordered to continue his convalescence at home. Deputy Prime Minister Simcha Ehrlich was appointed acting prime minister and chaired the remaining cabinet meetings of 1981.

Foreign Relations

The first ranking member of the new U.S. administration to visit Israel was Secretary of State Alexander Haig, who was in Jerusalem for one day early in April as part of a Middle East fact-finding tour. The talks, Haig said afterward, had produced "a convergence of outlook on important Middle East strategic issues." Speaking of Washington's desire to forge a unified anti-Soviet bloc in the Middle East, Haig asserted: "A strong Israel can play a central role against the threat of the Soviet Union and many of its surrogates." Israel, he declared, "is an ally whose strength and prosperity are in America's interest."

Haig's notion of a regional alliance notwithstanding, Israel came out strongly against the intention of the United States to conclude a major arms deal with Saudi Arabia. Israel, Haig was told, was particularly concerned about the planned sale of AWACS surveillance planes to the Saudis.

It was these two issues—the U.S. concept of a regional strategic bloc directed against the Soviet Union, and the U.S.-Saudi arms deal and its implications—that dominated Israeli-U.S. relations in 1981. Throughout the year the Israeli government made clear its stand on the AWACS issue; late in April the cabinet expressed its "profound regret and unreserved opposition" to the deal, but to no avail. The issue continued to simmer during the Israeli election campaign, and came to a boil when the U.S. administration formally notified Congress late in August of its intention to consummate the $8.5 billion deal. The matter was raised during Begin's official visit to Washington in the second week of September. Following the Senate's approval of the deal at the end of October—besides the AWACS planes, the package also included sophisticated offensive weaponry—the cabinet met in extraordinary session and issued a statement expressing "regret" at the deal and underscoring Israel's determination to "overcome" the threat it posed. President Reagan, in a letter to the prime minister, gave his "reassurance that America remains committed to help Israel retain its military and technological advantage." Noting that the "security of Israel" was an "essential factor" in U.S. strategic decision-making regarding the region, Reagan added, "This administration has a continued interest in working with Israel on a wide dimension of strategic issues, efforts which serve our mutual interests."

The notion of Israeli-U.S. strategic cooperation, the concept iterated by Haig in his April visit to Jerusalem, was itself the center of another controversy. Defense Minister Ariel Sharon, who accompanied Begin on his Washington visit in September, declared upon his return home that intensive consultations were to be held in the weeks ahead with the aim of concluding a "memorandum of understanding" on strategic cooperation between the two countries. After delaying a visit to the United States following the Senate's passage of the AWACS deal, and because of his perception of a tilt toward Saudi Arabia in U.S. foreign policy (see also Israel and the Middle East, below), at the beginning of December, Sharon went to Washington where he and Secretary of Defense Caspar Weinberger signed a "Memorandum of Understanding Between the Government of the United States and the Government of Israel on Strategic Cooperation." The accord, as its first article explained, was "designed against the threat to peace and security of the region caused by the Soviet Union or Soviet-controlled forces from outside the region introduced into the region." The rest of the brief agreement outlined the bilateral framework within which this purpose was to be achieved.

Four no-confidence motions against the agreement were introduced in the Knesset. The opposition speakers argued that the pact had been conceived in haste and actually jeopardized Israel's security by explicitly mentioning the Soviet Union and by making the Israeli army subservient to U.S. global interests. Defense Minister Sharon countered by declaring that the Israeli army would never be used "for a war that is not connected with Israel's survival or security." The coalition defeated the motions by a vote of 57–53.

However, just two weeks later (December 18) the United States announced that it was "suspending" the memorandum in the wake of Israel's passage of the Golan Heights law (see The Administered Areas, below). Prime Minister Begin reacted to this two days later by informing U.S. ambassador to Israel Samuel Lewis that he regarded the suspension announcement as tantamount to U.S. "abrogation" of the memorandum.

Begin took the unusual step of having the government secretary read out to the press the text of his remarks to Lewis, which effectively summed up the rocky course of Israeli-U.S. relations in 1981. He noted that this was the third time within six months that the United States had punished Israel. The first two instances had involved temporary suspensions of the delivery of U.S. warplanes to Israel—once following Israel's destruction of the Iraqi nuclear reactor in June, and again after Israeli planes leveled PLO headquarters in Beirut. "What kind of expression is this 'punishing Israel'?" Begin asked. "Are we a vassal state of yours? Are we a banana republic?" Assailing the U.S. for its infliction of civilian casualties in World War II and in Vietnam and for "an ugly campaign of antisemitism" around the AWACS controversy, invoking the Inquisition, the Holocaust, and the Jewish resistance movements, the prime minister concluded by making it clear that "no force on earth" could bring about the Golan law's rescission.

Israel's relations with Western Europe were somewhat smoother in 1981 than in the previous years, as the EEC member-states virtually abandoned the "Middle East initiative" which had irked Israel. (See AJYB, Vol. 81, 1981, p. 258; Vol. 82, 1982, p. 249.) Nonetheless, the Knesset in November again rejected the Venice declaration which formed the basis of that initiative when it adopted the government's general policy statement at the opening of the Knesset's winter session.

In May Prime Minister Begin welcomed François Mitterrand's victory in the French presidential elections. Early in December French foreign minister Claude Cheysson paid a one-day visit to Jerusalem, meeting with his Israeli counterpart Yitzhak Shamir. Upon Cheysson's departure, Shamir said that "a new era" in Israeli-French relations had begun.

Relations with West Germany were not so cordial. Following a statement made by Chancellor Helmut Schmidt, after he had visited Saudi Arabia, to the effect that Germany had a moral commitment to the Palestinians, Prime Minister Begin early in May denounced Schmidt fiercely, accusing him of "callous" disregard of the Holocaust, of "unbridled greed and avarice," and of indifference to whether Israel was annihilated by the Arabs. Begin added that Schmidt had remained "a loyal officer to Hitler until the last moment of World War II."

Following an August 29 terrorist attack on a Vienna synagogue, killing two persons and wounding 19, foreign ministry officials charged that the Kreisky regime's lenient policy toward the PLO facilitated that organization's activities in Austria.

Foreign Minister Shamir met with his Soviet counterpart, Andrei Gromyko, when both were in New York in late September for the UN general assembly session. In an interview, Shamir explained that the meeting was important, even though it produced no concrete results. It was the first encounter between the two countries at this level in six years.

Israel's relations with most of the Latin American countries continued on a firm footing; Shamir visited several countries in that region during the year.

Foreign press reports of a secret visit to a number of African countries by Defense Minister Ariel Sharon were confirmed by Israel early in December. The apparent breakthrough in relations with some countries in black Africa was linked to the fact that Israel was about to sign a strategic cooperation accord with the United States, an act which, according to Jerusalem officials, placed Israel "on a higher plane" in the perception of these pro-Western African nations. Zaire president Mobutu Sese Seko stated that there were no longer any obstacles to his country's resumption of diplomatic ties with Israel. At year's end, however, it was unclear what effect the passage of the Golan Heights law would have on this new African opening.

Lebanon

The situation in Lebanon deteriorated seriously in the first half of 1981, nearly precipitating a major eruption of hostilities. Early in the year the terrorists intensified their sporadic katyusha rocket attacks from Lebanese territory against Israel's northern settlements. In Lebanon itself, the Syrian army fiercely bombarded Christian strongholds, with the heaviest attacks coming against the town of Zahleh, on the Beirut-Damascus road. Israel expressed its deep concern about this Syrian military activity. Foreign Minister Shamir declared on April 5, "Israel cannot sit idly by, with arms folded, and watch Syrian troops massacre Lebanese Christians." After a large-scale Israeli army strike against terrorist targets a week later, Shamir said the attack had also been directed at the Syrians "because these terrorist organizations are all supported by Syria." The subject was raised with U.S. Secretary of State Haig during his visit to Israel in April.

As the Syrians continued their offensive, senior Israeli military sources in mid-April revealed publicly for the first time that Israel was "supplying the Lebanese Christians with means and equipment to protect themselves," but denied that Israel had military advisers in northern Lebanon or ran training bases there.

Tensions reached a new peak on April 28, when Israel shot down two helicopters that were enroute to reinforce a heavy Syrian offensive against Lebanese Christian troops on Mount Lebanon. Syria immediately responded by moving mobile Soviet-made SAM ground-to-air missiles into Lebanon's Beka'a valley, posing a threat to Israeli aircraft. As intensive diplomatic activity began to defuse the crisis, Prime Minister Begin explained that Israel's more "direct" action in Lebanon had been taken only after diplomatic efforts had failed to deter the Syrians. "We will not tolerate a Syrian takeover in Lebanon," he asserted, "and we will not let Syria wipe out the Christians there." Nonetheless, Israel, he said, had no desire to go to war with Syria. In an Independence Day interview—broadcast the same day, May 7, that Philip Habib, the special envoy appointed by President Reagan to try to resolve the crisis, began his mission in Beirut—Begin said Israel was demanding a return to the *status quo ante* and would not give up its right to make reconnaissance flights over Lebanon. Against the backdrop of a cabinet vote to give Habib more time to find a solution to the crisis and the Syrians' downing of an Israeli pilotless drone over Lebanon (they were to down three more such unmanned craft in the coming month), Begin touched off a public furor when he revealed in the Knesset that he had ordered the chief of staff to have the air force destroy the Syrian missile batteries in Lebanon on April 30, but the strike had been called off three times that day due to adverse weather conditions. Various civilian and military circles charged that Begin had given away military secrets by making public the conditions in which the Israeli air force could not operate.

As Habib continued to shuttle between Jerusalem, Beirut, Damascus, and Riyadh, the cabinet rejected a call by Labor party chairman Peres that the government hold informal consultations with the opposition on the Lebanese crisis. Labor's criticism of the government's handling of the crisis was excoriated by a number of ministers, who, as the election campaign entered its crucial stage, charged that Labor was being "unpatriotic" and "shameless" in "exploiting a national emergency for its own narrow political ends." At the beginning of June Yitzhak Rabin presented an Alignment motion for the agenda in the Knesset criticizing Israel's undertaking to provide the Lebanese Christians with air cover against attack by Syrian planes. During the debate it emerged that in 1978 Begin, along with Foreign Minister Moshe Dayan and Defense Minister Ezer Weizman, had given such a commitment to the Christians in Lebanon, and that Israel had reaffirmed its guarantee in April 1981. Rabin argued that the government had in effect given a foreign party the power to determine when and how the Israeli air force would be employed. The motion was defeated by a vote of 52–36.

Habib's first round of talks concluded on May 27. When he returned to the region two weeks later, Prime Minister Begin told him he would be given "ample time" to resolve the crisis. However, the prime minister noted, he had also told Habib, "and not for the first time," that his mission could not go on indefinitely: "There is a national consensus in Israel that if the diplomatic way does not bring positive results, Israel . . . will use military means to get rid of these missiles."

Israel resumed its attacks on terrorist targets in Lebanon on Friday, July 10— its first such attack since June 2 and the first since the Knesset elections. Habib was at this time back in Beirut on his third round of talks. Several hours after the Israeli strike, a barrage of katyusha rockets hit Kiryat Shemona, destroying a synagogue and other buildings and wounding 14 persons in the northern development town. This, it soon turned out, was but the prelude to a two-week flareup of violence across the northern border of sufficient scale and intensity to be dubbed a "mini-war." On July 12 Israeli aircraft attacked terrorist positions south of Beirut. Two days later Israeli pilots downed a Syrian fighter when it tried to interfere in an Israeli operation over Lebanon. On July 15 the terrorists pounded the entire north of Israel, killing three people and wounding 25 in the coastal resort town of Nahariya. The following day the Israeli air force destroyed five bridges in southern Lebanon to block the terrorists' ability to move arms into the area.

On July 17 Israeli planes bombed Palestinian terrorist headquarters located in a Beirut residential area. The terrorist targets were leveled, but heavy civilian casualties also resulted. Air force commander David Ivri said later that the pilots had made every effort to hit only the highrise buildings in which the terrorists had their command posts, and to spare the surrounding buildings. In reaction to the Beirut attack, the United States postponed the delivery to Israel of six F-16 fighter planes.

In Israel's north, sporadic shelling continued after the Beirut attack. Throughout the area residents slept in shelters, resort sites were deserted, children were evacuated to the country's center, and commercial life came to a virtual standstill.

It was to take another five days of violence, during which another three Israeli civilians were killed, before Philip Habib was able to negotiate a cease-fire. The July 24 announcement heralding the end of the violence was carefully worded to prevent the impression that any Israeli-PLO negotiations had taken place. "At 13:30 hours local time," the statement read, "all hostile military action between Lebanese and Israeli territory in either direction will cease."

The cease-fire held throughout the rest of the year, although Israeli spokesmen charged from time to time that the PLO was violating it by undertaking a major arms buildup in southern Lebanon, by attacking positions in Major Saad Haddad's Israeli-supported enclave in southern Lebanon, and by perpetrating terrorist acts inside Israel and against Jewish targets abroad. Speaking in the Knesset in mid-December, Defense Minister Sharon said that if Israel's northern settlements were again shelled by the terrorists, Israel would "react differently" than it had in July.

Terrorism

In 1981, 17 persons were killed, including 11 civilians, and 157 wounded in Arab terrorist attacks in Israel and abroad, and in Israeli army actions in Lebanon. About 205 terrorists were killed and 250 wounded in Israeli operations.

Following a raid by Israeli forces on an Arab Liberation Front base in southern Lebanon in February, the chief of staff stated that the attack was in retaliation for the terrorist outrage in April 1980 at Kibbutz Misgav Am (see AJYB, Vol. 82, 1982, p. 252). "In this operation," Lieutenant General Rafael Eitan said, "we settled our account with the group that attacked Misgav Am. They set out from this point and we returned to kill all the terrorists there." In 1981 there were no instances in which terrorists seized hostages in Israel.

Vigilance by the security forces and alertness by the public succeeded in foiling numerous terrorist attempts to set off explosives in public places. Buses were the targets of two grenade attacks in the Jerusalem area during the year; tourists in East Jerusalem were the victims in two other instances. In July the military governor of Gaza was killed when an explosive charge went off. The following month one soldier was killed and eight others were wounded when two military vehicles hit landmines which had been laid by infiltrators from Jordan south of Beit She'an.

Israeli security forces had several successes in uncovering terrorist cells in the administered areas, notably a Fatah "liquidators squad" responsible for a series of violent acts in the Ramallah area. Terrorist activity in the Gaza Strip declined sharply after Israeli forces killed "the most wanted terrorist" there in a firefight.

Trials of captured terrorists continued throughout the year. One of the most closely followed trials was that of the four perpetrators of the outrage on the Jewish worshippers in Hebron in May 1980 (see AJYB, Vol. 81, 1981, p. 264; Vol. 82, 1982, pp. 253–254). In November they were convicted and sentenced to life imprisonment. The presiding judge noted that two of the three judges wished to impose the death penalty, but this required a unanimous ruling.

In September three Arab residents of the western Galilee village of Shfaram became the first persons to be convicted under a 1980 amendment to the Prevention of Terrorism ordinance (see AJYB, Vol. 82, 1982, p. 253). They had been detained for distributing leaflets of the outlawed "Sons of the Village" movement. Later that month two Arab students at the Hebrew University were sentenced to three months in prison for producing and distributing a booklet supporting the PLO's struggle against the "Zionist entity."

Abroad the worst incident occurred in Vienna, where a synagogue was attacked (see Foreign Relations, above). In September an Israeli-owned shipping firm in Cyprus came under grenade attack by a youth who said he was a Palestinian, and in late December a Palestinian terrorist organization claimed responsibility for a fire that broke out aboard a Greek passenger liner as it was about to enter Haifa port. A ship's officer died in the blaze.

The Administered Areas

In the waning days of the first Begin government, efforts by Deputy Prime Minister Yigael Yadin to reverse government decisions on the establishment of new settlements by appeal to the Knesset's defense and foreign affairs committee were unsuccessful—notably in the case of three new settlements which, Yadin told the committee in January, were "designed to close off political options to any future solution of the problem of Judea and Samaria, and are superfluous from any other aspect."

In March Matityahu Drobless, the co-director (on behalf of Herut, along with Labor's Raanan Weitz) of the WZO's and the Jewish Agency's land settlement departments, told reporters that there were 18,500 Jews living in Judea and Samaria, as compared with 5,000 when the Likud took office in 1977. A senior defense establishment source told the press that 24,000 dunams (6,000 acres) had been seized in the preceding four months for settlement purposes. These moves were part of a plan to bring the Jewish population of Judea and Samaria to 25,000 by the end of 1981. According to figures released in April by the Israel Information Center, a total of 200,000 dunams (50,000 acres) had been allocated for Jewish settlement in Judea and Samaria. In the pre-election period, with the polls indicating a close vote, Ariel Sharon, then agriculture minister, launched a drive to complete work on a series of new settlements before the new government took office. Termed "unprecedented" in its intensity by a WZO official, the project was financed by a special allocation of IS50 million.

Speaking to a crowd of 35,000 people at the Samaria settlement of Ariel on Independence Day (May 7), Prime Minister Begin took a vow: "I, Menachem, the son of Ze'ev and Hasia Begin, do solemnly swear that as long as I serve the nation as prime minister, we will not leave any part of Judea, Samaria, the Gaza Strip, or the Golan Heights."

On May 22 the new Jewish quarter of Hebron was officially dedicated as two Jewish families moved into a restored building and 30 yeshiva students took up residence in the adjacent Avraham Avinu synagogue. Late in June the first municipal court in Judea and Samaria with special jurisdiction over Israeli settlers—and applying Israeli law in its rulings—opened in Kiryat Arba, the urban center bordering Hebron.

Shortly after the formation of the new Begin government in August, Ariel Sharon, now defense minister and as such responsible for the administered areas, launched what was touted by defense establishment officials as a liberalization program in the areas designed to end various restrictions on the local population and get local leaders to join the autonomy talks. As Sharon held a series of meetings with leading figures in the areas, the defense ministry in September announced a plan for the separation of civilian and military authority in Judea and Samaria. Following the cabinet's approval of the plan, Professor Menachem Milson, lecturer in modern Arabic literature at the Hebrew University and a former adviser on Arab affairs to the military government, was appointed head of the civilian administration in Judea and Samaria. Milson's appointment was effective from November 1, one month before the official commencement of the reorganized governing apparatus in the areas. The Sharon-Milson concept was based on the cultivation of the village leagues in the areas. The rural districts, it was pointed out, accounted for 70 per cent of the population there, and their inhabitants were considered less radical in outlook than their urban counterparts. The defense establishment also let it be known that while the Israeli authorities would cooperate with those Palestinians who sought to lead quiet, peaceful lives, they would react harshly to any attempts to disrupt order.

Following widespread disturbances in Judea and Samaria on the 64th anniversary of the Balfour Declaration (November 2)—intensified by the inhabitants' opposition to the civilian administration, which they believed to be a prelude to Israeli annexation of the territories—the military government closed down Bir Zeit University. A spate of protest demonstrations followed. In contrast to past years, however, the violence did not abate. Late in November the PLO claimed responsibility for the ambush murder of the chairman of the Ramallah district village league and his son. The military government demolished the homes of three families in Beit Sahur, a Christian village near Jerusalem, after the sons of the families had reportedly admitted hurling firebombs at Israeli patrols. (The bombs did not explode.) Two more houses were leveled elsewhere. Major General Danny Matt, coordinator of activities in the administered areas, who was reported to be displeased with recent actions taken under the aegis of the incipient civilian administration, told Defense Minister Sharon that he was resigning at the end of the year.

At the funeral of the murdered Ramallah district village league head, his counterpart in the Hebron district, Mustapha Dudin, castigated the PLO for having committed the deed: "The murderers will never represent the Palestinian nation." The defense ministry revealed in December that it had issued arms to the Arab village leagues for self-defense against PLO assassination attempts.

Some observers believed the Israeli moves were being taken with an eye to April 26, 1982—the date of the final withdrawal from Sinai—after which, according to the prevailing view in Israel, intense pressure would be exerted to get Jerusalem to agree to a compromise solution in the territories. According to this theory, Israel wished to have moderate Palestinians, beholden to the civilian administration, installed in the areas so that they could negotiate on behalf of the inhabitants there.

At the very end of the year an event electrified the nation and the world—the application of "Israeli law, jurisdiction, and administration" on the Golan Heights. In mid-March the Knesset had defeated a bill to extend Israeli sovereignty to the area (see AJYB, Vol. 82, 1982, p. 255). During the year heavy pressure by Druze religious leaders on the Golan and by Syria led most Golan Druze who had opted for Israeli citizenship to return their identity cards to the interior ministry.

On the morning of December 14 Prime Minister Begin summoned various ministers to tell them he wished to have the Knesset apply Israeli law on the Golan that very day. In his view, the time had come to implement the clause in the government's policy guidelines referring to the Golan Heights. Begin argued that, given the superpowers' preoccupation with the Polish crisis, Philip Habib's failure to resolve the missile crisis, the blow the United States had dealt Israel in the AWACS sale, and a reported statement made by Syrian president Hafez Assad that his country would never recognize Israel even if the PLO did, the time was propitious for enacting the required legislation.

Begin immediately convened the cabinet plenum, won approval for his plan, and the government submitted the bill to the Knesset that very afternoon. After the House Committee waived the required waiting periods between readings, the bill became law late on the evening of December 14, following a six-hour Knesset session. The vote was 63–21. Supporting the bill were the coalition factions (excluding Agudat Israel, which did not vote), Tehiya, and eight Alignment-Labor members. Opposing it were Shinui, Telem, the DFPE, and 13 Alignment members, seven from Labor and six from Mapam. The debate and vote exposed the divisions within the Alignment on policy vis-à-vis the areas. In fact, all the Alignment members who voted broke ranks, since the faction had decided to boycott the vote.

The legislation drew a furious U.S. response, resulting in the suspension of the just-concluded memorandum of strategic understanding between the two countries. In Israel 10,000 people on December 19 staged a demonstration against the new law under the slogan of "Zionism without annexation." Following fierce Syrian denunciations of the law, Israel stepped up its military deployment on the Golan Heights as a preventive measure. The chief of staff, who was on an official visit to Egypt at the time, was recalled to supervise the military preparations. As the year ended, the Israeli-Syrian border was quiet, legal experts were debating whether the new law was actually tantamount to outright annexation of the Golan Heights, and the Druze residents there were waiting to see what, if any, practical consequences the new law would have for them.

Israel and the Middle East

Certain Israeli actions and pronouncements during the year pointed to the emergence in Jerusalem of a comprehensive security outlook vis-à-vis the Middle East.

On June 8 Israel stunned the world by announcing that its planes had, the previous day, bombed and destroyed Iraq's Tammuz 1 nuclear complex situated at Tuwaitha, 17 kilometers south of Baghdad. Explaining the move, Prime Minister Begin said that by July, or September at the latest, the reactor would have been "hot," meaning that an attack, by unleashing deadly radiation, would have endangered the lives of untold numbers in Baghdad. "No Israel government would have bombed under those circumstances," Begin stated. Dismissing as "not credible" reports that the Iraqi reactor was being constructed for peaceful purposes, he cited Israeli intelligence information as having determined that the plant would manufacture Hiroshima-type atomic bombs for use against Israel. When those bombs were ready, in four or five years, Iraqi president Saddam Hussein would have had "no hesitation" in dropping them on Israel, causing incalculable loss of life. Given this scenario, the prime minister said, the air force's attack was "literally a life-saving operation." Neither the United States nor Egypt had had any advance information about the attack, Begin emphasized. "For the past two years," he pointed out, Israel had tried to persuade France to withdraw from the Iraqi nuclear project. (See also AJYB, Vol. 82, 1982, p. 249.)

At a subsequent press conference, the prime minister gave public expression to a fundamental tenet of Israeli Middle East policy when he asserted that Israel would "not tolerate" the acquisition of nuclear weapons by any Middle East country. He reiterated that Israel would not be the first country to introduce nuclear weapons into the Middle East and said Israel would sign the nuclear non-proliferation treaty after the Arab states signed a peace treaty with Israel.

Following a ruling by U.S. officials that Israel had violated the arms exports control act by using American-built planes in the attack, the United States announced a suspension of the delivery of four F-16 aircraft to Israel. Speaking at an election rally on June 11, the prime minister charged that U.S. secretary of defense Caspar Weinberger was "the culprit who attempted to deny Israel all military aid" in the wake of the attack. In contrast, he said, Secretary of State Haig had shown himself to be "a true friend of Israel."

Not only foreign governments were critical of the operation. The Labor party charged it had been timed with a view to the June 30 Knesset elections. (A public opinion poll conducted shortly after the attack showed gains for the Likud at the Alignment's expense, apparently due to the popularity of the Iraqi operation. A subsequent poll found 82.9 per cent approval of the operation among the Israeli public, with 11.4 per cent against and the rest undecided.) The party asserted that the Israeli government need not have claimed responsibility for the attack and had done so solely to win votes. Labor party leader Shimon Peres said the reactor would not have been "hot" until September and that Israel could have taken advantage of the change of government in France to persuade Paris to halt its supply of weapons-grade uranium to Baghdad.

On June 19 the United States joined the other members of the UN security council in a resolution "strongly" condemning the Israeli attack which had come "in clear violation of the United Nations charter and the norms of international conduct," and asserting that Iraq was "entitled to appropriate redress for the destruction it has suffered, responsibility for which has been acknowledged by Israel." Two days later the Israeli government, noting with "deep regret" that the United States had "joined in the serious injustice done to Israel," asserted that "Israel, believing in the justice of its cause, will continue with all the means available to it to protect its people and prevent its enemies from developing weapons of mass destruction. That is its sacred duty."

At the end of September the International Atomic Energy Agency voted to deny Israel technological assistance because of the attack. The Israeli foreign ministry termed the decision "arbitrary, discriminatory, and unjustified."

The course of events in 1981—particularly the U.S.-Saudi arms deal—led Israel on a number of occasions to express its attitude toward the regime in Riyadh. At the beginning of August the foreign ministry rejected an eight-point Middle East peace plan put forward by Saudi Arabia which called for Israeli withdrawal from the administered areas and the creation of a Palestinian state with Jerusalem as its capital. The plan was termed a "plot to liquidate Israel by stages." Israeli television, however, quoted certain cabinet ministers as saying that the plan's clause guaranteeing the right of all states in the region to "live in peace" constituted implicit Saudi recognition of Israel's right to exist; as such, they said, the plan, while unacceptable as a whole, might be a turning point in the search for a Middle East peace. Late in October Prime Minister Begin, referring to U.S. administration statements indicating growing support for the Saudi plan, said its adoption would constitute "a great obstacle to the peace process," as it would be a "complete deviation from the Camp David agreements."

Defense Minister Sharon was reported to regard Saudi Arabia as a full-fledged "confrontation state" in view of the immense quantities of arms it was receiving from the United States. Early in November the Knesset rejected the Saudi peace plan when it adopted a government policy statement made by the prime minister at the outset of the winter session. The Alignment and the Likud agreed to send a bipartisan parliamentary delegation to the United States to explain Israel's opposition to the plan.

Israel informed the United States that it would not desist from carrying out reconnaissance flights over Saudi Arabia. The U.S. had raised the matter with Israel following a Saudi complaint that Israel had carried out such a mission on November

9. Israel was particularly concerned about the Saudis' construction of a major military base and airfield at Tabuk, about 200 kilometers from Eilat. At the end of November officials in Jerusalem said Israel was ready to begin negotiations with Saudi Arabia "without preconditions, any time, any place," if the Saudis were sincere about making peace. Prime Minister Begin told an interviewer he would be willing to meet with Saudi King Khalid only if the monarch made it clear that his peace plan did not entail Israel's destruction.

Late in September Prime Minister Begin proposed an Israeli-Jordanian "confederation." Begin said he had a "vision" of a time when there would be peace "between us and the ruler of East Transjordan." Israel would then be able to give Jordan a free port on the Mediterranean, either in Ashdod or in Haifa. . . . We will be able to establish what I may today call a free confederation . . . between the free eastern and western Land of Israel." Jordan rejected the idea in its Hebrew-language television newscast.

Toward the end of the year Defense Minister Ariel Sharon gave expression to a broad-based Israeli security view. Sharon spoke of "red lines" whose violation by Arab states would bring about an armed Israeli reaction. These included the manufacture or acquisition of nuclear weapons, the movement of Syrian troops into southern Lebanon, the entry of Iraqi forces into Syria or Jordan, or the movement of Egyptian troops into the Sinai demilitarized zone. With respect to Syrian or Iraqi troop movements, "Israel would find itself at war immediately," Sharon said. Regarding Egypt, he was less specific, though he did note that Israel had "made it very clear" it would not acquiesce in "any violation of the agreement—large or small."

Normalization of Relations with Egypt

In 1981 the process of normalization of relations between Israel and Egypt was put to the test in the wake of President Sadat's assassination. The year's events until then, which included two summit meetings, indicated that relations were on a solid footing. However, as the second full year of peaceful ties ended, the attitude in Israel was one of wait-and-see.

Toward the end of February, as the second anniversary of the signing of the peace treaty approached (see AJYB, Vol. 80, 1980, p. 262), the foreign ministry summed up the assets and liabilities in the first year of the normalization process. The former included full diplomatic relations, open borders, regular flights between the two countries, and "fairly" complete observance of the treaty's military provisions. Among the liabilities were an Egyptian "tendency" to slow down the pace of normalization and link it with progress in the autonomy talks, tardiness in ratifying agreements, the small numbers of Egyptians visiting Israel, and continued publication of anti-Israeli, sometimes antisemitic, literature in Egypt. In riposte, Foreign Minister Kamal Hassan Ali declared that, while Egypt was fully honoring its commitments, Israel had been guilty of "many practices which conflict with Egyptian and American efforts to achieve a just and comprehensive Middle East peace settlement." He was referring, apparently, to the Israeli attitude on Jerusalem and the establishment of Israeli settlements in the West Bank and the Gaza Strip.

In mid-May Agriculture Minister Ariel Sharon paid a six-day visit to Egypt. Following a meeting with President Sadat, it was announced that the Egyptian leader had approved two projects involving Israeli assistance—a cattle-breeding farm and a land cultivation scheme. That same week, Israel's second ambassador to Cairo, Moshe Sasson, presented his credentials to President Sadat. Sasson, a career diplomat fluent in Arabic, replaced Eliahu Ben-Elissar, who had resigned in order to run on the Likud list in the Knesset elections.

On June 4 President Sadat and Prime Minister Begin held a one-day summit meeting at Ofira (Sharm el Sheikh). Coming less than a month before the Knesset elections, the event took senior government officials in both countries by surprise and drew charges of "electioneering" from opposition ranks in Israel. At a joint press conference following a 90-minute meeting, Prime Minister Begin said that he and President Sadat had achieved "important agreements and serious solutions" in their talk, but had agreed not to divulge details. Replying to a question about what effect possible Israeli-Syrian hostilities would have on the peace process—the summit meeting took place at the height of the missile crisis in Lebanon (see Lebanon, above)—Sadat noted that this had been one of the major topics he and Begin had discussed, and added, "We have pledged together that the October war would be the last war, and we have agreed upon this today also." Both Sadat and Begin condemned the Syrian presence in Lebanon and both reaffirmed their commitment to the Camp David process.

The good taste of the Ofira summit was, as it were, retroactively soured when Israel destroyed the Iraqi nuclear reactor just three days later. President Sadat termed the Israeli action "unlawful" and "provocative," and said such moves could produce "grave consequences." In a special session of the Egyptian parliament, Foreign Minister Ali, amid deputies' cries for a suspension of relations with Israel, described the attack as "shameful and irresponsible" and fraught with "enormous dangers" for the region. The ferocity of the Egyptian reaction was taken in Jerusalem as a reflection of Cairo's embarrassment over the fact that the attack had occurred so soon after the Begin-Sadat summit.

Nonetheless, on June 25 Egypt and Israel were able to reach agreement on the nature of the multinational force which, by the terms of the peace treaty, was to be set up to monitor the security arrangements following Israel's withdrawal from Sinai in April 1982. Initialed in a ceremony in London on July 17 by Israeli, Egyptian, and American representatives, the agreement was ratified by the Knesset later that month. The Multinational Force and Observers (MFO) was to be comprised of 2,000 troops and another 1,000 service and logistics personnel. A diplomatic tangle arose in connection with the MFO's European unit, in the wake of a statement by the Europeans that they would operate within the framework of the EEC's Venice declaration (see also Foreign Relations, above), a position Israel found unacceptable and which led to a lightning one-day visit to Washington by Foreign Minister

Shamir in November for talks with Haig. At the beginning of December, however, Israel and the United States issued a joint statement which was expected to pave the way for European participation in the MFO. The statement, which had Egyptian approval as well, asserted that the "basis for participation in the MFO" was the Israeli-Egyptian peace treaty which "originated in the Camp David accords."

A second Begin-Sadat summit meeting took place in Alexandria on August 26 —the final one, as it turned out, between the two men who had been the partners in the first Arab-Israeli peace agreement. Its main outcome was an agreement that the autonomy talks would be resumed the following month (see below). Significantly, Sadat gave a "no comment" reply when asked at a joint press conference for his reaction to Israel's destruction of the Iraqi reactor. Begin noted only, "I provided the president with facts and dates." The two leaders agreed to expand the normalization process, particularly in trade, culture, and tourism. Accompanying Begin was Defense Minister Ariel Sharon, who announced that the two countries had decided to set up several committees to deal with the Sinai withdrawal and various normalization issues.

September saw the resumption of the autonomy talks, meetings between Israeli and Egyptian transport experts, and the first direct transport to Egypt of goods from Israel in semi-trailer trucks (without the goods having to be reloaded onto Egyptian vehicles at the border checkpoint). At the beginning of October a number of agreements were worked out by the Israel-Egypt trade committee, which met in Cairo.

On October 6, following Cairo's confirmation of the death that day of President Sadat at the hands of assassins during a military parade to mark the eighth anniversary of the 1973 war, Prime Minister Begin said, "I have lost today not only a partner in peace but also a friend." Recalling Sadat's Jerusalem visit in 1977 as "one of the great events of our time," Begin concluded, "The people of Israel share in the mourning of the people of Egypt." On Friday, October 9 (the day after Yom Kippur) Prime Minister Begin, accompanied by senior cabinet ministers, flew to Cairo to attend the funeral. Shortly after their arrival, Vice President Hosni Mubarak received the prime minister for a 40-minute talk. Upon his return to Israel the following evening, Begin told reporters that "in a very simple, dramatic moment" he and Mubarak had shaken hands "and pledged to each other peace forever." Begin emphasized that all the meetings on autonomy and normalization would be held as scheduled. Subsequently a Labor party delegation went to Egypt to express condolences, and in mid-November President and Mrs. Navon paid a one-day visit during which they laid a wreath on Sadat's grave and met with President Mubarak. Navon said the Egyptian president had accepted an invitation to visit Israel, although no date had been set for the visit.

Israel monitored Egyptian policy statements during the rest of the year, to ascertain whether the new administration was introducing any changes in Egypt's basic positions. Israeli and Egyptian negotiators concluded agreements on tourism in Sinai for the period following the Israeli withdrawal, on communications, and on transport, specifically cooperation between the airport in Eilat and the nearby

Etzion field, which was to be handed over to Egypt. Toward the end of the year it was announced that two of the new Israeli air bases being built in the Negev to replace the Etzion and Eitam sites in Sinai were already operational.

Addressing the World Agudat Israel executive late in December, Foreign Minister Yitzhak Shamir summed up the current Israel posture vis-à-vis Egypt. Israel, he said, required "a few years" to determine whether the peace with Egypt was genuine "and whether our sacrifices were worthwhile." Thus, Israel "must not make any more concessions until this peace is firmly established." Jerusalem, he added, was also concerned over a perceptible "change of mood" in Cairo, President Mubarak's assurances notwithstanding.

The Autonomy Negotiations

Following some 18 months of near-total inactivity (see AJYB, Vol. 81, 1981, pp. 255–256; Vol. 82, 1982, p. 251), the autonomy negotiations were resumed at the ministerial level in Cairo on September 23, in the wake of an agreement reached at the Begin-Sadat summit the previous month. A joint communiqué issued after the two-day session stated that the parties—Israel, Egypt, and the United States—had pledged themselves "to move as rapidly as possible toward agreement . . . on understandings and principles." However, foreign ministry director-general David Kimche told the press that "approximately fifteen major issues" still remained unresolved.

A nine-day round of talks was held in Tel Aviv toward the end of October. Prime Minister Begin said afterward that he believed a "breakthrough" could be achieved in the next session if the negotiators concentrated on certain key issues. Specifically, he suggested, they should focus on "the composition, authority, and manner of election to the administrative council" which was to be created in the areas. Foreign Minister Shamir said that both Israel and Egypt wished to have the autonomy talks wrapped up by the end of April 1982, consonant with Israel's final withdrawal from Sinai.

The two-day round of talks held in Cairo on November 11–12 failed to produce a "breakthrough." An effort to reach agreement on elements of a "declaration of principles" failed. A joint statement which "instructed the working team to . . . present a draft agreement on understandings and principles for the ministers' consideration" indicated that little progress was being made. Egyptian foreign minister Kamal Hassan Ali said pointedly that no "target date" existed for concluding the talks.

Addressing a Young Herut gathering at year's end, Foreign Minister Shamir said he thought the United States would make a "special effort" in the immediate future to achieve progress in the autonomy talks. As for Israel, it would "make no compromises." Shamir elaborated, "At Camp David we reached the final and absolute limit. We will honor the Camp David commitments, but the world had better know that we will take no more risks."

Economic Developments

The "proper economy" of Finance Minister Yoram Aridor, who late in January was named to succeed Yigael Hurvitz, dominated events on the economic front. Shortly after he took office, Aridor reduced prices on various durable goods (notably color televisions and small cars), instituted a policy of moderate price increases in government-controlled commodities and services (in some cases their prices were actually reduced), and introduced a "mini-tax reform" in which tax brackets were adjusted to lower the income tax rates of most Israelis and a number of taxes were eliminated altogether. Since Aridor took office virtually at the end of the Israeli fiscal year (March 31), he was compelled to work with a budget his predecessor had drawn up. The cabinet approved a third budget for the current fiscal year early in February, in order to adjust for inflation outlays, and the Knesset on March 30 passed the government's IS206 billion budget for 1981/82.

The new finance minister narrowly missed his self-proclaimed goal of reducing the inflation rate from triple- to double-digit inflation by the end of 1981. The annual inflation rate was 101.5 per cent, down from 132.9 per cent the previous year and 114 per cent in 1979.

The devaluation of the shekel against the U.S. dollar continued to outstrip the inflation rate. The shekel was devalued by 106.7 per cent against the dollar in 1981, though only by 82 per cent against a basket of other major foreign currencies. During the four years of the Likud government's tenure, the shekel had been devalued by 914 per cent relative to the dollar and by 868 per cent relative to other foreign currencies.

The gross national product rose by five per cent in 1981, due largely to intensified commercial activity. Real wages were up by ten per cent, and per capita private consumption rose by nine per cent after a decline the previous year. Industrial output grew by seven per cent and agriculture by four per cent, while construction fell by three per cent. The average weekly unemployment rate for the year stood at 5.1 per cent, or about 68,000 persons, the highest rate in a decade. The civilian balance of payments debt decreased by $102 million, but still stood at $2,017 million. The overall deficit, including defense imports, totalled $4,364 million. The country's external debt stood at $22,153 million, while its foreign currency reserves totalled $8,517 million. Exports increased by 5.5 per cent but were more than offset by a 10.2 per cent jump in imports. For the first time in a single year, exports to the United States exceeded $1 billion, with state-of-the-art technological products accounting for much of this figure.

There was friction during the year between the governor of the Bank of Israel, Arnon Gafny, and the treasury. Gafny, who was informed by Aridor that his five-year tenure would not be renewed when it expired at the end of the year—because of their conflicting views on the Bank of Israel's role in the economy—said that there had been no reduction in government spending during his term. He noted that on many occasions he had made known to the government his view that Israel's economic problems could be solved if state spending were cut. This, however, had remained steady at about one-third of the GNP since 1973. Gafny said that the annual inflation rate had been achieved by increasing subsidies and allowing the state deficit to grow. Particularly worrisome in 1981, he added, were the growth in government spending and the massive printing of money.

El Al, the national airline, was in the headlines again in November (see also AJYB, Vol. 82, 1982, p. 258). In reaction to a management decision to make 18 flight engineers "redundant," the company's workers launched a wildcat strike. It was only after Deputy Prime Minister David Levy assured the workers that the original redundancy letter was null and void that the strike was called off. El Al's chairman of the board Avraham Shavit resigned to protest what he termed Levy's intervention and his undercutting of management's authority. The 12-day strike cost the company $12 million in immediate losses and an incalculable amount in long-term damage. Nahman Perl, a diamond dealer and a member of the Herut secretariat, was named acting El Al board chairman.

Other Domestic Matters

Israel's population stood at 3,977,000 as the year ended—3,320,000 Jews (83.5 per cent) and 657,000 non-Jews (16.5 per cent)—an overall increase of 1.4 per cent over the previous year. In the decade ending in 1981 Israel's population grew by about 900,000 persons, of whom 700,000 were Jews.

The country was shocked when Sheikh Hamad Abu Rabia, a Bedouin Knesset member, was shot to death on January 12 in front of the Jerusalem hotel in which he was staying. He had stood for election in 1977 as a candidate in the United Arab List—which had won only one seat—on the understanding that he would resign in favor of the Druze Sheikh Jabar Muaddi, the next on the list, in the middle of the Knesset term. He had refused to resign, however, citing the urgent problems facing the Bedouin in the Negev. Muaddi's three sons were arrested and charged with the murder. Their motive, according to the police charge sheet, was to enable their father to enter the Knesset. (Sheikh Muaddi was sworn in as an MK shortly after the murder.) The three sons pleaded not guilty when they appeared in court early in April. Despite fears of reprisal in accordance with the Bedouin tradition of the blood feud, and Druze resentment at the arrests, both sides were persuaded to let justice take its course. The trial was in its final stages as the year ended.

Violence erupted a number of times on the new road to the Ramot suburb on Jerusalem's western outskirts, when residents of the religious neighborhood overlooking the road, joined by other ultra-Orthodox groups, sought to prevent its use on the Sabbath. The construction of a bypass (see AJYB, Vol. 81, 1981, pp. 271–272) failed to solve the problem, as the road was not a top-grade one and, moreover, many Ramot residents refused to use it on principle, holding that it was the duty of the authorities to ensure their safety and free passage on the main highway. The issue led to a major riot in March in Jerusalem's Orthodox Me'a She'arim quarter. The demonstrations peaked on the Sabbath following the riot when 15,000 ultra-Ortho-dox Jews gathered on the Ramot road to protest its use by motorists on the day of rest.

Notable legislation passed by the outgoing ninth Knesset in 1981 included the protection of privacy law, which was voted through despite press protestations that it would restrict freedom of expression; the equal employment opportunities law, banning discriminatory hiring practices due to an applicant's sex, marital or paren-tal status; and a law enabling the prime minister to dismiss a cabinet minister without the entire government dissolving as a result.

The Israeli merchant marine suffered the worst disaster in its history when the MS *Mezada* sank in a storm off Bermuda on March 8, resulting in the death of 26 crew members. A board of inquiry found that the cause of the tragedy was "ac-cumulated human errors combined with rough seas."

In April Prime Minister Begin, as defense minister, cited the 1945 defense (emer-gency) regulations in a proclamation banning the National Coordinating Committee which, according to the prime minister's adviser on Arab affairs, represented about a hundred Israeli Arab activists who had "set as a goal war against the State of Israel and Zionism" and aimed to create "in the Land of Israel a Palestinian state under the leadership of the PLO." An all-Arab congress had been banned four months earlier (see AJYB, Vol. 82, 1982, p. 261).

Happier events included the official dedication, late in June, of the Hebrew University's restored Mount Scopus grounds, site of its original campus which opened in 1925 but had been in Jordanian hands from 1948 until the Six Day War of 1967. The 11th Maccabiah Games—the "Jewish olympics"—were held in July, with the participation of 3,500 athletes from 35 countries.

A major dispute broke out in July between archaeological authorities and ultra-Orthodox elements concerning a site in Jerusalem's City of David. As a fourth season of excavations got underway, Orthodox Jews overran the area, protesting that it was in fact an ancient Jewish cemetery. Work was suspended while the chief rabbis investigated the matter; they ruled that the site was indeed a burial ground, and therefore barred from excavation work. Early in September the supreme court ruled that work at the site could be resumed, since the rabbinate could not interfere in state policy. The attorney general also decreed that the rabbinate had no standing in the matter. In reaction, the supreme rabbinical council issued a proclamation affirming the "eternal nature of Jewish religious law and its primacy in the State of Israel over civil law."

On June 26, virtually the eve of the Knesset elections, Yaacov Meridor, slated for a senior cabinet post if the Likud won (he was subsequently named chief economic coordinator), announced that scientists working for him had discovered a previously unknown energy source which could solve Israel's, and the world's, energy prob-lems. Thanks to this discovery, Meridor asserted, Israel would become an "eco-nomic power" and would have "the world's strongest currency, eliminating all its debts within five to seven years." In subsequent interviews he refused to divulge details of the device, although on June 29 he promised that "within six or seven months" a power station would be constructed based on the new invention. By the end of the year the new energy source was still a secret, but Meridor vowed to reveal it by mid-March 1982.

As the date approached for Israel's final withdrawal from Sinai (April 26, 1982), tension rose in the northern Sinai agricultural settlements and in the urban center of Yamit. Despite the government's proclaimed readiness to compensate the settlers with what many thought a lavish hand, no compensation agreement had been worked out with most of them. Tension in the area was heightened by the presence of members of the Movement to Stop the Sinai Withdrawal—in the main, settlers from Judea and Samaria or students from religious academies—who had moved into empty houses in the various settlements, saying they would not budge. As the settlers received letters from the Prime Minister's office stating that they would have to vacate the area by March 31, 1982, there were scenes of hysteria and violence in Yamit, with the residents shutting the town in a self-imposed siege. Compensation talks with the government had resumed by the end of the year, but the situation remained explosive.

Following the elections, Project Renewal, which the first Likud government had set in motion with the aim of rehabilitating slum areas in the country, was transferred to the housing ministry under the charge of the deputy minister, Moshe Katzav (Herut). At Katzav's initiative, the Jewish Agency agreed to eliminate the duplication of functions between it and the government, a factor which had mired the project in bureaucratic red tape. In a cabinet discussion of Project Renewal late in October, Katzav reported that the government had contributed IS1.2 billion to the project, whereas the Jewish Agency—which was responsible for collecting contributions from Diaspora Jewry—had paid in just IS300 million. The Agency responded by saying that the funds had been collected but would be handed over only after specific neighborhood schemes had been formally approved.

Israel and World Jewry

Jewish immigration to Israel in 1981 totalled 12,300, the lowest figure since the establishment of the state, with the exception of 1953. The main reasons for this poor record were, on the one hand, a drop in the number of Jews allowed to leave the Soviet Union (9,451) and, on the other, a rise in the "dropout" rate: only 1,808 of the Jews who left the USSR chose to go on to Israel; the rest proceeded to other destinations, chiefly the United States, from the Vienna transit center. Efforts by the Jewish Agency to reach an agreement with the Hebrew Immigrant Aid Society (HIAS) whereby the latter would assist only Soviet Jewish emigrants with close relatives in the United States, proved largely unsuccessful. The problem was at least partially mired in the morass of Israeli politics; late in the year the coalition and the Alignment were unable to agree on a draft resolution following a Knesset debate on immigration and emigration.

The emigration problem continued to generate public debate. Emigrants outnumbered immigrants by about 10,000 persons in 1981. The total number of emigrants since 1948 was authoritatively estimated at approximately 300,000. Early in the year the director-general of the Jewish Agency, Shmuel Lahis, whose report on emigration had caused a furor in 1980 (see AJYB, Vol. 82, 1982, p. 261), had resigned his post, explaining that he had not received backing from Jewish Agency chairman Arye Dulzin in his efforts to combat emigration. Lahis subsequently established a group called Citizens for the Prevention of Emigration. The government also seemed to feel that the issue called for more intensive handling. In August MK Dov Shilansky, a deputy minister in the prime minister's office, was named to head the fight against emigration.

Early in 1981 over 500 delegates gathered in Jerusalem for the seventh plenary session of the World Jewish Congress. A report prepared for the WJC and released at the Jerusalem meeting asserted that Diaspora Jews should have the right to be critical of Israel. The report, whose authors included the newly-elected WJC president, Edgar Bronfman of Montreal, as well as some leading Israeli academic and business figures, took its own advice and offered a list of "differences and doubts" that Diaspora Jews had vis-à-vis certain Israeli policies and ideologies. Among these were Israeli settlement policy in the territories, the country's atomized political structure, and its "growing materialism."

Following a three-day closed retreat in Caesarea in February, the "non-Zionist" members of the Jewish Agency's board of governors joined with the board's Zionist members to affirm the centrality of Israel in Jewish life and the importance of *aliyah* (immigration). "We are all Zionists," the group declared. The tenth annual Jewish Agency assembly opened in Jerusalem on August 29. President Yitzhak Navon told the 340 delegates that world Jewry must give top priority to *aliyah* and to Jewish education in the Diaspora.

The 30th anniversary conference of the Israel Bonds Organization took place in Israel in August. The highlight of the gathering was a one-day seminar, devoted to Israel's energy problems, held in the Negev development town of Arad. Those among the conference's 600 participants who had committed themselves to purchasing at least $100,000 in bonds in 1981 as "founders" of the Mediterranean-Dead Sea canal (see AJYB, Vol. 82, 1982, p. 258) signed a parchment scroll to be sealed in a time capsule and embedded in the power station planned for construction near Arad as part of the canal's energy-producing capability.

A unique and moving event took place in Jerusalem in June when over 10,000 Jews from around the world attended a four-day World Gathering of Jewish Holocaust Survivors. There were emotional scenes as friends and relatives who had not seen each other in decades—who had not, in some cases, even known that persons dear to them had survived the Holocaust—were reunited. The climax of the event occurred when all the participants assembled at the Western Wall to reaffirm their belief in life, Israel, and the Jewish people, and to take a solemn oath "never to let the memory of the six million be erased."

Personalia

Justice Haim Cohen retired from the supreme court in March after 21 years, having reached the mandatory retirement age of 70. Major General Amir Drori succeeded Major General Avigdor Ben-Gal as O.C. northern command, in September. Major General Uri Orr took over in November as O.C. central command, replacing Major General Moshe Levy; Levy was appointed deputy chief of staff. Moshe Arens was appointed by the cabinet as Israel's ambassador to the United States, on November 29; he was to replace Ephraim Evron early in 1982. The cabinet also extended the term of the chief of staff, Lieutenant General Rafael Eitan, for another year, his fifth. Major General Haim Erez was named to succeed Dan Shomron as O.C. southern command, effective January 1, 1982. Yitzhak Nebenzahl, 75, retired at the end of 1981 after serving 15 years as state comptroller.

Personalities who died during the year included: Cecil Hyman, former diplomat and journalist, on January 21, aged 80; MK Hanna Mwais, a veteran member of the Communist party in Israel, on February 13, aged 68; Lea Ben Dor, former editor of the Jerusalem *Post,* on March 12, aged 68; Yonatan Ratosh, poet and leader of the "Canaanite" movement, on March 24, aged 73; Uri Zvi Greenberg, poet and man of letters, on May 8, aged 87; Yitzhak "Antek" Zuckerman, a leader of the Warsaw Ghetto revolt in 1943, on June 17, aged 66; Meyer Levin, American-Israeli novelist, on July 9, aged 75; Josef Goldschmidt, former MK and deputy interior minister, on July 25, aged 74; Rabbi Yitzhak Nissim, former Sephardi chief rabbi, on August 9, aged 85; Rivka Aharonson, member of the Nili spy ring in World War I, on August 22, aged 89; Faye Schenk, head of the WZO's organization department and former president of Hadassah, on August 17, aged 72; Avraham Regelson, prize-winning poet, on August 21, aged 84; Rivka Guber, noted educator and social worker, on September 10, aged 79; Haim Landau, former cabinet minister and Irgun leader, on October 6, aged 65; Moshe Dayan, soldier and statesman, on October 16, aged 66; Eliahu Eliachar, Sephardi communal leader and worker for peace, on October 30, aged 82; Yosef Kremerman, industrialist and former Herut MK, on November 12, aged 56; and Avraham Zabarsky, a builder of the cooperative economic system, on November 27, aged 84.

RALPH MANDEL

South Africa

National Affairs

I N THE GENERAL ELECTIONS held in April 1981, the key issues were the government's racial policies, the economic situation, and the detention without trial of persons alleged to pose a threat to state security. The National party (NP), under the leadership of Pieter Botha, was returned to power with 131 seats, while the Progressive Federal party (PFP), the official opposition, led by Fredrik van Zyl Slabbert, obtained 26 seats, and the New Republic party (NRP) eight seats. Although the right-wing Herstigte Nationale party (HNP) gained no seats, it received 191,249 votes (13.1 per cent of all votes cast), a 10.5 per cent increase over its 1977 performance. Most commentators saw the election as indicative of much greater polarization among the electorate than had been the case in recent years. On the other hand, the NP (despite the loss of seven seats) received massive electoral endorsement of its policies.

The country was plagued by an increase in acts of sabotage and terrorism. These included a grenade and rifle attack at Fort Jackson near East London; an attack on a Ciskei police patrol; the blowing up of the train lines from Soweto to Johannesburg and from Durban to Umlazi; the detonation of a bomb at the Durban cenotaph; 15 explosions in the Eastern Transvaal which damaged power stations at Arnot, Camden, Delmas, and Rietvlei; a rocket attack on the Voortrekkerhoogte military base in Pretoria; the blowing up of the Durban South electricity supply sub-station; and a bomb blast in East London. The African National Congress claimed responsibility for most of the attacks; the weapons used were almost uniformly of Russian origin. The South African police reported uncovering secret "terror" bases and arms caches near Johannesburg and other Rand cities.

The South West Africa–Namibia issue remained unresolved, despite the endeavors of the contact group formed by West Germany, Britain, Canada, France, and the United States. Much, however, was achieved by Chester Crocker, U.S. assistant secretary for African affairs, who proposed a constitutional conference to be followed by elections, along the lines of the Lancaster House conference that had done so much to resolve the Zimbabwe problem. This was a significant departure from UN security council resolution 453, which the South West African Peoples Organization (SWAPO) strongly backed. Various attempts by African nations to have the

UN impose a total ban on ties with South Africa were foiled by the Western powers. Subsequent to his mid-year meeting with U.S. secretary of state Alexander Haig and U.S. president Ronald Reagan in Washington, South African foreign minister Roelof (Pik) Botha expressed the view that progress toward a solution of the SWA–Namibia problem was possible. Indeed, this seemed to be the case when first-round discussions of an American-proposed settlement plan were held in London.

At the end of August the South African defense forces launched a four-pronged search and destroy mission against SWAPO strongholds in Southern Angola, during which more than 450 SWAPO members and Angolan soldiers were killed, and radar and anti-aircraft installations were destroyed. Ten members of the South African defense forces died in the raid. Minister of Defense Magnus Malan announced that several Russian military officers had also been killed and a Russian warrant officer captured during the operation. The United States used its veto to block a UN security council draft resolution condemning South Africa for its Angolan operation.

A sharp decline in the price of gold had a deleterious effect on the economy. Strict economic policies, including a steeply hiked interest rate, helped to slow down inflation to 13.9 per cent, from 15.7 per cent in 1980. The country's trade deficit totalled 436.2 million rands as against a surplus of 5.27 billion rands in the previous year.

Relations with Israel

On a week-long visit to South Africa as guest of the Israel United Appeal (IUA), Abba Eban, Israel's former foreign minister, noted that "the Israel government need not necessarily agree with South Africa's internal policies to maintain diplomatic and trade links." Professor Marcus Arkin, director-general of the South African Zionist Federation (SAZF), pointed out that both Israel and South Africa "confront in-built hostility from the UN, . . . are indirectly threatened by their neighbors, and . . . are menaced by Soviet diplomatic and strategic designs."

Israel's destruction of an Iraqi nuclear reactor generated a mixed response in South Africa, with most commentators recognizing the defensive need for the action, but expressing caution about its overall implications. Widespread discussion of the extent of cooperation on nuclear research and development between South Africa and Israel followed the Israeli raid, particularly after Iraq charged that the two countries had twice secretly exploded nuclear devices off the South African coast.

Ariel Sharon, who was then serving as Israel's minister of agriculture, visited South Africa in April to discuss ways of expanding cooperation between the two countries.

Nathan Meron, the counsellor at the Israeli embassy, stated that South Africa provided a "progressive and healthy market for the Israeli exporter," a description well-supported by the continuing growth of trade and commercial links between the two countries. South Africa was Israel's second fastest growing trade partner. Abe Barron, chairman of the South Africa–Israel Chamber of Economic Relations, reported that South African exports to Israel in 1980 (not including 500 million rands' worth of diamonds) were valued at 74 million rands, while imports from Israel were worth 48 million rands. Israel's purchases from South Africa represented two per cent of its imports, while Israel's exports represented 0.5 per cent of South Africa's total imports. A more cautious note was sounded by W.J. Saayman, the South African trade counsellor in Tel Aviv, who pointed out that the strengthening of the rand and economic progress in South Africa had seriously lowered the amount of South African exports to Israel during the year.

Cultural and scientific contacts between South Africa and Israel included the following: a tour of Israel by the 43-member Stellenbosch University wind ensemble orchestra; the participation in the International Choir Festival in Israel of the Baragwanath Hospital Choir, the Pretoria Boys and Girls Choir, the Potchefstroom University Choir, and the East Rand Youth Choir, which was placed third in the contest; an archeological tour of Israel by Professor F.N. Lion Cachet and 40 students from the theological school at Potchefstroom University for Christian Higher Education; and a visit to South Africa by five Israeli scholars who attended a conference on biosolar energy conversion organized by the South African society of the Weizmann Institute of Science and the Council for Scientific-Industrial Research.

The Israeli ambassador to South Africa, Josef Harmelin, completed his tour of duty and was succeeded by Eliahu Lankin.

Antisemitism

While there were some manifestations of antisemitic activity, they were restricted to extreme right-wing fringe groups and such notorious journals as the *SA Observer,* edited by S.E.D. Brown. Other papers, such as the Herstigte Nationale party's *Die Afrikaaner,* continued their anti-Jewish and anti-Zionist propaganda.

The *Zionist Record* reported that a number of members of parliament had received antisemitic publications published in the United States and mailed from Pakistan.

A sensational development was the arrest of a number of members of the extreme right-wing Wit Kommando organization, and the subsequent trial on charges of sabotage and terrorism of Massimo Domingo Bollo and Fabio Miriello, who were sentenced, respectively, to 52 and 42 years in prison. In effect, Bollo would serve ten years in jail and Miriello, five years. Miriello was the editor of a viciously antisemitic South African Italian paper, *Noi Europa.* A cache of arms was discovered in the possession of the convicted men, who were reported to have links to terrorist organizations in Italy and elsewhere in Europe.

It was reported that the leader of the extreme right-wing Afrikaanse Weerstandsbeweging (AWB), Eugene Terre Blanche, was warned by the authorities that his activities were being observed. The AWB announced that it had formed Blitskommando, an action group.

A new umbrella organization, Action Save White South Africa, was formed to unite such groups as AWB, Aksie Eie Toekoms, the National Conservative party, the SA First Campaign, and the Kappie Kommando into a political party. Among the leaders of the organization were Lieutenant General Colin Royden Cockcroft, former surgeon general of the South African defense force, and Professor Alkmaar Swart of the University of South Africa; Willie Lubbe was elected chairman.

Rudolf and Ingrid Schmidt, leading members of various antisemitic and neo-Nazi groups, including the Anglo-Afrikaner Bond and its youth arm, the Odal Clan, left South Africa to establish a settlement of like-minded people on land allocated to them by the government of Paraguay. The Schmidts announced that they were emigrating because they felt that the right-wing cause was lost in South Africa. Their departure was considered a serious setback to the radical right.

JEWISH COMMUNITY

Communal Activities

While South African Jews continued to benefit from the general wave of prosperity within the country, this was not reflected in Jewish communal coffers, which were adversely affected by the high inflation rate. To deal with its urgent financial problems, the South African Board of Jewish Education (SABJE) ran an emergency campaign to raise R5 million; it was launched in May by Rabbi David Rosen, chief rabbi of Ireland. In preparation for the 17th United Communal Fund (UCF) campaign—launched by Professor Irwin Cotler, president of the Canadian Jewish Congress—*Jewish Affairs,* the journal of the South African Jewish Board of Deputies (SAJBD), published a special edition which detailed the financial problems of local Jewish community organizations. In Cape Town, the guest of honor at the opening of the campaign was Eugene Louw, administrator of the Cape. He noted with satisfaction that 70 per cent of UCF's income was allocated to education, and added that the provincial administration would contribute R140 per pupil per year to private schools in the province. Louw used the occasion to laud the contribution made by South African Jews (3.5 per cent of the total white population) to various professional fields. Jews, he noted, constituted 21 per cent of all doctors, dentists, and veterinary surgeons, 17 per cent of auxiliary medical workers, 11 per cent of accountants, 10 per cent of jurists, and 12 per cent of teachers.

Archie Shandling, the outgoing chairman of the SAJBD Cape committee, caused a stir in the community when he stated that mounting right-wing extremism would result in a major exodus of South African Jews, and that all Jews would be out of the country by the year 2000. Shandling called on the Jewish community to pursue its usual activities, but argued that large-scale and costly projects be eschewed.

While the SAJBD national executive disassociated itself from Shandling's remarks, some Jewish leaders, including Frank Bradlow, national vice-president of SAJBD, did express concern about increased antisemitic activity.

At the November inter-provincial conference of SAJBD, Judge David Melamet presented a report on the functioning of the Board. Melamet, acting as a one-man commission, had taken extensive evidence from a wide spectrum of people, ranging from private individuals to communal leaders, throughout the country. The major recommendation was that the structure of the Board be altered to provide for the establishment of a truly national executive council, constituted on the basis of proportional representation, that would meet every two months to deal with national matters exclusively. In addition, a Transvaal committee would be formed to deal with regional concerns. A council of chairmen of leading organizations would convene regularly to keep the Board in touch with various communal groups. Melamet also recommended that some of the Board's current activities be transferred to other organizations that were better equipped to handle the job. It was decided to adopt the recommendations on an experimental basis and to evaluate them in one year's time.

The Johannesburg branch of the Union of Jewish Women celebrated its 50th anniversary with gala events. The group received many congratulatory messages lauding its achievements.

An association was established to promote the interests of professionals in Jewish communal work.

At the Yad Vashem memorial center in Johannesburg, Israel consul general Gershon Gera presented a certificate of honor to Lilo Hellenbrandt in recognition of the work done by her parents in saving Jewish doctors and their families in Poland during World War II.

The SAJBD Cape committee, in a well-publicized declaration, associated the Jewish community with a statement in which church leaders condemned the eviction and subsequent arrest of colored families from the Langa bachelor barracks.

Zionism

The Jewish community continued to express its deep Zionist commitment through the work of the various societies and departments of the South African Zionist Federation (SAZF), which organized lecture series, discussion groups, information services, and tours to Israel. SAZF maintained routine institutional relationships with major communal organizations, including SAJBE, SAJBD, and student and youth groups.

One of the major tasks undertaken by SAZF was the organization of the IUA biennial campaign, which was launched in 1981 by Abba Eban, who spoke in the major cities. The impact of Eban's visit was reflected in the number of important meetings held for him and in the media coverage that ensued. The central focus of IUA was Project Renewal. Other IUA emissaries included David de Rothschild of France and Mordechai Gur, member of the Knesset and former Israeli chief of staff.

Ruth Izakson of Israel, chairman of World WIZO, was one of the guests of honor at the 24th South African women's biennial Zionist conference. She was accompanied by Yosef Mendelevich, the recently-released Soviet Jewish activist. Mendelevich was accorded a hero's welcome wherever he appeared, and was the subject of profiles in leading newspapers throughout the country.

SAZF organized various activities around the country celebrating Israel's Independence Day.

The Jewish community celebrated the 15th anniversary of the reunification of Jerusalem at Jerusalem Day functions. In Johannesburg, Israeli chief rabbi Shlomo Goren was the main speaker.

South Africa sent its largest team ever to the Maccabiah games in Israel. Although the visit was somewhat marred by the Mexican team's refusal to play soccer against the South Africans, the latter were applauded for winning the third highest number of medals at the games.

Religion

Writing in the *SA Jewish Times'* New Year annual, Alek Goldberg, executive director of SAJBD, noted a general impression of strengthened religious life in Johannesburg, visible in an increase in regular synagogue attendance, a growing number of *shiurim* (religious study groups), and increased utilization of available *kashrut* facilities.

Reacting to a statement by Abba Eban, that if the Labor party came to power, it would, *inter alia,* legalize the status of Conservative and Reform rabbis, Bernard Casper, chief rabbi of the Federation of Synagogues of South Africa (FSSA), condemned the proposal. With the backing of the South African Rabbinical Association, the Lubavitch Foundation, and the United Mizrachi Organization, he argued that such recognition would lead to "destruction . . . of a magnitude . . . not even contemplated by the enemies of the Jewish people and certainly not achieved by them in spite of all the diabolical attempts made to do so." Naturally offended by this statement, Reform Jews gave public expression to their anger in a communiqué issued by Rabbi Walter Blumenthal, chairman of the central ecclesiastical board of the South African Union for Progressive Judaism. Israel Abramowitz, chairman of SAJBD, expressed regret that the verbal strife, centered on an Israeli political matter, had become the cause of Orthodox–Reform friction in South Africa and had overflowed into the general press.

Both the Orthodox and Reform groups held major conferences during the year. FSSA's conference had as its theme "challenge, change, and continuity" and was opened by Israeli chief rabbi Shlomo Goren. Among other matters, it dealt with the escalating Jewish divorce rate, the crisis in Jewish family life, and the role of the synagogue in a changing world. The 50th anniversary of the establishment of the Reform movement in South Africa was celebrated at a conference with the theme "roots in a moving stream." The Reform conclave was attended by large delegations from Israel and the United States; among the participants were Gerald Daniel and Rabbi Richard Hirsch, respectively president and executive director of the World Union for Progressive Judaism, and Rabbi Jerome Malino, president of the Central Conference of American Rabbis. Another important guest of the South African Reform group was its founder, Rabbi Moses Cyrus Weiler, who had been living in Israel for over twenty years.

Rabbi Solomon Gaon, spiritual leader of the World Sephardi Federation, dedicated the Shalom synagogue, the first Sephardi synagogue in Cape Town.

Jewish Education

The Lubavitch movement in Johannesburg launched a new school, the Torah Academy, located on a 22-acre piece of land, formerly the Good Shepherd convent, in the central residential area of Orchards. Extensive renovation and building converted the complex into one of the most up-to-date educational institutions in the country. In some quarters, concern was expressed that the existing Jewish day schools in the community would suffer because the new school would draw pupils away. On the other hand, SAJBE spokesmen referred to growing waiting lists of would-be students at its network of schools.

In Cape Town, M.H. Goldschmidt, who had undertaken to contribute R500,000 toward a major construction program at the city's Herzlia School, led the ground-breaking ceremonies. The project was to include 21 classrooms, six specialist rooms, a major hall, and an administrative complex.

The *yeshiva gedola* of Yeshiva College in Johannesburg welcomed its new director, Rabbi Aharon Pfeuffer.

The Cape Town Jewish community bid farewell to Meyer Katz, for many years the principal of Herzlia School and one of the country's leading educators, upon his *aliyah* to Israel. Upon her retirement, Miriam Fendel was honored by the Jewish community for 28 years of service as principal of the Rondebosch Hebrew school.

Jewish Culture

The contribution of Jews to every aspect of theatrical life in South Africa continued to be noteworthy. Leonard Schach, living in Israel for a number of years, returned to South Africa to direct Arthur Miller's *After the Fall,* to much critical acclaim. *Zayde,* written by Henry Rootenberg, and starring Molly Seftel, had its premiere. The first play by art critic Natalie Knight, *There's No Sugar Left,* was staged at the Market Theater in Johannesburg. Henry Goodman received the South

African Television Arts award for best actor in a television play, Geraldine Aron's *Mickey Harris Caught My Eye.*

Two Israeli ballet companies, Bat Sheva and the Kibbutz Ballet, toured South Africa.

There were numerous exhibitions of works by Jewish artists, among them Rachelle Lipschitz, the late Sidney Goldblatt, Michael Muchnik of New York, David Goldblatt, Barbara Arenson, Na'ama Nothman, Myra Bloomberg, and Chaim Menashehaff of Israel.

Newly-published books by Jewish authors included *The Inverted Pyramid* by Rose Zvi, *July's People* by Nadine Gordimer, *Passport to Life* by Henia Brazg, and *Beikvei Haggim uMoadim* by Rabbi Eugene Duschinsky.

The Cape Council of Adult Jewish Education organized a successful symposium on the Jewish contribution to South African performing arts.

An evening of music and readings celebrated the 40th anniversary of SAJBD's *Jewish Affairs.*

Professor Piet Cillie, head of the department of journalism at Stellenbosch University, was the main speaker at the tenth anniversary celebration of SAJBD's Afrikaans journal, *Buurman.* The event drew much congratulatory comment in the press.

The Israeli ambassador to South Africa, Joseph Harmelin, opened the Israel exhibition arranged by the South African Union of Jewish Students at the University of Witwatersrand.

The fifth anniversary of the founding of Swazi radio's "Jewish Sound," a weekly program of Jewish affairs, was celebrated.

SAJBD organized a lecture tour by the Brandeis University historian Bernard Wasserstein.

The Kaplan Center for Jewish Studies at the University of Cape Town continued to offer stimulating programs, including "Origins of South African Jewry." The Center also inaugurated a Jewish oral history project.

Personalia

People appointed to communal offices included: Solly Kessler, chairman, Cape committee of SAJBD; Colin Jankelowitz, chairman, eastern province committee of SAJBD; David Orelowitz, national chairman, SAUJS; Mervyn Braude, chairman, Jewish Students Association, University of Cape Town; Melissa Elion, chairman, SAUJS, Rhodes University; Steven Warb, chairman, SAUJS, Stellenbosch University; Stephen Cohen, assistant to the executive director, SAJBD; Professor Yossi Gamzu, chairman, department of Hebrew, Witwatersrand University.

Lazar Druion, finance director of SAJBD, retired after 47 years of service. Eve Davis, secretary to the executive director of SAJBD, retired after more than 30 years of service.

Recipients of important awards and appointments included: Percy Amoils, senior ophthalmologist at the Johannesburg Hospital, the Medal of Honor for research in cryosurgery by the Massachusetts Institute of Technology; Edward Epstein, the establishment of a research fellowship in his name by the American Intraocular Society, in recognition of his work in lens transplants; Jack Barnett, Gold Medal of the Institute of South African Architects; Phillip Tobias, dean of the faculty of medicine at Witwatersrand University, the Paul Harris Fellowship award of the Rotary Foundation, for his "outstanding ability and devoted application to the science of mankind"; Morris Hellman, president of the Medical Association of South Africa, Cape Western branch; Harry Nelson, Merit Award for service to the Medical Association of South Africa; Lionel Goldes, Orange Free State commissioner for St. Johns ambulance brigade; Helen Suzman, member of Parliament, special medal for "heroism" by Edward Koch, mayor of New York City; David Lazarus, honorary life member of the Hebrew Order of David; Aviva Pelham, Nederburg Prize for Opera and Ballet; Cyril Adler, curator of the Adler Museum of History of Medicine, the University of Witwatersrand alumni honor award; Henry Gluckman, honorary doctor of laws by Witwatersrand University; Nadine Gordimer, the Commonwealth Award in Literature for her contribution to modern literature, by the Modern Language Association of America; J.S. Levy, chairman of the Rhodes University council; Sylvia Kaplan, national president of the South African Association of Arts; and Mendel Kaplan, treasurer of the World Jewish Congress.

A number of Jews were returned to Parliament, including Harry Schwartz, Ruben Sive, Helen Suzman, and Alf Widman, all of the Progressive Federal party. Theo Aronson was not reelected, but was returned to Parliament as a nominated member of the National party. Simon Chilchik, Alan Gadd, Herbert Hirsh, Irene Menell, Joel Mervis, and Samuel Moss were elected as provincial councillors. Jews elected to local government office included: Louis Kreiner, mayor of Cape Town for a second term; S.J. Gross, mayor of Vereeniging; H. Wolder, mayor of Fochville for a second term; Peter Ucko, mayor of Edenvale; Ivor Katz, junior mayor of Johannesburg; Dave Milner, mayor of Newcastle.

Individuals achieving honors in sports included: Greta Glaser, winner of the South African women bowlers' singles championship; Alan Chait, table tennis champion, chosen as Western province sportsman of the year; Charmaine Gale, *Fair Lady* sportswoman of the year; Antony Wainer, skier, Maccabi junior sportsman of the year; Mandi Yachad, cricketer, Maccabi sportsman of the year; and Peter Lindenberg, water-skier, the State President's Award for 1981.

Among prominent Jews who died during the year were: Norman Addelson, lawyer, sportsman, journalist, governor of Rhodes University, and communal leader in the Cape Border region, in February; Philip Lapin, veteran Pretoria lawyer, in April; Philip Bernstein, Cape Town lawyer and sportsman, in April; Maurice Porter, lawyer, Jewish communal leader, and past president of SAJBD, in June; Harry

Sneech, freeman of Edenvale, businessman and philanthropist, in July; Barney Shapiro, Vereeniging Jewish communal leader, in October; Rebecca Ostrowiak, educator, in October; Phyllis (Inkey) Lopert, national director SAZF Jewish National Fund Charitable Trust, in October; Shlomo Mandel, cantor of Berea Hebrew Congregation for 30 years, prior to his *aliyah* to Israel, in October; Louis Franklin Freed, scientist, author, and civic worker, in December; Solly Leibman, founder of Pretoria Progressive Jewish Congregation, in December; Professor Michael Moshal, director, South Africa Medical Research Council Institute for Diseases in Tropical Environments, in January; Ruth Hayman, civic and social worker, in January.

DENIS DIAMOND

World Jewish Population

THE 1982 AMERICAN JEWISH YEAR BOOK (AJYB) CONTAINED new estimates of the Jewish population in various countries of the world at the end of 1980, as well as background information and analysis. The statistical tables are reprinted here, without the accompanying text. Changes have been made in one respect only. While the estimates for Jews in the 1982 AJYB related to the end of 1980, the data for the general population of the respective countries reproduced the United Nations estimates as of mid-year 1979. This time the updated United Nations estimates as of mid-year 1980 have been used for the total population,[1] and the proportion of Jews per 1,000 of the respective country's total population has been recomputed accordingly.

The 1984 AJYB will present updated and, where necessary, revised Jewish population estimates for the countries of the world at the end of 1982.

In Tables 4-8 the following rating of the Jewish population estimates has been given: (A) base figure derived from countrywide census or reliable Jewish population survey; updated on the basis of full or partial information on Jewish population movements in intervening period; (B) base figure derived from somewhat less accurate countrywide Jewish population investigation; partial information on population movements in intervening period; (C) base figure derived from less recent sources and/or partial geographical coverage of Jewish population in country; updating according to demographic information illustrative of regional demographic trends; and (D) base figure essentially conjectural; no reliable updating procedure. In categories (A) and (B) the year for which the principal base figure was obtained is also reported. The time elapsed since that date provides an additional yardstick to assess reliability of data.

U. O. SCHMELZ
SERGIO DELLAPERGOLA

---

[1]United Nations, Department of International Economic and Social Affairs, Statistical Office, *Population and Vital Statistics Report: Data Available as of January 1, 1982.* (ST/ESA/STAT/SER. A/139).

TABLE 1. WORLD JEWISH POPULATION, 1970–1980 (ROUGH ESTIMATES)

	In Thousands			Per Cent		% Change
	1970	1975	1980	1970	1980	1970–1980
Diaspora	10,242	10,020	9,745	79.9	74.8	− 4.8
Israel	2,582	2,959	3,283	20.1	25.2	+ 27.1
World	12,824	12,979	13,028	100.0	100.0	+ 1.6

TABLE 2. CHANGES IN WORLD JEWISH POPULATION, 1970–1980 (ROUGH ESTIMATES)

Type of Change	1971–1980	1971–1975	1976–1980
	In Thousands		
Diaspora, total change	− 497	− 222	− 275
Natural and affiliative	− 280	− 82	− 198
Net *aliyah*	− 217	− 140	− 77
Israel, total change	+ 701	+ 377	+ 324
Natural	+ 484	+ 237	+ 247
Net *aliyah*	+ 217	+ 140	+ 77
World, total change[a]	+ 204	+ 155	+ 49

[a]I.e., natural change in Diaspora and Israel, affiliative change in Diaspora.

TABLE 3. ESTIMATED JEWISH POPULATION, BY CONTINENTS AND MAJOR
GEOGRAPHICAL REGIONS, 1980

Region	Number	Per Cent
America, Total[a]	6,491,950	49.8
North[b]	5,998,000	46.1
Central	44,050	0.3
South	449,200	3.4
Europe, Total[a]	2,969,500	22.8
West	1,119,500	8.6
East & Balkans[c]	1,848,500	14.2
Asia, Total	3,327,900	25.5
Israel	3,282,700	25.2
Rest[c]	45,200	0.3
Africa, Total	164,550	1.3
North	21,050	0.2
South	109,550	0.8
Rest[d]	33,950	0.3
Oceania	74,000	0.6
World	13,027,900	100.0

[a]Including "Other countries."

[b]U.S.A. and Canada.

[c]The Asian territories of USSR and Turkey are included in "East Europe and Balkans."

[d]Including Ethiopia.

TABLE 4. ESTIMATED JEWISH POPULATION DISTRIBUTION IN THE AMERICAS, 1980

Country	Total Population	Jewish Population	Jews per 1,000 Population	Accuracy Rating
Canada	23,941,000	308,000	12.9	A 1971
U.S.A.	227,658,000	5,690,000	25.0	B 1971
Total Northern America		5,998,000		
Bahamas	237,000	500	2.1	B 1970
Costa Rica	2,245,000	2,500	1.1	C
Cuba	9,833,000	1,000	0.1	D
Dominican Republic	5,431,000	200	0.0	D
El Salvador	4,813,000	350	0.1	C
Guatemala	7,262,000	1,100	0.2	C
Haiti	5,009,000	150	0.0	D
Jamaica	2,192,000	250	0.1	D
Mexico	71,911,000	35,000	0.5	C
Netherlands Antilles	266,000	700	2.6	C
Panama	1,837,000	2,000	1.1	C
Trinidad	1,139,000	300	0.3	D
Total Central America[a]		44,050		
Argentina	27,064,000	242,000	8.9	B 1960
Bolivia	5,600,000	1,000	0.2	C
Brazil	123,032,000	110,000	0.9	B 1960
Chile	11,104,000	25,000	2.2	D
Colombia	27,093,000	7,000	0.3	B 1977
Ecuador	8,354,000	1,000	0.1	D
Paraguay	3,067,000	700	0.2	C
Peru	17,780,000	5,000	0.3	C
Surinam	389,000	500	1.3	C
Uruguay	2,899,000	40,000	13.8	D
Venezuela	13,913,000	17,000	1.2	D
Total Southern America[a]		449,200		
Other		700		
Total		6,491,950		

[a]Total of countries reported in detail.

TABLE 5. ESTIMATED JEWISH POPULATION DISTRIBUTION IN EUROPE, 1980

Country	Total Population	Jewish Population	Jews per 1,000 Population	Accuracy Rating
Austria	7,505,000	8,000	1.1	A 1971
Belgium	9,857,000	33,000	3.3	C
Bulgaria	8,862,000	3,500	0.4	B 1965
Czechoslovakia	15,312,000	9,000	0.6	D
Denmark	5,123,000	7,000	1.4	C
Finland	4,779,000	1,200	0.2	A 1976
France	53,713,000	535,000	10.0	B 1972–78
Germany, East	16,737,000	1,000	0.1	D
Germany, West	61,561,000	33,500	0.5	A 1970
Gibraltar	33,000	550	16.7	A 1970
Great Britain	55,945,000	390,000	7.0	C
Greece	9,559,000	5,000	0.5	A 1978
Hungary	10,713,000	65,000	6.1	D
Ireland	3,401,000	2,000	0.6	B 1971
Italy	57,042,000	32,000	0.6	B 1965
Luxembourg	358,000	750	2.1	A 1971
Netherlands	14,144,000	27,000	1.9	B 1966
Norway	4,086,000	900	0.2	A 1970
Poland	35,578,000	5,000	0.1	D
Portugal	9,933,000	600	0.1	C
Rumania	22,201,000	33,000	1.5	B 1977–79
Spain	37,430,000	12,000	0.3	D
Sweden	8,311,000	15,000	1.8	C
Switzerland	6,373,000	21,000	3.3	A 1970
Turkey[a]	44,438,000	22,000	0.5	B 1965
USSR[a]	265,542,000	1,700,000	6.4	B 1979
Yugoslavia	22,344,000	5,000	0.2	B 1971–72
Other		1,500		
Total		2,969,500		

[a]Including Asian regions.

TABLE 6.   ESTIMATED JEWISH POPULATION DISTRIBUTION IN ASIA, 1980

Country	Total Population	Jewish Population	Jews per 1,000 Population	Accuracy Rating
Hong Kong	5,068,000	250	0.0	D
India	663,596,000	4,500	0.0	B 1971
Iran	37,447,000	32,000	0.8	C
Iraq	13,084,000	200	0.0	D
Israel	3,921,700a	3,282,700	837.1	A 1980
Japan	116,782,000	700	0.0	D
Lebanon	3,161,000	200	0.1	D
Philippines	48,400,000	200	0.0	D
Singapore	2,391,000	450	0.2	D
Syria	8,979,000	4,500	0.5	D
Yemen	5,926,000	1,200	0.2	D
Other		1,000		
Total		3,327,900		

aEnd 1980.

TABLE 7.   ESTIMATED JEWISH POPULATION DISTRIBUTION IN AFRICA, 1980

Country	Total Population	Jewish Population	Jews per 1,000 Population	Accuracy Rating
Algeria	18,594,000	300	0.0	D
Egypt	42,201,000	250	0.0	D
Ethiopia	31,065,000	32,000	1.0	B 1976
Kenya	16,402,000	450	0.0	D
Morocco	20,242,000	18,000	0.9	B 1970
South Africa	29,285,000	108,000	3.7	A 1970–74
Tunisia	6,369,000	2,500	0.4	D
Zaire	28,291,000	200	0.0	D
Zambia	5,834,000	300	0.1	D
Zimbabwe	7,360,000	1,550	0.2	C
Other		1,000		
Total		164,550		

TABLE 8.   ESTIMATED JEWISH POPULATION DISTRIBUTION IN OCEANIA, 1980

Country	Total Population	Jewish Population	Jews per 1,000 Population	Accuracy Rating
Australia	14,616,000	70,000	4.8	A 1971–76
New Zealand	3,100,000	4,000	1.3	A 1971
Total		74,000		

TABLE 9.   COUNTRIES WITH LARGEST JEWISH POPULATION (100,000 JEWS AND ABOVE), 1980

Rank	Country	Jewish Population	% of Total Jewish Population: In the Diaspora	In the World
1	United States	5,690,000	58.4	43.7
2	Israel	3,282,700	-	25.2
3	Soviet Union	1,700,000	17.4	13.1
4	France	535,000	5.5	4.1
5	Great Britain	390,000	4.0	3.0
6	Canada	308,000	3.2	2.4
7	Argentina	242,000	2.5	1.9
8	Brazil	110,000	1.1	0.8
9	South Africa	108,000	1.1	0.8
	Total 8 Largest Diaspora Communities	9,083,000	93.2	69.7
	Total 9 Largest World Communities	12,365,700	-	94.9

Directories
Lists
Necrology

National Jewish Organizations[1]

UNITED STATES

Organizations are listed according to functions as follows:

COMMUNITY RELATIONS

AMERICAN COUNCIL FOR JUDAISM (1943). 307 Fifth Ave., Suite 1006, N.Y.C., 10016. (212)889-1313. Pres. Clarence L. Coleman, Jr.; Sec. Alan V. Stone. Seeks to advance the universal principles of a Judaism free of nationalism, and the national, civic, cultural, and social integration into American institutions of Americans of Jewish faith. *Issues of the American Council for Judaism; Special Interest Report.*

AMERICAN JEWISH ALTERNATIVES TO ZIONISM, INC. (1968). 133 E. 73 St., N.Y.C., 10021. (212)628-2727. Pres. Elmer Berger; V. Pres. Mrs. Arthur Gutman. Applies Jewish values of justice and humanity to the Arab-Israel conflict in the Middle East; rejects nationality attachment of Jews, particularly American Jews, to the State of Israel as self-segregating, inconsistent with American constitutional concepts of individual citizenship and separation of church and state, and as being a principal obstacle to Middle East peace. *Report.*

AMERICAN JEWISH COMMITTEE (1906). Institute of Human Relations, 165 E. 56 St., N.Y.C., 10022. (212)751-4000. Pres. Maynard I. Wishner; Exec. V. Pres. Donald Feldstein. Seeks to prevent infraction of civil and religious rights of Jews in any part of the world; to advance the cause of human rights for people of all races,

---

[1]The information in this directory is based on replies to questionnaires circulated by the editors. Inclusion does not necessarily imply approval of the organizations by the publishers; nor can they assume responsibility for the accuracy of the data.

creeds, and nationalities; to interpret the position of Israel to the American public; and to help American Jews maintain and enrich their Jewish identity and, at the same time, achieve full integration in American life; includes Jacob and Hilda Blaustein Center for Human Relations, William E. Wiener Oral History Library, Leonard and Rose Sperry International Center for the Resolution of Group Conflict. AMERICAN JEWISH YEAR BOOK (with Jewish Publication Society of America); *Commentary; Present Tense; What's Doing at the Committee.*

AMERICAN JEWISH CONGRESS (1918). Stephen Wise Congress House, 15 E. 84 St., N.Y.C., 10028. (212)879-4500. Pres. Howard M. Squadron; Exec. Dir. Henry Siegman. Works to foster the creative religious and cultural survival of the Jewish people; to help Israel develop in peace, freedom, and security; to eliminate all forms of racial and religious bigotry; to advance civil rights, protect civil liberties, defend religious freedom, and safeguard the separation of church and state. Maintains the Martin Steinberg Center for Jewish arts and artists. *Congress Monthly; Judaism; Boycott Report; Jewish Arts Newsletter.*

ANTI-DEFAMATION LEAGUE OF B'NAI B'RITH (1913). 823 United Nations Plaza, N.Y.C., 10017. (212)490-2525. Nat. Chmn. Maxwell E. Greenberg; Nat. Dir. Nathan Perlmutter. Seeks to combat antisemitism and to secure justice and fair treatment for all citizens through law, education and community relations. *ADL Bulletin: Face to Face; Fact Finding Report; Israel Backgrounder; Law Notes; Rights; Law; Research and Evaluation Report; Discriminations Report.*

ASSOCIATION OF JEWISH CENTER WORKERS (1918). 15 E. 26 St., N.Y.C., 10010. (212)532-4949. Pres. Bernard T. Rosen; Exec. Dir. Herman L. Zimmerman. Seeks to enhance and improve the standards, techniques, practices, scope, and public understanding of Jewish community center and kindred work. *The Kesher; Viewpoints.*

ASSOCIATION OF JEWISH COMMUNITY RELATIONS WORKERS (1950). 155 Fifth Ave., N.Y.C., 10010. (212)533-7800. Pres. Muriel Bermar; Exec. Dir. Ann Plutzer. Aims to stimulate higher standards of professional practice in Jewish community relations; encourages research and training

toward that end; conducts educational programs and seminars; aims to encourage cooperation between community relations workers and those working in other areas of Jewish communal service. Quarterly newsletter.

CENTER FOR JEWISH COMMUNITY STUDIES (1970). 555 Gladfelter Hall, Temple University, Philadelphia, Pa., 19122. (215)787-1459. Chmn. Daniel J. Elazar; V. Chmn. Charles S. Liebman. Worldwide consortium of scholars devoted to the study of Jewish community organization, political thought and public affairs, past and present, in Israel and throughout the world. Publishes original articles, essays, and monographs; maintains library, archives, and reprint series. *Jerusalem Letter/Viewpoints; Tefutsot Israel.*

COMMISSION ON SOCIAL ACTION OF REFORM JUDAISM (1953) (under the auspices of the Union of American Hebrew Congregations). 838 Fifth Ave., N.Y.C., 10021. (212)249-0100. Chmn. Alex Ross; Dir. Albert Vorspan; Assoc. Dir. David Saperstein. Develops materials to assist Reform synagogues in setting up social-action programs relating the principles of Judaism to contemporary social problems; assists congregations in studying the moral and religious implications in social issues such as civil rights, civil liberties, church-state relations; guides congregational social-action committees. *Issues of Conscience; Newsletter.*

COMMITTEE TO BRING NAZI WAR CRIMINALS TO JUSTICE IN U.S.A., INC. (1973). 17 Fort George Hill Ave., N.Y.C., 10040. (212)942-8071. Pres. Charles H. Kremer; Treas. Jacob Zonis. Compiles and publicizes records of Nazi atrocities and labors to bring to justice the perpetrators of those crimes. Remains committed to preserving the memory of all victims of the Holocaust, and actively opposes antisemitism wherever and however it is found.

CONFERENCE OF PRESIDENTS OF MAJOR AMERICAN JEWISH ORGANIZATIONS (1955). 515 Park Ave., N.Y.C., 10022. (212)752-1616. Chmn. Howard M. Squadron; Exec. V. Chmn. Yehuda Hellman. Coordinates the activities of 34 major American Jewish organizations as they relate to American-Israeli affairs and problems affecting Jews in other lands. *Annual Report; Middle East Memo.*

CONSULTATIVE COUNCIL OF JEWISH OR-
GANIZATIONS-CCJO (1946). 135 William
St., N.Y.C., 10038. (212)349-0537. Co-
Chmn. Basil Bard, Jules Braunschvig,
Joseph Nuss; V. Chmn. Arnold Franco;
Sec.-Gen. Moses Moskowitz. A nongov-
ernmental organization in consultative sta-
tus with the UN, UNESCO, International
Labor Organization, UNICEF, and the
Council of Europe; cooperates and con-
sults with, advises and renders assistance
to the Economic and Social Council of the
United Nations on all problems relating to
human rights and economic, social, cultural, educational, and related matters pertaining to Jews.

COORDINATING BOARD OF JEWISH ORGAN-
IZATIONS (1947). 1640 Rhode Island Ave.,
N.W., Washington, D.C., 20036. (202)857-
6545. Pres. Jack J. Spitzer (B'nai B'rith),
Greville Janner (Board of Deputies of British Jews), David K. Mann (South African
Jewish Board of Deputies); Exec. V. Pres.
Daniel Thursz (U.S.). As an organization
in consultative status with the Economic
and Social Council of the United Nations,
represents the three constituents (B'nai
B'rith, the Board of Deputies of British
Jews, and the South African Jewish Board
of Deputies) in the appropriate United Nations bodies for the purpose of promoting
human rights, with special attention to
combatting persecution or discrimination
on grounds of race, religion, or origin.

COUNCIL OF JEWISH ORGANIZATIONS IN
CIVIL SERVICE, INC. (1948). 45 E. 33 St.,
N.Y.C., 10016. (212)689-2015. Pres. Louis
Weiser. Supports merit system; combats
discrimination; promotes all Jewish inter-
est projects; sponsors scholarships; is mem-
ber of Greater N.Y. Conference on Soviet
Jewry, Jewish Labor Committee, America-
Israel Friendship League, N.Y. Jewish
Community Relations Committee, N.Y.
Metropolitan Coordinating Council on
Jewish Poverty. *CJO Digest.*

INSTITUTE FOR JEWISH POLICY PLANNING
AND RESEARCH (see Synagogue Council of
America, p. 303).

INTERNATIONAL CONFERENCE OF JEWISH
COMMUNAL SERVICE (1966). 15 E. 26 St.,
N.Y.C., 10010. (212)683-8056. Pres.
Ralph I. Goldman; Sec.-Gen. Solomon H.
Green. Established by Jewish commu-
nal workers to strengthen their under-
standing of each other's programs and to
communicate with colleagues in order to
enrich quality of their work. Conducts
quadrennial international conferences in
Jerusalem and periodic regional meetings.
*Proceedings of International Conferences;
Newsletter.*

JEWISH LABOR COMMITTEE (1934). Atran
Center for Jewish Culture, 25 E. 78 St.,
N.Y.C., 10021. (212)535-3700. Pres. Donald Slaiman; Exec. Dir. Emanuel Murav-
chik. Serves as a link between the Jewish
community and the trade union movement; works with the AFL-CIO and others
to combat all forms of racial and religious
discrimination in the United States and
abroad; furthers labor support for Israel's
security and Soviet Jewry, and Jewish communal support for labor's social and economic programs; supports Yiddish cultural institutions. *JLC News.*

———, NATIONAL TRADE UNION COUNCIL
FOR HUMAN RIGHTS (1956). Atran Center
for Jewish Culture, 25 E. 78 St., N.Y.C.,
10021. (212)535-3700. Chmn. Wilbur
Daniels; Exec. Sec. Martin Lapan. Works
with trade unions on programs and issues
affecting both labor and the Jewish community.

———, WOMEN'S DIVISION OF (1947).
Atran Center for Jewish Culture, 25 E. 78
St., N.Y.C., 10021. (212)535-3700. Nat.
Chmn. Eleanor Schachner. Supports the
general activities of the Jewish Labor Committee; provides secondary school and college scholarships for needy Israeli students; participates in educational and
cultural activities.

———, WORKMEN'S CIRCLE DIVISION OF
(1939). Atran Center for Jewish Culture,
25 E. 78 St., N.Y.C., 10021. (212)535-
3700. Chmn. Bernard Rifkin; Co-Chmn.
Abraham Finesilver. Promotes aims of,
and raises funds for, the Jewish Labor
Committee among the Workmen's Circle
branches; conducts Yiddish educational
and cultural activities.

JEWISH WAR VETERANS OF THE UNITED
STATES OF AMERICA (1896). 1712 New
Hampshire Ave., N. W., Washington,
D.C., 20009. (202)265-6280. Nat. Comdr.
Robert M. Zweiman; Nat. Exec. Dir. Harris B. Stone. Seeks to foster true allegiance
to the United States; to combat bigotry and
prevent defamation of Jews; to encourage
the doctrine of universal liberty, equal

rights, and full justice for all; to cooperate with and support existing educational institutions and establish new ones; to foster the education of ex-servicemen, ex-servicewomen, and members in the ideals and principles of Americanism. *Jewish Veteran; The JWV Washington Report.*

————, NATIONAL MEMORIAL, INC; NATIONAL SHRINE TO THE JEWISH WAR DEAD (1958). 1712 New Hampshire Ave., N.W., Washington, D.C., 20009. (202)265-6280. Pres. Ainslee R. Ferdie; Treas. Cornelius Schneider. Administers shrine in Washington, D.C., a repository for medals and honors won by Jewish men and women for valor from Revolutionary War to present; maintains *Golden Book* of names of the war dead.

NATIONAL CONFERENCE ON SOVIET JEWRY (formerly AMERICAN JEWISH CONFERENCE ON SOVIET JEWRY) (1964; reorg. 1971). 10 E. 40 St., Suite 907, N.Y.C., 10016. (212)679-6122. Chmn. Theodore R. Mann; Exec. Dir. Jerry Goodman. Coordinating agency for major national Jewish organizations and local community groups in the U.S., acting on behalf of Soviet Jewry through public education and social action; stimulates all segments of the community to maintain an interest in the problems of Soviet Jews by publishing reports and special pamphlets, sponsoring special programs and projects, organizing public meetings and forums. *Press Service; Leadership Wrap-Up Series; Activities Report.*

————, SOVIET JEWRY RESEARCH BUREAU. Chmn. Charlotte Jacobson. Organized by NCSJ to monitor emigration trends. Primary task is the accumulation, evaluation, and processing of information regarding Soviet Jews, especially those who apply for emigration.

NATIONAL JEWISH COMMISSION ON LAW AND PUBLIC AFFAIRS (COLPA) (1965). 71 Broadway, 6th fl., N.Y.C., 10006. (212)-269-0810. Pres. Howard Zuckerman; Exec. Dir. Dennis Rapps. Voluntary association of attorneys whose purpose is to represent the Orthodox Jewish community on legal matters and matters of public affairs.

NATIONAL JEWISH COMMUNITY RELATIONS ADVISORY COUNCIL (1944). 443 Park Ave. S., 11th fl., N.Y.C., 10016. (212)684-6950. Chmn. Bennett Yanowitz;

Exec. V. Chmn. Albert D. Chernin; Sec. Raymond Epstein. Consultative, advisory, and coordinating council of 11 national Jewish organizations and 108 local Jewish councils that seeks cooperatively the promotion of understanding of Israel and the Middle East; freedom for Jews in the Soviet Union; equal status and opportunity for all groups, including Jews, with full expression of distinctive group values and full participation in the general society. Through the processes of the Council, its constituent organizations seek agreement on policies, strategies, and programs for most effective utilization of their collective resources for common ends. *Guide to Program Planning for Jewish Community Relations.*

NORTH AMERICAN JEWISH YOUTH COUNCIL (1965). 515 Park Ave., N.Y.C., 10022. (212)751-6070. Chmn. Craig Wasserman; Exec. Dir. Donald Adelman. Provides a framework for coordination and exchange of programs and information among national Jewish youth organizations to help them deepen the concern of American Jewish youth for world Jewry; represents Jewish youth in the Conference of Presidents, United States Youth Council, etc.

STUDENT STRUGGLE FOR SOVIET JEWRY, INC. (1964). 210 W. 91 St., N.Y.C., 10024. (212)799-8900. Nat. Dir. Jacob Birnbaum; Nat. Coord. Glenn Richter. Provides information and action guidance to adult and student organizations, communities and schools throughout U.S. and Canada; assists individual Soviet Jews financially and by publicity campaigns; helps Russian Jews in the U.S.; aids Rumanian Jews seeking emigration; maintains speakers bureau. *Soviet Jewry Action Newsletter.*

UNION OF COUNCILS FOR SOVIET JEWS (1969). 1522 K Street, N.W., Suite 1110, Wash., D.C., 20005. Pres. Robert Gordon; Exec. Dir. Davida Manon. A confederation of 28 grass-roots organizations established in support of Soviet Jewry. Acts as a clearinghouse for information; organizes political and educational activities in support of Soviet Jews. *Alert.*

WORLD JEWISH CONGRESS (1936; org. in U.S. 1939). 1 Park Ave., Suite 418, N.Y.C., 10016. (212)679-0600. Pres. Edgar M. Bronfman; Chmn. No. Amer. Branch, Sol Kanee; Chmn. Amer. Sect. Arthur Schneier; Sec.-Gen. Gerhart M. Riegner

(Geneva); Exec. Dir. Israel Singer. Seeks to intensify bonds of world Jewry with Israel as central force in Jewish life; to strengthen solidarity among Jews everywhere and secure their rights, status, and interests as individuals and communities; to encourage development of Jewish social, religious, and cultural life throughout the world and coordinate efforts by Jewish communities and organizations to cope with any Jewish problem; to work for human rights generally. Represents its affiliated organizations —most representative bodies of Jewish communities in more than 65 countries and 21 national organizations in Amer. section—at UN, OAS, UNESCO, Council of Europe, ILO, UNICEF and other governmental, intergovernmental, and international authorities. Publications (including those by Institute of Jewish Affairs, London): *Christian Jewish Relations; Jewish Cultural News; News and Views; Boletín Informativo OJI; Batfutsot; Gesher; Patterns of Prejudice; Soviet Jewish Affairs.*

CULTURAL

AMERICAN ACADEMY FOR JEWISH RESEARCH (1920). 3080 Broadway, N.Y.C., 10027. Pres. Salo W. Baron; Sec. Isaac E. Barzilay. Encourages research by aiding scholars in need and by giving grants for the publication of scholarly works. *Proceedings, American Academy for Jewish Research.*

AMERICAN BIBLICAL ENCYCLOPEDIA SOCIETY (1930). 24 West Maple Ave., Monsey, N.Y., 10952. (914)425-8079. Pres. Leo Jung; Exec. V. Pres. Bernard Greenbaum; Author-Ed. Menachem M. Kasher. Fosters biblical-talmudical research; sponsors and publishes *Torah Shelemah* (the Encyclopedia of Biblical Interpretation) and related publications; disseminates the teachings and values of the Bible. *Noam.*

AMERICAN HISTADRUT CULTURAL EXCHANGE INSTITUTE (1962). 33 E. 67 St., N.Y.C., 10021. (212)628-1000. Nat. Chmn. Herbert Levine. Serves as a vehicle for promoting better understanding of the efforts to create in Israel a society based on social justice. Provides a forum for the joint exploration of the urgent social problems of our times by American and Israeli labor, academic, and community leaders. Publishes pamphlets and books on various Israeli and Middle East topics.

AMERICAN JEWISH HISTORICAL SOCIETY (1892). 2 Thornton Rd., Waltham, Mass., 02154. (617)891-8110. Pres. Ruth B. Fein; Dir. Bernard Wax. Collects, catalogues, publishes and displays material on the history of the Jews in America; serves as an information center for inquiries on American Jewish history; maintains archives of original source material on American Jewish history; sponsors lectures and exhibitions; makes available historic Yiddish films and audio-visual material. *American Jewish History; Newsletter.*

AMERICAN JEWISH PRESS ASSOCIATION (formerly AMERICAN ASSOCIATION OF ENGLISH JEWISH NEWSPAPERS) (1943). c/o Jewish Chronicle, 315 S. Bellefield Ave., Pittsburgh, Pa., 15213. (412)687-1000. Pres. Albert W. Bloom. Seeks the advancement of Jewish journalism, the attainment of the highest editorial and business standards for members, and the maintenance of a strong Jewish press in the U.S. and Canada.

AMERICAN SOCIETY FOR JEWISH MUSIC (1974). 155 Fifth Ave., N.Y.C., 10010. (212)533-2601. Pres. Albert Weisser; V. Pres.-Treas. Paul Kavon; Sec. Hadássah B. Markson. Seeks to raise standards of composition and performance in Jewish liturgical and secular music; encourages research in all areas of Jewish music; publishes scholarly journal; presents programs and sponsors performances of new and rarely heard works and encourages their recording; commissions new works of Jewish interest. *Musica Judaica.*

ASSOCIATED AMERICAN JEWISH MUSEUMS, INC. (1971). 303 LeRoi Road, Pittsburgh, Pa., 15208. Pres. Walter Jacob; V. Pres. William Rosenthall; Sec. Robert H. Lehman; Treas. Jason Z. Edelstein. Maintains regional collections of Jewish art, historical and ritual objects, as well as a central catalogue of such objects in the collections of Jewish museums throughout the U.S.; helps Jewish museums acquire, identify, and classify objects; arranges exchanges of collections, exhibits, and individual objects among Jewish museums; encourages the creation of Jewish art, ceremonial and ritual objects.

ASSOCIATION FOR THE SOCIOLOGICAL STUDY OF JEWRY (1971). Dept. of Sociology, Ohio State University, Columbus, Oh., 43210. (614)422-5658. Pres. Harold S.

Himmelfarb; V. Pres. Rela Geffen Monson; Sec. Treas. Abraham Lavender. Arranges academic sessions among social scientists studying Jewry; facilitates communication among social scientists studying Jewry through meetings, newsletter, and related materials. *Contemporary Jewry: A Journal of Sociological Inquiry; The ASSJ Newsletter.*

ASSOCIATION OF JEWISH LIBRARIES (1965). c/o National Foundation for Jewish Culture, 408 Chanin Bldg., 122 E. 42 St., N.Y.C., 10168. (212)490-2280. Pres. Philip Miller; V. Pres. Hazel Karp. Seeks to promote and improve services and professional standards in Jewish libraries; serves as a center for the dissemination of Jewish library information and guidance; promotes publication of literature in the field; encourages the establishment of Jewish libraries and collections of Judaica and the choice of Jewish librarianship as a vocation. *AJL Bulletin; Proceedings; AJL Newsletter.*

ASSOCIATION OF JEWISH BOOK PUBLISHERS (1962). 838 Fifth Ave., N.Y.C., 10021. (212)249-0100. Pres. Jacob Steinberg. As a nonprofit group, provides a forum for discussion of mutual problems by publishers, authors, and other individuals and institutions concerned with books of Jewish interest. Provides national and international exhibit opportunities for Jewish books.

CENTER FOR HOLOCAUST STUDIES, INC. (1974). 1605 Ave. J., Bklyn, N.Y., 11230. (212)338-6494. Dir. Yaffa Eliach; Chmn. Adv. Bd. Allen J. Bodner. Collects and preserves documents and memorabilia, oral histories, and literary works on the Holocaust period for purpose of documentation and research; arranges lectures and exhibits; maintains speakers bureau and audio-visual department. *Newsletter.*

CENTRAL YIDDISH CULTURE ORGANIZATION (CYCO), INC. (1943). 25 E. 78 St., N.Y.C., 10021. Pres. Noah Singman; Sec. Jona Gutkowicz. Promotes and publishes Yiddish books; distributes books from other Yiddish publishing houses throughout the world; publishes annual bibliographical and statistical register of Yiddish books, and catalogues of new publications. *Zukunft.*

CONFERENCE ON JEWISH SOCIAL STUDIES, INC. (formerly CONFERENCE ON JEWISH RELATIONS, INC.) (1939). 250 W. 57 St., N.Y.C., 10019. Pres. Jeannette M. Baron; Hon. Pres. Salo W. Baron; V. Pres. Joseph L. Blau, J. M. Kaplan. Publishes scientific studies on the Jews in the modern world, dealing with such aspects as antisemitism, demography, economic stratification, history, philosophy, and political developments. *Jewish Social Studies.*

CONGRESS FOR JEWISH CULTURE, INC. (1948). 25 E. 78 St., N.Y.C., 10021. (212)-879-2232. Pres. Joseph Landis; Exec. Dir. Hyman B. Bass. Seeks to centralize and promote Jewish culture and cultural activities throughout the world, and to unify fund-raising for these activities. *Bulletin fun Kultur Kongres; Zukunft; Leksikon fun der Nayer Yiddisher Literature; Pinkos far der Forshung fun der Yiddisher Literature un Presse; World of Yiddish.*

THE HEBREW ARTS SCHOOL (1952). 129 W. 67 St., N.Y.C., 10023. (212)362-8060. Bd. Chmn. Abraham Goodman; Pres. Philip Esterman; Dir. Tzipora H. Jochsberger; Sec. Benjamin W. Mehlman. Chartered by the Board of Regents, University of the State of New York. Provides children with training in music, dance, and art, combining instructions in Western culture with the cultural heritage of the Jewish people; adult division offers instrumental, vocal, dance, and art classes, music workshops for teachers, ensemble workshops, and classes of special interest covering many areas of music-making, dance, and art; has Jewish Music Teacher Training Institute, a part-time program for professional musicians or music majors; sponsors Hebrew Arts Chamber Players, Hebrew Arts Concert Choir, Young Musicians Concerts, Mendelssohn String Quartet, Great Cantors Series, Heritage Concerts. Hebrew Arts Music Publications; *Notes & Quotes.*

HEBREW CULTURE FOUNDATION (1955). 515 Park Ave., N.Y.C., 10022. (212)752-0600. Chmn. Milton R. Konvitz; Sec. Herman L. Sainer. Sponsors the introduction of the study of Hebrew language and literature in institutions of higher learning in the United States.

HISTADRUTH IVRITH OF AMERICA (1916; reorg. 1922). 1841 Broadway, N.Y.C., 10023. (212)581-5151. Pres. Alvin Kass; Exec. Dir. Shlomo Shamir. Emphasizes the primacy of Hebrew in Jewish life, culture, and education; aims to disseminate knowledge of written and spoken Hebrew in the Diaspora, thus building a cultural bridge between the State of Israel and Jewish communities throughout the world. *Hadoar; Lamishpaha.*

HOLOCAUST CENTER OF GREATER PITTS-BURGH (1980). 315 S. Bellefield Ave., Pittsburgh, Pa., 15213. (412)682-7111. Dir. Isaiah Kuperstein; Chmn. Alvin Rogal. Develops programs and provides resources to further an understanding of the Holocaust and its impact on civilization.

JEWISH ACADEMY OF ARTS AND SCIENCES, INC. (1925). c/o Sec'y, 123 Gregory Ave., West Orange, N.J., 07052. (201)731-1137. Headquarters: Dropsie University, Philadelphia, Pa., 19132. Pres. Jewish Center, N.Y.C. Leo Jung; Pres. Emeritus Dropsie Univ. Abraham I. Katsh. Scholarship, contributions, accomplishments of Jews in the arts and sciences; recognition by election to membership and/or fellowship; publishes papers delivered at annual convocations. *Annals.*

JEWISH INFORMATION BUREAU, INC. (1932). 250 W. 57 St., N.Y.C., 10019. (212)582-5318. Acting Dir. Grace S. Orgel; V. Chmn. Eleazar Lipsky. Serves as clearinghouse of information for inquiries regarding Jews, Judaism, Israel, and Jewish affairs; refers inquiries to communal agencies.

JEWISH MUSEUM (1904) (under auspices of Jewish Theological Seminary of America). 1109 Fifth Ave., N.Y.C., 10028. (212)860-1888. Dir. Joan Rosenbaum; Pres. Richard J. Scheuer. Main repository in western hemisphere of Jewish ceremonial objects. Collection ranges from Biblical archaeology to contemporary Judaica. Offers changing exhibitions of paintings, sculpture, and photography, in addition to films, lectures, and children's programs. Dedicated to exploring richness and diversity of past and present Jewish life; publishes catalogues of exhibitions.

JEWISH PUBLICATION SOCIETY OF AMERICA (1888). 1930 Chestnut St., Philadelphia, Pa., 19103. (215)564-5925. Pres. Muriel M. Berman; Ed. Maier Deshell; Exec. V. Pres. Bernard I. Levinson. Publishes and disseminates books of Jewish interest on history, religion, and literature for the purpose of helping to preserve

Jewish heritage and culture. AMERICAN JEWISH YEAR BOOK (with American Jewish Committee).

JUDAH L. MAGNES MEMORIAL MUSEUM—JEWISH MUSEUM OF THE WEST (1962). 2911 Russell St., Berkeley, Calif., 94705. (415)849-2710. Pres. Jacques Reulinger; V. Pres. Mathilde Albers; Dir. Seymour Fromer. Serves both as museum and library, combining historical and literary materials illustrating Jewish life in the Bay Area, the Western states, and around the world; provides archives of world Jewish history and Jewish art; repository of historical documents intended for scholarly use; changing exhibits; facilities open to the general public. *Magnes Museum News.*

JWB JEWISH BOOK COUNCIL (1942). 15 E. 26 St., N.Y.C., 10010. (212)532-4949. Pres. Robert Gordis; Dir. Ruth S. Frank. Promotes knowledge of Jewish books through dissemination of booklists, program materials; sponsors Jewish Book Month; presents literary awards and library citations; cooperates with publishers of Jewish books. *Jewish Book Annual; Jewish Books in Review.*

JWB JEWISH MUSIC COUNCIL (1944). 15 E. 26 St., N.Y.C., 10010. (212)532-4949. Chmn. Leonard Kaplan; Coord. Ruth S. Frank. Promotes Jewish music activities nationally, annually sponsors and promotes the Jewish Music Festival, and encourages participation on a community basis. *Jewish Music Notes* and numerous music resource publications for national distribution.

LEO BAECK INSTITUTE, INC. (1955). 129 E. 73 St., N.Y.C., 10021. (212)744-6400. Pres. Max Gruenewald; Sec. Fred Grubel. Engages in historical research, the presentation and publication of the history of German-speaking Jewry, and in the collection of books, manuscripts and documents in this field; publishes monographs. *LBI Bulletin; LBI News; LBI Year Book; LBI Library and Archives News.*

MEMORIAL FOUNDATION FOR JEWISH CULTURE, INC. (1964). 15 E. 26 St., N.Y.C., 10010. (212)679-4074. Pres. Nahum Goldmann; Exec. Dir. Jerry Hochbaum. Supports Jewish cultural and educational programs all over the world, in cooperation with universities and established scholarly organizations; conducts annual scholarship and fellowship program. *Annual Report.*

NATIONAL FOUNDATION FOR JEWISH CULTURE (1960). 1512 Chanin Bldg., 122 E. 42 St., N.Y.C., 10168. (212)490-2280. Pres. Amos Comay; Exec. Dir. Abraham Atik. Provides consultation, guidance, and support to Jewish communities, organizations, educational and other institutions, and individuals for activities in the field of Jewish culture; awards fellowships and other grants to students preparing for careers in Jewish scholarship and to established scholars; makes awards for creative efforts in Jewish cultural arts and for Jewish programming in small and intermediate communities; encourages teaching of Jewish studies in colleges and universities; serves as clearinghouse of information on American Jewish culture; administers Joint Cultural Appeal among local Jewish welfare funds in behalf of nine national cultural organizations, and administers Council for Archives and Research Libraries in Jewish Studies. *Jewish Cultural News.*

NATIONAL HEBREW CULTURE COUNCIL (1952). 1776 Broadway, N.Y.C., 10019. (212)247-0741. Pres. Frances K. Thau; Exec. Dir. Judah Lapson. Cultivates the study of Hebrew as a modern language in American public high schools and colleges, providing guidance to community groups and public educational authorities; annually administers National Voluntary Examination in Hebrew Culture and Knowledge of Israel in the public high schools, and conducts summer seminar and tour of Israel for teachers and other educational personnel of the public school system, in cooperation with Hebrew University and WZO. *Hebrew in Colleges and Universities.*

NATIONAL YIDDISH BOOK EXCHANGE (1980). P.O. Box 969, East Street School, Amherst, Ma., 01004. (413)253-9201. Pres. Joseph Marcus; Exec. Dir. Aaron Lansky. Collects used and out-of-print Yiddish books to distribute to individuals and libraries; offers courses in Yiddish language, literature, and cultural activities; publishes bimonthly *Catalogue of Rare and Out-of-Print Yiddish Books,* listing over 100,000 volumes for sale. *Der Pakntreger.*

RESEARCH FOUNDATION FOR JEWISH IMMIGRATION, INC. (1971). 570 Seventh Ave., N.Y.C., 10018. (212)921-3870. Pres. Curt C. Silberman; Sec. Herbert A. Strauss. Studies and records the history of the migration and acculturation of Jewish Nazi persecutees in the various resettlement countries; is in process of preparing worldwide biographical handbook of outstanding emigrés, in partnership with the Institut für Zeitgeschichte, Munich, Germany.

SEPHARDIC HOUSE (1978). 8 West 70 St., N.Y.C., 10023. (212)873-0300. Dir. Rabbi Marc D. Angel. Works to foster the history and culture of Sephardic Jewry by offering classes, programs, publications, and resource people; works to integrate Sephardic studies into the curriculum of Jewish schools and adult education programs; offers advice and guidance to individuals involved in Sephardic research. *The Sephardic House Bulletin.*

SOCIETY FOR THE HISTORY OF CZECHOSLOVAK JEWS, INC. (1961). 87-08 Santiago St., Holliswood, N.Y., 11423. Pres. Lewis Weiner; Sec. Joseph Abeles. Studies the history of the Czechoslovak Jews, collects material and disseminates information through the publication of books and pamphlets. *The Jews of Czechoslovakia* book series: Vol. I (1968), Vol. II (1971), Vol. III in prep. Annual reports and pamphlets.

ST. LOUIS CENTER FOR HOLOCAUST STUDIES (1977). 10967 Schuetz Rd., St. Louis, Mo. 63141. (314)621-8120. Dir. Warren Green. Develops programs and provides resources and educational materials to further an understanding of the Holocaust and its impact on civilization.

YESHIVA UNIVERSITY MUSEUM (1973). 2520 Amsterdam Ave., N.Y.C., 10033. (212)960-5390. Dir. Sylvia A. Herskowitz. Collects, preserves, interprets, and displays ceremonial objects, rare books and scrolls, models, paintings, and other works of art expressing the Jewish religious experience historically, to the present. A major thematic exhibition is mounted annually. Annual illustrated exhibition catalogue.

YIDDISHER KULTUR FARBAND—YKUF (1937). 853 Broadway, Suite 2121, N.Y.C., 10003. (212)228-1955. Pres. Itche Goldberg. Publishes a monthly magazine and books by contemporary and classical Jewish writers; conducts cultural forums and exhibits works by contemporary Jewish artists and materials of Jewish historical value. Organizes reading circles. *Yiddishe Kultur.*

YIVO INSTITUTE FOR JEWISH RESEARCH, INC. (1925). 1048 Fifth Ave., N.Y.C., 10028. (212)535-6700. Pres. Joseph Greenberger; Exec. Dir. Samuel Norich; Chmn. Morris Laub. Engages in Jewish social and humanistic research; maintains library and archives of material pertaining to Jewish life; serves as information center for organizations, local institutions, information media, and individual scholars and laymen; publishes books. *Yedies fun Yivo—News of the Yivo; Yidishe Shprakh; Yivo Annual of Jewish Social Science; Yivo Bleter.*

———, MAX WEINREICH CENTER FOR ADVANCED JEWISH STUDIES (1968). 1048 Fifth Ave., N.Y.C., 10028. (212)535-6700. Pres. Nathan Reich; Act. Dean Marvin I. Herzog. Trains scholars in the fields of Eastern European Jewish life and culture; the Holocaust; the mass settlement of Jews in the U.S. and other countries; Yiddish language, literature, and folklore through inter-university courses and seminars and its panel of consultants. *Annual Bulletin.*

OVERSEAS AID

AMERICAN COUNCIL FOR JUDAISM PHILANTHROPIC FUND (1955). 386 Park Ave. S., N.Y.C., 10016. (212)684-1525. Pres. Charles J. Tanenbaum. Through offices in Austria, France, Italy, and the United States, maintains programs offering freedom of choice and resettlement assistance in Western Europe and the United States to Jewish refugees from the Soviet Union, Eastern Europe and Arab countries.

AMERICAN FRIENDS OF THE ALLIANCE ISRAÉLITE UNIVERSELLE, INC. (1946). 135 William St., N.Y.C., 10038. (212)349-0537. Pres. Arnold C. Franco; Exec. Dir. Jack Kantrowitz. Helps networks of Jewish schools in Europe, Asia, Israel, and Africa. *Alliance Review; Bulletin.*

AMERICAN JEWISH JOINT DISTRIBUTION COMMITTEE, INC.—JDC (1914). 60 E. 42 St., N.Y.C., 10165. (212)687-6200. Pres. Henry Taub; Exec. V. Pres. Ralph I. Goldman. Organizes and finances rescue, relief, and rehabilitation programs for imperiled and needy Jews overseas; conducts wide range of health, welfare, rehabilitation, education programs and aid to cultural and religious institutions; programs benefiting

300,000 Jews in 30 countries overseas. Major areas of operation are Israel, North Africa, and Europe. *JDC Annual Report; JDC World.*

AMERICAN ORT FEDERATION, INC.—ORGANIZATION FOR REHABILITATION THROUGH TRAINING (1924). 817 Broadway, N.Y.C., 10003. (212)677-4400. Pres. Sidney E. Leiwant; Exec. V. Pres. Donald H. Klein. Teaches vocational skills in 26 countries around the world, maintaining 800 schools for over 100,000 persons annually, with the largest program of 70,000 trainees in Israel. The teaching staff numbers about 3,800. Annual cost of program is about $85 million. *ORT Bulletin; ORT Yearbook.*

———, AMERICAN AND EUROPEAN FRIENDS OF ORT (1941). 817 Broadway, N.Y.C., 10003. (212)677-4400. Pres. Simon Jaglom; Chmn. Exec. Com. Jacques Zwibak. Promotes the ORT idea among Americans of European extraction; supports the Litton ORT Auto-Mechanics School in Jerusalem.

———, AMERICAN LABOR ORT (1937). 817 Broadway, N.Y.C., 10003. (212)677-4400. Chmn. Edward Schneider; Hon. Exec. Sec. Samuel Milman. Promotes ORT program of vocational training among Jews.

———, BUSINESS AND PROFESSIONAL ORT (formerly YOUNG MEN'S AND WOMEN'S ORT) (1937). 817 Broadway, N.Y.C., 10003. (212)677-4400. Pres. Rose Seidel Kalich; Exec. Sec. Helen S. Kreisler. Promotes work of American ORT Federation.

———, NATIONAL ORT LEAGUE (1914). 817 Broadway, N.Y.C., 10003. (212)677-4400. Pres. Judah Wattenberg; Chmn. Exec. Bd. Jack Weinstein; Exec. V. Pres. and Sec. Jacob Zonis. Promotes ORT idea among Jewish fraternal *landsmanshaften*, national and local organizations, congregations; helps to equip ORT installations and Jewish artisans abroad, especially in Israel. *ORT Bulletin.*

———, WOMEN'S AMERICAN ORT (1927). 1250 Broadway, N.Y.C., 10001. (212)594-8500. Pres. Beverly Minkoff; Exec. V. Pres. Nathan Gould. Represents and advances the program and philosophy of ORT among the women of the American Jewish community through membership and educational activities; supports materially the vocational training operations of World

ORT; contributes to the American Jewish community through participation in its authorized campaigns and through general education to help raise the level of Jewish consciousness among American Jewish women; through its American Affairs program, cooperates in efforts to improve quality of education and vocational training in U.S. *Facts and Findings; Highlights; Insights; The Merchandiser; Women's American ORT Reporter.*

A.R.I.F.—ASSOCIATION POUR LE RÉTABLISSEMENT DES INSTITUTIONS ET OEUVRES ISRAÉLITES EN FRANCE, INC. (1944). 119 E. 95 St., N.Y.C., 10028. (212)-876-1448. Pres. Baroness Robert de Gunzburg; Sec.-Treas. Simon Langer. Helps Jewish religious and cultural institutions in France.

CONFERENCE ON JEWISH MATERIAL CLAIMS AGAINST GERMANY, INC. (1951). 15 E. 26 St., N.Y.C., 10010. (212)679-4074. Sec. and Exec. Dir. Saul Kagan. Utilizes balance of funds received from the German Federal Republic under Luxembourg agreement for relief to needy Jewish victims of Nazi persecution and needy non-Jews who risked their lives to help such victims. Periodic reports.

HIAS, INC. (1880; reorg. 1954). 200 Park Ave. S., N.Y.C., 10003. (212)674-6800. Pres. Edwin Shapiro; Exec. V. Pres. Leonard Seidenman. Worldwide Jewish migration agency with offices, affiliates, committees in United States, Europe, North Africa, Latin America, Canada, Australia, Israel, and New Zealand. Assists migrants and refugees from Eastern Europe, the Middle East, North Africa, and Latin America to find new homes in the United States and other countries. Assists, at the request of the U.S. Government, in the resettlement of Indochinese and other refugees. Responsible for premigration planning, visa documentation, consular representation and intervention, transportation, reception, initial adjustment and reunion of families; carries on adjustment of status and naturalization programs; provides protective service for aliens and naturalized citizens; works in the United States through local community agencies for the integration of immigrants; conducts a planned program of resettlement for Jewish immigrants in Latin America; has worldwide location service to assist in locating missing friends and relatives;

conducts educational campaigns on opportunities for migration and resettlement, with particular emphasis on family reunion. *HIAS Annual Report; HIAS Bulletin; Statistical Abstract.*

INTERNATIONAL LEAGUE FOR THE REPATRIATION OF RUSSIAN JEWS (1961). 315 Church St., Suite 200, N.Y.C., 10013. (212)431-6789. Sponsors employment and training program for East European immigrants.

JEWISH RESTITUTION SUCCESSOR ORGANIZATION (1947). 15-19 E. 26 St., N.Y.C., 10010. (212)679-4074. Pres. Maurice M. Bookstein; Sec. Saul Kagan. Acts to discover, claim, receive, and assist in the recovery of Jewish heirless or unclaimed property; to utilize such assets or to provide for their utilization for the relief, rehabilitation, and resettlement of surviving victims of Nazi persecution.

LEAGUE FOR YIDDISH (formerly FREELAND LEAGUE; 1935). 200 W. 72 St., Suite 40, N.Y.C., 10023. (212)787-6675. Pres. Nathan Turak; Exec. Sec. Mordkhe Schaechter. Promotes the development and use of Yiddish as a living language. *Afn Shvel.*

UNION OF COUNCILS FOR SOVIET JEWS (1970). 1411 K St., N.W., Ste. 402, Washington, D.C., 20005. (202)393-4117. Pres. Lynn Singer; Exec. Dir. Elaine Parker. Oldest national grassroots organization concerned with Soviet Jewry; works on behalf of Soviet Jews through public education, representations to Administration and Congress, letter writing, assistance, tourist briefing, speakers bureau, Adopt-A-Family, Adopt-A-Prisoner, Bar/Bat Mitzvah twinning, Tarbut, Congressional Vigil, briefings, and publications programming; maintains close links to groups in western Europe; subsidiary organizations include Soviet Jewry Legal Advocacy Center, Medical Mobilization for Soviet Jewry, International Committee for the Release of Anatoly Scharansky; *Alert.*

UNITED JEWISH APPEAL, INC. (1939). 1290 Ave. of the Americas, N.Y.C., 10019. (212)757-1500. Pres. Irwin S. Field; Nat. Chmn. Herschel W. Blumberg; Exec. V. Chmn. Irving Bernstein. Channels funds for overseas humanitarian aid, supporting immigration and settlement in Israel, rehabilitation and relief in 30 nations, and refugee assistance in U.S. through Joint Distribution Committee, United Israel Appeal, United HIAS Service, and New York Association for New Americans.

———, FACULTY ADVISORY CABINET (1975). 1290 Ave. of the Americas. (212)-757-1500. Chmn. Michael Walzer; Dir. Melvin L. Libman. To promote faculty leadership support for local and national UJA campaigns through educational and personal commitment; to make use of faculty resources and expertise on behalf of UJA and Israel.

———, RABBINIC CABINET (1972). 1290 Ave. of the Americas, N.Y.C., 10019. (212)757-1500. Chmn. Haskell M. Bernat; Dir. Melvin L. Libman. To promote rabbinic leadership support for local and national UJA campaigns through education and personal commitment; to make use of rabbinic resources on behalf of UJA and Israel.

———, UNIVERSITY PROGRAMS DEPT. (1970). 1290 Ave. of the Americas, N.Y.C., 10019. (212)757-1500. Dir. Judy Flumenbaum. Student Advisory Board. To crystallize Jewish commitment on the campus through an educational fund-raising campaign involving various programs, leadership training, and opportunities for participation in community functions.

———, WOMEN'S DIVISION OF (1946). 1290 Ave. of the Americas, N.Y.C., 10019. (212)757-1500. Pres. Peggy Steine; Nat. Chmn. Bernice Waldman; Dir. Nan Goldberg. *Ideas That Click; Right Now; Women's Division Record.*

———, YOUNG LEADERSHIP CABINET (1977). 1290 Ave. of the Americas, N.Y.C., 10019. (212)757-1500. Exec. Dir. Laurence H. Rubinstein; Chmn. Lawrence Jackier. Committed to the creative survival of Jews, Judaism, and Israel through dialogues with leading scholars and writers, and through peer exchanges at retreats, conferences, missions to Israel, and special programs. *Cabinet Communiqués.*

———, YOUNG WOMEN'S LEADERSHIP CABINET (1977). 1290 Ave. of the Americas, N.Y.C., 10019. (212)757-1500. Nat. Chmn. Bobi Klotz; Dir. Barbara P. Faske. Encourages young Jewish women to become involved with the organized Jewish community. *Cabinet Update.*

WOMEN'S SOCIAL SERVICE FOR ISRAEL, INC. (1937). 240 W. 98 St., N.Y.C., 10025. (212)666-7880. Pres. Rosi Michael; Sec. Dory Gordon. Maintains in Israel apartments for the aged, old age homes, nursing home, hospital for incurable diseases, rehabilitation department, department for bone injuries, soup kitchen. *Annual Journal; Newsletter.*

RELIGIOUS AND EDUCATIONAL

AGUDATH ISRAEL WORLD ORGANIZATION (1912). 5 Beekman St., N.Y.C., 10038. (212) 791-1835. Chmn. Rabbi Moshe Sherer, Rabbi Yehudah Meir Abramowitz. Represents the interests of Orthodox Jewry on the national and international scenes. Sponsors projects to strengthen Torah life worldwide.

AGUDATH ISRAEL OF AMERICA (1912). 5 Beekman St., N.Y.C., 10038. (212)791-1800. Pres. Moshe Sherer; Exec. Dir. Boruch B. Borchardt. Mobilizes Orthodox Jews to cope with Jewish problems in the spirit of the Torah; sponsors a broad range of constructive projects in fields of religion, education, children's welfare, protection of Jewish religious rights, and social services. *Jewish Observer; Dos Yiddishe Vort.*

———, CHILDREN'S DIVISION—PIRCHEI AGUDATH ISRAEL (1925). 5 Beekman St., N.Y.C., 10038 (212)791-1837. Pres. Shimon Katz; Nat. Dir. Joshua Silbermintz. Educates Orthodox Jewish children in Torah; encourages sense of communal responsibility; communal celebrations, learning groups, and welfare projects. *Darkeinu; Leaders Guide.*

———, GIRLS' DIVISION—BNOS AGUDATH ISRAEL (1921). 5 Beekman St., N.Y.C., 10038. (212)791-1818. Nat. Coordinator Shanie Meyer. Educates Jewish girls to the historic nature of the Jewish people; encourages greater devotion to and understanding of the Torah. *Kol Bnos.*

———, WOMEN'S DIVISION—N'SHEI AGUDATH ISRAEL OF AMERICA (1940). 5 Beekman St., N.Y.C., 10038. (212)791-1840. Pres. Esther Bohensky, Josephine Reichel. Organizes Jewish women for philanthropic work in the U.S. and Israel and for intense Torah education, seeking to train Torah-guided Jewish mothers.

———, YOUTH DIVISION—ZEIREI AGUDATH ISRAEL (1921). 5 Beekman St.,

N.Y.C., 10038. (212)791-1820. Pres. Joseph Ashkenazi; Exec. Dir. David Pitterman. Educates Jewish youth to realize the historic nature of the Jewish people as the people of the Torah and to seek solutions to all the problems of the Jewish people in Israel in the spirit of the Torah. *The Zeirei Forum; Am Hatorah, Daf Chizuk, Yom Tov Publications.*

AMERICAN ASSOCIATION OF RABBIS (1978). 350 Fifth Ave., Ste. 3308, N.Y.C., 10001. (212)244-3350. Pres. Rabbi David Schectman; Sec. Rabbi Robert Chernoff. An organization of rabbis serving in pulpits, and in the fields of education and social work. Provides rabbinical fraternity and placement services. *Quarterly Newsletter.*

ASSOCIATION FOR JEWISH STUDIES (1969). Widener Library M., Harvard University, Cambridge, Mass., 02138. (617)495-2985. Pres. Jane S. Gerber; Exec. Sec. Charles Berlin. Seeks to promote, maintain, and improve the teaching of Jewish studies in American colleges and universities by sponsoring meetings and conferences, publishing a newsletter and other scholarly materials, setting standards for programs in Jewish studies, aiding in the placement of teachers, coordinating research and cooperating with other scholarly organizations. *AJS Review; Newsletter.*

ASSOCIATION OF HILLEL DIRECTORS/JEWISH CAMP PROFESSIONALS (1949). 611 Langdon Street, Madison, WI, 53703. (608)256-8361. Pres. Alan B. Lettofsky; V. Pres. Gerald Serotta. Seeks to promote professional relationships and exchanges of experience, develop personnel standards and qualifications, safeguard integrity of Hillel profession; represents and advocates before National Hillel Staff, National Hillel Commission, B'nai B'rith Supreme Lodge, Jewish Federations and Welfare Funds.

ASSOCIATION OF JEWISH CHAPLAINS OF THE ARMED FORCES (1946). 15 E. 26 St., N.Y.C., 10010. (212)532-4949. Pres. Joseph I. Weiss; Sec. Norman Twersky. An organization of former and current chaplains of the armed forces of the U.S. which seeks to enhance the religious program of Jewish chaplains in the armed forces of the U.S. and in Veterans Administration hospitals.

ASSOCIATION OF ORTHODOX JEWISH SCIENTISTS (1947). 45 W. 36 St., N.Y.C., 10016. (212)695-7525. Pres. Lester Kaufman; Bd.

Chmn. Reuben Rudman. Seeks to contribute to the development of science within the framework of Orthodox Jewish tradition; to obtain and disseminate information relating to the interaction between the Jewish traditional way of life and scientific developments—on both an ideological and practical level; to assist in the solution of problems pertaining to Orthodox Jews engaged in scientific teaching or research. Two main conventions are held each year. *Intercom; Proceedings.*

BETH MEDROSH ELYON (ACADEMY OF HIGHER LEARNING AND RESEARCH) (1943). 73 Main St., Monsey, N.Y., 10952. V. Pres. Ira Miller; Chmn. of Bd. Arthur Sternfield. Provides postgraduate courses and research work in higher Jewish studies; offers scholarships and fellowships. *Annual Journal.*

B'NAI B'RITH HILLEL FOUNDATIONS, INC. (1923). 1640 Rhode Island Ave., N.W., Washington, D.C., 20036. (202)857-6600. Chmn. B'nai B'rith Hillel Com. Albert A. Spiegel; Internat. Dir. Oscar Groner; Chmn. Exec. Com. Seymour Martin Lipset. Provides a program of cultural, religious, educational, social, and counseling content to Jewish college and university students on 350 campuses in the United States, Australia, Canada, England, Israel, the Netherlands, South Africa, Switzerland, Italy, Colombia, Brazil, Venezuela, and Sweden. *Clearing House; Igeret; Hillel/Community; Commission Journal.*

B'NAI B'RITH YOUTH ORGANIZATION (1924). 1640 Rhode Island Ave., N.W., Washington, D.C., 20036. (202)857-6600. Chmn. Youth Com. Horace Stern; Internat. Dir. Sidney Clearfield. To help Jewish teenagers achieve self-fulfillment and to make a maximum contribution to the Jewish community and their country's culture; to help the members acquire a greater knowledge and appreciation of Jewish religion and culture. *BBYO Advisor; Monday Morning; Shofar.*

BRANDEIS-BARDIN INSTITUTE (1941). 1101 Peppertree Lane, Brandeis, Calif., 93064. (213)348-7201. Dir. Dennis Prager; Exec. Dir. Michael Harris; Pres. Jack I. Salzberg. Maintains Brandeis Camp Institute (BCI) for college students as a leadership training institute, Camp Alonim for children 8–16, Forum on Contemporary Values, and House of the Book Association weekend institutes for married adults, in an effort to instill an appreciation of Jewish cultural and spiritual heritage and to create a desire for active participation in the American Jewish community. *Brandeis-Bardin News.*

CANTORS ASSEMBLY (1947). 150 Fifth Ave., N.Y.C., 10011. (212)691-8020. Pres. Abraham B. Shapiro; Exec. V. Pres. Samuel Rosenbaum. Seeks to unite all cantors who are adherents to traditional Judaism and who serve as full-time cantors in bona fide congregations, to conserve and promote the musical traditions of the Jews, and to elevate the status of the cantorial profession. *Annual Proceedings; Journal of Synagogue Music.*

CENTRAL CONFERENCE OF AMERICAN RABBIS (1879). 21 E. 40 St., N.Y.C., 10016. (212)734-7166. Pres. Rabbi Herman E. Schaalman; Exec. V. Pres. Rabbi Joseph B. Glaser. Seeks to conserve and promote Judaism and to disseminate its teachings in a liberal spirit. *Journal of Reform Judaism; CCAR Yearbook.*

CENTRAL YESHIVA BETH JOSEPH RABBINICAL SEMINARY (in Europe 1891; in U.S. 1941). 1427 49 St., Brooklyn, N.Y., 11219. Pres. and Dean Jacob Jofen. Maintains a school for teaching Orthodox rabbis and teachers, and promoting the cause of higher Torah learning.

CLEVELAND COLLEGE OF JEWISH STUDIES (1964). 26500 Shaker Blvd., Beachwood, Ohio, 44122. (216)464-4050. Acting Pres., V. Chmn. Eli Reshotko. Trains Hebrew- and religious-school teachers; serves as the department of Hebraic and Judaic studies for Cleveland-area colleges and universities; offers intensive Ulpan and Judaic studies for community; serves as Jewish information center through its library; grants teachers diplomas and degrees of Bachelor of Hebrew Literature, Bachelor of Judaic Studies, Bachelor of Religious Education, Master of Science in Religious Education, and Master of Hebrew Literature, Hebrew Studies.

COALITION FOR ALTERNATIVES IN JEWISH EDUCATION (1976). 468 Park Ave. S., Rm. 904, N.Y.C., 10016. (212)696-0740. Nat. Dir. Eliot G. Spack; Chmn. Cherie Koller-Fox. Brings together Jews from all ideologies who are involved in every facet of Jewish education, and are committed to transmitting Jewish knowledge, culture, and experience; serves as a channel of communication for its membership to share resources and methods, and as a forum for exchange of philosophical and theoretical approaches to Jewish education. Sponsors programs and projects. *Mekasher; CAJE Jewish Education News.*

COUNCIL FOR JEWISH EDUCATION (1926). 114 Fifth Ave., N.Y.C., 10011. (212)675-5656. Pres. Rabbi Matthew Clark: Exec. Sec. Philip Jaffe. Fellowship of Jewish education profession, comprising administrators and supervisors of national and local Jewish educational institutions and agencies, and teachers in Hebrew high schools and Jewish teachers colleges, of all ideological groupings; conducts annual national and regional conferences in all areas of Jewish education; represents the Jewish education profession before the Jewish community; co-sponsors, with the Jewish Education Service of North America, a personnel committee and other projects; cooperates with Jewish Agency department of education and culture in promoting Hebrew culture and studies; conducts lectureship at Hebrew University. *Jewish Education; Sheviley Hahinuch.*

DROPSIE UNIVERSITY (1907). Broad and York Sts., Philadelphia, Pa., 19066. (215)-229-1566. Pres. Joseph Rappaport; Sec. Joseph B. Saltz. The only nonsectarian and nontheological graduate institution in America completely dedicated to Hebrew, Biblical, and Middle Eastern studies; offers graduate programs in these areas. Course study includes the cultures and languages of Arabic, Aramaic, Ugaritic, Akkadian, and ancient Egyptian peoples; offers Ph.D. degree. *Jewish Quarterly Review.*

———, ALUMNI ASSOCIATION OF (1925). Broad and York Sts., Philadelphia, Pa., 19132. (215)229-1566. Pres. Sidney B. Hoenig; Sec. Hanoch Guy. Enhances the relationship of the alumni to the University. *Newsletter.*

GRATZ COLLEGE (1895). 10 St. and Tabor Rd., Philadelphia, Pa., 19141. Chmn. Bd. of Overseers Daniel C. Cohen; Pres. Daniel Isaacman; Dean Saul P. Wachs. Prepares teachers for Jewish schools and teachers of Hebrew for public high schools; grants Master of Hebrew Literature, Bachelor of Hebrew Literature and Bachelor of Arts in Jewish Studies degrees; is accredited by the Middle States Association of Colleges and Secondary Schools and the Association of Hebrew Colleges; provides studies in Judaica and Hebraica; maintains a Hebrew high school, two college preparatory departments for cadet teachers, and a school of observation and practice; provides Jewish studies for adults; community-service division (central agency for Jewish education) coordinates Jewish education in the city and provides consultation services to Jewish schools of all leanings. *Alumni Newspaper; College Bulletin; DCS Bulletin; Gratz Chats; GC Annual of Jewish Studies; 75th Anniversary Volume; Kinnereth; Telem Yearbook; What's New.*

HEBREW COLLEGE (1921). 43 Hawes St., Brookline, Mass., 02146. (617)232-8710. Pres. Eli Grad; Assoc. Dean Michael Libenson. Provides intensive programs of study in all areas of Jewish culture from the high-school through college and graduate-school levels, also at branch in Hartford; maintains ongoing programs with most major local universities; offers the degrees of Bachelor and Master of Hebrew Literature, and Bachelor and Master of Jewish Education, with teaching certification; trains men and women to teach, conduct and supervise Jewish schools; offers extensive Ulpan program; offers courses designed to deepen the community's awareness of the Jewish heritage. *Hebrew College Bulletin.*

HEBREW THEOLOGICAL COLLEGE (1921). 7135 N. Carpenter Rd., Skokie, Ill., 60077. (312)267-9800. Pres. Rabbi Don Well; Bd. Chmn. Paul Rosenberg. An institution of higher Jewish learning which includes a division of advanced Hebrew studies, a school of liberal arts and sciences, a rabbinic ordination program, and a graduate school in Judaic studies. Trains rabbis, teachers, educational administrators, communal workers, and knowledgeable lay leaders for the Jewish community. *News; Annual Journal.*

HEBREW UNION COLLEGE—JEWISH INSTITUTE OF RELIGION (1875). 3101 Clifton Ave., Cincinnati, Ohio, 45220. (513)221-1875; Pres. Alfred Gottschalk; Exec. Dean Eugene Mihaly; Exec. V. Pres. Uri D. Herscher. Chmn. Bd. of Govs. Jules Backman. Academic centers: 3101 Clifton Ave., Cincinnati, Ohio, 45220 (1875), Samuel Greengus, Dean; One W. 4 St., N.Y.C., 10012 (1922), Paul M. Steinberg, Dean; 3077 University Ave., Los Angeles, Calif., 90007 (1954), Uri D. Herscher, Chief Adm. Officer; 13 King David St., Jerusalem, Israel (1963), Michael Klein, Dean. Prepares students for Reform rabbinate,

cantorate, religious-school teaching and administration, community service, academic careers; promotes Jewish studies; maintains libraries and a museum; offers bachelor's, master's and doctoral degrees; engages in archaeological excavations; publishes scholarly works through Hebrew Union College Press. *American Jewish Archives; Bibliographica Judaica; HUC—JIR Catalogue; Hebrew Union College Annual; Studies in Bibliography and Booklore; The Chronicle.*

———, AMERICAN JEWISH ARCHIVES (1947). Cincinnati. Dir. Jacob R. Marcus; Assoc. Dir. Abraham Peck. Maintained for the preservation and study of North and South American Jewish historical records. *American Jewish Archives.*

———, AMERICAN JEWISH PERIODICAL CENTER (1957). Cincinnati. Dir. Jacob R. Marcus; Co-Dir. Herbert C. Zafren. Maintains microfilms of all American Jewish periodicals, 1823–1925; selected periodicals, since 1925. *Jewish Periodicals and Newspapers on Microfilm (1957); First Supplement (1960).*

———, JEROME H. LOUCHHEIM SCHOOL OF JUDAIC STUDIES (1969). Los Angeles. Acting Dir. David Ellenson. Offers programs leading to M.A., B.S., B.A. and Associate in Arts degrees; offers courses as part of the undergraduate program of the University of Southern California.

———, EDGAR F. MAGNIN SCHOOL OF GRADUATE STUDIES (1956). Los Angeles. Dir. Stanley Chyet. Offers programs leading to Ph.D., D.H.S., and M.A. degrees; offers program for rabbinic graduates of the college leading to the D.H.L. degree; participates in cooperative doctoral programs with the University of Southern California.

———, NELSON GLUECK SCHOOL OF BIBLICAL ARCHAEOLOGY (1963). Jerusalem. Dir. Avraham Biran. Offers graduate-level programs in Bible, archaeology, and Judaica. Summer excavations are carried out by scholars and students. University credit may be earned by participants in excavations. Consortium of colleges, universities, and seminaries is affiliated with the school.

———, RHEA HIRSCH SCHOOL OF EDUCATION (1967). Los Angeles. Dir. Sara S. Lee. Offers B.S. degree and M.A. program in

Jewish and Hebrew education; conducts summer institutes and joint programs with University of Southern California; conducts certificate programs for teachers and librarians.

———, SCHOOL OF EDUCATION (1947). 1 W. 4 St., N.Y.C., 10012. (212)674-5300. Dean Paul M. Steinberg. Trains and certifies teachers and principals for Reform religious schools; offers M.A. degree with specialization in religious education; offers extension programs in various suburban centers.

———, SCHOOL OF GRADUATE STUDIES (1949). Cincinnati. Dean Herbert H. Paper. Offers programs leading to M.A. and Ph.D. degrees; offers program leading to D.H.L. degree for rabbinic graduates of the college.

———, SCHOOL OF JEWISH COMMUNAL SERVICE (1968). 3077 University Ave., Los Angeles, Calif., 90007. Dir. Gerald B. Bubis. Offers certificate and master's degree to those employed in Jewish communal services, or preparing for such work; offers joint M.A. in Jewish education and communal service with Rhea Hirsch School; offers M.A. and M.S.W. in conjunction with the University of Southern California School of Social Work and with the George Warren Brown School of Social Work of Washington University.

———, SCHOOL OF JEWISH STUDIES (1963). Jerusalem. Dean Michael Klein. Offers program leading to ordination for Israeli students; offers an academic, work-study year for undergraduate students from American colleges and universities; offers a one-year program in cooperation with Hebrew University for advanced students, and a one-year program for all first-year rabbinic students of the college and for master's degree candidates of the Rhea Hirsch School of Education.

———, SCHOOL OF SACRED MUSIC (1947). 1 W. 4 St., N.Y.C., 10012. (212)674-5300. Dean Paul M. Steinberg; Dir. Jon R. Haddon. Trains cantors and music personnel for congregations; offers B.S.M. and M.A. degrees. *Sacred Music Press.*

———, SKIRBALL MUSEUM (1913; 1972 in Calif.). 3077 University Ave., Los Angeles, Calif., 90007. Dir. Nancy Berman. Collects, preserves, researches, and exhibits art and artifacts made by or for Jews, or otherwise associated with Jews and Judaism. Provides opportunity to faculty and students to do research in the field of Jewish art.

HERZLIAH-JEWISH TEACHERS SEMINARY (1967). 69 Bank St., N.Y.C., 10014. Pres. Eli Goldstein; Exec. Dir. Aviva Barzel; V. Pres. for Academic Affairs Meir Ben-Horin. Offers undergraduate and graduate programs in Jewish studies; continuing education courses for teachers in Hebrew and Yiddish schools; academic and professional programs in major disciplines of Judaism, historic and contemporary, with emphasis on Hebrew language and literature; Yiddish language and literature, Jewish education, history, philosophy, and sociology.

———, GRADUATE DIVISION (1965). Dean Meir Ben-Horin. Offers programs leading to degree of Doctor of Jewish Literature in Hebrew language and literature, Yiddish language and literature, Jewish education, history, philosophy, and sociology. Admits men and women who have bachelor's degree and background in Hebrew, Yiddish, and Jewish studies. Annual Horace M. Kallen lecture by major Jewish scholars.

———, HERZLIAH HEBREW TEACHERS INSTITUTE, INC. (1921). V. Pres. for Academic Affairs Meir Ben-Horin. Offers four-year, college-level programs in Hebrew and Jewish subjects, nationally recognized Hebrew teachers diploma, preparatory courses, and Yiddish courses.

———, JEWISH TEACHERS SEMINARY AND PEOPLE'S UNIVERSITY, INC. (1918). V. Pres. for Academic Affairs Meir Ben-Horin. Offers four-year, college-level programs leading to Yiddish teachers diploma and Bachelor of Jewish Literature; offers preparatory courses and Hebrew courses.

———, MUSIC DIVISION (1964). Performing Arts Div. Dir. Cantor Marvin Antosofsky. Offers studies in traditional and contemporary music, religious, Yiddish, secular, and Hebraic; offers certificate and degree programs in Jewish music education and cantorial art, and artist diploma.

INSTITUTE FOR COMPUTERS IN JEWISH LIFE (1978). 845 N. Michigan Ave., Suite 843, Chicago, Ill., 60611. (312) 787-7856. Pres. Thomas Klutznick, Exec. V. Pres. Dr. Irving J. Rosenbaum. Explores, develops, and disseminates applications of computer technology to appropriate areas of Jewish life, with special emphasis on Jewish education; provides access to the Bar-Ilan University Responsa Project; creates educational software for use in Jewish schools; provides consulting service and assistance for national Jewish organizations, seminaries and synagogues. *Monitor.*

JEWISH CHAUTAUQUA SOCIETY, INC. (sponsored by NATIONAL FEDERATION OF TEMPLE BROTHERHOODS) (1893). 838 Fifth Ave., N.Y.C., 10021. (212)249-0100. Pres. Lawrence M. Halperin; Exec. Dir. Av Bondarin. Disseminates authoritative knowledge about Jews and Judaism; assigns rabbis to lecture at colleges; endows courses in Judaism for college credit at universities; donates Jewish reference books to college libraries; sends rabbis to serve as counselor-teachers at Christian Church summer camps and as chaplains at Boy Scout camps; sponsors institutes on Judaism for Christian clergy; produces motion pictures for public service television and group showings. *Brotherhood.*

JEWISH EDUCATION IN MEDIA, INC. (1978). P.O. Box 180, Riverdale Station, N.Y.C., 10471. (212)362-7633. Exec. Dir. Rabbi Mark S. Golub. Seeks to promote Jewish identity and commitment through the creation of innovative and entertaining media materials, including radio and television programming, film, and audio and video cassettes for synagogue and institutional use.

JEWISH EDUCATION SERVICE OF NORTH AMERICA, INC. (1981). 114 Fifth Ave., N.Y.C., 10011. (212)675-5656. Pres. Fred Sichel; Exec. V. Pres. Shimon Frost. Coordinates, promotes, and services Jewish education in federated communities of North America. Coordinating center for Jewish education bureaus; offers curricular advisement and maintains a National Educational Resource Center; runs regional pedagogic conferences; conducts evaluative surveys on Jewish education; sponsors the National Board of License and the Commission on Teaching About Zionism and Israel; engages in statistical and other educational research; provides community consultations. *Information Research Bulletins; Jewish Education News; Jewish Education Directory; Pedagogic Reporter; SAFRA: Jewish School Materials Review.*

JEWISH MINISTERS CANTORS ASSOCIATION OF AMERICA, INC. (1896). 3 W. 16 St.,

N.Y.C., 10011. (212)675-6601. Pres. David Rosenzweig. To further and propagate traditional liturgy; to place cantors in synagogues throughout the U.S. and Canada; to develop the cantors of the future. *Kol Lakol.*

JEWISH RECONSTRUCTIONIST FOUNDATION (1940). 31 E. 28 St., N.Y.C., 10016. (212)-889-9080. Pres. Ludwig Nadelmann; Chmn. of Bd. Charles D. Lieber; V. Pres. David A. Teutsch. Dedicated to the advancement of Judaism as the evolving religious civilization of the Jewish people. Coordinates all Reconstructionist activities and sponsors the Reconstructionist Rabbinical College, Reconstructionist Press, Reconstructionist Federation (congregations and *havurot*), Reconstructionist Rabbinical Assn., a women's organization, and university fellowship. *Reconstructionist.*

———, FEDERATION OF RECONSTRUCTIONIST CONGREGATIONS AND HAVUROT (1954). 432 Park Ave. S., N.Y.C., 10016. (212)889-9080. Pres. Jacob M. Snyder; Exec. Dir. Ludwig Nadelman. Services affiliated congregations and *havurot* educationally and administratively; fosters the establishment of new Reconstructionist congregations and fellowship groups. *Newsletter.*

———, RECONSTRUCTIONIST RABBINICAL ASSOCIATION (1975). 31 E. 28 St., N.Y.C., 10016. (212)889-9080. Pres. Rabbi Elliot Skiddell; V. Pres. Rabbi Kenneth Berger; Treas. Gary Gerson. Advances the principles of Reconstructionist Judaism; provides forum for fellowship and exchange of ideas for Reconstructionist rabbis; cooperates with Reconstructionist Rabbinical College, and Reconstructionist Federation of Congregations and Havurot. *RRA Newsletter.*

JEWISH TEACHERS ASSOCIATION—MORIM (1931). 45 E. 33 St., N.Y.C., 10016. (212)-684-0556. Pres. Beverly Lipschitz; Treas. William Leinwand. Promotes the religious, social, and moral welfare of children; provides a program of professional, cultural, and social activities for its members; cooperates with other organizations for the promotion of good will and understanding. *JTA Bulletin—MORIM.*

JEWISH THEOLOGICAL SEMINARY OF AMERICA (1886; reorg. 1902). 3080 Broadway, N.Y.C., 10027. (212)678-8000. Chancellor Gerson D. Cohen; Chmn. Exec.

Com. Alan M. Stroock. Organized for the perpetuation of the tenets of the Jewish religion, cultivation of Hebrew literature, pursuit of biblical and archaeological research, advancement of Jewish scholarship; maintains a library with extensive collections of Hebraica and Judaica, a department for the training of rabbis, a pastoral psychiatry center, the Jewish Museum, and such youth programs as the Ramah Camps and the OMETZ-Center for Conservative Judaism on Campus. *Conservative Judaism.*

——, AMERICAN STUDENT CENTER IN JERUSALEM (1962). P.O. Box 196, Jerusalem, Israel. Dean Shamma Friedman; Dir. Reuven Hammer. Offers programs for rabbinical students, classes in Judaica for qualified Israelis and Americans, and Midreshet Yerushalayim, an intensive program of Jewish studies for undergraduates. *News of the Israel Programs.*

——, CANTORS INSTITUTE AND SEMINARY COLLEGE OF JEWISH MUSIC (1952). 3080 Broadway, N.Y.C., 10027. (212)678-8038. Dir. Dean Morton M. Leifman. Trains cantors, music teachers, and choral directors for congregations. Offers programs leading to degrees of B.S.M., M.S.M., and D.S.M., and diploma of *Hazzan.*

——, DEPARTMENT OF RADIO AND TELEVISION (1944). 3080 Broadway, N.Y.C., 10027. (212)678-8020. Exec. Prod. Milton E. Krents. Produces radio and TV programs expressing the Jewish tradition in its broadest sense, with emphasis on the universal human situation: "Eternal Light," a weekly radio program; 7 "Eternal Light" TV programs, produced in cooperation with NBC; and 12 "Directions" telecasts with ABC; distributes program scripts and related reading lists.

——, FANNIE AND MAXWELL ABBELL RESEARCH INSTITUTE IN RABBINICS (1951). 3080 Broadway, N.Y.C., 10027. (212)678-8000. Co-Dirs. Louis Finkelstein, Saul Lieberman. Fosters research in rabbinics; prepares scientific editions of early rabbinic works.

——, INSTITUTE FOR ADVANCED STUDY IN THE HUMANITIES (1968). 3080 Broadway, N.Y.C., 10027. (212)678-8024. Dean Mayer Rabinowitz. A graduate program leading to M.A. degree in all aspects of Jewish studies and Ph.D. in Bible, Jewish education, history, literature, philosophy,

or rabbinics; offers dual degree in social work.

——, INSTITUTE FOR RELIGIOUS AND SOCIAL STUDIES (N.Y.C. 1938; Chicago 1944; Boston 1945). 3080 Broadway, N.Y.C., 10027. (212)678-8815. Pres. Gerson D. Cohen; Dir. Jessica Feingold. Serves as a scholarly and scientific fellowship of clergymen and other religious teachers who desire authoritative information regarding some of the basic issues now confronting spiritually-minded individuals.

——, MELTON RESEARCH CENTER (1960). 3080 Broadway, N.Y.C., 10027. (212)678-8031. Chmn. Eduardo Rauch; Chmn. Barry W. Holtz. Devises new curricula and materials for Jewish education; has intensive program for training curriculum writers; recruits, trains, and restrains educators through seminars and in-service programs; maintains consultant and supervisory relationships with a limited number of pilot schools. *Melton Newsletter.*

——, SCHOCKEN INSTITUTE FOR JEWISH RESEARCH (1961). 6 Balfour St., Jerusalem, Israel. Librarian Yaakov Katzenstein. Incorporates Schocken library and its related research institutes in medieval Hebrew poetry and Jewish mysticism. *Schocken Institute Yearbook (P'raqim).*

——, SEMINARY COLLEGE OF JEWISH STUDIES-TEACHERS INSTITUTE (1909). 3080 Broadway, N.Y.C., 10027. (212)678-8826. Dean Paula Hyman. Offers complete college program in Judaica leading to B.A. degree; conducts joint programs with Columbia University and Barnard, enabling students to receive two B.A. degrees after four years.

——, UNIVERSITY OF JUDAISM (1947). 15600 Mulholland Dr., Los Angeles, Calif., 90024. (213)476-9777. Pres. David L. Lieber; V. Pres. Max Vorspan, David Gordis. West Coast school of JTS. Serves as center of undergraduate and graduate study of Judaica; offers pre-professional and professional programs in Jewish education and allied fields, including a prerabbinic program and joint program enabling students to receive B.A. from UCLA and B.H.L. from U. of J. after four years, as well as a broad range of adult education and Jewish activities.

MACHNE ISRAEL, INC. (1940). 770 Eastern Parkway, Bklyn., N.Y., 11213. (212)

493-9250. Pres. Menachem M. Schneerson (Lubavitcher Rebbe); Dir., Treas. M.A. Hodakov; Sec. Nissan Mindel. The Lubavitcher movement's organ dedicated to the social, spiritual, and material welfare of Jews throughout the world.

MERKOS L'INYONEI CHINUCH, INC. (THE CENTRAL ORGANIZATION FOR JEWISH EDUCATION) (1940). 770 Eastern Parkway, Bklyn., N.Y., 11213. (212)493-9250. Pres. Menachem M. Schneerson (the Lubavitcher Rebbe); Dir., Treas. M.A. Hodakov; Sec. Nissan Mindel. The educational arm of the Lubavitcher movement. Seeks to promote Jewish education among Jews, regardless of their background, in the spirit of Torah-true Judaism; to establish contact with alienated Jewish youth, to stimulate concern and active interest in Jewish education on all levels, and to promote religious observance as a daily experience among all Jews; maintains worldwide network of regional offices, schools, summer camps, and Chabad-Lubavitch Houses; publishes Jewish educational literature in numerous languages and monthly journal in five languages: *Conversaciones con la juventud; Conversations avec les jeunes; Schmuessen mit kinder un yugent; Sihot la No-ar; Talks and Tales.*

MESIVTA YESHIVA RABBI CHAIM BERLIN RABBINICAL ACADEMY (1905). 1593 Coney Island Ave., Bklyn., N.Y., 11230. (212)377-0777. Pres. Sol Eiger; Bd. Chmn. Pincus Iseson; Admin. Tovia Rottenberg. Maintains elementary division in the Hebrew and English departments, lower Hebrew division and Mesivta high school, rabbinical academy, and postgraduate school for advanced studies in Talmud and other branches of rabbinic scholarship; maintains Camp Morris, a summer study camp. *Igud News Letter; Kol Torah; Kuntrasim; Merchav; Shofar.*

MIRRER YESHIVA CENTRAL INSTITUTE (in Poland 1817; in U.S. 1947). 1791–5 Ocean Parkway, Brooklyn, N.Y., 11223. Pres. and Dean Rabbi Shrage Moshe Klamanowitz; Exec. Dir. and Sec. Manfred Handelsman. Maintains rabbinical college, postgraduate school for Talmudic research, accredited high school, and Kollel and Sephardic divisions; dedicated to the dissemination of Torah scholarship in the community and abroad; engages in rescue and rehabilitation of scholars overseas.

NATIONAL COMMITTEE FOR FURTHERANCE OF JEWISH EDUCATION (1951). 824 Eastern Parkway, Brooklyn, N.Y., 11213. (212)735-0200. Pres. Alex M. Parker; Exec. V. Pres. Jacob J. Hecht; Sec. Morris Drucker. Seeks to disseminate the ideals of Torah-true education among the youth of America; aids poor, sick, and needy in U.S. and Israel; provides aid to hundreds of Iranian Jewish youth through the Iranian Children's Fund; maintains camp for underprivileged children; sponsors Hadar Ha Torah and Machon Chana, seeking to win back college youth and others to the fold of Judaism; maintains schools and dormitory facilities. *Panorama; Passover Handbook; Seder Guide; Spiritual Suicide; Focus.*

NATIONAL COUNCIL OF BETH JACOB SCHOOLS, INC. (1945). 1415 E. 7 St., Bklyn, N.Y., 11230. (212)979-7400. Chmn. of Bd. Shimon Newhouse; Sec. David Rosenberg. Operates Orthodox all-day schools from kindergarten through high school for girls, a residence high school in Ferndale, N.Y., a national institute for master instructors, and a summer camp for girls. *Bais Yaakov Digest; Pnimia Call.*

NATIONAL COUNCIL OF YOUNG ISRAEL (1912). 3 W. 16 St., N.Y.C., 10011. (212)-929-1525. Nat. Pres. Harold M. Jacobs; Exec. V. Pres. Ephraim H. Sturm. Maintains a program of spiritual, cultural, social, and communal activity towards the advancement and perpetuation of traditional, Torah-true Judaism; seeks to instill in American youth an understanding and appreciation of the ethical and spiritual values of Judaism. Sponsors kosher dining clubs and fraternity houses and an Israel program. *Viewpoint; Hashkofa Series; Masorah Newspaper.*

———, AMERICAN FRIENDS OF YOUNG ISRAEL SYNAGOGUES IN ISRAEL (1926). 3 W. 16 St., N.Y.C., 10011. (212)929-1525. Chmn. Jack Levy; Exec. V. Pres. Ephraim H. Sturm. Promotes Young Israel synagogues and youth work in synagogues in Israel.

———, ARMED FORCES BUREAU (1912). 3 W. 16 St., N.Y.C., 10011. (212)929-1525. Dir. Stanley W. Schlessel; Assoc. Dir. Sidney Weg. Advises and guides the inductees into the armed forces with regard to Sabbath observance, *kashrut*, and Orthodox behavior. *Guide for the Orthodox Serviceman.*

_____, EMPLOYMENT BUREAU (1912). 3 W. 16 St., N.Y.C., 10011. (212)929-1525. Exec. V. Pres. Ephraim H. Sturm; Employment Dir. Dorothy Stein. Operates an on-the-job training program under federal contract; helps secure employment, particularly for Sabbath observers and Russian immigrants; offers vocational guidance. *Viewpoint.*

_____, INSTITUTE FOR JEWISH STUDIES (1947). 3 W. 16 St., N.Y.C., 10011. (212)-929-1525. Pres. Harold M. Jacobs; Exec. V. Pres. Rabbi Ephraim H. Sturm. Introduces students to Jewish learning and knowledge; helps form adult branch schools; aids Young Israel synagogues in their adult education programs. *Bulletin.*

_____, INTERCOLLEGIATE COUNCIL AND YOUNG SINGLE ADULTS (formerly MASSORAH INTERCOLLEGIATES OF YOUNG ISRAEL; 1951). 3 W. 16 St., N.Y.C., 10011. (212)929-1525. Pres. Sidney Weg; Dir. Richard Stareshefsky. Organizes and operates kosher dining clubs on college and university campuses; provides information and counseling on *kashrut* observance at college; gives college-age youth understanding and appreciation of Judaism and information on issues important to Jewish community; arranges seminars and meetings; publishes pamphlets and monographs. *Hashkafa.*

_____, YISRAEL HATZAIR (reorg. 1968). 3 W. 16 St., N.Y.C., 10011. (212)929-1525. Pres. Jackie Goldstein; Nat. Dir. Richard Stareshefsky. Fosters a program of spiritual, cultural, social, and communal activities for the advancement and perpetuation of traditional Torah-true Judaism; strives to instill an understanding and appreciation of the high ethical and spiritual values and to demonstrate compatibility of ancient faith of Israel with good Americanism.

NATIONAL FEDERATION OF JEWISH MEN'S CLUBS, INC. (1929). 475 Riverside Dr., Suite 244, N.Y.C., 10115. (212)749-8100. Pres. Jacob C. Lish; Exec. Dir. David L. Blumenfeld. Promotes principles and objectives of Conservative Judaism by organizing, sponsoring, and developing men's clubs or brotherhoods; supports OMETZ-Center for Conservative Judaism on Campus; promotes Home Library of Conservative Judaism; sponsors Hebrew Literacy Adult Education Program; presents awards for service to American Jewry. *Torchlight.*

NATIONAL JEWISH HOSPITALITY COMMITTEE (1973). 201 S. 18 St., Rm. 1519, Philadelphia, Pa., 19103. (215)546-8293. Pres. Allen S. Maller; Exec. Dir. Steven S. Jacobs. Assists converts and prospective converts to Judaism, persons involved in intermarriages, and the parents of Jewish youth under the influence of cults and missionaries, as well as the youths themselves. *Our Choice.*

NATIONAL JEWISH INFORMATION SERVICE FOR THE PROPAGATION OF JUDAISM, INC. (1960). 5174 W. 8th St., Los Angeles, Calif., 90036. (213)936-6033. Pres. Moshe M. Maggal; V. Pres. Lawrence J. Epstein; Corr. Sec. Rachel D. Maggal. Seeks to convert non-Jews to Judaism and revert Jews to Judaism; maintains College for Jewish Ambassadors for the training of Jewish missionaries and the Correspondence Academy of Judaism for instruction on Judaism through the mail. *Voice of Judaism.*

NATIONAL JEWISH RESOURCE CENTER (1974). 250 W. 57 St., N.Y.C., 10107. (212)582-6116. Chmn. Irvin Frank; Dir. Irving Greenberg. Devoted to leadership education and policy guidance for the American Jewish community. Conducts weekend retreats and community gatherings, as well as conferences on various topics. *Newsletter.*

_____, ZACHOR: THE HOLOCAUST RESOURCE CENTER (1978). 250 W. 57 St., N.Y.C., 10107. (212)582-6116. Chmn. Irv Frank. Assoc. Dir. Michael Berenbaum. Disseminates information on the Holocaust to the American Jewish community; develops Holocaust memorial projects; advises communities and organizations on curricula and special projects; sponsors a Faculty Seminar on the Holocaust and a Task Force on Holocaust Liturgy. *Shoah: A Review of Holocaust Studies and Commemorations; Perspectives.*

NER ISRAEL RABBINICAL COLLEGE (1933). 400 Mt. Wilson Lane, Baltimore, Md., 21208. (301)484-7200. Pres. Rabbi Jacob I. Ruderman; V. Pres. Rabbi Herman N. Neuberger. Trains rabbis and educators for Jewish communities in America and worldwide. Offers bachelors, masters, and doctoral degrees in talmudic law, as well as Teachers Diploma. College has four divisions: Mechina High School, Rabbinical College, Teachers Training Institute,

Graduate School. Maintains an active community service division. Operates special program for Iranian Jewish students. *Ner Israel Bulletin; Alumni Bulletin; Ohr Hanair Talmudic Journal.*

OZAR HATORAH, INC. (1946). 411 Fifth Ave., N.Y.C., 10016. (212)684-4733. Pres. Joseph Shalom; Int. Pres. S.D. Sassoon; Exec. Dir. Rabbi Yoseph Milstein. Establishes and maintains elementary, secondary, and boarding schools, combining a program of religious and secular education for Jewish youth in Morocco, Iran, Syria, and France. *Bulletin.*

P'EYLIM—AMERICAN YESHIVA STUDENT UNION (1951). 3 W. 16 St., N.Y.C., 10011. (212)989-2500. Pres. Nisson Alpert; Dir. Avraham Hirsch. Aids and sponsors pioneer work by American graduate teachers and rabbis in new villages and towns in Israel; does religious, organizational, and educational work and counseling among new immigrant youth; maintains summer camps for poor immigrant youth in Israel; belongs to worldwide P'eylim movement which has groups in Argentina, Brazil, Canada, England, Belgium, the Netherlands, Switzerland, France, and Israel; engages in relief and educational work among North African immigrants in France and Canada, assisting them to relocate and reestablish a strong Jewish community life. *P'eylim Reporter; N'she P'eylim News.*

RABBINICAL ALLIANCE OF AMERICA (IGUD HARABONIM) (1944). 156 Fifth Ave., Suite 807, N.Y.C., 10010. (212)242-6420. Pres. Rabbi Abraham B. Hecht. Seeks to promulgate the cause of Torah-true Judaism through an organized rabbinate that is consistently Orthodox; seeks to elevate the position of Orthodox rabbis nationally, and to defend the welfare of Jews the world over. Also has Beth Din Rabbinical Court. *Perspective.*

RABBINICAL ASSEMBLY (1900). 3080 Broadway, N.Y.C., 10027. (212)678-8060. Pres. Rabbi Seymour J. Cohen; Exec. V. Pres. Rabbi Wolfe Kelman. Seeks to promote Conservative Judaism, and to foster the spirit of fellowship and cooperation among rabbis and other Jewish scholars; cooperates with the Jewish Theological Seminary of America and the United Synagogue of America. *Conservative Judaism; Proceedings of the Rabbinical Assembly.*

RABBINICAL COLLEGE OF TELSHE, INC. (1941). 28400 Euclid Ave., Wickliffe, Ohio, 44092. (216)943-5300. Pres. Rabbi Mordecai Gifter; V. Pres. Rabbi Abba Zalka Gewirtz. College for higher Jewish learning specializing in talmudic studies and rabbinics; maintains a preparatory academy including secular high school, a postgraduate department, a teachers training school, and a teachers seminary for women. *Pri Etz Chaim; Peer Mordechai; Alumni Bulletin.*

RABBINICAL COUNCIL OF AMERICA, INC. (1923; reorg. 1936). 1250 Broadway, Suite 802, N.Y.C., 10001. (212)594-3780. Pres. Bernard Rosensweig; Exec. V. Pres. Binyamin Walfish. Promotes Orthodox Judaism in the community; supports institutions for study of Torah; stimulates creation of new traditional agencies. *Hadorom; Record; Sermon Manual; Tradition.*

RECONSTRUCTIONIST RABBINICAL COLLEGE (1968). 2308 N. Broad St., Philadelphia, Pa., 19132. (215)223-8121. Pres. Ira Silverman; Dean Ronald Brauner. Co-educational. Trains rabbis for all areas of Jewish communal life: synagogues, academic and educational positions, Hillel centers, Federation agencies; requires students to pursue outside graduate studies in religion and related subjects; confers title of rabbi and grants degree of Doctor of Hebrew Letters. *Jewish Civilization: Essays and Studies.*

RESEARCH INSTITUTE OF RELIGIOUS JEWRY, INC. (1941; reorg. 1954). 471 West End Ave., N.Y.C., 10024. (212)874-7979. Chmn. Isaac Strahl; Sec. Marcus Levine. Engages in research and publishes studies concerning the situation of religious Jewry and its problems all over the world.

SHOLEM ALEICHEM FOLK INSTITUTE, INC. (1918). 3301 Bainbridge Ave., Bronx, N.Y., 10467. Pres. Burt Levey; Sec. Noah Zingman. Aims to imbue children with Jewish values through teaching Yiddish language and literature, Hebrew and the Bible, Jewish history, the significance of Jewish holidays, folk and choral singing, and facts about Jewish life in America and Israel. *Kinder Journal* (Yiddish).

SOCIETY FOR HUMANISTIC JUDAISM (1969). 28611 West Twelve Mile Road, Farmington Hills, Mich., 48018. (401)847-4794. Founder Rabbi Sherwin Wine; Exec. Dir.

Miriam Jerris; Pres. James Reiter. Established to promote a fourth alternative in Jewish life. Publishes educational and ceremonial materials; trains humanistic Jewish leaders; organizes humanistic congregations and groups; provides a public voice for humanistic Jews. *Humanistic Judaism.*

SOCIETY OF FRIENDS OF THE TOURO SYNAGOGUE, NATIONAL HISTORIC SHRINE, INC. (1948). 85 Touro St., Newport, R.I., 02840. (401)847-4794. Pres. Aaron Slom; Sec. Theodore Lewis. Assists in the maintenance of the Touro Synagogue as a national historic site. Illustrated brochure on Touro Synagogue.

SPERTUS COLLEGE OF JUDAICA (1925). 618 S. Michigan Ave., Chicago, Ill., 60605. (312)922-9012. Pres. David Wolf Silverman; Bd. Chmn. Ezra Sensibar; Dean Warren Bargad. Educates teachers of Judaica for secondary Jewish schools; certifies Hebrew teachers for public and private Illinois schools; provides Chicago area colleges and universities with specialized undergraduate and graduate programs in Judaica and serves as a Department of Judaic Studies to these colleges and universities; serves as Midwest Jewish information center through its Asher Library and Maurice Spertus Museum of Judaica; grants degrees of Master of Arts in Jewish Education, Jewish Studies, and Jewish Communal Service, Bachelor of Arts, and Bachelor of Judaic Studies.

SYNAGOGUE COUNCIL OF AMERICA (1926). 10 E. 40 St., N.Y.C., 10016. (212)686-8670. Pres. Rabbi Walter S. Wurzburger; Exec. V. Pres. Rabbi Bernard Mandelbaum. Serves as spokesman for, and coordinates policies of, national rabbinical and lay synagogal organizations of Conservative, Orthodox, and Reform branches of American Judaism. Sponsors Institute for Jewish Policy Planning and Research. *SCA Report; Analysis.*

———, INSTITUTE FOR JEWISH POLICY PLANNING AND RESEARCH OF (1972). 10 E. 40 St., N.Y.C., 10016. (212)686-8670. Chmn. Nathan S. Ancell. Seeks to strengthen American Jewry by conducting and promoting systematic study of major issues confronting its future vitality, for which it enlists informed academic and lay people; sponsors research and analysis on the subject and disseminates findings to synagogues and other Jewish organizations. *Analysis of Jewish Policy Issues; Background.*

TORAH SCHOOLS FOR ISRAEL—CHINUCH ATZMAI (1953). 167 Madison Ave., N.Y.C., 10016. (212)889-0606. Pres. Moshe Feinstein; Exec. Dir. Henach Cohen. Conducts information programs for the American Jewish community on activities of the independent Torah schools educational network in Israel; coordinates role of American members of international board of governors; funds special programs of Mercaz Hachinuch Ha-Atzmai B'Eretz Yisroel.

TORAH UMESORAH—NATIONAL SOCIETY FOR HEBREW DAY SCHOOLS (1944). 229 Park Ave. S., N.Y.C., 10003. (212)674-6700. Chmn. Nat. Bd. Sheldon Beren; Chmn. Exec. Com. David Singer; Nat. Dir. Rabbi Bernard Goldenberg. Establishes Hebrew day schools throughout U.S. and Canada and services them in all areas including placement and curriculum guidance; conducts teacher training institutes, a special fellowship program, seminars, and workshops for in-service training of teachers; publishes textbooks and supplementary reading material; conducts education research and has established Fryer Found. for research in ethics and character education; supervises federal aid programs for Hebrew day schools throughout the U.S. *Olomeinu—Our World; Tempo; Torah Umesorah Report; Machberet Hamenahel.*

———, INSTITUTE FOR PROFESSIONAL ENRICHMENT (1973). 22 E. 28 St., N.Y.C., 10016. (212)683-3216. Dir. Bernard Dov Milians. Provides enriched training and upgraded credentials for administrative, guidance, and classroom personnel of Hebrew day schools and for Torah-community leaders; offers graduate and undergraduate programs, in affiliation with accredited universities which award full degrees: M.A. in early childhood and elementary education; M.S. in family counseling; M.B.A. in management; M.S. in special education, reading; B.S. in education; B.A. in human relations, social sciences, education, gerontology. *Professional Enrichment News (PEN).*

———, NATIONAL ASSOCIATION OF HEBREW DAY SCHOOL ADMINISTRATORS (1960). 1114 Ave. J., Bklyn., N.Y., 11230.

Pres. David H. Schwartz. Coordinates the work of the fiscal directors of Hebrew day schools throughout the country. *NAHDSA Review.*

———, NATIONAL ASSOCIATION OF HEBREW DAY SCHOOL PARENT-TEACHER ASSOCIATIONS (1948). 229 Park Ave. S., N.Y.C., 10003. (212)674-6700. Nat. Pres. Mrs. Henry C. Rhein; Exec. Sec. Mrs. Samuel Brand; Chmn. of Bd. Mrs. Clarence Horwitz. Acts as a clearinghouse and service agency to PTAs of Hebrew day schools; organizes parent education courses and sets up programs for individual PTAs. *National Program Notes; PTA Bulletin; Fundraising With a Flair; PTA With a Purpose for the Hebrew Day School.*

———, NATIONAL CONFERENCE OF YESHIVA PRINCIPALS (1956). 229 Park Ave. S., N.Y.C., 10003. (212)674-6700. Pres. Rabbi Moshe Possick; Exec. V. Pres. Rabbi Joshua Fishman; Bd. Chmn. Nochem Kaplan. A professional organization of primary and secondary yeshiva day-school principals which seeks to make yeshiva day-school education more effective. *Machberet Hamenahel.*

———, NATIONAL YESHIVA TEACHERS BOARD OF LICENSE (1953). 229 Park Ave. S., N.Y.C., 10003. (212)674-6700. Bd. Chmn. Elias Schwartz; Exec. Consult. Zvi H. Shurin. Issues licenses to qualified instructors for all grades of the Hebrew day school and the general field of Torah education.

———, SAMUEL A. FRYER EDUCATIONAL RESEARCH FOUNDATION (1966). 229 Park Ave. S., N.Y.C., 10003. (212)674-6700. Chmn. Bd. of Trustees Jack Sable; Dir. Louis Nulman. Strengthens the ethics programs of Hebrew day, afternoon, and Sunday schools, summer camps, and Jewish centers through moral sensitivity-training program; provides extensive teacher-training program; publishes monographs, newsletter, and teachers' bulletin. *Newsletter.*

TOURO COLLEGE (1970). 30 W. 44 St., N.Y.C., 10036. (212)575-0190. Pres. Bernard Lander. Chartered by the N.Y. State Board of Regents to operate and maintain nonprofit, four-year college with liberal arts programs leading to B.A. and B.S. degrees, with an emphasis on the relevance of the Jewish heritage to the general culture of Western civilization. *Annual Bulletin.*

UNION OF AMERICAN HEBREW CONGREGATIONS (1873). 838 Fifth Ave., N.Y.C., 10021. (212)249-0100. Pres. Rabbi Alexander M. Schindler; Bd. Chmn. Donald S. Day. Serves as the central congregational body of Reform Judaism in the western hemisphere; serves its approximately 750 affiliated temples and membership with religious, educational, cultural, and administrative programs. *Keeping Posted; Reform Judaism.*

———, AMERICAN CONFERENCE OF CANTORS (1956). 838 Fifth Ave., N.Y.C., 10021. (212)249-0100. Pres. Murray E. Simon; Exec. Dir. Raymond Smolover. Members receive investiture and commissioning as cantors at ordination-investiture ceremonies at Hebrew Union College— Jewish Institute of Religion, Sacred School of Music. Through Joint Placement Commission, serves congregations seeking cantors and music directors. Dedicated to creative Judaism, preserving the best of the past, and encouraging new and vital approaches to religious ritual, music and ceremonies.

———, COMMISSION ON SOCIAL ACTION OF REFORM JUDAISM (see p. 284).

———, NATIONAL ASSOCIATION OF TEMPLE ADMINISTRATORS OF (1941). 838 Fifth Ave., N.Y.C., 10021. (212)249-0100. Pres. Henry E. Ziegler; Adm. Sec. William Ferstenfeld. Fosters Reform Judaism; prepares and disseminates administrative information and procedures to member synagogues of UAHC; provides and encourages proper and adequate training of professional synagogue executives; formulates and establishes professional ideals and standards for the synagogue executive; provides placement services. *NATA Journal.*

———, NATIONAL ASSOCIATION OF TEMPLE EDUCATORS (1955). 838 Fifth Ave., N.Y.C., 10021. (212)249-0100. Pres. Fred W. Marcus; V. Pres. Richard M. Morin. Represents the temple educator within the general body of Reform Judaism; fosters the full-time profession of the temple educator; encourages the growth and development of Jewish religious education consistent with the aims of Reform Judaism; stimulates communal interest in and responsibility for Jewish religious education. *NATE News; Compass Magazine.*

———, NATIONAL FEDERATION OF TEMPLE BROTHERHOODS (1923). 838 Fifth Ave., N.Y.C., 10021. (212)249-0100. Pres. David N. Krem; Exec. Dir. Av Bondarin. Promotes Jewish education among its members, along with participation in temple, brotherhood, and interfaith activities; sponsors the Jewish Chautauqua Society. *Brotherhood.*

———, NATIONAL FEDERATION OF TEMPLE SISTERHOODS (1913). 838 Fifth Ave., N.Y.C., 10021. (212)249-0100. Pres. Constance Kreshtool; Exec. Dir. Eleanor R. Schwartz. Serves more than 640 sisterhoods of Reform Judaism; inter-religious understanding and social justice; scholarships and grants to rabbinic students; braille and large-type Judaic materials for Jewish blind; projects for Israel, Soviet Jewry, and the aging; is an affiliate of UAHC and is the women's agency of Reform Judaism; works on behalf of the Hebrew Union College–Jewish Institute of Religion; cooperates with World Union for Progressive Judaism. *Notes for Now.*

———, NORTH AMERICAN FEDERATION OF TEMPLE YOUTH (NFTY; formerly NATIONAL FEDERATION OF TEMPLE YOUTH) (1939). 838 Fifth Ave., N.Y.C., 10021. (212)249-0100. Dir. Ramie Arian; Assoc. Dir. Daniel Freelander; Pres. Adina Baseman. Seeks to train Reform Jewish youth in the values of the synagogue and their application to daily life through service to the community and congregation; runs department of summer camps and national leadership training institute; arranges overseas academic tours and work programs, international student exchange programs, college student programs in the U.S. and Israel, including accredited study programs in Israel. *Ani V'Atah; The Jewish Connection.*

———, AND CENTRAL CONFERENCE OF AMERICAN RABBIS: COMMISSION ON JEWISH EDUCATION (1923). 838 Fifth Ave., N.Y.C., 10021. (212)249-0100. Chmn. Martin S. Rozenberg; Dir. Rabbi Daniel B. Syme. Develops curricula and teachers' manuals; conducts pilot projects and offers educational guidance and consultation at all age levels to member congregations and affiliates and associate bodies. *What's Happening; Compass; E³.*

———, AND CENTRAL CONFERENCE OF AMERICAN RABBIS: JOINT COMMISSION ON SYNAGOGUE ADMINISTRATION (1962). 838 Fifth Ave., N.Y.C., 10021. (212)249-0100. Chmn. Harold J. Tragash; Dir. Myron E. Schoen. Assists congregations in management, finance, building maintenance, design, construction, and art aspects of synagogues; maintains the Synagogue Architectural Library, consisting of photos, slides, and plans of contemporary and older synagogue buildings. *Synagogue Service.*

UNION OF ORTHODOX JEWISH CONGREGATIONS OF AMERICA (1898). 45 W. 36 St., N.Y.C., 10018. (212)563-4000. Pres. Julius Berman; Exec. V. Pres. Pinchas Stolper. Serves as the national central body of Orthodox synagogues; provides educational, religious, and organizational guidance to groups, and men's clubs; represents the Orthodox Jewish community in relationship to governmental and civic bodies, and the general Jewish community; conducts the national authoritative U Kashruth certification service. *Jewish Action; Jewish Life; Keeping Posted; U News Reporter.*

———, NATIONAL CONFERENCE OF SYNAGOGUE YOUTH (1954). 116 E. 27 St., N.Y.C., 10016. Pres. Sue Feuerstein; Nat. Dir. Baruch Taub. Serves as central body for youth groups of traditional congregations; provides such national activities and services as educational guidance, Torah study groups, community service, programs consultation, Torah library, Torah fund scholarships, Ben Zakkai Honor Society, Friends of NCSY; conducts national and regional events including week-long seminars, summer Torah tours in over 200 communities, Israel summer seminar for teens and collegiates, Camp NCSY in Israel for preteens. Divisions include Senior NCSY in 18 regions and 465 chapters, Junior NCSY for pre-teens, CYT-College Youth for Torah, B'nai Torah Day School and NCSY in Israel. *Keeping Posted With NCSY; Advisors' Newsletter; Mitsvos Ma'asiyos; Holiday Series; Jewish Thought Series; Leadership Manual Series; Texts for Teen Study.*

———, WOMEN'S BRANCH (1923). 84 Fifth Ave., N.Y.C., 10011. (212)929-8857. Pres. Mrs. Samuel A. Turk; Exec. Dir. Judy Paikin. Seeks to spread knowledge for the understanding and practice of Orthodox Judaism, and to unite all Orthodox women and their synagogal organizations; services affiliates with educational and programming materials, leadership and organizational guidance, and has an NGO representative at UN. *Hachodesh; Hakol.*

UNION OF ORTHODOX RABBIS OF THE UNITED STATES AND CANADA (1900). 235 E. Broadway, N.Y.C., 10002. (212)-964-6337. Pres. Rabbi Moshe Feinstein; Dir. Rabbi Hersh M. Ginsberg. Seeks to foster and promote Torah-true Judaism in U.S. and Canada; assists in the establishment and maintenance of *yeshivot* in the United States; maintains committee on marriage and divorce and aids individuals with marital difficulties; disseminates knowledge of traditional Jewish rites and practices and publishes regulations on synagogal structure; maintains rabbinical court for resolving individual and communal conflicts. *Hapardes.*

UNION OF SEPHARDIC CONGREGATIONS, INC. (1929). 8 W. 70 St., N.Y.C., 10023. (212)873-0300. Pres. The Haham, Solomon Gaon; Sec. Joseph Tarica; Bd. Chmn. Victor Tarry. Promotes the religious interests of Sephardic Jews; prepares and distributes Sephardic prayer books and provides religious leaders for Sephardic congregations.

UNITED LUBAVITCHER YESHIVOTH (1940). 841–853 Ocean Parkway, Brooklyn, N.Y., 11230. (212)859-7600. Pres. Eli N. Sklar; Chmn. Exec. Com. Rabbi S. Gourary. Supports and organizes Jewish day schools and rabbinical seminaries in the U.S.A. and abroad.

UNITED SYNAGOGUE OF AMERICA (1913). 155 Fifth Ave., N.Y.C., 10010. (212)533-7800. Pres. Simon Schwartz; Exec. V. Pres. Rabbi Benjamin Z. Kreitman. National organization of Conservative Jewish congregations. Maintains 12 departments and 20 regional offices to assist its affiliated congregations with religious, educational, youth, community, and administrative programming and guidance; aims to enhance the cause of Conservative Judaism, further religious observance, encourage establishment of Jewish religious schools; embraces all elements essentially loyal to traditional Judaism. *Program Suggestions; United Synagogue Review; Yearbook Directory and Buyers' Guide.*

——, ATID, COLLEGE AGE ORGANIZATION OF (1960, reorg. 1981). 155 Fifth Ave., N.Y.C., 10010. (212)533-7800. Dir.

Paul Freedman. Student Advisory Board. Seeks to develop a program for strengthening identification with Judaism, based on the personality development, needs, and interests of the collegian. *ATID Curricula Judaica; ATID Bibliography. ATID Bookmobile Project.*

——, COMMISSION ON JEWISH EDUCATION (1930). 155 Fifth Ave., N.Y.C., 10010. (212)533-7800. Chmn. Rabbi Joel H. Zaiman; Dir. Morton K. Siegel. Promotes higher educational standards in Conservative congregational schools and Solomon Schechter Day Schools and publishes material for the advancement of their educational program. Provides guidance and information on resources, courses, and other projects in adult Jewish education; prepares and publishes pamphlets, study guides, tracts, and texts for use in adult-education programs; publishes the Jewish Tract series and distributes El-Am edition of *Talmud.* Distributes black-and-white and color films of "Eternal Light" TV programs on Jewish subjects, produced by Jewish Theological Seminary in cooperation with NBC. *Briefs; Impact; In Your Hands; Your Child.*

——, JEWISH EDUCATORS ASSEMBLY OF (1951). 155 Fifth Ave., N.Y.C., 10010. (212)533-7800. Pres. Irving Skolnick; Admin. Herbert L. Tepper. Promotes, extends, and strengthens the program of Jewish education on all levels in the community in consonance with the philosophy of the Conservative movement. *Annual Yearbook; Newsletters.*

——, JOINT COMMISSION ON SOCIAL ACTION (1958). 155 Fifth Ave., N.Y.C., 10010. (212)533-7800. Co-chmn. Jerry Wagner, Dolly Moser; Dir. Muriel Bermar. Consists of representatives of United Synagogue of America, Women's League for Conservative Judaism, Rabbinical Assembly, and National Federation of Jewish Men's Clubs; reviews public issues and cooperates with civic and Jewish community organizations to achieve social action goals. *Judaism in Social Action.*

——, KADIMA OF (formerly PRE-USY; reorg. 1968). 155 Fifth Ave., N.Y.C., 10010. (212)533-7800. Int. Coordinator Carole Chapnick Silk; Dir. Amy Cytryn. Involves Jewish pre-teens in a meaningful religious, educational, and social environment; fosters a sense of identity and commitment to the Jewish community and Conservative movement; conducts synagogue-based chapter programs and regional Kadima days and weekends. *KADIMA; Mitzvah of the Month; Kadima Kesher; Advisors Aid Series; Chagim; Games.*

———, NATIONAL ASSOCIATION OF SYNAGOGUE ADMINISTRATORS OF (1948). 155 Fifth Ave., N.Y.C., 10010. (212)533-7800. Pres. Joseph M. Miller. Aids congregations affiliated with the United Synagogue of America to further aims of Conservative Judaism through more effective administration; advances professional standards and promotes new methods in administration; cooperates in United Synagogue placement services and administrative surveys. *NASA Newsletter; NASA Journal.*

———, UNITED SYNAGOGUE YOUTH OF (1951). 155 Fifth Ave., N.Y.C., 10010. (212)533-7800. Pres. Mark Davis; Exec. Dir. Paul Freedman. Seeks to develop a program for strengthening identification with Conservative Judaism, based on the personality development, needs, and interests of the adolescent. *AchShav; Advisors Newsletter; Tikun Olam; USY Alumni Assn. Newsletter; USY Program Bank.*

VAAD MISHMERETH STAM (1976). 4902-16 Ave., Brooklyn, N.Y., 11204. Exec. Dir. Rabbi David L. Greenfeld; Admn. Albert Sokol. A non-profit, consumer protection agency dedicated to preserving and protecting the halachic integrity of Torah scrolls, phylacteries, and *mezuzot.* Makes presentations and conducts examination campaigns in schools and synagogues. *A Guide to Mezuzah; The Halachic Encyclopedia of the Sacred Alphabet.*

WEST COAST TALMUDICAL SEMINARY (Yeshiva Ohr Elchonon Chabad) (1953). 7215 Warring St., Los Angeles, Calif., 90046. (213)937-3763. Pres. Abraham Linderman; V. Pres. Rabbi Shlomo Cunin; V. Pres. Rabbi Levi Bukiet. Provides facilities for intensive Torah education as well as Orthodox rabbinical training on the West Coast; conducts an accredited college preparatory high school combined with a full program of Torah-Talmudic training and a graduate Talmudical division on college level.

WOMEN'S LEAGUE FOR CONSERVATIVE JUDAISM (formerly NATIONAL WOMEN'S LEAGUE) (1918). 48 E. 74 St., N.Y.C., 10021. (212)628-1600. Pres. Goldie Kweller. Constitutes parent body of Conservative women's groups in U.S., Canada, Puerto Rico, Mexico, and Israel; provides them with programs in religion, education, social action, leadership training, Israel affairs, and community affairs; publishes books of Jewish interest; contributes to support of Jewish Theological Seminary and Mathilde Schechter Residence Halls. *Women's League Outlook.*

WORLD COUNCIL OF SYNAGOGUES (1957). 155 Fifth Ave., N.Y.C., 10010. (212)533-7693. Pres. Mordecai Waxman; Exec. Dir. Zipporah Liben. International representative of Conservative organizations and congregations (Hatenuah Hamasoratit); promotes the growth and development of the Conservative movement in Israel and throughout the world; supports new congregations and educational institutions overseas; holds biennial international convention; represents the world Conservative movement in the World Zionist Organization. *Newsletter.*

WORLD UNION FOR PROGRESSIVE JUDAISM, LTD. (1926). 838 Fifth Ave., N.Y.C., 10021. (212)249-0100. Pres. Gerard Daniel; Exec. Dir. Richard G. Hirsch; Sec. Jane Evans; Nat. Adv. Bd. Dir. Paul Kushner. Promotes and coordinates efforts of Reform, Liberal, and Progressive congregations throughout the world; supports new congregations; assigns and employs rabbis overseas; sponsors seminaries and schools; organizes international conferences of Liberal Jews. *International Conference Reports; News and Views; Shalhevet* (Israel); *Teshuva* (Argentina); *Ammi.*

YAVNE HEBREW THEOLOGICAL SEMINARY (1924). 510 Dahill Road, Brooklyn, N.Y., 11218. (212)436-5610. Pres. Nathan Shapiro; Exec. Dir. Solomon K. Shapiro. School for higher Jewish learning; trains rabbis and teachers as Jewish leaders for American Jewish communities; maintains Machon Maharshal branch in Jerusalem for higher Jewish education and for an exchange student program. *Yavne Newsletter.*

YAVNEH, NATIONAL RELIGIOUS JEWISH STUDENTS ASSOCIATION (1960). 25 W. 26 St., N.Y.C., 10010. (212)679-4574. Pres. Reena Wein; Exec. V. Pres. Michael Edelstein. Seeks to promote religious Jewish and Zionist education on the college campus, to facilitate full observance of halakhic Judaism, to integrate the insights gained in college studies, and to become a force for the dissemination of Torah Judaism in the Jewish community; initiated *kiruv* programs aimed at drawing into the established Jewish community alienated and assimilated Jewish students; publishes occasional monographs in *Yavneh Studies Series;* conducts summer tours to Israel and an Eastern Europe holocaust study tour. *Kol Yavneh, Parshat Hashavua Series; Yavneh Shiron; Prayer: A Guide to the Philosophy and Meaning of Tefilah; Yavneh Dispatch.*

YESHIVA UNIVERSITY (1886). 500 W. 185 St., N.Y.C., 10033. (212)960-5400. Pres. Norman Lamm; Chmn. Bd. of Trustees Herbert Tenzer. The nation's oldest and largest private university founded under Jewish auspices, with a broad range of undergraduate, graduate, and professional schools, a network of affiliates, publications, a widespread program of research, community service agencies, and a museum. Curricula lead to bachelor's, master's, doctoral, and professional degrees. Undergraduate schools provide general studies curricula supplemented by courses in Jewish learning; graduate schools prepare for careers in medicine, law, mathematics, physics, social work, education, psychology, Semitic languages, literatures, and cultures, and other fields. It has six undergraduate schools, eight graduate schools, and three affiliates, with its four main centers located in Manhattan and the Bronx. *Inside Yeshiva University; Yeshiva University Report.*

Undergraduate schools for men at Main Center: Yeshiva College (Dean Michael Hecht) provides liberal arts and sciences curricula; grants B.A. degree. Merkin College of Hebraic Studies (Dean Jacob M. Rabinowitz) awards Hebraic Studies and Hebrew Teacher's diplomas, B.A., and B.S. James Striar School of General Jewish Studies (Dir. Morris J. Besdin) grants Associate in Arts degree. Mazer School of Talmudic Studies (Dir. Zevulun Charlop) offers advanced course of study in Talmudic texts and commentaries.

Undergraduate schools for women at Midtown Center, 245 Lexington Ave., N.Y.C., 10016; Stern College for Women (Dean Karen Bacon) offers liberal arts and sciences curricula supplemented by Jewish

studies courses; awards B.A., Jewish Studies certificate, Hebrew Teacher's diploma. Teachers Institute for Women (Dir. Walter Orenstein) trains professionals for education and community agency work; awards Hebrew Teacher's diploma and B.S. in Education.

Sponsors two high schools for boys and two for girls (Manhattan and Brooklyn).

Auxiliary services include: Stone-Saperstein Center for Jewish Education, Sephardic Studies Program, Brookdale Foundation Programs for the Aged, Maxwell R. Maybaum Institute of Material Sciences and Quantum Electronics.

———, ALBERT EINSTEIN COLLEGE OF MEDICINE (1955). Eastchester Rd. and Morris Pk. Ave., Bronx, N.Y., 10461. (212)430-2000. Dean Ephraim Friedman. Prepares physicians and conducts research in the health sciences; awards M.D. degree; includes Sue Golding Graduate Division of Medical Sciences (Dir. Jonathan R. Warner), which grants Ph.D. degree. Einstein College's clinical facilities and affiliates encompass five Bronx hospitals, including Bronx Municipal Hospital, Montefiore Hospital and Medical Center, and the Rose F. Kennedy Center for Research in Mental Retardation and Human Development. *AECOM News; AECOM Newsletter.*

———, ALUMNI OFFICE, 500 West 185th Street, N.Y.C., 10033. Dir. Richard M. Joel. Seeks to foster a close allegiance of alumni to their alma mater by maintaining ties with all alumni and servicing the following associations: Yeshiva College Alumni (Pres. Joseph Applebaum); Erna Michael College of Hebraic Studies Alumni; James Striar School of General Jewish Studies Alumni; Stern College Alumnae (Pres. Zelda Braun); Teachers Institute for Women Alumnae (Pres. Rivka Brass Finkelstein); Albert Einstein College of Medicine Alumni (Pres. Seligman Rosenberg); Ferkauf Graduate School Alumni (Pres. Alvin I. Schiff); Wurzweiler School of Social Work Alumni (Pres. Neva Rephun, Norman Winkler); Bernard Revel Graduate School—Harry Fischel School Alumni (Pres. Bernard Rosensweig); Rabbinic Alumni (Pres. Haskel Lookstein); Benjamin N. Cardozo School of Law Alumni (Pres. Wayne Halper); Alumni Council (Chmn. Abraham S. Guterman) offers guidance to

Pres. and Bd. of Trustees on university's academic development and service activities. *Alumni Review; AECOM Alumni News; Jewish Social Work Forum; Alumnews.*

———, BELFER GRADUATE SCHOOL OF SCIENCE (1958). 500 W. 185 St., N.Y.C., 10033. Dir. Dr. David Finkelstein. Offers programs in mathematics and physics, including college teaching in those areas; conducts advanced research projects; confers M.A. and Ph.D. degrees.

———, BELFER INSTITUTE FOR ADVANCED BIOMEDICAL STUDIES (1978). Eastchester Rd. and Morris Pk. Ave., Bronx, N.Y., 10461. Dir. Ernest R. Jaffe. Offers postdoctoral program that coordinates projects for research fellows and associates, and the development of new training programs; awards certificate at term's completion.

———, BENJAMIN N. CARDOZO SCHOOL OF LAW (1976). 55 Fifth Ave., N.Y.C., 10003. Dean Monrad G. Paulsen. Prepares students for the professional practice of law or other activities in which legal training is useful; grants L.L.D. degree.

———, BERNARD REVEL GRADUATE SCHOOL (1937). 500 W. 185 St., N.Y.C., 10033. Dean Sid Z. Leiman. Offers graduate work in Judaic studies and Semitic languages, literatures, and cultures; confers M.S., M.A., and Ph.D. degrees.

———, CANTORIAL TRAINING INSTITUTE. Dir. Macy Nulman. Provides professional training of cantors and other music personnel for the Jewish community; awards Associate Cantor's Certificate and Cantorial Diploma.

———, CAROLINE AND JOSEPH S. GRUSS INSTITUTE IN JERUSALEM. Ed. Supervisor Aharon Lichtenstein. A center in Israel for advanced Talmudic studies; offers programs for pre-semikhah, semikhah, and post-semikhah students.

———, FERKAUF GRADUATE SCHOOL OF HUMANITIES AND SOCIAL SCIENCES (1957). 55 Fifth Ave., N.Y.C., 10003. Dean Morton Berger. Offers graduate programs in education, psychology, Jewish education, and special education; grants M.S., M.A., Specialist's Certificate, Doctor of Education, Doctor of Psychology, and Ph.D. degrees.

———, HARRY FISCHEL SCHOOL FOR HIGHER JEWISH STUDIES (1945). 500 W. 185 St., N.Y.C., 10033. Dean Sid Z. Leiman. Offers summer graduate work in Judaic studies and Semitic languages, literatures, and cultures; confers M.S., M.A., and Ph.D. degrees.

———, MARCOS AND ADINA KATZ KOLLEL. Rosh Kollel Rabbi Hershel Schachter. Institute for advanced research in rabbinics. Provides intensive training in Talmudic scholarship.

———, (affiliate) RABBI ISAAC ELCHANAN THEOLOGICAL SEMINARY (1896). 2540 Amsterdam Ave., N.Y.C., 10033. Chmn. Bd. of Trustees Charles H. Bendheim; Dir. Rabbi Zevulun Charlop. Offers comprehensive training in higher Jewish studies; grants semikhah (ordination) and the degrees of Master of Religious Education, Master of Hebrew Literature, Doctor of Religious Education, and Doctor of Hebrew Literature; includes Kollel (Institute for Advanced Research in Rabbinics; Dir. Rabbi Hershel Schachter) and auxiliaries. Cantorial Training Institute (Dir. Macy Nulman) provides professional training of cantors and other musical personnel for the Jewish community; awards Associate Cantor's certificate and cantorial diploma. Sephardic Community Activities Program (Dir. Rabbi Herbert C. Dobrinsky) serves the specific needs of 70 Sephardi synagogues in the U.S. and Canada; holds such events as annual Sephardic Cultural Festival; maintains Sephardic Home Study Group program. *American Sephardi.* Community Service Division (Dir. Victor B. Geller) makes educational, organizational, programming, consultative, and placement resources available to congregations, schools, organizations, and communities in the U.S. and Canada, through its youth bureau, department of adult education, lecture bureau, placement bureau, and rabbinic alumni. National Commission on Torah Education (Dir. Robert S. Hirt); Camp Morasha (Dir. Zvi Reich) offers Jewish study program; Educators Council of America (Dir. Robert S. Hirt) formulates uniform educational standards, provides guidance to professional staffs, rabbis, lay leaders with regard to curriculum, and promotes Jewish education.

———, SOCIETY OF THE FOUNDERS OF THE ALBERT EINSTEIN COLLEGE OF MEDICINE (1953). 55 Fifth Ave., N.Y.C., 10003.

Exec. Dir. Harold Blond. Seeks to further community support of Einstein College.

_____, WOMEN'S ORGANIZATION (1928). 55 Fifth Ave., N.Y.C., 10003. Pres. Ann Arbesfeld; Dir. Malkah Isseroff. Supports Yeshiva University's national scholarship program for students training in education, community service, law, medicine, and other professions, and its development program. *YUWO News Briefs.*

_____, WURZWEILER SCHOOL OF SOCIAL WORK (1957). 55 Fifth Ave., N.Y.C., 10003. Dean Lloyd Setleis. Offers graduate programs in social casework, social group work, community social work; grants Master of Social Work, Master of Professional Studies, and Doctor of Social Welfare degrees. Includes Block Education Program (Dir. Samuel M. Goldstein), which offers practical training in fieldwork at Jewish communal agencies.

_____, YESHIVA UNIVERSITY GERONTO-LOGICAL INSTITUTE. Dir. Celia B. Weisman. Fosters and coordinates gerontological research; offers post-Master's Certificate in Gerontology.

_____, (affiliate) YESHIVA UNIVERSITY OF LOS ANGELES (1977). 9760 West Pico Blvd., Los Angeles, Calif., 90035. (213)-553-4478. Bd. Chmn. Samuel Belzberg; Co-chmn. Roland E. Arnall; Dean of Admin. Rabbi Marvin Hier. With Menachem Begin School of Jewish Studies, Yeshiva Program, Beit Midrash Program, Kollel; students pursue B.A. or B.S. degree at college of their choice. Includes Simon Wiesenthal Center for Holocaust Studies (Coordinator, Ephraim J. Zuroff).

YESHIVATH TORAH VODAATH AND MESIVTA RABBINICAL SEMINARY (1918). 425 E. 9 St., Brooklyn, N.Y., 11218. (212)-941-8000. Pres. Henry Hirsch; Chmn. of Bd. Fred F. Weiss; Sec. Earl H. Spero. Offers Hebrew and secular education from elementary level through rabbinical ordination and post-graduate work; maintains a teachers institute and community-service bureau; maintains a dormitory and a nonprofit camp program for boys. *Chronicle; Mesivta Vanguard; Thought of the Week; Torah Vodaath News.*

_____, ALUMNI ASSOCIATION (1941). 425 E. 9 St., Brooklyn, N.Y., 11218. (212)941-8000. Pres. Marcus Saffer; Chmn. of Bd. Seymour Pluchenik. Promotes social and cultural ties between the alumni and the schools through fund-raising; offers vocational guidance to students; operates Camp Torah Vodaath; sponsors research fellowship program for boys. *Annual Journal; Hamesivta Torah Periodical.*

SOCIAL, MUTUAL BENEFIT

AMERICAN ASSOCIATION FOR ETHIOPIAN JEWS (1974). 304 Robin Hood Lane, Costa Mesa, Calif., 92627. (714)851-2049. Pres. Howard M. Lenhoff; Exec. V. Pres. Graenum Berger. Provides educational material in North America on Ethiopian Jews, and support for Ethiopian Jews in Africa and in Israel.

AMERICAN FEDERATION OF JEWISH FIGHTERS, CAMP INMATES AND NAZI VICTIMS, INC. (1971). 823 United Nations Plaza, N.Y.C., 10017. (212)697-5670. Pres. Solomon Zynstein; Exec. Dir. Ernest Honig. Seeks to perpetuate memory of victims of the Holocaust and make Jewish and non-Jewish youth aware of the Holocaust and resistance period. *Martyrdom and Resistance.*

AMERICAN FEDERATION OF JEWS FROM CENTRAL EUROPE, INC. (1942). 570 Seventh Ave., N.Y.C., 10018. (212)921-3871. Pres. Curt C. Silberman; Exec. V. Pres. Herbert A. Strauss; Exec. Sec. Joan C. Lessing. Seeks to safeguard the rights and interests of American Jews of Central European descent, especially in reference to restitution and indemnification; through its Research Foundation for Jewish Immigration sponsors research and publications on the history of Central European Jewry and the history of their immigration and acculturation in the U.S.; sponsors a social program for needy Nazi victims in the U.S. in cooperation with United Help, Inc. and other specialized social agencies. Undertakes cultural activities, annual conferences, publication, and lecture programs. Member, Council of Jews from Germany.

AMERICAN SEPHARDI FEDERATION (1972). 225 W. 34 St., Rm. 1505, N.Y.C., 10122. (212)563-4625. Pres. Liliane L. Winn; Exec. Dir. Gary Schaer; Chmn. Bd. of Dirs. Morrie Yohai. Seeks to preserve the Sephardi heritage in the United States, Israel, and throughout the world by fostering and supporting religious and cultural activities of Sephardi congregations, organizations and communities, and uniting them in one overall organization; supports Jewish institutions of higher learning and those for the training of Sephardi lay and religious leaders to serve their communities everywhere; assists Sephardi charitable, cultural, religious and educational institutions everywhere; disseminates information by the publication, or assistance in the publication, of books and other literature dealing with Sephardi culture and tradition in the United States; organizes youth and young adult activities throughout the U.S.; supports efforts of the World Sephardi Federation to alleviate social disparities in Israel. *Sephardi World; Sephardi News Bulletin; Sephardi Spotlight; Sephardic Connection.*

AMERICAN VETERANS OF ISRAEL (1949). c/o Samuel E. Alexander, 548 E. Walnut St., Long Beach, N.Y., 11561. (516)431-8316. Pres. Louis Brettler; Sec. Samuel E. Alexander. Maintains contact with American and Canadian volunteers who served in Aliyah Bet and/or Israel's War of Independence; promotes Israel's welfare; holds memorial services at grave of Col. David Marcus; is affiliated with World Mahal. *Newsletter.*

ASSOCIATION OF YUGOSLAV JEWS IN THE UNITED STATES, INC. (1940). 247 W. 99 St., N.Y.C., 10025. (212)865-2211. Pres. Sal Musafia; Sec. Mile Weiss. Assists members and Jews and Jewish organizations in Yugoslavia; cooperates with organization of former Yugoslav Jews in Israel and elsewhere. *Bulletin.*

BNAI ZION—THE AMERICAN FRATERNAL ZIONIST ORGANIZATION (1908). 136 E. 39 St., N.Y.C., 10016. (212)725-1211. Pres. Sidney Wiener; Exec. V. Pres. Herman Z. Quittman. Fosters principles of Americanism, fraternalism, and Zionism; fosters Hebrew culture; offers life insurance, Blue Cross hospitalization, and other benefits to its members; sponsors settlements, youth centers, medical clinics, and Bnai Zion Home for Retardates in Rosh Ha'ayin, Israel. Program is dedicated to furtherance of America-Israel friendship. Has Young Leadership Division—TAMID. *TAMID Outlet; Bnai Zion Foundation Newsletter; Bnai Zion Voice.*

BRITH ABRAHAM (1887). 136 E. 39 St., N.Y.C., 10016. Grand Master Herb Fink. Protects Jewish rights and combats antisemitism; supports Israel through Bnai Zion

Found. and other Jewish organizations; maintains foundation in support of Soviet Jewry; aids Jewish education and Camp Loyaltown for Retarded. Section in *Voice.*

BRITH SHOLOM (1905). 3939 Conshohocken Ave., Philadelphia, Pa., 19131. (215)878-5696. Nat. Pres. David Saner; Nat. Exec. Dir. Joshua Eilberg. Fraternal organization devoted to community welfare, protection of rights of Jewish people and activities which foster Jewish identity and provide support for Israel; sponsors Brith Sholom House for senior citizens in Philadelphia and Brith Sholom Beit Halochem under construction in Haifa, a rehabilitation center for Israel's permanently warwounded. *Community Relations Digest; Brith Sholom News.*

CENTRAL SEPHARDIC JEWISH COMMUNITY OF AMERICA (1940). 8 W. 70 St., N.Y.C., 10023. (212)787-2850. Pres. Solomon Altchek; Sec. Isaac Molho. Seeks to foster Sephardic culture, education, and communal institutions. Sponsors wide range of activities; raises funds for Sephardic causes in U.S. and Israel.

FREE SONS OF ISRAEL (1849). 932 Broadway, N.Y.C., 10010. (212)260-4222. Grand Master Hyman H. Robinson; Grand Sec. Murray Birnback. Promotes fraternalism; supports State of Israel, UJA, Soviet Jewry, Israel Bonds, and other Jewish charities; fights antisemitism; awards scholarships. Local lodges have own publications. *National Reporter; Digest.*

JEWISH LABOR BUND (Directed by WORLD COORDINATING COMMITTEE OF THE BUND) (1897; reorg. 1947). 25 E. 78 St., N.Y.C., 10021. (212)535-0850. Exec. Sec. Jacob S. Hertz. Coordinates activities of the Bund organizations throughout the world and represents them in the Socialist International; spreads the ideas of Socialism as formulated by the Jewish Labor Bund; publishes pamphlets and periodicals on world problems, Jewish life, socialist theory and policy, and on the history, activities, and ideology of the Jewish Labor Bund. *Unser Tsait* (U.S.); *Foroys* (Mexico); *Lebns-Fragn* (Israel); *Unser Gedank* (Australia); *Unser Shtimme* (France).

JEWISH PEACE FELLOWSHIP (1941). Box 271, Nyack, N.Y., 10960. (914)358-4601. Pres. Naomi Goodman. Unites those who believe that Jewish ideals and experience provide inspiration for a nonviolent philosophy and way of life; offers draft counseling, especially for conscientious objection based on Jewish "religious training and belief"; encourages Jewish community to become more knowledgeable, concerned, and active in regard to the war/peace problem. *Shalom;* Quarterly Newsletter.

JEWISH SOCIALIST VERBAND OF AMERICA (1921). 45 E. 33 St., N.Y.C., 10016. (212)-686-1536. Pres. Meyer Miller; Nat. Sec. Maurice Petrushka. Promotes ideals of democratic socialism and Yiddish culture; affiliated with Social Democrats, USA. *Der Wecker.*

ROUMANIAN JEWISH FEDERATION OF AMERICA (1956). 17 Fort George Hill Ave., N.Y.C., 10040. (212)942-8071. Pres. Charles H. Kremer; Treas. Jacob Zonis. Interested in protecting the welfare, preserving the culture, and easing the plight of Jews of Roumanian descent throughout the world. Works to influence the Roumanian government to grant freedom of worship to Jews and permission for their immigration to Israel.

SEPHARDIC JEWISH BROTHERHOOD OF AMERICA, INC. (1915). 97–29 64th Rd., Rego Park, N.Y., 11374. (212)459-1600. Pres. Nick Levi; Sec. Jack Ezratty. Promotes the industrial, social, educational, and religious welfare of its members, offers funeral and burial benefits, scholarships and aid to needy. *Sephardic Brother.*

UNITED ORDER TRUE SISTERS, INC. (1846). 150 W. 85 St., N.Y.C., 10024. (212)362-2502. Nat. Pres. Nana Klein; Nat. Sec. Fran Goldman. Philanthropic, fraternal, community service; nat. projects; cancer service; aids handicapped children, deaf, blind, etc. *Echo.*

WORKMEN'S CIRCLE (1900). 45 E. 33 St., N.Y.C., 10016. (212)889-6800. Pres. Israel Kluger; Exec. Dir. Nathan Peskin. Provides fraternal benefits and activities, Jewish educational programs, secularist Yiddish schools for children, community activities, both in Jewish life and on the American scene, cooperation with the labor movement. *The Call; Kinder Zeitung; Kultur un Lebn.*

———, DIVISION OF JEWISH LABOR COMMITTEE (see p. 285).

SOCIAL WELFARE

AMERICAN JEWISH CORRECTIONAL CHAPLAINS ASSOCIATION, INC. (formerly NATIONAL COUNCIL OF JEWISH PRISON CHAPLAINS) (1937). 10 E. 73 St., N.Y.C., 10021. (212)879-8415. (Cooperating with the New York Board of Rabbis and Jewish Family Service.) Pres. Irving Koslowe; Exec. Dir. Paul L. Hait; Assoc. Dir. Allen S. Kaplan. Provides religious services and guidance to Jewish men and women in penal and correctional institutions; serves as a liaison between inmates and their families; upgrades the quality of correctional ministrations through conferences, professional workshops, and conventions. *Bulletin.*

AMERICAN JEWISH SOCIETY FOR SERVICE, INC. (1949). 15 E. 26 St., Rm. 1302, N.Y.C., 10010. (212)683-6178. Pres. E. Kenneth Marx; Exec. Dir. Elly Saltzman. Conducts four voluntary work service camps each summer to enable young people to live their faith by serving other people. *Newsletter.*

AMC CANCER RESEARCH CENTER AND HOSPITAL (formerly JEWISH CONSUMPTIVES' RELIEF SOCIETY, 1904; incorporated as AMERICAN MEDICAL CENTER AT DENVER, 1954). 6401 West Colfax Ave., Lakewood, Colo., 80214. (303)233-6501. Dir. Manfred L. Minzer, Jr.; Chmn. Bd. of Trustees, Randolph B. Heller. A national cancer hospital that provides the finest specialized treatment available to patients, regardless of ability to pay; pursues, as a progressive science research center, promising leads in the prevention, detection, and control of cancer.

———, NATIONAL COUNCIL OF AUXILIARIES (1904; reorg. 1936). 6401 W. Colfax, Lakewood, Colo., 80214. (303) 233-6501. Pres. Lillian Solomon. Provides support for the AMC Cancer Research Center and Hospital program by disseminating information, fund-raising, and acting as admissions officers for patients from chapter cities throughout the country. *Bulletin.*

ASSOCIATION OF JEWISH FAMILY AND CHILDREN'S AGENCIES (1972). 200 Park Ave. S., N.Y.C., 10003. (212)674-6659. Pres. Helene Cohen; Exec. Dir. Martin Greenberg. The national service organization for Jewish family and children's agencies in Canada and the United States.

Reinforces member agencies in their efforts to sustain and enhance the quality of Jewish family and communal life. *Newsletter; Directory.*

BARON DE HIRSCH FUND (1891). 386 Park Ave. S., N.Y.C., 10016. (212)532-7088. Pres. Ezra Pascal Mager; Mng. Dir. Theodore Norman. Aids Jewish immigrants and their children in the U.S., Israel, and elsewhere by giving grants to agencies active in educational and vocational fields; has limited program for study tours in U.S. by Israeli agriculturists.

B'NAI B'RITH INTERNATIONAL (1843). 1640 Rhode Island Ave., N.W., Washington, D.C., 20036. (202)857-6600. Pres. Jack J. Spitzer; Exec. V. Pres. Daniel Thursz. International Jewish organization with affiliates in 42 countries. Programs include communal service, social action, and public affairs, with emphasis on preserving Judaism through projects in and for Israel and for Soviet Jewry; teen and college-age movements; adult Jewish education. *The National Jewish Monthly; Shofar; International Jewish Monthly.*

———, ANTI-DEFAMATION LEAGUE OF (see p. 284).

———, CAREER AND COUNSELING SERVICES (1938). 1640 Rhode Island Ave., N.W., Washington, D.C., 20036. (202)857-6600. Chmn. Milton W. Kadish; Nat. Dir. Max F. Baer. Conducts educational and occupational research and engages in a broad publications program; provides direct group and individual guidance services for youths and adults through professionally staffed regional offices in five population centers. *B'nai B'rith Career and Counseling Services Newsletter; Catalogue of Publications; Counselors Information Service; College Guide for Jewish Youth.*

———, HILLEL FOUNDATIONS, INC. (see p. 324).

———, INTERNATIONAL ASSOCIATION OF HILLEL DIRECTORS (see p. 323).

———, YOUTH ORGANIZATION (see p. 324).

B'NAI B'RITH WOMEN (1897). 1640 Rhode Island Ave., N.W., Washington, D.C., 20036. (202)857-6670. Pres. Dorothy Binstock; Exec. Dir. Edna J. Wolf. Participates in contemporary Jewish life through youth and adult Jewish education programs, human rights endeavors, and community-service activities; supports a variety of services to Israel; conducts community service programs for the disadvantaged and the handicapped, and public affairs programs. *Women's World.*

CITY OF HOPE—A NATIONAL MEDICAL CENTER UNDER JEWISH AUSPICES (1913). 208 W. 8 St., Los Angeles, Calif., 90014. (213)626-4611. Pres. M. E. Hersch; Exec. Dir. Ben Horowitz. Admits on completely free, nonsectarian basis patients from all parts of the nation suffering from cancer and leukemia, blood, heart, and respiratory ailments, and certain maladies of heredity and metabolism including diabetes; makes available its consultation service to doctors and hospitals throughout the nation, concerning diagnosis and treatment of their patients; as a unique pilot medical center, seeks improvements in the quality, quantity, economy, and efficiency of health care. Thousands of original findings have emerged from its staff who are conducting clinical and basic research in the catastrophic maladies, lupus erythematosus, Huntington's disease, genetics, and the neurosciences. *Pilot; President's Newsletter; City of Hope Quarterly.*

CONFERENCE OF JEWISH COMMUNAL SERVICE (1899). 15 E. 26 St., N.Y.C., 10010. (212)683-8056. Pres. Gerald B. Bubis; Exec. Dir. Matthew Penn. Serves as forum for all professional philosophies in community service, for testing new experiences, proposing new ideas, and questioning or reaffirming old concepts. Concerned with advancement of professional personnel practices and standards. *Concurrents; Journal of Jewish Communal Service.*

COUNCIL OF JEWISH FEDERATIONS, INC. (1932). 575 Lexington Ave., N.Y.C., 10022. (212)751-1311. Pres. Morton L. Mandel; Exec. V. Pres. Robert I. Hiller. Provides national and regional services to 200 associated federations embracing 800 communities in the United States and Canada, aiding in fund-raising, community organization, health and welfare planning, personnel recruitment, and public relations. *Directory of Jewish Federations, Welfare Funds and Community Councils; Directory of Jewish Health and Welfare Agencies* (triennial); *Jewish Communal*

Services: Programs and Finances (1977); Yearbook of Jewish Social Services; Annual Report.

HOPE CENTER FOR THE RETARDED (1965). 3601 E. 32 Ave., Denver, Colo., 80205. (303)388-4801. Pres. Al Perington; Exec. Dir. George E. Brantley; Sec. Lorraine Faulstich. Provides services to developmentally disabled of community: preschool training, day training and work activities center, speech and language pathology, occupational arts and crafts, recreational therapy, and social services.

INTERNATIONAL COUNCIL ON JEWISH SOCIAL AND WELFARE SERVICES (1961). 200 Park Ave. S., N.Y.C., 10003. (N.Y. liaison office with UN headquarters.) (212)674-6800. Chmn. David Young; V. Chmn. Kenneth Rubin; Second V. Chmn. Henry Taub; Exec. Sec. Leonard Seidenman; Dep. Exec. Sec. Theodore D. Feder. Provides for exchange of views and information among member agencies on problems of Jewish social and welfare services, including medical care, old age, welfare, child care, rehabilitation, technical assistance, vocational training, agricultural and other resettlement, economic assistance, refugees, migration, integration and related problems, representation of views to governments and international organizations. Members: six national and international organizations.

JEWISH BRAILLE INSTITUTE OF AMERICA, INC. (1931). 110 E. 30 St., N.Y.C., 10016. (212)889-2525. Pres. Jane Evans; Exec. V. Pres. Gerald M. Kass. Seeks to serve the religious and cultural needs of the Jewish blind by publishing braille prayer books in Hebrew and English; provides Yiddish, Hebrew, and English records for Jewish blind throughout the world who cannot read braille; maintains worldwide free braille lending library. *Jewish Braille Review; JBI Voice.*

JEWISH CONCILIATION BOARD OF AMERICA, INC. (1930). 120 W. 57 St., N.Y.C., 10019. (212)582-3577. Pres. Lewis Bart Stone; Exec. Dir. Beatrice Lampert. Evaluates and attempts to resolve conflicts within families, organizations, and businesses to avoid litigation; offers, without charge, mediation, arbitration, and counseling services by rabbis, attorneys, and social workers; refers cases to other agencies, where indicated.

JWB (1917). 15 E. 26 St., N.Y.C., 10010. (212)532-4949. Pres. Esther Leah Ritz; Exec. V. Pres. Arthur Rotman. Major service agency for Jewish community centers and camps serving more than a million Jews in the U.S. and Canada; U.S. Government accredited agency for providing services and programs to Jewish military families and hospitalized veterans; promotes Jewish culture through its Book and Music Councils, JWB Lecture Bureau, Jewish Media Service, and Jewish educational, cultural and Israel-related projects. *JWB Circle; Zarkor; Contact; JWB Personnel Reporter.*

————, COMMISSION ON JEWISH CHAPLAINCY (1940). 15 E. 26 St., N.Y.C., 10010. Chmn. Rabbi Herschel Schachter; Dir. Rabbi Joseph B. Messing. Recruits, endorses, and serves Jewish military and Veterans Administration chaplains on behalf of the American Jewish community and the three major rabbinic bodies; trains and assists Jewish lay leaders where there are no chaplains, for service to Jewish military personnel, their families, and hospitalized veterans.

————, JEWISH BOOK COUNCIL (see p. 289).

————, JEWISH MUSIC COUNCIL (see p. 289).

LEO N. LEVI NATIONAL ARTHRITIS HOSPITAL (sponsored by B'nai B'rith) (1914). 300 Prospect Ave., Hot Springs, Ark., 71901. (501)624-1281. Pres. Harry Levitch; Adm. D. E. Wagoner. Maintains a nonprofit nonsectarian hospital for treatment of sufferers from arthritis and related diseases.

NATIONAL ASSOCIATION OF JEWISH FAMILY, CHILDREN'S AND HEALTH PROFESSIONALS (1965). 1 Pike Dr., Wayne, N. J. 07470. (201)595-0111. Pres. Abraham Davis; V. Pres. Lee Kalik, Arnold Marks. Brings together Jewish caseworkers and related professionals in Jewish family, children, and health services. Seeks to improve personnel standards, further Jewish continuity and identity, and strengthen Jewish family life; provides forums for professional discussion at national conference of Jewish communal service and regional meetings; takes action on social policy issues; provides a vehicle for representation of Jewish caseworkers and others in various national associations and activities. *Newsletter.*

NATIONAL ASSOCIATION OF JEWISH HOMES FOR THE AGED (1960). 2525 Centerville Road, Dallas, Texas, 75228. (214)327-4503. Pres. Gerald N. Cohn; Exec. V. Pres. Herbert Shore; Pres. Elect Maurice May. Serves as a national representative of voluntary Jewish homes and housing for the aged. Conducts annual meetings, conferences, workshops and institutes. Provides for sharing information, studies and clearinghouse functions. *Directory; Progress Report.*

NATIONAL ASSOCIATION OF JEWISH VOCATIONAL SERVICES (formerly Jewish Occupational Council) (1940). 386 Park Ave. S., N.Y.C., 10016. (212)685-8355. Pres. J. William Baros, Jr.; Exec. Dir. Harvey P. Goldman. Acts as coordinating body for all Jewish agencies in U.S., Canada, and Israel, having programs in educational vocational guidance, job placement, vocational rehabilitation, skills-training, sheltered workshops, and occupational research. *Newsletter;* information bulletins.

NATIONAL CONGRESS OF JEWISH DEAF (1956; inc. 1961). 9102 Edmonston Court, Greenbelt, Md., 20770. (301)345-8612. Exec. Dir. Alexander Fleischman; Pres. Alvin Klugman. Congress of Jewish congregations service organizations and associations located throughout the U.S. and Canada, advocating religious and cultural ideals and fellowship for the Jewish deaf. *Quarterly.*

NATIONAL COUNCIL OF JEWISH PRISON CHAPLAINS, INC. (see AMERICAN JEWISH CORRECTIONAL CHAPLAINS ASSOCIATION, INC.)

NATIONAL COUNCIL OF JEWISH WOMEN (1893). 15 E. 26 St., N.Y.C., 10010. (212)-532-1740. Nat. Pres. Shirley I. Leviton; Exec. Dir. Dadie Perlov. Operates programs in education, social and legislative action, and community service for children and youth, the aging, the disadvantaged in Jewish and general communities; concerns include juvenile justice system as basis for legislative reform and community projects; deeply involved in women's issues; promotes education in Israel through NCJW Research Institute for Innovation in Education at Hebrew University, Jerusalem. *NCJW Journal; From the President's Desk; Washington Newsletter; NACS Newsletter.*

NATIONAL JEWISH COMMITTEE ON SCOUTING (1926). 1325 Walnut Hill La., Irving, Texas, 75062. (214)659-2000. Chmn. Marshall M. Sloane; Exec. Dir. Rabbi William H. Kraus. Seeks to bring Jewish youth closer to Judaism through Scouting programs. Works through local Jewish committees on Scouting to organize Cub Scout packs, Boy Scout troops, and Explorer posts in synagogues, Jewish community centers, and other Jewish organizations wishing to draw Jewish youth. *Ner Tamid for Boy Scouts and Explorers; Scouting in Synagogues and Centers.*

NATIONAL JEWISH HOSPITAL/NATIONAL ASTHMA CENTER (1899). 3800 E. Colfax Ave., Denver, Colo., 80206. (303)388-4461. Pres. Richard N. Bluestein; Exec. V. Pres. Michael K. Schonbrun; Nat. Chmn. Andrew Goodman. Largest, leading medical center for study and treatment of chronic respiratory diseases and immune system disorders. Clinical emphasis is placed on asthma, emphysema, tuberculosis, chronic bronchitis, interstitial lung diseases, and cystic fibrosis; immune system disorders such as juvenile rheumatoid arthritis, systemic lupus erythematosus, and immune deficiency disorders. *New Directions.*

WORLD CONFEDERATION OF JEWISH COMMUNITY CENTERS (1947). 15 E. 26 St., N.Y.C., 10010. (212)532-4949. Pres. Esther Leah Ritz; Exec. Dir. Haim Zipori. Serves as a council of national and continental federations of Jewish community centers; fosters development of the JCC movement worldwide; provides a forum for exchange of information among centers. *Newsletter.*

ZIONIST AND PRO-ISRAEL

AMERICA-ISRAEL FRIENDSHIP LEAGUE (1971). 134 E. 39 St., N.Y.C., 10016. (212)-679-4822. Pres. Herbert Tenzer; Exec. Dir. Ilana Artman. Seeks to further the existing goodwill between the two nations on a people-to-people basis, through educational exchange programs, regional conferences, and dissemination of information. *News;* bulletins.

AMERICAN ASSOCIATES OF BEN-GURION UNIVERSITY OF THE NEGEV (1973). 342 Madison Ave., Room 1923, N.Y.C., 10017. (212)687-7721. Pres. Robert H. Arnow; Chmn. Exec. Com. Bobbie Abrams; Chmn. Bd. Dirs. Richard B. Stone. Serves as the University's publicity and fund-raising link to the United States. The Associates are committed to publicizing University activities and curricula, securing student scholarships, transferring contributions, and encouraging American interest in the University. *AABGU Reporter.*

AMERICAN COMMITTEE FOR SHAARE ZEDEK HOSPITAL IN JERUSALEM, INC. (1949). 49 W. 45 St., N.Y.C., 10036. (212)-354-8801. Pres. Charles Bendheim; V. Pres. Morris Talansky; Bd. Chmn. Ludwig Jesselson; Sec. Isaac Strahl; Treas. Norbert Strauss. Raises funds for the various needs of the Shaare Zedek Medical Center, Jerusalem, such as equipment and medical supplies, a nurses training school, research, and construction of the new Shaare Zedek Medical Center. *Shaare Zedek News Quarterly.*

AMERICAN COMMITTEE FOR THE WEIZMANN INSTITUTE OF SCIENCE, INC. (1944). 515 Park Ave., N.Y.C., 10022. (212)752-1300. Pres. Norman D. Cohen; Chmn. of Bd. Morris L. Levinson; Exec. V. Pres. Harold Hill. Secures support for basic and applied scientific research. *Interface; Rehovot; Research.*

AMERICAN FRIENDS OF HAIFA UNIVERSITY (1969). 206 Fifth Ave., 4th fl., N.Y.C., 10010. (212)696-4022. Exec. Dir. Rebecca Gallers; Pres. Sigmund Strochlitz. Supports the development and maintenance of the various programs of the University of Haifa, among them the Center for Holocaust Studies, Arab Jewish Center, Yiddish Department, Bridging the Gap project, Department of Management, School of Education, kibbutz movement, and Fine Arts Department; arranges overseas academic programs for American and Canadian students. *Newsletter.*

AMERICAN FRIENDS OF THE HEBREW UNIVERSITY (1925; Inc. 1931). 11 E. 69 St., N.Y.C., 10021. (212)472-9800. Pres. Harvey M. Krueger; Exec. V. Pres. Leonard A. Waldman; Chmn. of Bd. Julian B. Venezky; Chmn. Exec. Com. Stanley M. Bogen. Fosters the growth, development, and maintenance of the Hebrew University of Jerusalem; collects funds and conducts programs of information throughout the United States, interpreting the work of the Hebrew University and its significance; administers American student programs and arranges exchange professorships in the United States and Israel. *American Friends Report; News from the Hebrew University of Jerusalem; Scopus Magazine.*

AMERICAN FRIENDS OF THE ISRAEL MUSEUM (1968). 10 E. 40 St., N.Y.C., 10016. (212)683-5190. Pres. Romie Shapiro; Exec. Dir. Michele Cohn Tocci. Raises funds for special projects of the Israel Museum in Jerusalem; solicits contributions of works of art for exhibition and educational purposes. *Newsletter.*

AMERICAN FRIENDS OF THE JERUSALEM MENTAL HEALTH CENTER—EZRATH NASHIM, INC. (1895). 10 E. 40 St., N.Y.C., 10016. (212)725-8175. Pres. Anita Blum; Exec. Dir. Nancy S. Gitman; Bd. Chmn. Irwin S. Meltzer. Supports research, education, and patient care at the Jerusalem Mental Health Center, which includes a 250-bed hospital, comprehensive outpatient clinic, drug abuse clinic, geriatric center, and the Jacob Herzog Psychiatric Research Center; Israel's only non-profit, voluntary psychiatric hospital; is used as a teaching facility by Israel's major medical schools. *Progress Reports; Ezrah.*

AMERICAN FRIENDS OF THE TEL AVIV MUSEUM (1974). c/o M.J. Schubin, 425 Park Ave., N.Y.C., 10022. (212)407-8287. Pres. Roy V. Titus; Chmn. Leon L. Gildesgame. Solicits contributions of works of art to enrich the Tel Aviv Museum collection; raises funds to support development, maintenance, and expansion of educational work of the museum.

AMERICAN FRIENDS OF THE TEL AVIV UNIVERSITY, INC. (1955). 342 Madison Ave., N.Y.C., 10017. (212)687-5651. Bd. Chmn. Jack Cummings; Pres. Walter B. Stern; V. Pres. Nitza Drori. Supports development and maintenance of the Tel Aviv University. Sponsors exchange student programs and exchange professorships in U.S. and Israel. *Tel Aviv University Report; AFTAU Newsletter.*

AMERICAN-ISRAEL CULTURAL FOUNDATION, INC. (1939). 485 Madison Ave., N.Y.C., 10022. (212)751-2700. Bd. Chmn. Isaac Stern; Pres. William Mazer; Exec. Dir. Stanley Grayson. Membership organization supporting Israeli cultural institutions, such as Israel Philharmonic and Israel Chamber Orchestra, Tel Aviv Museum, Rubin Academies, Bat Sheva Dance Co., Omanut La'am, and Tzlil Am; sponsors cultural exchange between U.S. and Israel; awards scholarships in all arts to young Israelis for study in Israel and abroad. *Hadashot.*

AMERICAN ISRAEL PUBLIC AFFAIRS COMMITTEE (1954). 444 North Capitol St., N.W., Suite 412, Washington, D.C., 20001. (202)638-2256. Pres. Lawrence Weinberg; Exec. Dir. Thomas A. Dine. Registered to lobby on behalf of legislation affecting Israel, Soviet Jewry, and arms sales to Middle East; represents Americans who believe support for a secure Israel is in U.S. interest.

AMERICAN-ISRAELI LIGHTHOUSE, INC. (1928; reorg. 1955). 30 E. 60 St., N.Y.C., 10022. (212)838-5322. Nat. Pres. Mrs. Leonard F. Dank; Nat. Sec. Mrs. L.T. Rosenbaum. Provides education and rehabilitation for the blind and physically handicapped in Israel to effect their social and vocational integration into the seeing community; built and maintains Rehabilitation Center for the Blind (Migdal Or) in Haifa. *Tower.*

AMERICAN JEWISH LEAGUE FOR ISRAEL (1957). 595 Madison Ave., N.Y.C., 10022. (212)371-1583. Hon. Pres. Seymour R. Levine; Chmn. Exec. Com. Eleazar Lipsky; Chmn. of Bd. Samuel Rothberg. Seeks to unite all those who, notwithstanding differing philosophies of Jewish life, are committed to the historical ideals of Zionism; works, independently of class or party, for the welfare of Israel as a whole. Not identified with any political parties in Israel. *Bulletin of the American Jewish League for Israel.*

AMERICAN MIZRACHI WOMEN (formerly MIZRACHI WOMEN'S ORGANIZATION OF AMERICA) (1925). 817 Broadway, N.Y.C., 10003. (212)477-4720. Nat. Pres. Roselle Silberstein; Exec. Dir. Marvin Leff. Conducts social service, child care, and vocational-educational programs in Israel in an environment of traditional Judaism; promotes cultural activities for the purpose of disseminating Zionist ideals and strengthening traditional Judaism in America. *The American Mizrachi Woman.*

AMERICAN PHYSICIANS FELLOWSHIP, INC. FOR MEDICINE IN ISRAEL (1950). 2001 Beacon St., Brookline, Mass., 02146. (617)232-5382. Pres. Leo Kaplan; Sec. Manuel M. Glazier. Helps Israel become a major world medical center; secures fellowships for selected Israeli physicians and arranges lectureships in Israel by prominent American physicians; supports Jerusalem Academy of Medicine; supervises U.S. and Canadian medical and paramedical emergency volunteers in Israel; maintains Israel Institute of the History of Medicine; contributes medical books, periodicals, instruments, and drugs. *APF News.*

AMERICAN RED MAGEN DAVID FOR ISRAEL, INC. (1941). 888 7th Ave., N.Y.C., 10019. (212)757-1627. Nat. Pres. Louis Rosenberg; Nat. Exec. V. Pres. Benjamin Saxe. An authorized tax exempt organization; the sole support arm in the United States of Magen David Adom in Israel with a national membership and chapter program. Educates and involves its members in activities of Magen David Adom, Israel's Red Cross Service; raises funds for MDA's emergency medical services, including collection and distribution of blood and blood products for Israel's military and civilian population; supplies ambulances, bloodmobiles, and mobile cardiac rescue units serving all hospitals and communities throughout Israel; supports MDA's 73 emergency medical clinics and helps provide training and equipment for volunteer emergency paramedical corps. *Chapter News; Lifeline.*

AMERICAN TECHNION SOCIETY (1940). 271 Madison Ave., N.Y.C., 10016. (212)889-2050. Pres. Jack E. Goldman; Exec. V. Pres. Saul Seigel. Supports the work of the Technion-Israel Institute of Technology, Haifa, which trains nearly 10,000 students in 20 departments and a medical school, and conducts research across a broad spectrum of science and technology. *ATS Newsletter; ATS Women's Division Newsletter; Technion Magazine.*

AMERICAN ZIONIST FEDERATION (1939; reorg. 1949 and 1970). 515 Park Ave., N.Y.C., 10022. (212)371-7750. Pres. Joseph P. Sternstein; Exec. Dir. Karen Rubinstein. Consolidates the efforts of the existing Zionist constituency in such areas as public and communal affairs, education, youth and *aliyah,* and invites the affiliation and participation of like-minded individuals and organizations in the community-at-large. Seeks to conduct a Zionist program designed to create a greater appreciation of Jewish culture within the American Jewish community in furtherance of the continuity of Jewish life and the spiritual centrality of Israel as the Jewish homeland. Composed of 16 national Zionist organizations; 10 Zionist youth movements; individual members-at-large; corporate affiliates. Maintains regional offices in Pittsburgh, Denver, Los Angeles, Chicago, Boston, Cleveland, Detroit, and New York. *Issue Analysis.*

AMERICAN ZIONIST YOUTH FOUNDATION, INC. (1963). 515 Park Ave., N.Y.C., 10022. (212)751-6070. Bd. Chmn. Bernard S. White; Exec. Dir. Donald Adelman. Sponsors educational programs and services for American Jewish youth including tours to Israel, programs of volunteer service or study in leading institutions of science, scholarship and arts; sponsors field workers who promote Jewish and Zionist programming on campus; prepares and provides specialists who present and interpret the Israeli experience for community centers and federations throughout the country. *Activist Newsletter; Guide to Ed. and Programming Material; Programs in Israel.*

————, AMERICAN ZIONIST YOUTH COUNCIL (1951). 515 Park Ave., N.Y.C., 10022. (212)751-6070. Chmn. David Kornbluh, Bruce Rudolph. Acts as spokesman and representative of Zionist youth in interpreting Israel to the youth of America; represents, coordinates, and implements activities of the Zionist youth movements in the U.S.

AMPAL—AMERICAN ISRAEL CORPORATION (1942). 10 Rockefeller Plaza, N.Y.C., 10020. (212)586-3232. Pres. Michael Jaffe; Chmn. of Bd. Jacob Levinson. Finances and invests in Israel economic enterprises; mobilizes finance and investment capital in the U.S. through sale of own debenture issues and utilization of bank credit lines. *Annual Report; Prospectuses.*

ARZA—ASSOCIATION OF REFORM ZIONISTS OF AMERICA (1977). 838 Fifth Ave., N.Y.C., 10021. (212)249-0100. Pres. Roland B. Gittelsohn; Exec. Dir. Ira S. Youdovin. Individual Zionist membership organization devoted to achieving Jewish pluralism in Israel and strengthening the Israeli Reform movement. Chapter activities in the U.S. concentrate on these issues, and on strengthening American public support for Israel. *ARZA Newsletter.*

BAR-ILAN UNIVERSITY IN ISRAEL (1955). 527 Madison Ave., N.Y.C., 10022. (212)-751-6366. Pres. Emanuel Rackman; Chmn. Bd. of Trustees Phillip Stollman;

Pres. Amer. Bd. of Overseers Mrs. Jerome L. Stern. A liberal arts and sciences institution, located in Ramat-Gan, Israel, and chartered by Board of Regents of State of New York. *Bar-Ilan News; Academic Research; Philosophia.*

BRIT TRUMPELDOR BETAR OF AMERICA, INC. (1935). 41 E. 42 St., Ste. 617, N.Y.C., 10017. (212)687-4502. Pres. Mitch Chupak. Teaches Jewish youth love of the Jewish people and prepares them for *aliyah;* emphasizes learning Hebrew; keeps its members ready for mobilization in times of crisis; stresses Jewish pride and self-respect; seeks to aid and protect Jewish communities everywhere. *Herut; Etgar.*

DROR—YOUNG KIBBUTZ MOVEMENT— HABONIM (1948). 114 Fifth Ave., N.Y.C., 10011. (212)675-1168. Pres. Israel Karni. Fosters Zionist program for youth with emphasis on *aliyah* to the Kibbutz Hameuchad; stresses Jewish and labor education; holds annual summer workshop in Israel; sponsors two *garinim* to Israel each year. *New Horizons.*

————, CHAVURAT HAGALIL (1978). Pres. Israel Karni; Nat. Coordinator Cecelia Ronis. Aids those between ages of 27–35 in making *aliyah* to an Israeli kibbutz. *Newsletter.*

————, GARIN YARDEN, THE YOUNG KIBBUTZ MOVEMENT (1976). Pres. Israel Karni; Nat. Coordinator Cecelia Ronis. Aids those between ages of 20–26 interested in making *aliyah* to an Israeli kibbutz; affiliated with Kibbutz Hameuchad. *New Horizons.*

EMUNAH WOMEN OF AMERICA (formerly HAPOEL HAMIZRACHI WOMEN'S ORGANIZATION) (1948). 370 Seventh Ave., N.Y.C., 10001. (212)564-9045. Nat. Pres. Shirley Billet; Exec. Dir. Shirley Singer. Maintains and supports 180 educational and social welfare institutions in Israel, including religious nurseries, day-care centers, vocational and teacher training schools for the underprivileged in Israel. *The Emunah Woman.*

FEDERATED COUNCIL OF ISRAEL INSTITUTIONS—FCII (1940). 1475–47 St., Brooklyn, N.Y., 11219. (212)853-6920. Chmn. Bd. Z. Shapiro; Exec. V. Pres. Julius Novack. Central fund-raising organization for over 100 affiliated institutions; handles and executes estates, wills, and bequests for the traditional institutions in Israel; clearinghouse for information on budget, size, functions, etc. of traditional educational, welfare, and philanthropic institutions in Israel, working cooperatively with the Israel government and the overseas department of the Council of Jewish Federations and Welfare Funds, New York. *Annual Financial Reports and Statistics on Affiliates.*

FUND FOR HIGHER EDUCATION (1970). 1500 Broadway, Suite 1900, N.Y.C., 10036. (212)354-4660. Pres. Amnon Barness; Sec. Richard Segal; V. Pres., Nat. Campaign Dir. Joel R. Erenberg. Supports, on a project-by-project basis, institutions of higher learning in Israel and the U.S.

HADASSAH, THE WOMEN'S ZIONIST ORGANIZATION OF AMERICA, INC. (1912). 50 W. 58 St., N.Y.C., 10019. (212)355-7900. Dir. Aline Kaplan. In America helps interpret Israel to the American people; provides basic Jewish education as a background for intelligent and creative Jewish living; sponsors Hashachar, largest Zionist youth movement in U.S., which has four divisions: Young Judaea, Intermediate Judaea, Senior Judaea, and Hamagshimim; operates eight Zionist youth camps in this country; supports summer and all-year courses in Israel. Maintains in Israel Hadassah–Hebrew University Medical Center for healing, teaching, and research; Hadassah Community College; Seligsberg/Brandeis Comprehensive High School; and Hadassah Vocational Guidance Institute. Is largest organizational contributor to Youth Aliyah and to Jewish National Fund for land purchase and reclamation. *Update; Headlines; Hadassah Magazine.*

———, HASHACHAR (formerly YOUNG JUDAEA and JUNIOR HADASSAH; org. 1909, reorg. 1967). 50 W. 58 St., N.Y.C., 10019. (212)355-7900. Pres. of Senior Judaea (high school level) Steven Eisenbach; Nat. Coordinator of Hamagshimim (college level) David Posner; Nat. Dir. Rabbi Avi Zabolcki. Seeks to educate Jewish youth from the ages of 10–30 toward Jewish and Zionist values, active commitment to and participation in the American and Israeli Jewish communities, with *aliyah* as a prime goal; maintains summer camps and summer and year programs in Israel. *Hamagshimim Journal; Kol Hat'una; The Young Judaean; Daf L'Madrichim.*

HASHOMER HATZAIR, INC. 150 Fifth Ave., Suite 1002, N.Y.C., 10011. (212)929-4955.

———, AMERICANS FOR PROGRESSIVE ISRAEL (1951). (212)255-8760. Nat. Chmn. Bernard Harkavy; Exec. Dir. Linda Rubin. Affiliated with Kibbutz Artzi. Believes Zionism is the national liberation movement of the Jewish people; educates members towards an understanding of their Jewishness and progressive values; promotes dignity of labor, social justice, and the brotherhood of nations. *Background Bulletin; Progressive Israel; Israel Horizons.*

———, SOCIALIST ZIONIST YOUTH MOVEMENT (1923). Nat. Sec. Tuvia Liberman; Dir. Shlomo Margolit. Seeks to educate Jewish youth to an understanding of Zionism as the national liberation movement of the Jewish people. Promotes *aliyah* to kibbutzim. Espouses socialist ideals of peace, justice, democracy, industry, and brotherhood. *Youth and Nation; Young Guard; La Madrich; Hayasad; Layidiatcha.*

HEBREW UNIVERSITY—TECHNION JOINT MAINTENANCE APPEAL (1954). 11 E. 69 St., N.Y.C., 10021. (212)988-8418. Dir. Clifford B. Surloff. Conducts maintenance campaigns formerly conducted by the American Friends of the Hebrew University and the American Technion Society; participates in community campaigns throughout the U.S., excluding New York City.

HERUT-U.S.A., INC. (UNITED ZIONIST-REVISIONISTS OF AMERICA) (1925). 41 E. 42 St., N.Y.C., 10017. (212)687-4502. Chmn. Eryk Spektor; Exec. Dir. Hagai Lev. Supports Jabotinskean Herut policy in Israel for peace with security. Seeks Jewish unity for Israel's defense. Preaches Zionist commitments; *aliyah,* Jewish education, and mobilization of Jewish resources. Advocates historic right to Eretz Israel and to Jewish residency throughout the land. Subsidiaries: Betar Zionist Youth; Young Herut; Concerned Jewish Youth; Tel-Hai Fund, Inc. *Zionism Today; Herut.*

THEODOR HERZL FOUNDATION (1954). 515 Park Ave., N.Y.C., 10022. (212)752-0600. Chmn. Kalman Sultanik; Sec. Isadore Hamlin. Cultural activities, lectures, conferences, courses in modern Hebrew and

Jewish subjects, Israel, Zionism, and Jewish history. *Midstream.*

———, THEODOR HERZL INSTITUTE. Chmn. Jacques Torczyner; Dir. Sidney Rosenfeld. Program geared to review of contemporary problems on Jewish scene here and abroad; presentation of Jewish heritage values in light of Zionist experience of the ages; study of modern Israel; and Jewish social research with particular consideration of history and impact of Zionism. *Herzl Institute Bulletin.*

———, HERZL PRESS. Chmn. Kalman Sultanik; Editor Mordecai S. Chertoff. Publishes books and pamphlets on Israel, Zionism, and general Jewish subjects.

ICHUD HABONIM LABOR ZIONIST YOUTH (1934). 114 Fifth Ave., N.Y.C., 10011. (212)255-1796. Sec.-Gen. David Kornbluh; Program Dir. Nomi Segal; Editor Jonathan Shevin. Fosters identification with pioneering in Israel; stimulates study of Jewish life, history, and culture; sponsors community-action projects, seven summer camps in North America, programs in Israel, and *garinei aliyah* to Kibbutz Grofit and Kibbutz Gezer. *Bagolah; Haboneh; Hamaapil; Iggeret L'Chaverim.*

ISRAEL MUSIC FOUNDATION (1948). 109 Cedarhurst Ave., Cedarhurst, N.Y., 11516. (516)569-1541. Pres. Oscar Regen; Sec. Oliver Sabin. Supports and stimulates the growth of music in Israel, and disseminates recorded Israeli music in the U.S. and throughout the world.

JEWISH NATIONAL FUND OF AMERICA (1901). 42 E. 69 St., N.Y.C., 10021. (212)-879-9300. Pres. Charlotte Jacobson; Exec. V. Pres. Samuel I. Cohen. Exclusive fund-raising agency of the world Zionist movement for the afforestation, reclamation, and development of the land of Israel, including the construction of roads and preparation of sites for new settlements; helps emphasize the importance of Israel in schools and synagogues throughout the world. *JNF Almanac; Land and Life.*

KEREN OR, INC. (1956). 1133 Broadway, N.Y.C., 10010. (212)255-1180. Pres. Ira Guilden; V. Pres. and Sec. Samuel I. Hendler; Exec. Dir. Jacob Igra. Funds the Keren-Or Center for Multi-Handicapped Blind Children; participates in the program for such children at the Rothschild Hospital in Haifa; funds entire professional staff and special programs at the Jewish Institute for the Blind (established 1902) that houses, clothes, feeds, educates, and trains blind from childhood into adulthood. *Newsletter.*

LABOR ZIONIST ALLIANCE (reorg.; formerly FARBAND LABOR ZIONIST ORDER; now uniting membership and branches of POALE ZION—UNITED LABOR ZIONIST ORGANIZATION OF AMERICA and AMERICAN HABONIM ASSOCIATION) (1913). 575 Sixth Ave., N.Y.C., 10011. (212)989-0300. Pres. Allen Pollack; Exec. V. Pres. Bernard M. Weisberg. Seeks to enhance Jewish life, culture, and education in U.S. and Canada; aids in building State of Israel as a cooperative commonwealth, and its Labor movement organized in the Histadrut; supports efforts toward a more democratic society throughout the world; furthers the democratization of the Jewish community in America and the welfare of Jews everywhere; works with labor and liberal forces in America. *Alliance Newsletter.*

LEAGUE FOR LABOR ISRAEL (1938; reorg. 1961). 575 Sixth Ave., N.Y.C., 10011. (212)989-0300. Pres. Allen Pollack; Sec. Bernard M. Weisberg. Conducts labor Zionist educational, youth, and cultural activities in the American Jewish community and promotes educational travel to Israel.

NATIONAL COMMITTEE FOR LABOR ISRAEL —ISRAEL HISTADRUT CAMPAIGN (1923). 33 E. 67 St., N.Y.C., 10021. (212)628-1000. Pres. Aaron L. Solomon; Exec. V. Pres. Bernard B. Jacobson. Provides funds for the social welfare, vocational, health, and cultural institutions and other services of Histadrut to benefit workers and immigrants and to assist in the integration of newcomers as productive citizens in Israel; promotes an understanding of the aims and achievements of Israel labor among Jews and non-Jews in America. Fund-raising arms are: Israel Histadrut Campaign, Israel Histadrut Foundation.

———, AMERICAN TRADE UNION COUNCIL FOR HISTADRUT (1947). 33 E. 67 St., N.Y.C., 10021. (212)628-1000. Chmn. Matthew Schoenwald; Nat. Dir. Herbert A. Levine. Carries on educational activities among American and Canadian trade unions for health, educational, and welfare activities of the Histadrut in Israel. *Shalom.*

PEC ISRAEL ECONOMIC CORPORATION (formerly PALESTINE ECONOMIC CORPORATION) (1926). 511 Fifth Ave., N.Y.C., 10017. (212)687-2400. Pres. Joseph Ciechanover; Sec.-Asst. Treas. William Gold. Finances and administers business enterprises in Israel. *Annual Report.*

PEF ISRAEL ENDOWMENT FUNDS, INC. (1922). 342 Madison Ave., N.Y.C., 10173. (212)599-1260. Pres. Sidney Musher; Sec. Burt Allen Solomon. Uses funds for Israeli educational and philanthropic institutions and for constructive relief, modern education, and scientific research in Israel. *Annual Report.*

PIONEER WOMEN, THE WOMEN'S LABOR ZIONIST ORGANIZATION OF AMERICA, INC. (1925). 200 Madison Ave., N.Y.C., 10016. (212)725-8010. Pres. Phyllis Sutker; Exec. Dir. Shoshonna Ebstein. Supports, in cooperation with Na'amat, a widespread network of educational, vocational, and social services for women, children, and youth in Israel. Provides counseling and legal aid services for women, particularly war widows. Authorized agency of Youth Aliyah. Foremost in women's rights efforts. In America, supports Jewish educational, youth, cultural programs; participates in civic affairs. *Pioneer Woman.*

POALE AGUDATH ISRAEL OF AMERICA, INC. (1948). 156 Fifth Ave., N.Y.C., 10010. (212)924–9475. Pres. David B. Hollander; Presidium: Alexander Herman, Anshel Wainhaus. Aims to educate American Jews to the values of Orthodoxy, *aliyah,* and *halutziut;* supports kibbutzim, trade schools, *yeshivot,* teachers' college, civic and health centers, children's homes in Israel. *Achdut; PAI Views; PAI Bulletin.*

_____, WOMEN'S DIVISION OF (1948). Presidium: Ethel Blasbalg, Sarah Iwanisky, Bertha Rittenberg. Assists Poale Agudath Israel to build and support children's homes, kindergartens, and trade schools in Israel. *Yediot PAI.*

RELIGIOUS ZIONISTS OF AMERICA. 25 W. 26 St., N.Y.C., 10010. (212)889-5260.

_____, BNEI AKIVA OF NORTH AMERICA (1934). 25 W. 26 St., N.Y.C., 10010. (212)-338-7247. Exec. Pres. Danny Mayerfield; V. Pres. Alan Silverman; Sec. Yitzchak Fuchs. Seeks to interest youth in *aliyah* to Israel and social justice through pioneering

(halutziut) as an integral part of their religious observance; sponsors five summer camps, a leadership training camp for eleventh graders, a work-study program on a religious kibbutz for high school graduates, summer tours to Israel; establishes nuclei of college students for kibbutz or other settlement. *Akivon; Hamvaser; Pinkas Lamadrich; Daf Rayonot; Ma'Ohalai Torah; Zraim.*

_____, MIZRACHI-HAPOEL HAMIZRACHI (1909; merged 1957). 25 W. 26 St., N.Y.C., 10010. (212)689-1414. Pres. Hermann Merkin; Exec. V. Pres. Israel Friedman. Dedicated to building the Jewish State based on principles of Torah; conducts cultural work, educational program, public relations; sponsors NOAM and Bnei Akiva; raises funds for religious educational institutions in Israel. *Horizon; Kolenu; Mizrachi News Bulletin.*

_____, MIZRACHI PALESTINE FUND (1928). 25 W. 26 St., N.Y.C., 10010. Chmn. Joseph Wilon; Sec. Israel Friedman. Fund-raising arm of Mizrachi movement.

_____, NATIONAL COUNCIL FOR TORAH EDUCATION OF MIZRACHI-HAPOEL HAMIZRACHI (1939). 25 W. 26 St., N.Y.C., 10010. Pres. Israel Shaw; Dir. Meyer Golombek. Organizes and supervises *yeshivot* and Talmud Torahs; prepares and trains teachers; publishes textbooks and educational materials; conducts a placement agency for Hebrew schools; organizes summer seminars for Hebrew educators in cooperation with Torah department of Jewish Agency; conducts *Ulpan.*

_____, NOAM-HAMISHMERET HATZEIRA (1970). 25 W. 26 St., N.Y.C., 10010. (212) 684-6091. Chmn. Stuart Apfel; Exec. Dir. Sarah Craimer. Sponsors five core groups to settle in Israel; conducts summer and year volunteer and study programs to Israel; organizes educational programs for young adults in the U.S., through weekly meetings, *Shabbatonim,* leadership seminars, etc. *Bechol Zot; B'Darche Noam.*

SOCIETY OF ISRAEL PHILATELISTS (1948). 1125 E. Carson St., #2, Long Beach, Ca., 90807. (213)595-9224. Pres. Howard Novitch. Exec. Sec. Irvin Girer. Promotes interest in, and knowledge of, all phases of Israel philately through sponsorship of

chapters and research groups, maintenance of a philatelic library, and support of
public and private exhibitions. *Israel Phila-
telist.*

STATE OF ISRAEL BONDS (1951). 215 Park
Ave. S., N.Y.C., 10003. (212)677-9650.
Gen. Chmn. Sam Rothberg; Pres. Yitz-
hack Rager; Exec. V. Pres. Morris Sipser.
Seeks to provide large-scale investment
funds for the economic development of the
State of Israel through the sale of State of
Israel bonds in the U.S., Canada, Western
Europe, and other parts of the free world.

UNITED CHARITY INSTITUTIONS OF JER-
USALEM, INC. (1903). 1141 Broadway,
N.Y.C., 10001. (212)683-3221. Pres. Zevulun Charlop; Sec. Sam Gabel. Raises funds
for the maintenance of schools, kitchens,
clinics, and dispensaries in Israel; free loan
foundations in Israel.

UNITED ISRAEL APPEAL, INC. (1925). 515
Park Ave., N.Y.C., 10022. (212)688-0800.
Chmn. Jerold C. Hoffberger; Exec. V.
Chmn. Irving Kessler. As principal benefi-
ciary of the United Jewish Appeal, serves
as link between American Jewish community and Jewish Agency for Israel, its operating agent; assists in resettlement and
absorption of refugees in Israel, and supervises flow of funds and expenditures for
this purpose. *Briefings.*

UNITED STATES COMMITTEE SPORTS FOR
ISRAEL, INC. (1948). 341 S. 18 St., Philadelphia, Pa., 19106. (215)546-4700. Pres.
Robert E. Spivak. Sponsors U.S. participation in, and fields and selects U.S. team for,
World Maccabiah Games in Israel every
four years; promotes physical education
and sports program in Israel and total
fitness of Israeli and American Jewish
youths; provides funds, technical and material assistance to Wingate Institute for
Physical Education and Sport in Israel;
sponsors U.S. coaches for training programs in Israel and provides advanced
training and competition in U.S. for Israel's national sports teams, athletes and
coaches; offers scholarships at U.S. colleges to Israeli physical education students;
elects members of the Jewish Sports Hall of
Fame, Wingate Institute, Natanya, Israel.
Report; Journal of the U.S. team in Israel's
Maccabiah Games.

WOMEN'S LEAGUE FOR ISRAEL, INC. (1928).
1860 Broadway, N.Y.C., 10023. (212)245-
8742. Pres. Marilyn Schwartzman; Chmn.
Exec. Bd. Trudy Miner. Promotes the welfare of young people in Israel; built and
maintains Y-style homes in Jerusalem,
Haifa, Tel Aviv, and Natanya; in cooperation with Ministry of Labor and Social Betterment, operates live-in vocational training center for girls, including handicapped,
in Natanya, and weaving workshop for
blind. *Bulletin; Chapter News and Views.*

WORLD CONFEDERATION OF UNITED ZION-
ISTS (1946; reorg. 1958). 30 E. 60 St.,
N.Y.C., 10022. (212)371-1452. Co-Presi-
dents Charlotte Jacobson, Kalman Sultanik, Melech Topiol. The largest dias-
pora-centered Zionist grouping in the
world, distinguished from all other groups
in the Zionist movement in that it has no
association or affiliation with any political
party in Israel, but derives its inspiration
and strength from the whole spectrum of
Zionist, Jewish, and Israeli life; supports
projects identified with Israel; sponsors
non-party *halutzic* youth movements in
the diaspora; promotes Zionist education
and strives for an Israel-oriented creative
Jewish survival in the diaspora. *Zionist Information Views.*

WORLD ZIONIST ORGANIZATION-AMERI-
CAN SECTION (1971). 515 Park Ave.,
N.Y.C., 10022. (212)752-0600. Chmn.
Charlotte Jacobson; Exec. V. Chmn. Isadore Hamlin. As the American section of
the overall Zionist body throughout the
world, it operates primarily in the field of
aliyah from the free countries, education in
the diaspora, youth and *hechalutz,* organization and information, cultural institutions, publications; conducts a worldwide
Hebrew cultural program including special
seminars and pedagogic manuals; disperses
information and assists in research projects
concerning Israel; promotes, publishes,
and distributes books, periodicals, and
pamphlets concerning developments in Israel, Zionism, and Jewish history. *Israel
Scene.*

———, DEPARTMENT OF EDUCATION AND
CULTURE (1948). 515 Park Ave., N.Y.C.,
10022. (212)752-0600. Seeks to foster a
wider and deeper knowledge of the Hebrew
language and literature and a better understanding and fuller appreciation of the role
of Israel in the destiny of Jewry and Judaism, to introduce the study of Israel as
an integral part of the Jewish school curriculum, and to initiate and sponsor

educational projects designed to implement these objectives.

———, NORTH AMERICAN ALIYAH MOVEMENT (1968). 515 Park Ave., N.Y.C., 10022. (212)752-0600. Pres. Zipporah Liben; Exec. Dir. Moshe Berliner. Promotes and facilitates *aliyah* and *klitah* from the U.S. and Canada to Israel; serves as a social framework for North American immigrants to Israel. *Aliyon.*

———, ZIONIST ARCHIVES AND LIBRARY OF THE (1939). 515 Park Ave., N.Y.C., 10022. (212)752-0600. Dir. and Librarian Sylvia Landress. Serves as an archives and information service for material on Israel, Palestine, the Middle East, Zionism, and all aspects of Jewish life.

ZIONIST ORGANIZATION OF AMERICA (1897). ZOA House, 4 E. 34 St., N.Y.C., 10016. (212)481-1500. Pres. Ivan J. Novick; Nat. Exec. Dir. Paul Flacks. Seeks to safeguard the integrity and independence of Israel by means consistent with the laws of the U.S., to assist in the economic development of Israel, and to foster the unity of the Jewish people and the centrality of Israel in Jewish life in the spirit of general Zionism. *American Zionist; Public Affairs Memorandum; ZINS Weekly News Bulletin; ZOA in Review.*

PROFESSIONAL ASSOCIATIONS*

AMERICAN CONFERENCE OF CANTORS (Religious, Educational)

AMERICAN JEWISH CORRECTIONAL CHAPLAINS ASSOCIATION, INC. (Social Welfare)

AMERICAN JEWISH PRESS ASSOCIATION (Cultural)

AMERICAN JEWISH PUBLIC RELATIONS SOCIETY (1957). 234 Fifth Ave., N.Y.C., 10001. (212)697-5895. Pres. Avi Feinglass; Treas. Hyman Brickman. Advances professional status of workers in the public-relations field in Jewish communal service; upholds a professional code of ethics and standards; serves as a clearinghouse for employment opportunities; exchanges professional information and ideas; presents awards for excellence in professional attainments, including the "Maggid Award"

for outstanding literary or artistic achievement which enhances Jewish life. *The Handout.*

ASSOCIATION OF JEWISH CENTER WORKERS (Community Relations)

ASSOCIATION OF JEWISH CHAPLAINS OF THE ARMED FORCES (Religious, Educational)

ASSOCIATION OF JEWISH COMMUNITY RELATIONS WORKERS (Community Relations)

CANTORS ASSEMBLY OF AMERICA (Religious, Educational)

COUNCIL OF JEWISH ORGANIZATIONS IN CIVIL SERVICE (Community Relations)

EDUCATORS ASSEMBLY OF THE UNITED SYNAGOGUE OF AMERICA (Religious, Educational)

INTERNATIONAL ASSOCIATION OF HILLEL DIRECTORS (Religious, Educational)

INTERNATIONAL CONFERENCE OF JEWISH COMMUNAL SERVICE (Community Relations)

JEWISH MINISTERS CANTORS ASSOCIATION OF AMERICA, INC. (Religious, Educational)

JEWISH TEACHERS ASSOCIATION—MORIM (Religious, Educational)

NATIONAL ASSOCIATION OF JEWISH CENTER WORKERS (Community Relations)

NATIONAL ASSOCIATION OF SYNAGOGUE ADMINISTRATORS, UNITED SYNAGOGUE OF AMERICA (Religious, Educational)

NATIONAL ASSOCIATION OF TEMPLE ADMINISTRATORS, UNION OF AMERICAN HEBREW CONGREGATIONS (Religious, Educational)

NATIONAL ASSOCIATION OF TEMPLE EDUCATORS, UNION OF AMERICAN HEBREW CONGREGATIONS (Religious, Educational)

NATIONAL CONFERENCE OF JEWISH COMMUNAL SERVICE (Social Welfare)

*For fuller listing see under categories in parentheses.

NATIONAL CONFERENCE OF YESHIVA PRINCIPALS (Religious, Educational)

NATIONAL JEWISH WELFARE BOARD COMMISSION ON JEWISH CHAPLAINCY (Social Welfare)

WOMEN'S ORGANIZATIONS*

AMERICAN MIZRACHI WOMEN (Zionist and Pro-Israel)

B'NAI B'RITH WOMEN (Social Welfare)

BRANDEIS UNIVERSITY NATIONAL WOMEN'S COMMITTEE (1948). Brandeis University, Waltham, Mass., 02254. (617)-647-2194. Nat. Pres. Elaine R. Lisberg. Responsible for support and maintenance of Brandeis University libraries; sponsors University on Wheels and, through its chapters, study-group programs based on faculty-prepared syllabi, volunteer work in educational services, and a program of New Books for Old Sales; constitutes largest "Friends of a Library" group in U.S. *Imprint.*

HADASSAH, THE WOMEN'S ZIONIST ORGANIZATION OF AMERICA, INC. (Zionist and Pro-Israel)

NATIONAL COUNCIL OF JEWISH WOMEN (Social Welfare)

NATIONAL FEDERATION OF TEMPLE SISTERHOODS, UNION OF AMERICAN HEBREW CONGREGATIONS (Religious, Educational)

PIONEER WOMEN, THE WOMEN'S LABOR ZIONIST ORGANIZATION OF AMERICA (Zionist and Pro-Israel)

UNITED ORDER OF TRUE SISTERS (Social, Mutual Benefit)

WOMEN'S AMERICAN ORT FEDERATION (Overseas Aid)

WOMEN'S BRANCH OF THE UNION OF ORTHODOX JEWISH CONGREGATIONS OF AMERICA (Religious, Educational)

WOMEN'S DIVISION OF POALE AGUDATH OF AMERICA (Zionist and Pro-Israel)

WOMEN'S DIVISION OF THE AMERICAN JEWISH CONGRESS (Community Relations)

WOMEN'S DIVISION OF THE JEWISH LABOR COMMITTEE (Community Relations)

WOMEN'S DIVISION OF THE UNITED JEWISH APPEAL (Overseas Aid)

WOMEN'S LEAGUE FOR CONSERVATIVE JUDAISM (Religious, Educational)

WOMEN'S LEAGUE FOR ISRAEL, INC. (Zionist and Pro-Israel)

WOMEN'S ORGANIZATION OF HAPOEL HAMIZRACHI (Zionist and Pro-Israel)

YESHIVA UNIVERSITY WOMEN'S ORGANIZATION (Religious, Educational)

YOUTH AND STUDENT ORGANIZATIONS*

AMERICAN ZIONIST YOUTH FOUNDATION, INC. (Zionist and Pro-Israel)

———, AMERICAN ZIONIST YOUTH COUNCIL

ATID, COLLEGE AGE ORGANIZATION, UNITED SYNAGOGUE OF AMERICA (Religious, Educational)

B'NAI B'RITH HILLEL FOUNDATIONS, INC. (Religious, Educational)

B'NAI B'RITH YOUTH ORGANIZATION (Religious, Educational)

BNEI AKIVA OF NORTH AMERICA, RELIGIOUS ZIONISTS OF AMERICA (Zionist and Pro-Israel)

BNOS AGUDATH ISRAEL, AGUDATH ISRAEL OF AMERICA (Religious, Educational)

DROR YOUNG ZIONIST ORGANIZATION (Zionist and Pro-Israel)

HASHACHAR—WOMEN'S ZIONIST ORGANIZATION OF AMERICA (Zionist and Pro-Israel)

HASHOMER HATZAIR, ZIONIST YOUTH MOVEMENT (Zionist and Pro-Israel)

ICHUD HABONIM LABOR ZIONIST YOUTH (Zionist and Pro-Israel)

JEWISH STUDENT PRESS-SERVICE (1970)— JEWISH STUDENT EDITORIAL PROJECTS, INC. 15 East 26 St., Suite 1350, N.Y.C., 10010. (212)679-1411. Editor Neil Barsky;

---

*For fuller listing see under categories in parentheses.

Admin. Dir. Evelyn Sucher. Serves all Jewish student and young adult publications, as well as many Anglo-Jewish newspapers, in North America, through monthly feature packets of articles and graphics. Holds annual national and local editors' conference for member publications. Provides technical and editorial assistance; keeps complete file of member publications since 1970; maintains Israel Bureau. *Jewish Press Features.*

KADIMA (Religious, Educational)

MASSORAH INTERCOLLEGIATES OF YOUNG ISRAEL, NATIONAL COUNCIL OF YOUNG ISRAEL (Religious, Educational)

NATIONAL CONFERENCE OF SYNAGOGUE YOUTH, UNION OF ORTHODOX JEWISH CONGREGATIONS OF AMERICA (Religious, Educational)

NATIONAL FEDERATION OF TEMPLE YOUTH, UNION OF AMERICAN HEBREW CONGREGATIONS (Religious, Educational)

NOAR MIZRACHI-HAMISHMERET (NOAM) —RELIGIOUS ZIONISTS OF AMERICA (Zionist and Pro-Israel)

NORTH AMERICAN JEWISH STUDENTS APPEAL (1971). 15 E. 26 St., N.Y.C., 10010. (212)679-2293. Pres. Susan Grossman; Exec. Dir. Roberta Shiffman. Serves as central fund-raising mechanism for five national, independent, Jewish student organizations; insures accountability of public Jewish communal funds used by these agencies; assists Jewish students undertaking projects of concern to Jewish communities; advises and assists Jewish organizations in determining student project feasibility and impact; fosters development of Jewish student leadership in the Jewish community. Beneficiaries include local and regional Jewish student projects on campuses throughout North America; current constituents include Jewish Student Press Service, North American Jewish Students Network, Student Struggle for Soviet Jewry, *Response,* and Yugntruf; beneficiaries include the Student Coalition for Soviet Jewry (Brandeis); Israel Activities Committee of Indiana U.; and *Zamir,* an Israel-oriented radio program in Amherst, Mass.

NORTH AMERICAN JEWISH STUDENTS' NETWORK (1969). One Park Ave., # 418, N.Y.C., 10016. (212)689-0790. Pres. David Makovsky; Exec. Dir. Blythe Sherry. Coordinates information and programs among all Jewish student organizations in North America; promotes development of student-controlled Jewish student organizations; maintains contacts and coordinates programs with Jewish students throughout the world through the World Union of Jewish Students; runs the Jewish Student Speakers Bureau; sponsors regional, national, and North American conferences. *Network.*

NORTH AMERICAN JEWISH YOUTH COUNCIL (Community Relations)

STUDENT STRUGGLE FOR SOVIET JEWRY, INC. (Community Relations)

UNITED SYNAGOGUE YOUTH, UNITED SYNAGOGUE OF AMERICA (Religious, Educational)

YAVNEH, NATIONAL RELIGIOUS JEWISH STUDENTS ASSOCIATION (Religious, Educational)

YUGNTRUF YOUTH FOR YIDDISH (1964). 3328 Bainbridge Ave., Bronx, N.Y., 10467. (212)654-8540. Chmn. Paul Glasser; Editor Itzek Gottesman. A worldwide, nonpolitical organization for high school and college students with a knowledge of, or interest in, Yiddish. Organizes artistic and social activities. Offers services of full-time field worker to assist in forming Yiddish courses and clubs throughout the U.S.A. *Yugntruf.*

ZEIREI AGUDATH ISRAEL, AGUDATH ISRAEL OF AMERICA (Religious, Educational)

CANADA

CANADA-ISRAEL SECURITIES, LTD., STATE OF ISRAEL BONDS (1953). 1255 University St., Montreal, PQ, H3B 3W7. Pres. Allan Bronfman; Sec. Max Wolofsky. Sale of State of Israel Bonds in Canada. *Israel Bond News.*

CANADIAN ASSOCIATION FOR LABOR ISRAEL (HISTADRUT) (1944). 4770 Kent Ave., Rm. 301, Montreal, PQ, H3W 1H2. Nat. Pres. Bernard M. Bloomfield; Nat. Exec. Dir. Bernard Morris. Raises funds for Histadrut institutions in Israel, supporting their rehabilitation tasks. *Histadrut Foto News; Histadrut Review.*

CANADIAN B'NAI B'RITH (1964). 15 Hove St., Suite 200, Downsview, Ont. M3H 4Y8.

(416)633-6224. Pres. Morley Wolfe; Exec. V. Pres. Frank Dimant. Canadian Jewry's largest service organization; makes representations to all levels of government on matters of Jewish concern; promotes humanitarian causes and educational programs, community volunteer projects, adult Jewish education and leadership development; dedicated to human rights; sponsors youth programs of B'nai B'rith Youth Org. Hillel. *Covenant; Communiqué.*

———, LEAGUE FOR HUMAN RIGHTS (1970). Nat. Chmn. Ted Greenfield. Dedicated to the monitoring of human rights, combating racism and racial discrimination, and preventing bigotry and antisemitism, through education and community relations. Sponsors Holocaust Education Programs, the R. Lou Ronson Research Institute on Anti-Semitism; distributor of Anti-Defamation League materials in Canada. *The Reporter; Christians & Jews Today.*

CANADIAN FOUNDATION FOR JEWISH CULTURE (1965). 150 Beverly St., Toronto, Ont., M5T 1Y6. (416) 977-3811. Pres. Joseph L. Kronick; Exec. Sec. Edmond Y. Lipsitz. Promotes Jewish studies at university level and encourages original research and scholarship in Jewish subjects; awards annual scholarships and grants-in-aid to scholars in Canada.

CANADIAN FRIENDS OF THE ALLIANCE ISRAÉLITE UNIVERSELLE (1958). 5711 Edgemore Ave., Montreal, PQ, H4W 1V8. (514)487-1243. Pres. Harry Batshaw; Exec. Sec. Marlene Salomon. Supports the educational work of the Alliance.

CANADIAN FRIENDS OF THE HEBREW UNIVERSITY (1944). 208-1 Yorkdale Road, Toronto, Ont. M6A 3A1. (416)789-2633. Nat. Pres. Ralph Halbert; Exec. Dir. Jonathan Livny. Represents and publicizes the Hebrew University in Canada; serves as fund-raising arm for the University in Canada; processes Canadians for study at the University. *Scopus; Ha-Universita.*

CANADIAN JEWISH CONGRESS (1919; reorg. 1934). 1590 Ave. Docteur Penfield, Montreal, PQ, H3G 1C5. (514)931-7531. Pres. Irwin Cotler; Exec. V. Pres. Alan Rose. The official voice of Canadian Jewry at home and abroad. Acts on all matters affecting the status, rights, and welfare of Canadian Jews. *I.O.I.; Quarterly Report;*

Background & Analysis; Congress Memorandum.

CANADIAN ORT ORGANIZATION (Organization of Rehabilitation Through Training) (1942). 5165 Sherbrooke St. W., Suite 208, Montreal, PQ, H4A 1T6. (514)481-2787. Pres. J.A. Lyone Heppner; Exec. Dir. Mac Silver. Carries on fund-raising projects in support of the worldwide vocational-training school network of ORT. *Canadian ORT Reporter.*

———, WOMEN'S CANADIAN ORT (1948). 3101 Bathurst St., Suite 404, Toronto, Ont., M6A 2A6. (416)787-0339. Pres. Ruth Druxerman; Exec. Dir. Diane Uslaner. *Focus.*

CANADIAN SEPHARDI FEDERATION (1973). 1310 Greene Ave., 8th Floor, Montreal, PQ, H3Z 2B2. (514)934-0804. Pres. Joseph Benarrosh; Exec. Dir. Shlomo Levy. Preserves and promotes Sephardic identity, particularly among youth; works for the unity of the Jewish people; emphasizes relations between Sephardi communities all over the world; seeks better situation for Sephardim in Israel; supports Israel by all means. Participates in *La Voix Sépharade, Le Monde Sépharade,* and *World Sephardi.*

CANADIAN YOUNG JUDAEA (1917). 788 Marlee Ave., Toronto, Ont., M6B 3K1. (416)787-5350. Nat. Pres. David Shapiro; Exec. Dir. Stephen M. Baron. Strives to attract Jewish youth to Zionism, with goal of *aliyah;* operates nine summer camps in Canada and Israel; is sponsored by Canadian Hadassah–WIZO and Zionist Organization of Canada, and affiliated with Hanoar Hatzioni in Israel. *Yedion; Judaean; The Young Judaean.*

CANADIAN ZIONIST FEDERATION (1967). 1310 Greene Ave., Westmount, Montreal, PQ, H3Z 2B2. (514)934-0804. Pres. Philip Givens; Exec. V. Pres. Leon Kronitz. Umbrella organization of all Zionist and Israel-oriented groups in Canada; carries on major activities in all areas of Jewish life through its departments of education and culture, *aliyah,* youth and students, public affairs, and fund-raising for the purpose of strengthening the State of Israel and the Canadian Jewish community. *Canadian Zionist; The Reporter.*

———, BUREAU OF EDUCATION AND CULTURE (1972). Pres. Philip Givens; Exec. V. Pres. and Dir. of Ed. Leon Kronitz. Provides counseling by pedagogic experts, in-service teacher training courses and seminars in Canada and Israel; operates teacher placement bureau, national pedagogic council and research center; publishes and distributes educational material and teaching aids; conducts annual Bible contest and Hebrew language courses for adults. *Al Mitzpe Hahinuch.*

HADASSAH—WIZO ORGANIZATION OF CANADA (1916). 1310 Greene Ave., 9th fl., Montreal, PQ, H3Z 2B8. (514)937-9431. Nat. Pres. Mrs. Allen Small; Nat. Exec. V. Pres. Lily Frank. Assists needy Israelis by sponsoring health, education, and social welfare services; seeks to strengthen and perpetuate Jewish identity; encourages Jewish and Hebrew culture in promoting Canadian ideals of democracy and pursuit of peace. *Orah.*

JEWISH IMMIGRANT AID SERVICES OF CANADA (JIAS) (1919). 5151 Cote Ste. Catherine Rd., Montreal, PQ, H3W 1M6. (514)-342-9351. Nat. Pres. Joseph Casse; Nat. Exec. V. Pres. Joseph Kage. Serves as a national agency for immigration and immigrant welfare. *JIAS Bulletin; JIAS News; Studies and Documents on Immigration and Integration in Canada.*

JEWISH NATIONAL FUND OF CANADA (KEREN KAYEMETH LE'ISRAEL, INC.) (1902). 1980 Sherbrooke St. W., Suite 300, Montreal, PQ, H3H 2M7. Nat. Pres. Alexander (Bobby) Mayers; Exec. V. Pres. Michael D. Yarosky. Fund-raising organization affiliated with the World Zionist Movement; involved in afforestation, soil reclamation, and development of the land of Israel, including the construction of roads, and preparation of sites for new settlements; helps to bring the message of "Keep Israel Green" to Jewish schools across Canada.

LABOR ZIONIST MOVEMENT OF CANADA (1939). 4770 Kent Ave., Montreal, PQ, H3W 1H2. (514)735-1593. Nat. Pres. Sydney L. Wax; Nat. V. Pres. Abraham Shurem. Disseminates information and publications on Israel and Jewish life; arranges special events, lectures, and seminars; coordinates communal and political activities of its constituent bodies (Pioneer Women, Na'amat, Labor Zionist Alliance, Poale Zion party, Habonim-Dror Youth, Israel Histadrut, affiliated Hebrew elementary and high schools in Montreal and

Toronto). *Canadian Jewish Quarterly; Viewpoints; Briefacts; Insight.*

MIZRACHI-HAPOEL HAMIZRACHI ORGANIZATION OF CANADA (1941). 5497A Victoria Ave., Suite 101, Montreal, PQ, H3W 2R1. (514)739-4748. Nat. Pres. Kurt Rothschild; Nat. Exec. Dir. Rabbi Sender Shizgal; Sec. Seymour Mishkin. Promotes religious Zionism, aimed at making Israel a state based on Torah; maintains Bnei Akiva, a summer camp, adult education program, and touring department; supports Mizrachi-Hapoel Hamizrachi and other religious Zionist institutions in Israel which strengthen traditional Judaism. *Mizrachi Newsletter; Or Hamizrach Torah Quarterly.*

NATIONAL COUNCIL OF JEWISH WOMEN OF CANADA (1947). 1111 Finch Ave. W., Suite 401, Downsview, Ont., M3J 2E5. (416)665-8251. Nat. Pres. Helen Marr; Exec. Sec. Florence Greenberg. Dedicated to furthering human welfare in Jewish and non-Jewish communities, locally, nationally, and internationally; provides essential services and stimulates and educates the individual and the community through an integrated program of education, service, and social action. *Keeping You Posted.*

NATIONAL JOINT COMMUNITY RELATIONS COMMITTEE OF CANADIAN JEWISH CONGRESS (1936). 150 Beverley St., Toronto, Ont., M5T 1Y6. (416)977-3811. Chmn. Rabbi Jordan Pearlson; Nat. Exec. Dir. Ben G. Kayfetz. Seeks to safeguard the status, rights, and welfare of Jews in Canada; to combat antisemitism and promote understanding and goodwill among all ethnic and religious groups.

UNITED JEWISH TEACHERS' SEMINARY (1946). 5237 Clanranald Ave., Montreal, PQ, H3X 2S5. (514)489-4401. Dir. A. Aisenbach. Trains teachers for Yiddish and Hebrew schools under auspices of Canadian Jewish Congress. *Yitonenu.*

ZIONIST ORGANIZATION OF CANADA (1892; reorg. 1919). 788 Marlee Ave., Toronto, Ont., M6B 3K1. (416)781-3571. Nat. Pres. Max Goody; Exec. V. Pres. George Liban. Furthers general Zionist aims by operating six youth camps in Canada and one in Israel; maintains Zionist book club; arranges programs, lectures; sponsors Young Judaea, Youth Centre Project in Jerusalem Forest, Israel.

Jewish Federations, Welfare Funds, Community Councils[1]

UNITED STATES

ALABAMA

BIRMINGHAM

BIRMINGHAM JEWISH FEDERATION (1935; reorg. 1971); P.O. Box 9157 (35213); (205)-879-0416. Pres. Fred Berman; Exec. Dir. Seymour Marcus.

JEWISH COMMUNITY COUNCIL (1962); P.O. Box 7377, 3960 Montclair Rd. (35223); (205)879-0411. Pres. Mayer U. Newfield; Exec. Dir. Harold E. Katz.

MOBILE

MOBILE JEWISH WELFARE FUND, INC. (Inc. 1966); 404 C One Office Park (36609); (205)-343-7197. Pres. Ed Zelnicker.

MONTGOMERY

JEWISH FEDERATION OF MONTGOMERY, INC. (1930); P.O. Box 1150 (36102); (205)-263-7674. Pres. Adolph Weil, Jr.; Sec. Barbara Marcus.

TRI-CITIES

*TRI-CITIES JEWISH FEDERATION CHARITIES, INC. (1933; Inc. 1956); Route 7, Florence (35632); Pres. Mrs. M. F. Shipper.

ARIZONA

PHOENIX

GREATER PHOENIX JEWISH FEDERATION (incl. surrounding communities) (1940); 1718 W. Maryland Ave. (85015); (602)249-1845. Pres. Shyrle Schaffer; Exec. Dir. Lawrence M. Cohen.

TUCSON

JEWISH COMMUNITY COUNCIL (1942); 102 N. Plumer (85719); (602)884-8921. Pres. Jack Cole; Exec. Dir. Charles Plotkin.

ARKANSAS

LITTLE ROCK

JEWISH FEDERATION OF LITTLE ROCK (1911); 221 Donaghey Bldg., Main at 7th (72201); (501)372-3571. Pres. Lee Ronnel; Exec. Sec. Nanci Goldman.

CALIFORNIA

LONG BEACH

JEWISH COMMUNITY FEDERATION (1937); (sponsors UNITED JEWISH WELFARE FUND); 3801 E. Willow Ave. (90815); (213)-426-7601. Pres. Emanuel Gyler; Exec. Dir. Oliver Winkler.

---

[1]This directory is based on information supplied by the Council of Jewish Federations and Welfare Funds. An asterisk (*) preceding a listing indicates an organization *not* affiliated with CJFWF.

LOS ANGELES

JEWISH FEDERATION–COUNCIL OF GREATER LOS ANGELES (1912; reorg. 1959); (sponsors UNITED JEWISH WELFARE FUND); 6505 Wilshire Blvd. (90048); (213)852-1234. Pres. Osias Goren; Exec. V. Pres. Ted Kanner.

OAKLAND

JEWISH FEDERATION OF THE GREATER EAST BAY (1918); 3245 Sheffield Ave. (94602); (415)533-7462. Pres. Marvin Weinreb; Exec. V. Pres. Melvin Mogulof.

ORANGE COUNTY

JEWISH FEDERATION OF ORANGE COUNTY (1964; Inc. 1965); (sponsors UNITED JEWISH WELFARE FUND); 12181 Buaro, Garden Grove (92640); (714)530-6636. Pres. Daniel Ninburg; Exec. Dir. Donald L. Gartner.

PALM SPRINGS

JEWISH WELFARE FEDERATION OF PALM SPRINGS-DESERT AREA (1971); 611 S. Palm Canyon Dr. (92262); (714)325-7281. Pres. Jim Greenbaum; Exec. Dir. Samuel J. Rosenthal.

SACRAMENTO

JEWISH FEDERATION OF SACRAMENTO (1948); 2351 Wyda Way (95825); (916)486-0906. Pres. Alex Fahn; Exec. Dir. Arnold Feder.

SAN BERNARDINO

SAN BERNARDINO UNITED JEWISH WELFARE FUND, INC. (1936; Inc. 1957); Congregation Emanu-el, 3512 N. "E" St. (92405). Pres. William Russler.

SAN DIEGO

UNITED JEWISH FEDERATION OF GREATER SAN DIEGO (1935); 5511 El Cajon Blvd. (92115); (714)582-2483. Pres. Pauline Foster; Exec. Dir. Steven M. Abramson.

SAN FRANCISCO

JEWISH WELFARE FEDERATION OF SAN FRANCISCO, MARIN COUNTY AND THE PENINSULA (1910; reorg. 1955); 254 Sutter St. (94108); (415)781-3082. Pres. Jerome I. Braun; Exec. Dir. Brian Lurie.

SAN JOSE

JEWISH FEDERATION OF GREATER SAN JOSE (incl. Santa Clara County except Palo Alto and Los Altos) (1930; reorg. 1950); 1777 Hamilton Ave., Suite 201 (95125); (408)267-2770. Pres. Ronald Sosnick; Exec. Dir. Nat Bent.

SANTA BARBARA

*SANTA BARBARA JEWISH FEDERATION; P.O. Box 3314 (93105); (805)962-0770. Pres. M. Howard Goldman.

STOCKTON

*STOCKTON JEWISH WELFARE FUND (1972); 5105 N. El Dorado St. (95207); (209)-477-9306. Pres. Joel M. Senderov; Treas. Harry Green.

VENTURA

*VENTURA COUNTY JEWISH COUNCIL—TEMPLE BETH TORAH (1938); 7620 Foothill Rd. (93003); (805)647-4181. Pres. Paul Karlsberg.

COLORADO

DENVER

ALLIED JEWISH FEDERATION OF DENVER (1936); (sponsors ALLIED JEWISH CAMPAIGN); 300 S. Dahlia St. (80222); (303)321-3399. Pres. Ralph Auerbach; Exec. Dir. Harold Cohen.

CONNECTICUT

BRIDGEPORT

JEWISH FEDERATION OF GREATER BRIDGEPORT, INC. (1936); (sponsors UNITED JEWISH CAMPAIGN); 4200 Park Ave. (06604); (203)372-6504. Pres. Jack Zaluda; Exec. Dir. Gerald A. Kleinman.

DANBURY

JEWISH FEDERATION OF GREATER DANBURY (1945); 54 Main St., Ste. E. (06810); (203)792-6353. Pres. Pearl Turk; Exec. Dir. Carol Rosengart.

HARTFORD

GREATER HARTFORD JEWISH FEDERATION (1945); 333 Bloomfield Ave., W., Hartford (06117); (203)232-4483. Pres. Daniel Neiditz; Exec. Dir. Don Cooper.

MERIDEN

*MERIDEN JEWISH WELFARE FUND, INC. (1944); 127 E. Main St. (06450); (203)235-2581. Pres. Joseph Barker; Sec. Harold Rosen.

NEW HAVEN

NEW HAVEN JEWISH FEDERATION (1928); (sponsors COMBINED JEWISH APPEAL) (1969); 1162 Chapel St. (06511); (203)562-2137. Pres. Marvin Lender; Exec. Dir. Arthur Spiegel.

NEW LONDON

JEWISH FEDERATION OF EASTERN CONNECTICUT, INC. (1950; Inc. 1970); 302 State St. (06320); (203)442-8062. Pres. Gary Motin; Exec. Dir. Eugene F. Elander.

NORWALK

JEWISH FEDERATION OF GREATER NORWALK (1946; reorg. 1964); Shorehaven Rd., East Norwalk (06855); (203)853-3440. Pres. Gary Oberst; Exec. Dir. Charles Vogel.

STAMFORD

UNITED JEWISH FEDERATION (Reincorp. 1973); 1035 Newfield Ave. (06905); (203)322-6935. Pres. Norma Mann; Exec. Dir. Steve Schreier.

WATERBURY

JEWISH FEDERATION OF WATERBURY, INC. (1938); 1020 Country Club Rd. (06720); (203)758-2441. Pres. Gloria Bogen; Exec. Dir. Albert G. Effrat.

DELAWARE

WILMINGTON

JEWISH FEDERATION OF DELAWARE, INC. (1935); 101 Garden of Eden Rd. (19803); (302)478-6200. Pres. Paul R. Fine; Exec. Dir. Morris Lapidos.

DISTRICT OF COLUMBIA

WASHINGTON

UNITED JEWISH APPEAL—FEDERATION OF GREATER WASHINGTON, INC. (1935); 6935 Arlington Rd., Bethesda, Md. (20014); (301)-652-6480. Pres. Melvin S. Cohen; Exec. V. Pres. Elton J. Kerness.

FLORIDA

BOCA RATON

SOUTH COUNTY JEWISH FEDERATION; 3200 N. Federal Hwy., Suite 124 (33431); (305)-368-2737. Pres. James B. Baer; Exec. Dir. Bruce S. Warshall.

DAYTONA

JEWISH FEDERATION OF VOLUSIA & FLAGLER COUNTIES, INC.; P.O. Box 5434, 504 Main St. (32018); (904) 255-6260. Pres. Clifford R. Josephson; Exec. Sec. Iris Gardner.

FT. LAUDERDALE

JEWISH FEDERATION OF GREATER FT. LAUDERDALE (1967); 8360 W. Oakland Pk. Blvd. (33321); (305)748-8200. Pres. Victor Gruman; Exec. Dir. Leslie Gottlieb.

HOLLYWOOD

JEWISH FEDERATION OF SOUTH BROWARD, INC. (1943); 2719 Hollywood Blvd. (33020); (305)921-8810. Pres. Robert Pittell; Exec. Dir. Sumner Kaye.

JACKSONVILLE

JACKSONVILLE JEWISH FEDERATION (1935); 5846 Mt. Carmel Terr. (32216); (904)733-7613. Pres. Ronald Elinoff; Exec. Dir. Gerald L. Goldsmith.

MIAMI

GREATER MIAMI JEWISH FEDERATION, INC. (1938); 4200 Biscayne Blvd. (33137); (305)576-4000. Pres. Harry A. Levy; Exec. V. Pres. Myron J. Brodie.

ORLANDO

JEWISH FEDERATION OF GREATER ORLANDO (1949); 851 N. Maitland Ave., P.O. Box 1508, Maitland (32751); (305)645-5933. Pres. Sonia Mandel; Exec. Dir. Paul Jeser.

PALM BEACH COUNTY

JEWISH FEDERATION OF PALM BEACH COUNTY, INC. (1938); 501 S. Flagler Dr., Suite 305, West Palm Beach (33401); (305)-689-5900. Pres. Jeanne Levy; Exec. Dir. Norman J. Schimelman.

PENSACOLA

*PENSACOLA FEDERATED JEWISH CHARITIES (1942); 1320 E. Lee St. (32503); (904)-438-1464. Pres. Gene Rosenbaum; Sec. Mrs. Harry Saffer.

PINELLAS COUNTY (incl. Clearwater and St. Petersburg)

JEWISH FEDERATION OF PINELLAS COUNTY, INC. (1950; reincorp. 1974); 302 S. Jupiter Ave., Clearwater (33515); (813)446-1033. Pres. Reva Kent; Exec. Dir. Gerald Rubin.

SARASOTA

SARASOTA JEWISH FEDERATION (1959); 1900 Main Bldg., Suite 315 (33577); (813)-365-4410. Pres. Jerome Kapner; Exec. Dir. Jack Weintraub.

TAMPA

TAMPA JEWISH FEDERATION (1941); 2808 Horatio (33609); (813)872-4451. Pres. Hope Barnett; Exec. Dir. Gary S. Alter.

GEORGIA

ATLANTA

ATLANTA JEWISH FEDERATION, INC. (1905; reorg. 1967); 1753 Peachtree Rd., N.E. (30309); (404)873-1661. Pres. Max Rittenbaum; Exec. Dir. Jay Rubin.

AUGUSTA

FEDERATION OF JEWISH CHARITIES (1937); P.O. Box 3251, Hill Station (30904); (404)-736-1818. c/o Hillel Silver, Treas.; Pres. Ira Schneider; Exec. Dir. Sheldon Sklar.

COLUMBUS

JEWISH WELFARE FEDERATION OF COLUMBUS, INC. (1941); P.O. Box 1303 (31902); (404)561-3953. Pres. Maurice Kravtin; Sec. David Helman.

SAVANNAH

SAVANNAH JEWISH COUNCIL (1943); (sponsors UJA-FEDERATION CAMPAIGN); P.O. Box 6546, 5111 Abercorn St. (31405); (912)-355-8111. Pres. Arnold J. Tillinger; Exec. Dir. Stan Ramati.

IDAHO

BOISE

*SOUTHERN IDAHO JEWISH WELFARE FUND (1947); 1776 Commerce Ave. (83705); (208)344-3574. Pres. Kal Sarlat; Treas. Martin Heuman.

ILLINOIS

CHAMPAIGN-URBANA

CHAMPAIGN-URBANA JEWISH FEDERATION (1929); P.O. Box 2936, Sta. A, Champaign (61820); (217)352-8044. Co-Chmn. Ira Wachtel, Mrs. Ralph Berkson.

CHICAGO

JEWISH FEDERATION OF METROPOLITAN CHICAGO (1900); 1 S. Franklin St. (60606); (312)346-6700. Pres. Herbert S. Wander; Exec. V. Pres. James P. Rice; Exec. Dir. Steven Nasatir.

JEWISH UNITED FUND OF METROPOLITAN CHICAGO (1968); 1 S. Franklin St. (60606); (312)346-6700. Pres. David Smerling; Exec. V. Pres. James P. Rice.

DECATUR

DECATUR JEWISH FEDERATION (member Central Illinois Jewish Federation) (1942); c/o Temple B'nai Abraham, 1326 West Eldorado (62522); Pres. Jerry Gliner; Sec. Marion Guggenheim.

ELGIN

ELGIN AREA JEWISH WELFARE CHEST (1938); 330 Division St. (60120); (312)741-5656. Pres. Fred Heinemann; Treas. Stuart Hanfling.

JOLIET

JOLIET JEWISH WELFARE CHEST (1938); 250 N. Midland Ave. (60435); (815)725-7078. Pres. Bernard Kliska; Sec. Rabbi Morris M. Hershman.

PEORIA

CENTRAL ILLINOIS JEWISH FEDERATION (1969); 3100 N. Knoxville, Suite 17 (61603); (309)686-0611. Pres. Marilyn Weigensberg; Exec. Dir. Peretz Katz.

JEWISH FEDERATION OF PEORIA (member CENTRAL ILLINOIS JEWISH FEDERATION) (1933; Inc. 1947); 3100 N. Knoxville, Suite 17 (61603); (309)686-0611. Pres. Saul Bork; Exec. Dir. Peretz A. Katz.

QUAD CITIES

JEWISH FEDERATION OF THE QUAD CITIES (incl. Rock Island, Moline, Davenport, Bettendorf) (1938; comb. 1973); 224-18th St., Suite 511, Rock Island (61201); (309)793-1300. Pres. Sam Gilman; Sec. Jay Gellerman; Exec. Dir. Judah Segal.

ROCKFORD

ROCKFORD JEWISH COMMUNITY COUNCIL (1937); 1500 Parkview Ave. (61107); (815)-399-5497. Pres. Eugene Levin; Exec. Dir. Daniel Tannenbaum.

SOUTHERN ILLINOIS

JEWISH FEDERATION OF SOUTHERN ILLINOIS (incl. all of Illinois south of Carlinville and Paducah, Ky.) (1941); 6464 W. Main, Suite 7A, Belleville (62223); (618)398-6100. Pres. Leonard Linkon; Exec. Dir. Bruce J. Samborn.

SPRINGFIELD

SPRINGFIELD JEWISH FEDERATION (member CENTRAL ILLINOIS JEWISH FEDERATION) (1941); 730 E. Vine St. (62703); (217)-528-3446. Pres. Stephen P. Stone; Exec. Sec. Lenore Loeb.

INDIANA

EVANSVILLE

EVANSVILLE JEWISH COMMUNITY COUNCIL, INC. (1936; Inc. 1964); P.O. Box 5026 (47715); (812)476-1571. Pres. Joel Lasker; Exec. Sec. Maxine P. Fink.

FORT WAYNE

FORT WAYNE JEWISH FEDERATION (1921); 227 E. Washington Blvd. (46802); (219)422-8566. Pres. Marvin Crell; Exec. Dir. Eli J. Skora.

INDIANAPOLIS

JEWISH WELFARE FEDERATION, INC. (1905); 615 N. Alabama St. (46204); (317)-637-2473. Pres. David Kleinman; Exec. V. Pres. Frank H. Newman.

LAFAYETTE

FEDERATED JEWISH CHARITIES (1924); P.O. Box 676 (47902); (317)742-9081. Pres. Francine Jacoby; Fin. Sec. Louis Pearlman, Jr.

MICHIGAN CITY

MICHIGAN CITY UNITED JEWISH WELFARE FUND; 2800 Franklin St. (46360); (219)874-4477. Pres. Nate Winski; Treas. Harold Leinwand.

MUNCIE

*MUNCIE JEWISH WELFARE FUND (1945); c/o Beth El Temple, P.O. Box 2792 (47302); (317)284-1497. Chmn. Edward J. Dobrow; Treas. Robert Koor.

NORTHWEST INDIANA

THE JEWISH FEDERATION, INC. (1941); reorg. 1959); 2939 Jewett St., Highland (46322); (219)972-2251. Pres. Irving Brenman; Exec. Dir. Barnett Labowitz.

SOUTH BEND

JEWISH FEDERATION OF ST. JOSEPH VALLEY (1946); 804 Sherland Bldg. (46601); (219)233-1164. Pres. Ronald Cohen; Exec. V. Pres. Harold Slutsky.

IOWA

CEDAR RAPIDS

*JEWISH WELFARE FUND OF LINN COUNTY (1941); 115 7 St. S.E. (52401); (319)366-3553. Chmn. Norman Lipsky; Treas. Jay Beecher.

DES MOINES

JEWISH FEDERATION OF GREATER DES MOINES (1914); 910 Polk Blvd. (50312);

(515)277-6321. Pres. Marvin Winick; Exec. Dir. Jay Yoskowitz.

SIOUX CITY

JEWISH FEDERATION (1921); 525 14 St. (51105); (712)258-0618. Pres. Henry B. Tygar; Exec. Dir. Doris E. Rosenthal.

WATERLOO

WATERLOO JEWISH FEDERATION (1941); c/o Congregation Sons of Jacob, 411 Mitchell Ave. (50702); Pres. Irving Uze.

KANSAS

TOPEKA

*TOPEKA-LAWRENCE JEWISH FEDERATION (1939); 101 Redbud Lane (66607); Pres. William Rudnick.

WICHITA

MID-KANSAS JEWISH WELFARE FEDERATION, INC. (1935); 400 N. Woodlawn, Suite 8 (67206); (316)686-4741. Pres. Nancy Matassarin.

KENTUCKY

CENTRAL

CENTRAL KENTUCKY JEWISH ASSOCIATION; 258 Plaza Dr., Ste. 208, Lexington (40503); (606)277-8048. Pres. Judith Levine.

LOUISVILLE

JEWISH COMMUNITY FEDERATION OF LOUISVILLE, INC. (1934); (sponsors UNITED JEWISH CAMPAIGN); P.O. Box 33035, 3630 Dutchman's Lane (40232); (502)451-8840. Frank Lipschutz; Exec. Dir. Norbert Fruehauf.

LOUISIANA

ALEXANDRIA

THE JEWISH WELFARE FEDERATION AND COMMUNITY COUNCIL OF CENTRAL LOUISIANA (1938); 1261 Heyman Lane (71301); (318)442-1264. Pres. Harold Katz; Sec.-Treas. Mrs. George Kuplesky.

BATON ROUGE

JEWISH FEDERATION OF GREATER BATON ROUGE (1971); P.O. Box 16420 A (70893); (504)343-1465. Pres. Justine Herzog; Exec. Dir. Lynn Weill.

MONROE

UNITED JEWISH CHARITIES OF NORTHEAST LOUISIANA (1938); 2400 Orrel Pl. (71201); (318)388-2859. Pres. Philip I. Roby; Sec.-Treas. Dennis S. Rosenzweig.

NEW ORLEANS

JEWISH FEDERATION OF GREATER NEW ORLEANS (1913; reorg. 1977); 211 Camp St. (70130); (504)525-0673. Pres. Joan Berenson; Exec. Dir. Jane Buchsbaum.

SHREVEPORT

SHREVEPORT JEWISH FEDERATION (1941); Inc. 1967); 2030 Line Ave. (71104); (318)-221-4129. Pres. Sylvia Goodman; Exec. Dir. David S. Abrams.

MAINE

BANGOR

*JEWISH COMMUNITY COUNCIL (1949); 28 Somerset St. (04401); (207)945-5631. Pres. George Z. Singal; Exec. Dir. Sanfred Pasternack.

LEWISTON-AUBURN

LEWISTON-AUBURN JEWISH FEDERATION (1947); (sponsors UNITED JEWISH APPEAL); 134 College St., Lewiston (04240); (207)786-4201. Pres. Bertha Allen; Exec. Dir. Howard G. Joress.

PORTLAND

JEWISH FEDERATION COMMUNITY COUNCIL OF SOUTHERN MAINE (1942); (sponsors UNITED JEWISH APPEAL); 66 Pearl St. (04101); (207)773-7254. Admn. Cecelia Levine; Pres. Richard D. Aronson.

MARYLAND

ANNAPOLIS

*ANNAPOLIS JEWISH WELFARE FUND (1946); 601 Ridgley Ave. (21401); Pres. Anton Grobani.

BALTIMORE

ASSOCIATED JEWISH CHARITIES & WELFARE FUND, INC. (a merger of the Associated Jewish Charities & Jewish Welfare Fund) (1920; reorg. 1969); 101 W. Mt. Royal Ave. (21201); (301)727-4828. Pres. Willard Hackerman; Exec. V. Pres. Stephen D. Solender.

MASSACHUSETTS

BOSTON

COMBINED JEWISH PHILANTHROPIES OF GREATER BOSTON, INC. (1895; reorg. 1961); 72 Franklin St. (02110); (617)542-8080. Pres. Ruth B. Fein; Exec. Dir. Bernard Olshansky.

FITCHBURG

*JEWISH FEDERATION OF FITCHBURG (1939); 40 Boutelle St. (01420); (617)342-2227. Pres. Elliot L. Zide; Treas. Allen I. Rome.

FRAMINGHAM

GREATER FRAMINGHAM JEWISH FEDERATION (1968; Inc. 1969); 76 Salem End Road, Framingham Centre (01701); (617)879-3301. Pres. Lawrence M. Stone; Exec. Dir. Lawrence Lowenthal.

HAVERHILL

*HAVERHILL UNITED JEWISH APPEAL, INC.; 514 Main St. (01830); (617)373-3861. Pres. Manuel M. Epstein; Exec. Dir. Joseph H. Elgart.

HOLYOKE

COMBINED JEWISH APPEAL OF HOLYOKE (1939); 378 Maple St. (01040); (413)534-3369. Pres. Herbert Goldberg; Exec. Dir. Dov Sussman.

LAWRENCE

*JEWISH COMMUNITY COUNCIL OF GREATER LAWRENCE (1906); 580 Haverhill St. (01841); (617)686-4157. Pres. Michael Baker; Exec. Dir. Irving Linn.

LEOMINSTER

LEOMINSTER JEWISH COMMUNITY COUNCIL, INC. (1939); 30 Grove Ave. (01453); (617)537-7906. Pres. Marc Levine; Sec.-Treas. Edith Chatkis.

NEW BEDFORD

JEWISH FEDERATION OF GREATER NEW BEDFORD, INC. (1938; Inc. 1954); 467 Hawthorn St., North Dartmouth (02747); (617)-997-7471. Pres. Joel Karten; Exec. Dir. Gerald A. Kleinman.

NORTH SHORE

JEWISH FEDERATION OF THE NORTH SHORE, INC. (1938); 4 Community Rd., Marblehead (01945); (617)598-1810. Pres. Gerald Ogan; Exec. Dir. Gerald S. Ferman.

PITTSFIELD

*JEWISH COMMUNITY COUNCIL (1940); 235 E. St. (01201); (413)442-4360. Pres. Rhoda Kaminstein; Exec. Dir. Jerry Niemand.

SPRINGFIELD

SPRINGFIELD JEWISH FEDERATION, INC. (1938); (sponsors UNITED JEWISH WELFARE FUND); 1160 Dickinson (01108); (413)737-4313. Pres. Alan Curtis; Exec. Dir. Robert Kessler.

WORCESTER

WORCESTER JEWISH FEDERATION, INC. (1947; Inc. 1957); (sponsors JEWISH WELFARE FUND, 1939); 633 Salisbury St. (01609); (617)756-1543. Pres. Morton H. Sigel; Exec. Dir. Melvin S. Cohen.

MICHIGAN

BAY CITY

*NORTHEASTERN MICHIGAN JEWISH WELFARE FEDERATION (1940); 1125 Orchard Rd., Essexville (48732); (517) 893-7779. Sec. Hanna Shiffman.

DETROIT

JEWISH WELFARE FEDERATION OF DETROIT (1899); (sponsors ALLIED JEWISH CAMPAIGN); Fred M. Butzel Memorial Bldg., 163 Madison (48226); (313)965-3939. Pres. Avern L. Cohn; Exec. Dir. Sol Drachler.

FLINT

FLINT JEWISH FEDERATION (1936); 120 W. Kearsley St. (48502); (313)767-5922; Pres. Malcolm Isaacs; Exec. Dir. Arnold S. Feder.

GRAND RAPIDS

JEWISH COMMUNITY FUND OF GRAND RAPIDS (1930); 1121 Keneberry Way S.E. (49506); (616)949-5238. Pres. Joseph N. Schwartz; Sec. Mrs. William Deutsch.

KALAMAZOO

KALAMAZOO JEWISH FEDERATION (1949); c/o Congregation of Moses, 2501 Stadium Dr. (49008); (616)349-8396. Pres. Martin Gall.

LANSING

GREATER LANSING JEWISH WELFARE FEDERATION (1939); P.O. Box 975, E. Lansing (48823); (517)351-3197. Pres. Anita Baron; Exec. Dir. Louis T. Friedman.

SAGINAW

SAGINAW JEWISH WELFARE FEDERATION (1939); 1424 S. Washington Ave. (48607); (517)753-5230. Pres. James Glazman; Fin. Sec. Mrs. Henry Feldman.

MINNESOTA

DULUTH

JEWISH FEDERATION & COMMUNITY COUNCIL (1937); 1602 E. 2nd St. (55812); (218)724-8857. Pres. R. L. Solon; Exec. Dir. Mrs. Arnold Nides.

MINNEAPOLIS

MINNEAPOLIS FEDERATION FOR JEWISH SERVICES (1929; Inc. 1930); 811 La Salle Ave. (55402); (612)339-7491. Pres. Morris Sherman; Exec. Dir. Herman Markowitz.

ST. PAUL

UNITED JEWISH FUND AND COUNCIL (1935); 790 S. Cleveland (55116); (612)690-1707. Pres. Donald Mains; Exec. Dir. Kimball Marsh.

MISSISSIPPI

JACKSON

*JEWISH WELFARE FUND (1945); 4135 N. Honeysuckle Lane (39211); (601)956-6215. Drive Chmn. Emanuel Crystal; Pres. Louis Shornick.

VICKSBURG

*JEWISH WELFARE FEDERATION (1936); 1210 Washington St. (39180); (601)636-7531. Pres. Richard Marcus.

MISSOURI

KANSAS CITY

JEWISH FEDERATION OF GREATER KANSAS CITY (1933); 25 E. 12 St. (64106); (816)421-5808. Pres. Albert Goller; Exec. Dir. Sol Koenigsberg.

ST. JOSEPH

UNITED JEWISH FUND OF ST. JOSEPH (1915); 2903 Sherman Ave. (64506); (816)-279-3436. Pres. Louis G. Becker; Exec. Sec. Ann Saferstein.

ST. LOUIS

JEWISH FEDERATION OF ST. LOUIS (incl. St. Louis County) (1901); 10957 Schuetz Rd. (63141); (314)432-0020. Pres. Harris J. Frank; V. Pres. Martin S. Kraar.

NEBRASKA

LINCOLN

LINCOLN JEWISH WELFARE FEDERATION, INC. (1931; Inc. 1961); P.O. Box 88014 (68501); (402)435-0230. Pres. Gerald Grant; Exec. Dir. Herbert F. Gaba.

OMAHA

JEWISH FEDERATION OF OMAHA (1903); 333 S. 132 St. (68154); (402)334-8200. Pres. Paul Cohen; Exec. Dir. Louis B. Solomon.

NEVADA

LAS VEGAS

JEWISH FEDERATION OF LAS VEGAS (1973); 1030 E. Twain Ave. (89109); (702)732-0556. Pres. Hon. Bill Hernstadt; Exec. Dir. Jerry Countess.

NEW HAMPSHIRE

MANCHESTER

JEWISH FEDERATION OF GREATER MANCHESTER (1913); 698 Beech St. (03104); (603)627-7679. Pres. Arnold Cohen; Exec. Dir. Robert D. Jolton.

NEW JERSEY

ATLANTIC COUNTY

FEDERATION OF JEWISH AGENCIES OF ATLANTIC COUNTY (1924); 5321 Atlantic Ave., Ventnor City (08406); (609)822-7122. Pres. Gerald Weinstein; Exec. Dir. Murray Schneier.

BAYONNE

BAYONNE JEWISH COMMUNITY COUNCIL; 1050 Kennedy Blvd. (07002); (201)436-6900. Pres. Raphael Levine; Exec. Dir. Alan J. Coren.

BERGEN COUNTY

UNITED JEWISH FEDERATION OF BERGEN COUNTY (1953; Inc. 1978); 111 Kinderkamack Rd., River Edge (07661); (201)488-6800. Pres. Arthur Joseph; Exec. V. Pres. James P. Young.

CENTRAL NEW JERSEY

JEWISH FEDERATION OF CENTRAL NEW JERSEY (sponsors UNITED JEWISH CAMPAIGN); (1940; expanded 1973 to include Westfield and Plainfield); Green Lane, Union (07083); (201)351-5060. Pres. Emanuel Pachman; Exec. V. Pres. Burton Lazarow.

ENGLEWOOD

UNITED JEWISH FUND OF ENGLEWOOD AND SURROUNDING COMMUNITIES (1952); 153 Tenafly Rd. (07631); (201)569-1070. Pres. Norman Gurman; Exec. Dir. Seymour J. Colen.

JERSEY CITY

UNITED JEWISH APPEAL (1939); 604 Bergen Ave. (07304); (201)433-4200. Chmn. Mel Blum; Exec. Dir. Arnold Piskin.

METROPOLITAN NEW JERSEY

JEWISH COMMUNITY FEDERATION (sponsors UNITED JEWISH APPEAL) (1923); 60 Glenwood Ave., East Orange (07017); (201)-673-6800. Pres. Clarence Reisen; Exec. V. Pres. Donald Feldstein.

MONMOUTH COUNTY

JEWISH FEDERATION OF GREATER MONMOUTH COUNTY (Formerly Shore Area) (1971); 100 Grant Ave., Deal (07723); (201)-531-6200. Pres. Ruth Rosenfeld; Exec. Dir. Marvin Relkin.

MORRIS COUNTY

UNITED JEWISH FEDERATION OF MORRIS-SUSSEX; 500 Route 10, Ledgewood (07852); (201)584-1850. Pres. Irwin Roseman; Exec. Dir. Michael P. Shapiro.

NORTH JERSEY

JEWISH FEDERATION OF NORTH JERSEY (formerly Jewish Community Council) (1933); (sponsors UNITED JEWISH APPEAL DRIVE); 1 Pike Dr., Wayne (07470); (201)-595-0555. Pres. Marge Bornstein; Exec. Dir. Leon Zimmerman.

NORTHERN MIDDLESEX COUNTY

JEWISH FEDERATION OF NORTHERN MIDDLESEX COUNTY (1975); (sponsors UNITED JEWISH APPEAL); 100 Menlo Park, Suite 101-102, Edison (08837); (201)494-3920. Pres. Gerald Grossman; Exec. Dir. Arthur Eisenstein.

OCEAN COUNTY

OCEAN COUNTY JEWISH FEDERATION; 301 Madison Ave., Lakewood (08701); (201)363-0530. Pres. Michael Levin; Exec. Dir. Abraham Mintz.

PASSAIC-CLIFTON

JEWISH FEDERATION OF GREATER PASSAIC-CLIFTON (1933); (sponsors UNITED JEWISH CAMPAIGN); 199 Scoles Ave. (07012). (201)777-7031. Pres. Morris Macy; Exec. Dir. Marden Prau.

RARITAN VALLEY

JEWISH FEDERATION OF RARITAN VALLEY (1948); 2 South Adelaide Ave., Highland Park (08904); (201)246-1905. Pres. Irwin Baker; Exec. Dir. Jonathan Spinner.

SOMERSET COUNTY

JEWISH FEDERATION OF SOMERSET COUNTY (1960); 11 Park Ave., P.O. Box 874,

Somerville (08876); (201)725-2231. Pres. Gilbert Pelovitz; Exec. Dir. Moshe M. Ziv.

SOUTHERN NEW JERSEY

JEWISH FEDERATION OF SOUTHERN NEW JERSEY (incl. Camden and Burlington Counties) (1922); (sponsors ALLIED JEWISH APPEAL); 2393 W. Marlton Pike, Cherry Hill (08002); (609)665-6100. Pres. Leonard Wolf; Exec. V. Pres. Stuart Alperin.

TRENTON

JEWISH FEDERATION OF THE DELAWARE VALLEY (1929); 999 Lower Ferry Rd., P.O. Box 7365 (08628); (609)883-9110. Pres. Martin Okean; Exec. Dir. Charles P. Epstein.

VINELAND

JEWISH FEDERATION OF CUMBERLAND COUNTY (1971); (sponsors ALLIED JEWISH APPEAL); 629 Wood St. (08360); (609)696-4445. Pres. David B. Rosenberg; Exec. Dir. Melvin May.

NEW MEXICO

ALBUQUERQUE

JEWISH COMMUNITY COUNCIL OF ALBUQUERQUE, INC. (1938); 600 Louisiana Blvd., S.E. (87108); (505)266-5641. Pres. Elvin Kanter; Exec. Dir. Allan Kaiser.

NEW YORK

ALBANY

GREATER ALBANY JEWISH FEDERATION (1938); (sponsors JEWISH WELFARE FUND); 19 Colvin Ave. (12206); (518)459-8000. Pres. Joan Rosenstein; Exec. Dir. Steven F. Windmueller.

BROOME COUNTY

THE JEWISH FEDERATION OF BROOME COUNTY (1937; Inc. 1958); 500 Clubhouse Rd., Binghamton (13903); (607)724-2332. Pres. Donald A. Bronsky; Exec. Dir. Stanley Bard.

BUFFALO

JEWISH FEDERATION OF GREATER BUFFALO, INC. (1903); (sponsors UNITED JEWISH FUND CAMPAIGN); 787 Delaware Ave. (14209); (716)886-7750. Pres. Mrs. Michael Kaplan; Exec. Dir. Morris Rombro.

ELMIRA

ELMIRA JEWISH WELFARE FUND, INC. (1942); P.O. Box 3087, Grandview Rd. (14905); (607)734-8122. Pres. Edward J. Grandt; Exec. Dir. Ernest G. Budwig.

GLENS FALLS

*GLENS FALLS JEWISH WELFARE FUND (1939); 16 Broadacres Rd. (12801); (518)792-4624. Chmn. Mrs. Sunny Buchman.

HUDSON

*JEWISH WELFARE FUND OF HUDSON, N.Y., INC. (1947); Joslen Blvd. (12534); (518)828-6848. Pres. Arthur T. Brooks.

KINGSTON

JEWISH FEDERATION OF GREATER KINGSTON, INC. (1951); 159 Green St. (12401); (914)338-8131. Pres. Joseph Cohen; Exec. Dir. Jane Myerson.

NEW YORK CITY

FEDERATION OF JEWISH PHILANTHROPIES OF NEW YORK (incl. Greater New York, Nassau, Suffolk, and Westchester Counties) (1917); 130 E. 59 St. (10022); (212)980-1000. Pres. Mrs. Laurence A. Tisch; Exec. V. Pres. William Kahn.

UNITED JEWISH APPEAL—FEDERATION OF JEWISH PHILANTHROPIES—JOINT CAMPAIGN (1974); 130 E. 59 St. (10022); (212)-980-1000. Pres. Lawrence B. Buttenweiser; Exec. V. Pres. William Kahn; Bd. Chmn. James L. Weinberg.

UNITED JEWISH APPEAL OF GREATER NEW YORK, INC. (incl. Greater New York, Nassau, Suffolk, and Westchester Counties) (1939); 130 E. 59 St. (10022); (212)980-1000. Pres. Stephen Shalom; Exec. V. Pres. Ernest W. Michel.

NEWBURGH-MIDDLETOWN

JEWISH FEDERATION OF NEWBURGH AND MIDDLETOWN, INC. (1925); 360 Powell Ave. (12550); (914)562-7860. Pres. Gerald Kreisberg; Exec. Dir. Lawrence Pallas.

NIAGARA FALLS

JEWISH FEDERATION OF NIAGARA FALLS, N.Y., INC. (1935); Temple Beth Israel Bldg. #5, College & Madison Ave. (14305); (716)-284-4575. Pres. Robert D. Wisbaum; Exec. Dir. Miriam Schaffer.

POUGHKEEPSIE

*JEWISH WELFARE FUND–DUTCHESS COUNTY (1941); 110 Grand Ave. (12603); (914)471-9811. Pres. Ruth Nosonwitz; Exec. Dir. Mark Baron.

ROCHESTER

JEWISH COMMUNITY FEDERATION OF ROCHESTER, N.Y., INC. (1937); 1200 Chestnut Plaza, 50 Chestnut St. (14604); (716)

325-3393. Pres. Irving Ruderman; Exec. Dir. Henry M. Rosenbaum.

SCHENECTADY

JEWISH FEDERATION OF GREATER SCHE-NECTADY (1938); (sponsors SCHENECTADY UJA AND FEDERATED WELFARE FUND); 2565 Balltown Rd., P.O. Box 2649 (12309); (518)393-1136. Pres. Neil Golub; Exec. Dir. Haim Morag.

SYRACUSE

SYRACUSE JEWISH FEDERATION, INC. (1918); P.O. Box 5004, 2223 E. Genesee St. (13201); (315)422-4104. Pres. Alan Burstein; Exec. Dir. Barry Silverberg.

TROY

TROY JEWISH COMMUNITY COUNCIL, INC. (1936); 2500 21 St. (12180); (518)274-0700. Pres. Louis Cohen; Exec. Dir. Gertrude Chesman.

UTICA

JEWISH COMMUNITY COUNCIL OF UTICA, N.Y., INC. (1933; Inc. 1950); (sponsors UNITED JEWISH APPEAL OF UTICA); 2310 Oneida St. (13501); (315)733-2343. Pres. Cecily Eidelhoch; Exec. Dir. Irving Epstein.

NORTH CAROLINA

ASHEVILLE

FEDERATED JEWISH CHARITIES OF ASHE-VILLE, INC.; 236 Charlotte St. (28801); (704)-253-0701. Pres. Ronald Goldstein; Exec. Dir. Robert Posner.

CHARLOTTE

CHARLOTTE JEWISH FEDERATION (1940); P.O. Box 220188 (28222); (704)366-0358. Pres. Richard Klein; Exec. Dir. Marvin Bienstock.

DURHAM-CHAPEL HILL

DURHAM-CHAPEL HILL JEWISH FEDERA-TION & COMMUNITY COUNCIL; 1721 Allard Rd. (27514); (919)929-4774. Pres. Symoine K. Laufe.

GREENSBORO

GREENSBORO JEWISH FEDERATION (1940); 713A N. Green St. (27401); Pres. Joanne Bluethenthal; Exec. Dir. Sherman Harris.

HIGH POINT

HIGH POINT JEWISH FEDERATION; P.O. Box 2063 (27261); (919)431-7101. Campaign Chmn. Harry Samet.

WINSTON-SALEM

WINSTON-SALEM JEWISH COMMUNITY COUNCIL; 710 Lichfield Rd. (27104); (919)-725-7576; Pres. Alan Andler.

OHIO

AKRON

AKRON JEWISH COMMUNITY FEDERATION (1935); 750 White Pond Dr. (44320); (216)-867-7850. Pres. Herman Rogovy; Exec. Dir. Steven Drysdale.

CANTON

JEWISH COMMUNITY FEDERATION OF CAN-TON (1935; reorg. 1955); 2631 Harvard Ave., N.W. (44709); (216)453-0133. Pres. Harriett Narens; Exec. Dir. Revella R. Kopstein.

CINCINNATI

JEWISH FEDERATION OF CINCINNATI AND VICINITY (merger of the Associated Jewish Agencies and Jewish Welfare Fund) (1896; reorg. 1967); 200 West 4th St. (45202); (513)-381-5800. Pres. Melvin Schulman; Exec. V. Pres. Harold Goldberg.

CLEVELAND

JEWISH COMMUNITY FEDERATION OF CLEVELAND (1903); 1750 Euclid Ave. (44115); (216)566-9200. Pres. Lawrence H. Williams; Exec. Dir. Stanley B. Horowitz.

COLUMBUS

COLUMBUS JEWISH FEDERATION (1926); 1175 College Ave. (43209); (614)237-7686. Pres. Bernard K. Yenkin; Exec. V. Pres. Ben M. Mandelkorn; Exec. Dir. Charles R. Schiffman.

DAYTON

JEWISH FEDERATION OF GREATER DAY-TON (1943); 4501 Denlinger Rd. (45426); (513)854-4150. Pres. Bernard Goldman; Exec. V. Pres. Peter Wells.

LIMA

FEDERATED JEWISH CHARITIES OF LIMA DISTRICT (1935); 2417 West Market St. (45805); (419)224-8941. Pres. Morris Goldberg.

STEUBENVILLE

JEWISH COMMUNITY COUNCIL (1938); P.O. Box 472 (43952); (614)282-9031. Pres. Morris Denmark; Exec. Sec. Mrs. Joseph Freedman.

TOLEDO

JEWISH WELFARE FEDERATION OF
TOLEDO, INC. (1907; reorg. 1960); P.O. Box
587, 6505 Sylvania Ave., Sylvania (43560);
(419)885-4461. Pres. John Bloomfield; Exec.
Dir. Alvin S. Levinson.

WARREN

JEWISH FEDERATION (1938); 3893 E. Market St. (44483); Pres. William Lippy.

YOUNGSTOWN

YOUNGSTOWN AREA JEWISH FEDERATION
(1935); P.O. Box 449 (44501); (216)746-3251.
Pres. Bert Tamarkin; Exec. Dir. Stanley
Engel.

OKLAHOMA

ARDMORE

*JEWISH FEDERATION (1934); 23 "B" St.,
S.W. (73401); Chmn. Ike Fishman.

OKLAHOMA CITY

JEWISH COMMUNITY COUNCIL (1941);
11032 Quail Creek Rd. #201 (73120); (405)-
524-4324. Pres. Maynard Greenberg; Exec.
Dir. Earnest Siegel.

TULSA

JEWISH FEDERATION OF TULSA (1938);
(sponsors TULSA UNITED JEWISH CAM-
PAIGN); 2021 E. 71 St. (74136); (918)495-
1100. Pres. Howard Raskin; Exec. Dir. Nathan Loshak.

OREGON

PORTLAND

JEWISH FEDERATION OF PORTLAND (incl.
state of Oregon and adjacent Washington
communities) (1920; reorg. 1956); 4850 S.W.
Scholls Ferry Rd., Suite 304 (97225); (503)-
297-8104. Pres. Jonathan Newman; Exec.
Dir. David Roberts.

PENNSYLVANIA

ALLENTOWN

JEWISH FEDERATION OF ALLENTOWN, INC.
(1938; Inc. 1948); 702 N. 22nd (18104);
(215)435-3571. Pres. Fred Sussman; Exec.
Dir. Ivan C. Schonfeld.

ALTOONA

FEDERATION OF JEWISH PHILANTHROPIES
(1920; reorg. 1940); 1308 17th St. (16601);
(814)944-4072. Pres. Ira B. Kron.

BUTLER

BUTLER JEWISH WELFARE FUND (incl. Butler County) (1938); 148 Haverford Dr.

(16001); (412)287-3814. Pres. Robert Brown;
Sec. Maurice Horwitz.

EASTON

JEWISH COMMUNITY COUNCIL OF EASTON,
PA. AND VICINITY (1939); (sponsors ALLIED
WELFARE APPEAL); 16th and Bushkill Sts.
(18042); (215)253-4235. Pres. Eugene Goldman.

ERIE

JEWISH COMMUNITY COUNCIL OF ERIE
(1946); 32 W. 8th St., Suite 512 (16501);
(814)455-4474. Pres. Herbert Appletree;
Exec. Dir. Mrs. Stefan Berger.

HARRISBURG

UNITED JEWISH COMMUNITY OF GREATER
HARRISBURG (1933); 100 Vaughn St.
(17110); (717)236-9555. Pres. Jay Maisel;
Exec. Dir. Avrom Fox.

HAZELTON

JEWISH COMMUNITY COUNCIL (1960); Lau-
rel & Hemlock Sts. (18201); (717)454-3528.
Pres. Herbert Schultz; Exec. Dir. Steven
Wendell.

JOHNSTOWN

UNITED JEWISH FEDERATION OF JOHNS-
TOWN (1938); 1334 Luzerne St. (15905);
(814)255-1447. Pres. Isadore Glasser.

LANCASTER

UNITED JEWISH COMMUNITY COUNCIL OF
LANCASTER, PA., INC. (1928); 2120 Oregon
Pike (17601); (717)569-7352. Pres. Norman
Axelrod; Exec. Dir. Lawrence Pallas.

LEVITTOWN

JEWISH FEDERATION OF LOWER BUCKS
COUNTY (1956; Inc. 1957); One Oxford Valley, Suite 602, Langhorne (19047); (215)757-
0250. Pres. Dorothy Dickstein; Exec. Dir. Elliot Gershenson.

NEW CASTLE

UNITED JEWISH APPEAL OF NEW CASTLE,
PA. (1967); P.O. Box 5050 (16105); (412)-
658-8389. Chmn. Ruth-Ann Fisher.

NORRISTOWN

JEWISH COMMUNITY CENTER (serving Cen-
tral Montgomery County) (1936); Brown and
Powell Sts. (19401); (215)275-8797. Pres.
Mark Hite; Exec. Dir. Harold M. Kamsler.

PHILADELPHIA

FEDERATION OF JEWISH AGENCIES OF
GREATER PHILADELPHIA (1901; reorg.
1956); 226 South 16 St. (19102); (215)893-

5600. Pres. Ronald Rubin; Exec. Dir. Robert Forman.

PITTSBURGH

UNITED JEWISH FEDERATION OF GREATER PITTSBURGH (1912; reorg. 1955); 234 McKee Pl. (15213); (412)681-8000. Pres. Leonard Rudolph; Exec. V. Pres. Howard Rieger.

POTTSVILLE

UNITED JEWISH CHARITIES (1935); 2300 Mahantongo St. (17901); (717)622-5890. Chmn. Henry Gilbert; Exec. Sec. Gertrude Perkins.

READING

JEWISH FEDERATION OF READING, PA., INC. (1935); (sponsors UNITED JEWISH CAMPAIGN); 1700 City Line St. (19604); (215)921-2766. Pres. Gerald Goodman; Exec. Dir. Roy Stuppler.

SCRANTON

SCRANTON-LACKAWANNA JEWISH COUNCIL (incl. Lackawanna County) (1945); 601 Jefferson Ave. (18510); (717)961-2300. Pres. Jack Plotkin; Exec. Dir. Seymour Brotman.

SHARON

SHENANGO VALLEY JEWISH FEDERATION (1940); 840 Highland Rd. (16146); (412)346-4754. Pres. Leon Bolotin; Treas. Irwin Yanowitz.

UNIONTOWN

UNITED JEWISH FEDERATION (1939); 406 W. Main St. (15401), c/o Jewish Community Center; (412)438-4681. Pres. Harold Cohen; Sec. Morris H. Samuels.

WILKES-BARRE

JEWISH FEDERATION OF GREATER WILKES-BARRE (1935); (sponsors UNITED JEWISH APPEAL); 60 S. River St. (18701); (717)824-4646. Pres. Eugene Roth; Exec. Dir. Monty Pomm.

YORK

YORK COUNCIL OF JEWISH CHARITIES, INC.; 120 E. Market St. (17401); (717)843-0918. Pres. Tim Grumbacher; Exec. Dir. Alan Dameshek.

RHODE ISLAND

PROVIDENCE

JEWISH FEDERATION OF RHODE ISLAND (1945); 130 Sessions St. (02906); (401)421-4111. Pres. Melvin Alperin; Exec. Dir. Elliot Cohan.

SOUTH CAROLINA

CHARLESTON

CHARLESTON JEWISH FEDERATION (1949); 1645 Millbrook Dr. (29407); P.O. Box 31298; (803)571-6565. Pres. David L. Cohen; Exec. Dir. Steven Wendell.

COLUMBIA

JEWISH WELFARE FEDERATION OF COLUMBIA (1960); 4540 Trenholm Rd. (29206); (803)787-2023. Pres. Jules Lindeau; Exec. Dir. Alex Grossberg.

SOUTH DAKOTA

SIOUX FALLS

JEWISH WELFARE FUND (1938); National Reserve Bldg. (57102); (605)336-2880. Pres. Richard M. Light; Exec. Sec. Louis R. Hurwitz.

TENNESSEE

CHATTANOOGA

CHATTANOOGA JEWISH WELFARE FEDERATION (1931); 5326 Lynnland Terrace (37411); (615)894-1317. Pres. Tom Trivers; Exec. Dir. Alan J. Hersh.

KNOXVILLE

JEWISH WELFARE FUND, INC. (1939); 6800 Deane Hill Dr., P.O. Box 10882 (37919); (615)690-6343. Chmn. Michael Feinman; Exec. Dir. Mike Pousman.

MEMPHIS

MEMPHIS JEWISH FEDERATION (incl. Shelby County) (1934); 6560 Poplar Ave., P.O. Box 38268 (38138); (901)767-5161. Pres. Samuel Weintraub; Exec. Dir. Howard Weisband.

NASHVILLE

JEWISH FEDERATION OF NASHVILLE & MIDDLE TENNESSEE (1936); 3500 West End Ave. (37205); (615)269-0729. Pres. Morris Werthan; Exec. Dir. Arthur Landa.

TEXAS

AUSTIN

JEWISH COMMUNITY COUNCIL OF AUSTIN (1939; reorg. 1956); 5758 Balcones Dr., Suite 104 (78759); (512)451-6435. Pres. Paul Gartner; Exec. Dir. Sheldon Sklar.

BEAUMONT

BEAUMONT JEWISH FEDERATION OF TEXAS, INC. (Org. and Inc. 1967); P.O. Box 1981 (77704); (713)833-5427. Pres. Edwin Gale; Dir. Isadore Harris.

CORPUS CHRISTI

CORPUS CHRISTI JEWISH COMMUNITY COUNCIL (1953); 750 Everhart Rd. (78411); (512)855-6239. Pres. Jack Solka; Exec. Dir. Andrew Lipman.

COMBINED JEWISH APPEAL OF CORPUS CHRISTI (1962); 750 Everhart Rd. (78411); (512)855-6239. Pres. Jule Pels; Exec. Dir. Andrew Lipman.

DALLAS

JEWISH FEDERATION OF GREATER DALLAS (1911); 7800 Northaven Rd., Suite A (75230); (214)369-3313. Pres. Ann Sikora; Exec. Dir. Morris A. Stein.

EL PASO

JEWISH FEDERATION OF EL PASO, INC. (incl. surrounding communities) (1939); 405 Mardi Gras, P.O. Box 12097 (79912); (915)-584-4437. Pres. Marvin J. Zimet; Exec. Dir. Howard Burnham.

FORT WORTH

JEWISH FEDERATION OF FORT WORTH (1936); 6801 Granbury Rd. (76133); (817)-292-3081. Pres. I. L. Freed; Exec. Dir. Norman A. Mogul.

GALVESTON

GALVESTON COUNTY JEWISH WELFARE ASSOCIATION (1936); P. O. Box 146 (77553); Pres. Mrs. E. I. Klein; Sec. Bernard Demoratsky.

HOUSTON

JEWISH FEDERATION OF GREATER HOUSTON, INC. (incl. neighboring communities) (1937); (sponsors UNITED JEWISH CAMPAIGN); 5601 S. Braeswood Blvd. (77096); (713)729-7000. Pres. Stephen Kaufman; Exec. Dir. Hans Mayer.

SAN ANTONIO

JEWISH FEDERATION OF SAN ANTONIO (incl. Bexar County) (1922); 8434 Ahern Dr. (78216); (512)341-8234. Pres. Allen Bassulk; Acting Dir. Hilda Heritch.

TYLER

*FEDERATION OF JEWISH WELFARE FUNDS (1938); P. O. Box 934 (75710); Pres. Ralph Davis.

WACO

JEWISH WELFARE COUNCIL OF WACO (1949); P. O. Box 8031 (76710); (817)776-3740. Pres. Mark Wolf; Exec. Sec. Mrs. Maurice Labens.

UTAH

SALT LAKE CITY

UNITED JEWISH COUNCIL AND SALT LAKE JEWISH WELFARE FUND (1936); 2416 E. 1700 South (84108); (801)581-0098. Pres. Bruce Cohne; Exec. Dir. Bernard Solomon.

VIRGINIA

NEWPORT NEWS

JEWISH FEDERATION OF THE VIRGINIA PENINSULA (1942); 2700 Spring Rd. (23606); P. O. Box 6680; (804)595-5544. Pres. Betty Levin.

NORFOLK

UNITED JEWISH FEDERATION OF TIDEWATER, INC. (1937); 7300 Newport Ave., P.O. Box 9776 (23505); (804)489-8040. Pres. Robert O. Copeland; Exec. Dir. A. Robert Gast.

RICHMOND

JEWISH COMMUNITY FEDERATION OF RICHMOND, INC. (1935); 5403 Monument Ave., P.O. Box 8237 (23226); (804)288-0045. Pres. S. Harold Horwitz; Exec. Dir. Roy Rosenbaum.

ROANOKE

JEWISH COMMUNITY COUNCIL; 2728 Colonial Ave., S.W. (24015); (703)982-2300. Chmn. Arnold P. Masinter; Exec. Dir. Debbie Kaplan.

WASHINGTON

SEATTLE

JEWISH FEDERATION OF GREATER SEATTLE (incl. King County, Everett and Bremerton) (1926); Securities Bldg., Suite 525, (98101); (206)622-8211. Pres. Francine Loeb; Exec. Dir. Murray Shiff.

SPOKANE

*JEWISH COMMUNITY COUNCIL OF SPOKANE (incl. Spokane County) (1927); (sponsors UNITED JEWISH FUND) (1936); 401 Paulsen Bldg. (99021); (509)838-2949. Pres. Samuel Huppin; Sec. Robert N. Arick.

WEST VIRGINIA

CHARLESTON

FEDERATED JEWISH CHARITIES OF CHARLESTON, INC. (1937); P. O. Box 1613 (25326); (304)342-6459. Pres. Robert Levine; Exec. Sec. Charles Cohen.

HUNTINGTON

FEDERATED JEWISH CHARITIES (1939); P. O. Box 947 (25713); (304)523-9326. Pres. William H. Glick; Sec. Andrew Katz.

WHEELING

UNITED JEWISH FEDERATION OF OHIO VALLEY, INC. (1933); 20 Hawthorne Court (26003); Pres. Harold Saferstein.

WISCONSIN

APPLETON

UNITED JEWISH CHARITIES OF APPLETON (1963); 3131 N. Meade St. (54911); (414)-733-1848. Co-Chmn. Arnold Cohodas and Dov Edelstein; Treas. Mrs. Harold Rusky.

GREEN BAY

GREEN BAY JEWISH WELFARE FUND; P. O. Box 335 (54305); Pres. Stuart Milson; Treas. Herman J. Robitshek.

KENOSHA

KENOSHA JEWISH WELFARE FUND (1938); 6537-7th Ave. (53140); (414)658-8635.

Pres. Elvin Kranen; Sec.-Treas. Mrs. S. M. Lapp.

MADISON

MADISON JEWISH COMMUNITY COUNCIL, INC. (1940); 310 N. Midvale Blvd., Suite 325 (53705); Pres. Stanley Mintz; Exec. Dir. Avrum Weiss.

MILWAUKEE

MILWAUKEE JEWISH FEDERATION, INC. (1938); 1360 N. Prospect Ave. (53202); (414)-271-8338. Pres. Esther Leah Ritz; Exec. V. Pres. Melvin S. Zaret.

RACINE

RACINE JEWISH WELFARE BOARD (1946); 944 Main St. (53403); (414)633-7093. Pres. Jess Levin; Exec. Sec. Betty Goldberg.

SHEBOYGAN

JEWISH WELFARE COUNCIL OF SHEBOYGAN (1927); 1404 North Ave. (53081); Sec. Mrs. Abe Alpert.

CANADA

ALBERTA

CALGARY

CALGARY JEWISH COMMUNITY COUNCIL (1962); 1607 90th Ave. S.W. (T2V 4V7); (403)263-5650. Pres. Joe A. Spier; Exec. Dir. Harry S. Shatz.

EDMONTON

EDMONTON JEWISH COMMUNITY COUNCIL, INC. (1954; Inc. 1965); 7200-156 St. (T5R 1X3); (403)487-5120. Pres. David Grossman; Exec. Dir. Hillel Boroditsky.

BRITISH COLUMBIA

VANCOUVER

*JEWISH COMMUNITY FUND & COUNCIL OF VANCOUVER (1932); 950 W. 41 Ave. (V5Z 2N7); (604)261-8101. Pres. Irvine E. Epstein; Exec. Dir. Morris Saltzman.

MANITOBA

WINNIPEG

WINNIPEG JEWISH COMMUNITY COUNCIL (incl. Combined Jewish Appeal of Winnipeg) (org. 1938; reorg. 1973); 370 Hargrave St. (R3B 2K1); (204)943-0406.

Pres. Marjorie Blankstein; Exec. Dir. Izzy Peltz.

ONTARIO

HAMILTON

HAMILTON JEWISH FEDERATION (incl. United Jewish Welfare Fund) (org. 1934; merged 1971); 57 Delaware Ave. (L8M 1T6); (416)528-8570. Pres. Leslie Lasky; Exec. Dir. Samuel Soifer.

LONDON

*LONDON JEWISH COMMUNITY COUNCIL (1932); 532 Huron St. (24), (N5Y 4J5); (519)-433-2201. Pres. Ralph Brooke; Exec. Dir. Sidney Indig.

OTTAWA

JEWISH COMMUNITY COUNCIL OF OTTAWA (1934); 151 Chapel St. (K1N 7Y2); (613)-232-7306. Pres. Joseph Lieff; Exec. V. Pres. Sol B. Shinder.

ST. CATHARINES

*UNITED JEWISH WELFARE FUND OF ST. CATHARINES; c/o Jewish Community Centre, Church St.; Pres. Jack Silverstein; Sec. Syd Goldford.

TORONTO

TORONTO JEWISH CONGRESS (1937); 150 Beverley St. (M5T 1Y6); (416)977-3811. Pres. Wilfred Posluns; Exec. V. Pres. Irwin Gold.

WINDSOR

JEWISH COMMUNITY COUNCIL (1938); 1641 Ouellette Ave. (N8X 1K9); (519)254-7558. Pres. Lottie Bernholtz; Exec. Dir. Joseph Eisenberg.

QUEBEC

MONTREAL

ALLIED JEWISH COMMUNITY SERVICES (merger of FEDERATION OF JEWISH COMMUNITY SERVICES AND COMBINED JEWISH APPEAL) (1965); 5151 Cote St. Catherine Rd. (H3W 1M6); (514)735-3541. Pres. Harvey Sigman; Exec. V. Pres. Manuel G. Batshaw; Exec. Dir. Emanuel Weiner.

Jewish Periodicals[1]

UNITED STATES

ARIZONA

ARIZONA POST (1946). 102 N. Plumer Ave., Tucson, 85719. (602)791-9962. Sandra R. Heiman. Fortnightly. Tucson Jewish Community Council.

PHOENIX JEWISH NEWS (1947). 1536 West Thomas Rd., Phoenix, 85015. (602)264-0536. Pearl R. Newmark. Biweekly.

CALIFORNIA

B'NAI B'RITH MESSENGER (1897). 2510 W. 7 St., Los Angeles, 90057. (213)380-5000. Gilbert E. Thompson. Weekly.

HERITAGE-SOUTHWEST JEWISH PRESS (1914). 2130 S. Vermont Ave., Los Angeles, 90007. Weekly. Dan Brin. (Also SAN DIEGO JEWISH PRESS-HERITAGE, San Diego [weekly]; CENTRAL CALIFORNIA JEWISH HERITAGE, Sacramento and Fresno area [monthly]; ORANGE COUNTY JEWISH HERITAGE, Orange County area [weekly].)

ISRAEL TODAY (1973). 10340 Reseda Blvd., Northridge, 91326. (213)786-4000. Phil Blazer. Biweekly. Hebrew.

JEWISH OBSERVER OF THE EAST BAY (1967). 3245 Sheffield Ave., Oakland, 94602. (415)533-7462. Lillian M. Bernstein. Fortnightly. Jewish Federation of the Greater East Bay.

JEWISH SPECTATOR (1935). P.O. Box 2016, Santa Monica, 90406. (213)829-2484. Trude Weiss-Rosmarin. Quarterly.

JEWISH STAR (1956). 693 Mission St., #305, San Francisco, 94105. (415)421-4874. Chet Swafford. Monthly.

SAN FRANCISCO JEWISH BULLETIN (1946). 870 Market St., San Francisco, 94102. (415)391-9444. Geoffrey Fisher. Weekly. San Francisco Jewish Community Publications.

WESTERN STATES JEWISH HISTORICAL QUARTERLY (1968). 2429 23rd St., Santa Monica, 90405. (213)399-3585. Dr. Norton B. Stern. Quarterly. Southern California Jewish Historical Society.

COLORADO

INTERMOUNTAIN JEWISH NEWS (1913). 1275 Sherman St., Suite 215–217, Denver, 80203. (303)861-2235. Miriam H. Goldberg. Weekly.

CONNECTICUT

CONNECTICUT JEWISH LEDGER (1929). P.O. Box 1688, Hartford, 06101. (203)233-2148. Berthold Gaster. Weekly.

JEWISH DIGEST (1955). 1363 Fairfield Ave., Bridgeport, 06605. (203)384-2284. Jonathan D. Levine. Monthly.

DISTRICT OF COLUMBIA

ALERT (1970). 1411 K St., N.W., Suite 402. Washington, 20005. (202)393-4117. Weekly. Union of Councils for Soviet Jews.

THE INTERNATIONAL JEWISH MONTHLY (1886 under the name MENORAH). 1640

---

[1]The information in this directory is based on replies to questionnaires circulated by the editors. Inclusion does not necessarily imply approval of the periodicals by the publishers of the AJYB. For organizational bulletins, see the directory of Jewish organizations.

Rhode Island Ave., N.W., Washington, 20036. (202)857-6645. Marc Silver. Ten times a year. B'nai B'rith.

JEWISH VETERAN (1896). 1712 New Hampshire Ave., N.W., Washington, 20009. (202)265-6280. Joan Alpert. Bi-monthly. Jewish War Veterans of the U.S.A.

JEWISH WEEK (1965). 774 National Press Building, Washington, 20045. (202)783-7200. Joseph M. Hochstein. Weekly.

MENORAH (1979). 1747 Conn. Ave., N.W., Washington, 20009. (202)483-7902. Arthur I. Waskow. Monthly. A Center for Jewish Renewal, Public Resource Center.

NEAR EAST REPORT (1957). 444 North Capitol St., N.W., Suite 412, Washington, 20001. (202)638-1225. Moshe Decter. Weekly. Near East Research, Inc.

FLORIDA

JEWISH FLORIDIAN (1927). P.O. Box 012973, Miami, 33101. (305)373-4605. Fred K. Shochet. Weekly.

JEWISH FLORIDIAN OF GREATER FORT LAUDERDALE. 8360 W. Oakland Park Blvd., Fort Lauderdale, 33321. (305)748-8200. Fred Shochet. Weekly. Jewish Federation of Fort Lauderdale.

SOUTHERN JEWISH WEEKLY (1924). P.O. Box 3297, Jacksonville, 32206. (904)355-3459. Isadore Moscovitz. Weekly.

GEORGIA

SOUTHERN ISRAELITE (1925). P.O. Box 77388, 188-15 St. N.W., Atlanta, 30357. (404)876-8248. Vida Goldgar. Weekly.

ILLINOIS

JEWISH COMMUNITY NEWS (1945). 6464 West Main, Suite 7A, Belleville, 62223. (618)398-6100. Bruce Joshua Samborn. Monthly. Jewish Federation of Southern Illinois.

SENTINEL (1911). 323 S. Franklin St., Chicago, 60606. 663-1101. J. I. Fishbein. Weekly.

INDIANA

INDIANA JEWISH POST AND OPINION (1935). 611 N. Park Ave., Indianapolis, 46204. (317)634-1307. Raanan Geberer. Weekly.

JEWISH POST AND OPINION. 611 N. Park Ave., Indianapolis, 46204. (317)634-1307. Gabriel Cohen.

IOWA

M'GODOLIM: THE JEWISH QUARTERLY. 621 Holt, Iowa City, 52240. (206)322-1431. Keith S. Gormezano. Quarterly.

KENTUCKY

KENTUCKY JEWISH POST AND OPINION (1931). 1551 Bardstown Rd., Louisville, 40205. (502)459-1914. Jeff Lebensbaum. Weekly.

LOUISIANA

THE JEWISH CIVIC PRESS (1965). P.O. Box 15500, New Orleans, 70175. (504)895-8785. Abner Tritt. Monthly.

JEWISH TIMES (1974). 211 Camp St., Suite 518, New Orleans, 70130. (504)524-3147. Joan D. Jacob. Biweekly.

MARYLAND

AMERICAN JEWISH JOURNAL (1944). 1220 Blair Mill Rd., Silver Spring, 20910. (301)-585-1756. David Mondzac. Quarterly.

BALTIMORE JEWISH TIMES (1919). 2104 N. Charles St., Baltimore, 21218. (301)752-3504. Gary Rosenblatt. Weekly.

MASSACHUSETTS

AMERICAN JEWISH HISTORY (1893). 2 Thornton Road, Waltham, 02154. (617)-891-8110. Henry L. Feingold. Quarterly. American Jewish Historical Society.

JEWISH ADVOCATE (1902). 251 Causeway St., Boston, 02114. (617)227-5130. Joseph G. Weisberg, Bernard M. Hyatt. Weekly.

JEWISH CHRONICLE–LEADER (1926). 340 Main St., Suite 551, Worcester, 01608. (617)752-2512. Sondra Shapiro-Davis. Semimonthly. Mar-Len Publications.

JEWISH REPORTER (1970). 76 Salem End Road, Framingham, 01701. (617)879-3300. Harvey S. Stone. Monthly. Greater Framingham Jewish Federation.

JEWISH TIMES (1945). 118 Cypress St., Brookline, 02146. (617)566-7710. JoAnn Edinburg. Weekly.

JEWISH WEEKLY NEWS (1945). P.O. Box 1569, Springfield, 01101. (413)739-4771. Leslie B. Kahn. Weekly.

THE JOURNAL OF THE NORTH SHORE JEW-ISH COMMUNITY CENTER. 209 Washington St., Salem, 01970. (617)741-1558. Alan J. Jacobs. Biweekly.

MOMENT (1975). 462 Boylston St., Boston, 02116. (617)536-6252. Leonard Fein. Monthly (except Jan.-Feb. and July-August). Jewish Educational Ventures.

MICHIGAN

JEWISH NEWS (1942). 17515 W. 9 Mile Rd., Suite 865, Southfield, 48075. (313)424-8833. Philip Slomovitz. Weekly.

MICHIGAN JEWISH HISTORY (1960). 24680 Rensselaer, Oak Park, 48237. (313)548-9176. Phillip Applebaum. Semiannual. Jewish Historical Society of Michigan.

MINNESOTA

AMERICAN JEWISH WORLD (1912). 4820 Minnetonka Blvd., Minneapolis, 55416. (612)920-7000. Norman Gold. Weekly.

MISSOURI

KANSAS CITY JEWISH CHRONICLE (1920). P.O. Box 8709, Kansas City, 64114. (913)-648-4620. Milton Firestone. Weekly.

MISSOURI JEWISH POST AND OPINION (1948). 8235 Olive St., St. Louis, 63132. (314)993-2842. Kathie Sutin. Weekly.

ST. LOUIS JEWISH LIGHT (1947). 10957 Schuetz Rd., St. Louis, 63141. (314)432-3353. Robert A. Cohn. Biweekly. Jewish Federation of St. Louis.

NEBRASKA

JEWISH PRESS (1921). 333 S. 132 St., Omaha, 68154. (402)334-8200. Morris Maline. Weekly. Jewish Federation of Omaha.

NEVADA

JEWISH REPORTER (1976). 1030 E. Twain Ave., Las Vegas, 89109. (702)732-0556. Jerry Countess. Monthly. Jewish Federation of Las Vegas.

LAS VEGAS ISRAELITE (1965). P.O. Box 14096, Las Vegas, 89114. (702) 876-1255. Don Tell. Biweekly.

NEW JERSEY

JEWISH COMMUNITY VOICE (1941). 2393 W. Marlton Pike, Cherry Hill, 08002. (609) 665-6100. Alex B. Einbinder. Biweekly. Jewish Federation of Southern N.J.

JEWISH HORIZON (1963). Green Lane, Union, 07083. (201)351-1473. Fran Gold. Weekly. Jewish Federation of Central N.J.

JEWISH JOURNAL (1956). 2 S. Adelaide Ave., Highland Park, 08904. (201)246-1905. Joan Kemeny Paru. Semi-monthly. Jewish Federation of Raritan Valley.

JEWISH NEWS (1947). 60 Glenwood Ave., East Orange, 07017. (201)678-3900. Charles Baumohl. Weekly. Jewish Community Federation of Metropolitan New Jersey.

JEWISH RECORD (1939). 1537 Atlantic Ave., Atlantic City, 08401. (609)344-5119. Martin Korik. Weekly.

JEWISH STANDARD (1931). 40 Journal Sq., Jersey City, 07306. (201)653-6330. Morris J. Janoff. Weekly.

JEWISH VOICE (1975). 100 Menlo Park, Suite 101–102, Edison, 08837. (201)494-3920. Arthur Eisenstein. Biweekly. Jewish Federation of Northern Middlesex County.

MORRIS/SUSSEX JEWISH NEWS (1972). 500 Route 10, Ledgewood, 07852, (201)584-1850. Edith K. Schapiro. Monthly. United Jewish Federation of Morris/Sussex.

NEW YORK

AFN SHVEL (1941). 200 W. 72 St., N.Y.C., 10023. (212)787-6675. Mordkhe Schaechter. Quarterly. Yiddish. League for Yiddish.

ALBANY JEWISH WORLD (1965). 1104 Central Ave., Albany, 12205. (518)459-8455. Sam S. Clevenson. Weekly.

ALGEMEINER JOURNAL (1972). 404 Park Ave. S., N.Y.C., 10016. (212)689-3390. Gershon Jacobson. Weekly. Yiddish.

AMERICAN JEWISH YEAR BOOK (1899). 165 E. 56 St., N.Y.C., 10022. (212)751-4000. Milton Himmelfarb, David Singer. Annual. American Jewish Committee and Jewish Publication Society.

AMERICAN MIZRACHI WOMAN (1925). 817 Broadway, N.Y.C., 10003. (212)477-4720. Micheline Ratzersdorfer. Eight times yearly. Hebrew. American Mizrachi Women.

AMERICAN ZIONIST (1910). 4 E. 34 St., N.Y.C., 10016. (212)481-1500. Carol Binen. Bimonthly. Zionist Organization of America.

AUFBAU (1934). 2121 Broadway, N.Y.C., 10023. (212)873-7400. Lawrence S. Leshnik. Weekly. English-German. New World Club, Inc.

BITZARON (1939). P.O. Box 798, Cooper Station, N.Y.C., 10003. (212)598-3209. Hayim Leaf. Bimonthly. Hebrew. Hebrew Literature Foundation.

BUFFALO JEWISH REVIEW (1918). 15 E. Mohawk St., Buffalo, 14203. (716)854-2192. Steve Lipman. Weekly. Kahaal Nahalot Israel.

THE CALL (1932). 45 E. 33 St., N.Y.C., 10016. (212)889-6800. Nathan Peskin. Bimonthly. Workmen's Circle.

COMMENTARY (1945). 165 E. 56 St., N.Y.C., 10022. (212)751-4000. Norman Podhoretz. Monthly. American Jewish Committee.

CONGRESS MONTHLY (1933). 15 E. 84 St., N.Y.C., 10028. (212)879-4500. Nancy Miller. Monthly (except July and August). American Jewish Congress.

CONSERVATIVE JUDAISM (1945). 3080 Broadway, N.Y.C., 10027. (212)678-8863. Harold Kushner. Quarterly. Rabbinical Assembly and Jewish Theological Seminary of America.

CONTEMPORARY JEWRY (1974 under the name JEWISH SOCIOLOGY AND SOCIAL RESEARCH). Dept. of Sociology, Queens College, 65-30 Kissena Blvd., Flushing, 11367. (212)222-3699. Steven M. Cohen, Samuel Klausner. Semiannual.

ECONOMIC HORIZONS (1953). 500 Fifth Ave., N.Y.C., 10036. (212)354-6510. Phil Opher. Quarterly. American-Israel Chamber of Commerce and Industry, Inc.

HADAROM (1957). 1250 Broadway, N.Y.C., 10001. Charles B. Chavel. Semiannual. Hebrew. Rabbinical Council of America, Inc.

HADASSAH MAGAZINE (1921). 50 W. 58 St., N.Y.C., 10019. (212)355-7900. Alan M. Tigay. Monthly (except for combined issues of June-July and Aug.-Sept.). Hadassah, Women's Zionist Organization of America.

HADOAR (1921). 1841 Broadway, N.Y.C., 10023. (212)581-5151. Itzhak Ivry. Weekly. Hebrew. Histadruth Ivrith of America.

U INSTITUTIONAL AND INDUSTRIAL KOSHER PRODUCTS DIRECTORY (1967). 116 E. 27 St., N.Y.C., 10016. (212)725-3415. Yaakov Lipschutz. Irregular. Union of Orthodox Jewish Congregations of America.

ISRAEL HORIZONS (1952). 150 Fifth Ave., Suite 1002, N.Y.C., 10011. (212)255-8760. Richard Yaffe, Yosef Gotlieb. Bimonthly. Americans for Progressive Israel.

ISRAEL QUALITY (1976). 500 Fifth Ave., N.Y.C., 10110. (212)354-6510. Beth Belkin, Laurie Tarlowe. Quarterly. American-Israel Chamber of Commerce and Government of Israel Trade Center.

JEWISH ACTION (1950). 45 W. 36 St., N.Y.C., 10018. (212)563-4000. Bracha Osofsky. Quarterly. Union of Orthodox Jewish Congregations of America.

JEWISH AMERICAN RECORD (1973). G.P.O. Box 317, N.Y.C., 10116. Alex Novitsky. Monthly.

JEWISH BOOK ANNUAL (1942). 15 E. 26 St., N.Y.C., 10010. (212)532-4949. Jacob Kabakoff. Annual. English-Hebrew-Yiddish. JWB Jewish Book Council.

JEWISH BOOKS IN REVIEW (1945). 15 E. 26 St., N.Y.C., 10010. (212)532-4949. Robert Gordis. JWB Jewish Book Council.

JEWISH BRAILLE INSTITUTE VOICE (1978). 110 E. 30 St., N.Y.C., 10016. (212)889-2525. Jacob Freid. Ten times a year. Jewish Braille Institute of America, Inc.

JEWISH BRAILLE REVIEW (1931). 110 E. 30 St., N.Y.C., 10016. (212)889-2525. Jacob Freid. Ten times a year. English-Braille. Jewish Braille Institute of America, Inc.

JEWISH CURRENT EVENTS (1959). 430 Keller Ave., Elmont, L.I., 11003. Samuel Deutsch. Biweekly.

JEWISH CURRENTS (1946). 22 E. 17 St., Suite 601, N.Y.C., 10003. (212)924-5740. Morris U. Schappes. Monthly.

JEWISH DAILY FORWARD (1897). 45 E. 33 St., N.Y.C., 10016. (212)889-8200. Simon Weber. Daily. Yiddish. Forward Association, Inc.

JEWISH EDUCATION (1929). 114 Fifth Ave., N.Y.C., 10011. (212)675-5656. Alvin I. Schiff. Quarterly. Council for Jewish Education.

JEWISH EDUCATION DIRECTORY (1951). 114 Fifth Ave., N.Y.C., 10011. (212)675-5656. Triennial. Jewish Education Service of North America, Inc.

JEWISH EDUCATION NEWS (1939). 114 Fifth Ave., N.Y.C., 10011. (212)675-5656. Gary Gobetz. Irregular. Jewish Education Service of North America.

JEWISH FRONTIER (1934). 114 Fifth Ave., N.Y.C., 10011. (212)243-2741. Mitchell Cohen. Monthly. American Labor Zionist Movement.

JEWISH GUARDIAN (1974). P.O. Box 2143, Brooklyn, 11202. (212)384-4661. Pinchus David. Quarterly. Neturei Karta of U.S.A.

JEWISH JOURNAL (1970). 16 Court St., Brooklyn, 11241. (212)238-6600. Sylvia Adelman. Weekly.

JEWISH LEDGER (1924). 1427 Monroe Ave., Rochester, 14618. (716)275-9090. Donald Wolkin. Weekly.

JEWISH LIFE (1946). 45 W. 36 St., N.Y.C., 10018. (212)563-4000. Yaakov Jacobs. Quarterly. Union of Orthodox Jewish Congregations of America.

JEWISH MUSIC NOTES (1945). 15 E. 26 St., N.Y.C., 10010. (212)532-4949. Irving S. Cohen. Semiannual. JWB Jewish Music Council.

JEWISH OBSERVER (1963). 5 Beekman St., N.Y.C., 10038. (212)791-1814. Nisson Wolpin. Monthly (except July and August). Agudath Israel of America.

JEWISH OBSERVER OF SYRACUSE (1977). P.O. Box 5004, Syracuse, 13250. (315)422-4104. Sherry Chayat, Barry Silverberg. Biweekly.

JEWISH POST OF NEW YORK (1977). 101 Fifth Ave., N.Y.C., 10003. (212)989-6262. Charles Roth, Jean Herschaft. Weekly.

JEWISH PRESS (1950). 338 3rd Ave., Brooklyn, 11215. (212)858-3300. Sholom Klass. Weekly.

JEWISH SOCIAL STUDIES (1939). 250 W. 57 St., N.Y.C., 10019. Tobey B. Gitelle. Quarterly. Conference on Jewish Social Studies, Inc.

JEWISH TELEGRAPHIC AGENCY COMMUNITY NEWS REPORTER (1962). 165 W. 46 St., Rm. 511, N.Y.C., 10036. (212)575-9370. Murray Zuckoff. Weekly.

JEWISH TELEGRAPHIC AGENCY DAILY NEWS BULLETIN (1917). 165 W. 46 St., Rm. 511, N.Y.C., 10036. (212)575-9370. Murray Zuckoff. Daily.

JEWISH TELEGRAPHIC AGENCY WEEKLY NEWS DIGEST (1933). 165 W. 46 St., Rm. 511, N.Y.C., 10036. (212)575-9370. Murray Zuckoff. Weekly.

JEWISH WEEK (1876; reorg. 1970). 1 Park Ave., N.Y.C., 10016. (212)686-2320. Philip Hochstein. Weekly.

JWB CIRCLE (1946). 15 E. 26 St., N.Y.C., 10010. (212)532-4949. Lionel Koppman. Bimonthly. JWB.

JOURNAL OF JEWISH COMMUNAL SERVICE (1899). 15 E. 26 St., N.Y.C., 10010. (212)-683-8056. Sanford N. Sherman. Quarterly. Conference of Jewish Communal Service.

JOURNAL OF JEWISH CONSERVATIVE EDUCATION (1942). 155 Fifth Ave., N.Y.C., 10010. Gabriel Schoenfeld. Quarterly. Jewish Educators Assembly and United Synagogue Commission on Jewish Education.

JOURNAL OF REFORM JUDAISM (1953). 21 E. 40 St., N.Y.C., 10016. (212)684-4990. Samuel E. Karff. Quarterly. Central Conference of American Rabbis.

JUDAISM (1952). 15 E. 84 St., N.Y.C., 10028. (212)879-4500. Robert Gordis. Quarterly. American Jewish Congress.

KINDER JOURNAL (1920). 3301 Bainbridge Ave., Bronx, 10467. (212)881-3588. Bella Gottesman. Irregular. Yiddish. Sholem Aleichem Folk Institute, Inc.

KINDER ZEITUNG (1930). 45 E. 33 St., N.Y.C., 10016. (212)889-6800. Joseph Mlotek, Jack Noskowitz, Saul Maltz, Mates Olitzky. Bimonthly. English-Yiddish. Workmen's Circle.

KOL HAT'NUAH (1943). 50 W. 58 St., N.Y.C., 10019. (212)355-7900. Jennifer Sylvor. Monthly (Nov.-June). Hashachar.

KOL YAVNEH (1960). 25 W. 26 St., N.Y.C., 10010. (212)679-4574. Rochel Gershon. Irregular. Yavneh, National Religious Jewish Students Association.

U KOSHER PRODUCTS DIRECTORY (1925). 116 E. 27 St., N.Y.C., 10016. (212)725-3415. Yaakov Lipschutz. Irregular. Union of Orthodox Jewish Congregations of America—Kashruth Div.

KULTUR UN LEBN—CULTURE AND LIFE (1967). 45 E. 33 St., N.Y.C., 10016. (212)-889-6800. Joseph Mlotek. Quarterly. Yiddish. Workmen's Circle.

LILITH—THE JEWISH WOMEN'S MAGAZINE (1976). 250 W. 57 St., N.Y.C., 10019. (212)757-0818. Susan Weidman Schneider. Quarterly.

LONG ISLAND JEWISH PRESS (1942). 95-20 63 Rd., Rego Park, 11374. Abraham B. Shoulson. Monthly.

LONG ISLAND JEWISH WORLD (1971). 115 Middle Neck Road, Great Neck, 11021. (516)829-4000. Jerome W. Lippman. Weekly.

MIDSTREAM (1954). 515 Park Ave., N.Y.C., 10022. Joel Carmichael. (212)752-0600. Monthly (bimonthly June-Sept.). Theodor Herzl Foundation.

MODERN JEWISH STUDIES ANNUAL (1977). Acad. 904, Queens College, 65-30 Kissena Blvd., Flushing, 11367. (212)520-7067. Joseph C. Landis. Annual.

MORNING FREIHEIT (1922). 22 W. 21 St., N.Y.C., 10010. (212)255-7661. Paul Novick. Weekly. Yiddish-English.

OLOMEINU—OUR WORLD (1945). 229 Park Ave. S., N.Y.C., 10003. (212)674-6700. Nosson Scherman, Yaakov Fruchter. Monthly. English-Hebrew. Torah Umesorah National Society for Hebrew Day Schools.

OR CHADASH (1981). 110 E. 30 St., N.Y.C., 10016. (212)889-2525. Gerald M. Kass. Two to four times a year. Hebrew. Jewish Braille Institute of America, Inc.

U PASSOVER PRODUCTS DIRECTORY (1923). 116 E. 27 St., N.Y.C., 10016. (212)725-3415. Yaakov Lipschutz. Annual. Union of Orthodox Jewish Congregations of America—Kashruth Div.

PEDAGOGIC REPORTER (1949). 114 Fifth Ave., N.Y.C., 10011. (212)675-5656.

Mordecai H. Lewittes. Quarterly. Jewish Education Service of North America, Inc.

PIONEER WOMAN (1926). 200 Madison Ave., N.Y.C., 10016. (212)725-8010. Judith A. Sokoloff. Five times a year. English-Yiddish-Hebrew. Pioneer Women/Na'amat, the Women's Labor Zionist Organization of America.

PRESENT TENSE (1973). 165 E. 56 St., N.Y.C., 10022. (212)751-4000. Murray Polner. Quarterly. American Jewish Committee.

PROCEEDINGS OF THE AMERICAN ACADEMY FOR JEWISH RESEARCH (1920). 3080 Broadway, N.Y.C., 10027. Isaac E. Barzilay. Annual. Hebrew-Arabic-English. American Academy for Jewish Research.

RABBINICAL COUNCIL RECORD (1953). 1250 Broadway, N.Y.C., 10001. (212)594-3780. Louis Bernstein. Quarterly. Rabbinical Council of America.

RECONSTRUCTIONIST (1935). 31 E. 28 St., N.Y.C., 10016. (212)889-9080. Ira Eisenstein. Monthly (Sept.-June). Jewish Reconstructionist Foundation, Inc.

REFORM JUDAISM (1972); formerly DIMENSIONS IN AMERICAN JUDAISM). 838 Fifth Ave., N.Y.C., 10021. (212)249-0100. Aron Hirt-Manheimer. Quarterly. Union of American Hebrew Congregations.

REPORTER. 500 Clubhouse Rd., Binghamton, 13903. (607)724-2332. Marc Goldberg. Weekly. Jewish Federation of Broome County.

RESPONSE (1967). 610 W. 113 St., N.Y.C., 10025. (212)222-3699. Steven M. Cohen. Quarterly. Jewish Educational Ventures, Inc.

SAFRA: JEWISH SCHOOL MATERIALS REVIEW (1980). 114 Fifth Ave., N.Y.C., 10011. (212)675-5656. Mordecai H. Lewittes. Semiannual. Jewish Education Service of North America, Inc.

SEVEN ARTS FEATURE SYNDICATE (see News Syndicates p. 351).

SHEVILEY HAHINUCH (1939). 114 Fifth Ave., N.Y.C., 10011. (212)675-5656. Matthew Mosinkis. Quarterly. Hebrew. Council for Jewish Education.

SH'MA (1970). Box 567, Port Washington, N.Y., 11050. (516)944-9791. Eugene B.

Borowitz. Biweekly (except June, July, Aug.).

SHMUESSEN MIT KINDER UN YUGENT (1942). 770 Eastern Parkway, Brooklyn, 11213. (212)493-9250. Nissan Mindel. Monthly. Yiddish. Merkos L'Inyonei Chinuch, Inc.

SHOAH (1977). 250 W. 57 St., Room 216, N.Y.C., 10107. (212)582-6116. Jane Gerber. Three times a year. National Jewish Resource Center.

SYNAGOGUE LIGHT (1933). 47 Beekman St., N.Y.C., 10038. (212)227-7800. Meyer Hager. Bimonthly. Union of Chassidic Rabbis.

SYRACUSE JEWISH OBSERVER (1978). P.O. Box 5004, 2223 E. Genesee St., Syracuse, 13250. (315)422-4104. Sherry Chayat. Biweekly. Syracuse Jewish Federation.

TALKS AND TALES (1942). 770 Eastern Parkway, Brooklyn, 11213. (212)493-9250. Nissan Mindel. Monthly (also Hebrew, French, and Spanish editions). Merkos L'Inyonei Chinuch, Inc.

TRADITION (1958). 1250 Broadway, Suite 802, N.Y.C., 10001. (212)594-3780. Walter S. Wurzburger. Quarterly. Rabbinical Council of America.

UNITED SYNAGOGUE REVIEW (1943). 155 Fifth Ave., N.Y.C., 10010. (212)533-7800. Marvin S. Wiener. Quarterly. United Synagogue of America.

UNSER TSAIT (1941). 25 E. 78 St., N.Y.C., 10021. (212)535-0850. Jacob S. Hertz. Monthly. Yiddish. World Jewish Labor Bund.

DER WECKER (1921). 45 E. 33 St., N.Y.C., 10016. (212)686-1538. Elias Schulman. Bimonthly. Yiddish. Jewish Socialist Verband of America.

WESTCHESTER JEWISH TRIBUNE (1942). 95-20 63 Rd., Rego Park, 11374. Abraham B. Shoulson. Monthly.

WOMEN'S AMERICAN ORT REPORTER (1966). 1250 Broadway, N.Y.C., 10001. (212)594-8500. Elie Faust-Lévy. Quarterly. Women's American ORT, Inc.

WOMEN'S LEAGUE OUTLOOK (1930). 48 E. 74 St., N.Y.C., 10021. (212)628-1600. Mrs. M. Milton Perry. Quarterly. Women's League for Conservative Judaism.

WORLD OVER (1940). 426 W. 58 St., N.Y.C., 10019. (212)245-8200. Stephen Schaffzin, Linda K. Schaffzin. Monthly. Board of Jewish Education, Inc.

YAVNEH REVIEW (1963). 25 W. 26 St., N.Y.C., 10010. (212)679-4574. Shalom Carmy. Annual. Yavneh, National Religious Jewish Students Association.

YEARBOOK OF THE CENTRAL CONFERENCE OF AMERICAN RABBIS (1890). 21 E. 40 St., N.Y.C., 10016. (212)684-4990. Elliot L. Stevens. Annual. Central Conference of American Rabbis.

YIDDISH (1973). Queens College, Acad. 904, 65-30 Kissena Blvd., Flushing, 11367. (212)520-7067. Joseph C. Landis. Quarterly. Queens College Press.

DI YIDDISHE HEIM (1958). 770 Eastern Parkway, Brooklyn, 11213. (212)493-9250. Rachel Altein, Tema Gurary. Quarterly. English-Yiddish. Agudas Nshei Ub'nos Chabad.

YIDDISHE KULTUR (1938). 1123 Broadway, Rm. 203, N.Y.C., 10010. (212)691-0708. Itche Goldberg. Monthly (except June-July, Aug.-Sept.). Yiddish. Yiddisher Kultur Farband, Inc.—YKUF.

DOS YIDDISHE VORT (1953). 5 Beekman St., N.Y.C., 10038. (212)791-1181. Joseph Friedenson. Monthly. Yiddish. Agudath Israel of America.

YIDDISHER KEMFER (1906). 114 Fifth Ave., N.Y.C., 10011. (212)675-7808. Mordechai Strigler. Weekly. Yiddish. Labor Zionist Letters, Inc.

YIDISHE SHPRAKH (1941). 1048 Fifth Ave., N.Y.C., 10028. (212)231-7905. Mordkhe Schaechter. Annual. Yiddish. Yivo Institute for Jewish Research, Inc.

YIVO ANNUAL OF JEWISH SOCIAL SCIENCE (1946). 1048 Fifth Ave., N.Y.C., 10028. (212)535-6700. David Roskies. Biannually. Yivo Institute for Jewish Research, Inc.

YIVO BLETER (1931). 1048 Fifth Ave., N.Y.C., 10028. (212)535-6700. Editorial board. Irregular. Yiddish. Yivo Institute for Jewish Research, Inc.

YOUNG ISRAEL VIEWPOINT (1952). 3 W. 16 St., N.Y.C., 10011. (212)929-1525. Yaakov Kornreich. Monthly (except July, August). National Council of Young Israel.

YOUNG JUDAEAN (1912). 50 W. 58 St., N.Y.C., 10019. (212)355-7900. Barbara Gingold. Monthly (Nov.-June). Hadassah Zionist Youth Commission.

YOUTH AND NATION (1933). 150 Fifth Ave., N.Y.C., 10011. (212)929-4955. Shlomit Segal. Quarterly. Hashomer Hatzair Zionist Youth Movement.

YUGNTRUF (1964). 3328 Bainbridge Ave., Bronx, 10467. (212)654-8540. Itzek Gottesman. Quarterly. Yiddish. Yugntruf Youth for Yiddish.

DI ZUKUNFT (1892). 25 E. 78 St., N.Y.C., 10021. Hyman Bass, J. Hirshaut. Monthly (bimonthly May-Aug.). Yiddish. Congress for Jewish Culture and CYCO.

NORTH CAROLINA

AMERICAN JEWISH TIMES—OUTLOOK (1934; reorg. 1950). P.O. Box 33218, Charlotte, 28233. (704)372-3296. Ronald Unger. Monthly.

OHIO

THE AMERICAN ISRAELITE (1854). 906 Main St., Room 505, Cincinnati, 45202. (513)621-3145. Henry C. Segal. Weekly.

AMERICAN JEWISH ARCHIVES (1947). 3101 Clifton Ave., Cincinnati, 45220. (513)221-1875. Jacob R. Marcus, Abraham J. Peck. Semiannually. American Jewish Archives of Hebrew Union College—Jewish Institute of Religion.

CLEVELAND JEWISH NEWS (1964). 13910 Cedar Road, Cleveland, 44118. (216)371-0800. Cynthia Dettelbach. Weekly. Cleveland Jewish Publication Co.

DAYTON JEWISH CHRONICLE (1961). 118 Salem Ave., Dayton, 45406. (513)222-0783. Anne M. Hammerman. Weekly.

INDEX TO JEWISH PERIODICALS (1963). P.O. Box 18570, Cleveland Hts., 44118. (216)321-7296. Jean H. Foxman, Miriam Leikind, Bess Rosenfeld. Semiannually.

OHIO JEWISH CHRONICLE (1921). 2831 E. Main St., Columbus, 43209. (614)237-4296. Milton J. Pinsky. Weekly.

STARK JEWISH NEWS (1920). P.O. Box 9112, Canton, 44711. (216)494-7792. Elaine M. Garfinkle. Five times a year.

STUDIES IN BIBLIOGRAPHY AND BOOKLORE (1953). 3101 Clifton Ave., Cincinnati, 45220. (513)221-1875. Herbert C. Zafren.

Irregular. English-Hebrew-German. Library of Hebrew Union College—Jewish Institute of Religion.

TOLEDO JEWISH NEWS (1951). 2506 Evergreen St., Toledo, 43606. Burt Silverman. Monthly. Jewish Welfare Federation.

YOUNGSTOWN JEWISH TIMES (1935). P.O. Box 777, Youngstown, 44501. (216)746-6192. Harry Alter. Fortnightly.

OKLAHOMA

SOUTHWEST JEWISH CHRONICLE (1929). 324 N. Robinson St., Suite 313, Oklahoma City, 73102. (405)236-4226. E. F. Friedman. Quarterly.

TULSA JEWISH REVIEW (1930). 2205 E. 51 St., Tulsa, 74105. (918)749-7751. Dianna Aaronson. Monthly. Tulsa Section, National Council of Jewish Women.

PENNSYLVANIA

JEWISH CHRONICLE (1962). 315 S. Bellefield Ave., Pittsburgh, 15213. (412)687-1000. Albert W. Bloom. Weekly. Pittsburgh Jewish Publication and Education Foundation.

JEWISH EXPONENT (1887). 226 S. 16 St., Philadelphia, 19102. (215)893-5740. Marc S. Klein. Weekly. Federation of Jewish Agencies of Greater Philadelphia.

JEWISH QUARTERLY REVIEW (1910). Broad and York Sts., Philadelphia, 19132. (215)-229-0110. Abraham I. Katsh. Quarterly. Dropsie University.

JEWISH TIMES OF THE GREATER NORTHEAST (1925). 2417 Welsh Road, Philadelphia, 19114. (215)464-3900. Leon E. Brown. Weekly. Federation of Jewish Agencies of Greater Philadelphia.

RHODE ISLAND

RHODE ISLAND JEWISH HISTORICAL NOTES (1954). 130 Sessions St., Providence, 02906. Albert Salzberg. Annual. Rhode Island Jewish Historical Assn.

TENNESSEE

HEBREW WATCHMAN (1925). 277 Jefferson Ave., Memphis, 38103. (901)526-2215. Herman I. Goldberger. Weekly.

TEXAS

JEWISH CIVIC PRESS (1971). P.O. Box 35656, Houston, 77035. (713)721-8901. Abner L. Tritt. Monthly.

JEWISH HERALD-VOICE (1908). P.O. Box 153, Houston, 77001. (713)661-3116. Joseph W. and Jeanne F. Samuels. Weekly.

TEXAS JEWISH POST (1947). P.O. Box 742, Fort Worth, 76101. (817)927-2831. 11333 N. Central Expressway, Dallas, 75243. (214)692-7283. Jimmy Wisch. Weekly.

VIRGINIA

UJF NEWS (1959). 7300 Newport Ave., Norfolk, 23505. (804)489-8040. Reba Karp. Weekly. United Jewish Federation of Tidewater.

WASHINGTON

JEWISH TRANSCRIPT (1924). Securities Building, Rm. 929, Seattle, 98101. (206)-624-0136. Philip R. Scheier. Bimonthly. Jewish Federation of Greater Seattle.

WISCONSIN

WISCONSIN JEWISH CHRONICLE (1921). 1360 N. Prospect Ave., Milwaukee, 53202. (414)271-2992. Lawrence Hankin. Weekly. Wisc. Jewish Publications Foundation.

NEWS SYNDICATES

JEWISH PRESS FEATURES (1970). 15 E. 26 St., Suite 1350, N.Y.C., 10010. (212)679-1411. Neil Barsky. Monthly. Jewish Student Press Service.

JEWISH TELEGRAPHIC AGENCY, INC. (1917). 165 W. 46 St., Rm. 511, N.Y.C., 10036. (212)575-9370. Murray Zuckoff. Daily.

SEVEN ARTS FEATURE SYNDICATE AND WORLD WIDE NEWS SERVICE (1923). 165 W. 46 St., Rm. 511, N.Y.C., 10036. (212)-247-3595. John Kayston. Semiweekly.

CANADA

BULLETIN DU CERCLE JUIF DE LANGUE FRANÇAISE DU CONGRES JUIF CANADIEN (1952). 1590 Avenue Docteur Penfield, Montreal, P.Q., H3G 1C5. (514)931-7531. M. Mayer Lévy. Quarterly. French. Canadian Jewish Congress.

CANADIAN JEWISH HERALD (1977). 17 Anselme Lavigne Blvd., Dollard des Ormeaux, P.Q., H9A 1N3. (514)684-7667. Dan Nimrod. Irregular.

CANADIAN JEWISH NEWS (1960). 562 Eglinton Ave. E., Suite 401, Toronto, Ont., M4P 1P1. (416)481-6434. Maurice Lucow. Weekly.

CANADIAN JEWISH OUTLOOK (1963). 2414 Main St., #4, Vancouver, B.C., V5T 3E3. (604)874-1323. Editorial Board. Monthly.

CANADIAN ZIONIST (1934). 1310 Greene Ave., Montreal, P.Q., H3Z 2B2. (514)934-0804. Dr. Leon Kronitz. Bimonthly (except July-Aug.). Canadian Zionist Federation.

JEWISH POST (1925). P.O. Box 3777, St. B, Winnipeg, Man., R2W 3R6. (204)633-5575. Matt Bellan. Weekly.

JEWISH STANDARD (1929). 67 Mowat Ave., Suite 319, Toronto, Ont., M6K 3E3. (416)-363-3289. Julius Hayman. Semimonthly.

JEWISH WESTERN BULLETIN (1930). 3268 Heather St., Vancouver, B.C., V5Z 3K5. (604)879-6575. Samuel Kaplan. Weekly.

JOURNAL OF PSYCHOLOGY AND JUDAISM (1976). 1747 Featherston Drive, Ottawa, Ont., K1H 6P4. (613)731-9119. Reuven P. Bulka. Semiannual. Center for the Study of Psychology and Judaism.

KANADER ADLER–JEWISH EAGLE (1907); 4180 De Courtrai, Suite 218, Montreal, P.Q., H3S 1C3. (514)735-6577. Mordechai Husid. Weekly. Yiddish. Combined Jewish Organizations of Montreal.

OTTAWA JEWISH BULLETIN & REVIEW (1936). 151 Chapel St., Ottawa, Ont., K1N 7Y2. 232-7306. Cynthia Engel. Biweekly. Jewish Community Council of Ottawa.

UNDZER VEG (1932). 272 Codsell Ave., Downsview, Ont., M3H 3X2. 636-4021. Joseph Kligman, Y. Tyberg. Quarterly. Yiddish-English. Achdut HaAvoda-Poale Zion of Canada.

WESTERN JEWISH NEWS (1926). P.O. Box 87, 400-259 Portage Ave., Winnipeg, Man., R3C 2G6. 942-6361. Pauline Essers. Weekly.

WINDSOR JEWISH COMMUNITY COUNCIL BULLETIN (1938). 1641 Ouellette Ave., Windsor, Ont., N8X 1K9. (519)254-7558. Joseph Eisenberg. Irregular. Windsor Jewish Community Council.

Necrology: United States[1]

ALT, HERSCHEL, psychologist, communal worker; b. (?), Ukraine, (?), 1897; d. N.Y.C., Nov. 16, 1981; in U.S. since 1923; staff mem., Toronto Fed. of Jewish Philanthropies, 1917–23; child welfare and mental health worker, Los Angeles and St. Louis, 1923–41; exec. v. pres., exec. dir., Jewish Bd. of Guardians, 1943–65; adviser, child welfare, Israeli govt.; consultant, mental health: UN World Health Org.; Welfare Adv. Group to the U.S. Com. for Unicef; Citizens Com. for Children of N.Y.; N.Y.C. Community Mental Health Bd.; chmn. adv. bd., U.S. Com., UN Internatl. Children's Emergency Fund; dir., Inst. for Research and Training in Child Mental Health, 1965–(?); mem., N.Y.C. Commission for the Foster Care of Children; faculty mem.: U. of Ca.; U. of Louisville; St. Louis U.; Wash. U., St. Louis; N.Y. School of Social Work, Columbia U.; author: *Forging Tools for Mental Health; Residential Treatment for the Disturbed Child; Russia's Children; The New Soviet Man.*

ALTCHEK, SOLOMON D., businessman, communal worker; b. Salonika, Greece, (?), 1904; d. N.Y.C., Sept. 19, 1981; in U.S. since 1914; volunteer mem., chmn., Selective Service Bd., Lower East Side, for 20 years since WWII; founder, pres., Albert Martin Assoc., Inc. printing co.; founding mem. bd. dirs., pres., Sephardic Jewish Center of Forest Hills, over 40 years; founding mem. bd. dirs., benefactor, Sephardic Home for the Aged; pres., Central Sephardic Jewish Community.

BICKERMAN, ELIAS J., historian; b. Kishiner, Russia, July 1, 1897; d. Tel Aviv, Israel, Aug. 31, 1981; teacher: U. Berlin, 1929–33; École Pratique des Hautes Études, 1933–40; Centre National de Recherche Scientifique, 1937–42; prof.: New School for Social Research, 1942–46; École Libre, 1942–46; special research fellow, Jewish Theological Seminary, 1946–50; visiting prof.: Columbia U., 1948–49; U. of Judaism, Los Angeles, 1950–52; U. of Ca. at Los Angeles, 1957; prof., ancient history: Columbia U., 1952–67; Inst. for Advanced Study, Princeton, 1967–68; Jewish Theological Seminary, 1968–81; author: *Der Gott der Makabaer* (1937); *Institutions des Seleucides* (1938); *The Maccabees* (1947); *From Ezra to the Last of the Maccabees* (1962); *Chronology of the Ancient World* (1967); *Four Strange Books of the Bible* (1967); *Studies in Jewish and Christian History, Vol. I* (1976); numerous articles in scholarly journals, on ancient and Jewish history; co-author, *The Latin History of Western Civilization* (1976); co-editor, *Revue Internationale des droits de l'Antiquité;* recipient: R. Kreglinger Triennial award, U. of Brussels, 1935; Lucas prize, U. of Tuebingen, 1976; fellow: Assoc. Études grecques, 1938; Guggenheim, 1949, 1959; Rockefeller Soc.; Amer. Acad. of Jewish Research; Brit. Acad.; Amer. Acad. of Arts and Sciences.

---

[1]Including Jewish residents of the United States who died between January 1 and December 31, 1981.

CELLER, EMANUEL, congressman, attorney; b. Brooklyn, N.Y., May 6, 1888; d. Brooklyn, N.Y., Jan. 15, 1981; congressman (Dem.), House of Representatives, 1922–72; chmn., House Judiciary Com., 1949–72; attorney, Wiesman, Celler, Spett, Modlin & Wertheimer firm, throughout life; wrote and sponsored passage of Civil Rights Act, 1957, and amendments in 1960, 1964, 1965, 1968, and 1970; mem. bd. dirs., Brookdale Hosp. Med. Center, Brooklyn, 1947–81; trustee, Oscar Strauss Memorial Fund; chmn., American Mogen Dovid for Israel, 30 years; mem.: Amer. Jewish Congress; Amer. Jewish Com.; B'nai B'rith; guest of honor, annual tribute ball, Brookdale Hosp. Med. Center, 1972.

CHAYEFSKY, PADDY (Sidney), writer; b. Bronx, N.Y., Jan. 29, 1923; d. N.Y.C., Aug. 1, 1981; serviceman, 104th Infantry Div., Germany, WWII; writer for television, stage, and film: *Middle of the Night; The Mother; Holiday Song; The Big Deal; The Americanization of Emily; Marty* (1953); *The Catered Affair* (1956); *The Bachelor Party* (1957); *The Goddess* (1958); *The Tenth Man* (1959); *Gideon* (1961); *The Passion of Joseph D.; The Latent Heterosexual; Hospital* (1971); *Network* (1976); *Altered States* (1979); council mem.: Writers Guild of Amer., East; Dramatists Guild, Inc.; mem., ASCAP; colleague, supporter, Writers and Artists for Peace in the Middle East; mem., contributor, Amer. ORT Fed.; supporter: Fed. of Jewish Philanthropies; ADL of B'nai B'rith; recipient, Motion Picture Acad. Awards (Oscars): *Marty* (1955); *Hospital* (1971); *Network* (1976).

DIXON, ARTHUR J., accountant, communal worker; b. (?), (?), 1924; d. Long Island, N.Y., Nov. 1, 1981; former pres., N.Y.S. Soc. of Certified Public Accountants; dir., former chmn., Law Alumni Assoc. of N.Y.U.; bd. mem., treas., mem. adv. com., Jewish Guild for the Blind; Fed. of Jewish Philanthropies: former v. pres.; chmn., distrib. com.; mem. exec. com.; mem. grants com.; mem., Fund for Jewish Ed. com.

EDELMAN, LILY P., editor, communal worker; b. San Francisco, Ca., Sept. 2, 1915; d. N.Y.C., Jan. 22, 1981; ed. dir., East and West Assn., 1941–50; editor, writer, State Dept. overseas info. program, 1951–53; exec. sec., Natl. Acad. for Adult Jewish Studies, United Synagogue of Amer., 1954–57; B'nai B'rith: dir., adult Jewish ed. dept., 1961–77; Natl. Program dir., since 1961; dir., lecture bureau, since 1977; editor: *ADL Bulletin* (monthly); *Face to Face* (an ADL quarterly); book editor, *B'nai B'rith Natl. Jewish Monthly;* co-editor, B'nai B'rith *Jewish Heritage Classics* series, 1961–73; translator (for Elie Wiesel): *Beggar from Jerusalem; One Generation After;* mem.: Phi Beta Kappa; Adult Ed. Assn., U.S.A.; Natl. Council of Jewish Audio-Visual Aids; bd. mem., Md. Assn. of Adult Ed.; author: *Japan in Story and Pictures* (1953); *Hawaii, U.S.A.* (1954); *The Sukkah and the Big Wind* (1956); *Israel: New People in an Old Land* (1958); manuals and journal articles on adult ed.

EFROS, ISRAEL I., professor; b. Ostrog, Volyn, Poland (Ukraine), May 28, 1891; d. Tel Aviv, Israel, Jan. 4, 1981; in U.S. since 1905; founder, dean, Baltimore Hebrew Coll. and Teachers Training School, 1918–28; prof., Hebrew and Jewish philosophy: Johns Hopkins U., 1916–28(?); U. of Buffalo, 1929–41; Jewish Theological Seminary of Amer., 1937–39; Hunter Coll., 1941–55; Dropsie U., 1941–75; Tel Aviv U.: first rector, 1955–59; prof., 1955–62; hon. pres., since 1959; past pres., Histadruth Ivrith of Amer.; co-editor, a Hebrew-English dictionary; translator (into Hebrew): Shakespeare's *Hamlet* (1942); Bialik's *Poetry* (1948); *Timon of Athens* (1953); *Coriolanus* (1959); author: *The Problem of Space in Jewish Medieval Philosophy* (1917); *The Bloody Jest* (1922); *Philosophical Terms in Moreh Nevuhim* (1924); *Shirim* (1932); *Maimonides' Treatise on Logic* (1938); *Ancient and Modern Jewish Philosophy,* two volumes (1965); four volumes of Hebrew verse (1966); *Studies in Medieval Jewish Philosophy* (1974); *Silent Wigwams;* several other scholarly and literary works in Hebrew; recipient: hon. DHL, Jewish Theological Seminary of Amer., 1937; Lamed poetry awards, 1942, 1954; Tchernichovsky award, 1961; JBCA award, 1965; Bialik award, 1966.

ELIASH, JOSEPH, professor; b. Jerusalem, Palestine, Oct. 25, 1932; d. Oberlin, Ohio, April (?), 1981; in U.S. since 1960's (?); asst. prof., U. of Ca. at Los Angeles, 1967–70; assoc. prof., dir. of Judaic and Near Eastern Studies, Oberlin Coll., since 1971; U.S. govt. consultant on Shi'i Islamic Law, during final Iran hostage negotiations;

editor and translator, portions of the Shi'i Muslim Corpus of Oral Tradition; recipient, numerous grants for research on Muslim law.

ENDZWEIG, SADIE, educator, communal worker; b. N.Y.C., Jan. 29, 1895; d. Brooklyn, N.Y., Aug. 2, 1981; teacher, 63 years (specializing in remedial reading): N.Y.C. public school system; Yeshiva of Flatbush; reading coordinator, instructor of teachers' in-service courses, N.Y.C. Bd. of Ed.; former principal, Shulamith School for Girls; past v. pres., Jewish Teachers Assn. of N.Y.; past pres., Brooklyn Business and Professional Chapter, Mizrachi Women's Org. of Amer.; mem., Young Israel of Flatbush; involved in philanthropic work; honored as an outstanding elementary school teacher of Amer., 1974.

EPSTEIN, BEINESH, writer, communal worker; b. (?) Lithuania, (?) 1896; d. N.Y.C., March 26, 1981; in U.S. since 1926; organizer, yeshiva student Zionist activities, Lithuania; publisher, Berlin, 1920's; teacher; journalist, Yiddish-language newspapers; writer, speaker for Zionist cause, throughout life; broadcaster, political commentary program, Radio Station WEVD; political analyst, Amer. foreign policy and internatl. affairs; head, Jewish Desk of the Republican party, during pres. campaigns, 1940's, 1950's; senior consultant, public affairs dept., Zionist Org. of Amer.; life mem. Actions Com., World Zionist Org.; mem., World Exec. body, Herut-Zionist Revisionists of Amer.; mem., former Amer. Zionist Council; recipient: Brandeis award, Zionist Org. of Amer., 1980; Jabotinsky centennial medal, presented by Prime Minister Begin, 1980.

FACHER, SEYMOUR, administrator; b. (?), (?) 1920; d. N.Y.C., Aug. 12, 1981; serviceman, U.S. Army, WWII; fund-raiser, campaign dir., dir. of development: Jewish Community Council of Metropolitan N.J.; Albert Einstein Coll. of Med.; Synagogue Council of Amer.; natl. campaign dir., ADL of B'nai B'rith, 1969–73; v. pres. of development and univ. relations, Brandeis U., 1974–80; dir., funding and building of new library, Jewish Theological Seminary of Amer., since 1980.

FREILICOFF, MORRIS, writer; b. Chernigov, Ukraine, (?), 1886; d. Wash., D.C., March 27, 1981; in U.S. since 1902; a founder, U.S. Labor Zionism movement; lecturer,

Yiddish literature; writer, *Day-Morning Journal,* 1925–63; active in: Jewish Cong.; war relief efforts for European Jews, WWI; author, essays and poetry in numerous Yiddish periodicals.

GNESHIN, JESSIE COHEN, communal leader; b. N.Y.C., May 28, 1898; d. N.Y.C., Oct. 20, 1981; yeoman, first class, U.S. Navy, WWI; mem. adv. bd., Veterans Admn.; pres., various U.S. pres. coms.; active in various state and municipal coms.; noted public speaker, 1936–69; Natl. Ladies Auxiliary of the Jewish War Veterans: mem., since 1932; Kings County pres.; N.Y.S. pres.; natl. pres., 1944; exec. dir., 1945–66; recipient: Freedom Found. medal, 1948; WWI veterans award, U.S. Navy; U.S. Veterans Admn. commendations; commendations from U.S. pres., from Roosevelt to Nixon; State of Israel commendations, from Pres. Weizman, Prime Minister Ben-Gurion, and others.

GOLDBERG, HANNAH L., communal worker; b. Boston, Mass., (?), 1902; d. Boston, Mass., March 26, 1981; attorney, Boston; writer, book reviewer, American-Jewish and general periodicals; mem. bd. dirs., exec. sec., Jewish Reconstructionist Found.; leader, Junior Hadassah; Senior Hadassah, Women's Zionist Org. of Amer.: v. pres., New England Region; mem. natl. bd., 1942–75; natl. exec. dir., 1953–71; asst. to pres., 1971–75; mem. editorial bd.: *The Reconstructionist* magazine; *Hadassah* magazine; delegate, World Zionist Congress, many years.

GOLDEN, HARRY L., author, publisher; b. Austria-Hungary, May 6, 1902; d. Charlotte, N.C., Oct. 2, 1981; in U.S. since childhood; reporter: N.Y. *Post,* 1932–36; N.Y. *Daily Mirror,* 1936–38; *Charlotte Observer,* 1939–40; *Hendersonville Times-News,* 1940–41; founder, editor, *Carolina Israelite,* 1941–68; mem.: bd. dirs., NAACP; N.C. Ed. Writers Assn.; Catholic Inter-Racial Soc.; Shakespeare Assn.; ADL of B'nai B'rith; Brith Abraham-Bnai Zion; Amer. Jewish Cong.; Temple Israel; author: *Only in America* (1958); *For 2 Cents Plain* (1959); *Enjoy, Enjoy* (1960); *Carl Sandburg* (1961); *You're Entitled* (1962); *Forgotten Pioneer* (1963); *Mr. Kennedy and the Negroes* (1964); *A Little Girl is Dead* (1965); *The Best of Harry Golden* (1967); *The Right Time* (autobiography, 1969); *So What Else is New?; The Spirit of the Ghetto; Ess, Ess, Mein Kind*

(Eat, Eat, My Child); *So Long as You're Healthy; The Israelis; Golden Book of Jewish Humor; The Greatest Jewish City in the World; Travels Through Jewish America; Our Southern Landsman; Long Live Columbus; America I Love You!;* co-author: *Jews in American History* (1950); *Five Boyhoods* (1962); recipient: man of the year award, Johnson C. Smith U., 1961; man of the year award, Temple Beth El, N.Y.C., 1962; literature award, N.C. Awards Commission, 1979; award, presented by Gov. Hunt and his Commission of Cultural Resources, 1979; honorary degrees: U. of N.C. at Charlotte; Theil Coll., Pa.; Belmont Abbey Coll., U. of N.C.

GOLDSTEIN, NATHANIEL L., attorney, communal leader; b. N.Y.C., (?), 1897; d. N.Y.C., March 24, 1981; infantry private, WWI; investigative aide, state legislative coms., N.Y.C.; accountant, since 1915; lawyer, since 1918; special counsel, Finley, Kumble, Wagner, Heine, Underberg & Casey law firm; N.Y.S. attorney gen., 1943–54 (three terms): led fight for Supreme Court revocation of a N.Y.S. Ku Klux Klan charter, 1946; reported on Ku Klux Klan and pro-Nazi German-American Bund links, for the FBI; prepared rent-control laws; led narcotics abuse investigations; alumnus, former bd. mem., N.Y. Law School; colleague: Brandeis U.; Pace Coll.; hon. alumnus, supporter, Benjamin N. Cardozo School of Law, Yeshiva U.; trustee, Fletcher School of Law and Diplomacy; legal counsel, officer, Wilkie Memorial of Freedom House, 35 years; colleague, counsel, The Lefrak Org.; founder, first chmn. bd. of overseers, chmn. emeritus of the bd., Albert Einstein Coll. of Med., Yeshiva U., since 1954; a leader, Israel Bond Org.; supporter, patron, Amer. Friends of Israel Museum; pres. emeritus, Amer. Friends of Hebrew U.; deputy chmn., Internatl. Bd. of Govs., Hebrew U.; chmn., bd. of overseers, Harry S. Truman Research Inst. for the Advancement of Peace, Hebrew U.; mem. bd. dirs., UJA of Greater N.Y.; helped establish child care agency, Fed. of Jewish Philanthropies; supporter, Chai founder, Amer. Friends of Boys Town Jerusalem; active in: Brooklyn Hebrew Orphan Asylum; Natl. Conf. of Christians and Jews; mem., Park Ave. Synagogue; recipient: hon. LLD, Brandeis U.; hon. PhD, Hebrew U.; 20th Anniversary Medallion, Albert Einstein Coll. of Med., Yeshiva U.; established in his honor:

Nathaniel L. Goldstein Chair in Forensic Medicine, A. Einstein Coll. of Med., Yeshiva U.; Nathaniel L. Goldstein Annual Lecture Series, Cardozo Law School, Yeshiva U.

GREENDALE, ALEXANDER, communal worker; b. Chicago, Ill., May 25, 1910; d. N.Y.C., Aug. 22, 1981; adjunct prof., social work, Adelphi U., 1960's; dir., Housing Div., Amer. Jewish Com., 1970–77; chmn., Inter-Religious Coalition of Housing, 1973; exec. dir., West Side Jewish Community Council, since 1977; playwright: more than 70 plays, including *Walk Into My Parlor* (1941), on Broadway; author, editor: *The Kipling Sampler* (1945); *Guidelines to Scatter Site Housing* (1971); *Life in Public Housing Equals Tenants Plus Management* (1971); *Are New Towns for Lower Income Americans, Too?* (1974); recipient: Rockefeller fellowship for playwriting, the Dramatists Guild, 1939; Theater Guild fellowship, 1940; Guggenheim fellowship, 1942; Amer. Acad. of Arts and Letters award, 1945.

GROSS, MURRAY S., labor leader; b. (?), Austria, May 17, 1907; d. N.Y.C., July 11, 1981; in U.S. since 1923; serviceman, U.S. Army, 1943–45; ILGWU: joined, 1926; mgr., complaint dept., Jt. Bd. of Dress & Waistmakers' Union, 1933–43; asst. gen. mgr., 1945–55; mgr., Local 66 Bonnaz Embroiderers' Union, 1955–69; internatl. v. pres., 1965–77; assoc. gen. mgr., Jt. Bd. of Dress & Waistmakers' Union, 1969–72; gen. mgr., since 1972; gen. mgr., Dressmaker Jt. Council, since 1972; natl. sec., Union for Democratic Action, 1941–43; v. pres., Workers Defense League, since 1945; natl. bd. mem., League for Industrial Democracy; mem., Human Rights Commission of N.Y.C., 1962–78; mem., natl. chmn., Amer. Veterans Com., 1962–64 (three terms); officer, governing bodies, Amer. ORT Fed., World ORT Union, and Labor ORT, over 30 years; founder, Lower Manhattan Men's ORT; mem., v. pres., United HIAS Service, since 1965; chmn., HIAS Trade Union Council of Orgs., since 1965; mem. bd. dirs., *Jewish Daily Forward,* since 1968; resident, founding dir., East River Housing Corp. project, ILGWU; chmn., Trade Union Council of the Bund Archives, Jewish Labor Mvmt.; mem. natl. com., Social Democrats U.S.A.; mem. bd. govs., Natl. Conf. on Soviet Jewry; active in: Natl. Com. for Labor

Israel; Amer. Trade Union Council for Histadrut.

HAGER, JOSEPH, rabbi; b. Radaviti, Rumania, Dec. 15, 1900; d. N.Y.C., May 4, 1981; in U.S. since 1913; founder, first rabbi, senior rabbi, Wall Street Synagogue, since 1929; founder: Hebrew Inst. of L.I. (Hi-Li); Yeshiva Day School of Spring Valley; founding publisher, editor, *Synagogue Light* monthly magazine, 1933-80; founder, past chmn. bd. dirs., Home of the Sages of Israel, N.Y.C., 1942-73; head, Kolel Radawitz (Inst. for Talmudic studies and research in Cabbala), Safed, Israel.

HALPERN, HARRY, rabbi; b. N.Y.C., Feb. 4, 1899; d. New Haven, Conn., June 10, 1981; rabbi, Jewish Communal Center of Flatbush, 1919-29; rabbi emeritus, East Midwood Jewish Center, Brooklyn, 1929-77; benefactor, teacher, Rabbi Harry Halpern Day School, East Midwood Jewish Center, 25 years; Yeshiva of Flatbush: a founder; benefactor; past chmn., bd. of ed.; past chmn., Eng. Dept, 1949; Jewish Theological Seminary of Amer.: past chmn., Rabbinic Cabinet; natl. co-chmn., planning com., since 1951; a founder, rabbinic counselor, pastoral counseling programs; visiting prof., homiletics; adjunct prof., pastoral psychiatry; past pres.: N.Y. Bd. of Rabbis; Rabbinical Assembly of Amer.; mem. bd. dirs.: Pride of Judea Mental Health Center; Rabbinic Cabinet of UJA of Greater N.Y.; a founder, life trustee, Commission on Synagogue Relations, Fed. of Jewish Philanthropies; trustee, Home for Blind, since 1975; past chmn.: Social Action Com., Conservative Judaism; Brooklyn Com., State of Israel Bonds Org., many years; Joint Commission on Social Action, United Synagogue of Amer., many years; senior mem. bd. dirs., Mt. Carmel Cemetery Assn.; colleague, Jewish Center of Kings Highway; advisor, Town League of Metropolitan Jewish Geriatric Center; pres.: Brooklyn Zionist region, Zionist Org. of Amer.; Midwood Lodge, B'nai B'rith; former bd. mem., Pride of Judea Children's Home; rabbi emeritus, founding mem., Kaddish Club; mem. exec. com.: Brooklyn Red Cross; Brooklyn Cancer Soc.; N.Y. Div., Natl. Conf. of Christians and Jews; former mem.: Kings County Adv. Council, N.Y.S. Commission Against Discrimination; N.Y.C. Commission on Human Rights, 1967-78; recipient: Colgate U. Medal,

1916; Lampert Homiletics Prize, Jewish Theological Seminary of Amer., 1930; Harry Halpern Fellowship in Talmud established in his honor, JTSA.

HIRSHHORN, JOSEPH H., businessman, philanthropist; b. Mitau, Latvia, Aug. 11, 1899; d. Wash., D.C., Aug. 31, 1981; in U.S. since 1907; office boy, stock chartist, *Magazine of Wall St.*, 1914-16; stockbroker: self-employed, with various partners, 1917-24; J.H. Hirshhorn Co., 1925-34; owner, dir.: Technical Mine Consultants, 1934-56; Internatl. Mine Services, 1954-81; bd. chmn., Callahan Mining Corp., 1954-81; hon. trustee, George Washington U., 1956-81; trustee: Archives of Amer. Art, N.Y., 1956-81; Aldrich Museum, Conn., 1966-73; Palm Springs Museum, Ca., 1968-77; donated entire art collection (valued at $50 million) to Wash., D.C., 1966; Hirshhorn Museum and Sculpture Garden, Wash., D.C.: founder, benefactor, 1974; trustee, 1977-81; regional dir., adv. council, Southeastern Center for Contemporary Art, N.C., 1976-81; recipient: Award of Merit, Lotus Club, N.Y., 1965; Annual Art Award, Arts Materials Trade Assn., 1967; James Smithson Award, Smithsonian Inst., 1973, 1977, 1979; Citation, Natl. Assn. of Schools of Art, 1975; Bicentennial Award, Amer. Jewish Cong., 1976; Horatio Alger Award, presented by Norman Vincent Peale, 1976; Gertrude Vanderbilt Whitney Award, Skohegan School of Painting and Sculpture, 1979; Award of Excellence, Friends of Moore Coll. of Art, 1980; Swan Award, Tenn. Botanical Gardens and Fine Arts Center, 1981; hon. DHL, Boston U., 1975; hon. DFA, Maryland Inst., Coll. of Art. 1975; hon. DFA, Wake Forest U., 1976; hon. LHD, Skidmore Coll., 1979; hon. DH, Pratt Inst., 1980.

HOFFMAN, ISIDOR B., rabbi, student counselor; b. Philadelphia, Pa., Aug. 4, 1898; d. Waterbury, Conn., Jan. 27, 1981; rabbi, Temple Beth El, Utica, N.Y., 1925-28; dir., Hillel Found., Cornell U., 1929-33; counselor to Jewish students, Columbia U., 1934-67; chmn., Social Justice Com., Rabbinical Assembly, 1939-40; mem. bd. dirs.: Religion and Labor Found., since 1939; Natl. Service Bd. for Religious Objectors; bd. chmn., Sane, since 1962; rep. bd. dirs., coordinator of Alternative Service, Synagogue Council of Amer., 1971-75; former exec. dir., hon. chmn., Jewish

Peace Fellowship, Nyack, N.Y.; active in coms. and internatl. relations insts., Amer. Friends Service Com.; recipient: hon. DHL, Columbia U., 1954; hon. DD, Jewish Theological Seminary of Amer., 1972.

HURWITZ, ABRAHAM B., educator, magician; b. (?), Lithuania, (?), 1905; d. Hollywood, Fla., Sept. 29, 1981; in U.S. since childhood; guidance counselor, Brooklyn Hebrew Orphanage, 1920's–(?); instructor, physical ed., City Coll. of N.Y., 1925–28; prof., physical ed., Yeshiva U., 1928–74; chmn., dept. of physical ed. & recreation, Yeshiva Coll., 1928–72; dir. of playgrounds, N.Y.C. Dept. of Parks, 1931–48; as official magician of N.Y.C., led traveling magic and puppet shows to parks, schools, and recreation centers in all five boroughs; instructor, magician and puppeteer skills; pres., Internatl. Guild of Prestidigitators; v. pres., Soc. of Amer. Magicians; mem., ed. com., Amer. Acad. of Television Arts & Sciences, 1958; dir., youth activities, Young Israel Synagogues of Parkchester and Crotona Park, Bronx, N.Y.; author, several books; co-author: *Games to Improve Your Child's English* (1970); *Barside Companion; Activity Games to Improve a Child's Mathematics; Games Children Play; Magic for Non-Magicians* (with daughter, Shari Lewis); recipient: every major citation in field of thaumaturgics, including the Star of Magic, Internatl. Brotherhood of Magicians; Supreme Knights Medal, Knights of Magic Internatl.

IUSHEWITZ, MORRIS, labor leader; b. (?), Ukraine, (?), 1902; d. N.Y.C., Sept. 18, 1981; in U.S. since 1903; serviceman, Canadian army, in France, Italy, and Palestine, WWI; worked for newspapers, Milwaukee, Chicago, 1920's; freelance reporter, cable editor, Jewish Telegraphic Agency, N.Y., 1930's; founding mem., Newspaper Guild; worked on union publications; union leader, several decades; research dir., N.Y.S. CIO Council, 1943; sec.-treas., N.Y.C. CIO Council, 1949; sec.-treas., Central Labor Council, N.Y.C. AFL-CIO; bd. mem., N.Y.C. Bd. of Ed., several years; trustee, State U. of N.Y.

JESSEL, GEORGE A., entertainer; b. N.Y.C., April 3, 1898; d. Los Angeles, Ca., May 24, 1981; vaudeville debut, Imperial Theater, N.Y., 1908; comedian, showman: in vaudeville tours, 1909–11; solo tours, 1911–23; Broadway star performer: *The Jazz Singer,* 1925; *The War Song,* 1928; *Sweet and Low,* 1930; *Joseph,* 1930; musical show producer: *Helen of Troy,* 1923; Little Old N.Y., 1939; *George Jessel's High Kickers,* 1941; several other shows; motion picture producer: *The Dolly Sisters,* 1944; *Nightmare Alley,* 1947; *I Wonder Who's Kissing Her Now,* 1948; *Dancing in the Dark,* 1950; *When My Baby Smiles at Me,* 1950; *Wait Till the Sun Shines Nellie,* 1951; *The I Don't Care Girl,* 1952; *Tonight We Sing,* 1952; *Meet Me After the Show;* a UJA film in Israel, 1953; film star, 1920's–50's: *Private Izzy Murphy,* 1926; *Yoshe Kolb;* television star: George Jessel Show, ABC-TV, 1953–(?); *Here Come the Stars;* playwright: *The War Song; High Kickers;* author: *So Help Me* (autobiography, 1942); *Elegy In Manhattan* (1961); song composer; helped raise millions of dollars for philanthropic causes, such as Israel Bonds Org. and City of Hope medical center; delivered hundreds of eulogies for famous personalities; recipient: 600 "thank-you" plaques; 200 City of Hope "torches"; Jean Hersholt Humanitarian Award, Acad. of Motion Picture Arts & Sciences, 1970; hon. mem., 188 synagogues; honored at numerous banquet dinners.

KAUFMAN, BENJAMIN, administrator; b. Buffalo, N.Y., March 10, 1894; d. Trenton, N.J., Feb. 5, 1981; first sergeant, U.S. Army, in France, WWI; Jewish War Veterans of the U.S.A.: natl. commander, 1941–43; natl. exec. dir., 1948–59; N.J. State commander, Disabled Amer. Veterans; natl. jr. v. commander, Legion of Valor; recipient: Congressional Medal of Honor, 1919; Croix de Guerre, France, WWI; eight other decorations for valor by allied govts.

LAPIDES, MAX, attorney, communal worker; b. Rochester, N.Y., (?), 1904; d. New Haven, Conn., Aug. 29, 1981; volunteer, U.S. army, WWII; exec. officer, counterintelligence div., U.S. strategic air force, Europe, WWII; staff mem.: N.Y.S. attorney general's office, under Gov. F.D. Roosevelt; Reconstruction Finance Corp., Wash., D.C.; U.S. Judge Advocate's office, Nuremberg Trials; served with: Jewish Agency for Israel (also in No. Africa and Geneva), 1948–68; United Israel Appeal; organizer, dir., Operation Magic Carpet, Aden, which brought 48,000 Yemenite Jews into Israel, Amer. Jewish Jt. Distrib. Com., 1949–52; conducted survey, Jewish conditions in Morocco, 1963; assisted in arrangements for bringing more Jews from Yemen to Israel, 1960's.

LAZRUS, OSCAR M., businessman, philanthropist; b. (?), Rumania, (?), 1888; d. N.Y.C., June 5, 1981; in U.S. since 1890; lawyer, Samuel Untermeyer law firm, N.Y., 1909–24; co-founder, pres., chmn., Benrus Watch Co., 1923–60; Natl. Conf. of Christians and Jews: past natl. sec.; sec. emeritus; established Paula K. Lazrus Library, 1955; donated $100,000 to establish Center for Interreligious Affairs, 1972; benefactor: Fed. of Jewish Philanthropies; UJA of N.Y.; active in fighting antisemitism and bigotry, and in promoting Amer. cultural ties with Israel; mem., Temple Emanu-El, N.Y.C.

LEVIN, MEYER, writer; b. Chicago, Ill., Oct. 8, 1905; d. Jerusalem, Israel, July 9, 1981; studied Hasidic lit., Paris, early 1920's; reporter, Chicago *Daily News,* 1922–28; correspondent, covered opening of Hebrew U., Jerusalem, 1925; worked on kibbutz near Haifa, 1928–29; writer, Jewish Telegraphic Agency, 1930–32; founder, head, experimental marionette theater, Chicago, early 1930's; assoc. editor, film critic, *Esquire* magazine, 1933–39; journalist, war correspondent: Overseas News Agency of JTA, 1944–46; Spanish Civil War (from Loyalist side); Arab riots in Palestine; staff mem., film work, Office of War Info., U.S. and England, WWII; served with Psych. Warfare Div., France, WWII; filmed *The Illegals,* a documentary on smuggling of Jews from Poland to Palestine, post-WWII; taught puppetry at New School, N.Y., 1950's(?); bd. mem., outspoken advocate for settlement of Falashas in Israel, Amer. Assn. for Ethiopian Jews; founding mem., Com. for Historical Truth; translator, Yiddish tales into English; author: *Reporter* (1929); *Frankie and Johnny* (1930); *Yehuda* (1931); *The Settlers; The Harvest; The Golden Mountain* (1932); *The New Bridge* (1933); *The Old Bunch* (1937); *Citizens* (1941); *My Father's House* (1945); *The Jewish Heritage* (nonfiction series, 1950); *The Search* (autobiography, 1950); *Diary of Anne Frank* (play, 1952); *Compulsion* (novel, 1956, play, 1959); *Eva* (1959); *The Fanatic* (1964); *The Stronghold* (1964); *Gore and Igor* (1968); *The Architect* (1981); recipient: first annual Joseph Handleman Prize in the Arts, Jewish Acad. of Arts and Sciences, 1980(?).

LEVINE, DOROTHY S., communal worker; b. N.Y.C., July 4, 1904; d. N.Y.C., Dec. 13, 1981; pres., Natl. Women's League of Bnai Zion, 1958–81; natl. v. pres., Bnai Zion, 1966–81; Jewish Natl. Fund chmn., Bnai Zion; natl. bd. mem., Amer. Zionist Fed., 1970–81; former bd. mem., Amer.-Israel Friendship League; mem. bd. dirs., Jewish Natl. Fund, 1975–81; pres., Dimona-Kadimah Chapter, Bnai Zion; a leader, Campaign Cabinet, Israel Bonds Org.; as rep. of World Confed. of United Zionists, attended World Zionist Cong. and WZO Actions Com. in Israel, numerous times since 1948; recipient, various awards from: Israel Bonds Org.; UJA; Jewish Natl. Fund; Bnai Zion Found.

LEVY, SOLOMON, rabbi; b. Tosh, Hungary, (?), 1894; d. Brooklyn, N.Y., Jan. 17, 1981; in U.S. since 1939; former Grand Rabbi, Hust, Czechoslovakia; founder, rabbi, cantor, conducted weekly lectures, Ohel Elimelech synagogue, Boro Park, Brooklyn, since 1939.

LIBOV, EDWARD, businessman, philanthropist; b. (?), (?), 1930; d. N.Y.C., Nov. 2, 1981; founder, pres., Ed Libov Assocs., N.Y.C., since 1964; leader in development of cooperative advertising; founding chmn. of bd., Amer. Friends of Boys Town in Jerusalem; mem., benefactor, Metropolitan N.Y. Coordinating Council on Jewish Poverty; a founder, the Mediterranean-Dead Sea Canal project; mem. bd. dirs., hon. chmn. of Toys and Allied Inds. Div., UJA-Fed. of Jewish Philanthropies Campaign; supporter, Brandeis U.; fund-raiser, chmn. of Golda Meir Leadership Award dinner, Israel Bond Org.; active in Youth Services of B'nai B'rith Found.; mem., Temple Emanu-El.

LINDER, HAROLD F., businessman, philanthropist; b. Brooklyn, N.Y., Sept. 13, 1900; d. N.Y.C., June 22, 1981; business positions, 1919–25; co-founder, Cornell, Linder & Co. finance mgmt. firm, 1925–33; partner, Carl M. Loeb, Rhoades & Co. banking firm, 1933–38; worked with Intergovt. Com. on Refugees, London, 1938–42; lieutenant cmdr., cmdr., U.S. Navy, WWII, in Europe; volunteer rep., v. chmn., Amer. Jewish Jt. Distrib. Com., London, 1945–48; adviser, Amer. delegation, Internatl. Refugee Org., London, 1945–48; involved in refugee aid programs, Europe and North Africa, 1945–48; pres., General Amer. Investment Co., Inc., 1948–55; deputy asst. sec., 1951; asst. sec.

of state for economic affairs, 1952–53; mem., Bd. of Natl. Estimates, CIA, 1955–56; pres., chmn. of bd., U.S. Export-Import Bank, Wash., D.C., 1961–68; ambassador to Canada, 1968–69; Inst. for Advanced Study, Princeton: trustee, since 1949; chmn. bd. of trustees, 1969–72; mem., Council on Foreign Relations; mem. finance com.: Smithsonian Inst.; Amer. Assn. for the Advancement of Science; consultant, Internatl. Finance Corp., World Bank Group, 1970–76; mem. adv. council, Faculty of Internatl. Affairs, Columbia U.; mem. Bd. of Overseers, Faculty of Arts and Sciences, U. of Pa.; council mem., School of Advanced Internatl. Studies, Johns Hopkins U.; mem.: John Jay Assocs. of Columbia Coll.; Cosmos Club, Wash., D.C.; White's Club, London; Benjamin Franklin fellow, Royal Soc. of Arts, London; active in: UJA-Fed. of Jewish Philanthropies; Jewish Guild for the Blind; Amer. Jewish Com.; mem., Temple Emanu-El; Harold F. Linder Professorship, School of Social Science, established in his honor, Inst. for Advanced Study; recipient, hon. LLD, U. of Pa., 1972.

LUBIN, EVELYN CRONSON, philanthropist; b. (?), (?), 1901; d. New Rochelle, N.Y., Sept. 30, 1981; teacher: Horace Mann School, 1925–26; School for Retarded Children, Pelham, N.Y., 1940's; volunteer worker, Einstein Coll. of Medicine, 1951–(?); chmn., Einstein Coll. Greater N.Y. Women's Div., 1960–(?); mem. Westchester Bd., Fed. of Jewish Philanthropies; mem. bd. trustees, Beth Abraham Home; benefactor: $1.3 million, Evelyn and Joseph I. Lubin Rehab. Center, Einstein Coll., Yeshiva U., 1966; Eisner & Lubin Auditorium, and medical center, N.Y.U.; Lubin Hall, Syracuse U.; Lubin House, Syracuse U. in N.Y.C.; Hebrew U., Jerusalem; $7.5 million, Lubin School of Business, and a Lubin graduate center, Pace U.; mem., past pres., Sisterhood, Park Ave. Synagogue; mem., Temple Israel of New Rochelle.

MARWICK, LAWRENCE, librarian, author; b. Sopockinie, Poland, Sept. 16, 1909; d. Bethesda, Md., Oct. 17, 1981; in U.S. since 1929; studied Arabic language and history, Egyptian Natl. U., Cairo, 1935–36; researched Semitic topics, in England, late 1930's; research asst., Dropsie Coll., 1937–40; special agent in charge, Counterintelligence Corp., U.S. army, 1941–45; asst. dir.,

Bd. of Jewish Ed., St. Louis, Mo., 1947–48; Library of Cong.: head, Hebraic section, since 1948; aided in acquisition of largest collection of its kind under govt. auspices; rep. to many internatl. meetings, including Internatl. Cong. of Orientalists, Turkey, 1951; hon. consultant in Hebraic bibliography; consultant to many internatl. ed. insts.; adjunct prof., Arabic and Islamic studies, Dropsie Coll., since 1954; adjunct prof., Hebraic and Arabic studies, N.Y.U., 1961–67; mem. bd. govs., Dropsie Coll., 1959–61; Amer. Friends of Hebrew U.: pres., Wash. chapter, 1951–55; mem., Acad. Council; chmn., natl. library com., 1958–63; pres.: Wash. Hebrew-Speaking Club; Chavruta, Wash., D.C., 1973–77; mem.: Amer. Acad. for Jewish Research; Amer. Oriental Soc. Assn. of Jewish Librarians; Neuman Prize Com. for Distinguished Hebrew Writing; author: *A Handbook of Diplomatic Hebrew* (1957); *Biblical and Judaic Acronyms* (1979); *Diplomatic Hebrew* (1980); *A Century of American Jewish Plays: A Bibliography* (1980); *Century of Yiddish Plays* (1981); *American Yiddish Folksongs* (bibliography, 1981); various articles on Judeo-Arabic commentaries and their authors; contributor, studies on the lives and Arabic writings of tenth-century Bible scholars; assoc. editor, *Jewish Book Annual,* since 1959; editor, *The Arabic Commentary of Salmon B. Yeruham on the Book of Psalms, Chaps. 42–72* (1956); co-editor, *Bloch Memorial Volume* (1960); recipient, Emma Lazarus fellowship, Dropsie Coll., 1930's; Library of Cong. Lawrence Marwick Memorial Gift, for commemorative planting, created in his honor.

MAYER, MORDECAI, rabbi; b. Chortkov, Poland, Jan. 28, 1915; d. N.Y.C., Jan. 26, 1981; in U.S. since 1936; rabbi, First American Roumanian Synagogue, N.Y.C., 20 years; conducted radio programs on Jewish topics, station WEVD, N.Y.C., 40 years; columnist, *Algemeiner Journal,* 1970's; author: *Israel's Wisdom in Modern Life* (1949); *Seeing Through Believing* (1973); other volumes in Hebrew and Yiddish; recipient, numerous honors and awards.

MEYEROWITZ, WILLIAM, artist, communal leader; b. Ekaterinoslav, Russia, July 15, 1895; d. N.Y.C., May 28, 1981; in U.S. since 1908; studied at Natl. Acad. of Design, 1912–16; painted scenes of Mass.,

Israel, and Jewish life on Lower East Side, N.Y.; perfected technique of color etching; art teacher, Metropolitan School of Self Expression, N.Y., 1933; produced film on etching, *The Magic Needle,* Fox Film Co.; etched portraits of several U.S. supreme court justices; draftsman; partner, architectural publ. co.; dir., summer art course, Mass., 1953; dir., Audubon Soc. of N.Y., 1950–54; past mem., Metropolitan Opera Chorus; paintings displayed in one-man shows, exhibitions, and permanent collections of numerous museums and ed. insts.: Metropolitan Museum of Art; Whitney Museum; Museum of Modern Art; Brooklyn Museum; Jewish Museum; Phillips Museum; Corcoran Gallery; Smithsonian Inst.; Library of Congress; Boston Museum of Fine Arts; Currier Art Gallery, Carnegie Inst.; Cone Collection, Baltimore Museum; Tel Aviv Art Museum; Bibliothèque Nationale, Paris; mem.: Natl. Acad. of Design; Artists Welfare Fund; N.Y. Artists Equity Assn.; Allied Artists of Amer.; Audubon Assn.; Rockport Art Assn.; Gloucester Art Assn.; Amer. Color Print Soc.; Amer. Soc. of Etchers; No. Shore Artists Assn.; Cape Ann Soc. of Modern Artists; Acad. of Political Science; B'nai Zion Found.; B'nai B'rith; past pres., Friends of Zion, #2, 1972–75; supporter, Jewish Natl. Fund; founding mem., Ohavei Zion; recipient: numerous awards and honors since 1914, including: Library of Cong. prize for etching, 1950; first prize for etching in color, Amer. Color Print Soc., 1950; Speyer prize for painting, 1965, and painting award, 1969, Natl. Acad. of Design; Grumbacher Purchase prize, 1966, Clair Layton prize for painting, Shore prize and citation, Audubon Soc. of Artists; Rotheburg award for painting, 1967; Vayana memorial prize, for musical theme, 1967; gold medal of honor, Rockport Art Assn., 1972, 1978; Salmagundi award, Allied Artists, 1979; Allied Artists of Amer. medal; gold medal, hon. mem., Italian Acad. of Art, Parma, 1980; first prize and medal for painting, first hon. mention, Prix de Rome.

OXENBURG, MINNIE, communal worker; b. (?), (?), 1887; d. Wash., D.C., Feb. (?), 1981; pres., auxiliary of the Hebrew Home of Greater Wash., 1927–30; bd. mem., Jewish Communal Center of Wash., since 1932; organizer, B'nai B'rith Women's Chapter, Wash., D.C.; past pres., Hadassah of Greater Wash.; past chmn., Hadassah's Constitution Com.; former mem.:

Natl. Council of Christians and Jews; Natl. Council of Jewish Women; mem. bd. of ed., Hebrew Acad. of Greater Wash.; choir mem., Congregation Adas Israel; hon. life mem., bd. dirs., Jewish Communal Center of Wash.; honored for Jewish community and library work, Hebrew Acad. of Greater Wash., 1968.

PICHENY, ELIAS, communal worker; b. Fostov, Ukraine, April 5, 1905; d. Berkeley, Ca., Aug. 23, 1981; in U.S. since 1913; social worker, exec. dir., Jacob Schiff Center, Bronx; mem. bd. dirs., Hebrew Teachers Union; mem. bd. dirs., Chicago chapter, and mem., Natl. Peace and Disarmament Com., Natl. Assn. of Social Workers; dir. research and community studies, community consultant, Natl. Jewish Welfare Bd., N.Y., 1942–67; field sec.; JWB midwest section, Chicago; organized JWB midwest teenage camp retreat inst.; consultant, studies dir., Social Ed. Research Dev., Inc., Wash., D.C., after 1967; co-founder, Social Workers for a Sane Nuclear Policy; contributor, articles in *JCC Program Aids, Jewish Currents,* and Amer. Library Assn. publications; editor, *The Right to be Different.*

PLOTKIN, BENJAMIN, rabbi; b. N.Y.C., (?), 1898; d. N.Y.C., May 9, 1981; founder, head rabbi, Congregation Emanu-El, Jersey City, N.J., more than 50 years; founder: (former) Amer. Jewish Alliance; Rabbinical Assn.; Jersey City chapter, Zionist Org. of Amer.; mem., Rabbinical Assembly.

POOL, TAMAR DE SOLA, communal leader; b. Jerusalem, Palestine, (?), 1890; d. N.Y.C., June 1, 1981; in U.S. since 1904; instructor, French, Latin, and Greek, Hunter Coll., 1914–17; pres., N.Y. chapter, Hadassah, 1929–35; organizer (with Henrietta Szold), Youth Aliya, to save Jewish children from the Holocaust, 1934; natl. pres., Hadassah, 1938–43; chmn., celebration of 100th anniversary of birth of Henrietta Szold, Hadassah, 1960; Hadassah chmn., Szold Inst.; author-in-residence, Ben-Gurion U. of the Negev, Beersheba, 1970's; dir., Natl. Council of Women of the U.S.; mem., gen. council, World Zionist Org.; past natl. pres., Amer. Mothers; trustee, Women's Div., Central Sephardic Jewish Community of Amer.; bd. mem.: Alliance Israélite Universelle Women's Div.; sisterhood of the Spanish and Portuguese Synagogue; Com. for Scholarship for Ed. in Israel;

Shearith Israel League; active in: UJA-Fed. Campaign; Sephardic Home for the Aged; Amer. Sephardi Fed.; Soc. of Jewish Science of N.Y. and Old Bethpage; Jewish Science Congregation of Agudat Shalva, Netanya, Israel; a founder, Fire Island Synagogue; benefactress: Yeshiva U.; Ben-Gurion U. of the Negev; editor, *Hadassah Newsletter*, ten years; author: *Israel and the United Nations: In the Spirit of '76* (a drama); *Triple Cord* (a novel); co-author (with husband, Rabbi David de Sola Pool): *An Old Faith in the New World: Portrait of Shearith Israel, 1654–1954; The Passover Haggadah: Is There an Answer? An Inquiry Into Some Dilemmas;* recipient, first internatl. fellowship to study at U. of Paris, 1913–14.

POSTAL, BERNARD, writer, communal worker; b. N.Y.C., Nov. 1, 1905; d. Freeport, N.Y., March 5, 1981; exchange editor, N.Y. *Times*, 1925–28; acct. exec., Guenther Law Adv. Agency, 1928; managing editor, *Grand Central Zone Tablet*, 1928–29; editor-in-chief, JTA *Daily Bulletin*, 1929–31; editor: Jersey City *Jewish Standard*, 1931–33; *Jewish War Veteran*, 1934–37; managing editor, *Seven Arts Features Syndicate*, 1933–38; natl. public relations dir.: B'nai B'rith, Wash., D.C., 1938–46; Natl. Jewish Welfare Bd., 1946–70; editor, *The Jewish Digest*, 1955–81; assoc. editor, *The Jewish Week*, 1970–81; founder, v. pres., Amer. Jewish Public Relations Soc.; founder, life mem., Amer. Jewish Press Assn.; founder, pres., Rockville Centre Jewish Community Council; former chmn. public relations: Assn. of Jewish Center Workers; Natl. Conf. of Jewish Communal Service; mem. exec. council, Jewish Book Council of Amer.; former mem. bd. trustees, chmn. religious ed. and adult ed. coms., Central Synagogue of Nassau County; v. pres.: Montgomery B'nai B'rith; Rocklyn Lodge B'nai B'rith; former mem.: B'nai B'rith Youth Com.; exec. council, Amer. Jewish Historical Soc.; mem.: B'nai B'rith Jewish Historical Com.; L. I. regional council of ADL; synagogue relations commission, Fed. of Jewish Philanthropies, N.Y.; co-author: *A Jewish Tourist's Guide to the U.S.* (1954); *Landmarks of a People* (1962); *Jewish Landmarks in New York* (1964); *Best of Ten Years of Jewish Digest* (1965); *Encyclopedia of Jews in Sports* (1965); *50 Year History of National Jewish Welfare Board* (1966); *And the Hills Shouted for Joy: The*

Day Israel Was Born (1972); *Traveler's Guide to Jewish Landmarks of Europe* (1973); *Jewish Tourist's Guide to Caribbean* (1974); *American Jewish Landmarks, Vol. 1* (1977); *Jewish Landmarks of New York* (1978); *Guess Who's Jewish in American History* (1978); *American Jewish Landmarks, Vol. 2* (1979); *Jewish Tourist's Guide to Mexico* (1980); *American Jewish Landmarks, Vol. 3* (1981); recipient: Amer. Jewish Tercentenary Award, for contrib. to Amer. Jewish history, Jewish Book Council of Amer., 1954; citation for contrib. to Amer. Jewish history, Amer. Jewish Historical Soc., 1973; citation, for Jewish historian and journalist career, Amer. Jewish Press Assn., 1979; Smolar Award, Council of Jewish Feds., 1979; Maggid of the Year Award, Amer. Jewish Public Relations Soc., 1980.

RAFEL, SOL, communal worker; b. N.Y.C., July 8, 1914; d. N.Y.C., April 20, 1981; Bronx House (Jewish community center): social worker, since 1939; exec. dir., since 1950; exec. dir., Bronx House Nursery School; mem. bd. dirs., Bronx House–Emanuel Camps, many years; past pres., Natl. Assn. of Jewish Center Workers, 1960–62; mem., exec. adv. council, Fed. of Jewish Philanthropies, 1976–81; bd. mem.: Pelham Parkway Mall Local Dev., 1976–81; Health System Agency–N.Y.C. Council F, 1976–81; chmn., UJA-Fed. Campaign, community service div., 1978–79; com. mem., Jewish Orientation Training Seminar; colleague: Altro Health and Rehabilitation Services, Inc.; Ruth Kirzon Group for Handicapped Children; recipient: Ruth Kirzon Group for Handicapped Children Humanitarian Award, 1967; Assn. for Help of Retarded Children, N.Y.C. Chapter Award, 1967; Naomi and Howard Lehman Award for Outstanding Professional Service in the Field of Child Care, 1976.

ROSENFELD, MAURICE, businessman, philanthropist; b. N.Y.C., Feb. 21, 1891; d. N.Y.C., June 25, 1981; Equitable Bag Co., Inc., N.Y.: founder, pres., bd. chmn., 1921–74; chmn. exec. com., since 1974; dir. recreational activities, N.Y.C. police dept., 1944–51; hon. deputy police commissioner, 1947–81; sponsor, N.Y.C. annual boxing tournaments for teenage boys, 1951–61; Youth Council Bureau of N.Y.C.: mem., 1947–52; v. pres., 1952–54;

pres., 1954–67; mem.: N.Y.S. Insurance Bd., 1948–54; Saratoga Springs Commission, since 1953; bd. dirs., Natl. Soc. for the Prevention of Juvenile Delinquency; bd. trustees, Natl. Council on Crime and Delinquency; trustee, Children's Center, N.Y.; Brooklyn Hebrew Orphan Asylum (Jewish Child Care Assn. of N.Y.): pres., 1942–49; hon. pres., 1949–60; dir., Brooklyn Jewish Hosp., many years until 1945; trustee, Long Island Coll. of Med., many years; special State Dept. rep. to Internatl. Film Festival, Scotland, 1954; Assay Commissioner, Annual Assay Commission, Mint, appointed by Pres. Eisenhower, 1959; mem., Natl. Adv. Council on the Ed. of Disadvantaged Children, appointed by Pres. Nixon, 1971–73; founder, Albert Einstein Coll. of Med., Yeshiva U.; hon. life trustee: UJA-Fed. of Jewish Philanthropies, since 1959; Jewish Child Care Assn. of N.Y., since 1960; Yeshiva of Crown Heights; Jewish Braille Inst. of Amer., since 1975; Union Temple of Brooklyn: mem., since 1940's; v. pres., 1945–50; hon. trustee, since 1950; mem., Westchester Jewish Center, Mamaroneck, N.Y.; benefactor, new room, Uris Bldg., Lenox Hill Hosp., 1976; recipient: first bronze plaque award of police coordinating councils, by N.Y.C. mayor for "outstanding service to youth," 1950; scroll in recognition of services to youth, N.Y.C. Parks Commissioner Robert Moses, 1961 (?); "Man of the Year, Benefactor of Youth" honor and plaque, Yeshiva of Crown Heights, 1960; honored with: plaque in playground, Temple Emanu-El, N.Y.C., 1964; Scroll of Honor, for philanthropic work, UJA, 1968; bronze plaque, A. Einstein Coll. of Med., 1969; scroll in recognition of services, Jewish Braille Inst. of Amer., 1975.

SALOMON, GEORGE, editor, communal worker; b. Hamburg, Germany, April 23, 1920; d. Great Neck, N.Y., May 8, 1981; in U.S. since 1937; senior editor, writer, translator, publications div., Amer. Jewish Com., 20 years; treas., AJC Staff Org., 1978–81; mem., Assn. of Jewish Community Relations Org. Workers; author: "Happy Ending—Nice and Tidy," *Kenyon Review,* 1962; "Journey to the Interior," *Present Tense,* 1974; co-author: "The Many Faces of Anti-Semitism," AJC; "The Ethnic Lobbying and American Tradition," AJC; editor: "Education and Attitude Change," AJC; "Jews in the Mind of America," AJC; numerous other papers

about prejudice; translator (expert at research and statistical data): *A Holocaust Reader* (1976); articles on Germany, *American Jewish Year Book,* many years; editor and/or translator: *People and Pianos* (1953); *How Catholics Look at Jews* (1974); *The Santa Claus Book* (1976); elected to Phi Beta Kappa, Swarthmore Coll., Phila., Pa.

SCHENK, FAYE LIBBY, communal leader; b. Des Moines, Iowa, Aug. 17, 1909; d. Jerusalem, Israel, Aug. 17, 1981; Hadassah: sec.; natl. treas.; past natl. v. pres.; natl. pres., 1968–72; founder, first pres., Wash. Heights group, N.Y. chapter; past pres., Brooklyn Parkway chapter; natl. chmn., Hadassah Medical Org.; pres.: Amer. Zionist Fed., 1974–78; Conf. of Natl. Jewish Orgs.; World Zionist Org., Jerusalem: mem., Actions Com.; chmn., Org. Dept., since 1977; mem. Exec., since 1978; mem. bd. govs.: Jewish Agency; Hebrew U., Jerusalem; mem. bd. dirs., Ampal —Amer. Israel Corp.; former mem. bd. dirs., United Israel Appeal; delegate, World Zionist Congs.; mem., hon. bd. of trustees, Amer. Friends of Hebrew U.; mem., bd. of overseers, The Jerusalem School, Hebrew Union Coll.–Jewish Inst. of Religion; colleague: Zionist Org. of Amer.; Americans for Progressive Israel; B'nai Zion; Amer. Jewish League for Israel; Emunah Women of Amer.; ARZA– Assn. of Reform Zionists of Amer.; Memorial Found. for Jewish Culture; Conf. on Jewish Material Claims Against Germany; recipient, hon. DHL, Hebrew Union Coll., 1974.

SHAPIRO, MANHEIM S., communal worker; b. Brooklyn, N.Y., Sept. 5, 1913; d. Wash., D.C., March 20, 1981; social worker: Benjamin Franklin High School, 1935–38; N.Y.C. Welfare Dept., 1938–43; U.S. army, 1943–46; dir.: programs and publications, B'nai B'rith Youth Orgs., 1946–49; Jewish communal affairs dept., Amer. Jewish Com., 1949–66; independent consultant, lecturer on Jewish sociology, for various Jewish organizations, since 1966; exec. dir., Bureau for Careers in Jewish Communal Service, 1968–69; adjunct prof., Jewish community studies, City Coll. of N.Y.; mem.: Natl. Conf. of Jewish Communal Service; Natl. Assn. of Jewish Center Workers; Assn. of Jewish Community Relations Workers; Amer. Sociological Assn.; Natl. Assn. of Social Workers;

Acad. of Certified Social Workers; Soc. of Professional Mgmt. Consultants; Adult Ed. Assn.; Internatl. Consultants Found.; Assn. of Intergroup Relations Officials; Council on Adult Ed., Amer. Assn. for Jewish Ed.; Soc. for Scientific Study of Religion; contributing editor, *National Jewish Digest*, since 1967; mem., editorial bd., *Reconstructionist;* contributor, articles in professional journals.

SHULTZ, LILLIE, journalist, communal worker; b. Phila., Pa., (?), 1904; d. N.Y.C., April 14, 1981; editor, English-language section, Phila. *Jewish World*, 1920's; reporter, cable editor, Jewish Telegraphic Agency, early 1930's; dir., Amer. Jewish Cong., 1933–44; organizer: boycott of goods from Nazi Germany, 1933–44; commission for investigation of economic discrimination against Jews, 1933–44; reporter for the UN, mem. editorial bd., *The Nation*, 1944–55; mem. bd. dirs., Nation Assocs., 1944–55; UN delegate and leading proponent of Palestine partition plan, Jewish Agency, 1940's–50's; founder, dir., Kenmore Assocs., public-relations firm whose main client was Israel, 1956–(?); dir. public-relations, Weizmann Inst. of Science in Israel, 1966–75; collaborated in preparation of Chaim Weizmann's memoirs, Amer. Friends of the Weizmann Inst. of Science.

STERN, CLARA, communal worker; b. Milwaukee, Wisc., (?), 1902; d. Bridgeport, Conn., Nov. 9, 1981; first exec. dir., Jewish Community Council of Greater Bridgeport, 1938–63; established: basis for intergroup relations dialogue in her region (encompassing Jewish, non-Jewish, civic, and labor orgs.); Conf. of Women's Orgs.; Council of Pres. of Greater Bridgeport; speaker on behalf of: Israel Bonds Org.; United Israel Appeal; active in: HIAS; Jewish Family Services Org.; YIVO Inst. for Jewish Research.

SWERDLIN, NATHAN, journalist, communal worker; b. Vilna, Poland, Dec. 7, 1907; d. Bronx, N.Y., June 9, 1981; in U.S. since 1933; writer, for Yiddish and Polish publications, Vilna, 1920's–30's; Yiddish journalist, N.Y., 1936–44; feature writer, drama editor, movie critic, *Jewish Day–Morning Journal*, 1945–71; part-time journalist, *Jewish Daily Forward*, 1971–(?); pres.: Film Critics Circle of the Foreign Language Press, N.Y., several terms, 1950's and 1960's; I.L. Peretz Yiddish

Writers' Union, many years; Jewish Writers' Assn., many years; delegate to Israel: as div. chmn., United Jewish Appeal, 1960; for Jewish Writers' Assn., 1961; recipient, award from Ben-Gurion, while delegate for UJA, 1960.

TAUSSIG, FRANCES, communal worker; b. Chicago, Ill., June 23, 1883; d. N.Y.C., Oct. 21, 1981; dir.: Jewish Social Service Bureau of Chicago, 1912–19; United Hebrew Soc., 1918; exec. dir., Jewish Family Service of N.Y., 1919–49; past pres.: Natl. Conf. of Jewish Welfare (Social Service), 1922–23; Amer. Assn. of Social Workers, 1930–32; Social Work Vocational Bureau; mem. bd. dirs.: Family Welfare Assn. of Amer.; Natl. Council of Jewish Women, after 1949; Jewish Bd. of Family and Children's Services (formerly the Jewish Family Service), after 1949; mem. bd. dirs., exec. com., Welfare Council of N.Y.C.; mem. bd. trustees, professional adv. bd., Training School for Jewish Social Work; bd. mem., officer, chmn. of casework com., N.Y. Assn. for New Americans.

TRUNK, ISAIAH, historian; b. Kutne, Poland, July 2, 1905; d. N.Y.C., March 28, 1981; in U.S. since 1954; instructor, history of Polish Jewry, Warsaw, 1927-1939; mem., historians' circle, YIVO, Warsaw, pre-WWII; assoc., Holocaust studies, Jewish Historical Commission in Warsaw, post-WWII; mem., Kibbutz Lochamei Hagetaot, 1950–52; dir., Peretz School, Calgary, Canada, 1953–54; YIVO Inst. for Jewish Research: research assoc., YIVO-Yad Vashem's documentary study of the Holocaust, 1954–70; chmn., research and planning commission; teacher; mem. bd. dirs.; chief archivist, since 1971; co-editor, *YIVO Bleter;* author: numerous articles and books in English, Yiddish, and Hebrew, on early life of Polish Jewish communities and on the Holocaust, including: "Ghetto Lodz," *News of YIVO*, 1962; *Judenrat: The Jewish Councils in Eastern Europe Under Nazi Occupation* (1972); *Jewish Responses to Nazi Persecution: Collective and Individual Behavior in Extremis* (1979); "YIVO and Jewish Historiography," *YIVO Bleter* (no. XLVI), 1981; numerous articles in other YIVO publications; recipient, National Book Award, for *Judenrat*, 1973.

WECHSLER, HARRY F., physician, communal worker; b. Jersey City, N.J., (?), 1899; d. N.Y.C., July 22, 1981; Lenox Hill Hosp.: intern, 1922–24; doctor, dept. of medicine, 1924–64; dir. of medicine, 1960–64; medical consultant, 1964–74; colonel, U.S. army medical corps, WWII; mem., Doctors Alumni Assn. of Lenox Hill Hosp.; former natl. v. pres., hon. v. pres., Zionist Org. of Amer.; delegate to Zionist Cong.; deputy mem., World Zionist Council; founder, past pres., hon. pres., Yorkville Zionist District, since 1929; supporter, fund-raiser, for student scholarships at Medical School, Hebrew U. of Jerusalem; pres., Class of 1919, Columbia Coll.; mem., John Jay Assocs. of Columbia Coll.; recipient: Alumni Medal, for work as internist, Columbia Coll.; the Columbia Lion, Columbia Coll.; Torch of Learning Award, for philanthropic work, 1981; Dr. Harry F. Wechsler Permanent Scholarship Fund established in his honor, Kfar Silver, Israel, Zionist Org. of Amer.

WEINSTOCK, GERARD, businessman, communal leader; b. N.Y.C., March 18, 1919; d. N.Y.C., Jan. 22, 1981; served in U.S. army, 1942–46; practiced law, N.Y.C., 1946–51; dir., exec. com., Merchants Bank of N.Y., 1949–(?); pres., Basic Foods baking manufacturers, 1951–73; past pres., mem., New Rochelle's Community Mental Health Clinic; trustee, treas., Windward School, White Plains, 1956–59; mem., Radio Free Europe delegation, Portugal, Germany, 1960; chmn., Amer. Field Service, New Rochelle, 1961–63; mem. bd. dirs.: Citizens for Public Ed., New Rochelle, 1961–65; Wildcliffe Childrens Museum, New Rochelle, 1963–65; trustee, Larchmont-Mamaroneck Center for Continuing Ed.; mem., Human Rights Commission, New Rochelle, 1963–65; v. pres., dir., Grossman Publishers, Inc., N.Y.C., 1964–68; lecturer on mergers and acquisitions, N.Y.U. School for Continuing Ed.; mem., admin. council, Jacob Blaustein Inst. for Advancement of Human Rights; mem., dir., Natl. Bakery Suppliers Assn., since 1970; pres., Guidance Center, New Rochelle, 1972–75; mem. adv. bd., Fed. Employment and Guidance Service, N.Y.C.; trustee, Amer. Schools for Oriental Research; mem., Amer. Soc. of Bakery Engineers; co-chmn., N.Y. area Harvard Campaign, Natl. Major Gifts Com.; Harvard U.: dir., Assn. Harvard Alumni; founder, chmn. Natl. Com., Harvard Center for Jewish Studies; mem., overseers com. on U. resources; mem., com. to visit Center for Middle Eastern Studies and Near Eastern Languages and Civilizations; mem., steering com., Friends of Harvard Judaica Collection, Widener Library; mem. bd. dirs., Children's Village, Dobbs Ferry, N.Y.; mem. publ. com., *Commentary* magazine; Amer. Jewish Com.: past natl. treas.; past co-chmn., com. on Middle East; pres., Westchester chapter; chmn., task force on the '80's; mem. bd. govs.; chmn. bd. of trustees; rep. at dedication of Knesset, Jerusalem, 1966; mem., leadership mission, Israel, 1967; mem., mission to Rumania, Yugoslavia, Austria, Germany, and England, where he attended Anglo-Jewish Assn. and Alliance Israélite Universelle meetings; trustee, Westchester County Jewish Community Services; mem., Natl. Jewish Welfare Bd.'s armed forces and veterans service com.

YABLOKOFF, HERMAN, actor; b. Grodno, Poland, (?), 1903; d. N.Y.C., April 3, 1981; in U.S. since 1924; actor in Yiddish theater, since age 12 in Poland; created and performed in Yiddish plays, Lower East Side, N.Y.C., 1930's and 1940's, including: *Der Payatz* (The Clown); *The King of Song; Goldela Dem Bakers; Mein Veise Blum; Der Dishwasher;* and *My Son and I,* in 1960; performed *Der Payatz* on N.Y. radio; European tours included performances at 94 Jewish refugee camps in Germany, Austria, and Italy, 1947; past pres.: United Hebrew Trades; Yiddish Theatrical Alliance; Hebrew Actors Union, N.Y., several terms, 1945–81; chmn., Yiddish Natl. Theater, N.Y.; author, *Around the World With Yiddish Theater* (two-volume memoirs); recipient: U.S. army Certificate of Merit, for performance tour to Jewish refugee camps; 1970 Zvi Kesel Prize for Yiddish literature.

ZUCKERMAN, ROSE, communal worker; b. Istanbul, Turkey, Nov. 15, 1888; d. Detroit, Mich., March 5, 1981; in U.S. since 1910; founder, pres., Jewish (European) Women's Economic Welfare Org., to aid immigrants, 1916; bd. mem., United Hebrew Schools; active in: Jewish Natl. Fund; United Jewish Appeal; Sinai Hosp. Guild; local Jewish and Zionist orgs.

Calendars

SUMMARY JEWISH CALENDAR, 5743–5747 (Sept. 1982-Sept. 1987)

HOLIDAY	5743 (1982)	5744 (1983)	5745 (1984)	5746 (1985)	5747 (1986)
Rosh Ha-shanah, 1st day	Sa Sept. 18	Th Sept. 8	Th Sept. 27	M Sept. 16	Sa Oct. 4
Rosh Ha-shanah, 2nd day	S Sept. 19	F Sept. 9	F Sept. 28	T Sept. 17	S Oct. 5
Fast of Gedaliah	M Sept. 20	S Sept. 11	S Sept. 30	W Sept. 18	M Oct. 6
Yom Kippur	M Sept. 27	Sa Sept. 17	Sa Oct. 6	W Sept. 25	M Oct. 13
Sukkot, 1st day	Sa Oct. 2	Th Sept. 22	Th Oct. 11	M Sept. 30	Sa Oct. 18
Sukkot, 2nd day	S Oct. 3	F Sept. 23	F Oct. 12	T Oct. 1	S Oct. 19
Hosha'na' Rabbah	F Oct. 8	W Sept. 28	W Oct. 17	S Oct. 6	F Oct. 24
Shemini 'Azeret	Sa Oct. 9	Th Sept. 29	Th Oct. 18	M Oct. 7	Sa Oct. 25
Simhat Torah	S Oct. 10	F Sept. 30	F Oct. 19	T Oct. 8	S Oct. 26
New Moon, Heshwan, 1st day	S Oct. 17	F Oct. 7	F Oct. 26	T Oct. 15	S Nov. 2
New Moon, Heshwan, 2nd day	M Oct. 18	Sa Oct. 8	Sa Oct. 27	W Oct. 16	M Nov. 3
New Moon, Kislew, 1st day	T Nov. 16	S Nov. 6	S Nov. 25	Th Nov. 14	T Dec. 2
New Moon, Kislew, 2nd day	W Nov. 17	M Nov. 7			W Dec. 3
Hanukkah, 1st day	Sa Dec. 11	Th Dec. 1	W Dec. 19	S Dec. 8	Sa Dec. 27
New Moon, Tevet, 1st day	Th Dec. 16	T Dec. 6	M Dec. 24	F Dec. 13	Th Jan. 1 (1987)
New Moon, Tevet, 2nd day	F Dec. 17	W Dec. 7	T Dec. 25		F Jan. 2
Fast of 10th of Tevet	S Dec. 26	F Dec. 16	Th Jan. 3 (1985)	S Dec. 22	S Jan. 11

	1983	1984	1985	1986	1987
New Moon, Shevat	Sa Jan. 15	Th Jan. 5	W Jan. 23	Sa Jan. 11	Sa Jan. 31
Hamishshah-'asar bi-Shevat	Sa Jan. 29	Th Jan. 19	W Feb. 6	Sa Jan. 25	Sa Feb. 14
New Moon, Adar I, 1st day	S Feb. 13	F Feb. 3	Th Feb. 21	S Feb. 9	S Mar. 1
New Moon, Adar I, 2nd day	M Feb. 14	Sa Feb. 4	F Feb. 22	M Feb. 10	M Mar. 2
New Moon, Adar II, 1st day		S Mar. 4		T Mar. 11	
New Moon, Adar II, 2nd day		M Mar. 5		W Mar. 12	
Fast of Esther	Th Feb. 24	Th Mar. 15	W Mar. 6	M Mar. 24	Th Mar. 12
Purim	S Feb. 27	S Mar. 18	Th Mar. 7	T Mar. 25	S Mar. 15
Shushan Purim	M Feb. 28	M Mar. 19	F Mar. 8	W Mar. 26	M Mar. 16
New Moon, Nisan	T Mar. 15	T Apr. 3	Sa Mar. 23	Th Apr. 10	T Mar. 31
Passover, 1st day	T Mar. 29	T Apr. 17	Sa Apr. 6	Th Apr. 24	T Apr. 14
Passover, 2nd day	W Mar. 30	W Apr. 18	S Apr. 7	F Apr. 25	W Apr. 15
Passover, 7th day	M Apr. 4	M Apr. 23	F Apr. 12	W Apr. 30	M Apr. 20
Passover, 8th day	T Apr. 5	T Apr. 24	Sa Apr. 13	Th May 1	T Apr. 21
Holocaust Memorial Day	S Apr. 10	S Apr. 29	Th Apr. 18	T May 6	S Apr. 26
New Moon, Iyar, 1st day	W Apr. 13	W May 2	S Apr. 21	F May 9	W Apr. 29
New Moon, Iyar, 2nd day	Th Apr. 14	Th May 3	M Apr. 22	Sa May 10	Th Apr. 30
Israel Independence Day	M Apr. 18	M May 7	F Apr. 26	W May 14	M May 4
Lag Ba-'omer	S May 1	S May 20	Th May 9	T May 27	S May 17
New Moon, Siwan	F May 13	F June 1	T May 21	S June 8	F May 29
Shavu'ot, 1st day	W May 18	W June 6	S May 26	F June 13	W June 3
Shavu'ot, 2nd day	Th May 19	Th June 7	M May 27	Sa June 14	Th June 4
New Moon, Tammuz, 1st day	Sa June 11	Sa June 30	W June 19	M July 7	Sa June 27
New Moon, Tammuz, 2nd day	S June 12	S July 1	Th June 20	T July 8	S June 28
Fast of 17th of Tammuz	T June 28	T July 17	S July 7	Th July 24	T July 14
New Moon, Av	M July 11	M July 30	F July 19	W Aug. 6	M July 27
Fast of 9th of Av	T July 19	T Aug. 7	S July 28	Th Aug. 14	T Aug. 4
New Moon, Elul, 1st day	T Aug. 9	T Aug. 28	Sa Aug. 17	Th Sept. 4	T Aug. 25
New Moon, Elul, 2nd day	W Aug. 10	W Aug. 29	S Aug. 18	F Sept. 5	W Aug. 26

CONDENSED MONTHLY CALENDAR
(1982–1984)

1981, Dec. 27–Jan. 24, 1982] ṬEVET (29 DAYS) [5742

Civil Date	Day of the Week	Jewish Date	SABBATHS, FESTIVALS, FASTS	PENTATEUCHAL READING	PROPHETICAL READING
Dec. 27	S	Tevet 1	New Moon, second day; Hanukkah, seventh day	Num. 28:1–15 7:48–53	
28	M	2	Hanukkah, eighth day	Num. 7:54–8:4	
Jan. 3	Sa	7	Wa-yiggash	Gen. 44:18–47:27	Ezekiel 37:15–28
5	T	10	Fast of 10th of Ṭevet	Exod. 32:11–14 34:1–10	Isaiah 55:6–56:8 (afternoon only)
9	Sa	14	Wa-yeḥi	Gen. 47:28–50:26	I Kings 2:1–12
16	Sa	21	Shemot	Exod. 1:1–6:1	Isaiah 27:6–28:13 29:22,23 *Jeremiah 1:1–2:3*
23	Sa	28	Wa-'era'	Exod. 6:2–9:35	Ezekiel 28:25–29:21

*Italics are for
Sephardi Minhag.*

1982, Jan. 25–Feb. 23]   SHEVAṬ (30 DAYS)   [5742

Civil Date	Day of the Week	Jewish Date	SABBATHS, FESTIVALS, FASTS	PENTATEUCHAL READING	PROPHETICAL READING
Jan. 25	M	Shevaṭ 1	New Moon	Num. 28: 1–15	
30	Sa	6	Bo'	Exod. 10: 1–13: 16	Jeremiah 46: 13–28
Feb. 6	Sa	13	Be-shallah (Shabbat Shirah)	Exod. 13: 17–17: 16	Judges 4: 4–5: 31 *Judges 5: 1–31*
8	M	15	Hamishshah–'asar bi-Shevaṭ		
13	Sa	20	Yitro	Exod. 18: 1–20: 23	Isaiah 6: 1–7: 6 9: 5, 6 *Isaiah 6: 1–13*
20	Sa	27	Mishpaṭim, (Shabbat Sheḳalim)	Exod. 21: 1–24: 18 Exod. 30: 11–16	II Kings 12: 1–17 *II Kings 11: 17–12: 17*
23	T	30	New Moon, first day	Num. 28: 1–15	

Italics are for Sephardi Minhag.

Civil Date	Day of the Week	Jewish Date	SABBATHS, FESTIVALS, FASTS	PENTATEUCHAL READING	PROPHETICAL READING
Feb. 24	W	Adar 1	New Moon, second day	Num. 28: 1–15	
27	Sa	4	Terumah	Exod. 25: 1–27: 19	I Kings 5: 26–6: 13
Mar. 6	Sa	11	Tezawweh (Shabbat Zakhor)	Exod. 27: 20–30: 10 Deut. 25: 17–19	I Samuel 15: 2–34 *I Samuel 15: 1–34*
8	M	13	Fast of Esther	Exod. 32: 11–14 34: 1–10	Isaiah 55: 6–56: 8 (afternoon only)
9	T	14	Purim	Exod. 17: 8–16	Book of Esther (night before and in the morning)
10	W	15	Shushan Purim		
13	Sa	18	Ki tissa' (Shabbat Parah)	Exod. 30: 11–34: 35 Num. 19: 1–22	Ezekiel 36: 16–38 *Ezekiel 36: 16–36*
20	Sa	25	Wa-yakhel, Pekude (Shabbat Ha-hodesh)	Exod. 35: 1–40: 38 Exod. 12: 1–20	Ezekiel 45: 16–46: 18 *Ezekiel 45: 18–46: 15*

*Italics are for
Sephardi Minhag.*

1982, Mar. 25–Apr. 23]   NISAN (30 DAYS)   [5742

Civil Date	Day of the Week	Jewish Date	SABBATHS, FESTIVALS, FASTS	PENTATEUCHAL READING	PROPHETICAL READING
Mar. 25	Th	Nisan 1	New Moon	Num. 28: 1–15	
27	Sa	3	Wa-yiḳra'	Levit. 1: 1–5: 26	Isaiah 43: 21–44: 24
Apr. 3	Sa	10	Ẓaw (Shabbat Ha-gadol)	Levit. 6: 1–8: 36	Malachi 3: 4–24
7	W	14	Fast of Firstborn		
8	Th	15	Passover, first day	Exod. 12: 21–51 Num. 28: 16–25	Joshua 5: 2–6: 1, 27
9	F	16	Passover, second day	Levit. 22: 26–23: 44 Num. 28: 16–25	II Kings 23: 1–9 21–25
10	Sa	17	Ḥol Ha-mo'ed, first day	Exod. 33: 12–34: 26 Num. 28: 19–25	Ezekiel 37: 1–14
11	S	18	Ḥol Ha-mo'ed, second day	Exod. 13: 1–16 Num. 28: 19–25	
12	M	19	Ḥol Ha-mo'ed, third day	Exod. 22: 24–23: 19 Num. 28: 19–25	
13	T	20	Ḥol Ha-mo'ed, fourth day	Num. 9: 1–14 Num. 28: 19–25	
14	W	21	Passover, seventh day	Exod. 13: 17–15: 26 Num. 28: 19–25	II Samuel 22: 1–51
15	Th	22	Passover, eighth day	Deut. 15: 19–16: 17 Num. 28: 19–25	Isaiah 10: 32–12: 6
17	Sa	24	Shemini	Levit. 9: 1–11: 47	II Samuel 6: 1–7: 17
23	F	30	New Moon, first day	Num. 28: 1–15	

1982, Apr. 24–May 22]   IYAR (29 DAYS)   [5742

Civil Date	Day of the Week	Jewish Date	SABBATHS, FESTIVALS, FASTS	PENTATEUCHAL READING	PROPHETICAL READING
Apr. 24	Sa	Iyar 1	Tazria', Mezora', New Moon, second day	Levit. 12: 1–15: 33 Num. 28: 9–15	Isaiah 66: 1–24
May 1	Sa	8	Ahare mot, Kedoshim	Levit. 16: 1–20: 27	Amos 9: 7–15 *Ezekiel 20: 2–20*
8	Sa	15	Emor	Levit. 21: 1–24: 23	Ezekiel 44: 15–31
11	T	18	Lag Ba-'omer		
15	Sa	22	Be-har, Be-hukkotai	Levit. 25: 1–27: 34	Jeremiah 16: 19–17: 14
22	Sa	29	Be-midbar	Num. 1: 1–4: 20	I Samuel 20: 18–42

1982, May 23–June 21]   SIWAN (30 DAYS)   [5742

Civil Date	Day of the Week	Jewish Date	SABBATHS, FESTIVALS, FASTS	PENTATEUCHAL READING	PROPHETICAL READING
May 23	S	Siwan 1	New Moon	Num. 28: 1–15	
28	F	6	Shavu'ot, first day	Exod. 19: 1–20: 23 Num. 28: 26–31	Ezekiel 1: 1–28 3: 12
29	Sa	7	Shavu'ot, second day	Deut. 15: 19–16: 17 Num. 28: 26–31	Habbakuk 3: 1–19 *Habbakuk 2: 20–3: 19*
June 5	Sa	14	Naso'	Num. 4: 21–7: 89	Judges 13: 2–25
12	Sa	21	Be-ha'alotekha	Num. 8: 1–12: 16	Zechariah 2: 14–4: 7
19	Sa	28	Shelah	Num. 13: 1–15: 41	Joshua 2: 1–24
21	M	30	New Moon, first day	Num. 28: 1–15	

Italics are for
Sephardi Minhag.

1982, June 22–July 20]   TAMMUZ (29 DAYS)   [5742

Civil Date	Day of the Week	Jewish Date	SABBATHS, FESTIVALS, FASTS	PENTATEUCHAL READING	PROPHETICAL READING
June 22	T	Tammuz 1	New Moon, second day	Num. 28: 1–15	
26	Sa	5	Koraḥ	Num. 16: 1–18: 32	I Samuel 11: 14–12: 22
July 3	Sa	12	Ḥukkat, Balak	Num. 19: 1–25: 9	Micah 5: 6–6: 8
8	Th	17	Fast of 17th of Tammuz	Exod. 32: 11–14 34: 1–10	Isaiah 55: 6–56: 8 (afternoon only)
10	Sa	19	Pineḥas	Num. 25: 10–30: 1	Jeremiah 1: 1–2: 3
17	Sa	26	Mattot, Mas‘e	Num. 30: 2–36: 13	Jeremiah 2: 4–28 3: 4 *Jeremiah 2: 4–28 4: 1, 2*

Italics are for Sephardi Minhag.

1982, July 21–Aug. 19]   AV (30 DAYS)   [5742

Civil Date	Day of the Week	Jewish Date	SABBATHS, FESTIVALS, FASTS	PENTATEUCHAL READING	PROPHETICAL READING
July 21	W	Av 1	New Moon	Num. 28: 1–15	
24	Sa	4	Devarim (Shabbat Ḥazon)	Deut. 1: 1–3: 22	Isaiah 1: 1–27
29	Th	9	Fast of 9th of Av	Morning: Deut. 4: 25–40 Afternoon: Exod. 32: 11–14 34: 1–10	(Lamentations is read the night before.) Jeremiah 8: 13–9: 23 Isaiah 55: 6–56: 8
31	Sa	11	Wa-etḥannan (Shabbat Naḥamu)	Deut. 3: 23–7: 11	Isaiah 40: 1–26
Aug. 7	Sa	18	'Eḳev	Deut. 7: 12–11: 25	Isaiah 49: 14–51: 3
14	Sa	25	Re'eh	Deut. 11: 26–16: 17	Isaiah 54: 11–55: 5
19	Th	30	New Moon, first day	Num. 28: 1–15	

1982, Aug. 20–Sept. 17]   ELUL (29 DAYS)   [5742

Civil Date	Day of the Week	Jewish Date	SABBATHS, FESTIVALS, FASTS	PENTATEUCHAL READING	PROPHETICAL READING
Aug. 20	F	Elul 1	New Moon, second day	Num. 28: 1–15	
21	Sa	2	Shofeṭim	Deut. 16: 18–21: 9	Isaiah 51: 12–52: 12
28	Sa	9	Ki teze'	Deut. 21: 10–25: 19	Isaiah 54: 1–10
Sept. 4	Sa	16	Ki tavo'	Deut. 26: 1–29: 8	Isaiah 60: 1–22
11	Sa	23	Nizzavim, Wa-yelekh	Deut. 29: 9–31: 30	Isaiah 61: 10–63: 9

1982, Sept. 18–Oct. 17] **TISHRI (30 DAYS)** [5743

Civil Date	Day of the Week	Jewish Date	SABBATHS, FESTIVALS, FASTS	PENTATEUCHAL READING	PROPHETICAL READING
Sept. 18	Sa	Tishri 1	Rosh Ha-shanah, first day	Gen. 21: 1–34 Num. 29: 1–6	I Samuel 1: 1–2: 10
19	S	2	Rosh Ha-shanah, second day	Gen. 22: 1–24 Num. 29: 1–6	Jeremiah 31: 2–20
20	M	3	Fast of Gedaliah	Exod. 32: 11–14 34: 1–10	Isaiah 55: 6–56: 8 (afternoon only)
25	Sa	8	Ha'azinu (Shabbat Shuvah)	Deut. 32: 1–52	Hosea 14: 2–10 Micah 7: 18–20 Joel 2: 15–27 *Hosea 14: 2–10* *Micah 7: 18–20*
27	M	10	Yom Kippur	Morning: Levit. 16: 1–34 Num. 29: 7–11 Afternoon: Levit. 18: 1–30	Isaiah 57: 14–58: 14 Jonah 1: 1–14: 11 Micah 7: 18–20
Oct. 2	Sa	15	Sukkot, first day	Levit. 22: 26–23: 44 Num. 29: 12–16	Zechariah 14: 1–21
3	S	16	Sukkot, second day	Levit. 22: 26–23: 44 Num. 29: 12–16	I Kings 8: 2–21
4–7	M-Th	17–20	Ḥol Ha-mo'ed	M Num. 29: 17–25 T Num. 29: 20–28 W Num. 29: 23–31 Th Num. 29: 26–34	
8	F	21	Hosha'na' Rabbah	Num. 29: 26–34	
9	Sa	22	Shemini 'Azeret	Deut. 14: 22–16: 17 Num. 29: 35–30: 1	I Kings 8: 54–66
10	S	23	Simḥat Torah	Deut. 33: 1–34: 12 Gen. 1: 1–2: 3 Num. 29: 35–30: 1	Joshua 1: 1–18 *Joshua 1: 1–9*
16	Sa	29	Be-re'shit	Gen. 1: 1–6: 8	I Samuel 20: 18–42
17	S	30	New Moon, first day	Num. 28: 1–15	

Italics are for
Sephardi Minhag.

Civil Date	Day of the Week	Jewish Date	SABBATHS, FESTIVALS, FASTS	PENTATEUCHAL READING	PROPHETICAL READING
Oct. 18	M	Ḥeshwan 1	New Moon, second day	Num. 28: 1–15	
23	Sa	6	Noaḥ	Gen. 6: 9–11: 32	Isaiah 54: 1–55: 5
30	Sa	13	Lekh lekha	Gen. 12: 1–17: 27	Isaiah 40: 27–41: 16
Nov. 6	Sa	20	Wa-yera'	Gen. 18: 1–22: 24	II Kings 4: 1–37 *II Kings 4: 1–23*
13	Sa	27	Ḥayye Sarah	Gen. 23: 1–25: 18	I Kings 1: 1–31
16	T	30	New Moon, first day	Num. 28: 1–15	

Civil Date	Day of the Week	Jewish Date	SABBATHS, FESTIVALS, FASTS	PENTATEUCHAL READING	PROPHETICAL READING
Nov. 17	W	Kislew 1	New Moon, second day	Num. 28: 1–15	
20	Sa	4	Toledot	Gen. 25: 19–28: 9	Malachi 1: 1–2: 7
27	Sa	11	Wa-yeze'	Gen. 28: 10–32: 3	Hosea 12: 13–14: 10 *Hosea 11: 7–12: 12*
Dec. 4	Sa	18	Wa-yishlaḥ	Gen. 32: 4–36: 43	Hosea 11: 7–12: 12 *Obadiah 1: 1–21*
11	Sa	25	Wa-yeshev, Hanukkah, first day	Gen. 37: 1–40: 23 Num. 7: 1–17	Zechariah 2: 14–4: 7
12–15	S-W	26–29	Hanukkah, second to fifth days	S Num. 7: 18–29 M Num. 7: 24–35 T Num. 7: 30–41 W Num. 7: 36–47	
16	Th	30	New Moon, first day; Hanukkah, sixth day	Num. 28: 1–15 7: 42–47	

Italics are for Sephardi Minhag.

1982, Dec. 17–Jan. 14, 1983] ṬEVET (29 DAYS) [5743

Civil Date	Day of the Week	Jewish Date	SABBATHS, FESTIVALS, FASTS	PENTATEUCHAL READING	PROPHETICAL READING
Dec. 17	F	Ṭevet 1	New Moon, second day; Ḥanukkah, seventh day	Num. 28: 1–15 7: 48–53	
18	Sa	2	Mi-ḳez, Ḥanukkah, eighth day	Gen. 41: 1–44: 17 Num. 7: 54–8: 4	I Kings 7: 40–50
25	Sa	9	Wa-yiggash	Gen. 44: 18–47: 27	Ezekiel 37: 15–28
26	S	10	Fast of 10th of Ṭevet	Exod. 32: 11–14 34: 1–10	Isaiah 55: 6–56: 8 (afternoon only)
Jan. 2	Sa	16	Wa-yeḥi	Gen. 47: 28–50: 26	I Kings 2: 1–12
8	Sa	23	Shemot	Exod. 1: 1–6: 1	Isaiah 27: 6–28: 13 29: 22, 23 *Jeremiah 1: 1–2: 3*

1983, Jan. 15–Feb. 13] SHEVAṬ (30 DAYS) [5743

Civil Date	Day of the Week	Jewish Date	SABBATHS, FESTIVALS, FASTS	PENTATEUCHAL READING	PROPHETICAL READING
Jan. 15	Sa	Shevaṭ 1	Wa-'era', New Moon	Exod. 6:2–9:35 Num. 28:9–15	Isaiah 66:1–24
22	Sa	8	Bo'	Exod. 10:1–13:16	Jeremiah 46:13–28
29	Sa	15	Be-shallaḥ (Shabbat Shirah) Hamishshah-'asar bi-Shevaṭ	Exod. 13:17–17:16	Judges 4:4–5:31 *Judges 5:1–31*
Feb. 5	Sa	22	Yitro	Exod. 18:1–20:23	Isaiah 6:1–7:6 9:5, 6 *Isaiah 6:1–13*
12	Sa	29	Mishpaṭim (Shabbat Sheḳalim)	Exod. 21:1–24:18 Exod. 30:11–16	II Kings 12:1–17 *II Kings 11:17–12:17 I Samuel 20:18, 42*
13	S	30	New Moon, first day	Num. 28:1–15	

Italics are for Sephardi Minhag.

1983, Feb. 14–Mar. 14]   ADAR (29 DAYS)   [5743

Civil Date	Day of the Week	Jewish Date	SABBATHS, FESTIVALS, FASTS	PENTATEUCHAL READING	PROPHETICAL READING
Feb. 14	M	Adar 1	New Moon, second day	Num. 28:1–15	
19	Sa	6	Terumah	Exod. 25:1–27:19	I Kings 5:26–6:13
24	Th	11	Fast of Esther	Exod. 32:11–14 34:1–10	Isaiah 55:6–56:8 (afternoon only)
26	Sa	13	Teẓawweh (Shabbat Zakhor)	Exod. 27:20–30:10 Deut. 25:17–19	I Samuel 15:2–34 *I Samuel 15:1–34*
27	S	14	Purim	Exod. 17:8–16	Book of Esther (night before and in the morning)
28	M	15	Shushan Purim		
Mar. 5	Sa	20	Ki tissa' (Shabbat Parah)	Exod. 30:11–34:35 Num. 19:1–22	Ezekiel 36:16–38 *Ezekiel 36:16–36*
12	Sa	27	Wa-yakhel, Pekude (Shabbat Ha-ḥodesh)	Exod. 35:1–40:38 Exod. 12:1–20	Ezekiel 45:16–46:18 *Ezekiel 45:18–46:15* Isaiah 66:1, 24

Italics are for
Sephardi Minhag.

1983, Mar. 15–Apr. 13] NISAN (30 DAYS) [5743

Civil Date	Day of the Week	Jewish Date	SABBATHS, FESTIVALS, FASTS	PENTATEUCHAL READING	PROPHETICAL READING
Mar. 15	T	Nisan 1	New Moon	Num. 28:1–15	
19	Sa	5	Wa-yikra'	Levit. 1:1–5:26	Isaiah 43:21–44:24
26	Sa	12	Ẓaw (Shabbat Ha-gadol)	Levit. 6:1–8:36	Malachi 3:4–24
28	M	14	Fast of Firstborn		
29	T	15	Passover, first day	Exod. 12:21–51 Num. 28:16–25	Joshua 5:2–6:1, 27
30	W	16	Passover, second day	Levit. 22:26–23:44 Num. 28:16–25	II Kings 23:1–19 21–25
Mar. 31	Th	17	Hol Ha-mo‘ed, first day	Exod. 13:1–16 Num. 28:19–25	
Apr. 1	F	18	Hol Ha-mo‘ed, second day	Exod. 22:24–23:19 Num. 28:19–25	
2	Sa	19	Hol Ha-mo‘ed, third day	Exod. 33:12–34:26 Num. 28:19–25	Ezekiel 36:37–37:14
3	S	20	Hol Ha-mo‘ed, fourth day	Num. 9:1–14 Num. 28:19–25	
4	M	21	Passover, seventh day	Exod. 13:17–15:26 Num. 28:19–25	II Samuel 22:1–51
5	T	22	Passover, eighth day	Deut. 15:19–16:17 Num. 28:19–25	Isaiah 10:32–12:6
9	Sa	26	Shemini	Levit. 9:1–11:47	II Samuel 6:1–7:17
13	W	30	New Moon, first day	Num. 28:1–15	

Civil Date	Day of the Week	Jewish Date	SABBATHS, FESTIVALS, FASTS	PENTATEUCHAL READING	PROPHETICAL READING
Apr. 14	Th	Iyar 1	New Moon, second day	Num. 28:1–15	
16	Sa	3	Tazria', Mezora'	Levit. 12:1–15:33	II Kings 7:3–20
23	Sa	10	Ahare mot, Kedoshim	Levit. 16:1–20:27	Amos 9:7–15 *Ezekiel 20:2–20*
30	Sa	17	Emor	Levit. 21:1–24:23	Ezekiel 44:15–31
May 1	S	18	Lag Ba-'omer		
7	Sa	24	Be-har, Be-hukkotai	Levit. 25:1–27:34	Jeremiah 16:19–17:14

Civil Date	Day of the Week	Jewish Date	SABBATHS, FESTIVALS, FASTS	PENTATEUCHAL READING	PROPHETICAL READING
May 13	F	Siwan 1	New Moon	Num. 28:1–15	
14	Sa	2	Be-midbar	Num. 1:1–4:20	Hosea 2:1–22
18	W	6	Shavu'ot, first day	Exod. 19:1–20:23 Num. 28:26–31	Ezekiel 1:1–28 3:12
19	Th	7	Shavu'ot, second day	Deut. 15:19–16:17 Num. 28:26–31	Habbakuk 3:1–19 *Habbakuk 2:20–3:19*
21	Sa	9	Naso'	Num. 4:21–7:89	Judges 13:2–25
28	Sa	16	Be-ha'alotekha	Num. 8:1–12:16	Zechariah 2:14–4:7
June 4	Sa	23	Shelah	Num. 13:1–15:41	Joshua 2:1–24
11	Sa	30	Korah, New Moon, first day	Num. 16:1–18:32 Num. 28:9–15	Isaiah 66:1–24 I Samuel 20:18,42

Italics are for Sephardi Minhag.

1983, June 12–July 10]   TAMMUZ (29 DAYS)   [5743

Civil Date	Day of the Week	Jewish Date	SABBATHS, FESTIVALS, FASTS	PENTATEUCHAL READING	PROPHETICAL READING
June 12	S	Tammuz 1	New Moon, second day	Num. 28:1–15	
18	Sa	7	Ḥukkat	Num. 19:1–22:1	Judges 11:1–33
25	Sa	14	Balak	Num. 22:2–25:9	Micah 5:6–6:8
28	T	17	Fast of 17th of Tammuz	Exod. 32:11–14 34:1–10	Isaiah 55:6–56:8 (afternoon only)
July 2	Sa	21	Pineḥas	Num. 25:10–30:1	Jeremiah 1:1–2:3
9	Sa	28	Maṭṭot, Masʻe	Num. 30:2–36:13	Jeremiah 2:4–28 3:4 *Jeremiah 2:4–28 4:1,2*

Italics are for Sephardi Minhag.

1983, July 11–Aug. 9]   AV (30 DAYS)   [5743

Civil Date	Day of the Week	Jewish Date	SABBATHS, FESTIVALS, FASTS	PENTATEUCHAL READING	PROPHETICAL READING
July 11	M	Av 1	New Moon	Num. 28:1–15	
16	Sa	6	Devarim (Shabbat Ḥazon)	Deut. 1:1–3:22	Isaiah 1:1–27
19	T	9	Fast of 9th of Av	Morning: Deut. 4:25–40 Afternoon: Exod. 32:11–14 34:1–10	(Lamentations is read the night before.) Jeremiah 8:13–9:23 Isaiah 55:6–56:8
23	Sa	13	Wa-ethannan (Shabbat Naḥamu)	Deut. 3:23–7:11	Isaiah 40:1–26
30	Sa	20	'Eḳev	Deut. 7:12–11:25	Isaiah 49:14–51:3
Aug. 6	Sa	27	Re'eh	Deut. 11:26–16:17	Isaiah 54:11–55:5
9	T	30	New Moon, first day	Num. 28:1–15	

1983, Aug. 10–Sept. 7]   ELUL (29 DAYS)   [5743

Civil Date	Day of the Week	Jewish Date	SABBATHS, FESTIVALS, FASTS	PENTATEUCHAL READING	PROPHETICAL READING
Aug. 10	W	Elul 1	New Moon, second day	Num. 28:1–15	
13	Sa	4	Shofeṭim	Deut. 16:18–21:9	Isaiah 51:12–52:12
20	Sa	11	Ki teze'	Deut. 21:10–25:19	Isaiah 54:1–10
27	Sa	18	Ki tavo'	Deut. 26:1–29:8	Isaiah 60:1–22
Sept. 3	Sa	25	Nizzavim, Wa-yelekh	Deut. 29:9–31:30	Isaiah 61:10–63:9

Civil Date	Day of the Week	Jewish Date	SABBATHS, FESTIVALS, FASTS	PENTATEUCHAL READING	PROPHETICAL READING
Sept. 8	Th	Tishri 1	Rosh Ha-shanah, first day	Gen. 21:1–34 Num. 29:1–6	I Samuel 1:1–2:10
9	F	2	Rosh Ha-shanah, second day	Gen. 22:1–24 Num. 29:1–6	Jeremiah 31:2–20
10	Sa	3	Ha'azinu (Shabbat Shuvah)	Deut. 32:1–52	Hosea 14:2–10 Micah 7:18–20 Joel 2:15–27 *Hosea 14:2–10* *Micah 7:18–20*
11	S	4	Fast of Gedaliah	Exod. 32:11–14 34:1–10	Isaiah 55:6–56:8 (afternoon only)
17	Sa	10	Yom Kippur	Morning: Levit. 16:1–34 Num. 29:7–11 Afternoon: Levit. 18:1–30	Isaiah 57:14–58:14 Jonah 1:1–4:11 Micah 7:18–20
22	Th	15	Sukkot, first day	Levit. 22:26–23:44 Num. 29:12–16	Zechariah 14:1–21
23	F	16	Sukkot, second day	Levit. 22:26–23:44 Num. 29:12–16	I Kings 8:2–21
24–27	Sa-T	17–20	Ḥol Ha-mo'ed	Sa Exod. 33:12–34:26 Num. 29:17–22 S Num. 29:20–28 M Num. 29:23–31 T Num. 29:26–34	Ezekiel 38:18–39:16
28	W	21	Hosha'na' Rabbah	Num. 29:26–34	
29	Th	22	Shemini 'Azeret	Deut. 14:22–16:17 Num. 29:35–30:1	I Kings 8:54–66
30	F	23	Simḥat Torah	Deut. 33:1–34:12 Gen. 1:1–2:3 Num. 29:35–30:1	Joshua 1:1–18 *Joshua 1:1–9*
Oct. 1	Sa	24	Be-re'shit	Gen. 1:1–6:8	Isaiah 42:5–43:10 *Isaiah 42:5–21*
7	F	30	New Moon, first day	Num. 28:1–15	

Italics are for Sephardi Minhag.

Civil Date	Day of the Week	Jewish Date	SABBATHS, FESTIVALS, FASTS	PENTATEUCHAL READING	PROPHETICAL READING
Oct. 8	Sa	Ḥeshwan 1	Noaḥ New Moon, second day	Gen. 6:9–11:32 Num. 28:9–15	Isaiah 66:1–24
15	Sa	8	Lekh lekha	Gen. 12:1–17:27	Isaiah 40:27–41:16
22	Sa	15	Wa-yera'	Gen. 18:1–22:24	II Kings 4:1–37 *II Kings 4:1–23*
29	Sa	22	Ḥayye Sarah	Gen. 23:1–25:18	I Kings 1:1–31
Nov. 5	Sa	29	Toledot	Gen. 25:19–28:9	I Samuel 20:18–42
6	S	30	New Moon, first day	Num. 28:1–15	

Civil Date	Day of the Week	Jewish Date	SABBATHS, FESTIVALS, FASTS	PENTATEUCHAL READING	PROPHETICAL READING
Nov. 7	M	Kislew 1	New Moon, second day	Num. 28:1–15	
12	Sa	6	Wa-yeẓe'	Gen. 28:10–32:3	Hosea 12:13–14:10 *Hosea 11:7–12:12*
19	Sa	13	Wa-yishlaḥ	Gen. 32:4–36:43	Hosea 11:7–12:12 *Obadiah 1:1–21*
26	Sa	20	Wa-yeshev	Gen. 37:1–40:23	Amos 2:6–3:8
Dec. 1–2	Th-F	25–26	Hanukkah, first to second days	Th Num. 7:1–17 F Num. 7:18–29	
3	Sa	27	Mi-keẓ, Ḥanukkah, third day	Gen. 41:1–44:17 Num. 7:24–29	Zechariah 2:14–4:7
4–5	S-M	28–29	Hanukkah, fourth to fifth days	S Num. 7:30–41 M Num. 7:36–47	
6	T	30	New Moon, first day; Ḥanukkah, sixth day	Num. 28:1–15 7:42–47	

Italics are for Sephardi Minhag.

1983, Dec. 7–Jan. 4, 1984] ṬEVET (29 DAYS) [5744

Civil Date	Day of the Week	Jewish Date	SABBATHS, FESTIVALS, FASTS	PENTATEUCHAL READING	PROPHETICAL READING
Dec. 7	W	Ṭevet 1	New Moon, second day; Hanukkah, seventh day	Num. 28:1–15 7:48–53	
8	Th	2	Hanukkah, eighth day	Num. 7:54–8:4	
10	Sa	4	Wa-yiggash	Gen. 44:18–47:27	Ezekiel 37:15–28
16	F	10	Fast of 10th of Ṭevet	Exod. 32:11–14 34:1–10	Isaiah 55:6–56:8 (afternoon only)
17	Sa	11	Wa-yeḥi	Gen. 47:28–50:26	I Kings 2:1–12
24	Sa	18	Shemot	Exod. 1:1–6:1	Isaiah 27:6–28:13 29:22–23 *Jeremiah 1:1–2:3*
31	Sa	25	Wa-’era’	Exod. 6:2–9:35	Ezekiel 28:25–29:21

Italics are for Sephardi Minhag.

Civil Date	Day of the Week	Jewish Date	SABBATHS, FESTIVALS, FASTS	PENTATEUCHAL READING	PROPHETICAL READING
Jan. 5	Th	Shevaṭ 1	New Moon	Num. 28: 1–15	
7	Sa	3	Bo'	Exod. 10: 1–13: 16	Jeremiah 46: 13–28
14	Sa	10	Be-shallaḥ (Shabbat Shirah)	Exod. 13: 17–17: 16	Judges 4: 4–5: 31 *Judges 5: 1–31*
19	Th	15	Hamishshah–'asar bi-Shevaṭ		
21	Sa	17	Yitro	Exod. 18: 1–20: 23	Isaiah 6: 1–7: 6 9: 5, 6 *Isaiah 6: 1–13*
28	Sa	24	Mishpaṭim	Exod. 21: 1–24: 18	Jeremiah 34: 8–22 33: 25, 26
Feb. 3	F	30	New Moon, first day	Num. 28: 1–15	

Italics are for Sephardi Minhag.

1984, Feb. 4–Mar. 4]   ADAR I (30 DAYS)   [5744

Civil Date	Day of the Week	Jewish Date	SABBATHS, FESTIVALS, FASTS	PENTATEUCHAL READING	PROPHETICAL READING
Feb. 4	Sa	Adar I 1	Terumah, New Moon, second day	Exod. 25: 1–27: 19 Num. 28: 9–15	Isaiah 66: 1–24
11	Sa	8	Teẓawweh	Exod. 27: 20–30: 10	Ezekiel 43: 10–27
18	Sa	15	Ki tissa'	Exod. 30: 11–34: 35	I Kings 18: 1–39 *I Kings 18: 20–39*
25	Sa	22	Wa-yaḳhel	Exod. 35: 1–38: 20	I Kings 7: 40–50 *I Kings 7: 13–26*
Mar. 3	Sa	29	Peḳude (Shabbat Sheḳalim)	Exod. 38: 21–40: 38 30: 11–16	II Kings 12: 1–17 *II Kings 11: 17–12: 17* I Samuel 20: 18, 42
4	S	30	New Moon, first day	Num. 28: 1–15	

Italics are for Sephardi Minhag.

1984, Mar. 5–Apr. 2]   ADAR II (29 DAYS)   [5744

Civil Date	Day of the Week	Jewish Date	SABBATHS, FESTIVALS, FASTS	PENTATEUCHAL READING	PROPHETICAL READING
Mar. 5	M	Adar II 1	New Moon, second day	Num. 28: 1–15	
10	Sa	6	Wa-yiḳra'	Levit. 1: 1–5: 26	Isaiah 43: 21–44: 24
15	Th	11	Fast of Esther	Exod. 32: 11–14 34: 1–10	Isaiah 55: 6–56: 8 (afternoon only)
17	Sa	13	Ẓaw (Shabbat Ẓakhor)	Levit. 6: 1–8: 36 Deut. 25: 17–19	I Samuel 15: 2–34 *I Samuel 15: 1–34*
18	S	14	Purim	Exod. 17: 8–16	Book of Esther (night before and in the morning)
19	M	15	Shushan Purim		
24	Sa	20	Shemini (Shabbat Parah)	Levit. 9: 1–11: 47 Num. 19: 1–22	Ezekiel 36: 16–38 *Ezekiel 36: 16–36*
31	Sa	27	Tazria' (Shabbat Ha-ḥodesh)	Levit. 12: 1–13: 59 Exod. 12: 1–20	Ezekiel 45: 16–46: 18 *Ezekiel 45: 18–46: 15*

Italics are for
Sephardi Minhag.

1984, Apr. 3–May 2]   NISAN (30 DAYS)   [5744

Civil Date	Day of the Week	Jewish Date	SABBATHS, FESTIVALS, FASTS	PENTATEUCHAL READING	PROPHETICAL READING
Apr. 3	T	Nisan 1	New Moon	Num. 28: 1–15	
7	Sa	5	Meẓora'	Levit. 14: 1–15: 33	II Kings 7: 3–20
14	Sa	12	Aḥare mot (Shabbat Ha-gadol)	Levit. 16: 1–18: 30	Malachi 3: 4–24
16	M	14	Fast of Firstborn		
17	T	15	Passover, first day	Exod. 12: 21–51 Num. 28: 16–25	Joshua 5: 2–6: 1, 27
18	W	16	Passover, second day	Levit. 22: 26–23: 44 Num. 28: 16–25	II Kings 23: 1–19 21–25
19	Th	17	Ḥol Ha-mo'ed, first day	Exod. 13: 1–16 Num. 28: 19–25	
20	F	18	Ḥol Ha-mo'ed, second day	Exod. 22: 24–23: 19 Num. 28: 19–25	
21	Sa	19	Ḥol Ha-mo'ed, third day	Exod. 33: 12–34: 26 Num. 28: 19–25	Ezekiel 36: 37–37: 14
22	S	20	Ḥol Ha-mo'ed, fourth day	Num. 9: 1–14 Num. 28: 19–25	
23	M	21	Passover, seventh day	Exod. 13: 17–15: 26 Num. 28: 19–25	II Samuel 22: 1–51
24	T	22	Passover, eighth day	Deut. 15: 19–16: 17 Num. 28: 19–25	Isaiah 10: 32–12: 6
28	Sa	26	Ḳedoshim	Levit. 19: 1–20: 27	Amos 9: 7–15 *Ezekiel 20: 2–20*
May 2	W	30	New Moon, first day	Num. 28: 1–15	

*Italics are for
Sephardi Minhag.*

1984, May 3–May 31]   IYAR (29 DAYS)   [5744

Civil Date	Day of the Week	Jewish Date	SABBATHS, FESTIVALS, FASTS	PENTATEUCHAL READING	PROPHETICAL READING
May 3	Th	Iyar 1	New Moon, second day	Num. 28: 1–15	
5	Sa	3	Emor	Levit. 21: 1–24: 23	Ezekiel 44: 15–31
12	Sa	10	Be-har	Levit. 25: 1–26: 2	Jeremiah 32: 6–27
19	Sa	17	Be-ḥuḳḳotai	Levit. 26: 3–27: 34	Jeremiah 16: 19–17: 14
20	S	18	Lag Ba-'omer		
26	Sa	24	Be-midbar	Num. 1: 1–4: 20	Hosea 2: 1–22

1984, June 1–June 30]   SIWAN (30 DAYS)   [5744

Civil Date	Day of the Week	Jewish Date	SABBATHS, FESTIVALS, FASTS	PENTATEUCHAL READING	PROPHETICAL READING
June 1	F	Siwan 1	New Moon	Num. 28: 1–15	
2	Sa	2	Naso'	Num. 4: 21–7: 89	Judges 13: 2–25
6	W	6	Shavu'ot, first day	Exod. 19: 1–20: 23 Num. 28: 26–31	Ezekiel 1: 1–28 3: 12
7	Th	7	Shavu'ot, second day	Deut. 15: 19–16: 17 Num. 28: 26–31	Habbakuk 3: 1–19 *Habbakuk 2: 20–3: 19*
9	Sa	9	Be-ha'alotekha	Num. 8: 1–12: 6	Zechariah 2: 14–4: 7
16	Sa	16	Shelaḥ	Num. 13: 1–15: 41	Joshua 2: 1–24
23	Sa	23	Ḳoraḥ	Num. 16: 1–18: 32	I Samuel 11: 14–12: 22
30	Sa	30	Huḳḳat, New Moon, first day	Num. 19: 1–22: 1 Num. 28: 9–15	Isaiah 66: 1–24 *Isaiah 66: 1–24* I Samuel 20: 18, 42

Italics are for
Sephardi Minhag.

1984, July 1–July 29]   TAMMUZ (29 DAYS)   [5744

Civil Date	Day of the Week	Jewish Date	SABBATHS, FESTIVALS, FASTS	PENTATEUCHAL READING	PROPHETICAL READING
July 1	S	Tammuz 1	New Moon, second day	Num. 28: 1–15	
7	Sa	7	Balak	Num. 22: 2–25: 9	Micah 5: 6–6: 8
14	Sa	14	Pineḥas	Num. 25: 10–30: 1	I King 18: 46–19: 21
17	T	17	Fast of 17th of Tammuz	Exod. 32: 11–14 34: 1–10	Isaiah 55: 6–56: 8 (afternoon only)
21	Sa	21	Mattot	Num. 30: 2–32: 42	Jeremiah 1: 1–2: 3
28	Sa	28	Mas'e	Num. 33: 1–36: 13	Jeremiah 2: 4–28 3: 4 *Jeremiah 2: 4–28 4: 1, 2*

Italics are for Sephardi Minhag.

1984, July 30–Aug. 28]   AV (30 DAYS)   [5744

Civil Date	Day of the Week	Jewish Date	SABBATHS, FESTIVALS, FASTS	PENTATEUCHAL READING	PROPHETICAL READING
July 30	M	Av 1	New Moon	Num. 28: 1–15	
Aug. 4	Sa	6	Devarim (Shabbat Ḥazon)	Deut. 1: 1–3: 22	Isaiah 1: 1–27
7	T	9	Fast of 9th of Av	Morning: Deut. 4: 25–40 Afternoon: Exod. 32: 11–14 34: 1–10	(Lamentations is read the night before.) Jeremiah 8: 13–9: 23 Isaiah 55: 6–56: 8
11	Sa	13	Wa-ethannan (Shabbat Naḥamu)	Deut. 3: 23–7: 11	Isaiah 40: 1–26
18	Sa	20	ʻEḵev	Deut. 7: 12–11: 25	Isaiah 49: 14–51: 3
25	Sa	27	Reʼeh	Deut. 11: 26–16: 17	Isaiah 54: 11–55: 5
28	T	30	New Moon, first day	Num. 28: 1–15	

1984, Aug. 29–Sept. 26]   ELUL (29 DAYS)   [5744

Civil Date	Day of the Week	Jewish Date	SABBATHS, FESTIVALS, FASTS	PENTATEUCHAL READING	PROPHETICAL READING
Aug. 29	W	Elul 1	New Moon, second day	Num. 28: 1–15	
Sept. 1	Sa	4	Shofeṭim	Deut. 16: 18–21: 9	Isaiah 51: 12–52: 12
8	Sa	11	Ki teze'	Deut. 21: 10–25: 19	Isaiah 54: 1–10
15	Sa	18	Ki tavo'	Deut. 26: 1–29: 8	Isaiah 60: 1–22
22	Sa	25	Niẓẓavim, Wa-yelekh	Deut. 29: 9–30: 20	Isaiah 61: 10–63: 9

Civil Date	Day of the Week	Jewish Date	SABBATHS, FESTIVALS, FASTS	PENTATEUCHAL READING	PROPHETICAL READING
Sept. 27	Th	Tishri 1	Rosh Ha-shanah, first day	Gen. 21: 1–34 Num. 29: 1–16	I Samuel 1: 1–2: 10
28	F	2	Rosh Ha-shanah, second day	Gen. 22: 1–24 Num. 29: 1–16	Jeremiah 31: 2–20
29	Sa	3	Ha'azinu (Shabbat Shuvah)	Deut. 32: 1–52	Hosea 14: 2–10 Micah 7: 18–20 Joel 2: 15–27 *Hosea 14: 2–10* *Micah 7: 18–20*
30	S	4	Fast of Gedaliah	Exod. 32: 11–14 34: 1–10	Isaiah 55: 6–56: 8 (afternoon only)
Oct. 6	Sa	10	Yom Kippur	Morning: Levit. 16: 1–34 Num. 29: 7–11 Afternoon: Levit. 18: 1–30	Isaiah 57: 14–58: 14 Jonah 1: 1–4: 11 Micah 7: 18–20
11	Th	15	Sukkot, first day	Levit. 22: 26–23: 44 Num. 29: 12–16	Zechariah 14: 1–21
12	F	16	Sukkot, second day	Levit. 22: 26–23: 44 Num. 29: 12–16	I Kings 8: 2–21
13	Sa	17	Ḥol Ha-mo'ed	Exod. 33: 12–34: 26 Num. 29: 17–22	Ezekiel 38: 18–39: 16
14-16	S-T	18-20	Ḥol Ha-mo'ed	S Num. 29: 20–28 M Num. 29: 23–31 T Num. 29:26–34	
17	W	21	Hosha'na' Rabbah	Num. 29: 26–34	
18	Th	22	Shemini 'Azeret	Deut. 14: 22–16: 17 Num. 29: 35–30: 1	I Kings 8: 54–66
19	F	23	Simḥat Torah	Deut. 33: 1–34: 12 Gen. 1: 1–2: 3 Num. 29: 35–30: 1	Joshua 1: 1–18 *Joshua 1: 1–9*
20	Sa	24	Be-re'shit	Gen. 1: 1–6: 8	Isaiah 42: 5–43: 10 *Isaiah 42: 5–21*
26	F	30	New Moon, first day	Num. 28: 1–15	

Italics are for Sephardi Minhag.

Civil Date	Day of the Week	Jewish Date	SABBATHS, FESTIVALS, FASTS	PENTATEUCHAL READING	PROPHETICAL READING
Oct. 27	Sa	Ḥeshwan 1	Noah, New Moon, second day	Gen. 6:9–11: 32 Num. 28: 9–15	Isaiah 66: 1–24
Nov. 3	Sa	8	Lekh lekha	Gen. 12: 1–17: 27	Isaiah 40: 27–41: 16
10	Sa	15	Wa-yera'	Gen. 18: 1–22: 24	II Kings 4: 1–37 *II Kings 4: 1–23*
17	Sa	22	Ḥayye Sarah	Gen. 23: 1–25: 18	I Kings 1: 1–31
24	Sa	29	Toledot	Gen. 25: 19–28: 9	I Samuel 20: 18–42

Civil Date	Day of the Week	Jewish Date	SABBATHS, FESTIVALS, FASTS	PENTATEUCHAL READING	PROPHETICAL READING
Nov. 25	S	Kislew 1	New Moon	Num. 28: 1–15	
Dec. 1	Sa	7	Wa-yeẓe'	Gen. 28: 10–32: 3	Hosea 12: 13–14: 10 *Hosea 11: 7–12: 12*
8	Sa	14	Wa-yishlaḥ	Gen. 32: 4–36: 43	Hosea 11: 7–12: 12 *Obadiah 1: 1–21*
15	Sa	21	Wa-yeshev	Gen. 37: 1–40: 23	Amos 2: 6–3: 8
19-21	W-F	25-27	Hanukkah, first to third days	W Num. 7: 1–17 Th Num. 7: 18–29 F Num. 7: 24–35	
22	Sa	28	Mi-ḳeẓ, Hanukkah, fourth day	Gen. 41: 1–44: 17 Num. 7: 30–35	Zechariah 2: 14–4: 7
23	S	29	Hanukkah, fifth day	Num. 7: 36–47	
24	M	30	New Moon, first day; Hanukkah, sixth day	Num. 28: 1–15 Num. 7: 42–47	

Italics are for Sephardi Minhag.

1984, Dec. 25–Jan. 22, 1985] ṬEVET (29 DAYS) [5745

Civil Date	Day of the Week	Jewish Date	SABBATHS, FESTIVALS, FASTS	PENTATEUCHAL READING	PROPHETICAL READING
Dec. 25	T	Ṭevet 1	New Moon, second day; Ḥanukkah, seventh day	Num. 28: 1–15 Num 7: 48–53	
26	W	2	Ḥanukkah, eighth day	Num. 7: 54–8: 4	
29	Sa	5	Wa-yiggash	Gen. 44: 18–47: 27	Ezekiel 37: 15–28
Jan. 3	Th	10	Fast of 10th of Ṭevet	Exod. 32: 11–14 34: 1–10	Isaiah 55: 6–56: 8 (afternoon only)
5	Sa	12	Wa-yeḥi	Gen. 47: 28–50: 26	I Kings 2: 1–12
12	Sa	19	Shemot	Exod. 1: 1–6: 1	Isaiah 27: 6–28: 13 29: 22, 23 *Jeremiah 1: 1–2: 3*
19	Sa	26	Wa-'era'	Exod. 6: 2–9: 35	Ezekiel 28: 25–29: 21

Italics are for Sephardi Minhag.

The Jewish Publication Society of America

REPORT OF NINETY-FOURTH YEAR

REPORT OF THE 94TH JPS ANNUAL MEETING

The 94th annual meeting of The Jewish Publication Society of America was held in Philadelphia on June 6, 1982 at the Hilton Hotel, with Dr. Muriel M. Berman presiding.

Bernard G. Segal, chairman of the Nominating Committee, presented the report and the following new trustees were elected: Paul Cowan of New York, journalist and author; Bernard Frank of Allentown, attorney, who was chairman of the Ombudsman Committee of the American and International Bar Association; Reuven Frank of New York, president of NBC News; Maxwell E. Greenberg of Los Angeles, attorney, who served as national chairman of the Anti-Defamation League; Leon J. Perelman, Philadelphia businessman, president of West Park Hospital and founder of the Perelman Antique Toy Museum; Charlotte Wilen, Atlanta, who was a member of the Federal Select Panel for Child Health and founding chairman of the Council of Maternal and Infant Health; and Sonia B. Woldow, Philadelphia, who served as president of Akiba Academy and is chairperson of the Federation of Jewish Agencies' Commission on the Elderly.

Reelected as trustees were Harold Cramer, Philadelphia; James O. Freedman, Iowa City; Irwin T. Holtzman, Detroit; Jack Lapin, Houston; Richard Maass, White Plains; Martin Meyerson, Philadelphia; Rela G. Monson, Philadelphia, and Jerry Wagner, Bloomfield, Connecticut.

Dr. Muriel M. Berman, Allentown, was reelected president. The following vice-presidents were reelected: Stuart E. Eizenstat, Washington; Norma F. Furst, Philadelphia; Norman Oler, Philadelphia; Robert S. Rifkind, New York; and Charles R. Weiner, Philadelphia. Robert P. Frankel, Philadelphia, was reelected treasurer; Marlene F. Lachman, Philadelphia, secretary, Robert P. Abrams, Philadelphia, chairman of the Executive Committee; Bernard I. Levinson, executive vice-president; and Maier Deshell, editor.

Following the report of the president, treasurer, and Nominating Committee, Yosef H. Yerushalmi, chairman of the Publication Committee, paid tribute to the late Gershom Scholem. Dr. Chaim Potok addressed the audience on "A Historic Moment: The New Translation of the Bible." Dr. Potok, special projects editor of JPS, was secretary of the committee of scholars who completed the translation of *The Writings-Kethubim,* the final portion of the Hebrew Bible.

From the Annual Report of JPS President Muriel M. Berman

An annual report could be prosaic, but this year has been an outstanding one for the Jewish Publication Society.

On Pesach, at the Seder, it is asked, "Why is this night different from any other night?," and you might ask us the same question, "Why is this year different from any other year?".

The answer is, of course, that this is the year we celebrated an important milestone in Jewish culture when we presented to the world a new translation of the Holy Scriptures. This is the first complete new translation since 1917, which was the first in the United States to be published in English. Our new translation, in the making since 1955, represents the latest in biblical scholarship and archaeological discoveries—including the Dead Sea Scrolls—and conveys the meaning of the original Hebrew text into modern, literary English.

This new translation is the product of a rich heritage and the indefatigable efforts of a committee comprised of renowned, learned, and distinguished professors, as well as rabbis representing the Orthodox, Conservative, and Reform traditions. The secretary to the committee was Dr. Chaim Potok, our own special projects editor.

Much devotion and inspiration were involved in the making of this magnificent work, years of stimulating and sometimes frustrating toil. Always the search for excellence, as well as truth and new scholarship, shines brilliantly from the pages of our new edition.

On Wednesday, the 26th of May, 1982—just twelve days ago—a significant and beautiful dinner was held in Philadelphia honoring the translators, the scholars, the rabbis, the past presidents, the board of trustees, the editors, and the Publication Committee. The honored guests read like a "Who's Who" of intellectual Jewry. A toast was proffered to our very special guests, the descendants of many famous people who had been involved in the original 1917 Bible project.

The theme of the evening was "Hope," and Elie Wiesel was our speaker. He is a man who lived through the horrors of the Holocaust, and who still expresses in his literary work confidence, solace, and inspiration derived from the meaning of the Torah. His very history is in itself a symbol of the continuity of our past, the living present, and the hope for the future of Judaism and all mankind. It was indeed an historic occasion, and a grand night to be remembered in the history of our Society.

Another celebration of the completion of the new JPS Bible was a scholarly and fascinating symposium hosted by New York University in cooperation with the Department of Near East Languages and Literature and the Humanities Council. More than 250 people attended. The featured participants were no less than three of the brilliant translators: Harry Orlinsky, H. L. Ginsberg, and Nahum Sarna. The program was moderated by Baruch Levine.

As president, I welcomed the participants and explained the history and goals of our Society to the New York audience. The subject of the symposium involved the intricacies of the translations such as the idiomatic expressions and the search for the true meaning of the individual words of the Bible from the Hebrew text.

The translators explained that hundreds of times in the footnotes they had to use the words "Hebrew obscure," "Hebrew unintelligible," or "probable translation," etc., proving that, even now, some explanations of words in the Bible are still a mystery.

Another event took place on March 10, 1982. The Jewish Publication Society cosponsored a book review featuring Blu Greenberg, the author of the controversial book entitled, *On Women and Judaism: A View from Tradition.* A large audience, including many Philadelphia members, attended the talk and reception at the UJA Federation building in New York City. A most worthwhile, interesting, and successful afternoon was spent highlighting one of the Jewish Publication Society's newest and successful publications. The reception was cosponsored by the Commission on Synagogue Relations of the Federation of Jewish Philanthropies.

A few words about the Commentary Project, headed by Jerome Shestack. Centuries ago, in 1475, the first printed Hebrew book appeared. It was Rashi's commentary on the Torah. Five hundred years later, in 1975, the Jewish Publication Society announced its plan for a new English language version of the Commentaries, with original thought, original comments, and the opinions of scholars involved today. Each person has his own idea of how a poem should be interpreted and what a painting denotes. Similarly, with the Bible, scholars through the ages have their own explanations and comments of their interpretation, expressing their personal perception of the meaning of the original texts.

To date more than 25 pledges of $5,000 each have been received for the project. The original funding plan was to have 70 contributors. The number 70 was based on the historical connection with the Septuagint, which refers to the 70 scholars originally involved in the translation of the Hebrew Bible into the Greek language centuries ago. We would welcome your participation as part of the new 70.

We are proud of the many awards our books have received:

First, and foremost, the *National Jewish Book Award,* for the completion of the new Bible translation by the Jewish Book Council.

Another, the *1981–1982 Outstanding Academic Books Award* for Andre Neher's book entitled *The Exile of the Word: From the Silence of the Bible to the Silence of Auschwitz.* This award was received from *Choice,* a publication that reviews books for academic libraries.

And yet another honor, the *Philadelphia Book Show Award,* for the highest standards of design, printing, and binding for the book *K'tonton in the Circus: A Hanukkah Adventure,* by Sadie Rose Weilerstein. *K'tonton,* the Jewish Tom Thumb, is a favorite with children. In his latest adventure, he goes to the circus, hobnobs with clowns, animal trainers, the fat lady, the human skeleton, and even snake charmers, but is safely returned in time to celebrate Hanukkah with his parents.

It was indeed a great honor to have *Cricket Magazine,* which specializes in children's works, use an excerpt from our publication *In the Shade of the Chestnut Tree,* written by Benjamin Tene. It is a poignant book of a young man who returns to Warsaw after the war, and finds and sits beneath his chestnut tree—the only familiar site still remaining in the city. He relives the laughter and the sorrow, remembering his dreams and frustrations with his childhood friends.

Commentary Magazine excerpted a section from Gershom Scholem's book *Walter Benjamin: The Story of a Friendship,* a rare intellectual drama about two of the century's most profound minds. And, I must mention that two of our copubs won *National Jewish Book Awards*: *The Art of Biblical Narrative* by Robert Alter and *Vichy France and the Jews* by Michael R. Marrus and Robert O. Paxton.

And, now to Jerusalem, where our centrally located office attracts many visitors. We have an enthusiastic and growing membership throughout Israel. We are represented at Israeli book fairs, and our Israel office sponsors book reviews and symposiums.

One of our authors, Dan Pagis, a noted Israeli poet, was featured in readings from his own work entitled *Points of Departure*, which we published. He is one of the leading poets of this generation; his work extends from grim vistas of genocide to lyrical medieval Hebrew poetry, and even includes science-fiction poems, where time is accelerated, distorted, and even reversed.

But the highlight of the Hebrew intellectual season in Israel this year was a symposium, again on the new translation of the Bible, including two of the three distinguished scholars who produced the translations, Moshe Greenberg and Jonas Greenfield, both of the Hebrew University. The third distinguished translator is here today in the audience, Dr. Nahum Sarna of Brandeis University.

Getting back to our United States activities, our public relations activities have been especially outstanding this year. We received reviews in the New York *Times* for Gershom Scholem's book *Walter Benjamin*, and have been interviewed by *Time Magazine* and the New York *Times* on our New York symposium. The Philadelphia *Inquirer* did almost a page, and press releases have gone throughout the country. Our translators have been interviewed by numerous radio stations, and one of the television stations even brought their cameras right into our office, on the 23rd floor. We have literally hundreds of book reviews a year—in the secular and Anglo-Jewish press—from California to New York and all points in between.

On Monday, the 24th of May, Mayor William Green honored the Jewish Publication Society with a Proclamation from the City of Philadelphia. Many of our board members attended the ceremony in his spacious office at City Hall. The completion of the new translations coincided with the celebration of Philadelphia's 300th anniversary, and the Jewish Publication Society will, officially, be forever a participant of Philadelphia's Century IV archives.

Now, from the sublime of books to an administrative situation: paramount was the real estate problem. Our lease was up and a decision had to be made. A Real Estate Committee was established, and the search was on. After many months, and in consultation with the Administration and Executive Committees and Board, no less than sixteen specific locations were examined and diagnosed by the Real Estate and Administration Committees. A prominent architect was consulted about feasability of space and our choice of location.

I can now announce that on September 15, our new address will be 1930 Chestnut Street—the entire 21st floor.

I am pleased to report that our membership has held its own. In order to raise the visibility of the organization throughout the nation a National Membership Committee is being formed. There are members on our board from at least eighteen important cities in the United States and Canada. Regional meetings are in the planning stage.

Some months ago a planning meeting was held in Washington, D.C., hosted by our vice-president Stuart Eizenstat, and a small, but prominent group of Washingtonians was invited. Your president and executive director also attended. The question was raised, "What can we do in Washington that we can't do in other cities?" So we investigated the possibility of a presentation of our new Bible to the president of the United States, and understand he is pleased with the idea. The White House is now trying to set a definite date. This will be the focal point for our D.C. event.

Los Angeles was next on the list, and Bernard Levinson has just returned from there, where he spoke on our behalf, and he will tell you about it himself.

Detroit hosted a JPS function on November 22, 1981. Allentown, Atlanta, and the University of Iowa have agreed to follow suit. With your cooperation, I am sure we can spread the word about our publications throughout the country.

And, lastly, in a few short years, we will celebrate the 100th Anniversary of this Society. I believe we must begin now to set the goals and initiate events, so they can come to fruition for this important event. We propose a year-long celebration. Among the projects already planned are: A book to be commissioned on the history of the organization—interesting, readable, and of the highest literary quality. We propose an anthology of the greatest Jewish writers—some pieces to be especially written in honor of the occasion, and some selected reprints from authors no longer living. Also, a wonderful JPS 100th Anniversary Weekend, comprising Sabbath services and Oneg Shabbats throughout the United States and Israel, featuring JPS books with authors reviewing their own works. An original lithograph for the occasion has already been discussed.

We are brimming with enthusiasm and ideas. We would like to hear your suggestions, and have your participation in this wonderful event. Please send your ideas to us.

And now, ladies and gentlemen, I would like to close by reading a note that Yehuda Blum, Israel's ambassador to the United Nations, sent to Bernard Levinson, our executive vice-president:

"I returned from an out-of-town engagement this morning to find your complimentary copy of the JPS Holy Scriptures on my desk. Please accept my grateful thanks for your thoughtful gesture, which I truly appreciate. You may be sure that I shall have many an opportunity to use it and quote from it in my statements both in the United Nations and elsewhere. It will no doubt also serve me well in my search for a suitable quotation to replace the one currently engraved in the Isaiah Wall facing the United Nations Headquarters."

JPS Treasurer's Report for 1981

I am pleased to report continued improvement in the financial picture of the Society. We reduced our operating deficit by 46 per cent and we increased the principal of our endowment funds by 35 per cent during 1981.

Income from sales of books and membership dues amounted to $1,038,470 while expenditures for printing and distributing our books came to $1,301,047. Fortunately, contributions and income from our special purpose funds of $213,413 reduced our operating deficit to $49,164, a significant drop from the 1980 deficit of $91,230.

In addition to the contributions the Society receives annually from welfare funds, federations, and individuals, during the past year we received gifts that have had a significant impact on our fiscal situation. It is my privilege to acknowledge them at this meeting. I would like to thank Joseph P. Mendelson and Prof. Jacob R. Marcus for their respective contributions of Israel Bonds to the Society.

Through the efforts of Muriel and Philip Berman and Joseph Mendelson, the number of sponsors of the JPS Bible Commentary project has more than doubled. We are indeed fortunate to be able to add new names to our growing list of patrons of this important undertaking.

We are grateful to Robert P. Abrams, the chairman of our Executive Committee, for his contribution in memory of his father, Peter Abrams. This gift helped us to underwrite the publication of *Spain, the Jews, and*

Franco, and this publication contains an appropriate inscription of Mr. Abrams's gift.

Finally, on behalf of a grateful society, on this occasion, I want to acknowledge again and thank Muriel and Philip Berman for their gift of $500,000 to our endowment fund. This magnificent gesture helps build a base to insure the future of the Society for coming generations.

Our endowment funds continue to be prudently invested so that we can remain confident of our ability to publish Jewish books of high quality.

JPS Publications

In 1981 JPS published the following new volumes:

Title and Author	*Printed*
THE BIROBIDZHAN AFFAIR: A Yiddish Writer in Siberia by Israel Emiot	3,000
SPIRITUAL RESISTANCE: Art from Concentration Camps 1940–1945 with Union of American Hebrew Congregations	2,000
JUDAISM AS A CIVILIZATION: Toward a Reconstruction of American-Jewish life by Mordecai Kaplan with the Reconstructionist Press	3,000
THE EXILE OF THE WORD: From the Silence of the Bible to the Silence of Auschwitz by Andre Neher	2,500
MA'ASEH BOOK: Book of Jewish Tales and Legends translated by Moses Gaster (paperback edition)	2,000
TANNA DEBE ELIYYAHU: The Lore of the School of Elijah translated by William G. Braude and Israel J. Kapstein	2,500
HEBREW BALLADS AND OTHER POEMS by Else Lasker-Schuler	2,000
IN LIGHT OF GENESIS by Pamela White Hadas	2,000
THE SYRIAN-AFRICAN RIFT AND OTHER POEMS by Avoth Yeshurun	2,000
K'TONTON IN THE CIRCUS: A Hanukkah Adventure by Sadie Rose Weilerstein	5,000
HERSHEL OF OSTROPOL by Eric A. Kimmel	3,000
IN THE SHADE OF THE CHESTNUT TREE by Benjamin Tene	4,000
AMERICAN JEWISH YEAR BOOK—Volume 81 edited by Milton Himmelfarb and David Singer (Co-published with the American Jewish Committee)	2,500
VICHY FRANCE AND THE JEWS by Michael R. Marrus and Robert O. Paxton (Co-published with Basic Books)	1,000

THE BOOK OF LIGHTS by Chaim Potok (Co-published with Alfred A. Knopf)	2,000
THE PENGUIN BOOK OF HEBREW VERSE edited by T. Carmi (Co-published with Viking Press)	1,750
THE ART OF BIBLICAL NARRATIVE by Robert Alter (Co-published with Basic Books)	1,500

1981 Reprints

During 1981 JPS reprinted the following books:

DONA GRACIA by Cecil Roth (2,000); THE FIVE MEGILLOTH AND THE BOOK OF JONAH (3,000); THE HANUKKAH ANTHOLOGY edited by Philip Goodman (2,000); THE HOLY SCRIPTURES (25,000); THE JEWISH CATA-LOG edited by Richard Siegel, Michael and Sharon Strassfeld (16,000); JEWISH COOKING AROUND THE WORLD by Hanna Goodman (2,000); THE JEWS OF ARAB LANDS by Norman A. Stillman (2,000); K'TONTON ON AN IS-LAND IN THE SEA by Sadie Rose Weilerstein (2,000); LEGENDS OF THE BIBLE by Louis Ginzberg (3,000); LEGENDS OF THE JEWS—Vol. VII by Louis Ginzberg (1,500); MANDARINS, JEWS, AND MISSIONARIES by Michael Pollak (2,000); SABBATH by Abraham E. Millgram (1,500); THE SECOND JEWISH CATALOG edited by Sharon and Michael Strassfeld (10,000); THE SHAVUOT ANTHOLOGY edited by Philip Goodman (2,000); THE THIRD JEWISH CATA-LOG edited by Sharon and Michael Strassfeld (10,000); THE TORAH (10,000); THE TREATISE TA'ANIT OF THE BABYLONIAN TALMUD edited by Henry Malter (2,000); WHAT THE MOON BROUGHT by Sadie Rose Weilerstein (2,000).

SPECIAL ARTICLES IN VOLUMES 51–82
OF THE AMERICAN JEWISH YEAR BOOK

OBITUARIES

Leo Baeck	By Max Gruenewald 59:478–82
Jacob Blaustein	By John Slawson 72:547–57
Martin Buber	By Seymour Siegel 67:37–43
Abraham Cahan	By Mendel Osherowitch 53:527–29
Albert Einstein	By Jacob Bronowski 58:480–85
Felix Frankfurter	By Paul A. Freund 67:31–36
Louis Ginzberg	By Louis Finkelstein 56:573–79
Jacob Glatstein	By Shmuel Lapin 73:611–17
Hayim Greenberg	By Marie Syrkin 56:589–94
Abraham Joshua Heschel	By Fritz A. Rothschild 74:533–44
Horace Meyer Kallen	By Milton R. Konvitz 75:55–80
Herbert H. Lehman	By Louis Finkelstein 66:3–20
Judah L. Magnes	By James Marshall 51:512–15
Alexander Marx	By Abraham S. Halkin 56:580–88
Reinhold Niebuhr	By Seymour Siegel 73:605–10
Joseph Proskauer	By David Sher 73:618–28
Maurice Samuel	By Milton H. Hindus 74:545–53
Leo Strauss	By Ralph Lerner 76:91–97
Max Weinreich	By Lucy S. Dawidowicz 70:59–68
Chaim Weizmann	By Harry Sacher 55:462–69
Stephen S. Wise	By Philip S. Bernstein 51:515–18
Harry Austryn Wolfson	By Isadore Twersky 76:99–111

Index